THE AUTHOR

Jack Lindsay was born in Victoria, Australia, in 1900 and studied at Brisbane Grammar School and Queensland University. He obtained a First Class Honours degree in Classics and drew on the ancient Greek world for writing poetry and historical novels. During the war he served first with the Signals Corps and then at the War Office.

The son of Norman Lindsay, he has written more than sixty books, including his novels in "The British Way" series and three volumes of autobiography. He lives in Castle Hedingham, Essex, with his wife and two children.

LEISURE AND PLEASURE
IN ROMAN EGYPT

OTHER WORKS BY JACK LINDSAY

Historical

SONG OF A FALLING WORLD
BYZANTIUM INTO EUROPE
CIVIL WAR IN ENGLAND
THE ROMANS WERE HERE
ARTHUR AND HIS TIMES
1764
THE WRITING ON THE WALL
SHORT HISTORY OF CULTURE

Biographical

MARC ANTONY
JOHN BUNYAN
CHARLES DICKENS
GEORGE MEREDITH

Autobiography

LIFE RARELY TELLS
THE ROARING TWENTIES
FANFROLICO AND AFTER

General

ANATOMY OF SPIRIT
A SHORT HISTORY OF CULTURE
HANDBOOK OF FREEDOM

HISTORICAL NOVELS

Ancient World

WANDERINGS OF WENAMEN
COME HOME AT LAST
(Short stories)
HANNIBAL TAKES A HAND
ROME FOR SALE
CÆSAR IS DEAD
LAST DAYS WITH CLEOPATRA
STORM AT SEA
(Golden Cockerel Press)
DESPOILING VENUS
BRIEF LIGHT
THE BARRIERS ARE DOWN

English History

THE GREAT OAK
FIRE IN SMITHFIELD
THE STORMY BARRIER
SUE VERNEY
1649
LOST BIRTHRIGHT
THE PASSIONATE PASTORIAL
LIGHT IN ITALY
MEN OF FORTY-EIGHT
ADAM OF A NEW WORLD
(Italy)

CONTEMPORARY NOVELS OF THE BRITISH WAY

END OF CORNWALL
WE SHALL RETURN
BEYOND TERROR
HULLO STRANGER
TIME TO LIVE
ALL ON THE NEVER-NEVER
CHOICE OF TIMES

BETRAYED SPRING
RISING TIDE
THE MOMENT OF CHOICE
LOCAL HABITATION
REVOLT OF THE SONS
THE WAY THE BALL BOUNCES
MASKS AND FACES

Translations of Theocritus, Aristophanes, Catullus, Longus, Apuleius,
Mediæval Latin Poets, etc.

Leisure and Pleasure in Roman Egypt

JACK LINDSAY

BARNES & NOBLE, INC.

PUBLISHERS · BOOKSELLERS · SINCE 1873

To V. S. Vakhrushev

At pregnant moons they also stared
and earth spilt into paradise
by blossomwinds. Their lavish hands
felt for a sudden permanence,
found it and lost it. They declared:
The sun's epiphany will suffice.

The light broke up in iris-moons;
the earth was fenced, a private thing;
secrecy darkened round the tree.
Mazed grew the irrepressible dance
that traced by winding pastoral tunes
the lost home, the forbidden spring.

The fountain gushed redeeming wine,
the apple flushed with innocent juice,
and all was well. The broken spell
stained earth with blood and cheats of guilt.
What god, what man might give the sign
to bring the true and bountiful truce?

Each garden is an eden still
and there the regular fall is found;
the ghostwind blows to claim the rose.
Now in our mouths the apples melt.
How harmonise our split will
till change and structure united fill
the accepted comprehended round
of time, and, as the tree upgrows,
we're standing firmly on the ground?

JACK LINDSAY

Contents

Line Illustrations

A*

Author's Foreword

THIS book deals in some detail with certain aspects of life in Roman Egypt—holidays, festivals and dances; the gymnasion and athletics including charioteering; hunting; the theatre and its organisation; gardens, their meaning and complex effects. Throughout the account there emerges the way in which the Dionysiac idea unifies all the activities and attitudes, the idea of a divine force making for joy, liberation, self-fulfilment, and ceaselessly transforming the earth into a sacro-idyllic garden, a *paradeisos*. So the inquiry finally moves into an account of the ways in which Alexander the Great and Dionysos became merged and the image of the Dionysiac Triumph entered Hellenistic and Roman political life as well as remaining a powerful element in popular hopes. We end with an examination of the 5th-century poet of Panopolis, Nonnos, in whose epic on Dionysos all these ideas come to a head. Nonnos has so far never been justly estimated as the poet of the breakdown of the ancient world and of the first medieval stages, of alchemic process and the vision of life as an endless series of transformations, with the Dionysiac earth of peace and plenty as the ultimate goal. A detailed analysis of his imagery and diction reveals his creative aims and values.

The book is thus complete in itself. However the reader will find, if he wishes, in my *Daily Life in Roman Egypt* the fuller background of these more specialised aspects. I have here cast my net more widely than in the first book, since it has been necessary often to set out the Hellenistic or even Pharaonic origins of the matters under discussion or to see those matters in the general perspective of the Roman empire. However, throughout, the focus is Egyptian and the effect is to show not only how Egypt took in and developed Greek forms, but also how it thus made a great contribution to the life of the empire and to the European future. The method is discursive; but the reader will find, I think, that the straying threads steadily come together and reveal a consistent pattern.

Alexander the Great invaded Egypt in 332 B.C., some ten years after the Persians had overthrown the last native Pharaoh. After his death, his general Ptolemaios, made himself king of Egypt, and his descendants reigned till the defeat and suicide of Cleopatra. In 27 B.C. the kingdom became a province of the Roman empire, though it kept many of its peculiar characteristics and had a special place in the Augustan system. With the reorganisations of Constantine we enter into the Byzantine epoch, which carried on till the Arab invasion in A.D. 639 (apart from a brief Palmyrean occupation, 269-71, and Persian rule 616-27). Our main interest here is the three Roman centuries; but some aspects of the Byzantine period intrude and Nonnos belonged to that period.

I hope to continue this series on Roman Egypt with several more studies of its life and culture.

JACK LINDSAY

There is no accepted and consistent scheme for transliterating Greek names as so many have been long familiarised in Latin forms. In so far as there is any tendency now among scholars, it is to get back to the correct Greek spelling, and I feel that this is a necessary step. Only laziness makes us keep to Latin forms. However, to make things easier, I have used the familiar forms for names such as *Alexander* the Great (*Alexandros*), *Cleopatra* (*Kleopatra*), *Athens* (*Athenai*); kept to C instead of K in well-known names like *Cyrene, Cappadocia, Canopos, Callimachos*. However, I have used the correct spelling for *Delphoi, Alexandreia* and names ending in *-on, e.g. Platon for Plato*; and while keeping to the clipped form, I have used the correct spelling *Ploutarch*, and so on. I have used the Greek form *gymnasion* instead of the Latin *gymnasium* in dealing with the Greek world, with *metropoleis* for the plural of *metropolis*, etc. In all these cases, though there may be a brief moment of surprise for the reader who knows no Greek, the forms are all immediately recognisable, so that I feel one is not asking too much in this effort to reach some sort of consistency and correctness in dealing with Greek names instead of accepting the Latin distortions as fixed for evermore. (Apollon I give as Apollo.)

J. L.

I

Holidays

ROMAN Egypt had a large number of festivals, celebrations, games, and entertainments. The free farmer or the well-off citizen could attend as many amusements as his duties and his work-calls permitted; but if we may judge from the apprentice-contracts, the men employed at the various trades in the workshops did not get a generous amount of holidays. There does not appear to be any list of specially important festivals which everyone attended and which were rated as national holidays, though no doubt every area had its own outstanding events. The main festivals celebrating Isis or the Nile perhaps came nearest to general holidays.

A papyrus dated A.D. 48 allows an apprentice boy three free days a month, thirty-six a year.[1] The method of computation shows the Egyptian division of the month into three *dechemeroi* or ten-day weeks. In a detailed contract of A.D. 183, made between Ischyrion and Heraklas, a weaver, the lad Thonis (probably Ischyrion's ward) is apprenticed for five years. Wages begin after 2 years 7 months and the weaver provides clothes on a rising scale. "The boy shall have 20 holidays a year on account of festivals without any deduction from his wages after wage-payment begins; but if he exceeds this number of days through idleness, bad health, disobedience, or any other reason, Ischyrion must produce him for the teacher for an equivalent number of days, during which he is to stay and carry out all his duties as aforesaid, without wages, fed by the said Ischyrion, because the contract has been made on these terms."[2]

The clause about the need to make up any absences is usual in these contracts; illness is generally not accepted as a reason for not working.[3] In another Oxyrhynchos papyrus of the late 2nd century a woman puts out her slave-girl to learn weaving:

Platonis, also called Ophelia, daughter of Horeion, of Oxyrhynchos, with her guardian, who is her full brother, Platon, and Loukios son of Ision and Tisasis, of the Aphrodeision in the Small Oasis, weaver, mutually acknowledge, Platonis also called Ophelia that she had apprenticed to Loukios her slave Thermouthion, who is under age, to learn the trade of weaving for a period of 4 years dating from the 1st of the coming month Tybi of the present year: for which period she is to feed and clothe the girl and produce her to her instructor daily from sunrise to sunset in the performance of all the duties to be imposed on her by him appertaining to the said trade, her pay being for the 1st year at the rate of 8 drachmai a month, for the 2nd year 12 dr. a month, for the 3rd year 16 dr. a month, and for the 4th year 20 dr. a month, and that the girl is to be allowed yearly 18 days' holiday on account of festivals, while, if there are any days on which she does no work or is ill, she shall remain with her instructor for a number equal to these at the period's end, the taxes upon the trade and imposts upon apprenticeship being chargeable to the instructor; and Loukios on his part . . . [4]

The papyrus probably went on to say that the weaver would thoroughly train the girl in his craft. Aphrodeision seems a village in the Small Oasis called after a shrine of Aphrodite (Hathor) rather than the temple itself; this Oasis had a metropolis, Psobthis, and so would include some villages. Platonis-Ophelia turns up in another contract, made with a woman Heras about an inheritance from Hermias. Hermias was the maternal grandfather of Heras and the father by adoption of Platonis' dead husband. Part of the inheritance was to go to Platonis' two sons; and the two women seem to be drawing up a settlement of claims.[5]

Further information is given by a document of the same period which at first was read as a list of festival days on which a priest took part in sacred processions in the area of Tentyris: a list used for calculating the compensation he could claim. A closer scrutiny has shown that it concerns an apprentice, but is not a contract. It is a list of the lad's absences through festivals, illnesses, and a visit. It records some 30 days thus spent away from the workshop. Presumably the absences were legitimate as there is no hint of indolence or truancy.[6] Despite gaps we can see that the document starts with a description of work; and as we find references to what seem a winecup, a necklace, a ring, the master must be a goldsmith or silversmith. The term used for cup is *baukalia*, which belongs to a group of words that includes *baukalis*, a vessel for cooling wine or water, and *baukalion* (*kaukalion*), a narrow-necked pot that gurgled as it was poured out. The baukalion is said to have been of Alexandrian origin.[7] Indeed the whole group seems Egyptian and *baukal-* entered through Latin into the Romance languages, surviving in Italian *boccale*, French and Spanish *bocal*. Athenaios, stating that the baukalis was "chiefly used in Alexandreia", cites the parodist Sopatros of Paphos for one "with four rings marked on it", and for a nonce-word:

> It's pleasant indeed to *baukalise*
> cups of the sweetness born through bees
> when thirsty under dawning skies
> from lastnight's overdose of boose.

He adds that Sopatros was a contemporary of Alexander the Great and "lived till the reign of the second King of Egypt, as he himself declares in one of his works"; it seems then likely that the poet lived in his later years in Alexandreia.[8]

Our papyrus-list would have point if a journeyman or hired worker had his pay based on things made and time spent at work. Contracts, however, contain only the barest statements about pay and its methods of computation. The most complicated one we know fixes the wages of dyers in a hemp-factory by the rate for a set number of bundles. Usually a worker just carried on, doing as he was told, and was then paid the basic wage he'd been promised.[9] Our list must then apply to an apprentice. All contracts stipulate that the master should properly teach his craft, and two of them add that he is to exhibit the apprentice at training's end before three good craftsmen.[10] A list of work done would prove that the master was carrying out obligations; a list of absences showed that he was watching the apprentice and taking care to get his full working-time. Also, it would serve the apprentice as a sort of certificate of training and ensure that no effort was made to keep him on working after he'd fulfilled his term.[11]

Other papyri deal only with the legal aspects of apprenticeship. They are contracts or registrations. A receipt proves that the tax on apprentices has been paid; a declaration states that a gild of hieroglyph-carvers includes no apprentices. Here alone do we get a glimpse of the apprentice at work and at play.

The holidays cited consist of a festival of Bes, the Typhonia, the Rhodophoria or Rose-bearing, and the Isia. One day was lost in *aedia*, which means some sort of illness, and two days in *karos*, which owns a wide range of medical meanings from drowsiness or lethargy to heavy stupor or coma after nausea and exhaustion, after too much food and drink.[12] Galen depicts the man with *karos*, stretched out insensible and motionless, breathing easily, with eyes closed, but unable to be roused; and compares him with the sufferer from apoplexy, with his hard breathing, or the cataleptic, whose eyes are open. There is no need however to suspect our apprentice of heavy drinking or the other troubles; he was probably just out of sorts.[13] He spent a day on a trip "with his mother" to Tentyris between 1st and 12th Epeiph, and four days in going to Tesenesis.[14] As the earliest definite date in the document is Hathur, the third month, and last is Mesore, the twelfth, the list may be taken as covering a whole year.

Whether the lad could have gone to more festivals if he had not been ill or using up time on trips, we do not know. But we have the interesting information of the four festivals he did attend. First, the Besia. We have no other references to it in the papyri and no clue to its date except that it seems in one of the first ten months of the year. Yet Bes was a very popular god, who increased his power in the Graeco-Roman era. He seems originally a figure representing puberty-initiation; an Old Kingdom relief shows some boys in play that certainly owns a ritual meaning: one, painted white, holds a lion mask (a Bes-mask), while others dance or are closed in a sort of hut. The boy with the mask has a stick ending in a hand, which is characteristic of the dwarfs and spirits analogous to Bes on the walls of the Saqqara mastabas. However, as the link with initiation broke down, Bes became a sort of guardian god in general. He was called a native of Punt, the rather mysterious region in the south-east, in the latitude of

Eritrea and Somaliland, which was famed for its sweet-smelling resins. He was shown as a grinning dwarf with big bearded head and large ears, shaggy brows and hair, long thick arms, bowed legs and tail: and he wore a lion, or panther, skin and a high-plumed crown. The crown resembles that of the goddess Satet, one of the triad at Elephantine; and this headgear suggests his connections with the Sudan. In Pharaonic days pygmies were fetched from the South to dance at court. Bes had become a

Bes (12th–18th dynasties); and Bes with Flowers.

dancer, musician, soldier with short belted tunic, short sword and shield.[15]

A happy, jesting figure, he had a strong prophylactic force and warded off evil influences, reptiles and malevolent beings. Dancing, he scared the demons by his grimaces and the rattling of his tambourine. He was carved on the handles of mirrors and stibium-tubes, on headrests and pillows of mummies.[16] Everyone smiled at his ridiculous figure. But while he often appears on stelai, vases, amulets, he is also found at times on formal monuments like temples. In the annexes added in the Late Period of the great sanctuaries where the yearly birth-rite of the child-god was per-formed, often with a peristyle enclosed to half its height by inter-columnar walls, the interior scenes showed the divine marriage and birth, while scenes of jollity and music were represented in the reliefs of abaci and propylaia. In these latter Bes might be

seen poking out his tongue, a beneficent spirit protecting women
in birth throes. Indeed at Tentyra, a locality mentioned in our
apprentice's list, figures of Bes adorned the Birth house of
Horsamto in the temple of Hathor.[17]

In the Egyptian board-games pieces are called *Dogs* in a demotic text; but in a set in the British Museum, ten have the heads
of Bes, ten have those of Anubis, the god of the dead who was
embodied in the wild dog or jackal roaming the cemeteries. Here
we seem to meet a ritual expression of the game of Life against
Death; and indeed it is clear that the board-game had many
ritual and magical associations. (Anciently the pieces were called

The scribe Ani at the boardgame.

dancers, as if the opposing sides were performers in a rite of death-
rebirth.[18]) In the papyrus of Ani we see the dead scribe seated in
a bower with a draughtboard set before him; his right hand is
raised above the board and he seems hesitating where to move the
piece that he holds. His wife sits behind, her right hand lifted as if
warning him against the move he proposes to make. The suggestion has been made that he plays with his wife; but much more
likely he is in a contest with an unseen adversary and his wife is
helping him. The gods played the game. "Hermes (Thoth) played
at draughts with the Moon and won the 72nd part of each one of
her lights," says Ploutarch, citing an astronomical myth, "out of
which he composed five days."[19] In the demotic tale Sethne seeks
to win a magical book from a dead man, who challenges him to
the boardgame. Sethne says, "I am ready."

They set before them the game-board with its dogs, they played at the game of Fiftytwo, and Neneferkaptah won one game from Sethne. He pronounced a spell to him, he supplemented it with the draught-board before them, he caused him to sink into the floor to his feet. He did the like by the second game, he won it from Sethne; he caused him to sink into the floor as far as his middle. He did the like by the third game; he caused him to sink into the floor as far as his ears.

After these things Sethne was in great straits at the hand of Neneferkaptah. Sethne called to Anherru his brother, saying, "Delay not to go up on earth and relate before Pharaoh all that is befalling me, and bring the amulets of Ptah my father and my books of magic."

Anherru delayed not to go up on earth and relate before Pharaoh what was befalling Sethne. And Pharaoh said, "Take him the amulets of Ptah and his books of magic." Anherru delayed not to go down to the tomb; he put the amulets on the body of Sethne, and at once Sethne sprang up high, and reaching forth his hand for the book he took it. And it came to pass that as Sethne came up out of the tomb, the light walked before him and the darkness walked behind him.[20]

It seems that the number 52 points to four games, each with 13 points. There seems a connection with the 13 lunar months of the solar year. (Modern packs of cards contain 52 in four sets of 13 each.) If Sethne had lost the fourth game, he would have been completely swallowed up by the earth.

Bes as a defender watched over sleepers and the dead. In Graeco-Roman times he rose from his minor status and became a rival of the high gods Isis, Osiris and Hor in the affection of the Egyptians. He even turned into an important oracular god and his mantic shrine at Abydos overshadowed even that of the great Osiris.[21] In a graffito in the temple of Sethos I at Abydos, on the east wall of the first court, we see a horoscope in a circle divided into twelve equal segments. The date seems 21 (or 22) September A.D. 353. At the end we read the name of the subject, Artemidoros, with the words, "Health [hygeia]! By Bes, may I not be wiped out!" Perhaps the cause for anxiety was the fact that the horoscope was in the house of Saturn; in any event the thoughts of Artemidoros turned to Bes as a saviour.[22]

Artemidoros may have been a Greek, an Egyptian or a Greek-Egyptian. Even though the Greeks in the Fayum and the metropoleis, with their gymnasia, held strongly to their own traditions, we see there too the unbroken persistence of the native gods. In areas like the Theban Memnonia the process of assimilating the Greeks was rapid. Thus, Hermias, a Greek, under the Ptolemy Euergetes 1, married an Egyptian Seminouthis, and their six children had Egyptian names. In 176 B.C. a Greek born in Egypt, son of Alexandros, bore the name of Ammonios and held land in Pestemenophis; in 113 another such Greek lent grain to the

Late forms of Bes.

choachytai of Memnonia—he was named Psen-Mon and had as son Pa-Thot.[23]

The oracle of Bes at Abydos became so popular that it was made use of by the imperial spy-system and led to much trouble under Constantius. Ammianus Marcellus tells us under the year A.D. 359:

There is a town called Abydos in the most remote corner of the Egyptian Thebais, where an oracle of the god known in that region by the name of Besa had formerly enjoyed some celebrity for its prophecies and had sacred rites performed at it with all the ceremonies anciently in use in the neighbouring districts. Some persons went themselves to consult this oracle, some sent documents containing their wishes by means of others and inquired the will of the deities with prayers couched in explicit language. The paper or parchment on which their wants were written, after the answer had been given, was sometimes left in the temple.[24]

Some of these papyri were collected and sent to the emperor, who, "being of a suspicious and petty temper", was enraged. He ordered "Paulus to proceed with all speed to the East, giving him authority, as to a chief of great eminence and experience, to try all the causes he pleased. And Modestus too, then Count of the East, a man well suited for such business, was joined with him in this commission. Hermogenes of Pontos, Prefect of the Praeto-

Bes drinking.

rium, was passed over as of too gentle a disposition." Paulus lost no time in inviting informers. "Numbers from all parts of the empire were brought before him, noble and lowborn alike; some of whom were condemned to imprisonment, others to instant death."

The town chosen for the proceedings was Skythopolis in Palestine: because it was little frequented and lay halfway between Antioch and Alexandreia, "from which many of those brought before the tribunal came". Among the victims was Parnasios, a man of "simple manners", who had been Prefect of Egypt; a long time past, when leaving his hometown Patrai in Achaia, he had dreamed of himself "conducted on his road by several figures in tragic robes". Demetrios, surnamed Chytras, a philosopher born in Alexandreia, who was now very old, was accused of "having often offered sacrifices in the temple of his oracle". He replied that he had done so from early youth, but not with any aim of raising his fortunes by the questions. Though put often on the rack, he stuck to this position and was at last allowed to retire to Alexandreia. Andronikos, well known for his "liberal accomplishments and poetry", put up a vigorous defence and was aquitted.

We do not hear of Bes during the trials; but it seems that the material gathered from his shrine at Abydos had started off a campaign against all efforts to see into the future through oracles.

If anyone wore on his neck a charm against the quartan ague or any other disease, or if through any information laid by his ill-wishers he was accused of having passed by a grave at nightfall and therefore of being a sorcerer and one who dealt in the horrors of tombs and the vain mockery of the shades that haunt them, he was found guilty and condemned to death.

The popularity of Bes is shown by such things as the listing of silver and bronze statues of him in an inventory of the Temple of Soknopaios at Soknopaiou Nesos, a Fayum village west of the Lake, in the 2nd century.[25] Valuable statues of the god, as well as terracottas, were also in private hands, as we learn from a document of A.D. 144, in which Diemous, daughter of Kollouthos, of Oxyrhynchos, complains to an official—a strategos, or a centurion or minor police-officer. The suggestion of a personal inspection points to the latter. "I shut up the door of my house and the door of the terrace, and on coming back home I found that a box I had on the terrace had been unfastened and there had been removed from it two gold bracelets of the weight of 4 minai, a gold figure of Bes, and two large silver bracelets—and that the terrace-door had been lifted. I have felt some suspicions against my neighbour Heras, son of Kalathos, weaver, and those who work with him, because my house is easy of access from his; so I present this petition and request, if you think fit, you should come for a personal inspection and Heras and his associates, whose names he will himself give, should be brought before you and the proper inquiry made, enabling me with your aid to recover what belongs to me." Bes continued to haunt the region of Abydos. An ostrakon of the XXII dynasty speaks of demons armed with knives that lurk in the darkness of the environs of that place. Bes, both as a good and troublesome spirit, is often shown armed with knives: and we find him continuing as a force, though now a wholly evil one, in the Christian epoch. A Coptic account tells how he was exorcised:

They prostrated themselves at the feet of our father apa Moisas and appealed to him; for there was a wicked demon named Bes who had entered into the temple situated to the north of the monastery. Under the effect of his blows some lost their sight, others felt their hands wither, others began to go lame, one man had a disfigured face, another became deaf and dumb. There was quite a host who saw him while he jumped on the floor in the temple, taking a thousand different forms.

St Moisas goes at eve into the place, then at midnight Bes cries out in pain, "How long will you make us suffer, Moisas." In vain he threatens and is driven out.[26]

The Rhodophoria must be the Latin Rosalia or Rose-Festival, the Greek Rhodismos. Here it seems to last seven days; or perhaps seven days were all that the lad could take off for it. It may well have been the chief festival of his area. For in the temple-accounts from Soknopaiou Nesos for 138, seventeen festivals are listed, ten of them lasting seven days, three lasting eight days, one nine days; the remaining three are the birthdays of the god of the temple, Soknopaios, and of Isis Nepherses (each nineteen days) and the Festival of the Rhodophoroi, lasting thirteen days. The accounts show a regular consumption of an artaba of wheat daily, which implies bread for a staff of thirty priests; on festivals four artaba daily were used, enough to feed some 120 persons. Revenue was doubtless got from the sale of bread to worshippers. For the Rose Festival, which began on 12 Mecheir (6 February), 52 artaba were used.[27]

The Romans celebrated two kinds of Rosalia: one connected with the cult of the dead and one welcoming-in spring and summer with feasting and merrymaking. For both kinds the idea of the rose as an emblem of renewed or reborn life was dominant.[28]

The rite at Tentyris was certainly the seasonal rite. Roses played an important part in both private and public rejoicings under the Empire.[29] They were displayed or strewn at the entry of notable persons into a city, as when Caracalla entered Alexandreia, during processions, and at the arrival of good news.[30] Tacitus tells us that at Rome in 69, in the midst of the festival of Ceres (which began on 19 April), news came of Otho's death and of the soldiers in the city swearing allegiance to Vitellius. "The spectators signified their applause. The people, with laurels and flowers, carried the images of Galba to the various temples and heaped their chaplets up in the form of a tomb on the spot near the lake of Curtius, which he had dyed with his blood."[31] As roses were regarded as the best material for wreaths or garlands, they played a main part in such flower-ceremonies. The flower-tomb of Galba represented a sort of apotheosis or rebirth: the general spring-rite of Ceres was spontaneously transformed into a specific action of homage, the magical renewal of an individual.

Sokrates the Rhodian in his *History of the Civil War* told of the entertainments by Cleopatra of Marcus Antonius in Cilicia. Every dish was of gem-inlaid gold, the walls were hung with embroideries of gold and purple; twelve triclinia were set out (to suggest the twelve high gods). Antonius, told to take everything he saw, was astonished at the splendour. Next day the queen invited him to a yet more lavish meal and told each of his captains to take his couch and goblet away, with further gifts of palanquins, slave-bearers, or horses, and Ethiopian torch-boys. Finally, on the last day "she paid more than a talant for roses, and the floor of the chamber for the men was strewn a cubit deep, nets being spread over the blooms."[32] The night of roses was the climax, a sort of paradisiac moment.

It was thus natural to pick out the Rose as the emblem of the festival of spring, though no clear line was drawn here between spring and summer.[33] Spring was pictorially represented with a crown or basket of roses.[34] The date of the first flowers varied from place to place. The calendar of Apollinopolis (Edfu), which had close religious ties with Tentyris, gave up 22 to 30 Mecheir for a rite celebrating the Germination of Divine Plants.[35] And as we saw that the Rose-festival at Soknopaiou Nesos occurred in the same month, we may be reasonably sure that the Tentyris rite was also then celebrated.

The Rosalia or Rhodophoria was an event in which Roman and Eastern elements met and harmonised. It was perhaps essentially a festival of city folk rejoicing at the flowers which reminded them of the earth's awakening.[36] At Rome the *macellum* or provision-market was festively decorated with flowers; and at Dura-Europos the standards of the legionaries had their rose-wreathing—the military form of the spring-ritual. The popularity of the festival is shown by its strong survival into Byzantine times.[37]

The garland played an important role in Greek life and had a sort of divinising value. At a banquet or a festival even the humblest person to some extent partook of the life of the gods if he were garlanded; he shared richly in what we may call the momentary eternity of the rite. And roses, with their strong association of love and beauty, lent out something of their own virtue at such a time. At the banquet—the occasion, Martial said, "when the Rose reigns"—the rose-wearer shared in the kingship.[38] Two of the Love-Letters of Philostratos (possibly a second-century member of a distinguished literary family) help to bring out the feelings that the rose evoked. The first mentions the festival at Rome:

Truly roses are Love's flowers. Like him they are young and lithe. Both he and they have golden tresses and share other traits. Roses have thorns for shafts, red blushes for torches, and petals for feathers; and neither Love nor Roses know Time. For that god is the foe of both the Autumn of Beauty and the Lingering of Roses.

At Rome I saw the Flowerbearers running and indicating by their speed how precarious is beauty's prime. For their running signified that that prime should be enjoyed. Hesitate and it's gone. A woman who loiters also withers with the roses. Don't delay, my beautiful. We'll wreathe ourselves with roses. Let's run on together.[39]

The ritual link makes the statement more than an appeal of *carpe diem;* we feel a hint of the Blakean call to kiss the flying joy and live in eternity's sunrise. Though there seems nothing Dionysiac

in the origins of the rose-festival, it took on a Dionysiac colouration through its link with banqueting and with wine (sometimes
specified in inscriptions as *profusiones*), and perhaps also through
its stress on rebirth.

The second letter brings out the mingling of erotic and religious
motives in such a festival as that of the Rose:

The roses, borne on their leaves like wings, have hastened to come to
you. Welcome them kindly as memorials of Adonis or as tincture of
Aphrodite or as Eyes of the Earth. Yes, a wreath of wild olive becomes
an athlete, an upright tiara the Great King, a helmet-crest a soldier,
but roses become a handsome boy, through the affinity of fragrance
and the distinctive hue. You won't wear the roses: they'll wear you.

The rose was said to spring from the blood of Adonis and to owe its
colour to Aphrodite's blood as her feet were pricked when she ran
about frantically on hearing of his death.

Egypt, a land that produced so many roses, could not but embrace
the Rhodophoria with enthusiasm. For the Dionysiac link we
may look at a mosaic at El-Djem in Tunisia where a rich carpet
of roses, in which are mingled birds, bacchic masks, panpipes,
serves as a field for the central medallion of Aphrodite and
Dionysiac Loves. (Other El-Djem mosaics of *xenia* or food-
droppings depict vegetables that could not have been eaten in
the locality but belong to Alexandreia: suggesting a Hellenistic
prototype from Egypt. Among the *xenia* are four bacchic masks
evoking the seasons.) The blood colour of the rose helped in
making it seem a life-source, able to revive the spring or bring
vitality to the dead as well as avert evil forces or witchcrafts, as
when it restored Lucius to human shape in the *Golden Ass*. It
owned, we are told, "something divine".[40]

With the Isia we come into the heart of Egyptian religion as it
survived in the Roman world. Isis had many festivals. Thus in the
temple accounts of Soknopaiou Nesos we meet the Birth of Isis
Nepherses, a rite lasting 19 days, and her Wedding (with Osiris),
lasting 9 days. Also, "to Priests of Soknopaios officiating at the
celebrations in honour of Isis Nephremmis and Harpokrates at the
Isle of Women, Thoth 19, 12 artaba. Tybi 1. Founding of the

shrine of Isis Nephremmis: 12 art. Mecheir 19, 12 art. Epeiph 9, 12 art. Total at Isle of Women, 48 art." Six keramia of wine were also used up at the Isle. Under revenue, we find listed "at Nilopolis: Altar of Isis Nepherses 500 dr. From this there is a balance of 90 dr. Altar of Isis Nephremmis 400 dr. From this there is no balance remaining."[41]

A widespread festival of Isis was the Ploiaphesia or Boat-launching, which took place on 5 March and seems limited to that

Isis as Queen of Sothis (Dogstar) and regent of the heavenly bodies and controller of the seasons.

day. We have a vivid account of it in Apuleius' *Golden Ass*.[42] But the Isia to which our apprentice went would most likely have been the great ritual at which the drama of the goddess was enacted: the murder of Osiris by his brother Seth-Typhon, Isis' lamentations and wanderings in search of the body, her discovery of it and her reunion with the resurrected brother-husband. There was a wild burst of rejoicing among her worshippers at the moment of discovery, a profound feeling that the restoration of life, happiness, family-harmony in the divine triad brought about a liberation for those participating in the rite. The devotees cried out that they too had found what they had lost, what they desired.[43]

By the Roman epoch the resurrection of Osiris was felt as a pledge for the fructification of the crops. Isis had come from the Delta, but her worship had long spread throughout Egypt, east to Koptos and south to Philai where was built the best preserved of her temples. Under the Ptolemies, though impeded by its dynastic bonds, her cult expanded outside Egypt; with the Empire a fuller diffusion all round the Mediterranean went on.

Myth and ritual had long been dislocated in Egypt by the Wandering Year, the result of a discrepancy in calendar calculations, which meant that only once in 1461 years did the New Year, 1 Thoth, coincide with the first rising of Sirius, 19 July in the Julian calendar. The festival of the Nile Flood was connected with the heliacal rising of Orion, 14 July, and that of Sirius, and thus should have provided a natural point for the distribution of festivals about the year. But the discrepancy upset the system. Various rulers seem to have tried to bring the festival back to its right moment; but religious conservatism resisted, with the result that in Graeco-Roman times many festivals were not in direct connection with the great myths of the Flooding and the calendar of the seasons. The Isiac festivals concerned with sowing and germinating were those of the month Choiak, and dealt with the loss and finding of Osiris. Osiris there appeared, not as the revived earth but as the buried seed that comes up in renewed vegetation. The *kikellia* or lamentations of 29 Choiak fell on 5 March in 304 B.C. but with the stabilising of the Wandering Year by the Romans in 30 B.C. (or 25), 28–9 Choiak became 24–5 December, and the festival was that of the winter solstice, the turn of the year, the revival of light out of darkness.[44]

We catch a glimpse of the festival's entertainments in a contract of A.D. 8–9, in which a performer was engaged for a year. He was to give his services "on the 9th and 10th of each month, and for two days at the Eisia (Isia) and at the time of the Stars of Hera" —another name for the planet Venus. Presumably some village was engaging the man; his salary suggests that he did not belong to the higher levels of his profession. No doubt he was a musician.[45]

Presents were exchanged at the Isia. The veteran Gemellus in

A.D. 110 writes to his steward, "Buy us some presents for the Isis Festival for the persons we're used to send them to, especially the strategoi. Buy the birds for the festival two days beforehand, and send them."[46] The occasion was used, it seems, to keep in well with the authorities, at least by men of property. Another letter of the early 2nd century mentions a night festival. Otherwise complete, it lacks the usual greeting at the start and the address:

The voyage past the Antaiopolite Nome is a great botheration. Every day I'm burdened on account of it and the thing has left me extremely worn out. If a gratuity must be given to the brother of the mother of Achillas' sons, please get some lotus for him from Sarapion at my charge. Don't forget the night-festival of Isis at the Sarapieion.[47]

We gain some idea of what the temples of Isis were like and how they were used, from the accounts in the Romances. In the *Aithiopiaka* the brigand chief dreams how he enters the temple at Memphis, his native city. The building is lighted up everywhere with a blaze of lamps; altars and braziers are laden with all kinds of animals and drenched with their blood; the portico and passages outside are crowded with people whose clatter and clamour fills the whole place.[48]

Later, amid a love-conflict, the old priest Kalasiris transmits his function to his son in the temple. He is conducted to the place "by the light of torches, while the tones of many panpipes and sacred flutes incited the more impetuous of the young folk to wild transports of dancing". There is a jostling throng. In the inner sanctuary Kalasiris prostrates himself, clasps the statue's feet, and stays thus "for a great length of time, in which he came very near to dying. The bystanders brought him to himself again; with some difficulty he stood up, poured a libation and offered prayers to the goddess. He then removed from his head the sacerdotal crown and set it on the head of his son Thyamis." Not long after he takes part in a banquet, at the end of which he offers up libations and prayers again to Isis; then goes to rest, warning his sons that the end is near. They keep a watch all night but at cockcrow he is found dead. The sacristan then announces,"We

have issued a summons for the attendance of the rest of the prophets and priests in the town, so that they may carry out the
funeral with the customary rites of their ancestral tradition. You
must therefore depart since it is not right for anyone, save the
persons invested with the holy functions, to offer sacrifice or even
set foot in the temple during the seven days after the decease."[49]

Achilleus Tatios tells how a rich Ephesian woman at Alexandreia, Melitte, falls in love with the hero, who thinks his beloved
is dead and at last succumbs to the widow's importunities."We
agreed that next day we'd meet at the temple of Isis to discuss
our future and take the goddess as witness of our troth. Menelaos
and Kleinias went there with us, and we took oaths, I to love her
honourably and she to make me her husband and declare me
master of all she owned." They then go to a banquet.[50]

We shall have more to say later of incense and fumigations;
but here we can glance at what Ploutarch in his treatise on Isis
and Osiris says of the symbolism. Resin, considered to be the
work of the sun, was burnt at night to purify the air which then
was thought to condense and weigh down the body while
making the soul misty, gloomy, heavy. Myrrh, considered to be
brought out of shrubs by the moon's influence, was burned at noon
when the sun drew exhalations from the earth; for it dispersed
the turbid element. The subtilising of the air was helped by burning woods of a dry nature: cypress, juniper, pine. The special
incense *kyphi* was made up of sixteen ingredients: honey, wine,
raisins, sweet-rush, resin, myrrh, frankincense, seselis, kalamos,
asphalt, thryon, dock, the less and the greater arceuthids, carda-
mon, orris-root: things believed to be nourished by cold airs,
shade, dews, moisture.

As for their number, it certainly looks like a square composed of a
square and alone containing the equal number of an equal number of
times, while bringing its external measurement exactly equal to its
area; this accidental circumstance must by no means be said to contribute nothing to its effect. The majority of the ingredients, owning
aromatical properties, send out a sweet breath and healthy exhalation
by which the air is changed and the body excited in the proper manner.
They lull people to sleep and own a seductive tendency, while they

loosen and untie the trouble and tension of our daily anxieties like so many knots. And they brighten and clarify the imaginative and prophetic part of dreams, as it were a mirror, to no less a degree than do the tunes on the lyre which the Pythagoreans used to play before going to sleep; thus charming down and doctoring the irrational and passionate portion of the soul.

For things smelt at once call back the failing sense and often on the other hand blunt and stupefy it, their evaporations diffusing themselves through the body on account of their subtilty, just as physicians say that sleep is brought on when the exhalations from food taken go creeping gently and as it were feeling their way round the inward parts, and thus cause a sort of tickling.[51]

Kyphi was taken both as a drink and as a pastille. As a drink it loosened the bowels and so was thought to purge the intestines.

We see then how incense was felt to make the temple a place of harmonious sense and spirit, of balanced elements: a paradisiac centre in a world of confusion and conflict. The scents and smells played an active part in restoring the unity of man and nature, and in raising nature to the heavenly level. In the temple-accounts of Soknopaiou Nesos we find:

For purchase of myrrh and balsam, 60 dr.
For purchase of spices for kyphi in honour of Harpokrates, 96 dr.
For purchase of incense and expenses at the nativity of the deified
   Augusti 40 dr.
For purchase of spices for kyphi in honour of Soknopaios, 500 dr.[52]

The local god seems to get by far the most incense. The worship of the State-powers, the Augusti, was clearly much more formal and unimportant than that of the native gods.

Ploutarch, we may note, had an Egyptian Ammonios as his teacher; he must have visited Egypt since he mentions his return from Alexandreia (in the late 1st or early 2nd century); his citation of Egyptian sayings suggests contacts with priests; his tracts on Isis and on Women were each dedicated to a priestess of Isis. He does not refer to Isiac practices as an initiate, though he seems to have had a genuine knowledge of many Egyptian attitudes. For instance his differentiation of two kinds of eternity conforms to the Egyptian ideas of a dynamic eternity and of a

B

constant one; the notion of receiving truth and giving truth in the opening of his work on Isis is also basically Egyptian.

We now come to the last of the festivals to which our apprentice went, the Typhonia. This is not known elsewhere and is an interesting example of local conservatism. Its existence brings out how stubborn were the native cults and how ancient were the roots of many. Typhon-Seth, patron of Ombos, had once been a great god whose thunders shook the earth. As lord of Upper

Seth and the Seth-animal.

Egypt he stood on a level with Osiris and Horos; but as the murderer of his brother in the complex conflict of cults and regional groups that produced the later Osirian system, he became in general the incarnation of evil. After Osiris' death he fought a bitter battle with Horos, and in the series of adventures that resulted Isis helped her son with her magical powers.[53]

Typhon's birthday fell on the epagomenal day and was considered unlucky; late calendars omitted it.[54] The learned priests saw him as the principle of dryness—of drought, famine, destruction; and he became the accomplice of black magicians. In the Osirian rituals he appeared as the condemned opponent;

and he did not normally have festivals of his own, even in areas where he once had had temples: Oxyrhynchos, the Great Oasis, Kynopolis, Hypsele, Ombos.[55]

Now and then a sacrifice might be made to him, but the act was given an offensive meaning. Red bulls without a single black or white hair were consecrated to him as the incarnations of the souls of impious men.[56] Even in his old domain of Upper Egypt, his sacred animals—donkey, crocodile, pig, antelope and certain typhonian birds and fishes—were periodically mutilated or otherwise destroyed.[57]

He had had his moments of rehabilitation. With the Hyksos invasion he was worshipped in the east Delta, at Tanis, Pelousion, Auaris; but that was because the Semitic intruders saw him as their own great Baal. At Heliopolis he was accepted in the divine ennead with Osiris and Isis, and stood with Thoth and Horos in the Sunship.[58] The Ramessides in general held him in honour. Under his patronage Sethos I and Ramses II restored the empire after its decline under Akhnaton. But Osiris and Horos kept rising, and towards the end of the dynastic age their supremacy was assured; by the Graeco-Roman period Osiris was the universal god of rebirth and fertility, while Seth-Typhon was a demon. Not that even then the latter was everywhere condemned. Thus, in a return of temple-property, dated A.D. 213–17 and drawn up by the priests of various temples at Oxyrhynchos and in the Oxyrhynchite and Kynopolite nomes, the deities worshipped consist of Zeus, Hera, the Semitic Atargatis Bethennun(is?), Kore, Dionysos, Apollo and Neotera. In the temple of Neotera (here probably Hathor-Aphrodite) we find an interesting collection of objects:

a representation of Our Lord the Emperor M. Aurelius Severus Antoninus Felix Pius Augustus and Julia Domna the Lady Augusta and his deified father Severus, some of the offerings being inscribed with the names of the dedicators . . . while in other cases we are ignorant of the dedicators, because the offerings have been in the temple from ancient times; a statue of Demeter, most great goddess, of whom the bust is of Parian marble and the other parts of the body of wood . . . was not disclosed to us. And with regard to other offerings, which were dedicated in accordance with ancient custom for vows or pious reasons . . . dedicated by Phragenes son of Horion a small bronze statue of Neotera, 5 rings dedicated by . . . son of Didymos, a green robe dedicated by the mother of An . . . , ... dedicated by Kastor son of Asklepiades, a small . . . on which is a statuette of Neotera, a stone . . . of wellcut stone, a rudder representing Neotera, a statue of . . . , of which the bust is of Parian marble and the amulets of plaster, a statue of Typhon, part of which . . . joined together in the middle.

Hellanikos of Lesbos, who visited Egypt late in the 5th century B.C., wrote an *Aigyptiaka* in which he mentioned a city on a river,

Horos slaying Crocodile-Seth; and Horos executing Donkey-Seth before Osiris.

called Tindion, a meeting-place of the gods, where, in the middle of the city, stood a large stone temple, with stone portals. Inside there grew black-and-white acacia trees on which wreaths of twined acanthus-blossoms, pomegranates, and grape-vines had been cast; these crowns were perpetually in bloom, but were "put away" by the gods on learning that Babys (more correctly Bebon), who was Typhon, ruled in Egypt. Here Typhon appears as the destroyer of the paradisiac harmony we noted in the incense-thick temples.[60]

In the magical papyri Isis holds supreme place; she makes Horos immortal and his father's successor.[61] Horos does not appear as conquering Seth, but their conflict is assumed in various formulas. A charm to be recited over burning wood runs: "O you that burned the godless Typhon, you fellow-combatant of Horos, you helper of Anubis, you guide of Isis. . . "[62] In a charm for opening a door, recited over the navel-string of a firstborn ram that had not touched the ground, we find: "Be opened, be opened, O bar, for I am Horos the great one, Archephrenepsou Phirinx, son of Osiris and Isis; and I want to escape from the godless Typhon quickly quickly at once at once."[63]

The second charm brings out the relation to the act of birth. Its power is aided by the navel-string of a ram that has not touched the ground—has not broken away from the potent sphere of the birth-moment. It breaks the bar, it carries out successfully the movement into a new space or dimension. It thus shows itself essentially a charm of rebirth. The other charm apparently holds a reference to the myth in which a burning tree is used in place of Horos in the immortalising rite. Myrrh seems to belong here. "The prayer addressed to Smyrna (the Myrrh-tree) reminds her in highly eulogistic style of the prominent parts which she played in the Osiris drama owing to her power of burning her enemies."[64]

Seth in these spells is the enemy. The black magician however feels himself drawn to Seth, who is "crowned with black ivy" and is "the headless demon with his sight in his feet".[65] The devotee burns Osiris' bones and cries to his patron, "I am he who has traversed the whole world with you and found the great Osiris whom I brought to you in chains." He threatens Horos: "I will take away the fatherless from the mother, the pole (of the heaven) will be borne away, and the two mountains will be one." He seeks the typhonic energy of revolt: "as Typhon is the adversary of the Sun, even so inflame the heart and soul of him. . . "[66] He wants to be identified with his hero who resists the whole frame of things. "Call me you, the headless god with his sight in his feet."[67] (Sight is allotted to the despised feet and the normal centre of thought is rejected, annihilated; the existing system is turned upside down. In such terms we see how in black magic is caught a blind impulse of revolt which cannot break outside a narrow hatred, an egoistic isolation.)

Elsewhere we find the Akephalos, the Headless Demon, who has his eyes in his shoulders; and in an incantation, *The Stele of Jeou the Painter*, he is taken as the creator of heaven and earth, day and night, and identified with Osiris-Onnophris, otherworld-ruler.[68] We are here merging into the world of the Gnostics—the

The All-God of the magicians, with the great typhonic animals enclosed in the snake on which he stands.

devotees of a given and esoteric Gnosis (Knowledge), who seem to have originated in the Syrian area but spread to Egypt in the reign of Hadrian.[69] In Egypt they found a fertile soil. One of the main sects was that of the Sethians, with books to which were attached the names of Seth and his Sons. Here Seth seems primarily the son of Adam, who was considered the inventor of astronomy.[70] Many Gnostics took the God of Genesis as an evil demiurge and in other ways also inverted the value of the Hebrew Bible, thus expressing in elaborate intellectual constructions the rejection of the ruling systems which we noted in black magic.

The Sethians did not use this transformation of values; but it was natural that in Egypt the Gnostic tendency to condemn a god who made the world as a worker of evil should take over Seth as the adversary of Osiris and make of him a supreme liberating deity. We find Seth-Typhon presiding over Judeo-Gnostic ritual in which Adam plays a leading part. There are Egyptian bronze figurines appropriate to such a cult: *e.g.* that which represents the god walking with hieratic gait, girt with loin-cloth and wearing an ass-head. The pedestal is engraved with the name Aberamentho, which denoted Jesus.[71] In a magical papyrus we see a drawing of Seth-Typhon-Aberamentho with cock's head; the text states that it is to be engraved with a bronze stylus on a leaden tablet, to accompany magical formulas.[72]

We meet then a strange mixture of Seth as a beneficent and as an evil force, a demiurge of the universe and an opponent of the demiurge.[73] There seems to have been a cult of Seth-Typhon in which various mysteries were celebrated.[74] A hermetic text sees in the Sons of Typhon the exponents of a topsy-turvy world. "Every soul, whether incarnated in a man or inhabiting the earth in some other form, knows where it ought to go, although certain Typhonioi come and tell us, my child, that a bull can pass its life in the depths of the sea or a tortoise in the air."[75]

It is worth noting that the site of the discovery of important Gnostic manuscripts about 1945 was at Chenoboskion in the region of Diospolis Parva. The Greek name suggests geese-breeding (though Alexandros Polyhistor in the 1st century A.D. tells us that there was no grassland in the area for geese, while the folk were said to have a great veneration for the abundant crocodiles).[76] The Coptic name however was Shenesit, Acacias of Seth. In the Roman period the town was occupied by a military garrison; but it became derelict, like the neighbouring villages, Phbou and Tabennisi. A Coptic chronicler of the 4th century wrote, "Shenesit-Chenoboskion was then a desert village, grilling in the intense heat. There were not many inhabitants; only a few."[77] Here about 320 the young Pachomios, freed from a Roman prison at Antinoopolis, was converted to Christianity and lived in a broken-down brick-kiln near the Nile. There were already some anchorites in the area, and they baptised him; but instead of carrying on with the hermit-way of life, he gathered other ascetics and devised the first monastic rule. From the Acacias of Seth the monastic discipline spread over Egypt and then the Near East. To the north of the town is the great abrupt cliff of Gebel el-Tarif. On the eastern slope of the mountain are Pharaonic tombs, in one of which a Coptic monk has painted in red the first words of several psalms; more to the north a pagan pilgrim, hardly earlier than the first monks, has inscribed a series of Greek invocations to Sarapis; and under the entries of the great tombs are the narrow deep cavities of the cemetery that served first for Diospolis Parva and then for Chenoboskion. In one of these lesser tombs the Gnostic library seems certainly to have been found, stored in a jar.[78] The name Shenesit shows that the region had once been devoted to the worship of Seth; and it is interesting that this Sethian environment nurtured both Gnostic Christianity and the first crucial steps of the monastic movement. (Monasticism, in its intense revulsion from the world and its rejection of marriage, had close links with certain aspects of Gnosticism and various heresies; but the Church managed to tame it and break down its threat, making it ancillary to the orthodoxy that accepted the need to carry on the business of the world and the institution of marriage.)

However, the Typhonia to which our apprentice went had certainly no connections with the pangs and rages of black magic, with the complex Gnostic constructions of esoteric myth and abstracted revolt.[79] His god was the old Ombite god whose cult had lost its high status but had resisted the influx of the Osirian myth.[80] As late as the last century B.C., a locality between Tentyris and Koptos kept the name of Typhonia (dedicated to Typhon), though at Tentyris the chief deity was Hathor, identified with Aphrodite and called Mother of Horos like Isis, and at Apollinopolis, not far off, Horos was the ruling god. Later still, the donkey, a typhonic animal, seems to have had rites at Diospolis Parva, the region of Chenoboskion.[81]

Before we pass on, we may glance at the Festival of the Nile in

Flood. On account of the way in which Osiris had become lord of fertility, with Typhon-Seth as the counter-principle of dryness and dearth, the Osirian myth, as we saw, had become linked with the Nile. The aretologies of Isis show her as mistress of the flooding. However, we do not seem to find any well defined names for the festival before the 2nd century A.D., when it is called Semasia, Festival of the Sign. Heliodoros in his romance, dealing with the area of Syene in Upper Egypt, declares, "The citizens had already given themselves up to merrymaking; for

The dual Hapy (Nile-god) tying stems of lotus and papyrus round the symbol of Union (North and South Egypt); the Nile-god in his cave under the mountains near Philai.

just at that time the Nile Festival, *Neiloia*, happened to be held, the greatest festival in Egypt. It is celebrated round about the summer solstice, when the rise of the river begins to show up, and is observed by the Egyptians more fervently than any other festival. That is because they deify the Nile and regard him as the greatest of their divinities." For the Nile does for them what the heavens do for other peoples; and "they regard the conjunction of the moist and the dry essences to be the principal cause of human existence and life"—Osiris representing the Nile, Isis the earth, and Typhon the enemy (dryness, dust-storms).[82] Diodoros, writing of the flood, stresses the flatness of the land, so that "cities and villages, as well as farms, lie on man made mounds" and the floodscene "comes to resemble the Cyclades"—clusters of small

B*

islands. Wild animals are drowned unless they escape to the higher grounds, but herds and flocks are kept in the villages and farm-houses, where fodder has been stored. "The masses of the people, relieved of their labours during the whole time of flooding, turn to recreation, feasting all the while and enjoying unhindered every device of pleasure." The Nilometer at Memphis measures the rise and fall of the flood, so that everyone is eased of anxiety and knows what the next harvest will be like, "the Egyptians having kept an accurate record of their observations of this kind over a long period of time".[83]

The pride of the Egyptians in the Nile is well put by Dion in addressing the Alexandrians: "If a man speaks in praise of water, he is praising, not men, but wells; if he talks of a good climate, he means that the land, not the people, is good; if he speaks of fish, he doesn't praise a city—how ridiculous—but the sea, a lake, a stream. Yet if anyone eulogises the Nile, you are always as elated as if you yourselves were rivers flowing from Aithiopia."[84] There was even a tale that the waters of the Nile were turned into wine.[85]

The Nile is always the Most Sacred, even when the cause of misfortune. In a legal petition of A.D. 131, a woman states that "news has reached me while staying here", at Alexandreia, "that all my property has been lost through the excessive rise of the Most Sacred Nile, buildings, lands, and dikes alike". In the second century an Oxyrhynchite papyrus gives a short list of articles that have been supplied to the strategos for the Neileia.

To the strategos, articles for the sacrifice to the Most Sacred Nile on 30 Pauni: 1 calf, 2 jars of sweet wine, 16 wafers, 16 garlands, 16 cones, 16 cakes, 16 green palmbranches, 16 reeds likewise, oil, honey, milk, every spice except frankincense.[86]

This document shows that the strategos was involved in the Nile-festivals of the towns in his area. Another papyrus of the same century tells of "a procession in honour of the Nile", costing no more than 20 drachmai. The persons taking part seem however to be part of a large festival in which there are others walking in a procession of the gods (at 56 dr.) as well as grooms, temple-

slaves, a boat for the slaves, a herald and a trumpeter. Charges
are added for the slaves' breakfast and for palms. No doubt the
komastai of the Nile carried out some sort of pageant in costume.
We hear also of the Neileia celebrated at the temple of Jupiter
Capitolinus in Arsinoe.[87]

2

More on Holidays and Festivals

APPRENTICES and perhaps hired craftsmen in general seem then to have the small allowance of some 30 days a year for their free time; but there was an abundance of events for those who were not so tied down. The festivals recorded in the accounts at Soknopaiou Nesos for A.D. 138 took up 154 days, or 156 if we add "as a special honour on the following occasions: Sarapaeia on Hadrianos 26 and a festival of Harpokrates on Tybi 16, I keramion [of wine] each day"; and this list does not include athletic or musical contests and the like.[1] There were many further days which could be made an excuse for a good time if a man had leisure.

Days on which no business was carried out were called *Hermes*. Thus, in a monthly report of customs, probably from some metropolis on the Nile in the Fayum where cargoes were re-shipped, in 104, we find blanks for the 10th, 12th, 26th. These days are labelled Hermes.[2] In another customs document, dated about 150, from Soknopaiou Nesos, which deals with goods probably going to Memphis—a journey of some five days—we find allotted to Hermes a large number of days: Hathyr 1–3, 7–12, 14–20, 24–5, 27–30; Choiak 1–3, 5–10, 13–15, 18–25, 28, 30; Tubi 1–4, 6–10, 12–20, 22–5, 28–30; and Mecheir 1–3, 6–11, 13, 15–24, 26–30. The customs officials there seem to have had an easy life.[3]

The irregular way in which Hermes-days turn up show that they depended solely on the chance of cargoes coming in. There was no holiday proper. It must have been in jest that the days without business were handed over to Hermes, who throughout the empire was the god of business, trade, and craft as well as of lucky windfalls. Heliodoros tells us, "They went off to the temple of Hermes, to whom Nausikles offered his sacrifice; for he had a special devotion for the god of trade and merchants. As soon as the victim had been immolated, Kalasiris observed their entrails a moment and showed by the play of his features that he read there a future full of mingled pleasures and pains." Again, Kalasiris says later of some departers, "May Hermes Trader and Poseidon Protector accompany and aid you. May they give you always a quiet sea and good wind, ports of easy access, towns that welcome merchants."[4]

The temples had monthly processions. In 215 at Arsinoe we find in the accounts of the temple of Jupiter Capitolinus: "to the overseer of the monthly procession, 12 dr.". Illuminations were popular. The same accounts show 4 to 8 dr. being continually paid for "oil for illumination in the grove", *sekos*: enclosure, also chapel or shrine. The shrine was no doubt kept permanently lighted. There was also "expenditures in fine oil for the illumination at the yearly festivals of the gods, 6 measures (? kotylai) daily, including the amount for anointing the priests of the five tribes in celebrations of the said gods, 6 measures of oil". Money was also spent on hiring asses loaded with trees and palm branches, oil for anointing all the bronze in the temple (a bronze worker being paid 8 dr. for the work), wreaths for the statues, shields, and images, and for "everything in the temple, oil for anointing all the statues".[5]

As another example of the sort of thing that went on at the religious festivals we may take a papyrus, probably of the late 3rd century, in which are parts of the accounts of two events, one of which was in honour of Sarapis. There is mention of a herald (twice), trumpeter, dancer (twice), comedian (twice), three trainers, a Homerist or epic reciter (twice), a Sarapis reader, the doorkeeper of that god's temple, two men, Heron and Spongos, who seem performers, and Sarapion and Amoitas pankratiasts.[6]

Comedian, *komoidos*, no doubt means someone who can do any sort of turn. The presence of trainers and pankratiasts (athletes who were both boxers and wrestlers) suggests athletic events; but the pankratiasts may merely have been present as honoured citizens. The entry about calf's blood is strange; for if it merely concerned a victim, we should find "a calf". The blood must have had some special use. Odd too is "gifts of the dogheaded one". A magical papyrus declares "the blood of the black dog-headed one shall be shed", but here the reference is probably to an official enacting the part of Anubis, the dogheaded guardian of Osiris, who might well be named simply as *kynokephalos*.[7]

A document, probably from the Fayum, of the 2nd century gives us accounts of expenses for various festivals—sucking pigs, hens, wine, crowns, and so on. Taxes are not mentioned. The festivals include the Souchia, Sarapeia, Kepouria, Isieia, Delia, Demetria, Rhodophoria, Panteleia, and an enigmatic Merobollia. Some of these are Greek. The Delia reminds us of the days when under the Ptolemies Egypt dominated the seas of the Eastern Mediter-ranean, and Delos was important. Demeter was identified with Isis by the Greeks of Egypt and elsewhere; but as the list includes a definite festival of Isis, the Demetria may have been generally Greek in character. The Rhodophoria we have already noticed. The Souchia celebrated the native Souchos, the crocodile-god. The Festival of Gardens and the Isis feast seem to represent a combination brought about by the goddess's role as patroness of cultivated plants, as *frugifera*. There is also a mutilated word *ame . . . sois*, which we may certainly read as the Amesysia or harvest-festival, which seems to correspond to a New Year celebra-tion or Wreath-bearing festival. The total effect is of a mixture of Greek and Egyptian elements, with the former dominant.

The term *Sponde* (or libation) *of Dionysos*, which occurs in a considerable number of documents, throws light on harvest-customs. Though we have no direct evidence, we may surmise that once the vine-dresser set aside some of the wine for Dionysos; by the time we find references to the *sponde* in documents, it appears as an extra-payment in various connections. But the likelihood that it was once a kind of firstfruits is increased by the fact that still in modern Egypt the firstfruits of the cornfield are treated with great respect. "Numbers of people are given presents of corn by the owner of the field; these gifts of the firstfruits are bestowed on some of the poorest people in the village, as well as on the barber, the *mueddin*, the *zummareh*-player, the carpenter, and the *fukaha* (poor men who recite the Koran in mosques, etc.)." The low ranks of the recipients is characteristic of a custom in the last stages of decay. The *Kornbraut* or cornbride existed from Pharaonic times and is still known to the fellahin; it is plucked by hand before any corn is cut.

Dionysos-Osiris was considered the inventor of wine, who taught men how to use it; Isis too had become connected with the vine. Among the Greeks Dionysos presided over the "early vintage" as well as the vintage proper. His share or libation had, however, become transferred to human beings. We find a sublessee obliged to "provide a pig worth 20 dr." at the vintage. In Byzantine times we meet "customery offerings and harvest gifts, *trygetika*", as well as "festival-gifts and *trygetika*" for a worker-slave. In A.D. 139 (or 149) a lessor stipulates an extra-payment of 2 dr. for the wine-press festival. A 6th-century document states that the tenants of vineland had to give the "customary libation" to the lessor from the first filled tub; and a similar allowance appears in the next century. Though these texts are late, they certainly deal with long-standing custom. The term used for the first wine, *protolena*, is found in a 3rd century ostrakon.

The tax called *apomoira* had affinities with the *sponde*. It was laid on vineyards and gardenlands from B.C. 264, the vineyard paying in kind (a sixth) and the *paradeisoi* in money to the cult of the Goddess Philadelphos. The change in the way the payments were made seems connected with the identification of the dead queen Arsinoe II with Isis-Aphrodite. The *sponde* was fixed at a definite sum, *oktadrachmos*, and finally paid in fractions of eight, being set down normally at the end of entries—whereas the *apomoira* was always calculated on the annual output. (Other *spondai* were that given by the charterer of a ship to the captain, *kybernetes*, and the *sponde Mempheos*, which may be connected with the ship's passage through the harbour of Memphis. In one papyrus the captain stipulates for actual wine, a *keramion*, for "libation" on arrival at the port of destination. Here we probably see a transference from ancient customs of sacrifice to the Nile.)

To return to harvests: we find a small item in some land-leases, "for the boys" (or children), which was later called simply *ta paidika*. Children were employed in lighter jobs—"sweeping up and carrying leaves", "gathering olives" (girls), "winnowing wheat", scaring birds and so on. Their remuneration is called *sponde* in a papyrus of A.D. 130, but by that time that term was used for gratuities of this sort in general. The children may be those of the lessor or other children, related or not; there were few slaves. What they got seems a traditional amount of corn or (later) a corresponding sum of money. In three Hermopolite papyri "the children" get ½ art. wheat (A.D. 125), or barley (A.D. 150). In vineyards the children also got some of the product:

The Nile (from an ossuary at Rome).

50 cadi from a place of 4 ar. in A.D. 569. The money sum (a *tetradrachmyos*) occurs in two papyri where the children deal with a grass-crop and a fowlhouse formerly a camel-stable—though in the latter case the additional payment consists of cocks, hens, eggs, and the children may have been paid in the same way.

What seems another traditional festival-payment commuted into money is the *thallos*, bough, which turns up with such various things as auction-bids and baby-nursing. The *thallos* was connected with the Amesysia, with a significance like that of the Roman *strena*—a token of good luck and new life. In the list of festivals mentioned above, the Amesysia gets two hens, 20 kotylai of rhaphanos-oil, and an extra keramion of Memphite wine. *Thallos* also was used of a porridge for festivals; in 188 B.C. it is described as wheat-porridge; and it is best known from the distributions made in Alexandreia on the anniversary of its foundation. "This is indicative of the popularity and extensive use of thallos at festivals; it has become a term for *heortika* in general (allowance made for gifts of wine generally designated by *sponde*)." We can sum up by saying that there is much evidence for festival-distributions at such important agricultural moments as harvest, but that much of our material comes from legal documents where the original nature of *sponde*, *thallos*, and so on, is disguised.[8]

There were various ceremonies and festivals connected with the imperial family. Holidays were proclaimed on the accession of an emperor. We have papyri dealing with Nero, Hadrian, Pertinax, Maximus. Sometimes the news took a good while to get around. The proclamation of Nero at Oxyrhynchos was dated 17 November, 35 days after Claudius' death, while at Elephantine the news was still unknown on 28 November.[9] A document connected with the accession of Hadrian in 117 from Heptakomia, the capital of the Apollonopolite Nome, shows that some sort of pageant was staged; for it gives us the text of a duet sung between the god Apollo and a representative of the citizens, perhaps personifying Demos. The choice of words and the style show that the text was for singing; and we may take it to be the work of some local poet.

> [*Apollon*]   Having just mounted aloft with Trajan in
> my white-horsed chariot, I come to you, People,
> no Unknown God, Phoibos, to proclaim
> the new Lord Hadrian whom all things serve
> because of his own virtue and the fate
> of his divine father.
>
> [*Demos*]   Let's make merry,
> let's kindle all our hearths in sacrifices,
> let's give up all our souls to laughter now,
> to the wine of the fountains and the unguents of
> the gymnasia: for all of which we're indebted
> to the reverence that our Strategos feels
> for this Our Lord, and to the zeal he shows
> on our behalf . . . [10]

The document is an official draft, coming from the archives of the strategos. The emperor's fate is his *tyche* or genius. Many of the listeners, it seems, would not know of Phoibos: hence his boost of himself as no unknown god. The relation of Hadrian to Trajan is perhaps stressed because rumours had spread all over the empire that the latter had not carried out Hadrian's adoption.[11] The fountains would be artificial constructions pouring out a doubtless limited amount of wine and beer.[12]

At Delphoi also, more appropriately, the citizens brought in Apollo to support the new ruler, as we learn from an inscription. Hadrian praises the city as ancient and noble, and goes on: "and not least because you showed your zeal by rejoicing at my accession to the rule and by invoking the Pythian god Apollo to bless me . . . I confirm your liberty and your autonomy and all the gifts granted to you of old, especially those granted by the divine Trajan."[13] All the cities and important societies hurried to send embassies and messages at an accession; and we have two more of Hadrian's replies, though they are not to Egyptians:

[To the magistrates, senate and people of Astypalaia] From your ambassador Petronios Herakon and from your enactment, I have learned that you were pleased at my taking over the paternal rule. I praise you for that.

[To the Synod of the Neoi in Pergamon] When I learned from your letter and your ambassador Klaudios Kyros that you expressed yourselves as sharing feelings of joy on our behalf, I thought it a proof of your being good men. Farewell.[14]

Clearly the imperial secretariate must have found it difficult to make up different replies to the vast number of congratulations.

Hadrian died in 138; but we find his cult persisting for many years. On 2 July 181 a man of Oxyrhynchos sent a request for a will to be opened—addressing not the strategos whom in other such documents appears as competent to do the opening, but two "ex-priests of the revered Hadrianeion, appointed for the opening of wills".[15] Then in 199 an ex-highpriest of Hadrian at Arsinoe issued formal notices to his wife and daughter, warning them that he meant to free some slaves and that if they caused any trouble the temple of Sarapis at Alexandreia would get a property which would otherwise be theirs. The slaves are to be freed "under sanction of Zeus, Earth, and Sun."[16]

A document of 163-4, from Oxyrhynchos, mentions a procession in honour of the emperors Antoninus and Verus. A sacred virgin, Taophryonis—represented by the priest of Athena-Thoeris, Isis, Sarapis and associated gods—has been chosen by the corporation, *plethos*, of priests to participate in the ceremony.[17]

Every month there were the August Days on which the accession and birthday of the emperor as well as the birthdays of other members of his house were honoured; but these can have been no more than formal matters without any effect on people in general.[18] In the Soknopaiou Nesos' accounts only one entry refers to the imperial cults: "For the purchase of incense and expenses at the Nativity of the deified Augusti, 40 dr." In the temple of Jupiter Capitolinus at Arsinoe there was naturally more attention paid to the State-cult:

(*In Choiak*) For the holiday, proclaiming Our Lord Caesar Marcus Aurelius Antoninus, 24 dr.

(*In one month*) 1st: Holiday on account of the 10th Anniversary and the victory of Our Lord the Emperor Severus Alexander: crowning in the temple the images, shields, and all statues . . . dr: oil for illumination, 4 dr. *19th*: Holiday because of the Victory of the God Severus Father of the Lord Emperor Severus Antoninus: crowning the statues in the temple 16 dr.: oil for illumination in the grove, 4 dr. *25th*: Holiday for the Safety and Everlasting Life of the Lord Emperor Severus Antoninus: crowning everything in the temple . . . oil for illumination in the grave.

(*Another month*) For the sale of iron from the winch built for raising the colossal divine statue of Our Lord the Emperor Severus Antoninus: 52 minai at 5 dr. per mina, 260 dr. *18th*: Holiday and festival for the raising of the statue of the Lord Emperor Severus Antoninus and for crowning everything on the shrine as above, 16 dr.; oil for illumination in the grove, 4 dr. *20th*: On the visit of the most illustrious Prefect Septimius Heraclitus: crowning everything, etc. Fee of Orator for making a speech in the presence of the most illustrious Prefect Septimius Heraclitus in acknowledgment of the Victory which he contributed to the possessions of the god, and of other gifts: 60 dr.

(*Another month*) 5th: Holiday for the Victory and Safety of the Lord

Emperor Severus Antoninus: crowning, etc. *9th*: Birthday of the Lord Emperor, etc. *12–3th*: Holidays for the Safety and Victory of the Lord Emperor, etc. *16th*: Birthday of the Divine Severus, etc. *19th*: Holiday for the Proclamation of Julia Domna as Mother of the Invincible Camps, etc. *26th*: Anniversary of the Foundation of Rome, etc.[19]

But even here the native crocodile god Souchos was not forgotten.

An amusing document dated about A.D. 200 mentions the Festival of the King, which is presumably the usual celebration of the emperor's birthday, though it might possibly be a holiday in honour of the accession of Caracalla (between November 197 and May 198). The writer seems to be trying out his hand and copies bits of documents: a petition to a prefect, a letter from the same prefect, a jingling proverbial statement, the start of a private letter by the man who made the petition, then on the verso another letter of the prefect.

To Magnius Felix Crescentillianus, prefect of Egypt, supplication from Ammonion also called . . .

Magnius Felix to the strategoi of the Heptanomia, greeting. I have assigned to the most high epistrategoi the appeals concerning the office of gymnasiarch and agoranomos, and an edict has been published about this in the Most Illustrious City of Alexandreia . . .

A little boy must eat bread, to nibble salt too is good, but sauce is not for the lad. And if wine he'd suck, give him your knuckles.

Greetings, Lady Diogenis, I Ammonion address you.

Magnius Felix to the strategoi of the Heptanomia and the Arsinoitte nome, greeting. I would have you know that the Most Divine Kings granted me the money from the so-called 8–drachma tax, and you have not yet up to the present made any payment. If then the centurions are long in your districts, let them speedily attend at the Most Illustrious City of the Alexandrians and celebrate the Festival of the King. Otherwise, if anyone disobeys this my order . . .

The appeal about the gymnasiarchy must be one of the many we know as the town-offices began to become crushing burdens. The part played by the centurion is not clear, as army-officers were not normally connected with the collection of taxes; but there may have been some special circumstances. Also, the order of recall to Alexandreia suggests some special importance in the festival. In the code of manners for small boys, the last sentence is found also in Souidas and the proverb-collectors.

At times the gymnasiarch paid for shows. In a regulation of 114–17, in which the prefect orders the reduction of the financial charges imposed on the gymnasiarchs of Hermopolis, we read that "the costs of the Torchlight Procession, which according to custom fell on the Gymnasiarchy, should be reduced more than that given by the . . . " Unfortunately here the papyrus breaks off. We have an order of the late 2nd or early 3rd century from a gymnasiarch for the payment of 600 dr. in connection with *theorika*, spectacles.[20] In the Byzantine period (7th century) we have an account of moneys received or expended. If the document records a collection, one column represents what has come in from the corporations of various trades, the other what has been got as the result of collecting by certain individuals, each from a particular street. The moneys appear to be meant for a festival; as the latter part of the accounts seems related to the Green Faction at the races, possibly the first part was related to the Blue Faction.[21]

On account of its lack of the usual municipal developments that went on in the rest of the empire in the first and second centuries A.D., Egypt seems to have had few civic benefactions in the towns. Citizens could contribute to festivals, but we have little record of such acts. The Horion who in 202 endowed the athletic games at Oxyrhynchos was exceptional.[22] A fragmentary copy of a petition seems to show a man wanting to make some benefaction to his hometown for the purposes of a festival of Antinoos.

The army had its Saturnalia and no doubt many other festivals of its own, such as are detailed in a papyrus from Dura-Europos on the Euphrates, which was found among military archives in the temple of Artemis Szzanathcona, dated 223–5. In its list is twice mentioned the *Rosalie Signorum*, which seems certainly the rose-festival of joyous fertility in its army application: the roses being wreathed round the standards, which always played an important part in army-rites and at times had sacrifices made to them.[24]

The veteran Gemellus, round about 100, writes, "Send 10 cocks for the Saturnalia, and for Gemella's birthday send some dainties . . . and an artaba of wheaten bread." A letter of the late 3rd or 4th century with some gaps runs: "From . . . s Gaianus, my good brother Agenor, I received at once, about the day of the Saturnalia, what you despatched to me. I should have myself sent more speedily to you if I had had more soldiers with me; but . . . went back and we cannot catch a single animal. I send for your use . . . I pray, my dear brother, for your lasting health and prosperity." Agenor is a prefect, probably of a legion; and the man who writes to him must be of high rank since he puts his own name first and uses a breezy familiar tone. He is used to having a number of soldiers at his disposal and his handwriting suggests that he was more accustomed to Latin than Greek. Apparently he had been out on an official hunt, using soldiers; the quarry would be beasts for the large shows, no doubt for transport to Rome.

A holiday brought in to celebrate some historical event might go on for quite a long time, because the reasons for its origin still remained significant or because people simply wanted any excuse for merrymaking. Thus, a petition of 200-2 reminds the emperor of "the loyalty, fidelity and friendship towards the Romans which the Oxyrhynchites have shown by helping them in the war against the Jews and in continuing till the present to celebrate the Day of Victory by a yearly festival". The strong term *polemos* is used for the war and it is not clear if the outbreak under Hadrian is meant. In any event, however, the wording shows that the Oxyrhynchites prided themselves on prolonging the festival over a considerable period. It also incidentally shows that they do not themselves feel "Romans", an integrated part of the empire.

Social clubs in towns and villages were common. They did much winedrinking and also played a part in organising local festivals. Country festivals were already well organised under the Ptolemies. A papyrus, dated about 250 B.C., deals with agricultural accounts and contributions for religious festivals. It has a list of *desmai* (bundles) made up on successive days by workers on a number of estates or *kleroi*. A damaged section sets out the contributions made by persons who seem to include an oikonomos and two secretaries, *grammateis*, for religious festivals; the contributors are Greek and so are the deities: Theos Soter and Basilissa (Queen: Berenike, wife of Ptolemaios I), Artemis, Aphrodite, Hermes, Herakles. In four cases there is a further entry, *to mousikon*, which is perhaps a contribution to a specific festival of the Muses, but more likely to the cost of the musical performances at all the festivals. Probably all the persons were members of an association or club that organised the celebrations. Another papyrus gives the letter of Kleon to his father Zenon, asking for some food (*opsinion*) and wine, and something (?the same) for the Hermaia and the Mouseia. "Everyone has already contributed." We also have the accounts of a synthiasos of 90 B.C. where, on the verso, various persons undertake to contribute such necessaries for a meeting as jars of wine, *mousika*, wreaths, oil, and so on.

A lease from Hermopolis of A.D. 139 (or 149) deals with a vineyard in which are also palms, olives and nuts. The lessor provides reeds, vine-supports, and water for irrigation in certain months; the yearly rent is 2 art. of dry pressed dates, the produce of one palm tree chosen by the lessor, 1 art. of bread, 1 load of dry wood, 10 loaves of bread, 2 kotylai of oil, and 2 dr. for the Festival of the Winepress. From the 2nd or 3rd century, of undefined locality, comes:

Account for Drinking Party: 3 jars (of wine) 42 dr. Meat: 21 dr. 2 ob. Total 63 dr. 2 ob. Divided among 5 men: 12 dr. 4 ob. each

This may belong to an occasional party or club. The clubs that we know of show some fifteen to twenty members in attendance; in one the members paid 100 dr. each and the balance was carried on to the club funds. Our document may indeed be merely the bill presented by some tavern-keeper.[25]

Philosophers and moralists tended to see only a riotous and demoralising waste of time in such matter. Philon of Alexandreia in the 1st century describes the passion for entertainment. In every festival and gathering of men the outstanding points are the way men relax and let go; they give themselves up to "drunkenness, deep drinking, revelry, luxury, amusement, music at the doors, nightlong banquets, violent acts of insolence, practices of intemperance, indulgence of folly, pursuits of shameful things, an utter destruction and renunciation of the good, wakefulness at night for the satisfaction of immoderate appetites, sleep by day when it is the right time to be awake, a topsyturvying of the laws of nature."[26] Such, he says, are the festivals of those who call themselves happy men—less guilty when carried on inside houses, but intolerable when made public spectacles in the temples:

performing unhallowed sacrifices, offering victims that ought not to be sacrificed, and prayers such as should never be accomplished; celebrating impious mysteries and profane rites, displaying a bastard piety, an adulterated holiness, an impure purity, a falsified truth, a debauched service of God.

They bathe bodies, but do not purify souls; they search victims for any flaw, but do not bother about polluted souls.

The idiom here should be noted. The image of a world turned upside down, in which nothing is what it seems and everything has been twisted into its opposite, will come up many times in our inquiry, especially when we come to the poet Nonnos, who summarises all the trends of the Graeco-Roman world in dissolution. We have already noted one form of the image in magical formulas.

Canopos, on the canal between Alexandreia and the Nile, was a spot that concentrated all the tendencies denounced by Philon. Before Alexandreia it had been the capital of the Menelaite nome and perhaps the leading port of the Delta; but when Alexandreia was founded, it lost its importance, while retaining a certain religious and mercantile prominence as well as being the pleasure-resort for the folk of the capital. It produced tissues, scents, salted fish, confectionaries, and sent out henna and the broad brimmed hats that the Alexandrians called *Kanobika petasa*. It had a celebrated temple of Sarapis, to which pilgrims came for cures; and nearby, at Menouthis, was a temple of Isis. According to Rufinos, these sanctuaries were even more splendid than those of Alexandreia. The Council of Priests held at Canopos to divinise the daughter of Ptolemaios III, dead at the age of nine, had its decree set out in the three scripts (hieroglyphic, demotic, Greek) and sent round to the most important temples: the copy known as the Rosetta Stone played an important part in the deciphering of hieroglyphic. Canopos thus successfully mingled piety and pleasure. Strabon describes the holiday boats of Eleusis and Canopos, the flute-playing and dances aboard, the many resorts along the banks.[27] Some four centuries later Ammianus Marcellinus wrote of it as "a place extremely well supplied with good inns, of a most wholesome climate, with refreshing breezes, so that anyone who resides in that district might think himself out of our world while he listens to the breezes murmuring through the sunny air."[28]

A mosaic found at Praeneste gives a panorama of Graeco-Roman Egypt, with emphasis on the festival aspects. (The original was perhaps of the early Ptolemaic period, the surviving mosaic seems late Hellenistic, but in essentials the picture shows us Roman Egypt as well.) The upper part is a kind of zoological atlas of the Sudan with its real and imaginary beasts. The lower part shows us Egypt—the Delta in particular—at the time of the flooding. In the right-hand corner we see a peasant's house with its dovecote. The man rushes out after his wife, who stands in the garden gazing at a boat in which are soldiers. Hippopotami and crocodiles fill the left-hand corner. Two buildings appear in the middle of the lower part. One is a splendid pavilion over the front of which hangs a large curtain; inside is a band of Roman soldiers preparing for a festival; drinking-horns and a big krater-bowl are set out. A laurel-wreathed officer sounds a horn, apparently as a signal to the soldiers coming up in an army rowing boat, *liburnica*; he is welcomed by a woman with a palm branch, who offers him a garland or diadem. Behind the pavilion is a tower-villa with a garden in an enclosure; and nearby is a group of civilians, some of whom are women, under the shade of a vine-covered pergola. These drink to a musical accompaniment, a

woman singing to a lyre (probably in honour of the victorious general).

Behind these buildings run two bands of decoration. In the middle one, a religious procession passes through a small shrine. Two men in front bear a stretcher with a sacred symbol. In the rear are standard-bearers and a congregation of devotees. Near the temple stands a statue of Anubis on a base. Behind the pergola is a sacred enclosure and an osier-barn, *moschotrophion*, where calves are perhaps reared for sacrifice. Before the barn-entrance two men chat, one of them holding a fork. A third man drives two oxen or calves to the water. Ibises fly round the barn.

Temples fill the last band. The biggest temple, behind the small shrine, owns two pylons and huge Egyptian statues near the main entry. Three other temples stand behind the pergola and the barn: an ibis-shrine, *ibieion*, a two-towered typical Egyptian shrine, a Graeco-Roman temple. The water is covered with animals, flowers, native canoes (one piled with lotuses), and two big cabined boats for pleasure and hunting.[29]

Apart from the public events there were many parties for birthdays and the like. The veteran Gemellus had a partiality for birthdays.[30] Letters show festival-matters entangled with the ordinary run of happenings and activities. Here are two of the 2nd century.

Korbolon to Herakleides, greeting. I sent you the key by Horion and the piece of the lock by Onnophris the camel-driver of Apollonios. In the former packet I enclosed a pattern of white-violet colour. Please be good enough to match it and buy me 2 dr.'s weight and send it along by any messenger you can find, for the tunic's to be woven at once. I got everything you told me to expect by Onnophris safely. By the same Onnophris I send you 6 quarts of good apples. I thank all the gods to think that I came on Ploution in the Oxyrhynchite nome.

Don't think I took no trouble about the key. The reason is that the smith's a long way from us. I'm surprised you didn't see your way to let me have what I asked you to send by Onnophris, especially when I wanted it for a festival. Please do buy me a silver seal and send to me as quick as you can. Take care that Onnophris buys me what Eirene's mother told him. I told him that Syntrophos said nothing more should be given to Amarantos on my account. Let me know what you've given him so I may settle accounts with him, otherwise I and my son will come and do it.

I had the big cheeses from Onnophris. But I didn't want big ones, I wanted small ones. Let me know of anything you want and I'll gladly do it. Farewell, 1 Pauni.

[PS] Send me an obol's worth of cake for my nephew.[31]

We see how camel drivers and persons moving about with a beast of burden were liable to be used as parcel-carriers. What is not clear is whether a man like Onnophris worked as such a carrier or was used by others while doing a job for his master (here Apollonios). In the next letter we see festivals across the worries caused by taxes, debts, and pawnings:

Dionysios to his mother Tetheus, greeting. I've had all the letters about which you write—and as for the wheat that the collectors have demanded from you, it's due all right but I'd forgotten to make any order for payment. However I've paid the naubion and other taxes in full. Don't be worried that the matter on which I wrote to Theon hasn't been carried out and that I've been so long taken up with Pausirion's business to no avail . . .

Please receive from Chairemon, bearer of this letter, 112 dr. of silver, of which you'll give to my friend Sarapion son of Apei 100 dr. and redeem my clothes, with 8 dr. to meet the interest, and keep 4 dr. for yourself for the festival's expenses. If I'd had more, I'd have forwarded a larger sum, but I've borrowed to send even this. So pay him the money and get my clothes back safe and put them in a secure place.

Don't be anxious about us, there's nothing the matter with us and we're on good terms with one another. Theonas salutes you. Salute the boys Apion and his brother Hermatois, Dionytas, those with Nike and little Thaisous, all those with . . . , Heras and his household, Leontas with his nose in the air and his household, those with Taamois, and Thermoutharion. Goodbye. 20th of month Kaisareios.

[PS] Send me word about this at once after the festival, whether you got the money and whether you recovered my clothes. Salute Dionytas and Theon.

A letter of the late 2nd century deals with a visit to a festival and arrangement made about a young girl, apparently the daughter of the man to whom the letter was written:

Greeting, my dear sir, Apolinarios, from Diogenes your friend. As I have encountered a man on his way to you, I greet you most kindly and pray all the gods for your safety . . . [some three lines missing] I came to the Great Festival. As for the little girl, I was present till she sailed, and everything was provided for her, so that on your return you'll bear me witness. Have no more anxiety about your household than if you were yourself there, I sent the letter to the little girl and made the night-strategos sleep on guard at the house. Salute my friend Ploutogenes. Sir, I pray for your health. If it's no bother, inquire of Antinoos if he bought the cloak for your child, and if he didn't, buy it. [Addressed] To Apolinarios . . . *presbeutes* [legate], from Diogenes, linen-merchant.

We know of night-strategoi at Hermopolis in the 4th century; and may assume that they existed in other large towns of Egypt. Where the present letter was written is uncertain. What is odd is to find the official guarding a private house; but possibly Apolinarios was a man of some importance.

From probably the 3rd century comes a letter in which again a festival appears casually:

Troilos to his sister Mazas [or Mazatis], greeting. Above all I pray you're doing well and the child too, bless him. I wanted to send the child a few presents, but a call for post-beasts had suddenly come up and the camel gone unexpectedly off. As for the vintage of your places, Sarmates took it lawfully with the knowledge of me and Aion, but the greater part through Aion, please sister hurry up making my tunic, so when I come to you after the festival I may find it done, Herakleides paying the wages. Get from Tamoun the 8 pounds . . .

Mazas is no doubt his wife. We have another letter of his, which is from Oxyrhynchos and mentions some of the same people. I cite it for the way it fills out the social picture of Troilos and his group:

Troilos to his sister Maz, greeting. You'll do well to have my white tunic made quick so I may find it made if I come to you. I've written to Herakleides too, so you may receive my tools and the weavers' wages, and I want to know how you're hurrying on its making. The

purple is put with the tools. Take care you send the latter to Thermouthion at Alexandreia, as we may be able to load 2 camels with
wheat for you and send them along. See that my slave-girl sticks to
her work, and if Tamoun bears a child make her look after it well.
Be sure you have my tunic properly made and see they put good
measure into it and no stinginess about the colouring. Buy a donkey
for Niketes so he'll be able to carry out your business, and reply to
me if you want anything. I salute Heras. I pray for your health.

[P.S.] I've written to Herakleides to give Tamoun 3000 dr.[32]

From the internal evidence this letter looks as if it had been

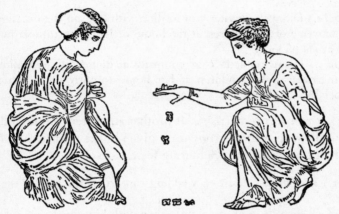

Two women playing kuncklebones (painting on marble from Herculaneum).

written shortly before the other. The remark about Tamoun
perhaps means that she must not expose the child.

We have many private invitations to parties. Often the hour
is the ninth: about 3 o'clock in the afternoon. And the day is
"tomorrow". Doubtless the notes merely formalised an invitation
already made by word of mouth. The places for the party vary
from the home to a temple or the gymnasion.[33] In one invitation
the gymnasion is the place and the occasion is the crowning of
a man's son (at entry into some town-office).[34] Sarapis' Temple
was a favourite place for parties, which were thus given a religious
tinge, a sense of the beloved god's participation. The dinner
merges with the communion.

(2nd c.) Chairemon requests your company at dinner at the Table of the Lord Sarapis at the Sarapieion tomorrow, 15th, at 9 o'clock.

(late 2nd or 3rd c.) The *dedarchos* invites you to his party on the 6th day before the Kalends at 8 o'clock.[35]

Here a cavalry officer gives the party, a *decurio*, who uses the Latin calendar. In the next, the meeting occurs at an official's house, but apparently because the groom is his son:

(2nd c.?) Agathos invites you to dine on the occasion of his daughter's wedding, tomorrow, 16th, at 2 o'clock, at the house of the Xystarch, where . . . lives.

(2nd c.) Dionysios invites you to dine with him on the occasion of the marriage of his children at the house of Ischyrion tomorrow the 30th at (?) o'clock.

(3rd c.) Herais requests your company at dinner in celebration of the marriage of her children at her house tomorrow the 5th at 9 o'clock.[36]

The last pair seems marriages of brother and sister; but no indication as to whom the persons are is given in the next item, which no doubt concerns the celebrating feast.

(3rd c.) Eros invites you to a wedding tomorrow the 29th at the 9th hour.[37]

(3rd c.) Heratheon invites you to dine with him on the occasion of his Examination, *epikrisis*, at his house tomorrow the 5th at the 9th hour.

(5th c.) To my Lord Makarios from Gennadios, speculator. Deign to gladden the Birthday Festival of my son Gennadios by dining with us on the 16th at 7 o'clock.[38]

After having undergone the *epikrisis* a youth was accepted into the gymnasion, into the privileged class. The normal age for the examination, which entailed proof that the youth in question came from parents of the privileged class, was at puberty, about 13 years, since at 14 he became liable to tax. The document here may have an address on the back ("to Chailamon, son of Elassios"), but as these words are in different hand thay may not belong to the invitation. Usually invitations were handed in direct and bore no address. The fifth-century letter shows the pompous style that came in with the Byzantine period, the acute sense of class differences. The speculator was originally an army scout, but in the empire he became a special adjutant, messenger, or body-guard of a general.

There is no need to detail here the minor games and pastimes of the Graeco-Roman world, in which Egypt shared. The Greeks brought in games like five-stones: tossing knucklebones up and catching them on the back of the hand—though simple games with bones, stones, nuts, and so on, are universal, and some Egyptian game of a like kind may well have existed. Flash-fingers (to use the Latin name) was another widespread game: two people simultaneously held up right hands with some of the fingers extended, and whoever first called out the total was winner. Nonnos mentions the Greek game of *kottabos*, in which a small amount of wine was thrown at a mark such as a saucer floating in a krater; but this game seems to have died out early in Hellenistic times, at least in Alexandreia; for Callimachos in his *Vigil* uses the term *kottabia* generally for prizes set up at night festivals.

> He that stays awake till the end will get the cake
> and a kiss from any girl in the party he'll take,
> or else from any lad, if he stays awake.

These cakes, provided for night parties in which everyone had to keep dancing in order not to fall asleep, were called happy-cakes "because the winners were happy to get them". Euboulos describes this sort of favour in some lines on the family festival held ten days after a birth, when the baby was given its name:

> Ladies, dance all night with open eyes—
> the baby's first day this is.
> Three ribbons I'll provide as the winning-prize,
> five apples and nine kisses.

Dionysios Chalkous (Bronze) in his *Elegies*, we may note, uses the kottabos game to describe a Dionysiac Gymnasion:

C

We the lovesick add a third kottabos prize
in Bromios' Gymnasion to stand
for you. All present, now insert their hands
inside the cups they use as balls, and first
measure with eyes the air beyond the couch:
see over how much space the drops must reach.[39]

Philon tells us, "Those who play with nuts are used, when setting three nuts on the floor, to set one more on top, producing a figure like a pyramid." At Memphis, we learn, what gave the answer to anyone consulting the oracle was the chance words heard outside from boys at play. "Lads at play announce the

Game of Morra or Flashfinger.

purpose of the god and this form of divination has proved to be free from falsehood."[40]

Dice were common throughout the Graeco-Roman world, and board-games were popular. We have already seen a board-game in a myth of death ritual; and Egypt has a strong claim for the origination of such games through magical practices. By far the oldest known board with pieces was found in a predynastic cemetery at El-Mahasna, some eight miles north of Abydos.

A large grave containing six burials, which had been partially plundered. At the south end of the grave were standing eight pottery vases, and the four clay objects were found with them. They are hollow and pierced for suspension, and when shaken make a noise like a rattle. They may have been part of the outfit of a medicineman, or may have been put to the more prosaic use of goat or sheep bells. The ivory comb was also found at this end of the grave . . . Bunches of imitation garlic and a large number of beads were found. At the other end of the grave was found a clay gaming-board. This is undoubtedly the origin of the sign "men" in the hieroglyphics. Ivory bracelets, clay objects of unknown use, and a fragment of a clay wand complete this group.

The board was about 7 by 2¾ inches, standing on two low cross-pieces, divided into 2 by 6 cells; there were 11 conical pieces, two of them some three times taller than the others (about 1 inch high). We see two board-games being played in wall-paintings of the 5th dynasty, in the tomb of a court-scribe; and again on the walls at Ben-hassan. One game is called *Sen't* and seems a race-game, and the other is called *Bowl*. A Theban inscription gives the name of a third game, *T'au*, robbers, which is also pictured in the *Book of the Dead*. It is the game that the dead man plays: at Medinat-Habu Ramses III is shown playing it with Isis. It was certainly a war-game. The race-game spread to Palestine, Sumer, Elam, and Assyria. A board at Thebai has ten carved ivory pins, half with dogheads, half with jackalheads. In the drawer of a board of Queen Hatshopu were 20 lionheaded men, ten of light wood, nine of dark, with one of ivory (doubtless a replacement). A conventionalised terra-cotta plaque of the Queen of Heaven found at Gezer in Palestine had a series of holes round the sides and up the middle, which would be identical in number with those in the Egyptian game, if the holes in the head were taken as one; several of the holes showed small circular spots of darker red as if pieces had been fixed in them.[41]

Platon, mentioning the games *petteia* and *kybeia* at Athenai, states that they had come from Egypt; and he was probably right in ultimate terms. He attributes their invention to Thoth. It is of interest that the term *dogs*, which we saw earlier as a name for pieces, carried on in Greece. The games Platon cites were no doubt not the only games played at Athens, but seem the ones that needed the most care and practice. They were probably particular games, not classes, though in time *kybeia* came to mean games with dices and *petteia* those without.[42] Again among the Romans, with dice or marked knucklebones, the term *dogs* comes up: the best throw (1.3, 4.6) was called Venus, the worst (1.1,1.1) the Dogs. Hence the lament of Propertius:

> While with the lucky dice I tried for Venus
> the cursed Dogs kept always turning up.

The bad throws are made prophetic of the love-disaster recorded in the following lines; they also express the impotence he feels

Boardgame (B.M. papyrus).

before the two girls with whom he is drinking. The very next lines run: "I was deaf to their singing, blind to their naked charms . . ." and two lines further on, Cynthia breaks in on the party.[43] A magical nexus is still obscurely felt.

As the Egyptians had their Robbers, so the Romans in their war-game had *Latrones*, Soldiers (the word later meaning Robbers or Brigands). Their race-game, *Twelve Lines*, is identical with the Egyptian game shown at Ak-hor.[44] It was carried by soldiers to the empire's frontiers. One of its boards was found at Holt in Denbyshire, dated the 1st century A.D., while another has come from tombs of Blemmyes kings and nobles at Qustul, a little north of the Nile's second cataract. The fine Qustul board had 30 pieces, half of ivory, half of ebony.[45] *Latrunculi*, the war-game, was also carried all over the empire by legionaries. Vopiscus says that the winner was hailed as *imperator*.[46]

A game that seems to have originated in Alexandreia involved the use of discs numbered 1–15; an ivory set in the British Museum has a design in relief on the obverse: for instance, two Muses or the head of the Sungod—on the reverse, the number in both Greek and Latin numerals and a description of the design, Mousai, Helios. Boards of Twelve-Lines are found with inscriptions in 36 letters, such as VICTOR VINCAS NABICE FEELIX SALBUS REDIAS (Victor, Conquerer, Sail Happy, Return Safe), PATRIA SANCTA FACIAS VTMEOS SALVOS VIDEAM (Holy Fatherland Ensure That I See My Own Ones Safe), VENARI LAVARI LVDERE RIDERE OCCEST VIVERE (Embrace Bathe Play Laugh That's Life). One found in a tomb near a gate at Rome summons up a picture of the Circus: CIRCVS PLENVS CLAMOR INGENS IANVAE TE (NSAE?) (Circus Full, Huge Shouting, Door Bursting). The contorniates or coinlike discs of bronze used as counters often have representations of such things as a chariot-race and a head of Alexander or a water-organ and a head of Nero. (Organs were played at the big shows.)[47]

The Twelve-Lines of the Roman game were in late times interpreted as standing for the zodiac. At Pompeius' third triumph in 61 B.C. a board-table, *alveus lusorius*, of gold and jewels was borne; in its centre was a golden moon of 30 lb weight. Such imagery may have drawn on a tradition, however vague now and confused, that games had once expressed the struggle of life and death, of cosmic conflict and renewal.[48]

Private festivals included celebrations of the dead on the date of their death, which thus became a sort of birth into a new life. Such celebrations were of incalculable importance in the early days of Christianity when the groups of the faithful took communion with their local martyr on the day of his death-birth. That development does not here concern us; but its preconditions in the pagan epoch are important. The divinisation of the rulers that became general in the Hellenistic period was accompanied with a tendency towards a lesser sort of apotheosis for all dead persons—or at least for those whose survivors could afford any sort of cult-celebration. In the last resort we must look to the

mystery-religions, in which the full devotee was to some extent
identified with the saviour god through various forms of initiation and communion, for the strongest driving-force in bringing
all this about. Especially rites of eating and drinking, in which the
desired communion with the divine figure or the world of divine
energies was achieved, were potent in providing the sense of
deification and of paradisiac translation. To examine all the forms
of communion with the divine in the Graeco-Roman world
would be a huge task; what we are concerned with is the particular traditions and developments in Egypt.

The feast of the dead appears among the rights of the *choachytai*
of the Memnonia—funerary priests who were above all connected with the liquid offerings made to the dead. The belief
in the hunger of the dead was general in this epoch, and a part of
the repast was set apart for them.[49] At Hermopolis it seems that
a brick stove in a vestibule of the ancient tomb of Petosiris was
used for sacrifices on the anniversary of the four burials, the dates
of which were scratched on the walls of a room of the *pronaos*
that had been taken over as a catacomb.[50]

A will states that the *taphos*, tomb, is delivered to the heirs
with *bomia*, an odd word which however presupposes a *bomos*,
altar. Such hearth-altars were installed in private chapels, as at
Tuna, or set along the public way, as at Zawiet el-Maietin.[51]
North of Deir el-Medineh, in the steep cliffside of a dried-out
wadi, at the foot of the first spur of the Mountain of Thebai, is
cut a tomb, probably of the 18th dynasty, which was turned later
into a catacomb. It was found full of mummies of the Roman
period, and on the wadi-sides were Greek graffiti of the same
period with names and dates of dead persons inscribed in what
one of the texts called the Hanging Tomb, *kremasterios taphos*.[52]
In the centre of the space outside was found a rock in a sort of
arch-shape, apparently made by nature, and nearby fragments of
stone, among which a piece of a table-of-offerings seemed of the
Roman period. Perhaps here was an altar for the cult of the dead
in the Hanging Tomb.[53]

An Hermopolite athlete, 138–61 A.D., allows in his will a
freedman 10 artaba a year, with money for clothing and "all

other expenses" as long as "on the high days of the cemeteries he goes to my tomb in the sand of the Sarapieion and carries out the customary rites for the dead"—high days, *episemoi hemerai*, outstanding days.[54] In 156 Akousilaos of Oxyrhynchos made a will. Dios his son was the heir, subject to a lifelong interest held by Aristous (Apollonarion) his wife; we have the official copy written out at a later date. At his death "the slaves Psenamounis also called Ammonios, and Hermas and Apollonous also called Demetria and her daughter Diogenis, and Diogenis another female slave", are to be set free "under sanction of Zeus, Earth and Sun, for their goodwill and affection towards me". Aristous, and at her death Dios, "shall give to my slaves and freedmen for a feast which they shall celebrate at my tomb on my birthday every year 100 dr. of silver to be spent".[55] A 3rd-century will lays down that a member of the testator's family shall come and sacrifice on his tomb, wearing a wreath.[56] Low stoves or furnaces still holding ashes seem to represent the sacrifice of animals.[57]

Such practices carried on into the Christian period. The will of Abraham, bishop of Hermonthis on the 7th–8th century, insisted: "I wish and command . . . *agapai* (love-feasts) and the high days of death to be performed."[58] We still meet *episemoi hemerai*. In many burials of monks were set baskets and goblets destined for the banquet to celebrate the day of resurrection.[59]

In effect every dead man became an Osiris, and sometimes the dead women became Hathors: we can show it in many of the demotic mummy-tickets and some of the Greek ones. Further the dead are associated with the high gods and profit from the offerings made to them. The woman Moutiritis, in whose honour was composed the short liturgy preserved for us in *P. dem. Cairo* 31170, received water, wine and milk when drink offerings were made to the gods of Amen-Re *mit erhabenem Sitz* and the great Osirises of Djêmé. The Dionysios (?) of the same collection received water on the table-of-offerings following "Osiris of the Lake". In the three texts cited by Blackman, the dead receive solid nourishments from Khonsu-Shu and water from Amenophis of Djêmé. In a dedication of Euergetes II on the second pylon of Karnak it is stated that the dead are not to worry about their food, for there is a great abundance on the altars of the Theban gods.[60]

Certain demotic texts—one of which was cited above—contain short elements of liturgies in honour of dead persons and show us the nature of the offerings from which the dead benefited.[61] Wine, milk, and especially water, were desired. The *choachytai* gained their Greek name from the ritual of offering liquids. At first the water was purificatory.[62] But the dead were thirsty, and the stress on thirst increased.[63] A stele on the time of Ptolemaios XI has the inscription: "Give me running water to drink." A Greek of Thebai (?) asks in an epitaph of Roman days for his friends and fellow-soldiers to spill on his tomb some drops of Nile water.[64] Some Greek inscriptions show the formula, with variations, "May Osiris give you cold water." In one we meet a mixture of Greek and Egyptian formulas:

> May Osiris then to you
> grant a light-weighing dust and cold water too.[65]

And in a catacomb of Kom ech-Chugafah sarcophagi were found in which by the heads of mummies were metal tubes meant to carry water to the mouth of the dead; in a corner of the catacomb was a cistern from which the water could be drawn. Burials of the Ptolemaic period do not show such customs, which come up under the Romans—revealing a stronger resurgence then of native conceptions.[66]

A strange text seems to deal with a burial rite rather than with a foundation-cult properly so called. It lays down that the mummy of the woman Artemis is to be set on its litter oriented to the four cardinal points, while persons wearing masks, it seems, are to play a sort of mystery-drama in which Horus destroys the enemies of his father Osiris.[67] Perhaps we can link this account with a passage in Diodoros, which has been taken as no more than an effort to rationalise and describe as a custom what was mythologically represented on tombs, temples, and funerary papyri.[68] (For instance, the relief in the southern chapel of the Ptolemaic temple at Deir el-Medineh shows Osiris enthroned—before him, the four funerary genii on a lotus-flower, the Devourer, and Harpokrates leant on a cross-staff. Thoth with his ibis-head writes down the judgment, Anubis and Horus weigh the dead man's heart, and two goddesses of Truth, with plumed heads, lead the dead man into the Hall of Judgment, where he makes his prayer to the forty-two judges.) However Diodoros had himself visited Egypt, and here he insists that Orpheus had actually seen the rites:

When the body is ready to be interred, the family announces the day of burial to the judges and to the relatives and friends of the dead man, and solemnly states that he who has just passed away—mentioning his name—"is about to cross the lake". Then, when the judges, forty-two in number, have assembled and taken seats in a semi-circle which has been constructed across the lake, the *baris* is launched, which has been prepared in advance by men specially engaged in that service and which is in charge of the boatman whom the Egyptians in their language call charon.

For this reason they insist that Orpheus, after visiting Egypt in ancient times and witnessed this custom, merely invented his account of Hades, partly reproducing this practice and partly making up his own account.

At any rate, after the *baris* has been launched into the lake, but before the coffin with the body is set in it, the law allows anyone who wishes to arraign the dead person. Now, if anyone comes forward and lays a charge and shows that the dead man has led a bad life, the judges announce the decision to all and the body is denied the customary burial; but if it comes out that the accuser has made an unjust charge, he is severely punished. When no accuser appears or the man who presented himself proves a slanderer, the relatives put aside their mourning and praise the dead. Of his ancestry indeed they say nothing, unlike the Greeks, since they hold all Egyptians to be equally wellborn; but first they tell of his training and education from childhood, then they describe his righteousness and justice after reaching manhood, his self-control and other virtues, and call on the gods of the lower world to receive him into the company of the righteous; and the multitude shouts its assent and extols the dead man's glory, as of one who is about to spend eternity in Hades among the righteous.

Those with private sepulchres lay the body in a vault reserved for it: but those without them construct a new room in their own house and stand the coffin upright against the strongest wall. Also those who are forbidden burial because of the accusations brought against them or because their corpses have been made security for a loan, are laid

C*

away in their own homes. And it at times happens that their sons' sons, having become prosperous and paid off the debt or cleared them of the charges, give them later a magnificent funeral.[70]

The account is matter-of-fact and is entangled with details that are certainly correct (*e.g.* the corpse as debt-security). Diodoros however is a consistent euphemeriser and rationaliser; and soon after this passage he argues that heaven and hell with other "fantastic conceptions current among the many, which are figments of imagination", were brought into Greece by Orpheus in imitation of Egyptian funeral customs. Still, it is possible that his account mingles what he heard in the interpretations of the pictures of the dead man's trial, and things he either saw or heard of a liturgic drama which was sometimes performed after the installation of the mummy in its tomb and in which the dead man was proclaimed "righteous of voice". The possibility of such a play is increased by what we know of the generally dramatic nature of Egyptian rite and liturgy, and by the accounts of the Munu of Bouto, who personified the funerary spirits and were thought to inhabit the nekropoleis where they welcomed in the dead man by their dances.[71]

An example of a Pharaonic rite carried on under the Ptolemies is the Festival of the Valley at Thebai. It was called in Greek the Crossing of the Great God Ammon into the Memnonia, and involved a passage over the Nile on to the left bank where the nekropolis lay. Its fame was widespread; a Homeric scholiast tells us that the removal of the Great God and his associated deities lasted for twelve days; and Diodoros knew of it. "The myths told about the dalliance of Zeus and Hera, and of their journey to Aithiopia, Homer also got from Egypt; for each year among the Egyptians the shrine of Zeus is borne across the river into Libya and then brought back some days later as if the god were arriving from Aithiopia. As for the dalliance of these deities, in their festal gatherings the priests carry the shrines of both to an elevation that has been strewn with flowers of every kind."[72] This account suggests that a sacred marriage was part of the rites; for Diodoros is thinking of the verses in the *Iliad* that tell of the flowers bursting out under the embracing deities:

"fresh new grass, dewy lotus, crocus and hyacinth thick and soft".
But he may be deducing the embrace from the Homeric picture.

A Greek text shows that the festival was still in 117 B.C. carried
on with a certain pomp. The epistrategos of the Thebaid, the
strategoi of Peri-Thebai and the neighbouring zones took part in
it, as once the Pharaoh had done.[73] The god went by boat to the
left bank and visited in turn the funerary shrines of the kings,
which provided halting-points; but there is no certainty as to the
itinerary. By Ptolemaic times many temples were in ruins or
quite broken down. Among those still in use, that of Hatshepsut
(a queen of the XVIII dynasty who ruled in her own right and
was a builder of magnificent monuments for Amun) was rather
decayed and saw only a popular pilgrimage to the upper court
and perhaps to a small sanctuary of Hathor. There was also the
temple of Deir el-Medineh, not a funerary temple but a place of
a deity of the dead; the Ptolemies there were *synnaoi* (shrine-
sharers) of Hathor; Medinet-Habu, where many cults, including
those of ancient Pharaohs, had taken refuge; and Kasr el-Aguz,
where again the Ptolemies were *synnaoi*.[74]

The Greek name of the Festival does not keep any memory of
the original name. The *choachytai* of the nekropolis were still
called "of the Valley" under the Persians.[75] Under the Ptolemies
they were called Pastophoroi of Amenophis in the West of
Thebai, even in demotic.[76] Perhaps the Festival survived the blow
of 88 B.C., when Soter II took Diospolis, but finally broke down
early under Roman rule when Gallus made his attack in 29.
Diodorus may be speaking only from hearsay; but as his visit to
Egypt can be dated 60/59 to 57/6 B.C., the ceremony may still
have been then carried on. Strabon, who visited the Thebaid,
says nothing of it. We may then surmise that the revolts of the
last century B.C. brought about the collapse of this ancient festival.
But that such a rite, even in a broken-down form, should persist
right into the Roman period is an interesting example of the
vitality of the old cults and of the continuity of certain deep-going
religious ideas and forms.

3

Dance of Life and Death

PERFORMERS for celebrations of all sorts could be hired by private persons, associations, villages or towns. Here is an order from the town-officials of Euergetis in the late 3rd century. The exegetes has an odd name, compounded of three deities, Hermes, Anubis, and Ammon, and the term used for mime is *biologos*. "Aurelios Agathos, gymnasiarch, prytanis in office, and Aurelios Hermanobammon, exegetes, and Aurelios Didymos, chief priest, and Aurelios Koprias, kosmetes, of the city of Euergetis: to Aurelios Euripas, mime-actor, and Aurelios Sarapas, Homeric reciter, greeting. Come immediately, in accordance with your practice of joining in the holiday, so as to celebrate with us our traditional festival on the Birthday of Kronos, the Greatest God. The spectacle will begin tomorrow the 10th and be held for the customary number of days, and you will receive the usual pay-ment and presents. Signed. I, Hermanobammon, pray for your health." Then come the signatures of Didymos and Koprias. (The latter has one of the names used for foundlings, babies picked off a dungheap, *kopria*.) The combination of mime and homerist seems popular.[1]

At times the youth acted as guards of honour and carried out manoeuvres. On 18 January 323 at Oxyrhynchos they displayed their athletic attainments in the assault-at-arms at a festival in which the traditional and distinguished character is stressed. Heliodoros, describing a festival at Delphoi, gives us some idea of what such a youth-group looked like. First came girls in two groups with girdles low in the waist and flowing hair; one group bore baskets of flowers and cakes on their heads—"they went linked in a figure of oblique lines and so were about to pace on and dance at the same time". The second group sang a hymn. "Behind the girls a mounted troop of youths led by their captain flashed along, presenting a vision of youth that prevailed over any charm of hearing. In number they amounted to fifty: divided into two companies of twenty-five and escorting the leader of their mission as he rode midway between them. They were shod with boots of red leather strapping interlaced and fastened above the ankle, and wore white cloaks gathered into their chests by gold clasps and edged all round with a border tinted blue." The high-spirited horses were adorned with silver or gilded head-bosses and frontlet.

In general musicians and dancers were most needed. A letter

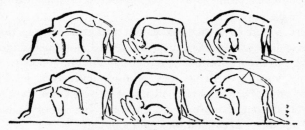

Dancers from the Chapel of Hatshepsut.

of the 2nd century mentions a dancer, though whether his journey is professional or not is unclear. The writing is clumsy and the wording obscure; the writer is leaving in haste to collect a loan. "Greeting. Kalokairos, I Kyrillos address you. I wasn't so un-feeling I left you for no reason, for though a man gets his interest tenfold in Tybi he still doesn't recover capital—I'm going up with the dancer, even if he wasn't going I'd not have broken my word. Farewell. [Addressed] Deliver to Kalokairos." He means that a man who wants the capital of his loan back won't be satisfied with any amount of interest.[2]

Festival dancing had ancient roots in Egypt.[3] At celebrations, large and small, there were all sorts of entertainers: jugglers, ropewalkers, conjurers, gymnasts, balancers, snake-charmers, animal-trainers, singers, and so on. "Men performing the leap crash with the fall their hanging body in a wretched disaster of death", says Firmicus Maternus. A conjurer appears in an Oxy-rhynchite festival.[4] The astrononomer Ptolemaios gives us the following combinations, which, whatever our view of their astrologic basis, illustrate the social attitudes of his epoch:

When two planets are found to rule action, if Hermes and Aphrodite take the rulership, they bring out action expressed by the Arts of the Muses, organs, melodies or poems, and rhythm, especially when they have changed places. For they produce people-of-the-theatre, actors, slave-dealers, organ-makers, choros-members, makers of strings, painters, dancers, weavers, and wax-moulders. And again, if Kronos testifies to them, he produces those of the cited callings as well as dealers in feminine finery. If Zeus testifies, he produces lawyers, supervisors of counting houses, public officers, teachers of children, leaders of the populace.

If Hermes and Ares together assume the lordship of action, they produce sculptors, armourers, makers of sacred monuments, modellers, wrestlers, physicians, surgeons, accusers, adulterers, evildoers, forgers. If Kronos testifies to them, they produce murderers, sneakthieves, burglars, pirates, cattlethieves, villains. If Zeus testifies, they produce war-lovers or singlehand-fighters, energetic clever busybodies, who meddle in others' affairs and thus gain a living.

But if Aphrodite and Ares together dominate action, they produce dyers, perfumers, workers in tin, lead, gold and silver, farmers, dancers-in-armour, druggists, physicians using drugs in their treatment. If Kronos testifies to them, they produce attendants of sacred animals, men who do burials, mourners, pipers at funerals, fanatics who resort to any place with mysteries, lamentations and bloody rites. But if Zeus testifies, temple-frequenters, omen-interpreters, bearers of sacred instruments, supervisors of women, interpreters of marriages and matches, who make a living by such occupations and are at the same time devoted to pleasure and reckless.[5]

Here however we shall concentrate on dancers. From the astrologic writers and other sources we see that they had a bad reputation; and Philon thus denounces their vogue. "In every quarter of the habitable globe, the theatres are every day filled with countless myriads of spectators. Being wholly under the domination of sounds and sights, and allowing ears and eyes to be carried away without restraint, they pursue harp-players and singers to the harp and every sort of effeminate unmanly music. More, eagerly receiving dancers and every other kind of actors—because they place themselves and move in all sorts of effeminate positions and motions—they are continually by their applause stirring up the factions of the theatre without thought for the propriety of their own conduct or that of the general body of citizens; but in their wretchedness they upset all their own plans of life for the sake of their eyes and ears."[6]

A horoscope, dated 3 January 123, tells us that the subject was "a dancer, and in his 25th year he was clapped in confinement in the course of a public riot, but was defended before the governor and set free through the aid of friends and the crowd's appeal, and became more esteemed". The planets' position indicated "there would be a riot and quarrelsomeness and rivalry through the affair." As a result "all the stars were operative in the 25th year. The nativity was precarious as regards loss of reputation and condemnation and danger of life. But Venus being found in the Horoscopos and the responsible sign, and Jupiter with the Sun, it had the best imaginable outcome and was successful in action." Later, "in the 32nd year he was deprived of honour and reputation and livelihood, and lived unhonoured". So, "he was to blame for his own fall, having become a braggart and a pretender. For the ruler of the daimon and the place of intellect, Mercurius, was in opposition to itself, that is, Gemini."[7] This dancer may well have been an Alexandrian; for around A.D. 148 (his 25th year) there were troubles in Alexandreia, an outbreak of rioting in which the prefect was killed. If the prefect in question was L. Munatius Felix, the riot occurred some time after 13 September 151, when a document shows him still alive; but there may have been lesser preluding discontents under the previous prefect, M. Petronius Honoratus, who was in office 147–8.[8]

Dion Chrysostom, in addressing the Alexandrians, stresses their self-abandonment at the theatre. "Some persons are insatiate and avid and all-aflutter over everything alike, while others take their part in the spectacle with decorum and quiet. Not so you. You sit thunderstruck, you jump up more violently than the hired dancers, you are tensed up with the songs. Other people are stirred by drink to song and dance, but with you the opposite is true. Song is the cause of your drunkenness, your frenzy. So, while wine's natural effect is as we have seen: begetting the inability to keep one's self-control and forcing those who use it stupidly and excessively to do many annoying things—yet men intoxicated by song are in a worse state than those wine-crazed—and what's more, from the outset, not by easy stages as at a drinking-party—such men are not to be seen elsewhere." He goes on to speak of a drug with effects like hasheesh. "Among some barbarians, it's true, we're told that a mild sort of intoxication is produced by the fumes of a burned incense. After inhaling it,

Middle Kingdom relief.

they are joyful, rise up and laugh, and behave altogether like men who've been drinking, yet without injuring one another. But of the Greeks you alone attain that condition through ears and voice, and talk more foolishly than those barbarians, and stagger worse and are more like men suffering from a debauch's after-effects." He compares the induced state with that brought on by music properly used, which produces harmony and orderliness. Song for the Alexandrians has exactly the opposite effect, and begets a Dionysiac exaltation. "It is not by the Muses, but by a kind of Korybantes you are possessed, and you make credible the mythologisings of poets; for they bring on the scene creatures called Bacchantes, maddened by song, and Satyrs too. No doubt with you the fawnskin and the thyrsos are lacking, nor do you, like the Bacchantes, bear lions in your arms; but in everything else you seem to be quite comparable with Nymphs and Satyrs.

For you are always in a merry mood, fond of laughing, fond of dancing. Only, in your case, when you are thirsty, wine doesn't bubble up of its own accord from some chance rock or glen, nor can you readily get milk and honey by scratching the ground with your fingertips. No, not even water comes to you of its own accord in Alexandreia, nor is bread yours to command, I suppose, except what you obtain from the hands of your superiors; and so, perhaps, it's about time you stopped your Bacchic revels and instead turned your attention on yourselves. However, at the moment, if you merely hear a harpstring twang, it's like the call of a bugle, you can no longer keep the peace."

This linking of the ecstasies induced by the arts of the epoch with the Dionysiac image of the earthly paradise has a great importance that will become clearer as we go on. Further, we may note the word used for the spontaneous growth and plenty of that paradise, *automatos*, which we shall find a keyword in Nonnos with his Dionysiac world.

Ammianus, depicting what he considers the decadence of the 4th century, states that at Rome the great houses, where there had once been a serious culture, now "re-echoed with the sound of vocal music and the tinkling of flutes and lyres. Instead of a philosopher, you'll find a singer; instead of an orator, some teacher of ridiculous arts is called; and the libraries are closed for ever, like so many graves; organs worked by waterpower are made, and lyres so vast in size as to look like wagons, flutes and ponderous machines for the exhibition of actors." Recently a famine had been feared, so all foreigners were expelled. "Those who practised liberal accomplishments and who were extremely small in number were sent out without a moment's breathing-space; yet the followers of actresses, and all who at the time claimed to be of that class, were let remain; and three thousand dancing girls had not even a question put to them, but stayed unmolested with the members of their choruses and a corresponding number of dancing masters."[9] The most admired dancers were the pantomimes. The origin of their art form is obscure. Athenaios states that it was introduced by two dancers Pylades and Bathyllos (in 22 B.C.):

The dance that is called the Tragic Dance, was first brought in by Bathyllos of Alexandreia who, according to Seleukos, danced "according to the laws" [of tragedy]. This is the Bathyllos, says Aristonikos, and Pylades as well, who wrote a treatise on dancing, made up the Italian Dance out of the comic one called the *kordax* together with the tragic one called the emmeleia and the satyric one called the sikinnis— hence the name of Sikinnistai for Satyrs. (The inventor of this latter dance was a barbarian named Sikinnos, though some say that he was a Cretan.)

Now the dance invented by Pylades was stately, pathetic, laborious; but that of Bathyllos was in a merrier style. For he added a sort of *hyporchema*.[10]

Hieroglyphs of dancers.

This involved statement is too concise to be helpful. The hyporchematic aspect has been explained a little earlier:

The Phaiakians in Homer had a dance connected with ballplaying and they danced very cleverly, alternating in figures with one another. That is what is meant by the phrase: "in frequent interchanges", while others stood by and made a clapping noise with their forefingers [called *lekein*]. The poet was also acquainted with the art of dancing so as to keep time with singing. While Demodokos was singing, youths on the edge of manhood were dancing; and in the book called the Making of the Arms, a boy played the harp, "danced round and sang in soft well-measured tune". In these passages the allusion is to that which is called the hyporchematic style, which flourished in the time of Xenodemos and Pindar. This kind of dance is an imitation of actions which are explained by words.[11]

Loukian says that the *hyporchemata* were songs for choirs like those of the boys on Delos, who moved and sang to flute and lyre while a selected number performed "an interpretative dance".[12] The two groups of girls dancing and singing at Delphoi, described by Heliodoros, were probably performing a *hyporchema*.

It is clear that the elements of the pantomime's dance were old. Loukian is certainly right in seeing that dance as the final expansion of certain traditional forms. Probably a new fusion was brought about by Bathyllos and Pylades, and it seems clear that Alexandreia played an important part in the development, though it was when the new art-form was taken to Italy that it burst triumphantly out and asserted itself as in many ways the dominant and most expressive mode of art under the empire.

Tragedy lost its vitality with the fall of the democratic *polis;* but efforts were made to perpetuate the form. An ordinance of the 4th century laid down that a play by Aischylos, Sophokles or Euripides should be produced each year at the Dionysia along with new tragedies. Athens was still the main seat of tragedy till about 300; then Alexandreia took over. Under Philadelphos (283–47 B.C.) there was a group known as the Tragic Pleiad. However tragedy went on declining. The intense closely-felt contradictions that had kept a mounting tension in democratic Athens were broken down in the different sphere of an absolutist monarchy. It was not till 217 A.D. that an edict of Caracalla abolished theatrical shows at Alexandreia; but long before that the pantomime had taken over from the tragic actor.

Loukian presupposes that his readers will know what a tragic performance was like. "Let us form our first opinion of its character from its outward semblance. What a revolting and at the same time fearful sight is a man tricked out to disproportionate state, mounted upon high clogs, wearing a mask towering above his head, with a mouth set in a huge yawn as if he meant to swallow the spectators, I forbear to mention pads for the breast and pads for the paunch, by means of which he assumes an additional counterfeit corpulence so that the disproportion in height won't give itself away more obviously in a slight figure. Then too, inside all this, you have the man bawling out, bending forward and backward, at times actually singing his lines, and, what is surely the climax of impropriety, melodising his calamities, holding himself answerable for nothing but his voice, as everything else has been attended to by the poets, who lived at some time in the distant past. Indeed, as long as he is an Andromache or a Hekabe, his singing can be borne; but when he comes on as Herakles in person and warbles a ditty, forgetting himself and lacking any shame for the lionskin he wears, or the club, a man with any sense may rightly call the whole thing a solecism."[13] Tragic performances, in fact, were certainly included in many games till the 2nd or 3rd century A.D., but vitality had long left the form.

The disintegration of tragedy, which Loukian illustrates by the intrusion of songs, can be traced back to Euripides, who

Male acrobat-dancer on cylinder seals of Old Kingdom.

introduced florid lyric solos sung by an actor on the stage.[14] It is however too simple to say that as the public lost interest in tragedy, separate parts came to be acted, especially the lyric solos. So the unity of the dramatic scene broke up; the action became dancing and the speech became song. Two performers were needed where there had been one.[15] Still, in some complicated way, this is what did happen; and it seems certain that the development occurred mainly at Alexandreia, where tragedy made the most strenuous efforts to survive. (In the Delian ritual dances cited above, we have the song already detached from the interpretative dance. So, in one sense, the art of the pantomime represented an intrusion or rebirth of earlier ritual elements on a sophisticated scene which transformed the whole thing.[16])

The relation to tragedy was genuine and deep, however indirect. One name, we saw, was the Tragic Dance. Inscriptions show a rather awkward effort to link pantomime and actor: "actor of tragic rhythmic movement", says one.[17] Loukian says, "The dancer's mask itself is very beautiful and suited to the drama that produces its theme; its mouth does not gape, as in tragedy and comedy, but is closed, for he has many people to do the singing for him. In the past indeed the actors both danced and sang; but later, as the panting produced by the movements disturbed their singing, it seemed better for others to accompany them with song. Tragedy and dance share common themes, in which there is no difference: except that the dance-themes are more varied, more unhackneyed, and contain endless vicissitudes [or changes]" *metabolai*. If the dance does not appear in contests, he holds that the reason lies in its importance and solemnity—though Neapolis in Italy "has added it by way of embellishment to the games held there".[18] He cites at length the themes, which cover the whole repertoire of tragic myth and legend. But while the audience had been drawn once more into participating in the dramatic experience, the tragic conflict and resolution had been dissipated and a lyrical excitement substituted. People sat "enthralled by the flute, watching a girlish fellow play the wanton with dainty clothes and bawdy songs, and imitate lovesick hussies, the most erotic of all antiquity, like Phaidra and Parthenope and Rhodope—the whole thing, in addition, accompanied by strumming and tootling and feet-tapping." The instruments used included flute, syrinx, various instruments of percussion (such as the iron-shoe, which marked time for dancer and singer).[19] The audience is again described as "a pack of effeminates and frenetics, clapping hands and shouting the most unbecoming words of praise to a nasty fellow who doubles himself up for no useful purpose".[20]

Though no doubt each important pantomime had his own style to some extent, there were definite systems of mime. Loukian remembered seeing a dancer who was miming the birth of Zeus (with Kronos eating his children) and who drifted into the role of Thyestes, in whose myth there was also a cannibalistic motive. Another dancer, enacting Semele, who perished under the thunderbolt, found himself playing Glauke, who was burned by the poisoned robe that Medeia sent her.[21] At times however a dancer let himself go and "exceeded the due limits of mimicry".

Something of that sort, I remember, I once saw done by a dancer who until then had been in truly high esteem, as he was intelligent in every way and really worth admiration; but by some bad luck, I don't know what, he wrecked his fortunes on an ugly piece of acting through exaggerated mimicry. In presenting Aias going mad straight after his defeat, he so overleaped himself that instead of feigning madness he himself went insane. He tore the clothes of one of the men beating time with the iron-shoe, snatched a flute from one of the accompanists, and with a vigorous blow cracked the head of Odysseus who was standing near and exulting in his victory. Indeed if his watchcap had not offered resistance and taken the brunt of the blow, poor Odysseus would have lost his life through coming in the way of a crazed dancer.

The pit however all went mad with Aias. They leaped and yelled and flung up their garments. For the riffraff, the wholly unenlightened, took no thought for propriety and couldn't distinguish good from bad, but considered that sort of thing a consummate mimicry of the affliction. To be sure, the politer sort understood, but were ashamed of what was going on; and so, instead of showing disapproval by silence, they themselves applauded, to cover up the absurdity of the dancing, though they clearly realised that the goings-on derived from the madness of the actor, not of Aias. For, not satisfied with what he'd done, the noble fellow did something else that was yet more ridiculous. He came down among the public and took his seat among the senators, between two ex-consuls who were very scared that he'd grab one of them and beat him, taking him for a wether.[22]

Macrobius tell us the following anecdotes about Pylades, whose pupil Hylas ended by becoming his rival in the time of Augustus. The people's suffrages were divided between the two dancers. Hylas one day danced a cantica, of which the culmination was the words "the great Agamemnon". He drew himself up to give the effect of a towering stature. Pylades heckled him from the pit, "You make yourself tall, not great." The people then forced him to act the same part, and at the crucial words he assumed a deeply meditative pose. While Hylas was enacting the role of the blinded Oedipus, Pylades called out, "You can see!"

When he acted as Hercules Furens, some spectators found that Pylades did not preserve well enough the gait of an actor, he doffed his mask and told his mockers, "Fools, I dance a madman", and at the same time he threw arrows among the people. Playing the same role by Augustus' order in a triclinium, he drew his bow and let an arrow fly; and the emperor was not offended that he acted with him just as he did with the Roman people. Pylades was considered to have replaced the artless dance of our ancestors by a new and much more graceful one. Augustus asked him what had been his procedure, and he replied, "I substituted the human voice for the flute." His rivalry with Hylas caused tumults among the people and angered Augustus, to whom he remarked, "Prince, you are ungrateful; let them concern themselves with us."[23]

Loukian as a panegyrist of the art stresses the extent of the panto-mime's skill and knowledge, equating him with the prophet who knows all that has been, is, and will be. "Beginning with Chaos and the primal origin of the world, he must know every-thing down to the story of Cleopatra the Egyptian"—which suggests that aspects of the latter's life and death may have been danced. Elsewhere in his essay Loukian definitely includes in the dance-repertoire events of post-Alexander history including a Seleukid love-affair. Further, he equates the dancer with the shapeshifter of myth. "It seems to me that the ancient myth about Proteus the Egyptian means nothing else than that he was a dancer, an imitative fellow, able to shape and change himself into anything, so that he could imitate even the liquidity of water and the sharpness of fire in the vivacity of his movement; yes, the ferocity of a lion, the rage of a leopard, the quivering of a tree—in short, anything he wished. Mythology however, in taking it over, described his nature in more paradoxical terms, as if he became what he imitated. Now, just that is typical of today's dancers, who certainly seem to be seen changing swiftly at the cue and imitating Proteus himself. And we must suppose that in Empousa [a bugbear associate of Hekate], who shifts into count-less forms, some such person has been handed down in mytho-logy." Further, "since Egyptian tales are rather mystical, the dancer will know them, but will present them more symbolically (than when he deals with historical events); I mean Epaphos and Osiris and the transformations of the gods into their bestial forms. But above all else he will know the stories of the god's loves, including those of Zeus himself and all the forms into which he changed himself, and also the whole *tragoidia* of Hades' realm, with the punishments and the reasons for each."[24]

There is much insight in these comments; for the imagery of transformation in myth does go back to the dances of tribal days in which the dancers represented animals and various aspects of the life of nature. Such dance-motives derived ultimately to a great extent from the dance-rituals of the shaman who enacted all

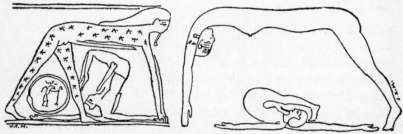

The sky-vault of Nut over the Earth.

sorts of transformations. But it was no mere capacity to imitate that seemed to beget the identity of dancer and thing represented; it was rather the whole complex of magic and ritual surrounding and penetrating the dance.

In the pantomime then a quite new aesthetic was expressed. It was no longer the tragic tension of Attic drama that dominated, but a lyrical verve of transformations. The essential point was that the conflict of man with man was eliminated and all experience concentrated in a single individual. "The dancer undertakes to enact characters and emotions, introducing now a lover and now an angry person, a man afflicted with madness, another with grief, and all this within set limits. Indeed the most astonishing thing is that on one day we are shown Athamas in a frenzy, then the next moment Ino in terror; presently the same person is

Atreus, and soon after Thyestes; then Aigisthos or Airope. Yet they are all only a single man."[25]

The tragic dance was the perfect form to express a world in which many of the contradictions that had rent the *polis* continued, but in expanded more complex forms, crushed and muffled under a worsening absolutism and yet deeply aware of great new potentialities in life. The individual was driven back in on himself and could not find the point outside, in society, from which to begin putting into action his enriched sense of the human universal. The great significance of the dance under the Roman Empire has been obscured by the fact that it attracted moral attacks and by its very nature has left no records except in literature. But literature and art alike were unable to encompass the achievements of the tragic dance of the pantomime because they could not find an adequate technique for expressing that dance's indriven intensity and its imagery of transformation. Only to some extent did Apuleius in his *Golden Ass* (correctly called the *Metamorphoses*) and Nonnos in his *Dionysiaka* succeed in catching the spirit of the dance and its method of successive transfigurations. After the direct Roman expression in poetry had reached its climax, its dead-end, in Juvenal, these two writers are the only ones of profound signficance.[26] Egypt had seen the tailing-off of tragedy and its devious rebirth in the art of the pantomime; it also produced the poet who most fully summed up the world of the tragic and transformative dance.

Nonnos, who was a native of Panopolis in Egypt, in the 5th century wrote a vast epic, the *Dionysiaka*, which, as we shall see, is one long dance of the pantomime. Here is a passage in which he directly describes a mimic dance. The occasion is the funeral rites of Staphylos, at which a dance-contest is held:

> Now who will contend, circling with skilful feet,
> and win the match of nimble feet, take up
> the golden bowl and the wine that's sweet inside it?
> But if a man staggers and totters on tripping feet
> and falls as worse dancer, the worse prize shall be his.
> . . . My turning-point
> is the dance, my starting-point is the skipping feet,

the beckoning hand, the pirouette, the twists
of the expressive features, the speaking silence
that twirls the signalling fingers, the dancer's whole face.[27]

Maron "danced with winding step, passing the changes right
over left and figuring a motley-storied silence with soundless
hand".[28] Seilenos "with wordless hand traced the art-symbols,
symbola techneenta, in all their mazy craft". (Nonnos loves the
paradox of the speaking silence, the wordless story.) With his
gesturing hands Seilenos enacts the contest of Dionysos and
Aristaios, the master of wine and the master of honey-drinks (not
fermented like mead). Dionysos in the mime wins:

Horned Seilenos wove his web with neathanded skill,
his right hand halted, fixing his gaze in the sky
he leaped with bounding shoe, now clapped both feet
then parted them, went hopping from foot to foot,
now on the floor twirled dancing round and round
upright upon his heels, in a circling sweep
spun round.
            Upon his right foot standing steady,
he held a toe of the other foot or bent
his knee and in his claspt hands grasped it, held
a thigh outstretched, the other leg kept straight,
heavy-kneed Seilenos. He raised his left foot coiling
up to the side, to the shoulder, twining it round
behind him, holding it up till he brought the sole
right round his neck. Then with a rapid turn
of the backswerving dance, he skilfully bent
himself well over, showing his belly outspread
and upcurved to the sky, while round and round
he spun on the one fixed spot.
                        His head hung down
as still he spun, as if it touched the ground
all the quick while, yet didn't graze the dust.
So with his hairy foot he scratched the ground
restlessly turning round in his wild capers.
At last his knees gave way. With shaking head
he slipped, fell down, rolled over on his back,
and at once became a river.[29]

The whole concept of Nonnos' *Dionysiaka* is of a universe animated by dance-energy, dance-magic, as we shall see later in some detail. The vast poem is an account of a great dance-mime, with Dionysos as the supreme dancer, capable of all transformations. Here the account of Seilenos' dance goes on:

> His body was water
> flowing with selfmoved ripples, his forehead changed
> to a winding current, the horns were waves, the swell
> in turbulence came to a crest on his head, in the sand
> his belly sank, a depth for fishes, his hair,
> as spread he lay, was turned to selfmade rushes
> and over the river his pipes made a selfborn tune
> shrilling as breezes touched them.[30]

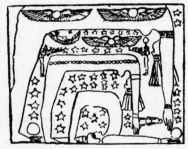 

The double-heaven of sun and moon over the earth, holding discs (moon rising and sun setting); figurine.

In this universe of dance-changes the adjective *poikilos* (translated *motley* above in the compound *poikilomythos*) and various adjectives expressing self-movement, self-creation, transformation initiated from within, are of prime importance. Here we have *automatos*, *autotelestos*, *autophyes*: self-moved, self-made (or completed), self-born (or growing).

Though the main stimulus towards the Nonnan image of the dance-mime came from the pantomime of the Roman Empire, which was pervasively popular, there is also an element that goes far back into the Egyptian past. In a hymn to the Nile we hear of men "singing with the hand".[31] In a painting of the Middle Kingdom five young girls give an acrobatic dance-performance entitled *The Song of the Four Winds*. The text is known only from religious formulas: "I have been given these winds", the girls cry. "It is the wind of life which comes from the North. I have been given it and I live on it."

Loukian, we saw, stressed the use of Egyptian motives by the pantomimes. The paradox of the Eloquent Silence of the dance-mime was widely spread; it went to the heart of the pantomime's aesthetic and was felt to be part of the deeply-riddling meaning intuited in the dance-image of the fettered, tormented, and yet liberated inner-energies. Loukian states that, in the words of the Delphic oracle, whoever beheld the dances must be able "to understand the dumb and hear the silent" dancer. He cites Demetrios the Cynic who had denounced the dance and yet after watching it could not help shouting, "I hear the story you are acting, man, I do not just see it. You seem to me to be talking with your very hands." Other anecdotes are added. A barbarian prince begged a pantomime from Nero, so that he could use him as interpreter. Loukian says, "I have heard a man express an extremely adventurous opinion as to the muteness of the dance-characters, to the effect that it was symbolic of a Pythagorean tenet." Athenaios, writing of the dancer Memphis, declared that "he discloses what the Pythagorean philosophy is, revealing everything to us in silence more clearly than those who profess themselves teachers of the art of speech". He calls the pantomime *philosophos orchestes* and says that at Rome he was given the name of Memphis by general assent, as he was compared for his bodily movement "with that most ancient and royal of cities, of which Bacchylides said: Memphis storm-exempt and reedy Nile." The epithet *acheimantos* suggests serenity of grace. Memphis seems to have been actually named Agrippa and to have been brought from the land of Parthians by L. Verus; but it is of interest that an Egyptian name was thus attached to him. Athenaios brings out further the universal language of the dance-silence by saying that the different nationalities congregated at Rome (Cappadocians and men of Pontis and Skythia) joined in acclaiming Memphis.[32]

The acrobatic dance often had cosmic imagery in Greece, but

the roots of such dances were especially strong and ancient in Egypt. The male acrobat doing the back-somersault appears already on cylinders of the Old Kingdom, though the form may owe something to influences from the Near East.[33] Later we see dancing girls in the same attitude in funerary rites, temple ceremonies and processions, festivals (*e.g.* those of Hathor), as well

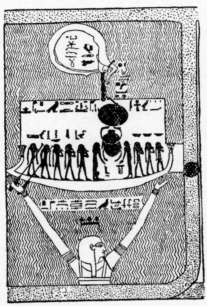

Sun in primeval ocean lifts the sunship; above, Nut takes the sun-disc from the scarab, standing on a male figure bent in a circle (Osiris encircling Tuat, the whole world): sarcophagus of Seti I.

as at secular entertainments.[34] A hieroglyphic sign reproduced the attitude.[35] The image of the backswung dance-tumbler appears in representations of the universe. Thus, under the human vault of Nut (here shown as ithyphallic), a figure lies bent back on itself, with feet brought round over the head. This figure too is ithyphallic and one of its horizontally-extended arms holds a disk surrounded by a serpent biting its tail.[36] Elsewhere, Nut appears as a woman in dual form (probably representing the double form of the heavens: that of the sun's course, and that, lower, of the moon). Below her is the backswung figure with disks of sun and moon—interpreted as Geb, the Earth, or as Tuat, the Underworld.[37] We need not explore such details; the general significance is clear—as on the sarcophagus of Seti I, where Nun the primeval abyss upholds the sun-boat, while, above, Nut receives the sun-disk, standing on a bent-round figure (described in an inscription as the Osiris whose body encircles the Tuat).[38]

The symbolism must have remained alive in Egypt, right into

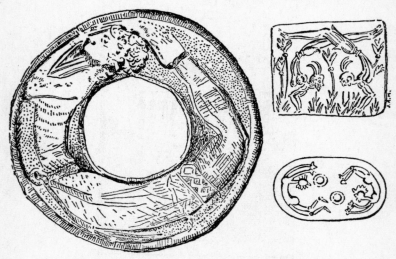

Sword-pommel from Mallia, Crete; and Minoan seals.

the Roman period. At Esna, where ruled Khnum, the ram-god who created the universe and modelled all the forms of life on the turning potter's wheel, ancient rituals continued through the Roman period. The ritual of 1 Phamenoth recalled the raising of the heaven above the earth and the putting of the wheel into action.[39] How strongly the cosmic image of the backswung figure continued in Egypt is shown by its survival into Christian days, when the monk Schnudi, at the end of the 4th century or early in the 5th, hoped for his enemy Gesios to be plunged into hell with his tongue attached to his toenails (*i.e.* in the acrobatic circle). Gesios died and Schnudi recounts how he duly saw him in hell in the acrobatic attitude. For the spinning dance (turning like the potter's wheel), which Nonnos' Seilenos also danced, we may compare a description in the *Aithiopika*, where it is however called Assyrian, "accompanied by flutes that played a tune with a lively cadence. At one moment the dancers jumped lightly into the air; at another they bent down close to the ground and turned on themselves like persons possessed."[40]

In Nonnos' poem, Seilenos dances the backswung dance in the Dionysiac form developed in Greece. On a psykter of Douris we see a seilenos bending back, with his arms upholding him behind, and with a kantharos balanced on his upstanding phallos.[41] This kind of acrobatic dance has here lost its cosmic force and is often linked with sword-dances and tumbling.[42] Thus Athenaios describes the wedding festivities of his friend Karanos in Makedonia: "There came in some ithyphallic dancers, and some jugglers, and some conjuring (*thaumatourgoi*) women as well, tumbling and standing on their heads on swords and vomiting fire out of their mouths, and they too were naked."[43] The magical aspects have been brought down to the entertainment-level. To dream of the sword-tumblers is, however, according to Artemidoros, a presage of death.[44]

The link with death is clear in ancient Egyptian ritual. The backswung dancers appear in funerary ceremonies, at the door of the tomb, before the dead man.[45] The leaps and somersaults are an integral part of the rite, as the texts prove: "The leaps of the Menju will be performed at the tomb's door", and "The leaps of the Nemiu will be performed for you at the door of the tomb." The determinative shows that the leaper will be someone who throws himself back, with arms touching the earth. "The leaps of Nemiu will be performed for me at the door of the tomb"— here the determinative shows a person who lets himself go down on to the earth.[46]

Homer preserves the image of the death-leap or somersault in the form of a simile. Patroklos has killed Kebrion, the charioteer of Hektor, who falls headfirst from the car. Patroklos calls:

Ho, look at the nimble man, how lightly he tumbles,
If only he were on the teeming sea, this fellow
would satisfy many, seeking for oysters, leaping
out of his ship, no matter how stormy the sea:
for now on the plain from his car he goes lightly tumbling
Ho, among the Trojans too there are tumblers indeed.[47]

The verb is *kybistan* and the noun *kybisteter*, which do not merely
refer to diving, as they are often made to do in this passage. The
Homeric *kybisteter* is the tumbler doing a handturn, touching the
ground with his feet and then his hands; and his art was almost
certainly inherited from Minoan Crete.[48] The religious nature of
the acrobatic dance carried on in certain cults, as with the Akro-

Ephebe and Seilenos in the balancing act (vase paintings).

batai of the Goddess, known till the 2nd century A.D. as forming
a fraternity of dancer-sacrificers in the service of the Ephesian
Artemis.[49] A devotee turns a somersault on a vase from the Kabiric
sanctuary near the Greek Thebai in homage to the god;[50] and
Loukian speaks of "the intense (*syntonos*) movement of the dance,
its twists and leaps and backflung poses (*hystiasmoi*)."

Nonnos shows abundantly that he is fully aware of the significance of the sacred somersault.[51] The physical attitude recurs. In
the Seilenic dance already noted its cosmic nature is stressed:
"Instead of the winepress you dance on the back of murmuring
Okean".[52] The account ends: "All wondered to see the winding
waters of Seilenos the pouring-out tumbler, *kybisteter*, the everturning river that was his likeborn likeness." Elsewhere, Seilenos,
"the old wanderer, challenged a satyr, twined hands and feet
together, and rolling himself in a ball, stooped and dived headfirst

into the stream from the heights".[53] And satyrs revel with gambols like *kybisteteres*.[54]

In the struggle with the Indians, the somersault becomes the Dance of Death. An Indian "with a somersault took a header like a tumbler".[55] Another, shot in the navel, "selfrolled, encountered death coming up to him". A third, "fell and somersaulted from an elephant".[56] Tektaphos gives a roll as he dies. A fifth Indian "rolled over and over in the dust and with a somersault took a header like a tumbler".[57] A Pan catches an Indian on his horns and flings him into the air where "he rolls back on himself like a tumbler". Yet another Indian is pierced by a spear through the middle and sent flying "till he fell through the air to the ground, headfirst crashing, and rolled over and over in the dust, and with a somersault took a header like a tumbler". Early in the poem the monster Typhon in death sends a severed hand "selfrolling over the ground in leaps, a maddened hand"; later an Indian is cut about, one arm "goes tumbling in a dancer's shake of death", and a hand goes "selfrolling in leaps".[58]

Agaue foresees the death of her son Pentheus; he is torn by beasts (who represent her and the other Bacchantes). "Pentheus fell tumbling over and over on himself." (Here and in the passages where "selfrolling" occurs, the word is *autokylostos*, which means rolling, turning, twisting in on oneself, in an involuntary contortion. Nonnos also makes much use of a similar word, *autoeliktos*.) When the time comes, Pentheus actually goes *autoeliktos* in a dancer's shake.[59]

Animals too die in the same way. In a seafight, a dolphin "leaped selftwisting in its usual curving course and half dead skipped with the jump of a dancing Fate. On all sides many fishes were dancing with pierced backs, *kybisteteres* of death." A bull, in an attack made by the Thyiades on the black cattle of Poseidon, "sank down half dead and twisted round on itself on its back". A Thyiad throws up two of his hooves "whirling round and round in the air".[60] Orontes attacks a Kentaur, "who half dead rolled headlong, tumbling about and brushing the dust with his ears; then lifting his body on to his feet with a last wild effort he danced a twist-footed horrible dance of death".[61]

D

The idea of the Dionysiac conflict as a dance is pervasive. The fighters "leap to bloody dance with frenzied foot, striking up a chant of death". And "so the dancers of cruel war fought all together. Round the car of Deriades they gathered in a ring of shields, beating their armour, and surrounded the tower in rhythmic battle and shield-bearing dance". (We have here an armoured dance like that of the Kouretes in Crete.) The slain Bassarids on the sea "go tumbling in the dance of death for Lyaios".[62]

Child of Medeia, turned back over an altar (vase painting).

The image could not be so deeply imbedded in Nonnos' whole conception without a powerful emotional association linked with the ritual forms we have discussed. He

utilises all the terms that evoke the idea of wheel, circle, ball, turning, and especially the epithets, *kymbachos*, *autokylistos*, *autoeliktos*, of which he is fond, this image of the body turning on itself, rolling itself into a ball with the head below. He compares it to the exercise of the *kybisteteres* as much when it is a question of the funerary dance of Seilenos and of his games as when it is a question of the convulsions and fall of a combatant, of a death-stricken animal. Between this acrobatic dance and death there is a close link; one imitates the other. Phlogios, favourite dancer of Dionysos, ends the tears of his master and his companions by miming the death of Phaethon, whom he represents "turning back on himself, all on fire". But he is slain by Morrheus, who, seeing him pant, cries out:

That was a different jig you danced by the table.
A merry dance you played by the mixing-bowl:
why pace a groaning dance on the battlefield?
If you're mad for a dancing-turn of Dionysos
take your mystery to Hades. You need no chalk,
the round of your face is well selfdusted. Or dance
if you like before Lethe the fancier-of-dirges,
please smileless Persephone with the sight of your capers."[63]

All that is very true; but by laying the whole emphasis on the
dance-leap as a death-symbol, it abstracts the complex of imagery

Sword-dances (from vases).

from the total effect in the poem. There life is an aspect of death,
but death is also an aspect of life. The deathleap is a leap into a
new life, a form of rebirth in a universe of ceaseless transformation. We saw how the spinning and backswung dance of Seilenos
leads into a rebirth as water, an elemental change. (The link with
water is not accidental. Homer's Kebrion in his death-somersault
is a deep-sea diver; Phaethon somersaults into water; Seilenos
flings himself as a ball into the Paktolos; Orontes rolls into
the river that bears his name. Silenos dances on the back of
Okean. There is on the one hand a link with the ritual-leap into
water, which is common in Greek ritual-myth and which goes
back to Minoan Crete in such figures as Britomartis and Glaukos;
and on the other hand a link with Osiris in his circular bent-back
form plunged into Nun.)[64] The circular bent-round posture may
indeed be ultimately identified with the child in the womb and
the associated leap or wheel-turn with the idea of rhythmic

birthpangs. The somersault or circular dance-turn is thus the expression of birth, rebirth, creation, transformation—death as an aspect of life and change.

Nonnos in his poem both takes up all the dominant concepts of his world—ranging from those of alchemy to those stirred by the residual elements of ritual in pantomimic dancing—and unites them with immemorial traditions of Egypt and Greece. In the sense of summing up a whole epoch in a highly original way, his epic is a great work despite its many weaknesses, above all its lack of effective structure. This point will become clearer with every step we take into the activities and ideas, the emotions and dreams, of his world of Roman Egypt.

4

The Gymnasion

WE now return to everyday life in a review of the Graeco-Roman Gymnasion, with special reference to Egypt. Physical training and sports were for the Greeks not something added to the normal course of existence but activities of the highest value, which did much to give a central and pervasive meaning to that course. Ailios Aristeides, describing the urban achievements in Asia under the empire, summed them up as gymnasia, fountains, propylaia, temples, craftsmen's shops, and schools. Dion of the Golden Mouth made a shorter list: agora (marketplace), theatre, gymnasion, and stoa (colonnade or piazza). He also tells how Anacharsis, the keen-eyed barbarian from the North, once remarked, "In every city of the Greeks there is a designated place where they daily go mad. I mean the gymnasion. When they go there and strip, they smear themselves with a drug."[1] The Greeks felt strongly that they excelled in health and beauty of body through the gymnasion, and that this bodily freedom and energy were inseparable from their intellectual and artistic achievements.[2]

The Greeks carried the gymnasion and all its connections into Egypt. Herodotos mentions some sort of large-scale games at Chemmis, a town that he visited—games held in honour, he says, of Perseus.[3] Diodoros however states that the Egyptians "hold that from daily exercises in wrestling their young men will gain, not health, but a vigour that is only temporary and indeed quite dangerous, while they consider music to be not only useless but even harmful, since it feminises the spirits of listeners."[4] Diodoros may be in part echoing the aristocratic contempt of the professionalism that had invaded sport and music in his day, though he may also be expressing an Egyptian concept of balance of body and mind that differed from the Greek one. In ancient days there had been a certain amount of sports. On the walls of their mastabas the Memphite lords watch contests by naked youths at wrestling or javelin-throwing; at Beni Hasan we see wrestlers catching or bracing themselves against one another according to definite rules; before the court of Ramses a quarter-staff contest between Egyptian and foreign soldiers, their heads and chins protected by leather, is represented. Hunting and fishing were sports of the nobles themselves; and most of the statues reveal trim waists and square-set shoulders.[5] The Macedonian nobles had their own ideals of hunting and charioteering; but the exclusion of the natives from the gymnasia may well have deepened the attitudes which Diodoros sets out.

The Romans themselves tended to look down on the palaistra and gymnasia. They were not Roman institutions, Vitruvius observed. Ploutarch said that even to his day the Romans considered the main cause of the Greeks falling into servitude and becoming effeminate to be the public places where they wrestled naked. Greek physical training begot waste of time, laziness, and lewdness, especially homosexuality, as well destroying bodily balance by its stress on particular actions. To such athletics the Romans, like the Spartans, opposed military training. Trajan wrote to Plinius who was administering Bithynia, "These Greeklings are I know immoderately fond of gymnastic diversions and therefore perhaps the citizens of Nicaea have planned a more significant building for this purpose than is necessary. However, they must be content with such as will be sufficient to answer the aim for which it was meant."[6] Though by the late Republic, wealthy men attached grounds for doing exercises to their villas and adorned them with works of art, the first public gymnasium was built at Rome by the philhellene emperor Nero. Another was later built by Commodus. But such institutions never gained any importance in comparison with baths, amphitheatres, circuses and the like.[7]

With the expansion of Greek culture after Alexander, the gymnasion spread all over the Near East and was the spearhead of Greek influence. Nationalists such as the author of *II Maccabees* tell indignantly how in the reign of Antiochos Epiphanes the high priest at Jerusalem "built a place of exercise under the tower itself and brought the chief young men under his subjection and made them wear a hat." The priests left the altar and the sacrifices of the Temple and "hastened to share in the unlawful allowance in the place of exercise, after the discus called them forth; not setting by the honours of their fathers, but liking the glory of the Grecians best of all". The larger cities of the Near East founded four-yearly games on the example of Olympia; by 175 B.C. the people of Tyre had such a festival in honour of their god Melkart

Horseman wearing chlamys (cup by Euphronios); youth with petasos and chlamys (vase painting).

(identified with Herakles).[8] Even in a backward area like Cappadocia we meet a gymnasiarch at Tyana near the end of the 2nd century.[9]

In Egypt the Ptolemaic kingdom saw the same process, but complicated by the fact that here the Greeks were a minority jealously trying to preserve their privileges and maintain the gymnasia as their sole prerogative. Gymnasia certainly existed at all sites where there were enough Greek settlers to need an exclusive place of education and the resulting club of ex-gymnasion members who dominated the locality. They are known for the cities, the metropoleis of the nomes, and even many villages.

The Egyptians preserved a strong nationalist spirit, right up to the last days of the Byzantine Egypt. There were revolts under the Ptolemies, for example in the reigns of Ptolemaios VI and Ptolemaios VIII. The feeling of the natives towards the Greeks may be read in the letters of Ptolemaios, son of a Macedonian settler Glaukias, who had become a devotee of Sarapis living in the Memphian precinct of the god. He suffered violence from the Egyptians in the temple "because he was a Greek" during the first revolt (under Dionysios Petosiris); in 163 he was again attacked in his cell and mishandled; in 158 he was yet again assaulted by Egyptians with "ass-drivers' sticks" through some dispute over reeds (for basketmaking?) bought from a reed-seller in the temple courts.[10] A letter written by an Egyptian or an Arab shows the way a sense of inferiority was driven in by the attitudes of the Greeks. "They look down on me because I'm a barbarian. So I beg you be good enough to bid them to let me have what's owing to me and for the future pay me regularly, so I shan't starve to death because I can't act the Greek"—or "be at home in Greek".[11] At the same time a continual assimilation of Greek and Egyptian occurred; by 130 B.C. an Egyptian, Paos, was governor in the Thebaid, commanding the royal army. Intermarriage went on; and a woman in the 2nd century B.C. writes of her son learning Egyptian in order to better his financial position.[12]

Still, with all the intermingling, a strong strain of Egyptian nationalism persisted. We can maybe trace the native contempt for Greek forms of athletics in an Aisopian fable, perhaps of the 2nd century, in which the Crocodile declared that his family was reckoned from the ancestors of the gymnasiarchs. The Fox interrupted with the comment that there was no need for him to make the claim since his skin showed that he had undergone many years of training in the gymnasion. That is, his rough horny skin suggested the battered faces of the upper classes who had boxed and wrestled on the training-grounds'[13]

Gymnasiarchs are common among the persons mentioned in the papyri; and we learn a fair amount about the various gymnasia.

At Alexandreia there seems to be several gymnasia and palaistrai (wrestling-grounds). One gymnasion at least was pre-eminent and appears in four historical incidents. The people dragged thither the king whom Sulla had imposed upon them; Cleopatra and Antonius sat there on thrones of gold with silver bases when they divided their realms among their children; Augustus gathered the people in the huge space there to announce his pardon for their resistance; two and a half centuries later Caracalla abused the people there for having mocked him, as a preliminary to the massacre he launched next day.[14]

Strabon cites only one gymnasion. "The city is full of civic and sacred edifices; but the most beautiful is the Gymnasion, which has porticoes more than a stadion in length. And in the middle are both the court of justice and the groves."[15] The intrusion of the lawcourts is odd, though we know of a council chamber, *bouleterion*, in the gymnasion of Elis; and gardens were often attached. However, though there is no known parallel, it is best not to try to amend the text.[16] Certainly a central gymnasion would have been built as one of the first constructions of the new city in the 3rd century B.C. There seems to be a reference to it and its trees in an epitaph of that century.[17]

> Philoxenos, no more your mother receives you
> and round your lovely neck casts lingering arms.
> No more you go with the lads to the famous city
> and rejoice in the gymnasion's shaded level.
> Your father Kaunos brought your strong bones here
> for burial after fire consumed the flesh.

In the eastern part of the city, near the Church of Alexandria, bases and capitals of granite columns of a pure Greek style have been found, which may have been part of its edifice.[18]

The plural term, gymnasia, is used in the *Bellum Alexandrinum*, the account of Julius Caesar's fighting in Egypt; and we hear of Marcus Antonius taking up his winter-quarters in the city and making private visits to its sanctuaries, gymnasia, and places where scholars gathered.[19] A papyrus of 124 B.C. preserves an edict concerning the proprietors of gymnasia in Alexandreia. The text is mutilated and may refer, not to buildings, but to associations

D*

or athletic colleges which were linked with the great Gymnasion and owned properties that fed their funds. At least it seems that such properties made up a part of their domains.[20]

Much the same obscurity shrouds the Palaistra. A letter of 257–6 B.C. shows a doctor Artemidoros who is afraid of being blamed by the king for the opening of the Palaistra, which had presumably been officially closed. He wants a certain Ptolemaios to take charge of the place.[21] Literary works provide two references. Polybios states that in 202, in the night-revolt against Agathokles, the latter fled by an underground passage between the Maiandros and the Palaistra. The scientist Ptolemaios mentions that in his time the Palaistra had a circle of bronze used for astronomical observations.[22] These accounts suggest that there was one pre-eminent Palaistra, but confuse its position. One author sets it south of the Gymnasion in the Broucheion; the other, to the west of the city, between the Theatre and the Library, at Rhakotis.[23]

The gymnasia of Ptolemaic Egypt were in the hands of private enterprise. Such a system was not the rule elsewhere in the Hellenistic world and came to an end with the Romans. Under the Hellenistic monarchies education generally became subject to official control—that of the city. The kings intervened in policy or administration only as patrons. The Ptolemaic gymnasia seem administered by associations of old-boys, those *ek tou gymnasiou*.[24] In some places the Greek residents made up a political organisation, as when at garrison-posts the soldiers constituted a *politeuma*; this association was then in close connection with the gymnasion-group. But if there was no *politeuma*, a sort of municipal system seems to have evolved round the gymnasion.

At Philadelpheia in 242–1 the garrison-cavalry asked for the use by the gymnasion-directors of a sum of 46 dr. which various donors had given to their predecessors. About a century later a Makedonian settler asked the komogrammateus to intervene with the gymnasiarch of the *neaniskoi* (youth) to get him exempted from a lampadarchy that had been incorrectly imposed upon him. A letter to the landowner Zenon requested him to have a young slave sent into the Little Palaistra, so that the gymnasion seems to be not the only educational establishment.[25] At Samareia in 221–0 Aristomachos, administrator of property held by Polykleitos, complains to the king that the gymnasion located on those lands and founded by the kleruch Apollodoros (of whom Polykleitos was the heir) had been improperly occupied by Dallos and his wife. He wanted the latter driven off and fined. Apollodoros as a private individual had built the gymnasion at his own charge, though dedicating it to the king. He did not however have the full control; for after his death some reconstruction was needed and Aristomachos had to get authorisation from the strategos. We gather that the interior was reached by a *prothyroma*, a monumental porch, in front of which was cut the dedicatory inscription. What changes were made is not clear; but Aristomachos had removed a structure above the gymnasion, which thus had an upper storey over at least one part of its extent.[26]

The ephebia or youth-association had generally declined in the Hellenistic epoch. Thus, at Athens the military aspect faded out and the importance of the exercise-master, *paidotribes*, increased. The ephebia, with its social basis narrowed, became an institution of physical education into which the rich and aristocratic lads entered. There they found a club with a miniature city-system: assembly, magistrates, debates, votes, and so on. As democratic activities were dying out of the city itself, the ephebia provided a democracy in club-form strictly limited to the upper classes. The trend was thus everywhere from a civic basis to a narrow aristocratic control, from a military to an athletic outlook. But here again Egypt was an exception. There was a close though indirect link of army and ephebia.[27]

This link has been denied, but the evidence confirms it. Apollodoros who built a gymnasion was an army-officer who had settled there. That might mean only that he was a rich landowner with a sense of enterprise. But the connection of army-officers and gymnasia is common. An inscription of 57–6 B.C. recording a decree of a gymnasion-club tells of Herodes, a cavalry-commander and benefactor, who, while gymnasiarch, held a reception in the gymnasion for the strategos and soldiers.[28] Another inscription of uncertain date and place mentions how a group of officers honoured Karadyses, fellow-soldier, *systratiotes*, and gymnasiarch.[29] Officers often carried out the gymnasiarch's work.[30]

In Egypt then the ephebia was concerned with the preservation of the Greek way-of-life in a world where that way could easily be swamped. Its problem was to integrate the individual in the Greek tradition rather than further his career; and it therefore acted as a more generally cohesive force for the whole Greek community than elsewhere. The Greeks clung to their athletics as the expression of their superiority, their difference from the

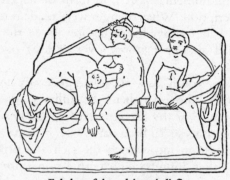

Ephebes of the palaistra (relief).

natives. But at the same time here too the ephebia had the effect of encouraging the emergence of an aristocracy and of consolidating it. This trend became even stronger under the Romans. In the imperial epoch the ephebia, as we have already noted, became an official institution, on which the whole town-system depended. The prefect laid down that no one was to be admitted unless he met the requirements. Though perhaps the ephebate lasted strictly for a year only, the members remained together in the same class, the Ptolemaic term for which, *hairesis*, now gave way to *symmoria*. At the head of the class was a symmoriarch.[31]

In an application of A.D. 224 for membership of the gymnasion the candidate is described as literate; but literacy was certainly not a condition and the claim to it here presumably reveals only a boastfulness.[32] Fathers put their sons' names down early. The motive was no doubt a keenness to make the quickest possible affirmation of his Greek character; but perhaps there was also a wish to share in the ephebia's expenses as the child became a sort of honorary ephebos.[33] We know of applications filed when the son was seven, three, or even one year old.

Here is an example of the application by a father for the epikrisis of his son as a preliminary to entering the gymnasion. The date is A.D. 98; and though the beginning is lost, we may assume that it was addressed to the strategos and the basilikogrammateus as the officials mainly responsible for the examination of epheboi of the country-towns at this time.

[I declare that I was passed at the *epikrisis* that took place under the] late strategos and Pamphilos, late basilikogrammateus, and the other proper officials in the 7th year of the God Vespasian in accordance with the proofs adduced in his lifetime by my aforesaid father Dionysios also called Amois, son of Psammis son of Ballaros, who was a member of the palaistra-guard, that his father Psammis son of Ballaros was in the list made in the 34th year of God Caesar of those . . . in the gymnasion;

and I myself declare that Thermouthion the mother of my son was married to me in the 2nd year of Domitian by an autograph contract which was also made public through the record-office in the following 3rd year, while her father Ploution son of Ploutarchos, registered at the South Square quarter, was in the 5th year of the God Vespasian placed by Sutorius Sosibius, then strategos, and Nikandros, then basilikogrammateus, and the other proper officials, in the class of persons selected by Quintius (?) Paulinus;

and I swear by the Emperor Caesar Nerva Trajanus Augustus Germanicus that I have made no false statement, and that Ploution is the son of myself and, Thermouthion by birth and not by adoption, nor is he supposititious, and that I have not availed myself of credentials belonging to others or identity of names. Otherwise may I be liable to the consequences of the oath.

The candidate needed to prove that all his ancestors had undergone the gymnasion-*epikrisis* since the procedure was set up; his physical traits were stipulated; his status as the son of a correct marriage was shown; and witnesses were required. The person declaring the details ended by swearing by the emperor's Tyche that the candidate was of full legitimacy. There was however a less rigorous *epikrisis* concerned with establishing that a candidate was of metropolitan status and so liable to reduced taxes (12 instead of 16 dr., it seems). Here is a document of A.D. 160–1:

From Hermippos also called Harpokration, son of Horion elder son of Hermippos, his mother being Thais daughter of Pekysis, of Oxyrhynchos, through his friend Dionysios son of Didymos.

In accordance with the orders concerning the selection of boys who have attained the age of 13 years if their parents on both sides are inhabitants of the metropolis rated at 12 dr., my son Ptolemaios by . . . daughter of A . . . on was listed in the Quarter of Teumenouthis as having reached the age of 13 in the past 23rd year; so, coming forward for his selection, I declare that he is a person rated at 12 dr. and that I am similarly rated at 12 dr. as registered in a polltax list of the past 23rd year at the Upper Camp Quarter, and that the father of the mother of my son, A . . . on son of Harpokration, his mother being Herakleia, was similarly rated at 12 dr.

Though it was not easy to squeeze into the metropolitan list, it was far more difficult to prove one's claim to the gymnasion. The administration had been drawn up, once for all, a full list of the Hellenes, from whom the magistrates were selected; and every effort was made to see that no one else intruded. In the metropolitan list, however, it was possible for new families to appear. Slaves and freedmen, for instance, by inheriting their master's privilege, could in effect create a new stratum of metropolitans. But such a development was impossible for the gymnasion-class or *tagma*.[34]

At Alexandreia, as no doubt elsewhere, the ephebate was the prerequisite of citizenship. Claudius at the start of his reign wrote to that city that no man who had been an ephebos would lose his citizenship unless he were of servile birth and so had had no right of entry.[35] In charge were the gymnasiarch and the kosmetes, both of whom were now among the regular town-authorities.[36] They managed things and also had to pay heavy contributions to the gymnasion and meet other charges of the metropolis. Here, as with all town-offices, the burdens increased; men tried to evade what had once been an honour; compulsions increased. Already under Trajan a prefect had to set a limit to the charges involved by the gymnasiarchy at Hermopolis; and by the mid-3rd century there was nothing surprising in the statement of a kosmetes and ex-gymnasiarch of that town that he had been bankrupted by his office.[37] At times attempts were made to divide the office among several persons; and at Koptos in the 3rd century we meet an under-gymnasiarch. The last record of the office is in 353, while the last reference to the ephebate is dated 323.[38]

The gymnasion was in effect the secondary school; but we shall not here examine the literary side of its education. However, though we are concerned primarily with the sports side, we had better glance at some of the varied uses made of gymnasia, since many of these throw light on the ways that leisure was spent as well as bringing out the central importance of the institution and its buildings. For this purpose we must consider the whole field of Hellenistic and Roman gymnasia; for not much evidence has come down from Egypt as to the wider functions.

First, the gymnasia were the main places of relaxation, lounging, small talk. There gossip, views on life, and serious matters were discussed. Some of the rooms round the enclosed inner area were sure to have marble seats and the sophists of the late 5th century B.C. realised the possibilities of such places as lecture-halls. Sometimes philosophical works had their first readings in this setting: Protagoras is said to have been introduced to the public by his book on the Gods being read by a pupil in the Athenian Lykeion.[39] Sokrates frequented the gymnasia as the best places to start arguments with young men and others; Prodikos of Keos was thrown out by a gymnasiarch for "uttering doctrines unsuitable for the young"; and another gymnasiarch wittily rebuked Karneades for his roaring voice.[40] It was thus no accident that the three great Athenian schools of philosophy were located in gymnasia: Plato's school in the Akademia; Aristotle's in the Lykeion; Antisthenes' Cynic school in the

Kynosarges. These three gymnasia seem the only ones that Athenai had in the 4th century, and they were all philosophic centres.[41]

This link of philosophy and gymnasia went on right through the Graeco-Roman epoch. Ploutarch describes his sons and other young men at Thespiai in their leisure-moments "philosophising in the palaistra". A philosopher or learned man, arriving in a strange place, had only to find the gymnasion and he was sure of an audience. Aristippos, wrecked on Rhodos, "headed straight for the gymnasion", where he proceeded to lecture on philosophy and was presented with gifts. Loukian on his way to Olympia looked in at the gymnasion of Elis and heard a Cynic launching a diatribe; and he describes his literary predecessor, the Cynic Menippos, as haunting the gymnasion:

"If anywhere you catch sight of the Menippos the Dog—and you'd probably find him at Korinth near the Kraneion [gymnasion] or in the Lykeion [at Athens], deriding the philosophers as they dispute with one another—say to him: Diogenes bids you come down below if you've mocked at things above ground enough . . . "

"Describe him, so I may know quite clearly what sort of man he looks."

"An old fellow, bald, with a little old cloak full of holes, exposed to every wind of heaven and variegated with rags and tatters; and he's forever laughing and for the most part he jeers at those loudvoiced philosophers."[42]

Hence architects had to shape the gymnasia more and more as places with a double function (physical training and general education) and added spacious exedras with seats for professor and students.[43] Both organised groups like the epheboi and the general public attended the lectures. Not only philosophers but also rhetors, physicians, musicians, literary scholars, and astronomers, are recorded as giving instruction in the gymnasia.[44] Poets read their poems there. At Delphoi about 132 B.C. a lad from Skepsis read an epic.[45] Ephebic examinations in oratory, rhetoric, music, geometry were held in gymnasia.[46] Libraries were often installed there; at least we know of them at Athens, Halikarnassos, Pergamon, Rhodes, Delphoi.[47] At Athens the epheboi in

123–2 B.C. were praised for their "faithful attendance at the lectures of Zenodotos in the Ptolemaion and Lykeion, and likewise of all the philosophers in the Lykeion and Akademia throughout the year".[48]

The Ptolemeion was the gymnasion presented by Ptolemaios

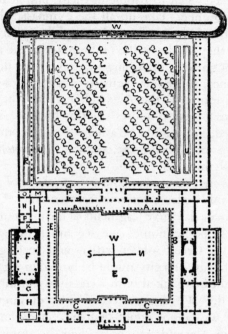

Gymnasium according to Vitruvius: peristyle; exedrae in porticoes ABC; ephebeum F; coryceum G (sack-exercise); dust-sprinkling H; cold bath L; anointing K; tepid bath L; sudatory N; hot bath P; three porticoes above; xystos R; open walks U; stadion W.

II of Egypt. Cicero, studying at Athens in 79 B.C., heard the eclectic Antiochos of Askalon lecturing there. In his dialogue on the Orator he makes Catulus say that the Greeks in their heyday "bore no resemblance to those who now force themselves on our ears, yet in their leisure they didn't avoid the kind of discourse and disputation" that he and his friends are carrying on. "The very portico where we walk, this field of exercise, and the seats in so many directions, all in some degree revive the remembrance of Greek gymnasia and disputes." Crassus replies, "I contemplate all these things in quite a different light; for I think that even the Greeks themselves originally contrived their palaestrae, their seats and porticoes, for exercise and amusement, not for disputation. For their gymnasia were devised many generations before the philosophers began to babble in them; and at this very day, when the philosophers take up all the gymnasia, their audience would still rather hear the discus than a philosopher; and as soon as it is heard, they all desert the philosopher in the middle of his discourse, though he is discussing matters of the utmost weight and consequence, to anoint themselves for exercise." Similarly Dion Chrysostom tells the Alexandrians that they should be ready to make a critical address of this festival-occasion, "and even if irritated, you should be ashamed to call out: When will the fellow stop? or, When is the conjurer (*thaumatopoios*) coming on? or any such thing."[49]

Gymnasia were also used as courtroom, places of judicial hearings, and assembly-places for public ceremonies.[50] Two papyri of a late Ptolemaic date give fragments of the diary of the strategos of the Herakleopolite nome; we see him visiting the village gymnasia of the Greek soldier-settlers and hearing their grievances.[51] Benefactors of a city might be buried in a gymnasion; or a lecturer might be thanked with a ceremony in the place where he had lectured.[52] We have no record of lectures in the gymnasia of Egypt, but we cannot doubt that they shared in such things, even though in Alexandreia scholars had the ample resources of the Mouseion and the Library at their disposal. Still, the gymnasia of the late Hellenistic world were already declining in cultural value and becoming more like Roman bathing establishments; and this tendency was speeded up under the Romans. We have abundant evidence for the extent to which the gymnasiarchs were concerned in Egypt with looking after the baths, supplying oil and fuel, and generally seeing that the baths functioned. Thus in A.D. 201:

To Sarapion also called Horion, gymnasiarch in office—represented because of his youth by his paternal grandfather Apion, ex-gymnasiarch, and Achillion, exegetes in office—represented by Achillion also called Sarapammon, his son and deputy—from Diogenes son of Sarapion and Loukios son of Hermias, both of Oxyrhynchos, appointed by the city-clerk in accordance with the decision of the council of magistrates to superintend the repairs and fixtures of the Baths of Hadrian.

We request that we may receive from the civic treasury 3 talants of silver on account to pay for the material. Total 3 talants of silver, of which we shall render due account. [Date and signatures.]

A poem of the middle or later part of the 3rd century from Oxyrhynchos, which stresses the oil-supply, is a valuable statement of the continuing devotion to Hermes and the gymnasion. Our manuscript may be that of an amanuensis, with corrections by the author; in any event it must date not long after the composition. The title was at first *Enkomion of Hermes*, but the god's name was washed out and an amendment entered higher up in the margin: to the *Archon* (magistrate). The first nine lines are indeed taken up with Hermes, but the real person celebrated is the youth Theon, whom we may take to have been a rich man's son, appointed at an early age to the office of gymnasiarch.

> Hermes, come haste to sing for me, I've prayed,
> your young interpreter. The bard now aid.
> The many-toned sevenstringed lyre with fingers skim:
> dropped at your mother's feet the lyre you made
> and gave Apollo, ransom for his oxen—
> serving the Muses, as we bards have told.
> You, herdsmen afield as pastoral god proclaim,
> athletes in stadia call you lord of games,
> and you as gymnasia-warden cities hymn.
> This youth too honours you in your hallowed folk,
> pouring the citizens out a fount of oil.
>
> Not newly do we know you, Theon, holding
> chief office among your comrades, but of old—
> anointing with oil-distilling flasks our limbs
> or sharing the gifts chaste Demeter bestows.
> Such blessings you gave the folk, everyone knows,
> and blessings more and better you gave the youth.

For those a rich man might provide in truth—
vainglorious the gifts of wealth may be; but these
derive from one made wise by Muses still.
Therefore for these we honour you more than those.
One set your father taught you, we may say,
the Muses taught the other, only they.

Following gifts of oil and corn, Theon was providing something
that could come only from a youth made wise by the Muses.
(The poet stresses Hermes' connection with music as well as with
the physical training.)[53] It is probably an example of the decline
of the gymnasiarchy in the 4th century, as part of the general
breakdown of the Graeco-Roman city-forms, that in 306, when

Hoops (from gems).

a considerable sum was needed for baths in the same town, it is
the prytanis (councillor, but here council-president) who writes
to the logistes, a special financial commissioner appearing in this
century.

To his dearest Aurelios Seuthis, also called Horion, Logistes of the
Oxyrhynchite nome, from Aurelios Hierakion, also called Noninos,
exgymnasiarch, exprytanis, councillor, prytanis in office of the
Illustrious and Most Illustrious City of Oxyrhynchos:
I request that orders may now be given to me to pay out of the
city's funds from the sums publicly apportioned . . . to be used for the
expenses in accordance with the letters of His Highness My Lord the
Prefect Clodius Culcianus, which I recently handed to you . . . a
further sum of 50 talants and 450 denars of silver. total 50 tal. 450 den.
I think it right that the curator of the civic chest should be sent to make
this payment to me, so that there may be no obstruction to the interests

of the Public Baths or to other interests of my Prytany. I pray for your health, dearest friend.[54]

Hierakion is at least an ex-gymnasiarch, but ten years later in an estimate for painting the Baths of Hadrian, which were again being repaired, a painter deals directly with the Logistes:

To Valerios Ammonianos also called Gerontios, Logistes of the Oxyrhynchite nome, from Aurelios Artemidoros son of Arsinoos, of the Illustrious and Most Illustrious City of Oxyrhynchos, a painter by profession.

In reply to the request of your grace for an inspection of the places that need painting in the Public Bath of the said city now auspiciously under repair at the warm baths of Trajan Hadrian, I hereby declare that for the painting of the parts that need it (the two coldwater-conductors and one vapour-bath and the entrances and exits of the whole colonnade and four passages round the vapour-bath in the outer colonnade and the other places) there is required for the cost of paint . . . thousand denars of silver, and of the . . . painting of the whole work 10,000 denars of silver.

The painter was illiterate and could not himself sign the report. *Zographos* means literally limner-of-live-things; but the extent of the work being contracted for makes evident that the job must have entailed much plain laying-on of paint. The term used for painting the whole premises is *zographia*. But *zographos* had come to be used very broadly; in one papyrus we meet the "painting" (decorating) of a garden with plants or trees. To paint may mean no more than to variegate (to make *poikilos*).

Further evidence of the way in which control was passing out of the hands of the gymnasiarch is to be found in a receipt of A.D. 324 from three komarchs of the village of Herakleides for money paid to them for charcoal supplied to the public bath of Oxyrhynchos. They make their acknowledgment to the strategos of the nome and were paid by Paulos, banker of public moneys. The payment was made as the equivalent in part of tow (a common article of trade in the Byzantine period) and in part of fine gold; the sum was 12 talants 4,575 drachmai. After the inflation of the later 3rd century the economy has lost its resilience, despite the stabilisations of Constantine. (That emperor's conquest of Egypt was not indeed effective before this year.[55])

Discussions went on in temple-precincts as well as in gymnasia. Heliodoros describes how an informed Egyptian abroad was listened to with the greatest interest. The priest Kalasiris goes to Delphoi, where he gains a favourable oracle from the Pythia:

> You've brought your steps from the rich land by the Nile
> in flight from what the spinning Fates portend.
> Keep on. I'll soon return you to the soil
> of darkfurrowed Egypt. Meanwhile be my friend.

And so "they gave their consent to my dwelling at pleasure in the temple-precincts and decreed my sustenance at the public charge. In short I enjoyed all advantages without stint. I took part in the ceremonies or officiated at the sacrifices daily offered by foreign as well as native peoples in large number and variety to gratify the god, or else I conversed with philosophers. For not a few of that way of life gathered about the temple of the Pythian Apollo. Indeed the city was quite a school of the Muses, inspired by Phoibos, the Muses' divine leader. For some time at first these persons plied me with questions on various matters. One asked how we Egyptians worship our country's gods, while another wanted to know how it came about that different animals were adored by different sections of our people, and what was the reason of each cult. Some wanted to know about the construction of the Pyramids, others about the Labyrinths under the earth. In brief, they omitted not a single point of interest in their inquiries about Egypt; for listening to any account of Egypt is what appeals most strongly to Greek ears."[56]

However, though no doubt a certain amount of serious discussion went on in the gymnasia of Egypt, in general under the Romans we may assume that they approximated more and more to places of unintellectual training and entertainment. In the later Hellenistic period Poseidonios complained that the Greeks of Syria were abandoned to luxury, "using the gymnasia as bathing-establishments and anointing themselves with costly olive-oil and scented unguents."[57] A spurious letter of the Cynic Diogenes, probably of Augustan or later date, scolded the Greeks because "both in the gymnasia at the time of the so-called Hermaia or Panathenaia, and in the midst of the agora, you eat and drink, get drunk and indulge in lewderies."[58] The gymnasia were converted more and more into clubs for amusement. Under Julian "they were thronged with gay and happy crowds".[59]

Though the letter of Diogenes was a forgery, the Cynics did in fact set themselves to denounce the use to which the gymnasia were put. On the day that Nero opened the gymnasium and warm baths in the Field of Mars at Rome, Demetrios the Cynic entered the gymnasium and harangued the senators and rich middle class there assembled on the immorality of the Roman style of baths. He nearly lost his life, but in the end was merely exiled.[60]

But while the gymnasion thus tended to lose both its athletic and its cultural qualities, and to become a club of the élite, its moral decline was linked with an expansion of its forms into the gardens and parks of the wealthy. The essential element of these garden-gymnasia was a portico with its annexes, giving on to a shady walk. *Xystos*, which in Greek had referred to the portico, here referred to the walks or approaches, which the Greeks called *paradromides*. (*Xystos* properly referred to the levelled ground, but had come to mean in Greek the whole gymnasion; in Latin it moved away again from the gymnasion, but in a different direction.) Thus the Roman *xystum* ended by designating any kind of terrace set up in a garden as long as it was related to a portico. And just as the gymnasia became a garden-form, so were stadia and hippodromes incorporated in the Roman gardens.[61]

5

Athletics

THE Hellenistic age then saw a great expansion of the gymnasia, their full incorporation in the civic and educational system of the city. But this development, though for a while it had rich cultural effects, did not bring about a general extension of athletic exercises—or at least any such effects were weakened with the decline of the gymnasia into clubs of entertainment linked with bathing establishments. Athletics became more and more the field of the professional, and mass-enthusiasm was directed, not towards participation in sports, but to the championing of various professionals, especially the local ones, and to the spectacles provided by these professionals at Games. The rise of Greek democracy had ended the aristocratic monopoly; but as the democratic *polis* broke down under its own unresolved inner conflicts, the ideal of a group of citizens, all striving for an active balance of bodily and mental faculties, gave way to the rise of professionals, who indeed continued the challenge to the aristocrats but at the cost of increasing exclusion of the people in general from athletic activities. An emotional excitement took the place of direct participation. In theory the full education, intellectual and physical, was open to all freemen; in fact only the rich could enjoy it, with the gifted professional coming up on the margin. (The inner conflicts of the *polis* included the division of free and enslaved, the deepening inequalities in property, the sinking in status of the free craftsman, the inferior position of women, the inability to extend democratic forms effectively outside the *polis*, and so on; but it is not our business here to analyse these conflicts in detail.)

The *paidotribes* superintended the palaistra and was the instructor in general physical education; the *gymnastes* was the coach for those intending to take up an agonistic career as professionals. As the career-aspects grew ever more important, the gymnast's status rose. Already Aristotle rated him above the paidotribes; five hundred years later, Galen saw the work of the paidotribes as quite secondary, something merely attached to the keywork of the gymnast.

The later 5th century B.C. brought about the need to develop the medical aspects of training. The pioneer was a paidotribes of Selymbria, Herodikos, who, himself a valetudinarian, worked out a system of exercises for health, calling it Gymnastics—though afterwards the terms Diet, *diaita*, and Hygiene, *hygiene*, were used. Platon jeered at the whole thing as a base trick for prolonging death, not life. Bathing was important in it, and so Herodikos and his system in the end helped to bring about the change of the Gymnasion into the huge Thermai or Public Baths of the Romans.[1]

Meanwhile the attack on the new athletics had begun. The Spartans, we saw, thought it made the breeding of good soldiers impossible. Platon thought it made the body very subject to disease and produced addicts, hard and brutal, who were unfit for social or political duties; Aristotle thought it a one-sided discipline, harmful to health, which weakened a man's capacity for procreation of children. Euripides in a long and passionate passage declared that "of all the myriad evils that press upon Hellas, there's no greater evil than the athletic folk".[2] This attitude carried on throughout the Roman times. Ploutarch voiced it and it found its most complete expression in the work of the physician Galen, who saw athletic training as a training in disease, reducing men to the level of brutes with its immoderate and unbalanced system of eating, drinking, and exertion.[3]

Philosophers and physicians might hold such views of athletics but had no effect on the popular passion or on the high esteem that city-authorities and imperial state alike showed for the winners at the big Games. In a world where the commoners were excluded from all share in the running of things, their thwarted desire to find some cause to which they could devote themselves had an outlet only in the sphere of sport. Also, sport was one of the very few ways in which a member of the lower classes could

achieve fame and success, a high social prestige and an easy life.
And we must recognise that the criticisms, though most of their
strictures were true enough, were made by members of the upper
class who resented the intrusion of the populace in any way into a
sphere that had once been an aristocratic preserve.

In Hellenistic times girls were admitted to the gymnasion at
several places, and, more rarely, slaves. (There were women professionals. Olympia had a race for women, with a track a sixth
shorter than the men's.) But we can be sure that in Egypt the
gymnasia were kept strictly for the males, on account of their
special function of maintaining the Greeks as a ruling-class.[4]
Philon indeed tells us:

As things are now, some women have reached such a degree of shame-
lessness that they not only, though they are women, give vent to
intemperate language and abuse among a crowd of men, but even
strike men and insult them, with hands practised in the works of the
loom and in spinning rather than in blows and assaults, like contestants in the pankration or wrestlers. And other things indeed may
be tolerable and such as one might easily bear, but it's a shocking thing
if a woman were to come to such a pitch of boldness as to grab the
genitals of one of the men in a brawl.[5]

He wants such a woman to have her hand cut off; and goes on:

It is right to praise those who have been the judges and directors of
gymnastic games, who have kept women from the spectacle, so that
they might not be thrown among naked men and thus spoil the
approved coinage of their modesty, neglecting the ordinances of
nature,

which he considers to forbid any mingling of the sexes when
naked.

An international centre in Hellenistic times was the mercantile
port of Delos, with its slave-trade. Here were several private
palaistrai, some of which were owned by foreigners (as at Athens).
One such owner was Nikeratos and his son, of Alexandreia.[6] A
paidotribes, Staseas, from Athens, had a class of 42 members, of
whom 22 were from Athens, with others from Rome, Chios,

Elea, Pitane (Aiolis), Salamis, Thera, Ephesos, Chalkis, Patara, Karpasia (Cypros), and Pelousion and Alexandreia in Egypt. These lads copied the organisation of their cities and called themselves priests, gymnasiarchs, lampadarchs (directors of torch-races) agonothetai (games-directors); they formed friendships and groupings that they carried on into the ephebeia. Though most of the lads were Athenians, there were others from all over the Mediterranean world. Among the paidotribai we find one from Alexandreia.[7]

The special gods of the palaistra and the gymnasion were Hermes and Herakles—though other deities might have their share of worship there, as well as the kings and emperors of the Hellenistic and Roman periods, and might have athletic festivals instituted in their honour.[8] Hermes was the main favourite.[9] Gymnasia often had *hermai* (statues composed of a four-sided pillar with a head on top, usually Hermes') of both Hermes and Herakles, and the two gods are at times linked in ephebic dedications.[10] But the dominant position of Hermes is brought out, for example, by an epitaph of Philokrates of Ikaria who died at the age of 12; he was sadly prevented from "casting the chlamys about his body and gazing on Hermes presiding over the gymnasion". That is, he was too young to enter the gymnasion, let alone the ephebic college which was symbolised by the chlamys, the short mantle.[11]

From the gymnasion of Delos we have an inventory of the 2nd century B.C., which cites 41 hermai in marble; and no doubt many more were added before the place was abandoned towards A.D. 90. We must visualise the colonnade of its court, as well as its various halls, as richly decorated with hermai in the last century B.C. One excavated head was very like another found in the gymnasion of the Ptolemies at Thera, with its long narrow eyes; it may be also compared with another Graeco-Egyptian head with heavy eyelids, which has been set among the works showing the last stage of Praxitelean influence at Alexandreia.[12]

Mostly the works at Delos show young heads, though one has the battered face of a near-professional. Inscriptions speak of actual portraits in the Hermes-heads only of persons of official rank: gymnasiarchs, paidotribai, or benefactors of the gymnasion. No text tells of epheboi represented as Hermes, yet the Delian sculptures are of lads not more than eighteen years. The heads are not strongly individualised and may be taken to depict Hermes and perhaps Herakles as ephebic ideals.[13]

As Hermes was the tutelary god of the palaistra and gymnasion, the planet Hermes was considered to endow men with their athletic powers. Ptolemaios states that in the child's first four years the Moon governs his growth; then for the next ten years Hermes takes over and "begins to articulate and fashion the intelligent and logical part of the soul, to implant certain seeds and rudiments of learning, and to bring to light individual peculiarities of character and faculties, awakening the soul at this stage by instruction, tutelage, and the first gymnastic exercises".[14] Then Aphrodite intrudes with puberty, the Sun next imparts purpose and desires for "substance, glory, and position". Ares for fifteen years rules with anxieties and struggles, and Zeus dominates in maturity for twelve years with the search for balance and understanding, followed by the passive declining phase of Kronos.[15]

Hermes appears in his gymnastic relations because he represents the growing lad who is preparing for the tests of puberty and manhood; and this astrologic position is in accord with the general ritual and mythological evidence. For later years Ptolemaios stresses Hermes as connected with practicality and ingenuity; in certain conjunctions he can produce "prophets who also make money":

Hermes, by himself taking the domination of the soul, in an honourable position makes those who are born under him wise, shrewd, thoughtful, learned, inventive, experienced, good calculators, inquirers into nature, speculative, gifted, emulous, beneficent, prudent, good at conjecture, mathematicians, partakers in mysteries, successful in attaining their ends. In the opposite position he makes them utter rascals, precipitate, forgetful, impetuous, lightminded, fickle, prone to change their minds, foolish rogues, witless, sinful, liars, undiscriminating, unstable, undependable, avaricious, unjust, and in general unsteady in judgment and inclined to evil deeds.[16]

Those "prone to athletic training, fond of competition", as well as those who are "lovers of the beautiful, of children, of spectacles, and of the domain of the Muses", and those who are "ambitious, glory-seekers, and in general gentlemanly", are dominated by Zeus in alliance with Aphrodite.

Under the Ptolemies in Egypt we find Herakles and Hermes linked in a gymnasion of the Pharbaithite nome, and a gymnasion-club called the Herakleion at Sebynnytos. In general discourse the link of Hermes and athletics remained till the end. Heliodoros writes of his hero as "a man trained from early years in the exercises of the gymnasia and thoroughly versed in the art of Hermes Enagonios", the Patron of Contests. Nonnos, playfully telling of the match between Dionysos and his lad Ampelos, says, "Mad

The stadion race, and the dolichos (vase paintings).

Love stood between them, a winged Hermes Enagonios, wreathing a lovegarland of daffodil and iris."[17]

Now let us look at the actual sports as they had been developed in the great days of Greek civilisation and carried on into the Hellenistic and Roman days. From the 8th century B.C. contenders were naked.[18] For hygienic and moral reasons a custom was brought in of tying the end of the prepuce to a belt; but this was unsuitable for violent movements.[19] The hair was shaved or cut in the bowl-crop, and Roman athletes tied their hair up in a knot. No shoes were used, the track being softened and laid with sand. Usually nothing was worn on the head even in the hottest weather, though a cap, apparently of dogskin, might be worn, with strings under the chin. Martial writes:

> So the foul oil your sleekbright locks may spare
> cover with this skincap your wellsoaked hair.[20]

The athlete carried a small bottle of oil. Before each exercise, he was massaged all over in a lukewarm room: first a dry rub, then oil applied with the bare hand in a more vigorous way—with youngsters, according to their age. After the exercise, there was again massage, and oil was used. The purpose was hygienic; any idea of making the body slippery in wrestling was an afterthought. For, after being oiled, the athlete covered himself with fine dust, which was thought to regulate the flow of sweat and protect the skin—perhaps from sun or wind.[21] We hear of five dusts, each with its own characteristics: mud-dust, a detergent; pottery-dust, evoking sweat (though Loukian says that dust inhibited sweat); asphalt-dust, giving warmth; black and yellow dust, feeding the skin, the yellow providing a handsome shine. Nile-dust had a high reputation. Suetonius tells us of Nero:

His unpopularity was increased by a scarcity of corn. For it happened in the midst of the famine a ship was announced with a cargo of dust for the court-wrestlers [instead of corn]. The general indignation was so stirred that he was treated to every sort of insult. On the top of his statue was set a knot, *cirrus*, with a Greek inscription: *Now indeed the wrestle is on, give up!*[22]

At the end of the exercises came a clean-up, begun with a scrape by a bronze currycomb. Philon gives us a detail about the oil: "In a gymnastic school oil is placed for the common use; but it often comes about that the master, through some civic necessity, changes the arrangement of the normal hours of exercise, so that some of those who want to anoint themselves turn up too late."[23] Elsewhere he says there could be an excessive supply. "It often happens, when the master of a gymnastic school has gone to extravagant expense, some of those who have no sense of decorum are bespattered with oil instead of water and let all the drops from them fall on the ground, so that a very slippery mud results."

The paidotribes wore a purple cloak, which he could throw off if he wanted to demonstrate. He also carried a long forked stick, for chastisement rather than for pointing out positions. Herodotos cites an exchange of witticisms before the battle of Salamis.[24] One Greek told Themistokles, "In the races the man who starts before the signal is whipped", and Themistokles replied, "Yes, but

those who start too late win no prizes." Loukian cites the warning,
"Look out, you'll get a lot more punishment if you don't do what
you're told." The gymnastes followed his pupils to the games,
made all the necessary preparations, and then stood by with words
of counsel, encouragement, or reproach; he expected implicit
obedience.[25] The *aleiptes* or anointer rose in status in later times
and was confused with the paidotribes; he came at times to pre-
scribe diet and even how it should be eaten. We find him dis-
approving of intellectual conversation, *philologein*, during meals.[26]

The dual patronage of Hermes and Herakles may in part have
been evolved as the expression of the division of contests into
light and heavy. Philostratos also mentions a division of athletes
into categories with names like lions, eagles, *schiziai* (laths or
sticks), bears, and so on. How such a classification arose is unclear.[27] Originally the diet is said to have been fresh cheese, dried
figs and wheat; such simple food was displaced by an over-
whelming emphasis on meat.[28] Pork was the main meat used, but
we hear also of beef and goat's flesh; no fish or cakes, but bread
slightly leavened and hardly baked. A breakfast of bread was
followed by exercises till evening, with only a few intervals;
then came a meat-dinner. Those under severe training ate vast
amounts of meat and became unable to do without these amounts
even for a day. The aim was to get sheer bulk and weight. Runners
naturally were trained to keep their weight down. On all athletes
the strictest continence was enjoined and was practised by some
during the whole period of training.[29] Besides the usual run of
exercises in palaistra and gymnasion we hear of athletes putting
heavy weights, bending iron bars, wrenching back the necks of
bulls, knocking suspended bags of sand to and fro with their
fists. They also worked with mattocks—work that was useful in
preparing the ground at Games.[30] Generally they concentrated
on one particular event.[31]

Races were run on a straight flat track. The stadion was a
basic length—some 600 feet, though the standard foot varied
in different cities. The runner started from a standing position,
his feet together, his body bent forwards. To avoid congestion,
heats with a final were used. The *diaulos*, a double-stadion—there

and back—was common; the four-lap, *hippios*, was less run;
we meet however races with 7, 12, 20 and (at Olympia) 24 laps.
Always the single stadion course was used, with a turn probably
round a post set up at the start or finish. Most Games included an
armed race, in which the runner had helm and shield; and torch-
races too were popular. At Olympia the winner of the stadion-
race gave his name to the Olympiad. Representations show the
stadion-runners swinging their arms backwards and forwards,
while in the *dolichos* or long-distance races they keep their elbows

The armed race; athlete washing hands (relief).

pressed against their sides. Cicero mentions runners shouting their
loudest; but he perhaps refers only to the stadion.[32]

Nonnos tells of a race of three runners, one of whom, Ampelos
(Vine), is the favourite of Dionysos:

> They stood in a row, trusting in the quick soles
> of their straightgoing feet. With a stormy movement
> Kissos went skimming the top of the ground he touched.
> Leneus went speeding at his rear as quick
> as heaven's winds, and with his breath he warmed
> the sprinter's back, still close behind the leader,
> his footstep in the other's footstep touched
> upon the dust as down it came: the space
> between them was no more than that the rod
> leaves open at the bosom of a girl
> who works a loom, before her firm young breast.
> Ampelos came on third and last.

So Dionysos breathed strength into him. Kissos (Ivy), striving hard, stumbled on a wet place and fell in the sandy slush. Leneus (personification of Lenos, winepress) had to check his course, his knees lost their swing, and Ampelos won the race.[33]

Heliodoros describes an armed race at the Pythian Games. The other events had been performed in magnificent style, "close-run races, clinches of wrestling and buffets of boxing", and the herald called, "Forward the armed men!" The heroine Charikleia went to the end of the stadion as devotee of Artemis, a torch in her left hand, a palmbranch in her right. Only one contestant appeared, a man who had been crowned in a number of contests. The officers were about to send him away, as without a contest he could not get the crown. He then insisted that the herald should call for anyone who offered to come out and contend. Theagenes, the hero, strode out, unable to bear the sight of anyone else getting a crown from Charikleia's hands and sure that he could win with the girl as goal. "He took his stand at the starting-line, panting and barely able in his impatience to wait for the signal of the trumpet." The herald proclaimed the names of the entrants.

When the cord was let drop and the race began at a speed almost defeating the quickest vision, the young girl could no longer keep still, her legs quivered, her feet danced, as if, to my thinking, her soul was floating away with Theagenes and zealously supporting him in the race. The spectators, to a man, were in suspense to see the result, and filled with a great anxiety, and I more than any . . . When he had completed half the course, he turned a little and looked askance at Ormenos [the other runner]. He then raised his shield on high, threw back his head, and, fixing his gaze full on Charikleia, he sped on like a dart to its mark, and came in so many yards ahead of the Arkadian that the measure of the interval was taken afterwards. He ran up to Charikleia, cast himself with intense fervour into her bosom, as though he could not check his impetus; and as he received the palm, I noticed that he kissed the girl's hand.

Philon however seems to know the armed race as a double-lap: "the warriors in the *diaulos* or the ebb and flow of the tides of the sea, returning to the point from which they originally set out".[34]

Athletes were keen on records; but through the lack of anything

E

like a stopwatch they could only claim to have been the first to win some sort of victory or combination of victories. In the 5th century a Spartan set out his victories at minor Peloponnesian festivals and claimed to have done "what no man alive has done". After that, phrases like "first of mankind" and "first of men at any time" keep turning up ever more often. A Milesian runner claimed to have been "the first and only man" to achieve one group of victories; for three others he is "first of all men", for another "first and only man from Asia", for another three "first of Ionians", for two others "the first Milesian". An inscription from Anazarbos in Asia Minor, mid-3rd century A.D., seems to claim that an athlete was "first of all men ever" to deadheat four times with the same man on the same day in the stadion-race.[35]

Jumping-weights (B.M.).

The only jump was the long jump. There was a short slow run, a firm take-off, probably at the starting-line, and a landing on levelled ground. Slides, falls and apparently even a landing with one foot ahead of the other were excluded. The two footprints must show clearly. Stone dumbells were held in the hand, weighing from 2 to 10 lb.; they were thought to balance the arms.[36]

From the end of the 5th century the discus was of bronze, weighing from 3 to 9 lb. (One of $12\frac{1}{2}$ lb. may be a votive offering.) The lighter ones are the older. The way in which the throw was made has to be deciphered from works of art.[37] The base was rounded on front and sides, but was not a circle; doubtless it was set at the starting-point of the race-track, as with the jump. The thrower held the discus in both hands, raised it to the level of his head, then pressed it with his hand tightly against his right forearm. He brought his right arm sharply down behind with his

head and body turning to follow the movement. His right foot
served as pivot, taking the full weight of his body. Then came
the throw, a sudden straightening of thigh and bent body supplying the force.[38]

The aim in javelin-throwing was distance. The sports-javelin
had no point, was body-length and thick as a finger. Weighted
at the end, it seems to have been very light. A leathern thong
was wound round the shaft near the centre of gravity; in the
terminating loop the athlete inserted the first two fingers of
his right hand. The loop kept the javelin on a straight course
and made it rotate (as a rifle-bore does a bullet); it had the effect of
lengthening the thrower's arm and outstretched fingers, and
doubled or trebled the length of throw. As with the discus, the
throw was preceded by a little spring and tensing of the body,
the head and trunk following the right arm as it was thrown back
as far as it would go.[39]

The fact that the runner gave the name to the Olympiad shows
the original importance of the foot-race; but wrestling had now
long become even more popular than running. Palaistra, which
means wrestling-ground, had become the sports-field and the
school of physical education. The ground was broken up by pick
or mattock as for jumping. The contestants were paired off by
lots. The aim was to throw one's opponent on to the ground
without falling; if one fell, the throw was not counted. There
were three rounds in a match. How the thrown man fell did not
matter—whether it was on his back, shoulder, or hip; but the
knees were not enough. Tripping, but not a leg-hold, seems
allowed; the permissible holds were on arms, neck, body. The
pentathlon (flat race, long jump, discus, javelin, and wrestling)
decided who was the best all-round athlete. The order and rules of
placing are not sure; but it seems that the race came first and wrestling at the end. The winner had to come first in at least three of
the events.[40]

Nonnos has two accounts of wrestling. I give these in prose as
the interest is only in the factual picture:

The athletes came forward naked but for body-belts that hid the unseen loins. They both began by grasping each other's wrists and wreathed this way and that, and pulled each other in turn over spread-out dust, holding the arms in a tight fingergrip. It was ebb-and-flow between them, man dragging man with evenly balanced pulls, dragging and dragged; for they hugged each other with both arms and bent the neck and pressed head to head on midforehead, pushing steadily downward. Sweat ran from the rubbed brows to show the hard struggle. The backs of both men were bent by the pull of the arms and pressed strongly by the two pairs of twined hands. Many a weal ran up of itself and made a purplish pattern with the hot blood, till their bodies were marked with it.

So, in their struggle, they showed all the varied tricks of the wrestling art. Then first Aristaios got his arms round his opponent and heaved him right up from the ground. But crafty Aiakos did not forget his cunning skill. With insinuating leg he gave a kick behind Aristaios' left knee and rolled him fully over, helpless on his back on the ground, exactly like a crashing cliff.

The people around all gazed with astonished eyes at Phoibos' son, so grand, so proud, so famed, taking a fall. Next Aiakos with an effort raised the huge son of Cyrene high above the ground . . . He held the man in his arms, without bending his back or his straight neck, carrying the man with both arms by the middle, so that they were like a pair of cross-rafters made by some carpenter to calm the stormy force of the winds. Then he threw him down at full length in the dust and got on his opponent's back as he lay there, thrust both legs along under his belly, and bent them in a close clasp just below the knees, pressing foot to foot and encircling the ankles. Quickly he stretched himself over the other's back and wound his two hands over each other like a necklace round the neck, interlacing his fingers, and so made his arms a fetter for the neck. Sweat ran in streams and soaked the dust. But he wiped away the pouring drops with dry sand, so that his opponent might not wriggle out of his enclosing grip through the streams of hot moisture that he exuded from his squeezed neck.

As he lay there in this tight embrace, the heralds came dashing up at full speed, men chosen as overseers of the games, so that the victor might not kill him with those strangling arms. For there was then no such law as in later days their successors devised, for the case when a man overcome by the suffocating pain of a noose round the neck testified to his opponent's victory by a significant silence, by tapping the victor with submissive hand.[41]

In this account the wrestling match has degenerated into the pankration or all-in wrestling.

In the other passage Nonnos playfully makes the wrestling of Dionysos and Ampelos into a love-play:

They stood forward as Athletes of the Loves. They joined their palms garlandwise over each other's back, packed at the waist with a knot-of-hands, squeezed the ribs with the muscles of their two forearms, raised each other alternately from the ground . . .

Ampelos enclosed the wrist of Bromios [Bacchos] in his palm. Then linking hands and tightening that intrusive grip, he interlaced his fingers and brought them together in a double-knot, squeezing the right hand of willing Dionysos.

Next Bacchos ran his two hands round the young man's waist, pressing his body with a loving grasp, and lifted him high. But Ampelos kicked Bacchos neatly behind the knee; and Euios [Bacchos] laughed merrily at the blows from his young comrade's tender foot and let himself fall on his back in the dust.

Thus, while Bacchos lay willingly on the ground, the lad sat across his naked belly; and Bacchos lay delighted at full length, sustaining the pleasant burden on his paunch. Then, raising one of his legs, he set the sole of the foot firmly on the sand and lifted his overturned back, but showed mercy in his strength as with the rival movement of a reluctant hand he dislodged his beloved burden.

The lad, no novice, turned sideways and rested his elbow on the ground, then jumped across on his adversary's back, then over his flanks with a foot behind one knee and another set on the other ankle he encircled the waist with a double bond, squeezed the ribs, and pressed straight out the lifted leg under his knee. Both rolled in the dust and the sweat poured out to announce their tiredness.[42]

Here too we find the pankration. The final hold is that called to-day the scissors.

In the *Aithiopika*, Theagenes has to wrestle with a giant Ethiopian. He "took up some dust and strewed it over his shoulders and arms, which were still moist from the bullhunt; shook off what did not stick, stretched out his hands in front of him, took his stand on firmly-planted feet, bent his knees, curved his shoulders and back, slightly inclined his neck, braced in his whole frame and stood chafing to get at grips". The Ethiopian watched with a sneering smile, an ironical nod; then ran up and heaved his arm on to Theagenes' neck. There was a loud smack, "and again he swaggered and laughed complacently to himself". Theagenes, though shaken, decided to rely on skill; pretended to be in more stress than he was; and laid the other side of his neck open to attack. The Ethiopian struck out again, and Theagenes feigned to be about to fall on his face. Then as the Ethiopian raised his arm for a third blow, Theagenes "suddenly crouched and darted in underneath, avoiding the downward stroke. With his right forearm he drove up his opponent's left, and staggered

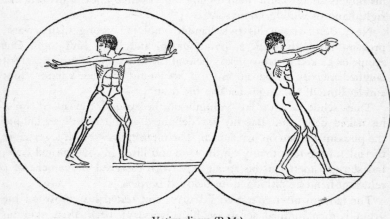

Votive discus (B.M.).

him as he was at the same time in part pulled groundwards by the sweep of his hand, which struck only empty air. Theagenes then came up under his armpits and got a strong hold from behind. Straining hard, he just engirdled the man's bulky middle, upset his footing by hard repeated hammerings with his heel at the joints and bones of the man's ankles, and so compelled him to sink down on to one knee. Then, bestriding him with feet apart, he thrust his legs into the region of the Ethiopian's groin, dislodged the wrists on which he was relying to uphold his chest, brought the man's forearms round to meet on his brows, drew them over to his back and shoulders, and so forced him to sprawl with belly on ground."[43]

We have already in these accounts moved from wrestling proper to the pankration, a brutal contest, in which almost anything was allowed: the usual boxing punches and wrestling grips, but also kicks in the stomach, twisting of arms and legs, bites, stranglings, and so on. Only, the fighters must not put their fingers in one another's eyes, nose, or mouth. Usually, after a few passes, they rolled on the ground, locked viciously, and fought on till one passed out or raised his arm. To make things worse, the ground was not only dug up but was also well watered, so that the rollings and writhings would go on in mud.

In wrestling, the contestants sometimes stayed entangled in their grips until the onlookers were bored. An Olympian inscription says of a pankratiast from Smyrna that "he stuck it out until nightfall" so that the stars caught up with him; he was "the first of men ever" to win a draw in the pankration there. (Loukilios the poet parodies such claims in an epigram about a long-distance runner still going fast at midnight.[44]) Draws in general seem common. A Magnesian wrestler of the 2nd century A.D. claimed to have won 29 times in games with crowns for prizes and 127 times in games with money-prizes; he drew at Olympia and on 18 other occasions.[45]

Heliodoros in the passage cited above contrasts the skilled athlete of normal proportions with the bulky type produced by the diet of meat and bread (though the Sudanese setting makes the latter out as brawny Ethiopian). The ideal heavy professional appears in an inscription from Antioch in Pisidia, in which a wrestler claims that "as soon as his opponents saw him stripped, they begged to be excused".[46]

In boxing there was no ring, no rounds. The men slogged on till one went down or gave up. The pace was slower than in modern boxing (as in the early barefist fights of England), with blows aimed mainly at the head. So the fighters used less clinching, kept a high guard and extended arm, and used stone-walling tactics. Under Titus there was a champion who could keep his guard up for two days and tire out his opponent without letting him get a single blow in. From the early 4th century B.C. soft bandages had given way to hard ones, a kind of mitten that left the fingers uncovered but went over the wrist and was tied below the elbow by a sheepskin band; the material was probably leather. The fingers had a bandage of their own, composed of three or five leather-strips held by laces.[47]

We know of a boxer of Hermopolis, Herminos of the later 2nd century A.D., whose nickname was Moros (dull, heavy, stupid). We can hardly think he would be proud of this name, but it appears in his diploma.[48] A festival account of Oxyrhynchos mentions two pairs of pankratiasts and boxers armed with the ball, *sphairomachoi*. (This *sphaira* seems an iron ball worn with padded covers.) Boxers appear later on Coptic textiles, showing that the matches must have had a popular appeal.[49] And we have the letter of Dios to his wife Sophrone; he had gone to Alexandreia to look for someone who had disappeared—probably a debtor—and "instead we found our lord the king", a visiting emperor. Games were held at the imperial command and Dios hopefully managed to get himself admitted "by an act of favour": presumably he was not qualified as the member of the correct athletic organisations. The professionals put him in his place by beating him badly in the pankration. Undaunted, he then challenged his own companions to some sort of all-in wrestling. No doubt he knew that he could tackle them with impunity; anyway he defeated them and was given a money-prize from the emperor while the others got clothes as consolation-prizes. He repeated his triumph on a day when the emperor led the procession to the Lagaion, honouring the memory of the first Ptolemy. "So don't be annoyed", Dios ends. "We haven't found the fellow, but fortune has given us something else."[50]

Nonnos describes a boxing match. Melisseus is faced by Eurymedon, "one to whom Hermes had given the gear of strong-limned boxing". The latter's brother sets his bodybelt by him, fits the girdle to his loins, and coils the leather-straps round his long hands. Then the boxer advances into the midst of the space, holding his left hand as a guard before his face.

All the while he kept on the defence before the dangerous attack of his opponent, so that the latter shouldn't get one in on brow or forehead, or draw blood by bashing his face, or smash his temple with a lucky blow, tearing away to the very centre of the busy brain, or with a hard hook over the temples tear the eyes from his blinded face, break his bloody jaw, and drive a long row of his sharp teeth in.

But as Eurymedon came with a rush, Melisseus landed one high up on the chest. Eurymedon countered with a lead at the face but missed. He hit only the air. Shaking with excitement, he skipped round the man past his chest with a side-step and brought home his right on the exposed breast under the nipple. Then they clinched together, shifting their feet a little, carefully, in short steps, hands making play against hands. As the blows fell in quick succession, the straps wreathed round

Athletics (mosaic of Tusculum).

their fingers made a terrible noise. Cheeks were torn, blooddrops stained the straps, jaws resounded under the blows, the round cheeks swelled and spread on the puffy face, the eyes of both were sunk in hollows.

Eurymedon was badly shaken by Melisseus and his tricky dodging. He had to stand with the sun shining intolerably on his face and blinding him. Melisseus rushed in, danced about with quickened twists and turns, and lashed in a sudden one on the jaw, under the ear. Eurymedon fell in distress on his back and rolled in the dust, helpless, fainting, like a man drunk. He inclined his head to one side and spat out a froth of thickish blood. His brother Alkon slung him on his back and glumly carried him off, stunned by the blow . . . [51]

Philon, who for all his rejection of festivals and games shows him-
E*

self well acquainted with them, remarks that a slave who is being punished exemplifies the passive reception of blows; the athlete in the pankration or a boxing-match exemplifies the active attitude. "As the blows fall on him, he brushes them off with either hand or he turns his neck this way and that thus evading the blows, or often he stretches up on tiptoes to his full height or draws himself in and forces his opponent to lash about in empty space, much as men do who are practising the movements."[52] Elsewhere he advises men not to take part in contests in badness; if however they cannot escape, to take care to be defeated. "And do not allow the herald or the judge to crown the foe as victor, but come forward and present the prizes and the palm, and crown him—'by your leave, sir'—and bind the headband round the head, and yourself make in a strong loud voice this announcement:

In the contest that was proposed in lust and wrath and licentiousness, in folly too and injustice, you spectators and stewards of the sports, I have been vanquished, and this man is the victor and has proved himself so vastly superior that even we his antagonists, who might have been expected to grudge him the victory, feel no envy."

Further, he says, do not count as holy contests "those which the States hold in their three-yearly Festivals and for which they have built theatres to hold many myriads of men; for in them the prizes are borne away by the man who has outwrestled someone and laid him on his back or on his face on the ground, or by the man who can box or combine boxing with wrestling, and who stops short of no act of outrage or unfairness. Some give a sharp strong edge to an ironbound thong and fasten it round both hands and lacerate their opponents' heads and faces, and when they manage to plant their blows, batter the rest of their bodies and then claim prizes and garlands for their pitiless savagery." As for the other contestants at sprinting or the pentathlon, what sensible person can help laughing at the zeal for records and victory? All sorts of animals can beat them, not only gazelles and stags, but even dogs and hares. What logic is there in fixing legal penalties against violence and then giving "garlands and public announcements and other honours" to men who commit outrages in public, at state-festivals and at the theatre? The true athletes are those who, though weakly in body, are stalwarts in spirit, and who strive for the virtues.[53]

Many loosening-up exercises were used, reaching their height in the 2nd and 3rd centuries A.D.—hiking, running 30 yards or so, running round in circles, skipping or jumping with the feet hitting the buttocks, kicking legs in the air, making arm-movements, climbing ropes, playing games with balls and hoops. Pick-handling came in through the need to prepare ground, then was used for muscle-strengthening. Boxers had to hold arms out or keep fists clenched a long time, hold an arm up while someone tried to drag it down; they used a punchbag of leather filled with sand or small seeds. Pankratiasts let the bag swing back on their heads or bodies to improve their balance. The oboe was used to give time; every establishment had its auletes.[54] Dion sarcastically tells the Alexandrians that the passion for music now affects teachers of rhetoric, politicians, lawyers, and the lecturers on philosophy and other subjects. "Since they note your interest in singing and your passion for it, they all sing now, public speakers as well as sophists, and everything's done to music. If you pass a courtroom, you can't easily tell if it's a drinking-party or a trial going on; and if there's a sophist's lecture-room near at hand, you won't be able to make out what he says. In my opinion people will soon go so far as to use song to accompany their gymnasion-exercise, yes, even to cure the sick. For already, when physicians discourse to you on their art, they chant."

Exercises also came to be used for health-reasons. A man walked tiptoe to prevent constipation and ophthalmia; he ran to relieve gonorrhea; he swam for dropsy.[55]

In wrestling the paidotribes taught the different positions or schemata in turn; then the athlete used them in an actual match. A papyrus of the 2nd century from Oxyrhynchos provides us with a fragment from a master's handbook; it is hard to translate in its concise jargon, but may be thus deciphered:

Get up close and stick right hand round his head.
You, put your arm round him.

You, grab hold of him from under.
You, move foreward and give him a hug.
You, grab hold of him from below with right arm.
You, put arm round him where he's got hold of you
    from below and bring left leg up to his side.
You, push him away with left hand.
You, change your place and clasp him.
You, turn round.
You, grab him by the balls.
You, bring your feet forward,
You, catch hold round his waist.
You, throw weight forward and bend him back.
You, bring body forward and straighten up, [pounce] on
    him and give as good as you get . . . [56]

There were many other games and sports, which did not provide events for the great festivals: swimming, weight-putting, archery, ball-games of many kinds—though some of these might be used for contests on lesser occasions. Nonnos has a charming account of a girl swimming and keeping her head well above water so that her hair is not wet; also he tells of a swimming race between Bacchos and Ampelos.[57] In an archery-contest a wild pigeon is tied to a ship's mast planted in sandy soil. The first marksman hits the cord and the bird flies free, but is then shot down. "The half-dead bird beat about in the dust with its wings, fluttering round the feet of danceweaving Dionysos."[58]

Balls varied in hardness, being stuffed with hair or feathers or airblown; racquets or bats seem unknown, though armguards were used. As medical authorities came to consider ballgames beneficial, a ball-room, *sphairisterion*, was added to gymnasia.[59]

6

Charioteers

WE CAN look more closely at the social trends expressed in athletics, and then turn to charioteering, to which a specially aristocratic colouration was attached. The criticisms of sports that we have noted were mainly made of the branches where professionals dominated, and concentrated on boxers and wrestlers. They indeed came largely from philosophic circles that were anti-democratic in attitude, and must be treated with some caution. But there were also the attacks by the Cynics, whose social views were often politically subversive and who expressed many of the emotions of the underdog, especially in the Hellenistic period.

Many of the charges against the Games had an undeniable element of truth; yet there were also great positive factors in the spreading of the spectacles and festivals. These factors have been summed up:

By introducing into the athletic games, some of which were known to the Egyptians, but only under the heading of amusements, a strict discipline that gave them a sort of dignity; by providing each man with a sort of aim in life, a victory in perspective and a possibility of attaining it; by making gleam in the humblest eyes a glory previously unsuspected; by exalting the individual and magnifying disinterested effort; by creating a domain where the distinctions of caste were replaced by a hierarchy of new values; by exhibiting to the eyes of all the human body in its beauty, force, suppleness, nudity; by turning out into the street, so to speak, the clamorous and moving troops of musicians, mimes, actors, conjurers, previously confined to the precincts of temples or lordly dwellings; by making pass before the marvelling eyes the host of shimmering imagery in Greek myths—

common life was enriched and great new potentialities created.

Despite the limiting and distorting factors in the situation, there is much truth in this claim.

The widespread passion for athletics is an undeniable fact. It has been remarked of the book by Artemidoros on the Interpretation of Dreams, "What, after the fear and respect of the gods, seems to have occupied the spirits of men were the representations of the circus and the theatre. On every page are mentioned Olympic Games, Nemean, combats of ferocious beasts, gladiators of all types, netfighters, *hoplomachoi*, *dimachoi*, athletes, acrobats, pugilists, actors, mimes, fluteplayers."[1] Much the same impression is given by the astrological writers—though, no doubt because of their considerable connection with the Egyptian scene, the gladiators loom less large.[2] Philon declared that men do not devote their leisure to a truce from all the everyday matters of making a living, but turn "to sports or shows of actors or dancers, for the sake of which those who madly pursue theatrical amusements suffer disasters and even meet wretched deaths".[3] Dion told the Alexandrians that "the organ of hearing of a people is the theatre, and into your theatre there enters nothing beautiful or honourable—or very rarely. But it is forever full of lyre-strummings and uproar, buffoonery and scurrility." The performers are usually:

> the mimes and dancers with earthbeating feet
> and men astride fast steeds who rouse to heat
> and strife the foolish childish crowds, and sprawl
> the cities down in ruin, one and all.

And he declares that someone has summed up the Alexandrians as "a people to whom you need only throw plenty of bread and a hippodrome-ticket, as they have no interest in anything else."[4]

The Hellenistic period, we must remember, in carrying the Greek city-forms far abroad, multiplied the gymnasia and the number of people interested in athletic contests. These people included not only the Greek settlers, but the natives who in varying degrees were Hellenised. All these groups were drawn into the great contests of the Greek world and felt the need to prove themselves the breeders and trainers of champions. In Greece itself the games had been contaminated, in the eyes of the aristocrats, by the influx of professionals; but in the outer Greek world the games now became the englamoured objects of the ambitions of many widespread groups. In the 2nd and 1st centuries B.C. the Olympic winners in large part come from Egypt, Asia Minor, Syria, Rhodes.[5] When in 216 the famous pankratiast Kleitomachos came up against Aristonikos, the special envoy of Ptolemaios IV, he rebuked the Greeks for applauding the Egyptian representative, saying that he himself was contesting for the honour of Greece.[6] Indeed all the ruling groups of Macedonia and Asia Minor as well

Race in Circus (mosaic of Lyons).

as those of Egypt were eager to win, not only in the chariot-races, but also in the other athletic events.

An outstanding example was Sosibios of Egypt, who in later life became an important minister under Ptolemaios IV. From the encomiast elegy by Callimachos we learn that he won the boys' double-length at some games (presumably the Ptolemaia established in honour of Ptolemaios I), then the men's contest in wrestling at the Panathenaian festival, though he was still under twenty, an *ageneios*, and finally, as a full adult, the chariot races at the Isthmian and the Nemean games. He was the first Egyptian Greek to win this double victory:

> The Nile as he brings his fertilising water
> yearly may say: "A beautiful reward
> has my nursling paid me back; for none till now

has brought a double trophy to the city
from these sepulchral festivals. I, though great,
with sources that no mortal man has known
in this one thing was less significant
than streams which the white ankles of women cross
easily and children pass on foot
with knees unwetted . . . "7

Callimachos seems trying to revive the ancient epinicean ode in elegiac couplets; but the narrowed court-basis of the celebration lacks the dynamic elements that gave the earlier odes their breadth and force.

The genre in which is found most abundantly agonistic reflections is the epigram, thus appropriate to the games: hence the elegy and the epyllion, literary forms dominating the epoch. Alexandrian poetry, further, imposes new aesthetic formulas on the ancient epic: Apollonios Rhodios, the chief of Alexandrian epic poets, does not introduce an account of entire contests, as Homer did, but selects a single event, such as boxing or wrestling, depicting it with accuracy and epical breadth, united to that love of detail which is so much recommended by Hellenistic aesthetes. The poets of the mimes, of the epyllion and of the pastorials keep indeed to this mode of procedure: as for the epigram, it had always been a genre used to set out a single characteristic element, in a very short and concise form.[8]

The agonistic element was used in a decorative and learned way, with the poets drawing on antiquarian lore and on technical manuals of sport; at the same time there was a genuine reflection of the attitudes and ways of life of the period. There was at one and the same time a growth of nationalist feeling in the various sections that made up Hellenistic civilisation with its many unifying factors, and a growth in individualism, an uprooting of the citizen. Professionalism in sport accompanied professionalism in war, an increase in the numbers of mercenaries.

The new positions found their expression, from the 4th century B.C. onwards, in the accumulation, sifting, and analysis of the material thrown up by the experiences of the preceding centuries in the field of sport. Technical manuals, medical treatises, and chronicles setting out the names and achievements of past athletes

from the earliest times, began to flourish. Local chronicles too
were consulted and used; and legends and marvellous tales were
taken up and developed. The permeation of daily life with agonistic ideas and images can be read in the philosophers. Zenon
excluded temples, lawcourts, and gymnasia from his ideal
Stoic State. Yet Stoic thought, accepting the unity of mind-
spirit-body, could not ignore the question of bodily wellbeing.
From Panaitios and Poseidippos to Musonius and Epiktetos the
athletic metaphor lies at the heart of the idea of the true sage; the
askesis of athletic training becomes the discipline of mind and
body in the philosopher, as later it becomes the ascetic way of
life of the Christian saint. The deepening and extending significance of this key-word brings out the extraordinary importance
of athletics in the ancient world, the way in which the conflict of
ideas that surrounded the agonistic sphere was felt as yielding the
supreme explanation of human destiny on earth. Either men found
a meaning in life through their self-identification with the contests,
or they had to reject those contests, and, in rejecting them, embrace them on a new level, in the sphere of the spirit. The agonistic conflict ceased to be a spectacle which conditioned men to
accept the world around; it was deeply absorbed within and
provided the basis for an inner drama of rejection and acceptance,
a rejection of all existing ways in a ceaseless *askesis* and an acceptance of the universe through the new point of harmony and understanding thus reached.[9]

The Cynics, speaking for lower level of society than did the
Stoics, attacked the sports-world in so far as it was based on professionalism and the rivalries of the rich and powerful. The setting
of their discourses was not the gymnasion of Platon but the workshops of craftsmen and cobblers.[10] Diogenes set out a dual *askesis*
and underlined the importance of physical exercises, but polem-
ised strongly against athletic training, which he emblematised in
the figure of heavy somnolent Herakles.[11] A fragment of Varro
serves to show the transition in the Stoic-Cynic diatribe from the
athletic *askesis* to the discipline of the philosophic dialectic; it
transfers the *agon epitaphios*, the grave-contest, to the paper
stadium (of literature and intellectual discussion) and finds value

in "the pankratium of the Stoics rather than that of the athletes".[12]

We should surmise on general grounds that Alexandreia (and to a lesser extent the other Greek cities or towns of Egypt) would abound with Cynics in the Roman period; and we have Dion's account to prove the point. He has stated that philosophers proper do not venture to appear in public and argue with the masses, though "some exercise their voices in what we call lecture-halls, where they gain an audience of men who are in accord with them and tractable". Then he has to admit that the Cynics alone brave the streets and common ways of life. "As for the Cynics, as they are termed, it is true that the city holds no small multitude of that sect, and that, as with anything else, this too has its harvest:

Eros in Circus with a dog-chariot (relief, B.M.).

persons whose tenets, indeed, include practically nothing spurious or ignoble, yet who must make a living—still, these Cynics, posting themselves at streetcorners, in lanes, at templegates, pass round the cap and play on the credulity of lads and sailors and crowds of that sort, stringing together rough jokes and a lot of tittletattle and a low badinage smacking of the marketplace. As a result, they do no good at all, but rather the worst possible harm; for they accustom thoughtless people to mock at philosophers in general, just as one might habituate lads to despise their teachers. When they ought to knock the insolence out of their listeners, these Cynics merely increase it." For a man of Dion's secure position, the Cynic message is hopelessly compromised by the fact its purveyors talk the language of the people and are pushed by need to ask for contributions. It is clear however that certain aspects of their harangues received strong popular support, putting in clearer form what the lower classes confusedly felt. Loukian, though no Cynic, found certain aspects of Cynic teach-

ing congenial and was much influenced by the satires of the early
Cynic Menippos. We may surmise that some of the jokes made
by the Cynic streetcorner-speakers were in the key of the following, which is put in the mouth of Anacharsis the Skythian (who
is used as 18th-century writers used the visiting Chinaman to
bring an innocently satirical eye to bear on the familiar scene).

And why are your young men behaving like this? Some are locked in
each other's arms and trip one another up, others choke and twist one
another, grovel together in the mud, wallow like swine. Yet at the
start, as soon as their clothes were off, they put oil on themselves and
took turns, rubbing each other down peacefully. I saw it. After that
I don't know what got into them, but they pushed one another about
with lowered heads and butted their foreheads like rams. And look
at that. One man picked the other up by the legs, then fell on him and
keeps him down, shoving him into the mud. Now he's wound his
legs round his waist and puts his forearm under his throat. He's
strangling the poor chap, who slaps him sideways on the shoulder—
begging him off, I suppose, to save himself from being quite choked.
Even out of consideration for the oil, they don't avoid getting dirty.
They rub the ointment off, plaster themselves with a mixture of mud
and sweat, and make themselves into jokes—to me, anyway—by
wriggling out of each other's hands like eels.

Another group's behaving the same way in the uncovered part of
the courtyard, though without the mud. There's a layer of deep sand
under them in the pit, as you see, they not only sprinkle one another
but of their own accord heap the dust on themselves like so many
cockerels — so that it'll be harder to break away in the clinches, I
presume, as the sand removes the slipperiness and provides a firmer
grip on a dry surface.

Others stand upright in a shroud of dust and attack one another
with blows and kicks. That fellow there looks as if he's going to spit
out his teeth, unlucky wretch, his mouth is so full of blood and sand.
As you see, he's had a blow on the jaw. But even the official nearby
doesn't part them and break up the fight—I gather from his purple
cloak that he's one of the officials. No, rather he urges them on and
praises the one that struck the blow.

Others in other parts are all exerting themselves. They jump up and
down as if running, but keep in the same spot. And they spring high
and kick the air.

So I want to know what's the good of doing all this. To me at least the thing looks more like sheer lunacy than anything else. I'd need very strong arguments to convince me that men who go on like this aren't out of their minds.[14]

The last-named exercise is that known nowadays as knees-up; it was called by the Romans the fuller's-jump from its likeness to the movement of the fuller jumping up and down on the clothes in his tub.[15]

The Cynic return-to-nature involved a glorification of the primeval days when men struggled directly with animals, especially in the hunt; and literary and philosophic expression of the interest in those days appeared in the emphasis on the old popular wisdom of fables, proverbs, legends. Man was helpless before the great beasts of prey; and yet man had triumphed somehow over Nature herself. This conclusion, understood in the narrowed perspective that interpreted it simply as the triumph of mind over matter, strengthened the idealist positions that separated mind from body and saw physical energy or force as purely animal. The comparison of man and animal, which had once been used for a popular criticism of aristocratic positions, was now used in a diametrically opposite way—against the professional athletes whom the aristocrats disdained, and in support of the intellectual scorn of game and festival.[16]

With the advent of the Roman Empire the spectacle of athletics further invaded Italy. Games with Roman names were founded, the Augusteia, the Capitolia, the Romaia, the Hadrianeia; and Hadrian established a fresh panhellenic festival at Athens under the name of Panhellenia. The general interest in athletics was shown in the writings of men like Ploutarch and Loukian; Phlegon compiled his new account of the Olympiads from 776 B.C. to A.D. 137; Philostratos and Galen from their different angles discussed training methods at length; the prose encomium, born in the Hellenistic period, expanded under the stimulus of rhetoric. Dionysios of Halikarnassos gives us the scheme for such encomia as developed in the 2nd century A.D., a period that saw a strong revival of athletics. It is significant that the intellectual attitude predominates in the schema, which

stresses the need of the athlete for the panegyrical word and thus
explains his position under the dual patronage of Herakles and
Hermes. The athlete who is proved to be corrupt, it is stressed, is
driven from the gymnastic world like a slave. And the ancient
days are recalled, when men competed without monetary rewards
and hence were heroised and even made *isotheoi*, the equals of gods.

The expansion of athletic games had, however, got well under
way by the 2nd century; it reached its climax in the 3rd; then in
the 4th, with the general weakening of the Graeco-Roman urban
systems, it went steadily into decline. The end is veiled in obscurity. The traditional date for the final collapse is A.D. 393; but

Circus races (Foligno).

the official closure of the games by Theodosius may not have
meant the end of all organised athletics. In the Code of Justinian
in the 6th century the laws about athletes are still included. Still,
the late 4th century certainly saw the general breakdown of the
old systems.

The participation of the rich and powerful families in the panhellenic games, which we noted under the Ptolemies, continued in
the Roman period. In Egypt and Asia Minor the upper classes
went on striving for victories. Instances are Markos Aurelios
Asklepiades also named Hermodoros; Herminos of Hermopolis;
Prosdektos of Mitylene; M. Aurelios Demetrios, pankratiast, of
Alexandreia; Quintilios Karpophoros of Ephesos, and many
others. Men of the high functionary class also took part in the

foot-races.[18] However, they were naturally attracted in particular to the chariot-races with their display and glamour.

In estimating the changes of the 2nd and 3rd centuries we must allow for certain liberalising factors at work. A monetary economy has a levelling effect from one aspect; all men tend to become equal before the law, though at the same time the stress on property-relations tends to reduce them to things. So a contrary movement is set up, a new set of social divisions determined by property. Under the empire there came about a lessened use of slave-labour, partly through drying-up supplies, partly through manumissions, and so on; as a result the stigma of manual work weakened. Further, the extending legal equality ended in the Antonine Constitution and the granting of full Roman status to the free population of the empire (apart from the *dediticii*). In Egypt the large numbers of Aurelioi met in the 3rd century must in considerable part represent the new citizens. "It is not even sure that all the Aurelioi have made use of their new status to frequent the gymnasion, in the cases where their access was previously forbidden; but it seems to me indisputable that such is indeed now their right." This point has important bearings on the civic system and its magistrates, and also on the use of and attitude to athletics. Social pressures would still work against the poorer citizens and we must not imagine any swamping of the gymnasia with the lesser Aurelioi and any democratic threat to the rich class's control of posts. (Those posts had anyway now become burdens and nobody was likely to push forward with claims for them.) The term *apo gymnasiou* persists through the century; what fades out is the term *metropolites*. However, when all allowances are made, the social effects in the Egyptian towns must have been large.[19]

By the time of the empire the chariot-race had become a very popular event, with an efficient organisation linked with the spectacles. The charioteers were generally slaves or men of the lowest class. They wore a short tunic laced round the body with leathern thongs, while other thongs bound the thighs. On the head was a tight-fitting cap. To enable the driver to cut himself free in the all-too-frequent accidents, he wore a curved knife stuck in his waistband. Those who managed to survive drove in large numbers of races. The *auriga* Diocles in mid-2nd century recorded that he had defeated winners of 3559, 2048, and 1467 races, while he himself, retiring at the age of 42, had won 3000 with two-horsed chariots and 1462 with larger ones. After Nero and Caligula set the example, upper-class Romans at times acted as charioteers.

The horses came mostly from Spain, Sicily, Mauretania, N. Greece and (later) Cappadocia. Usually a horse was not broken in till the age of three, and not raced till five; they thus had much stamina. A horse who won a hundred victories was called a *centenarius:* Diocles' inscription mentions a horse Tuscus that won 429 times. The initial or badge of the owner was branded on the flank. Almost all the names known for race-horses were male. In Egypt we hear of Cappadocian horses imported for the army; and horses and mules were exported to India as gifts for the princes, but we do not know if they had been reared in Egypt.

The chariot with two or four horses was the normal type in early days; but we now find chariots with three, six or seven horses. In a *biga* the horse was under a yoke; in the *quadriga* or bigger chariots, the middle horses were yoked, but those at the sides were merely held by traces. The chariots were light wooden structures bound with bronze, high in front and open behind. Up to twelve could take part in a race, which normally consisted of seven anti-clockwise laps. Rows of seven eggs or water-spouting dolphins, raised in stands over the centre of the course, kept the public informed of the number of laps completed: an egg being taken away, or a spout turned off, at the end of each lap.

A successful driver could win large sums of money; and at times, if a slave, was freed. In addition, in important races, where betting was heavy, he might get huge rewards from his backers. Under Domitian a driver won fifty purses of gold in an hour's racing; and a Moor named Crescens in ten years (A.D. 115–124) gained 1,556,346 sesterves with four horses, Circus, Acceptus, Delicatus, Cotynus.

Betting was permitted and large sums were laid. Race-cards were sold with lists of drivers and horses, which were also set out in advertisements painted on conspicuous walls, as have been found at Pompeii. On the mosaic from Lyon, *jubilatores* are shown galloping with the racers; they stimulated them with shouts and seem to have called the name of the winner. In some cases these attendants ran on foot.[20]

Nonnos has his account of charioteering. Aristaios advises his son to win by using his wits by keeping control of his horses, maintaining a straight course, watching the man in front, keeping close to the post and wheeling the car round without scratching the mark. "Tighten the guiding rein and swing the near horse full about and just clear the post, throwing your weight sideways." If however the post is struck with the axle, "you'll wreck both horses and car together". A man who is skilful enough can win even with inferior horses.

There are five contestants. They draw lots for position out of a helmet, then lift their leather whips and stand in a row. The umpire's main duty is to watch the way in which the post is turned. The race starts from the barrier. The men shake the reins and force along the horses with the jagged bit. A driver, coming up with another, crouches sideways, stretches himself, stands upright, "with bent hips urging on the willing horse, just a touch of the master's hand and a light whipflick". He keeps looking back; or checks his headlong horse and impedes the car at his rear. Another driver swerves from side to side to bar the man behind. The spectators sit on rows on a slope. One stands anxious, another beckons on a driver, a third feels his mad heart galloping along with the man he favours, another claps and shouts wretchedly, "cheering on, laughing, trembling, warning the driver".

In the last lap two drivers are close together. One of them touches up the flanks of his colts, draws level, and with his left hand catches at the mouth of his rival's horse, pulls at the bit, and forces the other car back. At the same time he lashes his own horses into a spurt. Then a third driver thinks of a trick. He manages to come up level with the car ahead, which he then scrapes with his own car; at the same time he hits a horse's legs with his wheel. The rival car is overturned. Three horses are caught in the wreckage, one lying on its flank, the second on its belly, the third on its neck—the fourth keeps on its feet, lifts the yokeband, and drags the car up again. There is a confused tangle on the ground, the driver rolls in the dirt beside a wheel, the skin of his forehead barked, his chin soiled, his arm outstretched in the dust, his elbow torn. He leaps up and flogs at a fallen horse. Another of the drivers, passing, taunts him. In rage he pulls at the tails of the sprawling horses and gets them up at last. One colt, which has struggled free, he refastens into the bridle; then he again mounts the car and whips his team on.

Now he himself meditates a trick as the drivers come up to a narrow passage. He drives up on to a competitor who is mocking

Chariot races (terracotta at Vienna).

him. The two chariots collide. The fouling driver hits the middle bolt of the other car with his axle and breaks it; the wheel rolls off and the car is immobilised. The fouler drives on. The spectators are mad with excitement, "all quarrelling and betting on the uncertain victory". Native quarrels with native, friend with comrade, old man with old and young with young, man with man. All take sides, "shouting in confusion".

Amid the uproar one of the drivers comes in first, "a near thing—ceaselessly lashing his horses right and left down from the shoulders". The horses are streaming with sweat, the driver spattered with dust. He wipes the sweat from his brow with his dress and quickly gets out of the car, resting his long whip against the yoke, while his groom unlooses the horses. Then he takes up the first prize.[21]

The two drivers who carry out dangerous fouls are meant to be admired; tactics aimed at making the other drivers crash seem to have been accepted as demonstrations of skilful driving. We hear of men who leap from the cars and "standing on the backs of the horses held themselves there with wonderful control, and who above all, borne on a horse, carry out military exercises-in-arms."[22] These however seem entertainers and acrobats rather than racers, perhaps giving displays in the intervals when acrobats, rope-dancers, and men skilled at feats of horsemanship took over. A Pompeian house shows a lady racing in an an antelope-chariot.

Philon bears testimony to the exitement of the spectators at Alexandreia. "I have seen at the horse-races persons acting in the most careless manner, who, when they should have sat still and watched the races in an orderly fashion, have stood in mid-course and been knocked down by the horses' hooves and the wheels, and who have met with a proper return for their folly."[23] Dion, addressing the Alexandrians, returns again and again to their passion for the horse-races. "As things are, if one of the charioteers falls from his chariot, you think it dreadful, the greatest of all disasters; but when you yourselves fall from the decorum that befits you, and the esteem you should enjoy, you are unconcerned." Again: "When you enter the stadion, who could describe the shouts you utter there, your hubbub and agony and bodily contortions and changes of colour, as well as the many horrible curses you let out? For if you were not merely watching the horses race—horses at that which are used to racing—but were yourselves driven by the whips of tragedy, you wouldn't exhibit such anguish. Why even Ixion you show up, I think, as a second-rater, the Ixion depicted by the poets as bound on the wheel and punished for some such impiety as yours. If in the midst of it all some god took his stand beside you and declared in a loud voice:

> Fools, you are mad. No more your spirit conceals
> your food and drink.

Why are you so violently perturbed? what's the excitement? what's the contest? It isn't Pelops driving, or Oinomaos, or Myrtilos, nor does a kingship, a wife, a death, hang in the balance. No, it's

only a contest of slaves for a paltry bit of silver, slaves who are
sometimes defeated, sometimes victorious—slaves in any case.'
If the god spoke thus, what would you reply? Or is it clear that
you wouldn't even listen at such a moment as that? . . . " He goes
on to say that just as Pasiphae in myth loved a bull and conceived
from it the Minotaur, "I myself am apprehensive that this passion
for horses which infects the city may in time bring forth for you
some strange and disastrous offspring." And he laughs at the way
they enact the races they watch. "Not a man of you keeps his seat
at the games. No, you fly faster than the horses and their drivers,
and it's comical to watch the way you drive and play the charioteer, urging the horses on and taking the lead and coming down
crash."[24]

He breaks out into a parody composed almost wholly of phrases
from the *Iliad*, which, though he attributes it to one of the
"feeble versifiers" of the Alexandrians, is probably his own. It
begins:

> At times the cars clung close to the abounding earth,
> at times bounced bounding broadly. The spectators
> gaping could neither stand nor sit at all,
> pallidly scared with fear, and keen to win
> they yelled and bellowed each to each and lifted
> their hands and vowed great offerings to all gods:
> just as the crank of cranes and croak of daws
> go up when they've imbibed too much of beer
> or wine, and clamouring they fly to reach
> the course: as a large cloud of starlings or daws
> swoop down with baleful screech, when they behold
> a horse come dashing, bearing death to fools.
> So those with roars went sprawling on each other . . . [25]

Seneca in Rome echoes the comment on the tumult of the scene.
"There now, the clamour of the races bursts out. My ears are
smitten with a sudden and universal shout. But this does not dis-
turb my thought or even break its progress. I can bear an uproar
with full patience. The medley of voices blurred into a single note
sounds to me like the crashing of waves or like the wind lashing
the treetops or like any other quite meaningless noise." A textile

from Achmîm has in its central medallion a frontal two-horsed chariot; the motive appears also on the bottom of two cups of the Christian epoch; the textile's horses look odd, perhaps through the necessary stylisation, but it is possible the medallion represents one of the grooms who ran out on to the horses' backs.[26]

At Oxyrhynchos we find a quarter of the town, amphodon, called "of the Hippodrome" in A.D. 22-25, and we may surmise that the race-course went back to Ptolemaic days.[27] In 195 at Her-

Circus race on lamp.

mopolis an ex-gymnasiarch, treasurer of the municipal and priestly funds, wrote to the koinon or collective of the kosmetai, which was acting through two men. He stated that he had today (19 Hathyr) paid out "to the accounts of the Horse Races" 5,600 silver drachmai "without prejudice to any right claimed by the city".[28] We know little about horse-raising in Egypt. There was a tax called diploma, which seems a licence-fee for the privilege of owning a horse.[29] Various contracts for the sale of horses have come down. In 134 in the Arsinoite nome a mare was sold for 80 dr. A letter of 256 from the same nome deals with working horses:

Syros to his dearest Heroninos greeting. Send another team of 4 donkeys to the city in place of Akes to carry fodder for the riding-donkeys and horses coming up. Let them have the older bundles. And when they come, let them bring up timber to the magistrate's house for delivery to Zosimos the driver. I pray for your health, dearest friend, 3rd year, 15 Tybi.

[PS] Have two beams (?) cut at once for oilpresses: to go to the press of Ammonios, oilmaker at Harmouthis.

An extract from the official survey-list of the early 3rd century kept in the public archives has been hastily copied out on the registration of a child (dated A.D. 209). Two entries have been extracted, both dealing with the properties of a charioteer, *enochios*:

Column 50, Senapta: Turning to the north, the house and court of Diogenes son of Heras, charioteer, by payment to . . . Publios (?), formerly the property of Ptolemaios son of Papontos, in accordance with a memorandum of the aforesaid Diogenes of the city of Oxyrhyn-chos, who declared that the aforesaid house and court belonged to him.

Turning to the east, the ruined house of Tazoilas daughter of Aphynchios in accordance with the men of Diogenes, charioteer, of the city of Oxyrhychos who declared that there belonged to him a quarter share which was formerly the property of his son Sarapion and before him of Teutheis and another quarter share which was formerly the property of Nechthenibis son of Horos . . . [30]

In the Byzantine world, racing gained a new impetus; once more there were seignorial lords whose prestige was connected with horses. In a contract of 550, Aurelios Serenos undertook to super-intend the racing stables of Flavios Serenos, Count, for a year. The terms were that (1) he was to discharge his duties regularly and with the utmost care, unless prevented by illness; (2) he was to be given for himself and the grooms 80 bushels of wheat, and 9 gold-solidi for barley and vegetables, 80 jars of wine, $\frac{1}{2}$ solidus for green stuff; (3) he was paid $4\frac{1}{2}$ solidi as earnest money, to be returned if he retired from the service before the year was out, and to be retained if he were dismissed without just cause. It seems that the town racecourse at Oxyrhynchos was now owned by the Apion family.[31]

A receipt of 552 states that the banker Anastasios had paid 1 solidus less 4 carats "for an embrocation needed by the horses of the public circus on the side of the Greens", and $\frac{1}{3}$ solidus less $1\frac{1}{2}$ carats for expenses. Another receipt, of 618, states that Georgios, a secretary, had paid $10\frac{5}{8}$ carats on the Alexandrian standard to two starters employed at the hippodrome on the side of the Blues as their wages for a month.[32]

A late 6th-century document deals with the lease of a stable. As an example of Byzantine horse-sales we may take a receipt of 618, stating that the banker Menas has paid 9 solidi for three horses from the inhabitants of Sephtha and given them to Victor, a land-agent. Another late receipt records the payment made by the monks of the monastery of Andreas to Serenos, a stableman, for carrying hay and chaff from the barn of the landlord to that of monks.

An account of the late 6th or early 7th century deals with horses and asses: their disposal, the changes brought about by sale and purchase, the losses through deaths. The use to which the animals were put is not stated; but it is possible that some of the horses were to be used for races. The great popularity of horse-racing at this time seems to have led to the import of foreign breeds. Note that one of the horses here has come from Constantinople. Some of the technical terms are difficult.

The two horses from Asklou were handed over to the groom. The horse from Ophis was delivered to the upper stable. The magistrate's horse was delivered to the same stable. The horse from Spania was delivered to the same stable. The small white horse was delivered to the groom. I gave Patrikios and the small gerates for the bay horse of the upper stable. I gave the white mare and the pelatos for the small horse that died. I sold the kentinos and bought the small black one that's in the stable. I sold the horse named Pleb for 3 solidi, which the revered Philoxenos has. I sold the two asses from Herakleopolis and the ass from Oureeiebt for $5\frac{2}{3}$ solidi, paid to the same. The magistrate's ass and the watercarrier's ass and its mate are dead. The dead mare belonged to Menas the official. Three asses were bought from Ophis for 8 solidi and another from Pallosis for 3 solidi. The she-ass of Karaneots is dead. The other she-ass of the said Karaneots and that belonging to the people from Loukiou and the small one I sold, and received 4 solidi for them.

A petition of 322 by the yearly superintendent of the express-post mentions only donkey-drivers; some of the asses here may have been used in the post.[33]

The factions of Blues and Greens were organisations of contractors who provided horses, drivers and other requisites for the games. Under the Roman Republic a few middle-class citizens had dealt with such matters and made all provisions; but with the rapid expansion of horse-racing under the Empire the *factio* soon emerged. The giver of the entertainment, *editor spectaculorum*, found the money; the *factio* did the rest. Each faction was distinguished by its colour, which was worn by all its performers. At first there were only the Reds and the Whites; then the Blues came in, probably at the time of Augustus; the Greens appeared soon after. Domitian added the Purples and the Golds. But the Blues and the Greens became the most important groups and carried on long into the Byzantine world. In the later empire the *factio* became an official *collegium* with a full bureaucratic system. A *familia quadrigaria*, a division of the *factio*, consisted of 25 *decuriones* (groups of ten): that is, at least 250 persons: drivers of four-horse chariots, grooms and assistants, saddlers, cobblers, tailors, pearl-embroiderers, surgeons, messengers, farm-servants concerned with fodder, watermen (who probably brought water for men and horse, and laid dust in the arena), *tentores* (who seem to have pulled the ropes opening the doors of the *carceres* or barriers in the circus), and *magistri* and *doctores*, who may have been trainers and instructors.[34]

Just as we saw the populace at Rome rioting in their championing of the pantomimes, so disturbances tended to gather round the factions. Spectators became devotees of one or other of the factions and were ready to fight in any dispute on its behalf. The astute remark of Pylades to Augustus showed that men were well aware that in conditions in which free political expression was stifled the brawls and arguments about sports and spectacles became an outlet for the frustrated social emotions, the needs of people to have some say in the running of their world. In the same way the passionate attachment to a side in sports served (as it still does today) to palliate and mask the lack of any social cause to which men might worthily attach themselves. Men always need the sense of belonging effectively to some larger whole than that

Four charioteers of the four factions, each with winning horse (mosaic from Fosti on the Via Cassia).

of their personal existence; and where genuine democratic expression is lacking, they find it in various fantasy-forms of thought and action. In due time, however, what had here begun as the expression of political frustration ended by begetting a new form of political struggle. In the Byzantine world the factions were transformed into political parties, or at least an organised outlet for

political positions, while still maintaining their aspect of sports-
excitement.

Some documents from Karanis give us a glimpse of the faction-
system in Egypt in the early 4th century.

Germanos and Ariston, komarchs of the village of Karanis, have
delivered in a boat belonging to Pausirios 28 art. 8 metra of barley
destined for Hephaistion; and through me, Herakles, an additional
29 art. 7 metra. [18 Aug. 315]

Aurelios Kollouthos shipmaster to Aurelios Ariston and Aurelios
Germanos, komarchs of the village of Karanis, greeting.

I have received and put on board the barley for Hephaistion, the
horsebreeder [*hippotrophos*], of Alexandreia, on account of the crop
of the 3rd Indiction, $21\frac{1}{2}$ art. of barley. I have issued this receipt in a
single copy, and in response to the formal question I have so declared
[11 Sept. 315] I, Aurelios Kollouthos, have written the whole document.[35]

The earlier part of this document consists of a list of names
described as *kephalaiotai* of Karanis, probably foremen in charge
of the donkey caravans which carried the barley from the
Karanis granary to a river port, where it was taken aboard ship
for delivery to Alexandreia. A further document brings out the
full role of Hephaistion:

Aurelios Ariston, son of Serenos, and Aurelios Germanos, acting
through his father Selpous, both komarchs, of the village of Karanis
in the 3rd Indiction, to Aurelios Herakles, son of Ploution, greeting.

We have received from you, in conformity with the orders issued
by the prefect's office, toward the price of the barley that we have
delivered, to the shipmaster Kollouthos, $21\frac{1}{2}$ art. of barley, and through
you, Herakles, $58\frac{1}{2}$ art., in all 80 art. of barley, destined for Hephaistion, chief of the Blues (*phaktionarios*) of Alexandreia, out of 13 talants
2000 dr., a total of 10 tal, of silver in all. The receipt is valid, and in
response to the formal question I have so declared.

I, Aurelios Neilammon, councillor, have written for them, as they
are illiterate, and I have drawn up the whole document. [16 Sept
315].[36]

Neilammon is probably a councillor of Arsinoe. This receipt is
dated five days after the previous one and is addressed to the

F

same Herakles who was responsible for the other. The barley is a special levy raised as a compensated-for requisition. Hephaistion is explicitly named as a leader of the Blue faction in Alexandreia. The name used for Blues is *Kallieinoi* (*Kallaïnoi*): coloured like the *kalaïs*, the topaz or chrysolite, a stone of greenish blue. Elsewhere we meet *Benetoi* as a transcription of the Latin *Veneti*.

We have already considered the excitable nature of the Alexandrians, which was liable to get out of control in theatre, stadion, hippodrome. Here is one more passage from Dion. "The Alexandrians are moderate enough when they offer sacrifice or go for a stroll or engage in any other pursuits. But when they enter the theatre or the stadion, as if maddening drugs lay buried there, they lose all consciousness of their former condition and aren't ashamed to say or do anything that occurs to them. And most distressing of all, despite their interest in the show, they do not really see, and, for all their wish to hear, do not hear, being evidently out of their senses, deranged—not only men, but even women and children. And when the dreadful exhibition is over and they are dismissed, the more violent aspect of their disorder is put away, but still at street corners and in alleys the malady goes on throughout the city for several days; just as when a great conflagration dies out, you see for a long time, not only the smoke, but also some parts of buildings still burning."[37]

The comparison with drugs may be meant to suggest the practice of burying charms, especially as necromantic charms connected with the dead in their tombs were considered to be characteristic of Egypt and the curse-tablets of lead were there as elsewhere at times used in the hope of magically affecting the events in the hippodrome. Such tablets, devoting some adversary to the dead, were buried.[38]

The hippodrome, like gymnasion and theatre, could become a place of sedition and riot, of political violence as well as of executions. Thus, Ptolemaios Philadelphos huddled the Jews in the Alexandrian hippodrome and had them trampled by elephants. One of the ways in which circus-factions later developed into parties with general ideas and principles was through the identification of the two main groups with the two great hostile sections in the Christian Church of the East. Right at the end of Byzantine Egypt, while Amr was besieging the imperial forces in Alexandreia, street-battles were going on between the Blues, led by the prefect of the Fayum, Domitianus, and the Greens under Menas the duke.[39] But these aspects are outside our scope here.

We may however glance at the symbolism that invaded the hippodrome and was linked with the colours of the factions. The circus came to be taken as a cosmic symbol, with the four seasons assimilated to the four factions; and as a result we find the genii of the seasons represented on winged horses as they order the cosmos in their strange course. The victorious charioteer becomes the lord of the sun.[40] A Carthaginian mosaic shows, under an outspread peacock tail (the sky), four horses decked with the colours of the factions, who browse on the plants of the four seasons; the green steed eats spring-roses. Such ideas were largely brought about by astrologic influence, though they reposed also on a very ancient substratum of thought, which, for instance, gave cosmic colours to the Babylonian ziqqurats—and, at even earlier levels, in tribal days linked colours with the four points of camp-orientation.[41] John Malalas linked the four colours with the origin of Rome and the four elements; and at Antioch the factions were linked with the four city quarters. In such matters immemorial systems of symbolism gain a new life on a more complex level.[42] Nonnos alludes to the theory that the twelve rounds of a chariot-race referred to the twelve months. "Arkas the traveller finds out the measure of the twelve months, and the sun's circuit, the mother of the years brought forth by his four-horse team."[43] Clement of Alexandreia sets out the common view of the faithful Christian as a spiritual athlete:

The athlete who has no hope of winning and gaining crowns does not even put his name down for the contest, while the other one who holds this hope in his heart but does not submit to hard training and exercises, and to a suitable diet, comes out uncrowned and quite misses the fulfilment of his hopes. Similarly, let not the man clad with this earthly covering [wealth] proclaim himself barred at the start from the Saviour's prizes—if, that is, he is faithful and surveys the magnificence of God's love to men; nor once again, let him hope, by remaining undisciplined and unused to conflict, to partake of the crowns of incorruption without dust and sweat. But let him come and subject himself to the Logos as trainer and to Christ as master of the contests (*agonothetes*). Let his appointed food and drink be the Lord's new covenant, his exercise the commandments, his grace and adornment the fair virtues of love, faith, hope, knowledge of the truth, goodness, gentleness, compassion, gravity, so that, when the last trumpet signals the end of the race and his departure from the present life as from a course, he may with good conscience stand before the judge a victor,

Eros as charioteer with four horses (two are Amandus and Frunitus); acclamations above (Dougga, Tunisia).

admitted to be worthy of the fatherland above, into which with angelic crowns proclamations he now ascends.

In this scheme of things Christ, as well as being *agonothetes*, is also charioteer. "Let us love Christ, the noble charioteer of men. He led the foal and its parent under the same yoke, and now, having yoked together the team of mankind, he shapes the course of his chariot for the goal of immortality."[43]

These ideas cohere in the image of the chariot-driver as expressing the apotheosis of the soul as on earth it expressed the triumphator and the hippodrome-victor. Its purely symbolic quality is brought out by the fact that on sarcophagi young children are shown as the drivers of quadrigae. Herakles as well as a Roman

Emperor ascended in a chariot in his apotheosis.[44] As one example
from the very large number thrown up under the Empire, the
rock-tomb of Aelia Arisuth in Tripolitania will serve. Her portrait in a roundel suggests with its intense expression the contemporary mummy-portraits.[45] Arisuth is called in an inscription
lea, lioness, which seems to mean that, though a woman, she
was a Mithraic initiate. At the end of the tomb-lid, over the head
of the dead, is a plaster basin with a hole in the bottom for liquid
offerings. The tomb-front and the adjoining parts of the wall are
painted with a circus-scene in which four chariots, each with a
faction-colour, are competing. White comes to grief, Green pulls
up just in time, Red is in the rear, Blue is winning and a blue
jubilator takes the prize-vase to him. Arisuth must have been a
supporter of the Blues in life, and she expects to be carried triumphantly into her future life by that faction.[46]

The Christians took the imagery over and put the chariot image
on the floors of their sanctuaries. For instance, in the Byzantine
church of El Mousassat the floor in front of the altar is filled with
talismanic pictures. Near a jewelled cross is a medallion from
which the horses of the four factions lift their heads towards the
cross, expressing its victory. In the Syrian church of Dar Solaib,
horses with beneficent names, Agathoperon and Nike, frame a
personification of Winter.[47] Finally we may note a Byzantine
diptych of the 5th century. The colossal statue of an emperor sits
enthroned in a shrine with two frontal columns, resting on wheels
and drawn by a quadriga of elephants; at the back is a bier with
eagles flying up; above them is a quadriga galloping to heaven
with the transformed ruler. Here the four-horse chariot represents
both the fourfold circling universe and the vehicle of transformation or divinisation.[48]

The collapse of the Graeco-Roman systems, with their main
stress on *polis* or *civitas* with varying degrees of self-government,
brought down the athletic training and the contests based on
palaistra and gymnasion. But the horse-race, with its strong
aristocratic tradition, survived the shock and found new life
from the rebirth of seignorial systems of land-holding.

A lucky chance enables us to see just what the charioteers

looked like, at least in the later period round 500. Part of a leaf of a
papyrus-book from Antinoe shows us a group in four main colours: light yellow, a sort of middle green, blue (now grown drab),
and red. White too is used, but only in very slight strokes or
points. The colour was laid on with the brush, then outlined by a
firm black stroke. The charioteers, with their hanging locks, belong to different factions. The first on the left in the front line

Apotheosis of Ruler
(ivory diptych).

has a short red tunic with yellow bands diagonally crossed and
with black and blue bindings. He stands to attention, left hand on
thigh, right hand and forearm raised; and was probably the central
figure—those on the left of the picture having been lost. Next,
there lounges a recognisable jockey, left hand on thigh, right hand
slightly raised and holding a whip. He turns a little to the right,
wearing a blue tunic, with red sleeves (an undergarment?) and
yellow cap.

To the right of these two important figures, and just a little
behind them, is a man in green tunic with yellow bands (vertical

and horizontal) and yellow cap with narrow blue border. He turns his head to one side and his tunic shows no bindings; he may not be a charioteer or is perhaps not yet ready for the games, but wears the jockey-cap.

Behind again is the head and bust of a fourth man in green tunic with bindings, red sleeves and blue-edged cap; his head also inclines to the left. Nearby are the head and shoulders of a fifth man in yellow cap, whose clothes are not visible and who seems to stand on a still higher level. On the left torn side appears part of a sixth man in green tunic and trousers, red sleeves; his head is gone.

There seem then to be three factions depicted: three Greens, one Red, one Blue. We may assume that one or more Whites appeared with more Reds and Blues on the lost part of the leaf. The drawing is bold and free, in Hellenistic style, with the figures balanced against one another. There is no perspective and no background except a band or arch, which may represent the arcade of the circus (the ropes for closing the circus-gates, the gate, or the barrier between spectators and arena). If a definite moment has been chosen, it may be that before the drawing of lots for places; but no doubt the composition is just a "group of charioteers". The faces are Greek, not Coptic. The left-inclination suggests textiles of the Graeco-Roman period or portrait-busts on two panels from Akhmîm (4th–5th centuries). The trick of showing the pupils in the corner of the eye or just above the lower lid also suggests a textile of the period, and we are reminded of Fayum portraits by the treatment of the noses—an almost straight black slope, or two at right angles, with a long vertical stroke on the shaded side and the other side lighted up.

The purpose of the illustration we can only guess at. The book from which it came must have treated chariot-racing in some way. The grouping of opposed factions in the same picture is not odd; for we know of the four factions uniting at times to honour some famous charioteer.[49]

Finally, as an example of the way in which athletic concepts, including those of charioteering, worked their way to the centre of philosophic thought, we may take what Philon has to say about *pneuma* (breath, spirit, life). He is applying the Stoic idea of a physical body as held together by *pneuma* in a state of motion, with all the various permeating *pneumata* constituting the *hexis* or structure, the sum of its physical qualities. The movements of the *pneuma* are tensional motions. Stobaios speaks of the *pneuma* "moving by itself to and fro, or moving forward and backward". Philon makes the notion yet more precise. He calls *hexis* "a very strong bond", and defines it as *pneuma* "turning back the way it comes". He amplifies the definition by saying: "It begins in the body's centre and extends outwards to its boundaries; and after touching the outermost surface it turns back till it arrives at the same place from which it started." This continuous double-course of the *hexis*, which he compares to the course of horse-races, is one that never decays. Thus the image of the horse-race enters into the deepest ideas of the structure and tensions of the universe.[50]

7

International Organisation of Athletes

THERE is yet one important aspect of athletics in the Roman world that we have not considered, the large-scale organisations that grew up in connection with the great games.[1] Winners known as the *hieronikai* or sacred victors are found already in the 2nd century B.C., but they do not seem organised. By the next century gilds appear to be emerging. A late Hellenistic inscription from Erythrai in the Ionian Dedekapolis mentions oecumenical athletes and sacred victors, who seem to participate in the award-ing of a crown to an Olympic winner. The oecumenical or world-athletes were probably those who took part in the games, whether they won or not; the sacred victors, those who had won in sacred games. The latter were naturally an exclusive gild in a position to press for recognitions and privileges.[2]

The first clear example of their definite status on a big scale occurs in 32–31 B.C. when they took advantage of the unsettled conditions to gain support from Marcus Antonius. He wanted to extend his popularity, and, further, the patronage of artistic or athletic gilds fitted in with his Dionysiac role. A copy of his re-script to the Koinon or Commonalty of the Hellenes in Asia has been found on the back of a medical papyrus:

Marcus Antonius, Imperator, Triumvir for the Restoration of the State, to the Koinon of the Hellenes in Asia, greeting.

On a previous occasion, when I gave audience in Ephesos to my friend the physical trainer [*aleiptes*], Marcos Antonios Artimedoros, together with Caropinos of Ephesos, eponymous priest of the Synod of Oecumenical Victors in the Sacred Games and Garlanded Victors, he asked me to confirm the inviolability of the existing privileges of the Synod and to make these further valuable grants:

F*

Exemption from military service, complete immunity from liturgies, freedom from billeting, and, for the duration of the festival, a truce and personal security, and the right to wear purple.

He asked me to agree to write to you immediately, and I assented through my friendship for Artemidoros and my wish to do a favour to their eponymous priest for the honour and expansion of the Synod.

And now again, in audience with me, Artemidoros has asked for them to have permission to set up a bronze tablet and engrave on it the aforesaid grants. As I wish not to disappoint him in any request, I allowed him to set up the tablet as he urged.

Such is my letter to you on these matter.[3]

There is no mention of athletes; but we may assume that the Synod was composed in part, or mainly, of them. Artemidoros is himself a trainer of athletes. The prize at musico-dramatic contests as well as athletic ones was the garland, and so *hieronikai* could also apply to winners who were members of the Dionysiac Artists' Gild.

A Milesian inscription of 20 B.C. mentions a professional athlete of the city who was first to win all the running events (stadion, diaulos, and armed race) in contests established by the oecumenical *hieronikai* and *stephanitai* (garland-crowned). The gild, then, itself could sponsor *panegyreis* or meetings. Ephesian inscriptions show that in the late first century B.C. the sacred victors had to pay 200 denars unless they won their crowns in the Epheseia, the great Augustan games of the city. An edict states that the *hieronikai*, "sacred to Artemis", are not to get further allowances from the goddess; while in another inscription, dealing with the construction of a ramp to join a stoa and an agora, one of the builders is Ischyrion, an Alexandrian of the tax-exempt *hieronikai* in the reign of Domitian.[4]

The relations of the athletes with the Dionysiac *mystai* and artists was close. In Asia we find synods that include them all. But the greater strength of the athletic sections is brought out by such terms as those used at Panamara, where we find "thymelic athletes" as well as "xystic"—*thymele* being the altar-shaped platform in the midst of the orchestra of the Athenian theatre, the adjective meaning "scenic" or "theatric", while *xyston* was the covered colonnade of the gymnasion, used for open-air exercises. Astrologic writers, too, link athlete and musician: "those who strive in contest and wrestling and thymele, and live at the public cost". We find a pankratiast of Alexandreia, several times victor, sharing in the communal food-system of the philosophers at the Mouseion; and we know of one case where an actor was a boxer. Apollogenes of the 3rd century B.C. acted the roles of Herakles, Achilleus, Antaios and Alexander in tragedy; he also won a boxing contest at Alexandreia. The paintings of the Casa dei Gladiatori at Pompeii show mime, pantomime (as Apollo-and-Marsyas, with four members of the singing choros), and athletes. (When

Pugilists (relief, Rome).

the amphitheatre was closed through the riot of A.D. 59, the athletes were transferred to the large theatre.)[5] In an Alexandrian papyrus of about A.D. 250 we meet a gymnasiarch-agonothetes who is honoured by "the sacred thymelic and xystic synods". A few decades later the emperors Diocletian and Maximian address a rescript to a synod of the same name (probably the one at Alexandreia) on the theme of privileges.[6] By this time the separate gilds of artists had dissolved, and the remnants joined in with the athletes. Earlier, the usual methods had been to allow the two sets of gilds to collaborate when convenient.[7]

Under the empire the gilds of athletes took ever more imposing titles. We meet the Sacred Gild of Roving Athletes Devoted to Herakles. This gild was oecumenical, with federated chapters. Each athlete might wander round, but was permanently based on his home-chapter. There was also the Entire Xystos or Portico.

It was the xystos at Elis that gave this new gild its name; the gild took in all athletes who were using a gymnasion and its grounds, and so in effect was a temporary gild of the men participating in some particular festival.[8]

Augustus upheld the privileges of athletes in general, as distinct from the sacred victors. Claudius, after his conquest of Britain in A.D. 46, received an embassy of three athletes with gold wreaths and the congratulations of the Gild of Wanderers; and he addressed the Gild with two short rescripts, first acknowledging the embassy and gifts, then (in 47) praising the Gild for good relations with the kings of Commagene and Pontos. Vespasian confirmed all the Claudian privileges.[9]

The athletes loved high-sounding titles and particularly glorified in the name of *paradoxos* (less commonly *paradoxonikes*). This title was at times assumed by musician winners too, but it specially designates a proud athlete. It suggests astounding, incredible victories.[10] We have seen how the winners loved to collect all sorts of records. An Egyptian is described on his epitaph as "Rouphos (Rufus) the Unforgettable Victor at Capitoline Olympic Pythian Isthmian Games, Astounding Victor in a Vast Number of Contests, Trainer, Wrestler, Boxer, Pankratiast, Xystarch. Be of Good Cheer." (The last words are addressed to the dead man.) Popular opinion took the athletes as heroic characters. The astrologers wrote of the "athlete who worthily attains the glories of nobility", of "athletes whom merits of illustrious virtues ennoble", of "the noble athlete". (The stress on nobility suggests the breakthrough into aristocratic preserves.) Vitruvius describes the triumphal procession of a victor entering his town. Loukian declares that his honours were those of a god; and we do hear of a boxer deified while alive.[11]

The 2nd century saw the increase in influence of the Greek or eastern elements in the empire, under philhellenic emperors. In Hadrian's reign, the highpriest of the Entire Xystos at Rome, M. Ulpius Domesticus, got together the sacred victors and athletes in general to ask for land in Rome on which to build a headquarters, plus an edifice for archives. On 5 May 134 Hadrian granted the request; but there were delays. Domesticus appealed again to Antoninus Pius in 143, and a rescript of 16 May of that year assigned a site near the Baths of Trajan.[12] The building was dedicated in 154 as Athletarum Curia. Rome thus became the administrative centre of the athletic world till the final breakdown of the gilds.[12] The dedication tells us:

The Sacred Gild of Athletes Devoted to Herakles, established in Imperial Rome since the time of their dissolution, honours M. Ulpius Domesticus, lifelong President and Highpriest of the Entire Xystos, Director of the Imperial Baths, their Patron who went in person and asked for the Precinct of the Entire Xystos.[14]

Elsewhere we learn that Domesticus had been a winner in the

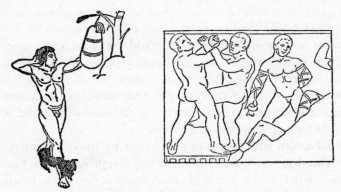

Korykos or sack (Ficoroni cista); pugilists (relief, Rome).

pankration and was a *parodonikes* or circuit-victor: he had won in the four great panhellenic games as well as the Acteia and Capitoline.[15] The Curia of the Athletes was a sacred precinct because of the cult of Herakles carried on there (as well perhaps as the imperial cult). Of the officials we know of two *archontes* or directors of the synod, and a secretary.[16]

Why a period of dissolution had intervened, we do not know. The previous centre must have been somewhere in Asia Minor, probably at Sardeis; but with the growth of centralisation, the emperors would naturally want an organisation more directly under their control.[17] Their favours continued on through the 3rd into the 4th century. The last rescript of which we know

is by Diocletian and characteristically shows an attempt to econo-
mise. Exemptions of athletes from civic duties are to apply only to
genuine professionals and lifelong competitors who without
bribery and corruption win three or more garlands in the sacred
games, at least one in Rome or ancient Greece.[18] A papyrus written in Diocletian's reign (in 292) gives us a letter from the council
of Oxyrhynchos to the strategos, which states that a man chosen to
attend the prefect's Immaculate Court at Alexandreia has claimed
exemption as a sacred victor in the games. The council therefore
appoints a substitute.[19]

The Gild was governed by a *nomos* or set of legal rules. A membership fee had to be paid (in 194 it was 100 denars). The member
was given a certificate stating that he was a paid-up member.
The Gild could deal with the emperor by means of letters,
officials, or chosen envoys; it could, with official sanction,
establish new festivals and give money-prizes (as at non-sacred
games at Aphrodisias).[20] It voted praises, honours, statues to its
own officers, to benefactors or generous emperors. One honour
it dispensed was the right to march at the head of the gild when
it made formal processions in Rome.

A successful athlete was in effect kept by his community, *e.g*
sitesis (food-ration, public maintenance) was provided for Turbon,
twice winner in the Antinoiia of Antinoopolis. These privileges
were salable; and Turbon did sell them to a man for his two sons.
A contract at Oxyrhynchos, dealing with the grinding of wheat
for bread to be supplied to the city, mentions in A.D. 199 "Tiberios
Klaudios Didymos, and however he is styled, a victor in the games
and exempt from taxation, member of the Dionyseion and the
Sacred Club". The Dionyseion we may take to have been a temple
of Dionysos at Oxyrhynchos, not at Alexandreia; the athlete's
connection with it—important enough to be noted in a civic
contract—is of interest. Another document shows the Oxyrhynchite Council notifying the record-office of the election of a man
to the syllogos, assembly, of a Sacred Club, which entitles him to
freedom from taxes. The statement of the man's claim cites a
rescript of Claudius Gothicus addressed to the world-society of
sacred and wreathed victors connected with Dionysos; apparently

he belonged to the theatrical not the athletic side. [21] A less important person was the athlete who petitioned the emperors (some time in the 3rd century) for the post of *keryx*, herald, in the Heptanomia. The keryx was the crier of public sales and the announcer of various public acts; and it is not clear exactly what the herald here was going to announce. The applicant has no high claims: he was a modest worker, no longer young, an old athlete. He states that the post of herald was reserved, by an imperial decision, for old athletes like himself; and makes an interesting justification of athletic privileges. The games where the athletes wear themselves out are offered to the gods for the victory and safety of the emperors. The post which is requested is specified as that of the Greek Herald—though the adjective is scored out. It would seem that a herald's functions were carried out also in Latin or in Egyptian.[22]

Three documents from the archives of the Oxyrhynchite Senate tell us much about the position of Dionysiac artist and athlete in the year 289. However, we must leave the main part of these papyri till we treat the Theatre. The third document, however, is from a pankratiast, Aurelios Ammon, son of Ammon, who seems to be a xystarch or chief-priest, *archiereus*, for life. Ammon is addressing the Senate:

Having exercised the skill of the pankratiast and ornamented my motherland, as is not unknown to you, I now desire to visit also places outside it, so that I may there too win victories in whatever games the Providence of the Gods, with the aid of your own Genius [Tyche], may permit me to adorn. Therefore I submit this petition asking you to consent and issue me the certificate necessary in these circumstances.

Despite his rank, Ammon has apparently not been abroad before.

The gild-finances were under a treasurer. One source of income was the entry-fee. The boxer Herminos of Hermopolis paid 50 denars for the privilege of acting as the gild's priest at the games of the Koinon of Asia in Sardeis. We may assume, then, that such temporary honours in general brought money in.[24] Patrons no doubt gave gifts.[25] Emperors must have helped from time to time, as with the Curia at Rome. Memorial gifts were made in honour of dead members.[26] In turn, money was expended in running the headquarters and in giving prizes in non-sacred games (where the awards had material value). Expenditure on any large scale seems to have been carried out by the whole Xystos, who erected statues, while the xystarch or president usually had to spend money in managing the games—though he was paid back by the city where the event took place.[27]

The Entire Xystos had a directorate of three men at Rome, and was kept occupied, arranging meetings there and all over the

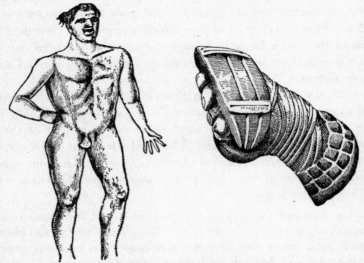

Athlete; late boxing-glove (terracotta fragment, B.M.).

empire. Each director had three titles: highpriest, life-xystarch, director of the imperial baths. Any one of them could go off to manage a show in another city. Thus, Demetrios of Alexandreia was sent in 198 to preside over the important Sebasta at Naples.[28] However, in general a highpriest was not necessarily a xystarch. The latter was the key-man for running a show; and though mostly appointed for life, he often had control of one festival, less often of all the athletic festivals of a city. Occasionally, he presided over a whole province. He was given his position by the emperor. While gymnasiarchs and agonothetai continued to be selected by their own communities, the xystarchs, a creation of the empire, were imperial nominees and represented the central government.[29]

They might be men of high rank, *e.g.* of a consular family— though they might also be athletes. They could get xystarchies for their sons: Domesticus of the Curia had a son who followed in his steps. The office might thus be kept in a family. We find three brothers as xystarchs at Oxyrhynchos.[30] An Alexandrian father and son were xystarchs at Rome.[31] The xystarch did not necessarily preside over his own city. There seems to have been a liking for the heavy athlete in the role. Of xystarchs whose athletic background is known we find many pankratiasts: at Smyrna (2), Aphrodisias, Magnesia (2), Ephesos (2), Kyme, Sardeis, Philippopolis. In Egypt there was a pankratiast, Demetrios of Alexandreia, who was also a wrestler. Of other xystarchs: two were wrestlers, two were long-distance runners. Some were sacred victors, others *periodonikai*. The xystarch was spokesman and signatory for the xystos; he wore a wreath and purple robe while performing his functions; and honours were lavished on him. We find xystarchs as councillors, priests or highpriests, and so on.

Besides the xystarch and highpriest (often the same man), there was a secretary and a doctor. We find doctors being given oil at a festival. They presumably dealt with bruises or other injuries to athlete or spectator. In 368 the emperors ceased to appoint the archiater: apparently a sign of lessening interest.[32] In the curia, in the years 384–92, a last statue was set up, of the wrestler Johannes of Smyrna; Theodosius authorised the act, but there was no reference to a gild.[33] The ending of the Olympic games completed the collapse. (The Greek character of the xystos is shown by the fact that there is no sign of it in Africa, Spain, Britain and Gaul, save slightly in Provence.)

We catch glimpses of athletes and officials in their daily life. In 227 the pankratiast Aurelios Phoibammon made a loan to Aurelios Kornelios of Hermopolis.[34] At Oxyrhynchos in 250 an ex-president of the games carried out a property deal. We have the receipt issued by a public bank for payment of the *enkyklion*, the tax on sales, mortgages and the like. The transaction here may have been a transfer:

Second Year of the Emperor and Caesar Gaius Messius Quintus Trajanus Decius Pius Felix and Quintus Herennius Etruscus Messius Decius and Gaius Valens Hostilianus Messius Quintus the Most August Caesars, Augusti, Choiak 19.

Paid to Aurelios Apollonios and his associate, both senators of the city of Oxyrhynchos, public bankers, to the account of the sales tax by Tiberios Claudios Diogenes, son of Tiberios Claudios Diogenes, exkosmetes, ex-president of the games, senator of the city of Oxyrhynchos, on account of the half share of an old house and all its appurtenances belonging to him in the said city in the North Quay Quarter, which [he bought?] from his fosterchild's mother Aurelia Ammonia daughter of . . . and Techosous, of the said city, in accordance with a privately drawn contract made in the said month of Choiak by an irrevocable transfer, on the valuation which he has made of the said halfshare of the house, namely 3.5 dr. 5½ obols, in payment for libation-money and the sales tax 73 dr. 5½ obols.

[signed] I Aurelios Apollonios, exgymnasiarch, senator, public banker, have certified the 73 dr. 5½ obols.

The rate of the *enkyklion* in Roman times is known as ten per cent; the rate here seems remarkably high. *Sponde* or libation-money is the extra-charge at times found in association with taxes; and we should expect it to be a small sum. Agonothetes is an unusual title to find in a provincial town; at Alexandreia it often occurs, linked with the gymnasiarchy.[35]

Athletes of any standing travelled a great deal. Astrologic texts speak of them as "wanderers over the whole wide earth meeting in contests with opponents", or as "men unconquered in all contests but carried about to various places for the sake of domicile". And they are linked with soldiers as liable to fall into dangerous traps and chances.[36] Certainly one of the purposes of synod and xystos was to make it easier for members to travel in groups to the various festivals of the Greek world. We know of over 200 such festivals which drew in more than local entries in the 2nd century. Possibly each association arranged a circuit yearly for its members to fit the year's festival programme.[37] At times, however, an athlete went around on his own initiative, as seems the case with Aurelios Ammon whose petition was cited above.[38] A letter found at Oxyrhynchos (dated 2nd–3rd centuries) had been written in Antioch by Sarapammon to his mother and another woman. He mentions an *agon* and thus seems to be on an athletic trip.[39]

We noticed how the athletes and the Dionysiac artists were associated in Roman times. It is of interest, then, to look back at the Ptolemaic festival, described by Kallixenos, which seems certainly to have taken place on the second occasion of the Ptolemaia at Alexandreia, in 274. These games had been instituted by Philadelphos in honour of his father: a five-yearly world-event to which contestants came from all over the Greek world. Here a newly-devised sacred game, based on a tomb, was given a strong Dionysiac tincture; and many of its aspects will be found to link with elements developed in the culture of Roman Egypt.

A great tent was set up in the circuit of the citadel, able to hold 130 couches set round in a circle. Five wooden pillars on each side, fifty cubits high, held up the roof; a sort of canopy was made by a scarlet veil with white fringe, with beams on each side "covered over with turreted veils, on which were placed canopies embroidered all over the centre. And four of the pillars were made to represent palmtrees, with a representation of thyrsoi in the middle". Outside them ran a portico, with a peristyle on three sides and vaulted roof. Here was a place for feasters, with scarlet curtains surrounding the interior. In the middle were hides of beasts suspended, strange in size and in variegated colour. In the open around were myrtles and daphnes and other such shrubs. As for the floor, it was strewn with all sorts of flowers.

Egypt, through the temperate nature of the atmosphere surrounding it, produces in great abundance and all the year round those plants which are rarely found in other lands, and then only at particular seasons. Roses and white lilies and countless other flowers never lack there. So, though the entertainment took place in midwinter, there was a show of flowers that foreigners found incredible. Flowers of which one could not have easily found enough in another city to make

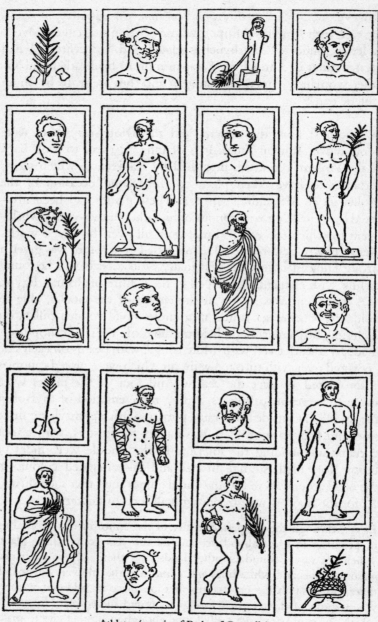

Athletes (mosaic of Baths of Caracalla).

one chaplet were here supplied in the utmost profusion, to make chaplets for every guest and were strewn thickly over the whole floor of the tent, so that truly it gave the appearance of a most divine meadow.

The tent was decorated inside with animal carvings, paintings, cloaks gold-embroidered with portraits of Egyptian kings, gold and silver shields, with twenty caves above, eight cubits high. In the caves were "representations of feasting parties opposite one another, of tragic, comic, and satyric animals dressed in real clothes". In many of the caves were placed nymphaia. Huge golden eagles faced one another on the highest part of the roof.

Many processions went through the stadion in the city. First that of the Morning Star, which began as the star itself appeared; then that of the king's parents; then those "sacred to each of the gods, with arrangements suited to each god's story"; finally that of the Evening Star. In the Dionysiac procession, which seems to have dominated the day, Silenoi in purple and scarlet cloaks went first, clearing the way; then Satyrs, twenty in each division of the stadion, came with gilded lamps of ivywood; then golden-winged Victories with incense-burners six cubits in height, their tunics embroidered with animal figures. Next came a double altar, six cubits high, decorated with gilt ivy-leaves and a gold crown of vineleaves, enveloped in bandages with white centres. Then came boys in purple, with frankincense, myrrh, and saffron, on gold dishes, and forty Satyrs with gold ivy-garlands and bodies painted purple, vermilion, and other colours. Then two Seilenoi in purple cloaks with white fringes, one with petasos (broad-brimmed cap) and gold caduceus, and the other with a trumpet. Between them went a man four cubits high(? on stilts) in tragic dress and ornaments, with the golden horn-of-plenty; he was Eniautos (the Returning Year). After him came a beautiful woman of more than normal height, holding a garland of peach-blossoms and palmbranch; she was Pentereris (Five Years). Then came the four Seasons dressed in character, with two more big incense-burners and a square golden altar. Then more Satyrs, with gold winejars or goblets. Then "marched Philiskos the poet, who was priest of Bacchos, and with him all the artists concerned with the service of Bacchos. Next to them were carried the Delphic tripods, as prizes for the trainers of athletes: one, nine cubits high, for the trainer of boys, and one, twelve cubits, for the trainer of men."

Then came a fourwheeled waggon, fourteen cubits long, drawn by 180 men. In it was an image of Bacchos, ten cubits high, pouring libations of wine from a golden goblet and clad in purple. Round him were various golden objects (including an incense-burner and two bowls full of cassia and saffron) and a cover decorated with leaves of ivy and vines, with wreaths, fillets, thyrsoi, drums, turbans, and tragic, comic, satyric masks. Then marched the priests and priestesses and newly-initiated votaries, companies of every nation and people with the mystic van; then the bacchantes with dishevelled hair and garlands of snakes, yew, vine and ivy, and holding daggers or snakes. Next came another waggon, drawn by sixty men, with a statue of Nysa (the mount where Dionysos was reared). A mechanism made the statue rise up, pour libations of milk, and sit again. Over the statue was a parasol, and at the four corners of the waggon were four golden lamps. A third waggon, drawn by 300 men, showed sixty Satyrs treading grapes and singing a song of praise of the winepress to the flute. Seilenos presided here and the new wine streamed over the road. Wine too flowed from a sack made of sewn leopard-skins, that held 3000 measures. There followed 120 garlanded Satyrs and Seilenoi, with casks, bowls, goblets. A fourth waggon held a silver vessel with 600 measures of wine, engraved with animal figures, and two huge silver goblets with figures in relief, as well as many other vessels, tripods, wine-coolers and so on. Men followed with articles of gold plate connected with wine, altars, sideboards, tripods; then 1600 white-tunicked boys, wreathed with ivy or pine, carrying more vessels of gold and silver or others painted in every colour, which were used to give drinks to the spectators.

Among further representations was one of Semele's bedchamber on a waggon, with statues clad in golden tunics, inlaid with precious stones.

And it would not be right to pass over this fourwheeled waggon, 22 cubits by 14, drawn by 500 men. On it was a cave extremely deep, overgrown with ivy and yew, and out of it flew doves, pigeons and turtledoves, all along the road, as the wagon went on—their feet tied with slight threads so that the spectators might easily catch them. Out of the cave there also rose two fountains, one of milk, one of wine, and around it all the nymphs had garlands of gold, and Hermes had a golden herald's-wand and very superb raiment.

On another wagon the Return of Bacchos from the Indians was depicted. Here there was a figure of Bacchos 12 cubits high, riding on an elephant, clad in a purple robe, crowned with golden leaves of vine and ivy, and holding a thyrsos-like spear also of gold. He wore sandals embroidered with golden figures. Before him, on the elephant's neck, sat a Satyr 5 cubits high, crowned with a wreath of golden pineleaves and holding in his right hand a goat's horn of gold, with which he seemed to be blowing signals. The elephant had golden furniture, and on his neck a crown of ivyleaves made of gold; and he was followed by 500 maidens in purple tunics with gold girdles. The hundred in front wore gold crowns of pineleaves; and after them came 120 Satyrs in complete armour, of silver or of bronze. After them marched five troops of asses on which rode Seilenoi and Satyroi all wearing crowns.

After them came 24 chariots drawn by four elephants, 60 drawn by pairs of goats, 12 drawn by antelopes, 7 by oryxes, 15 by buffaloes, 8 by pairs of ostriches, 7 by gnus, 4 by pairs of zebras, and 4 by four zebras each. Boys dressed as charioteers rode all these animals, wearing petasoi and pine-wreaths; and by them went smaller boys with little pelta-shields and thyrsos-spears, wearing ivy leaves. Next came camels, mules, palanquins with women from India and other lands, dressed as prisoners. The camels bore large quantities of frankincense, myrrh, saffron, cassia, cinnamon, iris, and 200 other spices. Then came Aithiopians with 600 tusks, 2000 faggots of ebony, gold and silver goblets, golddust. Then 200 hunters with gold-tipped spears, and 2400 dogs, Indian, Hyrcanian, Molossian and other breeds. Then 150 men with trees from which hung birds and beasts of all lands; and cages with parrots, peacocks, guineafowls, Aithiopian birds in great numbers. Then 130 Aithiopian sheep, 300 Arabian sheep, 20 Euboian sheep, white hornless cattle, 26 Indian cows, 8

Aithiopian oxen, an immense white bear, 14 leopards, 16 panthers, 4 lynxes, 3 *arcetoi*, a cameleopard (giraffe), and a rhinoceros from Aithiopia. Then an image of Bacchos fleeing from Hera to Rhea's altar, Priapos and Hera herself; images of Alexander the Great and the first Ptolemaios with gold ivy leaves; a statue of Virtue beside the latter, as also a statue of the City of Korinth. Then trooped women sumptuously representing the cities of Ionia and other Greek cities: "as many as, occupying the islands and the Asian coast, were made subject to the Persians, and all wore golden crowns. On other chariots were borne a gold thyrsos 90 cubits long and a silver spear 60 cubits; on another a gold phallos

Triumph of Dionysos (sarcophagus, Vatican).

120 cubits long, chased all over and wreathed with golden garlands, with a gold star at the end, 6 cubits in circumference."

Kallixenos pauses at this point to say that he has been mentioning only articles of gold and silver in this procession, and that many other things were included—vast numbers of beasts and horses, and 24 enormous lions; many wagons with statues of kings and images of gods; a band of 600 men, half of whom were harp-players, goldcrowned with harps of pure gold; 2000 bulls all of the same colour with gold decorations. Then came a procession in honour of Zeus and many other gods; then one in honour of Alexander, with a gold statue on a chariot drawn by elephants, Victory and Athena on each side.

Kallixenos goes on to detail a large number of other golden articles, a throne, crowns, incense-burners, stoves, tripods, palm-trees, a herald's-staff 45 cubits long, horns, an immense number of gilded animal figures, mostly 12 cubits high, "and beasts of enormous size and eagles 20 cubits high". There were 200 gold crowns as well, and "a separate mystic crown of gold studded with precious stones, 80 cubits high: this was the crown placed at the door of Berenike's temple; and there was a gold aigis too". Of the vast number of gold chaplets, one, borne by richly-dressed girls, was 2 cubits high and 16 around. There was further much armour of gold and silver, some of huge size, and much gold plate, "all of which was carried in the procession of Bacchos". There were 400 wagons of silver plate, 20 wagons of gold plate, and 700 of perfumes and spices. Then came the soldiers, 57,600 infantry and 23,200 cavalry. Ptolemaios and Berenike were crowned with 23 golden crowns, "standing on golden chariots in the sacred precincts of Dodona". Philadelphos, their son, who gave the show, "was crowned with 20 golden crowns, two of them on golden chariots, and one 6 cubits high on a pillar, and five of them 5 cubits, and six 4 cubits".

This account has been given in a full summary because it is of great importance in bringing out the Dionysiac attitudes which began to spread in the post-Alexander world. The image of triumph has here become a Dionysiac revel, with Alexander's victorious march transposed into the Bacchic conquest of India. Though Zeus and other gods may get a quota of homage, in effect Dionysos is made the god of the new dispensation, and the struggles in both the athletic and the musical or dramatic spheres are associated with his progresses. What had once been attached only to drama and to certain kinds of song-music like the dithyramb has now extended its reach to take in the whole of culture—or rather those spheres of culture in which a direct activity, witnessed by spectators, is the key-thing. Philadelphos is expressing in a grandiose way the trends which brought about the association of athlete and Dionsyiac artists; and he is using imagery which came more and more to embody the deepest ideas and emotions of the people of the Hellenistic and Roman epochs. (This statement omits Christianity, in which a counter-trend finds an increasingly powerful expression—one which has certain links with what we may call the Dionysiac Way, but which also radically opposes that Way.) These points will become clearer as we go on with our inquiry.

There is yet one more point raised by the great Ptolemaic pageant, which will link with what we have to say of the Roman Garden and its architectural associations. This is the huge round tent with its canopy. Here we have a cosmic image. That image reappears in diminutive form in the parasol over Mount Nysa. (Here the divine birthplace becomes a cosmic mount and takes over the parasol from Dionysos himself.[41]) For the moment it is enough to indicate the connection of the Ptolemaic tent with the tent of Alexander—the golden canopy or *ouraniskos* (heaven-

Pulvinar at Theoxenia (Dioscures above); pulvinar of lectisternum.

cover) set over this throne, which he used on his campaigns for the reception of envoys and as a banqueting pavilion with a hundred feasting couches and a throne in the midst. The Achaimenid kings of Persia lived in palaces of brick and stone, but held audiences and festivals in a cosmic tent. Ploutarch says, "The Son of Heaven had a magnificent tent made with fifty gilded posts which carried a sky of rich workmanship." And Hesychios, dealing with ouranos, says that the Persian "royal tents and courts of round awnings were called heavens". Alexander borrowed the custom after defeating the Persians. He was imitating such a tent as that of Dareios, which he captured and which was "worthy of admiration for its height and size".[42] Henceforth the heavenly *skene* or tent was associated with him and became a symbol of power in the Hellenistic and Roman world. Plinius, describing the statues in his tent, calls the tent *tabernaculum*.[43]

In fact, however, in Alexander's *ouraniskos* there was a fusion of Greek and Persian ideas. In setting up a precedent for the fusion of the sacred meal with the palace-rites of the ruler-cult, and for the linking of the kingly world-banquet with the domical cosmic tent, he was also carrying into a new dimension the ideas inherent in the Greek hero-cult with its round tomb, in the *theoxenia* (taken over by the Romans as *lectisternium*) and in the common custom of a meal eaten round a tomb in communion with the dead.[44] The theoxenia or sacred meal could be linked with the games; a Greek vase shows the sacred couch at such a meal, with

Funeral banquet: note snake and horse of the death-journey; and offerings at tomb in form of heroon (relief and vase-painting).

the Dioskouroi above and with the palmbranch of an Olympic victor offered up on the couch.[45] Further, in Egypt the religious banquet was an ancient part of both temple-ceremonies and the palace-ritual of the ruler-cult.

The closest link of the Hellenistic cosmic tent is perhaps with the *heroon*, traditionally a *tholos* or *skias* (circular structure or parasol) in which the inside was presumably covered with a replica of the heavenly *skene* and where the celebrants feasted with the ancestor or hero.[46] And in the Ptolemaic banquet-tent (which also has its link with a sepulchral ritual, that of Ptolemaios Soter) there may well be also a memory of ancient Egyptian usages, which the learned priests would bring to the notice of the court. The tent as a place of advent goes back to early days in the cult of Horus-King. The king was identified with the Master of the Sky and adored as Son of the Sun, making his ritual appearances under three kinds of covers: the primitive bundle of reeds and matting under which he was presented as a god in one of the palace-temple ceremonies: the golden pavilion of the Window of Appearances; the *heb-sed* tent with its four posts and curved canopy. The last-named was used for the Jubilee which celebrated the renewal of his divine life. After a rite of purification he went to the festival hall or platform in the court, and took a seat under each of the two tent canopies representing Upper and Lower Egypt. (As usual in such rites in Egypt a dual form was used.) Since the ceremony was celebrated through "the entire earth", it also involved the presentation and adoration of the king's statues, each under the celestial *heb-sed* canopy in all parts of his realm. A papyrus of the Middle Kingdom shows Senowsret visiting his towns in a ceremonial fashion which may be compared with the epiphany and *adventus*-receptions of Hellenistic kings and Roman emperors.[47] He made his appearances as the living Horus under a baldachin that resembled the *heb-sed* tent. There is every reason to believe that the Ptolemies were aware of such Pharaonic rituals.[48]

8

Men and Animals in the Arena

IN EGYPT, as throughout the Greek East, the bloody combats of the arena were not popular. The gladiatorial fight did indeed at times gain a footing in Greek areas; but the scorn with which Dion Chrysostom speaks of such a development was always a strong element in the attitudes of the Greek world. He states that the Athenians have come to emulate the Korinthians in their zeal for gladiatorial shows, and have surpassed them. For the Korinthians watched the shows outside the city in a large glen— a dirty place, "such that no one would even bury there any free-born citizen". (He seems to refer to a rocky hollow at the foot of a hill east of the new town, which later was turned into a proper amphitheatre and was called a splendid construction in the 4th century.[1]) But the Athenians hold their shows in the very theatre "where they bring Dionysos into the orchestra and stand him up, so that often a fighter is slaughtered among the very seats where the Hierophant and the other priests must sit". A philosopher rebuked them, but they ignored his counsel and did not even applaud; in fact he "was forced to leave the city and preferred to go and live somewhere else in Greece".[2] This man, whom Dion calls a wellborn Roman, must have been the Stoic Musonius Rufus.

Dion held to the old ideal of a harmonious development of mind and body.[3] And despite the dominance of professionalism and the many bad systems of training which the medical writers analysed, despite the failure of the *polis, municipium* or *civitas*, to develop democratically the system of the gymnasion in a situation of worsening social inequalities, the old ideal never died out and to some extent found a new life in the extended possibilities that emerged under the empire.

The gladiatorial fights, however, represented the worst aspects of the imperial situation, a bloody appeasement of the emotions of frustrated aggression and hatred that the oppressions and limitations of freedom stirred up. Local bronzes and terracottas in Egypt show that the combats were not altogether without some appeal, at least in Alexandreia. On a vase-handle we see a stricken gladiator let his sword drop; and we meet on a vase a gladiator who seems a net-fighter.[4] A papyrus of the 2nd century shows that songs were made up in which gladiators figured. Here we have a monody, a complaint from a woman abandoned by her lover, a *mirmillo* (a gladiator who wore a helmet with a fish-crest

Combat of Women Gladiators at Halikarnassos: Amazon and Achillia, "discharged".

—hence his name—and who often was opposed to a netfighter or a Thracian); on the other side is a tax-account from the Arsinoite nome. The lament is in lyric stanzas.

> At the command of a proud man, *mirmillo*
> among the netfighters, alas you are gone,
> gripping in strong hands a sword your sole weapon;
> and me you have left in my anguish alone.

The girl then addresses an attendant:

> Why weave those rosegarlands? It's you I am calling.
> Terrible things happen now to our lad.
> They've coaxed him to fight with vile beasts on his own.
> Zeus, hear my voice, let me not cry unheard.

> Go, servant, then, with your mistress's gold,
> unpurse it, persuading a loud violent man.
> And you've purple clothing in plenty as well—
> swear that you'll bring him as much yet again.[5]

There must have been gladiatorial shows now and then at the amphitheatre in Alexandreia on important imperial occasions. The city had a *ludus* or imperial training-school, and we know of various gladiators who came from it. An inscription mentions a procurator of it, L. Bovius Celer.[6] In A.D. 260 we find clothing requisitioned on its behalf:

.... Aurelios Achilleus, registered in the east ward of the city [Hermopolis], named by the city-secretaries at the time for the oversight, preparation, and convoy of garments for the contests of fighters in single combat in the preceding 7th year of the sovranty preceding this, I swear by the Tyche of Our Lords Macrianus and Quietus, Augusti, to transport and deliver in the month Epeiph of the current 1st year to the office of the excellent Juridicus or to whomsoever I am ordered to deliver them, the half of the amount requisitioned from our city:

147 pairs of tunics, ... pairs of ...., and 87 Syrian [garments] for the past 7th year.

And I shall take the customary receipts for delivery for your inspection (?), or may I be liable to the penalty of my oath. Being interrogated, I agreed.[7]

At Ephesos a base found near the theatre shows a gladiator throwing himself to the right, belted, probably with a greave on his left leg, a dagger in his right hand and a small shield in his left. The inscription tells us: "I was born at the mouth of the Nile. Rhodios my name . . . My might destroyed many men." It probably means that he came from Alexandreia.[8]

Other inscriptions mention M. Antonius Exochus *natione Alexandrinus;* Macedon, *Alexandrinus;* Generosius, a netfighter, *natione Alexandrinus.*[9] We meet also a Thracian-fighter, Aptus *nat(ione) Alexandrinus,* of 37 fights.[10] Faustus from the Alexandrian *ludus* was in Spain.[11]

The magical papyri mention gladiators among those doomed to cruel deaths. "They turn out dying violently and tombless."[12]

We have the horoscope of a youth born on 6 April 113, who brought about the destruction of himself and his family. "The damage would come to a person because Mars was in a human-shaped sign [Aquarius]. He was erotic and fond of gladiators, erotic through Venus and Jupiter, fond of gladiators because Mars was in Epanaphora with respect to midheaven and Mercurius was in the house of Mars. He died about his 25th year, in a bad way, because this [number] and the rising time of Aquarius were the same." The death would thus have taken place in 137–8. The youth has been identified with Pedanius Fuscus whom Hadrian executed in 136, together with his parents, for sedition.

Circus Games (plaques).

Dion Cassios however says that Fuscus' age was then eighteen; the horoscope does not suggest any crime as important as sedition; and the rising time of Aquarius as 25 degrees applies to Alexandreia. The youth may have been of that city.[13]

Inscriptions tell us also of the organisation in the East of spectacles from Rome. Africa and the east provided animals for the big Roman shows. We have seen a Roman officer on the hunt for animals. As late as 8 July 483 an astrologer, Palchos, was approached with the query: "About a small lion whether he will be tamed." We have the horoscope, in which "Aphrodite being in the Horoscopos and Zeus in the [11th locus] Agathos Daimon, about to receive the contact of the Moon, indicated tameness and especially the third (?) of the Moon and the seventh (?) from

Aphrodite: all this showed that it would be tamed and brought up with man; and that the Moon and the Lot of Fortune happened to be in the setting sign showed that it would go abroad on a ship because the setting sign was watery. And that the Moon had left contact with Aphrodite to make contact with Zeus joined the fortunes of the sender and the receiver; for the sender was to become consul and the receiver was consul." In this year the consul in the West was Acilius Aginatius Faustus, the consul in the East Flavius Trocondus. Palchos was probably an Egyptian. He dealt with a ship sailing from Palestine to the Hellespont and himself travelled to Athens; but he was in Smyrna at the time a ship came in from Alexandreia, and one of his horoscopes certainly deals with an Egyptian subject: Theodoros the prefect (horoscope 17 March 486), who "began well and caused prosperity, was truthful and in good repute in the city [Alexandreia] but was soon dismissed in disgrace and under punishment for thievery."[14]

On a Tunisian mosaic are depicted bull, ostrich, boars, bears, with names that include Nilus and Alecsandra. (Each beast of the amphitheatre had its name.)[15] Strabon tells us of crocodiles exhibited in spectacles at Rome, with men from Tentyra bravely handling them.[16] We shall have more to say of Egyptian animals when we come to hunting; here it will suffice to point out the change in meaning that came over the word kynegos (hunter, dog-leader). Under the Ptolemies the kynegoi were hunters, especially dealing with the capture of elephants, and they seem organised on a quasi-military basis. In the Roman period the kynegos was a man who participated in kynegesia (kynegia) of the amphitheatre.[17]

The Egyptians had their own tradition of bullfights. At Memphis, Strabon heard about them though he does not mention having seen one of the fights, in which bull attacked bull.[18] Philon writes as if he had witnessed bullfights in the arena. "In the battles that take place with wild beasts, the bulls do not at once gore their adversaries, but stand well apart. They relax their necks to some extent, bend their heads on one side, and then looking fierce (as it were) after a truce, they rush on with the determination of persevering in the contest. This sort of behaviour

G

is called 'sparring' by men who have the habit of inventing new
words: a sort of sham attack before the real one."[19] Heliodoros
describes a bullfight, which he sets in Meroe. This is not a set
fight, but the result of a sacrificial bull being scared by a giraffe.
Theagenes grabs a piece of cleft wood and mounts a horse, then
gives chase. Coming up level, he leaps on to the bull's neck.

He then laid his face down between the horns, and, encircling them
with his hands as with a wreath, he locked his fingers on the bull's
forehead. The rest of his body was slung on the bull's right shoulder.
Hanging thus, he was carried along, tossed only a little by the bull's
bounding. But when he felt it begin to gasp under his weight and its
muscles weakening their extreme tension—at the moment it came
round to where Hydaspes sat in state—he swung himself over to the

Doors of Carceres opened by Slaves (relief at Velletri).

front, thrust his feet against its legs, and kept knocking on its hooves
till he astutely hindered its movement. Finding its onrush hampered
and overborne by the young man's strength, it gave way at the knees
and all of a sudden stumbled headlong. Then crashing on to its shoulders, it rolled on its back and for long lay outstretched, upside down,
its horn stuck fast in the ground and so driven in that the head could
not move. Its legs kicked in useless prancing and thrashed the empty
air in the wild anguish of its defeat.

Theagenes leans on it with his left arm, raises his right hand
heavenward, and waves it. The bull's bellows serve as a trumpet
to proclaim his victory; and the people reply with a wordless
yell of acclamation.[20]

A 3rd-century drawing on a papyrus gives us some idea of acro-
batics at an animal spectacle. An athlete, facing right, seems
swinging on a trapeze; only his thighs, legs and booted feet are
left. He seems meant to be male from his reddish-brown hue—

though some inkstrokes above can be read as part of a word ending *-ersosis:* the termination suggesting a woman. On the left—
with marks apparently meant to suggest rapid movement in
towards the acrobat—a bear of a deep dull brown rears up. In the
top centre is a violet ring, garland, or hoop, which seems travelling leftwards (as indicated by tangential strokes on the lower
right). The picture is best interpreted as showing an athlete
swinging on a trapeze above a bear and preparing to launch himself through a ring that is thrown towards him.[21]

We can now return to the symbolism of man and animal, man
against animal, men themselves imaged as animals—a symbolism
that had become entangled with the opposition of body and soul
(or mind), professional athlete and philosopher, especially in
Aisopian fable and Cynico-Stoic diatribe. Galen provides an
important expression of this conflict of animal and man in the
sphere of ideas. In his *Exhortation* he discusses beauty and strength.
He goes on to argue that the athlete's strength is useless as it
does not help in agriculture or in war; the professionals cannot
endure heat or cold, and, though they talk of emulating Herakles,
they cannot even sleep in the open. With their boasted might they
are at times unable in palaistra or gymnasion to defeat cobblers,
masons, carpenters. (This statement is of the greatest interest
in showing how, despite all the limitations of the situation,
there were democratic elements present in the later 2nd century.)
Galen then draws on tales of the ancient athlete Milon, who was
eaten by wolves after being caught in a tree which he was trying
to split open with his hands. This death expresses the weakness
of man before the forces of nature; it makes nonsense of the
vauntings of the athletes—what the Christian Tertullian elsewhere called the Vanity of the Xystos.[22]

Galen goes on to cite a fragment of a parody. He gives it in
prose, though it was originally in verse. The poet-parodist was
drawing on the positions of Cynics like Diogenes, which had yet
earlier roots in popular jests and satires. The point of the parody is
that if the games were thrown open to animals as well as men, the
former would win in all events. The horse would win the en-

durance-test, the hare would win the stadion-race, the gazelle would win the double-length. No Olympic winner, however he bragged of being the successor of Herakles, could defeat the elephant and lion in strength. The bull would win the boxing contest, as indeed also the donkey, using its wooden clogs. (The chronicle of the 21st Olympic would have verified that once a man was defeated by an ass.[23])

Philon was aware of this sort of satire. Before Galen, he had written: "What athlete would be a match for the bull's might or the elephant's strength? What runner could equal the speed of hound or hare? The man of keenest eyesight is very shortsighted in comparison with the power of vision owned by hawks or eagles. In hearing and scent the irrational creatures are much our superiors. Even the ass, regarded as the dullest among living creatures, if he were tested with us, would make our hearing appear deafness, while a dog, with his great rapidity of scent, reaches to such an enormous distance as to rival the range of the eyes and to prove a nose to be a superfluous part of the human frame."[24]

With these points in mind, we can review with a new insight some works of art belonging to the period of conflict between Octavianus (later Augustus) and Marcus Antonius, between the Roman world and the Greek East (especially Egypt). In a Pompeian brothel, or rather on three external pilasters of its structure, paintings were made. On the left is Bacchus giving drink to the panther at his side; on the right Mercurius goes with petasus and winged sandals, purse and caduceus—a very common representation for shops. But on the middle pilaster is shown an ithyphallic Ass who sexually assaults and subjects a Lion, rewarded by a crown from a Victory who holds a palmbranch in the other hand.[25]

Beyond a doubt this picture represented the triumph of Octavianus, the Ass, over Marcus Antonius, the Lion, at the Battle of Actium. Suetonius tells us: "At Actium, while on the way down to his fleet to engage the enemy, he (Octavianus) was met by an ass with an ass-driver: the man's name was Eutychus and the beast's name was Nicon. After the victory he erected a bronze statue to each of them, in a temple built on the spot where he had encamped."[26] (The names suggested Good Fortune and Victory.) Ploutarch repeats the story.[27]

There was thus reason enough for identifying Augustus with an ass. Antonius in turn was linked with lions. He struck an aureus with a lion holding a sword; the date was probably the end of 37 B.C., after he had married Cleopatra, cut himself off from the west, and called his son Helios (a coin with a radiate head of the Sun seems of the same date). The Lion is a symbol for Alexander in the Sybilline Oracles; but it seems also to have been Antonius' genethliac sign. Ploutarch's tale of his driving lions in his chariot may have come from a rationalisation of the astrological connection—though it is possible that such a flamboyant person might

Pompeian Graffito.

have sought to bring out his Lion-aspect by some such pageantry. In the Sybilline poems he appears as the Lion whom Cleopatra marries. And in his Heraklean manifestation (he claimed descent from Herakles) he may have seen himself as the slayer of the Nemean Lion. On the aureus there is a star over the lion's back; probably it is the *Julium Sidus*, the sign of Julius Caesar in his apotheosis. Antonius was starting off on his Parthian campaign, and he doubtless wished to combine his own Lion-aspect with a favouring Julian influence.

Further animal symbolism appears in a Pompeian graffito: *Taurus Octavianus Victoriae*, which makes Augustus a bull and again links him with Victory. The ass-lion struggle suggests both fable and parody; the victorious bull suggests the battles of the arena. The symbolism is further complicated by Sibylline references. One prophetic poem is *The Battle of the Stars*, in which the zodiacal constellations fight together, and Orion and his Dog join in; finally heaven throws them all out and they fall to the earth, which they set on fire. The poem tells then of world-end.

In it the New Bull fights and kills Capricorn. The New Bull, if a god, must be Dionysos; and the epithet *Neos* suggests some recent manifestation. Whom else but Antonius? Especially as Capricorn was the badge of Augustus. Suetonius says that early in his life, during retirement at Apollonia, he was "adored" by the astrologer Theogones. "Not long after, Augustus was so confident of the greatness of his destiny that he published his horoscope and struck a silver coin with the sign of Capricorn, under whose influence he was born." The poem thus appears

Boscoreale Cup.

to have been composed before the Battle of Actium. It has further the line "The Virgin charged with the fate of the Twins in the Ram", which may refer to Cleopatra and the renaming of her twins—the boy becoming Alexander (Alexander the Great in the Romance is born under the Ram).[28]

We can enlarge these suggestive glimpses of popular symbolism by considering some contemporary works of art found not far away at Boscoreale.[29] Two cups from the treasure show animal themes. One has a lion and an elephant; the other has a pantheress and an ass. The lion is ridden by a young drunken Satyr with thyrsos and wine-crater in an orgiastic pose, and by a young Love, who guides him. Another Love familiarly holds his tail and a third faces him with a pipe. On two small columns hang the masks of satyr and bacchante; on the ground is a syrinx and an overturned kantharos. The elephant is ridden by two Loves, one of whom holds a mask. A third Love raises a stick and wants to take the mask, which he grasps by the beard. A fourth fondly holds the elephant's trunk. A Dionysiac chest, from which emerges the head of a serpent, hangs on high; and from two small columns hang masks of a horned Pan and a satyress. In these erotic-Dionysiac representations the theme is that Love Conquers All Things, even such mighty beasts as Lion and Elephant. The specific application seems to Antonius, the lion-lover of Cleopatra in a Dionysiac setting. The elephant has been taken to represent Africa, but we must also recall that the skin of the elephant-head is characteristic of certain portraits of Alexander and was used by the Ptolemies as a symbol of their power, their inheritance from him. Thus, on a coin of Ptolemaios I,

Boscoreale Cup.

struck at Cyrene, we see Alexander with the attributes of Zeus Ammon in a quadriga drawn by elephants; and on other coins he appears as an oriental Herakles with elephant-skin instead of lion-skin. (Note his effigy in an elephant-drawn chariot in the Ptolemaic procession cited in the last chapter, where Dionysos further appears on elephant-back.) The tradition was still alive under the empire. Coins of Augustus show him as triumphator in a biga drawn by elephants; Alexandrian coins under Domitian, Trajan, and Hadrian, show the emperor in an elephant-quadriga. Many Roman sarcophagi depict Dionysos in a car drawn by elephants. As he lunges forward to indicate the start of his Indian campaign, the elephants tug at the traces and he himself looks up and back with his mantle bellying above. He is here a Lightbringer.[30]

On the second cup the Pantheress is ridden by a child Bacchos over whom a Love holds a parasol; another Love leads the beast while a third holds her tail; rattles and tympanon lie on the earth; masks of a seilenos and a bacchante hang on columnettes. On the other side, the Ass introduces the first note of discord in the series. He stands with neck outthrust and ears lowered, muzzle turned to the earth, refusing to move despite the efforts of two Loves on his back and two others on the ground, who pull his tail and beat him. Again there is the Dionysiac environment, masks of Satyr and Bacchante on columnettes; syrinx, drinking horn, mask. The theme here is that Love does not conquer all things; for while the Pantheress-Kleopatra proudly makes her progress, the Ass-Octavianus refuses to fit into this scheme of things.

A silver patera from the same treasure shows a central emblema, a bust-relief of a woman who has been generally taken to represent Africa or Alexandreia. Her head is covered with an elephant skin and tusks; she holds an uraeus and a cornucopia bursting with grapes and fruits crowned by a crescent that is attached to a cedar-cone (attribute of the saviour-god Attis). On the horn is represented a bust of Helios, the sun-eagle, and the two stars of the Disokouroi. Fruits (grapes, pomegranates, figs, cedar-cones, etc.) fill her lap, and among the fruit is a peacock (Hera's bird and also a sky-symbol). Stepping over the fruit is a large figure of a pantheress. Corresponding to the horn of the gods of light on the left are symbols of Herakles on the right: lion, club, bow, quiver. (These symbols are large like the uraeus, panther, horn.) On the left is the sistron of Isis; under the right hand, a sea-emblem (waves and dolphin); under the fruit, the tongs of the smith Hephaistos and the snake-sceptre of Asklepios. Right of the horn is Apollo's lyre.

We see that this woman is under the protection of the Egyptian gods; she is Queen of Egypt (the uraeus is symbol of Egyptian royal power). Of her other protectors, the chief is Dionysos (the pantheress), while her prosperity and fertility are the gift also of the gods of light and of the great civilising hero Herakles (who could represent both Alexander and the Macedonian line which was supposed to descend from him). Other emblems stress the sea-trade, the healthy site, the flourishing industry and art of Alexandreia, of the Egyptian kingdom.[31]

While thus a good case can be made out for seeing the woman as a personification of Alexandreia, an even stronger case can be made for her as Cleopatra. The Dionysiac and royal complex of symbols suits that queen's reign, and would hardly have been acceptable after the Augustan annexation of Egypt. For the same reason we must surely attribute the patera, like the cups described above, to workshops of Alexandreia and not of Campania.[32] In any event the symbolism in general belongs to the epoch of Cleopatra and Antonius. (For the Sun and Moon we must remember Alexandros Helios and Cleopatra Selene, the children of those two.[33]) The Boscoreale treasure we may take to represent part of the loot of Alexandreia after the occupation by the Romans, which had passed into imperial possession.[34]

With these points in mind we may look at two other cups that were found at Pompeii. One depicts a Dionysiac scene, in which a winged Love takes part, riding a pantheress; on the other side is a large goat, also ridden and guided by a Love. Here the symbolism that exalts the love of Antonius and Cleopatra on the Boscoreale cups is twisted into a depreciation of Antonius. Another cup, also Dionysiac in its scenes, shows a young bull ridden by a winged Love on one side; on the other, a haughty Love-ridden Lion. Here we seem to have the rivalry of Octavianus and Antonius represented, so that we are able to fill out the graffito *Taurus Octavianus Victoriae* with something like *Leone Antonio devicto munera cepit*: Bull Octavian, with Lion Antonius defeated, accepted the rewards of Victory—though Antonius may have been Caper, the Bacchic Goat: in which case the emblems of the Sibylline Star-poem would have been reversed. Such a reversal would no doubt have been possible in the complicated exchanges and ironies of the period's propaganda.[35] The graffito's use of the name Octavianus suggests that it and no doubt the ass-painting belong to the years close to Actium.

Maybe the man who painted the picture of the Ass raping the Lion was not really glorifying Octavian, but was using the ass-association of Actium to satirise the victor. His picture would then be an assertion that an ass-power had balefully defeated the lion-hero. It would be going too far to make any direct connection between the conquering Ass-Roman and the villainous Seth of Egyptian myth; but we must remember that both the Jews and the Christians were said by maligners to worship ass-gods or

G*

gods with ass-heads. It is legitimate then to claim that there was a general notion floating about in this world of the ass as an emblem of perversity, of the principle of destruction. The painting of Ass raping Lion was obliterated; and it has been suggested that this was done in the reign of Claudius (son of a daughter of Antonius). It is perhaps more likely that the obliteration was done

Emblema of Patera, Boscoreale.

earlier by someone who recognised the dubious compliment to Augustus.

The likelihood that the Ass here had an aspect of malevolence is increased if we consider further the nature of Seth-Typhon in his ass–character. According to Ploutarch, he effected nothing by his union with Nephthys, but, after escaping on an ass, he became the father of two. He was invoked on love-charms; twice in the

myths he has his way with Horos, anally penetrating him; he
takes his pleasure with Anat in a way that reminds us of this feat;
and he is shown as madly in love with Isis when she appears as a
beautiful maid. Ass-coition occurs in *The Golden Ass* and the
Lucianic *Lucius*, and is common on obscene lamps. In magic Seth
seems connected with abortions. From the XXII dynasty we meet
curses against stele-violation in which the malefactor, his wife and
children, are threatened with sexual assault by the Ass (whom we
may take to be Seth). The same motive has turned up on Indian
stelai, where a relief shows an ass raping a woman. Two amulets
command the Metra or Womb (the dangerous Womb considered
the cause of pains in stomach, bowels, heart or chest, and even of
suffocation) to give up its roaming about on pain of being punished
by Typhon (Seth); we may assume that the punishment would
consist of the ass-rape. A haematite gem shows the blessed Metra
of fertility on one side, protected by the Khnoubis-serpent; on
the other side is Seth as a warning that the Womb must not become troublesome. A second gem shows ram-headed Khnum
with solar disc on head, holding the Metra with the key in his
right hand and sitting on a tripod between Isis and Horos-Har-
pokrates (who emerges from a Bes-figure); on the reverse ass-
headed Seth stands upon the Metra. A third gem, which thus
depicts Seth on the Womb, describes him in the inscription as
Typhon who has taken possession of it.

There is good reason then to attribute to the Ass-figure in
an anally-ravishing pose an aura of evil and to see in the Pompeian example at least a distant reflection of Seth-Typhon,
whether or not the artist was hailing him.[36]

It is of interest to note how in general there was a series of
charges and countercharges in the propaganda-war between
Octavianus and Antonius. Suetonius tells us that the former once
gave a private party, commonly called the Supper of the Twelve
Gods, which caused much comment. Antonius took the episode
up in his letters and an epigram circulated:

> When lately in a dinner masquerade
> Twelve Gods in well-matched pairs had Mallia puzzling,
> the role of Phoebus Caesar foully played:

in new adulteries the gods lay guzzling.
From earth depart the outraged deities
and from his golden throne Jove headlong flees.[37]

If the dinner ever happened, it seems an imitation of the *lectisternum* or the *epulum Jovis*. (Later Domitian probably celebrated the Dinner of Jove, with himself in Jove's role, in the rectangular and apsidal triclinium of the Domus Augustana.[38]) The time of the story about Octavianus was probably the famine-scare caused by Sextus Pompeius' blockade, when the populace were outraged and cried, "the gods have eaten up all the corn, Caesar is indeed Apollo, Apollo the Torturer." (There was a shrine of Apollo Tortor in Rome, probably in the Suburra.) The men who started off the effective phrase about Apollo were no doubt Antonius' agents at Rome; for we find exactly the same sort of twist used against him as Dionysos. Yes, said the counter-propaganda, he was indeed Dionysos, but the Ravager, not the Bringer-of-plenty. We must recall too the twelve triclinia at the Cilician festivities of Antonius, mentioned in our first chapter; and, as another obvious instance of Roman propaganda the tale of Dionysos abandoning the defeated Antonius, with Bacchic music in the night.

How thoroughly political ideas and propaganda penetrated the art of the period is exemplified by Pompeii, a provincial town outside the main stream of events and struggles.

The many episodes from the Taking of Troy must, like the second book of the *Aeneid*, have been inspired by a reawakened interest in the Trojan ancestry of the Romans; the pictures of the loves of Mars and Venus recall the honour in which these patron gods of the Julian race were held in Rome; two paintings show the one the group of Aeneas with Anchises and Iulus, the other Romulus shouldering the spoils of Acron, both evident copies of the statues in the Forum of Augustus described by Ovid; ornamental details, the tripods and other Apollinine emblems, the dolphins and the ships so profusely introduced among the "fantasies" of the Pompeian Fourth Style, obviously refer to the Augustan cult of Apollo and the naval victories of Actium. Still another Pompeian picture—a landscape of the Third Style offers a glorified version of the Romulean legend of the Palatine exalted by Augustus.[39]

There seems every reason, then, to take the Boscoreale cups and emblema, as well as the two Pompeian cups, as works of art deeply involved in the struggle of ideas and images that went on between Octavian and Antonius. The Boscoreale works must have come from Alexandrian artists in Cleopatra's reign. They show a fusion of royal and Dionysiac symbolism with popular elements derived from fable and satire, and an oblique but powerful link with the arena and the conflict of ideas in the sphere of athletics.

9

Hunts and Zoological Collections

HUNTING on a grand scale is a natural expression of a society dominated by great lords or landholders. We find it among the Ptolemies with such big landowners as the Apollonios whom Zenon served, and again in Byzantine Egypt with its baronial estates. The imagery of the boar-hunt shows the transition from the classical attitudes to the seigneurial. Classical representations or accounts depict a hunt on foot, in which dogs may help but do not control the kill. The eastern princely imagery shows the lordly cavalier chasing the boar alone, or with a crowd of servitors and the pack. This Persian mode was taken up by the nobles after Alexander. He himself had dangerously wanted to kill a lion alone; the Macedonians had demanded that he should hunt on horseback, surrounded by friends. Quintus Curtius adds that it was the Persian princely custom not to hunt on foot or without a select body of comrades and lords. After that the Persian mode became the rule of the Greek kings in Syria, Egypt, Macedonia; and the Roman nobles, who would have disliked the idea of imitating orientals, were ready to follow a Macedonian example after the defeat of king Perseus. A new life came into the princely hunt in the later empire and its art.

On contorniate medallions of Caracalla's epoch, and perhaps also on the Palermo mosaic, the memory of Alexander is linked with both the combat on horseback and on foot against the boar ... At Dresden on a sarcophagus of the real "imperial" hunt the boar is attacked by horsemen; and naturally hunts of Hippolytos, Atalanta, or Meleagros at times adopt horseback for the fight against the Kalydonian monster. The pavement of the Antiquarium which recalls the hunts of a high functionary of the Constantinian epoch, constitute a good example of

the transposition into "seigneurial" hunting of the classical theme
with three characters (man, boar, dog) of the fight with the boar.[1]

In the aristocratic mind the hunt was closely linked with warfare.
Platon and Xenophon stress the point. Philon repeats the tradition.

Hunting is a good training-ground for warlike natures; for those who
are trained for generalship practise themselves first in the chase.

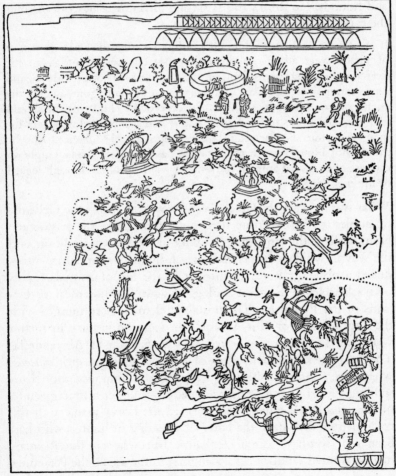

Nilotic Scene (mosaic at El Alia, Tunisia).

Unreasoning animals are made to serve as material with which to practice in government for the emergencies of both peace and war. For the hunting of wild beasts is a drill ground for the general in fighting the enemy; and the care and management of tame animals is a schooling for a king on dealing with his subjects. For this reason kings are called Shepherds of their People.[2]

Elsewhere he states that the custom among both Greeks and barbarians is to share out the flesh of the slain beasts among hunters and hounds. He thinks this is wrong as the Mosaic code forbids the eating of bodies torn by beasts.

If a man who has devoted himself wholly to meditation and the practice of virtue were all of a sudden to grow enamoured of gymnastic exercises and hunting, looking on the hunt as a sort of prelude to, and representation of, the wars and dangers to be undergone against the enemy, then, whenever such a man succeeded in his sport, he should give the slain beasts to his dogs as a feast and as a reward or wages for their victorious boldness and their irreproachable alliance. But he should not himself touch them, as he has been previously taught in the case of irrational animals the sentiments he should hold with regard to his enemies.[3]

What was new for the Greeks was the way in which the Hellenistic nobles tried to keep up their own tradition of the aristocratic hunt, while at the same time drawing in the Persian tradition, and the way in which a deepened sense of distance from nature introduced a nostalgic note, an interest in the life of animals for its own sake. Hence the great zoological, as well as botanical, collections of the Ptolemies. The nostalgic element here merges with the new growth of post-Aristotelian scientific inquiry in such a writer as Theophrastos, which was carried on at Alexandreia. The Ptolemies had their corps of hunters under an *archikynegos*, who were concerned both to keep off the hippopotamoi from spoiling the crops and to make expeditions under a strategos into Nubia after the elephants that formed the heavy artillery of the royal army.[4] We have the letter of a soldier or hunter who had been sent south to catch elephants. But whereas the Romans mainly wanted wildbeasts for slaughter in the arena, the Ptolemies wanted to stock their collections. And not only the Ptolemies, but their great lords also wanted to build up impressive zoological gardens.[5] Alexander, however had set an example of pleasure in the spectacle of animals fighting one another: while on the other hand in the days of the late Republic rich Romans took up the practice of animal collections, at times linking them (e.g. through the symbolism of Orpheus) with the paradisiac parks we shall later discuss. A philhellenic emperor like Nero had a collection of exotic animals for his Golden House.

Many Egyptian traditions helped to intensify the interest in beasts and birds. Animals were mummified and given their own tombs right into the Roman period. A large Ptolemaic tomb at Drah abu'l-Neggah was a "house of repose for ibis and falcons", as a papyrus says.[6] We meet in 284 B.C. a *taricheutes* of the monkeys of Thoth.[7] There were cat-tombs in an area called the Sopheis, apparently in the Memnonia.[8] We hear of animal mummies set side by side with those of the human clients of the chaochytai. The variety of animals thus treated was considerable: bulls, jackals, rams, crocodiles, snakes, dogs, cats, horned vipers, and so on.[9]

We have some letters, dated A.D. 13, which deal with the sale of persea and acacia wood, which had no private owner and thus belonged to the idiologos. The would-be buyer applies to that official, who sends his application to the basiliskogrammateus of the nome with instructions to verify details and value the wood. There is then a regular descent in the official scale, to the topos-secretary and then to the village-secretary, who finally has to supply the required details to the treasury. What interests us here is the part played by the tomb of sacred animals as convenient spots for official use. The topos-secretary tells the village-secretary: "Go to the objects specified as concerning Didymos son of Herakleides, namely a branch of a live persea-tree at the Thoereion of Osorphnas, and two dry branches of a living persea-tree in the temple of Harpebekis at the Tomb of the Sacred Animals, and see whether they are dry and ought to be appropriated by the privy purse in accordance with the tariff, add the true value, with a signed declaration and report clearly, making it your aim that nothing be concealed or done by favour, knowing that you will

be held accountable in any inquiry about facts that remain unknown." Didymos' original application is attached and declares:

I wish to buy in the Oxyrhynchite nome from the privy purse some
dried logs which have no owner and ought to be appropriated by
the privy purse in accordance with the tariff, namely at the village of
Kerkeura in the middle toparchy in the Thoereion of Osorphnas a
single branch of a small persea-tree, dried and worth 6 dr., and in the
Temple of Harpebekis on the Tomb of the Sacred Animals two dried
branches of a living persea-tree worth 2 dr., and at the village of
Peënno in the same toparchy in the Temple of Ammon a dried branch
of a living persea-tree worth 2 dr., and near the same village in the
holding of Melanthios in the cutting made in the great dyke 2 fallen
acacia-trees worth 8 dr.[10]

A considerable fuss for the purchase of a small amount of wood.
Harpebekis means Horos the Hawk; and Osorphnas seems an
unknown, deified animal.

Animals were also kept in temples. For example, lions were still
fed and venerated in the temple of Leontopolis.[11] Diodoros
describes a wall-representation of a lion fighting beside a pharaoh
and adds that some persons interpret it as a real lion, others as an
emblem of the king's courage, his spiritual state.[12] In the temple
of Ramses III in the Memnonia a lion paces by the king in his
chariot, and at Deir el-Bahari Hatshepsut is depicted with a lion-
head destroying the foe.[13] Following the Pharaohs, the Ptolemies
kept lions at court. Berenike had one, who licked her face to
wipe out the wrinkles and participated at her dinners.[14] Antonius
the Lion with his lion-chariot fits well into the Egyptian scene.

The idea of the Sacred Hunt went far back in Egyptian thought.
Temples showed the rite of the Seth-born oryx having its throat
cut, the hippopotamos dismembered, fishes caught—"fish which
are the Nubians, birds which are rebellious Asiatics, hostile bulls
and rebellious ibex". All game, whether birds, beasts, fish, were
considered to be dedicated to the evil powers. The very act of the
hunt cast spells on foreigners, demons, magicians, public or private
enemies. For the king the hunt was above all a trial of strength
and a proof of his continued youth or vitality. By a ritual privilege

he could face lions. Amenophis III in ten years killed 102 of them; his annals (on temple-walls) tell of his victories over the bulls of the marshes, the Syrian wild-asses, the elephants of the Orontes, and a great rhinoceros met by chance on an expedition into the Sudan.[15]

The Ptolemies carried on the tradition of the sacred hunt. For example, in wall-representations and texts at Edfu.[16] The walls show us Horos standing in a small boat, with Isis, about to pierce the Sethian hippopotamos, while the king, Ptolemaios XI, followed by his sons in guise of harpooners, shares in the divine act from the riverbank. (The image of Horos or the King killing the

Sacrifice of the Oryx (temple at Luxor).

beast of evil underlies the Byzantine and medieval iconography of St George or St Michael slaying the dragon.[17])

Of interest too is the very ancient sacrifice of the oryx. This seems to originate in the 26th nome of Upper Egypt, which had in the late period on its standard an oryx with a falcon on its back. At least in that late period there seems an assimilation of the oryx to Seth-Typhon, so that Horos, the ancient warrior of Hebenu, becomes the foe and conqueror of the place's primitive emblem.[18] In the Ptolemaic Speos of Elkab a representation of the oryx-sacrifice occurs.

The development seems as follows. The antelope-hunt gave birth to a liturgy linked with the preparation of certain sacred boats. The sacrifice was a technical rite that involved the killing of the creature while bleeding it, cutting it up, and using the hide. The 26th nome in its traditions kept some traits of this rite. Meanwhile the rite had been given a symbolic interpretation and taken into astronomic liturgies that sought to control the return of sun and moon; the antelope become consecrated to Sokaris (a god with strong solar character) whose boat was decorated with its head.

The study of the oryx-sacrifice enables us to throw light on a curious process of composition used by the decorators of the late temples, by which they established subtle correspondences of one scene with another, in a suggestive way, as of echoes, whether by playing on the likeness of certain signs, or whether by exploiting the possibilities of substituting partially-equivalent symbols. It is in some sort the transposition of procedures in the decoration that have long been recognised in Ptolemaic writing, and the result of a systematic exploition pushed to the limits of its possibilities in the fundamental principles that allowed the birth of Egyptian writing itself. This exploitation was only the application to a precise end of the unconscious rules of analogic thought to which we owe all the cosmological and theological systems of the ages before Greek rationalism.[19]

We have here a valuable example of the way in which ancient traditions survived: how they were broken up, revalued, given fresh associations inside an expanding system, and yet at the same time revealed a stubborn strength of rebirth.

Some of the Ptolemies had names as hunters; and we may be sure that the Egyptian clergy did not leave them ignorant of their own religious interpretation of such activities. A painting by Antiphilos represented the hunt of Ptolemaios Soter.[20] Ptolemaios IV was proud of his reputation as a bold and skilful hunter: and these qualities of his, together with his adroitness on horseback and with arms, were vaunted by the Egyptian ambassador before Philopoimen.[21]

Before we pass on to the Roman period, we may profitably look at a poem roughly inscribed on an irregularly shaped stone, not prepared for such a use—no doubt a draft copy. For while giving us some interesting sidelights on to Ptolemaic elephant-

hunts, it also brings out some aspects of Min-Pan of Panopolis, a
city that will later concern us as the birthplace of the poet Nonnos.
The poem runs:

> To Pan! hunt-helper and friendly, who led me safe
> from the Troglodyte Land where I suffered heavy hardships
> on two toils, from the holy Myrrhland and the Koloboi
> O you saved me as we wandered the Sea, sending
> a fair wind to ships whirled in the waves and piping
> shrill blasts from your reeds till you brought us to Ptolemais,
> piloting with the sure grasp of your hunter's-hands.
>
> Now, kindly god, save the City of Alexander
> most famed, founded long past on Egypt's coast;
> and I'll proclaim your power, dear Pan, when I safely
> come through to Ptolemaios and Arsinoe . . .

There are the remains of two more lines. The stone probably
came from Redesîeh, a village on the east side of the Nile, some
five miles from Edfu (Apollonopolis Magna). Five other inscriptions from there record someone being "saved from the Troglo-
dytes"; and there are some twenty inscriptions to Pan *Euagros*
(hunt-helper), *Epekoos* (hearkener) or *Euodos* (helper-on-the-way),
which come mostly from the same site—one from near Koptos
(Wadi Abad) and one from Philai—with one to Ares. Some 37
miles almost due east from Redesîeh, in the desert, lies a rock
temple built by Seti I of the XIX Dynasty in connection with a
watering-station on the way to the mines of Jebel Zubara, and
dedicated to Amon-Re. The site was repaired, doubtless under
Ptolemaios II, as a station on the caravan-road from Apollonopolis to some port on the Red Sea, presumably Berenike. A Greek
inscription, found near the temple, speaks of it as a Paneion over
against Apollonopolis; graffiti on walls, columns, architectural
fragments and the near cliffs show that the frequenters were
mainly Ptolemaic, but that the place was used down to Roman
times.

The dedicator of our poem seems the leader of an elephant-
hunt. The epithet given to Pan, *euagros*, suggests this. The inscription of Alexandros, second in command to Charimortos, the

strategos on an elephant-hunt, is dedicated to Ares *euagros*;
Satyros, known as an elephant-hunter, made a dedication at the
temple near Redesîeh; and Strabon mentions elephant-hunts in
each of the regions named in the third line of our poem. Ptolemaios Philadelphos began explorations of the Troglodytic coast
with a view to arranging a steady supply of elephants; and Ptolemais Harbour was created for this reason. Our dedicator with his
ships (which suggest a hunt rather than trading) was probably
busy between 217 and 203; his appeal for the safety of Alexandreia is best taken as referring to this period with its fourth Syrian
war, rebellions among the natives and revolt in the City. He seems
to have made two landings, with expeditions after elephants, and
now to have been making his way to Alexandreia. We may

African Landscape (relief, Vatican).

assume that he was a high official. The Min-Pan of his dedication
cared for travellers across the desert on their way to Punt, for
hunters and sailors making for the Red Sea; from the XI Dynasty
he was connected with Wadi Hammamat on the caravan route
from Koptos to the coast; from the XII Dynasty with Punt and
the Red Sea.[22]

Hunting in the Roman period must have been much stimulated
by the continual need of animals for shows. Like Asia and the rest
of Africa, Egypt was ransacked. The demand had already begun
under the Republic. In 58 B.C. Scaurus at his games had 500 felines
(a record at that date) together with a hippopotamos and five
crocodiles of the Nile swimming in an euripus. Four centuries
later, as we see in Ammianus Marcellinus, the shock was still

registered. In 55 B.C., Pompeius had in the arena a Gallic lynx (probably got through Caesar), a rhinoceros from Egypt, and an Ethiopian monkey.[23]

We get some idea of the part played by the army in connection with wild beasts from the correspondence of Flavios Abinnaios in mid-4th century. Meios, who seems a Christian church-dignitary of some kind, to judge by his chatter of pious sentiments and the way he treats Abinnaios as an equal, is bothered by gazelles:

To my Beloved Brother Abinnaios, the priest Meios greeting in the Lord. I give thanks to God for your wellbeing: may he deliver you from ... We know your Excellence and your Love for us. It is on behalf of God that you must act, and I pray to Him to requite you for the Love you manifest, because you act for Him.

Then I'll write to you, Brother. For I've heard there are nets stored at the Standards. If it is possible, send them to me for a few days. The gazelles are devastating the sown crops. But if you haven't got them at the Standards, perhaps you may find them somewhere else. Anyhow, send me a few, and I'll quickly return them to you, for I know you do more than I've asked. I've sent you by Sais a hyena's skin. Greetings individually to everyone in your House. May the Lord God preserve you. [2nd hand] The priest Meios. [1st hand] Health to you in the Lord.[24]

Meios or his scribe wrote the letter in capitals. Abinnaios was a cavalry-officer commanding the camp at Dionysias in the Arsinoite nome. The Standards of a unit were kept at the headquarters, where they had a special religious significance; hence they came to signify the HQ itself. In another letter, where the opening is mutilated (though the address "Beloved Brother" can be made out), we again seem to meet Meios, who is putting in some special pleading for his wife's brother.

... a drink of water to one of these little ones shall not lose his reward. Let not your soul be vexed at your being upset, but trust in God and stop. I'm writing to you about my wife Naomi's brother. He's a soldier's son and has been enlisted to go as a soldier. If you can release him again, you'll have done a good deed, first of all on God's behalf, secondly on mine, because his mother is a widow and has nobody but him. Still, if he must serve, please save him from being sent abroad with the draft for the field-army, and may God repay you for your charity and raise you up to greater things.

As I left your presence (?), I took Sp.amios with me. He asked that he might come for his gear, but delayed lest ... coming till ... if you know he doesn't want to come with frankness as we, the ... agreed ... with you that not only he, but anything only ... authority, and as I said to you, send the huntsman.

I greet you and all in your house. May God preserve you. [Addressed] To his Beloved Brother Abinnaios . . .[25]

In a third letter, Thareotes writes in a very bad hand, also with a recommendation, which he backs up with gifts. He too is interested in hunting.

To my Master and Patron, the Praepositus Castrorum of Dionysias, Thareotes, greeting in God. First I pray for you that you may receive my letter in good spirits; for I pray also to the Lord for the health of Constantius and Domnus (sons of Abinnaios).

I beg of you, my Master, for Syrion, my brother's son, whom I present to you. He requests and begs of you that you'll show him the same consideration (?) as to me.

For this is what I said: Whatever you need of, my Master supplies you with it there. I've sent you by Ammonios the cobbler 2 jars of quails, 1 pot of fishpaste, 1 flagon of grapesyrup. I didn't do a letter for him, but I've given the chickens by way of earnest money. Don't worry about them, the chickens are inside. Now as they are still small and white . . . let them grow big, and I'll come to visit you in Phamenoth; and keep the hempen cords ready, for I'll bring the huntsmen when I come, so that we may make the nets.

I'm sending you also the camels from the middle farm with a letter letting you know whatever is needed by the men in charge of the chickens, so you may give them instructions, for many persons are doing them harm, and may help to keep them safe. I won't let them go . . . I pray for your health . . . [Addressed] To my Master the Praepositus, Thareotes.[26]

It seems that Abinnaios has quite a lot to do with hunters, though we have no other indication of their purpose than crop-protection.

Hunting could be useful for producing hides or for adding to the food-supply, especially at moments of festival. A papyrus of Mesore, 250 B.C., deals with the expenses of transporting ani-

mals which were being sent as gifts to the king for the festival
of the Arsinoiia (this year on 16 October). Though hunting
is not directly mentioned, the wild boars that are being sent
must have been caught by hunters, and one item of expenditure is
for workmen unloading animal-cages, *galeagrai*, from ships.[27]

The governmental control of hunting established by the
Ptolemies was carried on by the Romans. The State exercised its
control through public hunters, *demosioi kynegoi*. Hunting rights
were farmed out, and the tax was collected by the farmers. We

Mule and Camel (Theodosian Column).

have several documents dealing with concessions. Here is one for
A.D. 87–8 from Theadelpheia:

I wish to lease the pastures that lie in the swamp of Theadelpheia with
the right of hunting, fishing, trapping of wild . . . , gathering the floss
of the reeds, papyrus, and . . . as in my former lease. This lease is only
for the current 7th year of the emperor Caesar Domitianus Augustus
Germanicus at a total rental of 11,000 silver dr., which includes . . . dr.
for the swamp of Theadelpheia and Polydeukeia and i, 348 dr 1 ob.
for the estate of Dionysodoros . . .[28]

One wonders how that single obol strayed in. At Theadelpheia
again in 154–5, Horsiesis, whose father was unknown and whose
mother was Tapsupsitis, offered to two men "and their associates
in the overseeing of the mere of the village" 32 silver dr. for the
right to hunt and snare "wild fowl of all kinds" for four months.
Aged 47, he was to pay the money in two equal instalments. In
the same year Heron son of Apollonios, "registered in the Cilician
Quarter, a huntsman and a Persian-of-the-Epigone", applied for

similar rights for a whole year, at the charge of 40 dr., which was to be paid down as a lump sum in Phamenoth. "I shall have with me two assistants, if you consent to the concession." It is hard to understand the disparity in the bids, unless the four months from Pachon to Mesore (late April to late July) were by far the best season.[29]

From the Herakleopolite nome, in the 3rd century, we have a complaint from the lessee of the hunting concession (of the whole nome?) to the dedarch in charge of the nome's peace. He is Aurelios Apion. "Horos, son of . . . , hunter from the village of Thmoiamounis and Papnoutis son of Tasonps . . . , also a hunter from the village of Paraperiph . . . , display great disobedience and disregard of law by refusing to pay the taxes established by order of the most distinguished Juridicus. Though I again and again approach them, they drive me off with insults and abuse, almost with blows. They oppress others and defraud the revenues derived from hunting. Compelled by necessity, I appeal to you, paying as I do ten talants . . . dr. yearly, and I lodge this information so that they may be brought before you to give an account of their arrogance and disobedience."[30]

A hunter's work inevitably had many hazards. We find a daughter in A.D. 216 writing in fear of what may have happened to her huntsman father.[31] The astrologers stress the dangers and wretched ends of hunters. "They meet with wild beasts or die on journeys or become hunters." "Hunters who suffer violent deaths." "Hunters always blaspheming the god." "Always malign and owning the ways of woodland beasts." "Preparing traps for wildbeasts they are torn to pieces by their fangs."[32] Deaths through wildbeasts seem common. Among the horoscopes that have come down, we find a man who appears to have been born on 4 April 91: "Locus of death in Cancer, Saturn the ruler of the fullmoon turning away; also Mars in opposition to his own house. This person was killed by wildbeasts." Again of a man born 26 December 115, "The (8th) Locus of Death was in Taurus and Saturn is there. This person was killed by wildbeasts."[33] And of a child, born on 14 August 158 and dying in May 161, we read: "At the end of the 8th month, and during part of the 9th, he was subject to convulsions lacking little of being dangerous. And there were indications for the other months, being controlled by the maleficent [stars]; and he was afflicted by eruptions and eczema namely in the 15th, 17th, and 23rd [month], and in rest, but especially in the 27th month. And supposedly he fell into an animal snare and was struck in parts of his body." More convulsions lead to death.[34]

Sometimes men came on an animal by chance and killed it, as did four Ptolemaic mercenaries who caught a fox in the cella of Horos at Abydos.[35] But hunting was mostly well organised. Gazelles

Three late types of Opet: third as Queen of Heaven.

or antelopes were hunted in the desert areas by quick greyhounds, escorted by men on foot. From prehistoric days the Egyptians used the lasso. We see hunters represented on a palette, preparing to seize or already having seized antelopes.[36] The lasso, wielded by Egyptians or Libyans to catch beasts for the arena, was used also in the arena by gladiators and *bestiarii*.[37]

The hippopotamos could cause much damage to crops and so appears as an incarnation of evil force. On the walls of mastabas we see dead nobles killing the creature. Steering through papyrus-thickets in frail skiffs, the hunters come on a herd and hurl their harpoons in their jaws. (Nilotic Negroes still use the same sort of harpoons against hippopotami.) The hunt-leader holds the

ropes attached to the harpoons, and with them the stricken hippopotamos is dragged out of the water, killed, and ceremonially cut
up. At Edfu, town of Horos, sacred harpooners were maintained.
However, while the male hippopotamos seems feared and hated,
the female "was practically always a benign and good divinity, a
form of the mother-goddess". The hippopotamos is shown on some
predynastic palettes, but it would not be safe to infer at this early
period anything like the later goddess. She appears as a friend in
the Book of the Dead, and large numbers of blueglazed figures of
hippopotami have been found in Middle Kingdom tombs, decorated with waterplants and flowers. The great creature with broad
shining flanks had come to symbolise fecundity and was worshipped as the White One, Opet, and the Great One, Thoueris.[38]
Opet may have grown in importance through confusion with
another Opet, personification of the Luxor temple, from whose
cult some of her later epithets seem to derive. It is doubtful however if her name of Mother-of-Osiris came from the same source;
for Ipy in pyramid texts is described as suckling the dead king
and may be taken as prototype of Opet, the childbirth-helper of
the Mother of the Gods, kings, and ordinary mortals. Figures,
statues, amulets, and temple-representations of Thoueris show
her on her hind feet, leaning on the magic knot. Documents
ranging from the Saite to the Ptolemaic period reveal a series of
twelve hippopotamus-goddesses who preside in a definite order
over the twelve months of the year. Most of the names of these
goddesses reappear in the names of women in documents of
the late period. Thoueris too plays her part in names of that period;
women turned to her in childbirth and at other moments of crisis
in their lives.[39] Once again we find ancient elements persisting
potently into Roman Egypt.

Nonnos erroneously states that hippopotami exist also in the
river Hydaspes of India:

> There swims the roaming riverhorse through the water
> cleaving with his hoof the blackpebbled stream
> just like the dweller in my own Nile who cuts
> the summergotten flood and with long jaws
> travels the depths. He climbs ashore and splits

the wooded ridges with sharp-pointed teeth;
with only a wet ungraven jaw for looting
the fruits, he cuts with his makeshift sickle the harvest,
a reaper of sheafbearing crops who owns no steel.[40]

Ammianus tells us that he loses no chance of sallying out of the
dense reeds to ravage the crops. When gorged, "he walks backward and makes many tracks, to prevent any enemies from follow-

Egyptian Landscape (plaque).

ing the straight road and so finding and easily killing him". When
his belly is swollen, he rolls in the reeds till blood flows from his
thighs and legs, then he smears the wounds with clay.[41] Achilleus
Tatios is hardly more accurate. "It happened that some men were
hunting a riverbeast that is well worth seeing, the Nile Horse as the
Egyptians call it." His description seems aimed at giving a mon-
strous mythological effect. The belly and feet are like a horse's,
though the hooves are cloven; the size is about that of the biggest
ox, the tail short and hairless; indeed the whole body is hairless;
the big round head is cheeked like a horse's, wide nostrilled and

breathing out hot vapour, the jaws enormous, the mouth gaping up to the temples, the eye-teeth crooked and about three times a horse's.

The hunters note the tracks, then dig a pit which they roof with straw and earth. Under this contraption of thatch, they set at the bottom a wooden box with its cover open up to the pit-top. Then they wait for the beast to fall in. When it comes along, it crashes down and the box takes it like a trap. The hunters rush out, close the lid, and gain possession of their prey. He's too strong for anyone to master by mere force. Not only is he very powerful, but his hide, as you may see, is of great thickness and cannot be pierced by steel.[42]

The Nilotic scene in Graeco-Roman days appears on a large number of mosaics, many of which include pygmies. The types must have originated in Alexandreia, though they were doubtless used and modified in various places by artists who had no direct connection with Egypt.[43] An example from Quasr el-Lebia in Libya, found in a Christian church of the 6th century, deserves a word. Here are 50 panels. The Four Rivers of Paradise are shown: Geon, Physon, Tigris and Euphrates. Geon, identified with Nile, is bearded and holds a sistron. There are three Nilotic scenes of waterfowl, lotus and fish; two of lions and two of ostriches; one of a duck on an oddly-shaped crocodile; two of striped beast, probably a zebra. There is a satyr, and the nymph Kastalia as well —perhaps standing for pagan testimony to Christ, but more likely repeating, even in A.D. 539, the tradition of Delphoi's part in Cyrene's foundation some twelve centuries before. A panel shows the Pharos or Lighthouse of Alexandreia, foreshortened to bring in the bronze statue of Helios pointing to what may be the great iron mirror. In a room at the east end of the north aisle another mosaic has hunt-scenes in one corner, amid a lively panorama of plants and beasts. Two hounds strain at the leash held by their master; they want to catch three foxes, one of which has already entered a burrow so that only its head sticks out. In the centre is a Nilotic scene in a panel. A crocodile tries to pull a cow into the river, while the cow's owner hangs on to her tail; on the other side men fish from a small flow. (The motive of cow, crocodile and man also appears at Cyrene in the 6th-century mosaic floors of the cathedral.[44])

The crocodile, like the hippopotamos and many other beasts, had a dual nature. He was a foe, liable to snap at a bather or some-one from an overturned boat, or to drag away children at play, women filling waterpots, or the washerman. Herdsman had magical songs to spell him while their beasts crossed a ford. Indeed there were many spells against crocodiles. The devotees of Osiris and Horos saw them as allies of Seth. In fact, however, crocodiles did not seek out human beings to kill and eat; they slept on the banks, half-hidden in thick waterplants, and plunged with great speed after fish, their main food. Like the Sun, the crocodile emerged from the primordial water, while fish were the concealed enemies of the Sun. So the crocodile was worshipped: Sobek (Souchos). From the marshes of the Delta to the sandy shores of Silsileh, Ombos, Gebelein, he had many temples and was popular from the time of the Middle Kingdom. He was the great lord of Crocodilopolis in the Fayum and all round Lake Karun.[45]

Ploutarch sets out the dark side. Speaking of typhonic animals, he says that Seth is identified with the most stupid of tame animals, the ass, and the most savage of wild ones, the crocodile and hippopotamos.

At Hermopolis they show as a figure of Typhon a hippopotamos, on which stands a hawk fighting a serpent; by the hippopotamos signifying Typhon, by the hawk power and virtue, which Typhon often gains by force and never gives up being disturbed by his own wickedness and disturbing others. So, when they sacrifice on 7 Tybi, which they call the Coming of Isis out of Phoinikia, they stamp on the consecrated cakes the figure of a hippopotamos bound. At Apollinopolis it is the custom that everyone must by all means eat [yearly] a piece of crocodile. On one day they catch and kill as many crocodiles as they can, and lay them out in front of the temple, saying that when Typhon ran away from Horos he changed himself into a crocodile— thus making out that all animals, plants and feelings which are harmful and bad, are the productive parts and instigations of Typhon.[46]

Achilleus Tatios tries to build a terrifying picture of a crocodile along the same lines as the one he gave of a hippopotamos; but Heliodoros introduces the creature into his narrative effectively as an everyday incident.

They had scarcely left the village and were passing along the banks of the Nile when they noticed a crocodile that crawled across their path from right to left and with a sudden rush plunged into the flowing waters. The others saw nothing disturbing in this common sight, though Kalasiris for his part declared that it portended some obstacle to be encountered on their way. But Knemon was very alarmed. The creature had not shown itself distinctly to him, but had rather slid past like a shadow along the ground; and he was on the edge of running off.

Nausikles couldn't restrain a loud laugh, while Kalasiris remarked, "Knemon, I thought you found only the night a place of terrors, scaring you with the least noise in the dark. But here in broad daylight you show yourself just as brave. Not only the mentioning of names but now sights of an ordinary and harmless sort strike you with dismay."[47]

The ichneumon, a small weasel-like thing related to the mongoose, was noted for its destruction of crocodile eggs. We have a receipt of A.D. 104, which shows that it was requisitioned for shows. "Julius Eutyches acknowledges the receipt of 24 ichneumons, 1 dead, from Claudios Erasos strategos of the division of Themistes in the Arsinoite nome, through Herakleidion son of Dios, who brought them down."

Boar-hunts seem fairly common. We have two epigrams on a young untrained dog, *skylax*, who died of wounds defending his master Zenon, the agent of the finance-minister of the Ptolemaioi Philadelphos and Euergetes, who had been sent to the Fayum (the Arsinoite nome) to superintend the work on a great estate given to Apollonios. The poems were no doubt the work of some professional poet of Alexandreia, inscribed on the dog's tombstone. Often thus two epitaphs in different metres were composed:

> This tomb proclaims that Indian Tauron here
> lies dead. His slayer went to Hades first.
> Like a wild relic of Kalydon's great boar,

on Arsinoe's rich plain, immoveable, he grew,
shaking his manes in masses in his lair
and dashing froth from his broad jaws around.
Charging the fearless dog, he gashed his breast
and laid at once his own neck on the ground.
Gripping the massive nape, the mane and all,
Tauron held fast till Hades got the Boar.
Untrained, the hunter Zenon he saved and now,
buried, has earned his thanks for evermore.

> Tauron, a dog, lies in this grave.
> Faced with a killer, he still was brave.
> In battle he met a boar, which, white
> with froth and jawpufft, in its might
> tore a deep furrow in his breast.
> Straight on its back two feet he pressed,
> gashed the bristling monster in midchest,
> sent down the murderer he'd defied
> and then like a good Indian died.
> He saved the hunter Zenon who led him.
> So here in this light dust we've laid him.[48]

Indian dogs were known before Alexander. Xenophon speaks of them as "strong, big, swift, courageous". But after the invasion of India and Alexander's Indian dog, the gift of the kings Sopeithos and Poros, they must have become more common. We noted above the Palermo mosaic of the boar-hunt of Alexander.

A letter of A.D. 262 written in the Arsinoite nome shows the boarhunt still going strong. "From Alypios. Take care to supply everything necessary to the huntsmen whom I've sent to hunt wild boars for various needs—all that is they're accustomed to get, they themselves and their animals, so that they may put full zeal into the hunt. Give them one spirited donkey out of those in your charge, as I've kept for my own use the mule they had. I pray for your health, honoured friend. To Hieroninos, steward of Thraso. 9th year, 25 Pachon." Thraso was a village of the Fayum. Alypios was a large landowner, many of whose letters have been preserved.[49]

Achilleus Tatios in his romance includes a tale told by an

H

Egyptian Menelaos on returning to his homeland. "I loved a handsome youth who was a passionate hunter. I did my best to hold him back, but all my efforts were no use. Then, as he wouldn't heed me, I used to accompany him on his expeditions. One day we were both out hunting on horseback. At first we had some good luck, routing out only small beasts. But all of a sudden a boar burst from the woodland. The lad gave chase. The boar turned and faced him, making a direct charge. But he wouldn't

Gladiators and Beasts (relief from Theatre of Marcellus).

give way. I shouted and yelled, 'Pull in your horse, turn the reins, the beast's dangerous.' The boar made a spring and plunged straight at him. They closed. At the sight I was unnerved—scared that the creature would get in first and wound the horse. I poised my javelin and without careful enough aim I let fly. The lad crossed the line and got the point full in his body. What do you think my feelings were? If I had any at all, they were those of a living death. More pitiful still, while he still breathed faintly, he stretched out his hands and clasped me. There in his death-throes, he whom I'd slaughtered didn't shrink from me, but gave up the ghost embracing my murderous hand. His parents dragged me, not at all reluctant, to the lawcourt. I made no defence and proposed the death-penalty. So the jury pitied me and passed a sentence of three years' exile. This period is now over and I'm returning to my own country."[50]

In the 3rd century homicide was in fact punished by voluntary exile, though in the next century sentences had become harsher and homicide in anger earned *damnatio in metallum*, heavy labour in the mines, while common homicide brought crucifixion.[51] Exile also appears in an edict (A.D. 367–70) of the prefect Flavius Entolmius Tatianus dealing with abuses of military jurisdiction. Civil litigants have been turning to military praepositi. "Should anyone be found out leaving his proper court and having recourse to unauthorised persons, if he is a man of common rank, I order him to be deported; if a senator, I subject him to confiscation of property." The differentiation between *humiliores* and *honestiores* is typical of the post-Constantine world.[52]

10

Lions, Birds, Cats

LIONS could be met on the Libyan side of Egypt. Hadrian set out
to deal with a famous lion, the Marousian, which, according to
Athenaios, had ranged all over Libya. The lion was killed near
Alexandreia, where a minor poet Pankrates celebrated the event.
Hadrian was a zealous hunter. Once with a single blow he killed
a huge boar. He hunted in Spain, Italy and elsewhere, and "so
loved horses and dogs that he had tombs erected for them".
For his horse Borysthenes "he constructed a tomb, set up a
stele, and engraved epitaphs". The verses were his own. These
attitudes were linked with the trends that sought to see a sort of
Heraklean civilising power in the emperor and to revive the
image of Herakles-Alexander.

We have already noted the episode of Alexander and his lion-
hunt. A bronze statuette (in the Museo Nazionale, Naples) shows
him on a rearing horse; he looks back after having hurled a wea-
pon. Lysippos is known to have made two large dedicatory
bronze groups with Alexander as their centre: one of the battle
near the Granikos, the other of a lionhunt (this latter was done
with Leochares for Delphoi). The statuette reflects one or other of
these groups. The lionhunt also appears on the Alexander-sar-
cophagus from Sidon (now in Istanbul).

Athenaios tells us that Hadrian was so pleased with Pankrates
that he awarded him free keep at the Mouseion. For long we
knew only four lines of his poem, which we may assume was
read in public to the emperor. Athenaios cited these lines as "not
inelegant"; though claiming the poet as an acquaintance, he was
careful not to praise his work beyond this cautious phrase.

Speaking of Alexandreia, I know that in that fine city there is a wreath called Antinoeios made from the lotus there bearing that name. This lotus grows in the marshes, in the summer; there are two colours, one resembling the rose; it is from this that the wreath called Antinoeios is twined; the other is called *lotinos* [lotus] and its colour is blue. Pankrates, a poet of the region, with whom I was acquainted, showed the emperor Hadrian on his visit to Alexandreia the rosy lotus as a great wonder, declaring that it was the one that should be called Antinoeios, since it sprang, so he said, from the earth when it received the blood of the Morousian Lion that Hadrian had killed while hunting in the part of Libya near Alexandreia. It was a huge creature that had long ravaged the whole of Libya, of which it had made many places

Hylas and Nymphs (sarcophagus, Rome).

uninhabitable. Hadrian therefore, pleased at the originality and novelty of the thought, granted him the favour of maintenance in the temple of the Muses. The comic poet Kratinos also called the lotus a water-plant in *Odysseis*, since all leafy plants are spoken of as waterplants by the Athenians.[1]

Then come the four lines:

> Wooltufted thyme, white lily, hyacinth of purple,
> flowers of blue celandine, yes, and the roses unfolding
> to zephyrs of spring, but surely never before
> has earth brought to bloom the flower from Antinoos named.

However, a papyrus has given us what is certainly a fairly long passage from the narrative section of the poem. The papyrus-sheet had been used as cover for a glass bottle and wrapped about its mouth. Some 27 lines of a first column are lost. Then comes the second column:

> . . . and swifter than Adrastos' horse that once
> preserved the king who fled in battlethrong:
> on such a steed Antinoos sat awaiting
> the deadly lion, bridle in his left hand,
> in his right was poised a spear with adamant shod.
> First Hadrian cast his brass-tipped spear and wounded
> the beast, but not with mortal wound, of purpose
> he missed the mark, wanting to test in full
> the certainty of aim Antinoos owned.

That seems a courtly attempt to cover up bad marksmanship on the emperor's part. It also allows Pankrates to continue with a forcible-feeble account of the irritated lion.

> Stricken, the beast raged worse, and in his wrath
> tore up the rough ground with his paws, the dust
> rising in such a cloud it dimmed the sun.
> He furied like a wave of the surging sea
> when Zephyr's stirred after the blast of Strymon,
> straight rushed upon them both, scourging his haunches,
> his side, with his fierce tail. Beneath his brows
> the eyes glared terrible fire. From ravening jaws
> foam slavered down on earth and loudly inside
> the teeth were gnashing. On his mighty head
> and shaggy neck the hair stood bristling out.
> On his other limbs as bushy as trees it showed
> and on his back was spiked like whetted spearpoints.
> Thus on the Glorious God and on Antinoos
> he came, like Typhoeus in olden times
> on Zeus the Slayer of Giants . . . [2]

The rest of the column is fragmentary and only a few words of a third column are left. The lines, which have a few Homeric reminiscences, are weaker even than the sample in Athenaios would suggest. Pankrates was not at his best in describing action.

We may pause here to glance at the cult of Antinoos, the Bithynian favourite of Hadrian, who was drowned in the Nile during the voyage upstream. Some mystery surrounded his death or was added to it by the popular reaction to Hadrian's grief. It is unclear whether the drowning was accidental or whether the youth threw himself into the river in disgust or from a belief that he would thus avert some calamity from the emperor. Hadrian sought to perpetuate his memory in all possible ways. He founded in his honour a town which was intended to serve as a fresh centre of Greek influence in Egypt. Laid out on a Greek plan with regularly numbered blocks, it was given a constitution of the Greek kind, with a senate. Though Naukratis, the oldest Greek settlement in Egypt, was the main model, the tribes and demes of the new city were named after the Roman imperial house.

Hylas and Nymphs (ex-voto, Rome).

Settlers were largely drawn from Ptolemais, the sole place in Upper Egypt where the Greek way-of-life was firmly rooted. Antinoos was turned into a local god. But for all Hadrian's philhellene attitudes, there was no exclusion of Egyptian influences. The deified youth was worshipped as Osirantinoos—seemingly with the normal hierarchy of Egyptian priests, prophets, and other temple-servitors. There are also traces of an identification with Bes, who had been the local god before the city was built. Also, Antinoites were permitted to marry Egyptians—a right that did not exist for the Greeks of Naukratis. We may surmise then that Hadrian had in mind a city and a cult that would work out as drawing the Egyptians into a Greek way of life.

Temples were also built outside Egypt—for instance at Mantineia: and statues of Antinoos set up all over the empire. At one of his sanctuaries oracles were given in his name. A star was declared to have been noticed for the first time between the Eagle and the Zodiac, and was proclaimed as his soul. It still bears his name. Greek cities, though not Rome or Roman colonies, struck medals or coins in his honour. For instance, that at Bithynion, Hadrian's birthplace, had the inscription, "His fatherland [worships] the God Antinoos". He appears as Iacchos and Neos Iacchos; and a link with Hermes was somehow made; Hermes with bull appears on the reverse of the Bithynian coin, and a Greek inscription from Italy (? Rome) calls Antinoos *Neos Theos Hermaon*.[3] Games were celebrated, Antinoeia. They were yearly or five-yearly, and we meet them at Athens, Eleusis, Argos, Mantineia, as well as in Bithynia and Egypt. It is hard to say how long they were carried on, but we find a reference to them in the mid-3rd century.[4]

A large number of works of art depicted the beautiful lad in an idealised form and played a considerable part in the hellenising art-trends of the time.[5] The divinisation of a man or woman because of their beauty was in some ways in key with the thinking of Hadrian's world. Loukian in his *Charidemos* takes up the point and insists, "No sooner do we see beautiful persons than we are captivated, we adore them and do not hesitate to serve them with all our power, as superior beings."[6] Especially instructive is the romance by Chariton, of much the same date. Here the heroine is continually being taken as a sort of goddess, and this divine aspect of her beauty plays an integral part in the story. "Haven't you heard the poets say that beautiful persons are the children of the gods?"[7] Kallirhoe is carried off and sold as a slave. When a man speaks of her master, Dionysios (who has bought her) strikes him. "Blasphemer, do you address the gods as if they were men?" When her empty tomb is found, Chaireas cries, "Which one of the gods is it who has become my rival and carried her off?" She is taken as an incarnation of Aphrodite. King Artaxates sees her as Artemis. When she appears in public, she seems more beautiful than the Homeric goddesses "of the white arms and the fair ankles". Indeed, "not a soul in the crowd could withstand

the radiance of her beauty. Some turned their heads away as if
sunlight had fallen on their eyes, others bowed low in reverence,
and even the children were affected."

There seems also an Egyptian note in the divinisation of someone drowned in the Nile. Herodotos tells us: "If anyone, Egyptian
or foreigner, is found drowned in the river or killed by a crocodile,
there is the strongest obligation on the people of the nearest town
to have the body embalmed in the most elaborate way and buried
in a consecrated burial-place; no one is allowed to touch it but
priests of the Nile, not even relatives or friends; the priests alone

Birth of Aphrodite (relief, Rome).

prepare it for burial with their own hands and set it in the tomb,
as if it were something more sacred than the body of a man."
Josephos, protesting that the Jews do not honour asses, states
that they are unlike the Egyptians, who honour and attribute
divine powers to crocodiles and snakes, "when they consider
anyone stung or crocodile-seized to be blessed and worthy as
a god." These attitudes seem late in origin; under the XXI
Dynasty drowning was a punishment at Thebai. We have from
the nekropolis at Hermopolis the tomb of a girl, Isidora, aged
fifteen, more or less the contemporary of Antinoos, who is
presented in a sort of apotheosis or divinisation in which the Nile
plays a part. There is no mention of drowning in the inscription,
but the Nymphs of the Nile are said to have made the funerary

H*

thalamos or chamber, while the eldest of them was responsible for the shell modelled on the vault of the niche where the mummy rested. Later we shall note the way in which the shell-cover of a niche or apse was often merged with the image of the ribbed sky-tent. Here however the shell, while representing a cosmic cover, has definite water-relations and so may be linked with Aphrodite's shell. Venus was "born out of the *concha*", says Plautus; and here the niche is "such as the Nile owns in its depths", though the Oreads (apparently from the near high ground) have had their hand in the *thalamos*. Drowning is strongly suggested by the intrusion in Isidora's epitaph of the nymph Kreneia, who raped Hylas as husband (drew him down to drown) and who made the two twisted columns that frame the niche and turn it into a grotto, *speos*. The plainest interpretation of Isidora's death-apotheosis is then that she was drowned and the drowning was conceived as a marriage with the elements, transforming her into a sort of goddess like the nymphs themselves.

Both shell-decoration and twisted column have an earlier history, but it is about this time that they grow widely popular. We must assume that with the 2nd century A.D. their symbolism became generally understood and was further elaborated. The shell-decoration became much used on aedicula and sarcophagus, first by pagans and then by Christians.

The twisted column has a long past, originating perhaps in such forms as the support of a three-headed twisted snake for the tripod at Delphoi made from the Persian spoils after Plataia. It appears in full-fledged form in a fresco of Dura-Europos dated about A.D. 75; and though an Egyptian origin has been claimed for the developed pillar, we can say no more than that it appears in the Near East and Egypt under the empire as an important new architectural form. It appears often on Coptic stelai. Behind the column however lie such forms as the serpent-entwined tree, stake, wand, support. The snake-entwined tree guards the earthly paradise (Hesperides) or otherworldly-treasure (Golden Fleece). Hence the strong psychopomp colouration of the caduceus. The snake-wand guides into the spirit world and has a redemptory power, as with a god like Asklepios. The twined snakes guard the door of the otherworld, the secret door, the door of initiation. A stele from Samothrace shows a temple-front and door; snakes are rolled round the doorframe: the inscription tells how Asklepiades of Kyzikos, an initiate of the highest grade, has gone in accordance with the embassy of the Samothracian people to undertake the temple-construction and the sacred Hermai. The idea of time and eternity is brought out in the Mithraic lionheaded Aion, round

Mithraic Time-figure (Modena); ex-voto to Demeter after a dream: note snake round column-staff (from Philippopolis).

whom snakes entwine. Part of a statuette, perhaps from Apollinopolis, shows the lionheaded man with part of the mane covering his breast; a snake winds over his shoulders, and via his armpits ties itself into a knot over his breast. A relief shows Aion with four wings, a nimbus with radiate crown on his lion's head, his lower body from the hips covered with shaggy hair to the cloven feet; in each hand he holds a key, with a torch also in his right hand; between his thumb is an object that seems to represent lightning. A snake hangs from each hand, one over a krater, the other over a small burning altar, while a third comes from between his teeth and creeps to the altar. Aion indeed seems to have iconographically originated in Egypt; we have seen the multiple figure

of the magician's god and we find, for instance, Bes in the 23rd
Dynasty represented with scarab wings, with four arms, with the
plumes of Amon-Re, the hawk-wings of Horos, crocodile-tail
of Sebek, ramhorns of Khnum, Min's phallus, and Anubis-heads
for feet.

The twisted snakes on a post or wand, the selftwisted column,
representing a guide or doorway into the spirit world, is connected in turn with the stress on helical or twining forms which
we shall later find in the paradise or garden and which the poet
Nonnos brings out in several ways as part of his Dionysiac
universe of spontaneous life and energy. Ultimately behind the

The House of Death with Twisted Columns: Urn of C. Magius Heraclidus (from
Frascati, in B.M.).

imagery there lies a concept of process as a spiralling movement
with points of nodal change. This is an alchemic viewpoint, and
if we were to analyse at length the mathematical treatment of the
helix by ancient scientists we could show an inability to break
from the idea of closed systems (circle, parabola, conic section,
sphere, and so on) which marked their limitations and against
which alchemy was chafing. But this would lead into abstruse
dimensions, and we must keep our investigation to the concrete.[8]

We may note a variant, under direct Dionysiac influence, of
the twisted column, in which bands of spiral fluting alternate with
bands of all-over vintage-scrolls. Good examples are those in
St Peter's, Rome, which in medieval times were thought to have
come from the Temple of Solomon, but which in fact were
Greek products. Ordinary columns with vine-scroll ornament

appeared on sarcophagi in Rome. Figured vine-scroll columns, rare in Italy, were common in Gaul. (One colonnette in Ostia museum shows high-relief carvings of putti vintaging among a spiralling vine.)

To return to Isidora: her tomb has three epigrams. The first, in which the father speaks, tells of the girl's rape by the nymphs who drowned Hylas. The second identifies the girl herself as a nymph, who is to be worshipped:

> No longer I'll sacrifice to you, my daughter,
> lamenting. Now I know a nymph you appear.
> With libation and sacrifice glorify Isidora!
> nymph-snatched to be a nymph for evermore.
> Hail, child, be named a nymph: as the Seasons pour
> gifts for you in the fullness of Isis' year.

The third epigram describes the flowers, wine and honey to be offered in season: milk and olive oil in winter, with a wreath of narcissus; honey and rosebuds in spring; summer a cup of new wine and a wreath of grapes. Thus Isidora "is assimilated to the immortals" and lamentations must cease.

A 2nd-century epitaph from Rome says that a young wife has been raped by the Nymphs, not by Death:

> For there was Charm in her sweetcomplexioned face
> to keep her in the Aither's immortal home.

Here Beauty, *Charis*, seems the passport, as in an epitaph from Egypt of the same century: "Kyrilla, like the gods in shape, be of good cheer: in the peaceful place of the immortals now you dwell." The general theme of an apotheosis of the dead person, found at this period throughout the empire, was well known to the folk of Egypt. From Alexandreia comes the dialogue-epitaph: "I'm unwithering, no mortal. I'm wonderstruck: who are you? Isidora."

Though there is no hint of Dionysiac associations in Pankrates' poem (which looks rather to the Alexander-Herakles complex), a strong link of Dionysos and the hunt had grown up. On the one hand there was an old association of the god as well as Artemis with the Wild Hunt; his beast-tearing mainads, both in myth and in cult-fact, bring out the association. And on the other hand there was the identification with Alexander as warrior and hunter, as victorious hero, to merge athletics, drama, music, and hunting all together as expressions of the Dionysiac way of life. This aspect merged in turn with the triumphal imagery.

For Nonnos the element of the wild-hunt remains as a reminder of the terrible things the god can do, of the ambushes that lie about us, ready to release the beast-force in treacherous and tragic transformations. The terms are ancient and traditional, but the angle of reference is modern and subtle. The changes belong to the dream-undertow that is liable, if vigilance is relaxed

Birth of Aphrodite (sarcophagus, Rome, Lateran).

for a moment, to introduce into everyday life its dangerous confusions: face and false-face, customary reality and the hidden suppressed truths under its surfaces, become hopelessly entangled. Thus Autonoe laments:

> Your unhappiness, Agaue, I envy and want;
> for the darling face of Pentheus still you kiss,
> you kiss the dear eyes and the hair of your son.
> You're happy, sister, though, mother, you slew your son.
> But I'd Aktaion to mourn, his body was changed,
> I wept for a fawn, instead of the head of my son
> I buried the long antlers of a *bastard* stag.
> It's a small relief in your pain that you beheld
> no *alien type* of your son, no fell of a fawn,
> no unprofitable hoof you raised, no horn. Alone
> I saw my son a *bastard* corpse and mourned
> the *image of a shape alienborn dappled voiceless.*
> I am called the mother of a stag, not of a son.
> But I pray to you, spinsterish daughter of Zeus, now
> glorify your Phoibos who fathered my husband and change

my mortal shape to a deer. Do grace to Apollon.
Give wretched Autonoe also as a prey
to the same dogs as Aktaion or my own hounds.
Let Kithairon see the mother after the son
dogtorn; but when I'm changed to the same horned shape
as all your deer, don't yoke me to your car,
unhappy, but fiercely lash me with your whip.[9]

Later we shall see the strange emotional force and the complicated network of ideas that Nonnos weaves round the words I have italicised.

The Triumph of Dionysos was known in Egyptian works of art. On a mosaic is represented a procession in his honour; he

Hylas and Nymphs (situla from Dorogoï, Moldavia).

stands in a car drawn by centaur and centauress.[10] On a Coptic textile he holds a bowl in his right hand and a duck in his left as he stands in a car drawn by spotted panthers.[11] On two other textiles the car is drawn by rampant panthers or lions.[12] Elsewhere mosaics, silver plate, and sarcophagi show lionesses, tigers, panthers, elephants drawing the chariot; and at times lions accompany the god. The child Dionysos is set astride both a lion and a panther on Ptolemaic sculptures of Memphis.[13] A relief on an Alexandrian ivory pyxis depicts Dionysos in a car drawn by panthers, while he fights with Indians, a torch in his right hand and a shield in his left.[14] In a mosaic from Acholla in N. Africa he is drawn by galloping centaurs, a kantharos in his right hand, in his left a spear such as was used in hunting.[15] Such spears are shown as carried by bacchantes: on a Coptic textile of a Triumph and in a

Pompeian wall-painting of the dismemberment of Pentheus.[16]

In Libya, panthers were captured by means of wine. The hunters sought out a small pool in the midst of a desert. "There at the rising of dawn come panthers to drink; in the dusk twenty amphoras of strong wine are poured in; then the men hide themselves some way off under skins of beasts or their nets. For there are no trees, says the poet, on that arid African earth. In the morning the panthers, drawn by thirst and attracted by the smell, drink . . . You'd think them then drunken men. They stagger, roll on the ground, and are taken without resistance."[17]

It has been remarked:

Such a story is not without relation to the *legomena* and *dromena* of Dionysiac rites, which show the feline companions of the god drinking in kraters. Still, there is no reason to reject it as a real technique of the hunt.[18]

We hear also of panthers being caught through aromatics.[19]

Wild elephants had abounded in N. Africa in Punic days; but they were wiped out under the empire, no doubt in large part through the hunters. They survived for some time in Mauretania; a Volubilis inscription of Caracalla's reign mentions the "heavenly animals" that the forests had provided for the imperial menageries —but it is not sure whether lions or elephants are meant.[20] Elephants from Troglodytika and Indika probably came through the ports of the Red Sea for importation to Rome.[21] Achilleus Tatios has a long account of Indian elephants, during which the Egyptian Menelaos remarks, "I once saw an extraordinary sight. A Greek put his head right into the midst of the animal's jaws. It kept its mouth open and breathed on." The man told him afterwards that he had paid a fee for the experience, "as the beast's breath was only less sweet than the scents of India, and a sovran cure for headache. The elephant knows he owns this healing power and won't open his mouth for nothing; he's one of those rascally doctors who insist on fee down first. When you give it, he graciously agrees, opens his jaws wide, and keeps them stretched as long as man wants; he knows he has hired out the sweetness of his breath." The reason is that he feeds on the Indian black rose (apparently the clove) nurtured close to the sun.[22]

Seneca tells us of the shows. "The trainer puts his hand into the lion's mouth; the tiger is kissed by his keeper. The tiny Ethiopian orders the elephant to sink down on its knees or to walk a rope."[23] Ailian says that Philadelphos received from India a young elephant that had learned to understand Greek.[24] We hear also of elephants throwing weapons and a dozen of them dancing and dining.[25]

If the lion-hunt represents the heroic aspects of the king or hunter, the Heraklean triumph of man over the strongest and fiercest of animals, the bird-hunt introduces an idyllic element. In ancient representations, such as those on the walls of the funerary temple of Userkaef, the birds fly above the papyrus-thicket where the king gives himself up to the sport of hunting and fishing. We see them caught in their tree by the fowler's net. They show no disquiet and the artist uses the net, mostly reduced to a contour, as a frame for a charming picture. "The treatment of the theme is already idyllic or elysian." The birds in one fragment have a special reason for ignoring what goes on; they have given themselves up to pleasure with interlaced beaks. "How their contentment is conveyed cannot be made out. One has to believe that in the handling of the eye there are imperceptible expressive nuances. And a movement of the plumage prolongs this eye in a way that would be on a human face that of a smile. Finally the perfect symmetry of this pretty couple increases our impression of a jubilant exchange." We may add that

the unreal grouping of the family around the father in the slight-boat of hunting and fishing scenes proves that the sport-theme was largely left behind. The essential was to reunite the family in a delightful milieu, such as one desired for the natural frame of a better world. In the hyogeum of Knumhotep III at Beni-Hassan it is quite a bouquet of birds that presents itself, encircled by a net, above the niche of the background, facing the entry. Immeasurable love for a simple scene of tenderness. The pleasant motive is there justified because it evokes a dreamworld where one would like to be resurrected. Recall that the "nilotic" landscape, so much in vogue at Pompeii and in the Roman world, reappears in the mosaics of the dome of Ste Constanza at

Rome and of St Stephan of Gaza, where it could only evoke the Christian paradise.

Here we see the continuity between the ancient hunting-paradise and the afterworld dream of the later pagan and the Christian worlds. (The birds being snared, it seems, are songbirds destined for aviaries.)

From the most ancient days birds were snared in large numbers. The delta, lakes and marshes abounded in waterfowl, especially the Bitter Lakes. Quail, magpie, and francolin were much esteemed by epicures.[26] We have seen the host of birds in the

Camel and Rhinoceros (Naples, Mus. Borb.).

procession of Philadelphos. Hipparchos, in his *Egyptian Iliad*, a work about which we know nothing, had the lines:

> The Egyptian way-of-life I cannot follow:
> they pluck the chennia, which they salt and swallow.[27]

The chennion was a small sort of quail; and the character of the couplet suggests that the poem belonged rather to the line of parodies. Sokrates in his treatise on Boundaries, Places, Fire, and Stones, has an odd tale:

The quail was transported from Lydia into Egypt and let loose in the woods there. For some time it made noises like a quail. But after the River got low and a great scarcity came along, in which many of the country's folk died, they [the quails] never ceased crying out, as they do to this day, in a voice more distinct than that of the very clearest-speaking children: Threefold evils to the evildoers. And when caught, they not only couldn't be tamed, but even gave up making any sound at all. Yet, if let go again, they recover their voice.[28]

Athenaios tells us that Ptolemaios Physkon (Euergetes II) in his

Commentaries, speaking of the palace at Alexandreia and the animals kept there, remarked, "Also the kind of pheasants they call tetaroi; not only did he [probably Philadelphos] procure these from Media, but by mating Numidian birds [guineafowls] he produced quantities of them for food; for it is asserted that they make a very rich dainty." Athenaios adds, "Here you have the word of the most illustrious king, who admits that he never so much as tasted a pheasant, but kept the very birds we have here [at dinner] as a carefully-hoarded treasure. If he had seen each of us today served with a whole pheasant as well as the food already consumed, he'd have filled up another book to add to the famous tales in his *Commentaries*, now consisting of twenty-four books."

Birds were tamed and taught to speak. The Alexandrians were particularly skilled at taming animals and teaching them tricks. Olympiodoros, born at Thebai in Egypt in the 5th century A.D., had a pet parrot for twenty years; when it died, he wrote affectionately that it could imitate practically anything men do, and especially could dance, sing, and call him by his name. Philon mentions Maltese dogs as extremely tame and affectionate tail-waggers who fawned on their masters. From Martial we learn that ichneumons were kept as pets in Rome; in the same epigram he tells of a woman burying her nightingale under a tomb, *tumulus*.[29]

We cannot linger much more over animals; but before we pass on, we shall glance at pets and at pigeons—the latter serving as a link with the Gardens we shall soon explore. Clement draws a picture of the fine lady of Alexandreia and states that her pets were an important element in her establishment. A pup or a parrot, a peacock or a monkey, received lavish attention; but when they grew boring, she welcomed visitors. (Loukian tells of a rich woman with a philosopher in her train; she bade him to look after her favourite dog.) Clement suggests that the solicitude over pets would be better turned on to the aged or the poor.[30]

The first reference to a domestic cat occurs about 2100 B.C.; representations are common from the Middle Kingdom on; and mummies begin to appear. The cat had probably been brought in as a curiosity from the west and south. (A wild species was known from prehistoric times, thickset and short-tailed. This was the "Great Cat who is in Heliopolis" of the *Book of the Dead*: an ancient solar being who protected men and tore to pieces at the foot of the sacred tree the evil serpent.) The cat was used in marsh-hunts by fowlers to put up the game from the papyrus-thickets; it was also used to keep down mice and rats. Satirical pictures, illustrating tales or fables on ostraka or papyri, show the cat as the slave of the mouse or an army of mice attacking a cat-force blockaded in a fortress, a cat herding geese or a seated mouse whom another mouse fans from behind while a

Egyptian Battle of Cats and Rats.

cat respectfully presents a palm branch. Here we have the theme of the topsyturvy world and gain some inkling of the extent to which the animal fable developed in Egypt.

In the cultworld the small newcomer, the cat, somehow managed to take over the role of the liongoddess. The myth told how the Eye of the Sun, Re's daughter, became enraged and was changed into a lioness, then ran off to Nubia; an attempt was made to appease her and the lioness of fire assumed the characteristics of Bastet, feline but smiling. Bastet, the lioness become cat, had her great temple at Boubastis. Hundreds of bronze images from there show a catheaded woman, Bastet suckling her kittens, Bastet a jewelled queen-cat on a throne.

Probably the cat reached the west from Egypt via Greece. Coins and vase-paintings show the cat in South Italy by the 5th century B.C.; but Seneca and the elder Plinius are the first to men-

tion the cat in Latin in a way that suggests it was kept in houses
in their time. No remains of cats have been found at Pompeii
and Herculaneum. However, we find a cat represented on a
tombstone of the early empire at Rome; and a relief shows a cat
being trained, apparently to dance on its hind legs to music—a
couple of birds being hung over its head to encourage it. Seneca,
arguing that there is such a thing as instinctive understanding,
asks why chickens fear a cat and not a dog; and Plinius writes,
"How silently and with what light steps they creep up to birds;
how covertly they watch before springing out on mice."[31]

In the Hellenistic and Roman worlds the migration of the cat
may well be bound up, at least in part, with the expansion of the
cult of Isis. The advent of the cat in Gaul seems connected with
Egyptian trade and religious contacts in the 2nd–4th centuries
A.D.[32]

With doves and pigeons we reach a territory that includes both the
pleasure-garden and the farm worked for profit. Philon, writing
as an Alexandrian Jew, declared that, "passing over the infinite
variety of birds, God chose only two kinds out of them all, the
turtle-dove and the pigeon: for the pigeon is by nature the most
gentle of all domesticated and gregarious birds, and the turtledove
the most gentle of all that love solitude."[33] Doves seem exported
to Rome. Columella says that chicks should be kept together
after hatching. "If this isn't done, at any rate birds of different
breeds, such as the Alexandrian and the Campanian, shouldn't
be mated; for they feel less affection for hens unlike themselves
and so have little intercourse with them and don't often produce
offspring." He and Plinius both mention the pigeon-craze at
Rome. Aristotle states that "when the chicks are hatched, the
cockbird spits on them to avert the evil eye; and the hen lays two
eggs, the first producing a cock, the second a hen. They lay at
every season of the year, so that they lay ten or eleven times yearly,
and in Egypt they lay ten times."[34]

Pigeon-houses and towers were a common part of the Egyptian landscape. We have many paintings that show them; and
whether the paintings were the work of Alexandrian artists, they

belong to an Alexandrian tradition of *topia*. In one from Herculaneum we see three farms on the banks of a canal. That on the left is composed of two towerlike buildings and is surrounded by a brick wall. The central farm consists of a pylon, a high tower, and the main buildings (farmhouse and tower) with trees at the rear and with shaduf and well to the left. The third farm on the other side of the canal is similar: its rear-garden is surrounded by palisades.[35]

References to pigeoncotes in property-documents are common and help us to realise how true to fact was such a landscape as that at Herculaneum. In A.D. 83 the lessee of such a cote receives the dung and pays a rental of a hundred pigeons a year. Some 1st-century memoranda conjure up the scene:

Concession. Ptolemaios son of Tees. Slave(?) Certificate for Tisichis. Another for Thrage. Horion . . . Machinery of the wheel for cutting. Refusal . . . Receipt. Relating to Philon. Green (? garment). Missive of Hierax to Kro . . . villager. Water-channel pigeonhouse. Receive the account of Herodes. For Hermaios the cellarer.[36]

At Oxyrhynchos in 183 there was leased an upper room in which was a pigeoncote, for 4 years, at 60 dr. a year. At Karanis in 192 a cote was leased for 4 months at 100 dr., and the sum of 240 dr. was received as rent of cotes by Bacchiotes. A Fayum document of the 1st-2nd centuries records the sale of a house with attached pigeoncote for 1300 drachmai; another, the lease of a tower and two waterchannels for 140.[37] Here is a document of 214 in full: an agreement of four persons, two of whom are minors, acting together to divide the usufruct of a pigeonhouse; the minors get usufruct of two years together, the others a single year each. (Divisions of property were common, but not those of usufruct.)

Markos Aurelios Andronikos, also called Mithres, and however he is styled, and Aurelia Dionysias also called Chairemonis, through her husband Aurelios Ammonios, gymnasiarch elect, senator of Oxyrhynchos, and Didyme also called Apollonia, and Letodoris also called Dionysotheonis, both minors, through their mother Ptolema daughter of Dionysiotheon, ex-gymnasiarch of the said city of Oxyrhynchos, herself acting through Epikrates son of Didymos:
    mutually acknowledge that they have divided up among them-

selves the usefruct of the excellent productive pigeonhouse owned by
them in equal shares in the farmstead of their vineyard called Perkops,
for a further period of 4 years from 1 Thoth of the present 23rd year,
and the minors had had allotted to them the usufruct of two years,
namely the present 23rd and 25th year, Aurelia Dionysias also called
Chairemonis that of the coming 24th year, and Aurelios Andronikos
also called Mithres similarly that of the 26th year, and each party . . .
the dung is to go yearly to their aforesaid vineyard, and each party is
to deliver to the other the said pigeonhouse on the first of the inter-
calary days in productive condition, none of the parties having the
right to molest another during his aforesaid period.

  This agreement done in triplicate in order that each party may have
a copy is valid.[38]

The dung was a valuable part of a productive cote. At Oxyrhynchos in 256 a cote was leased for five years; the lessor provided

Boy with Dog (Egyptian relief: Ny-Carlsberg).

an artaba of lentils and of wheat monthly for food, and got half
the dung and six pairs of pigeons for the first year; after that he
got two-thirds of the dung yearly and a specified number of
pigeons as rental; the lessees were to care for the pigeons, feed
them regularly, and return the cote at the lease's end with supply
of breeding pigeons. At Hermopolis in 276 we meet the sale of a
cote and stable. At Oxyrhynchos again, in the 3rd century, two
cotes and cella were leased for three years at 400 dr. yearly.[39]

  The love of pigeoncotes carried right on into modern times. A
traveller, in a book published in 1873, remarked that the pigeons
were far better housed than the villagers then were in their
mud-huts. "The only storey that is ever raised above ground
floor—which is of the ground as well as on it—is the dovecote.

This, therefore, is the only object in a village which attracts the eye of the passer-by. In the Delta the fashion appears to be to raise a rude roundish mudtower, full of earthenware pots for the pigeons to breed in. These are inserted—of course, lying horizontally—in the mud of which the tower is built. In Upper Egypt these towers have assumed the square form, about twelve feet each side. Three or four tiers of branches are carried round the building for the pigeons to settle on; these are stuck into the wall, and as the branches depart from the straight line, each according to its own bent, each belt of branches presents a very irregular appearance. No village is without its dovecotes. From the summit of the propylaea of the grand Ptolemaic temple of Edfou, I counted about forty of these dovecotes on the tops of the mud hovels below me. The number of domestic pigeons in Egypt must be several times as great as that of the population."[40]

11

Plays and Players

TRAGEDY could not effectively survive the death of the democratic *polis*; we have seen how elements of it made a strange survival in the art of the pantomime. Comedy lost its strong links
with ritual and became the comedy of manners in Menandros
and others. Oddly, the new form took over certain underlying
patterns of tragedy, but thinned them out and romanticised them.
The theme of the threatened and outcast child, which had once
led to such tragic situations as that of Oidipous, was now used to
provide entangled plots, with a happy ending: the disinherited
heir who comes into his own, and so on. Many of these elements
spilled over into romance proper; the theme of the lost children
ending with the delightful pastoral utopia of *Daphnis and Chloe*.
But there is no need for us here to dwell in detail on such developments; for under the Empire there were only two significant
stage-forms—the dance-mime we have considered, and the
comical mime with words.[1]

The mime-players were generally of low repute, but were
great favourites of the populace. They inevitably varied from the
famous performers appearing at the large towns to the strollers
living in a hand-to-mouth way. Certain stock themes were no
doubt general; but again there must have been wide divergences
between the stars with their polished and sophisticated satire and
troupes who set out to gain laughs from a village-audience. At
times one of the important dancers or actors went into the provinces. Thus Caracalla, to please his compatriots of Lepcis in
North Africa, sent the leading pantomime of the day, his freedman Agrippa, to perform before them. (This Agrippa was made
an honorary town-councillor at Verona and Vicentia, and Milan

admitted him to its youth-club.)[2] Fair-sized towns like Certa in Africa had their own municipal troupe; we have the epitaph of a clown (*stupidus*) of the Troupe of the Four Colonies.[3]

Most comment by literary men tends to look down on actors of all kinds. Philostratos speaks of actors as undisciplined and conceited: Loukian depicts their wretched state—whipt at the audience's pleasure, hissed, wandering about in beggary after they doffed their fine stage-costumes. Yet successful actors could

Funeral Monument of Septumia Spica, with hare and jugglers (Mantua).

gain large sums and might win the esteem of their fellow-citizens, as appears in the acrostic epitaph of Vincentius found at Timgad:

> Vincentius is here, the Pantomimes' Glory,
> In people's mouths he lives, an undying story.
> Not only was he for the scenic role
> Cherished by all, but for his upright soul:
> Ever reliable, true. As for his art:
> Notably when he danced a favourite part,
> The Theatre was spelled till the Stars filled the Skies.
> In the earth before the ramparts now he lies.
> Till his twenty-third year he flourished, his time well spent
> Still more in life than in art shown eloquent.[4]

Outside Alexandreia, we find few references to theatres in the other cities or metropoleis. However, they certainly existed. In a report or petition to the strategos of the Memphite nome, probably of the first half of the 3rd century, a theatre appears with some objects, *thyrones*, which can mean halls or antechambers but here seems to mean detachable doors or some sort of stage-scenery:

To Aurelios Heraklammon, strategos of the Memphite Nome, from Aurelios Paeis Diogenes of Memphis, former overseer and key-warden of the theatre there.

When, at the time of the visit to the people there of Aurelios Anoubion the Frumentarius, who had been appointed for the . . . , of thyrones, you sent for me and inquired whether any thyrones had been stored away in the theatre, I protested that I had not taken any over from the previous overseer nor . . . [5]

The sites of the theatres at Oxyrhynchos and Antinoopolis have been found; and no doubt the mimes we meet in records of Oxy-rhynchite festivals performed in the town-theatre. In a late 1st-century letter from Neilos to his father Theon there is an obscure reference to "the matter of the theatre". Neilos is studying in Alexandreia and incidentally seems to have smashed up the family-chariot; his embroilment with the theatre we can only guess at.[6] In municipal accounts of the late 2nd century we find a disburse-ment for a procession held during the tenure of the office of exe-getes, a popular festival or *panegyris* held in the theatre, repairs and heating of baths, and sacrifices in the theatre. In other accounts of the same period occurs the entry: "To Kallinikos son of Epimachos and the associated contractors for hangings"—the word is a Greek transliteration of the Latin *vela* and doubtless refers to hangings or awnings for the theatre.

An Alexandrian statuette shows an actress on kothornoi or tragic highboots; and actors in general are fairly common in art-representations. A textile shows the declamatory gestures of a stage-warrior.[7] Dionysiac elements, grapebunches and masks also are common in art, and show that scenic attributes were popular in Egypt as elsewhere.[8]

Hence the way in which we find theatric references extremely common even in writers who considered themselves opposed to such entertainments. Philon cannot refrain from using the phrase "the theatre of the universe", though in the context of heavenly enjoyments. Clement denounces, "You have made the heaven a stage, *skene*, and the divine has become drama for you; you make the holy into comedy with the masks of daimons."[9] (Tertullian's vision of the Last Judgment is essentially one of the great spectacles of Rome with the roles reversed: the Christians sitting happy and honoured in the seats and the pagan philosophers or poets being tortured and burned.) The romancer Heliodoros shows how stage-ideas haunted him, both in the construction of his plot and treatment of characters. Near the beginning of his tale the heroine appeals to brigands, "Deliver us from the sufferings that harass us, by killing us and bringing to a close the drama of our destiny." She spoke in high tragic vein, *epetragoidei*. Near the end, we read "Finally, to crown their good deeds and as the culminating point of the drama they made this young Greek appear, in whom has been revealed the betrothed of your daughter." Heliodoros thus shows his awareness of the link between the romance-theme or parted lovers or lost heirs and the discovery-motives in tragedy or Menandrian comedy. The words that follow suggest the link with tragedy, indeed they suggest that Heliodoros has an intuition of the way in which tragic conflict is based in violent social contradictions and changes fought out in ritual terms: "Come, let us recognise the divine miracle that has been wrought, and become collaborators in the gods' purpose. Let us proceed to the holier oblations and banish human sacrifice for all time." Further, the term he used for "concluding point" seems a bit of theatrical slang, *lampadion*. According to Pollux, this was the mask of a young courtesan, in which the coiffure rises up to a point. Why this mask should be used to emblematise the end of a play, we have no idea. The *lampadion* is the last enumerated in Pollux' list of stage-courtesans and appears to be the youngest; she is the Little Lamp or Torch, it seems, because her hair stands up in a bunch like a flame.[10] Elsewhere Heliodoros says, "A plot, the beginnings of which have been laid out by the deity with many complications, must needs be brought to its conclusion through detours of some length; and especially where a great lapse of time has blurred the story, it isn't clarified to effect at one sharp stroke, above all when the prime mover in the whole scheme affecting us, she on whom the whole sequence of complica-

tion and recognition depends, my mother I mean, is missing."
The characters go on to discuss tokens left with the heroine when
she was exposed as a baby. Twice elsewhere Heliodoros uses
the metaphor of the stage-machine to express a sudden change
in fortune; in one he refers definitely to the crane that swung
people about: "How is it likely for a woman to be transported
from the middle of Greece into a remote corner of Egypt, as if by
a stage-machine?"[11]

The theatre, like the arena, was one of the few places in which
large numbers of people could gather under the empire without
being considered a seditious mob. As a result it was in the theatre
or arena that sedition could alone effectively show itself at
moments of great strain or suffering. However, in this book we
are not treating matters of a direct political bearing; and so we
must leave this important aspect of the theatre for treatment
elsewhere. What does concern us here is the forms of organisation
found among the actors and musicians.

The stages by which the Gild of Artists was formed is obscure.
During the 4th century B.C. gilds or colleges of musical and
dramatic performers had grown up at Athens.[12] In the second
half of the century small groups toured the demes of Attica and
famous actors went round the Greek world. They visited the
courts of the Macedonian kings and were even used as accredited
diplomatists by both Athens and King Philip. They thus gained
freedom of travel and immunity from hostile action: this position
being regularised by decrees of the Amphiktyonic Council. By
277 B.C. we find that definite gilds were organised, and the
priority of the Athenians is asserted.[13] The Council gave the Athenian *technitai* freedom from arrest in war or peace, exemption
from military and naval service, safety of person and property;
any offender among them, and even the city where the offence
was committed, was held responsible to the Amphiktyon. The
story, recorded by Diodoros, that Dionysos himself had invented
musical festivals and the privileges of artists, was no doubt the
official myth of the gild.[14]

A considerable expansion must have gone on by the mid-2nd
century. In the great procession of Ptolemaios Philadelphos, of

which Kallixenos has left the account, we saw the gild at Alexandreia led by the poet Philiskos, priest of Dionysos: that is, the gild's president. An inscription, dated about 240 B.C. shows the gild active at Ptolemais:

Be it resolved by the Gild of Artists devoted to Dionysos and the Brother Gods [Philadelphos and his sister-wife Arsinoe, now dead] and by those who share membership in the Gild, that Dionysios, son of Mousaios, who is a prytanis for life, is hereby authorised to adorn himself, in accordance with native custom, with the crown of ivy, in recognition of his generosity to the City of the Ptolemaians and to the Gild of Artists devoted to the great Dionysos and the Brother Gods.

The crowning is to take place publicly at the Dionysia, and this resolution shall be inscribed upon a stele and set up in front of the Temple of Dionysos. The cost of the stele shall be paid by the Treasurer, Sosibios.[15]

We have seen how Marcus Antonius seems to have made the final step in completing an international organisation of artists and athletes. His rescript does not specify athletes; neither does it mention artists. But it is best taken as intended to draw over on to his side both influential groups. In 32 B.C. he had summoned the Dionysiac *technitai* from the whole of the Greek world to assemble at Samos and entertain Cleopatra and himself. In any event the first clear reference to a world-organisation of artists is made by Claudius, though we safely surmise that the granting of privileges on a world scale goes back to Augustus.[16] The next references to a world-synod come under Trajan. At Gerasa a decree is recorded in honour of T. Flavius Gerrenus who had served as agonothetes on a great occasion. It refers to the *technitai stephanitoi* and *synagonistai* (who had been crowned and taken part in the great contests) and from it and other inscriptions we may surmise that these groups kept to some extent a separate existence inside the comprehensive society—just as local gilds may have carried on or been gradually absorbed.[17] A census return of Oxyrhynchos dated A.D. 145–6 mentions a house in the topos called *Of the Technitai of Dionysos*, which suggests that the local gild had its centre there. We also hear of theatre-guards in the town. A decree in honour of a gymnasiarch, about mid-2nd century, praises him among other things for contributing to theatrical displays, *theorika*: and we hear also of proceedings in the theatre "at the general assembly in Tybi and Pachon.[18]

The world-H.Q. was at Rome.[19] The epithet *peripolistike* that turns up from the period of Antoninus Pius (or a little earlier) shows that the members travelled round, like the athletes; the epithet *neokoros* connotes the guardianship of a cult's sanctuary —generally that of the divine emperor: here it refers especially to the central cult at Rome. Each local gild had its own set of regulations or *nomoi*. It had something of a minor independent state about it in the way in which cities received its envoys; its *proxenoi* were recognised by states and other gilds; and it sent its envoys or *theoroi* to appear with those of the cities at the great festivals. Officers were yearly appointed by the koinon, which also voted statues and crowns to famous actors or benefactors. Doubtless the authority of the koinon lay behind such acts as the infliction of fines on actors who failed to show up at festivals to which they had been sent. How such actors were selected, we do not know; but they seem considered as representatives of the gild.[20] The chief officer was normally the priest of Dionysos, who was eligible for re-election at the year's end; he might be, but was not necessarily, a performing artist. There was also a treasurer and a secretary.[21] Under the empire a commissionr, *logistes*, seems appointed by the emperor to keep an eye on what was going on inside the gild.[22]

The gild might have its own *panegyris* yearly, not to mention monthly feasts, celebrations of rulers or benefactors, common dinners, wine-parties. It participated in the public sacrifices of sanctuaries and towns, and marched in processions, dressed in purple and gold. Its members consisted of poets working in epic, drama, or lyric, actors in tragedies, comedies or satyric plays, singers in choruses, instrumentalists, rhapsodes, and, in due time, reciters of enkomia and the like, and trainers of choroi (actors or singers).[23] Names of members occur from time to time both as trainers, *didaskaloi*, and as chorus-members, *choreutai*. We meet also *hypodidaskaloi*, probably at first sub-producers

under poets who had the full charge, but later apparently pro-
ducers of old plays. Costumiers also seem to be members; but it
is doubtful whether the heralds or the trumpeters who announced
the start of each event at an *agon* were accepted.[24] Mimes were
certainly refused. The way in which an artist almost always has
the name of his homeland attached to his own name suggests he
remained a citizen with full rights however much he wandered.
Payments obviously varied considerably according to the importance of a festival and the status of an artist. We find festivals
distinguished as *thematikoi* (money-down), *argyrikai* (silver), half-
talant, and talant, in a rising order of remuneration.

Like the athletes, the artists were vain about their victories.
They too were called sacred victors when they won in sacred
games or belonged to a holy synod. A victor in all four great
festivals of Greece called himself *periodoneikes*; if he broke records,
he was *pleistoneikes;* and he liked the epithet *paradoxos*.[25]

Important Oxyrhynchite documents of A.D. 289 deal with the
privileges of Athletes and Dionysiac Artists. They are three and
formed part of a stuck-together roll in the archives of the Oxyrhynchos Senate. The first has only the ends of lines left, but
was perhaps the letter that Aurelios Hatres had sent in with his
credentials. The second is a certificate demonstrating that he is
a member of the Dionysiac Artists. What Hatres wants is exemption from taxes and liturgies; and so he includes copies of imperial letters and decrees that confer such privileges on the society.
These copies consist of a letter from Claudius to the society
allowing *eikones* or statues to be set up and confirming the
privileges granted by Augustus; a decree of Hadrian on those
privileges; a letter of Severus thanking the society for its good-
wishes on his accession and confirming privileges; a letter of
Alexander confirming the decisions of Caracalla and Severus; an
open letter of the society to its members certifying Hatres'
appointment at Oxyrhynchos as its highpriest and his payment of
the necessary fees; an elaborate ratification of this letter, dated by
the Games at Panopolis and the current officers of the society,
witnessed by all these officers and countersigned by the organisers
of the Panopolite Games. Finally comes a decree of the society

and the covering letter to the Oxyrhynchos Senate. The date is 26 July 289. (The scribe's hand is professional, but he reveals a careless ignorance.) The third document is from a pankratiast and has already been cited in chapter seven.[26]

A few passages from Hatres' claim will illustrate the tone of the documents. Under Claudius the society is "the Dionysiac Artists of the Empire, Victors in the Sacred Games, Wearers of the Garland, and their Associates". By the late 3rd century, it has become, "The Dionysiac Artists of the Empire and the Holy Artistic (*mousike*), Travelling, Worldwide, Grand Society of Dionysiac Artists. Victors in the Sacred Games, Wearers of the Garland, under the Patronage of Diocletian and Maximian, Pious, Auspicious, August." The privileges defined by Hadrian were "inviolability, seating precedence, exemption from military service, immunity from public duties, the right to keep untaxed all that they earn from private business or the Games (?) . . . not to supply guarantors, exemption from special taxes, communal sacrifice, not to be forced to supply billets for foreigners, not to be imprisoned (?) . . . , or liable to the death penalty." Hatres' fees are 850 denarii "and the payments for the temples of the emperors." Here are the signatures of some of the Panopolites:

First Officer: The Astounding (*paradoxos*) M. Aurelios Herakleios Komodos, Citizen of Antinoopolis and Panopolis, Victor in the Olympic, Pythian and Capitoline Games, Victor of Many Games.

Second Officer and Secretary: The Astounding Agathokles called Asterios, Kitharode, Citizen of Alexandreia, Antinoopolis, and Lykopolis, Victor in the Pythian Games, Victor of Many Games.

Officer in Charge of the Constitution: The Astounding Aurelios Kasyllas, Citizen of Panopolis and Antinoopolis, Trumpeter, Victor in the Olympic and Pythian Games, Victor of Many Games.

I the Astounding Aurelios Herakleios called Nikantinoos, citizen of Antinoopolis and Panopolis and Hermopolis and Lykopolis and Oxyrhynchos, Victor in the Olympic, Capitoline and Pythian Games, Victor of Many Games, First Officer of the Sacred Artistic Grand Society, under the Patronage of Diocletian and Maximian, have signed and sealed for Aurelios Hatres, son of Peteesios, son of Nechthenibis, an Oxyrhynchite, on his enrolment as Highpriest in my Presence in the Most Noble City and Most August City of the Panopolites, in the

I

7th Pythiad, during the Presentation of the Sacred Eiselastic International Dramatic and Scenic Games of Perseus of the Sky at the Great Festival of Pan.

Another signatory, a trumpeter, states that he is a citizen of Hermopolis, Antioch "and citizen of many other cities". Though Panopolis had been the city of Min, who was identified with Pan, Herodotos associated the place with Perseus and says that its people held athletic games in the Greek fashion in that hero's honour. The papyrus thus authenticates what Herodotos says, but leaves us still unclear as to why Perseus had this connection and how his celebrations were linked with the great Festival of Pan.[27]

A document of A.D. 163 shows us a member of the Dionysiac gild in everyday life. Permission was needed if a landowner wanted to change the kind of cultivation used on his land. Here we find an application for olive-groves to be converted into cornland. Generally olive-groves would be more remunerative than corn; here the trees must have been very old, otherwise it is hard to explain why the work of removing them would be undertaken. The petition merely says they'd grown unproductive.

To the village-secretary of Lagis from Heron, son of Hermanoubion son of Heron, belonging to the tribe of Theometor and the deme of Eusebeios, and a member of the Sacred Gild of Dionysos, Victor in the Sacred Games and immune from taxes, and from his sister Hermitarion also called Sarapias, resident of the City.

Since both are absent, this petition is presented through the agent they have appointed, in accordance with a writ of agency approved by the prytanies of Alexandreia in the preceding month Tybi, the agent appointed being Heron son of Ammonios son of Sotas, from the Syrian Quarter.

We wish to transfer to cornland the 10 ar. of olivegrove from the 13 ar. called the Postemian Lot belonging to us in common and in equal shares in the katoikic classification in one section near the aforesaid village of Lagis, 4 ar. out of the 7 ar. called the Allotment of Menas in another section, 2 ar. from another section called the Lot of Sacred Zeus, in another section $2\frac{7}{8}$ ar. from 3 ar. called the Lot of Kolokynthon, 1 ar. in another section, and $1\frac{3}{4}$ ar. from 2 ar. which belong to Heron alone in the Lot called that of Sacred Zeus. In all, 21⅝ ar. or as many as they may be.

These fields we wish to convert to cereal culture from the current 3rd year of Antoninus and Verus, Our Lords, because they have become unproductive. Therefore we present this petition that the proper procedure as in like cases may be followed.[28]

A fee was charged for the permit. Heron resided with his sister in Alexandreia.

Puppetshows seem to have been popular at Alexandreia. Philon uses them in a simile, asking what value the senses would be without the invisible mind, like a juggler or puppeteer, *thaumatopoios*, "to prompt its faculties, sometimes relaxing and giving them a free rein, sometimes forcibly pulling and jerking them back, and thus causing its puppets, *thaumasia*, at one time to move in harmony, at another to rest". The Greek terms suggest that the motions of puppets must have been a source of great wonder to the populace.[29] (Herodotos tells of village-women parading on what he calls Dionysiac festivals with puppets whose huge genitals they worked with strings.)

One point worth noting is the way that plays and players became connected with the tomb as emblems of a significant and happy afterlife. One aspect of the breakdown of tragedy and the selection of scenes, especially monologues, for use on social occasions, is found in the appearance of the tragic actor at funerals. Thus, at Caesar's funeral in 44 B.C. songs from Pacuvius' *Contest for the Arms of Achilles* and scenes from Atilius' *Electra* were presented. Wall-paintings in a grave at Cyrene show a group of tragic actors, a kithara-player and a flautist (each with a choros of seven young men), two solo kitharists, and a solo flautist. One tragic actor has the club of Herakles, the other has a herald's staff and may be Hermes—at his side is a table with wreaths and palm-branches for victors. Dramatic and lyric performances combined appear on the tomb of the young Flavius Valerius at Rome in the early 3rd century. Behind the lad is a small shrine with ancestral figures; a youth plays a water-organ; the main tragic actor declaims with club in hand.[30]

As our next theme is the Garden, we may make the transition here by pointing out the part played by theatral decoration in the garden and its representations. Vitruvius says that tragedy was set in the *regiae*, before columns decorated with statues; comedy before the façades of private houses; satyric drama in a scene "ornamented with trees, grottos, mountains and other country-elements composed to make an *opus topiarium*"—that is, to form a landscape-garden. When this scene is painted on a housewall, it becomes the reproduction of a stage-set in which landscapes are inserted between the columns of a portico.

The salon of Boscoreale villa illustrates Vitruvius; for there we find a palace with *tholos*, a street-scene, and a garden with grotto and fountains. In the Pompeian house of the Centenario are represented two aediculae, with door open on both sides, behind which we surmise a large park, a sacred wood. Further, because both garden and theatre share all sorts of Dionysiac forms of decoration, such as masks, the garden itself becomes a stage for an incessant mythological drama, which converts it into a sacro-idyllic landscape. Take for example the reliefs in the peristyle of the so-called House of the Golden Loves at Pompeii.

We see that they are in large part dionysiac and that, spread about in the midst of twists of ivy (as they were probably in antiquity), they evoke insistently the cult of the god: everywhere there are theatral masks, bacchic hermai and allusions to satyric drama. For instance, the plaque that presents on one of its faces a mask of Pan and another of a Mainad sets them between two hermai on a rocky background; a burning torch separates them. It is easy to see that these accessories symbolise an open-air scene, the special topiary countryside that the satyric drama requires. On the other face, the sacrifice of fruits (among them a pinecone) offered by a Silenus, while at the same rustic altar a Satyr lights a bough, seems indeed an allusion to the Roman Liberalia.[31]

This house had two lararia, one with traditional Roman deities, one with Egyptian gods. The abundance of masks has suggested an actor; but the fact seems simply a consistent Dionysiac setting. The persistence of the Egyptian idea appears in an early 3rd-century inscription which tells how a fraternity, the Spirae, have rebuilt in marble their sanctuary of Liber "with a chapel and columns", with a court and small garden "called Memphis in honour of the Nymphs"—note the jingle, *Memphis, Nymphis*. We are reminded of the pantomime called Memphis for his serene grace.[32]

12

Gardens and their Traditions

THE gardens of Roman Egypt had a long tradition behind them, into which many new elements flowed after Alexander. By the time of the New Kingdom pleasure-gardens were common, generally with a pond. Not that these gardens of the XVIII Dynasty had developed without some Asian influences which came in after the imperial expeditions of the Pharaohs.[1] Still, there were certain native ideas and images, connected with gardens and their flowers, which were tenaciously deep-rooted. Take for instance the association of lotus and pond. Nard-receptacles were made in lotus-shape. A form that evoked the scents of nature was linked with an artificial scent. Duck-shaped spoons with girls swimming to push them on (as handles) are familiar. We find also a wooden spoon representing three lotuses with stalks wound round in a circle as handle; the cavity is cut in the flower and the two buds framing it. From the flower emerges a rounded shape: fruit or rising sun. Nard and flower blend in an image of revival, or rebirth.[2]

The image of a cup as an opening flower is charmingly expressed in an alabaster cup from the subterranean chambers of a stepped pyramid at Saqqarah, which represents the perfection of a type. Many-lobed circles ripple out on the white basis in rosy tints that shade from mauve to amber. The cup "has retained to this day the freshness of an opening flower. And the motive is not limited to this resemblance. The dawn-tints which, circle on circle, reach that cup's rim, ray out beyond. This unreal grace goes far past what one expects of a definite object. Without doubt the floral and solar play, which the maker was able to draw on to the surface, appeared to him to possess a meaning that made worth while a great art-effort to the point of effacing every trace of effort under the purity achieved."[3]

The numerous cups of faience or gold in lotus-form of the New Kingdom receive their explanatory commentary in the vignette of *the Book of the Dead* in which the dead man is shown being reborn from a similar sort of flower.[4] Right from the first dynasty, cups imitated the lotus; and the original aspect of fertility developed its facet of salvation or personal renewal, and was heightened through its link with the solar cults given prominence by Imhotep, highpriest of Hermopolis, under the pharaoh Zoser (about 2800 B.C.).[5] We see the fusion of cults in the myth of the sun enclosed at night in the lotus, under the primordial water, and released into the upper air in the morning out of the open corolla.[6] The flower-vases give to men the promise of a similar release into a new day, while the dead (assimilated more and more to the nightsun) find in them a token of resurrrection into a world of light.

The symbolism is further clarified by a consideration of the lotiform chalices made by the 18th Dynasty, and the relief chalices that come up with the 22nd. The lotus had two species, the blue (*Nymphaea caerulea*) and the white (*Nymphaea lotus*). The blue lotus was the one mainly used in art. Both blue and white flower from December to March, the latter through the night till about eleven A.M: the former from sunrise to noon, rising a little above water, then opening and closing daily without sinking, till the withered flower is drawn down. Each blue lotus has four green sepals almost as clear as the petals; but as it expands, only three are visible from any of the four viewpoints—three spikes symmetrically divided, with many petals showing between.[7]

The earliest dateable representation of a blue-lotus chalice is in the south Hall of Offerings at Deir el-Bahari. Nearly contemporary are the representations on the Halls of Annals at Karnak, where among the offerings of gold brought to Amun by Tuthmosis from his Syrian campaign appears such a chalice called Lotus of Offering; there is another of silver, and others of gold, lapis, and malachite. In the tomb of Rekhmireh at Thebai two metal chalices are found among the offerings of temple-furniture and three chalices among the provisions for a special rite (perhaps the Beautiful Festival of the Valley); but none turns up in the equipment for daily meals. The same point applies to other representatations. A chalice filled with vegetable offerings is set before the Hathor-cow welcoming the resurrected dead-man at the Gates of the Mountain of the West and thrusting her head through a papyrus-thicket.[8] We may then generalise that "the caerulea chalice, unlike the alabaster lotus chalice, is never shown being used for drinking, but is frequently shown as a cult vessel in the ritual of the dead."[9] Its significance is one of revivification and rebirth.

Some examples will bring out the imagery drawn from nature

Chalice-cup from Saqqara.

on these chalices of new-life; they also help to fill in the Nilotic hunting scene. On the narrow rim-zone of a chalice from Saqqara is a frieze of birds with fluttering or closed wings in alternation, and with a nest of two eggs above the bird; in the main zone are marsh reeds with alternate leaves, though at one point instead of three reeds are three papyri with buds on shorter culms between them and a bird or a nest with two eggs above the bud; the bottom of the cup has the four petals and three intervening leaves of caerulea; the stem and foot have inverted leaves with incised veins.[10] On another cup two geese tend goslings while a fluttering duck between them watches in excitement its two eggs in a nest; in a boat a calf lies in the bow and a girl sits on the sternpost pulling a papyrus to propel the boat; a man walks on the bank hold-

ing a nest with a chick; a girl punts a boat with two plumed ser-
pent-deities in the bow and a bird (perhaps a pigeon) fluttering
overhead; fish swim below. A third chalice shows a duck-hunt,
a man brandishing a boomerang; a fourth depicts the hunt in
detail:

In the small rim-zone, bordered by single relief lines, two geese face
each other and eat from the same bin. To either side a pattern begins,
with two ducks and a nest, and for the rest of the scene geese pick
from the ground and geese flutter in varying attitudes and directions,
with no set pattern. Of six ducks' nests, four have two eggs each, one
has two chicks with two more below it, and in the sixth a chick seems
to emerge from the egg.

  In the main zone two boats move to right, bow to stern. In the front
boat a man stands to right in the stern, punting and looking back to
fend off the boat behind from making a bump. In the middle of the
boat a cow lies with forelegs folded. On the prow a man balances
firmly with right foot, his left foot delicately set forward on a lotus
which is tied round the neck of a cow in the water; he leans his weight
back, right hand brandishing a boomerang and left hand holding
forward a decoy (heron?). Above the cow in the boat three papyrus
heads are bending downwards, and two nests with two eggs in each
rest on them, and a third nest seems to have a chick. In front of the
boat, with mouth touching the fowler's front toes, the cow is struggling
out of the marsh, front legs stretched forward, A man stands behind
the cow to left, lifting it by a horn and its neck; and next to him
another man stands idly looking to left, holding across his shoulders a
punt-pole from which a basket hangs. Behind these two men four
papyri bend, two to left and two to right, to make a group with the
men.

  In the rear boat a man stands in the bow holding with outstretched
hands a triangular net. To his right a cow's head emerges out of the
papyrus thicket behind. In the stern a man kneels to left, looking back
to right, with left hand pushing straight behind. In the stern a man
kneels to left, looking back to right, with left hand stretched back to
hold his companion for balance, and right arm reaching out to lift a
cow which is jumping forward from the water. Another man stands
in the water behind the cow, left hand helping the cow and right hand
prodding a pole in the water. All the men wear kilts.[11]

In the background are two close-set rows of papyri. In the care-

I*

fully organised scene of vigorous action, on either side of the central point between the two boats, are four men, two cows, and the two boats themselves; in the third narrower zone two horses struggle to rise out of the water and a crocodile between them jumps on the back of the leading horse. On either side of this central group of three figures is another group of three, all moving to right: in one a man struggles out of water, brandishing a stick, and drives two horses out, while in the other a man similarly drives two cows. The cup-bottom has the sepals and petals of caerulea; on stem and foot are inverted palm-leaves.

In these Nilotic scenes we see imagery which through various

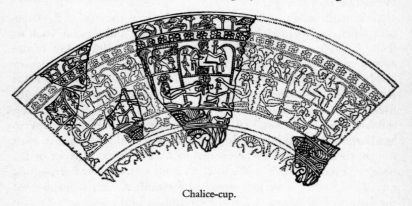

Chalice-cup.

channels carries on into the motives of cow, crocodile and man in the late mosaics of Cyrene and Quasr el-Lebia.

In another chalice a man with a lasso urges on a cow that lifts its head in a moo; in a second group a man holds one hand to the mouth of a Hathor-cow with disk between its horns, and the other hand to a calf running for her milk. On some chalices Bes appears. On one of them three Bes-figures dance, the first holding a big flower (?) behind him, the second a cymbal, the third with arms akimbo; a fourth Bes grips by two feathers the head of a small hook-nosed prisoner, who has been given only one leg. Each Bes wears an apron and has a long tail and single feather on his head. (It has been suggested that the three dance in honour of the one who has caught his foe.) On another chalice four Bes figures grasp the tails of two monkeys who climb up after the headfeathers.[12] There is also an important connection with the infant sungod. On one chalice he squats on a caerulea, flanked by winged cobras twisted round a papyrus-culm, one with red crown, one with white; at the back are papyri with ducks busy at their nests on the umbels. Another chalice has five zones. Its fragments show ducks in a papyrus-marsh, six-petalled rosettes, fish nibbling pairs of lotus-stems, a black-rumped cow suckling her calf, lotus with buds and palmettes. In the third or main zone:

The god of the Inundation, Hapy, black-wigged and kilted, with papyrus clump on his head, squats to right clasping in each outstretched hand a notched palm branch which curves inwards to the king above, and as usual the tadpole of 100,000 under each palmbranch inwards. On Hapy's left elbow stands an 'ankh-sign. On each side of him, outside the palmbranch, a similar Hapy squats facing inwards, holding the palm with his nearer hand and reaching forward his farther hand in adoration. Enthroned on a relief line above the central Hapy, the king faces right, wearing the blue crown with uraeus and a heavy necklace but no trace of a robe. In his right hand he holds the flail over his shoulder and in his left he holds forward a curving sceptre or scimitar.

In front of him, presented by the palmbranch, are two 'ankhs, and behind him an 'ankh and a sceptre. The two side-Hapys are taller than the central one, and above each a Bes dances towards the king, holding out the uadjat-eye, with 'ankh below. From his tail rises a papyrus-umbel and above his head is a long feather. Generally Heb, the God of Eternity, holds the palmbranches, and Bes, as we have seen, attends births. Here the Nilegod offers millions of years of life and power in a scene that may commemorate a coronation or a sed festival. (On a foursided ivory unguent basin, probably of the XVIII Dynasty, two Hapys hold a lotus-nibbling fish in a rite of protection; Hapy as protector appears in the Book of the Dead; and in the tomb of Queen Nefertari he holds the notched palm and protects the ovoid germ in which the falcon's egg is figured. On the basin the fish is Inet, image of being, in gestation before birth, protected by the spirits of primeval water and nibbling the lotus that represents the first plantgrowth of the world's dawn and symbolises the reborn sun.) A text states: "At the dawn the god abandons his form of mummy and is reborn in the sanctuary as in the eastern sky as a young man, a child rising from the lotus, a milking calf." (On another side of the basin a man punts a calf in a boat.)[13]

The centre of production seems at Hermopolis. The sacred area of the Primeval Hill set in the Isle of Flame has been found there. In one tradition the Hill rose up out of the sea which had laid since eternity in darkness and the Young Sun appeared on a lotus. The New Year Festival was held in the area of the Hill, comme-morating afresh the action of Creation. The birth of the Sun in Creation and his victorious fight against his enemies were de-picted in a mystery-play. A sacred garden was connected with the site. A little to the north of the structure built in the Middle Kingdom, Ramses II founded a temple of the sungod, which was carried out by Merneptah and completed by Sethos II. According to an inscription on a pylon, Merneptah gave the temple a park with fruit-trees and ponds in which lotus and papy-rus grew: a park which was restored by Petosiris after sight-seers and intrusive commoners damaged it.[14] "I protected the enclosure of the park to stop it being trampled on by the people. For it is the place where all the gods were born at the beginning of the world, and the common people trampled on it. There was indignation because of it in the whole land, and it did no good to Egypt."[15]

The phase of Egyptian art represented by the chalices is of great interest and may be said to have anticipated certain aspects of Greek art;

For a moment the Egyptian allowed himself on his pottery the descrip-tive scenes of men in action which played so tremendous a role in Greek art, and in that moment he anticipated the Greeks by some 200 years. The Greek potters of the early Orientalising period may have been stirred to paint scenes of action as much by the epic narra-tives which were brought across the Aegean in their day as by the ivory and metal objects brought to them by the Phoenicians. Two hundred years earlier Shoshenq's potters had been stirred to use the marsh scenes which their forbears had loved, and the reasons for their exuberance may have been the pageantry of the Hermopolis Festivals and a quickened interest in the ivory craftsman's skill. But it was momentary, and the conventional figures of dogma soon replaced the lively men in their punts. Not by mere chance are these chalices so rare.[16]

Though there must have been some particular social circumstances allowing this breakthrough of a fresh and lively art in the chalices, we must also allow for an inspiring element in the festival of rebirth at Hermopolis at this moment, with its imagery of a world-hill and a sacred or primeval garden. The complaint about damage suggests a strong popular response to the shrine.

But though we have here an especially striking example of the power of the lotus-imagery of rebirth, we must realise that the imagery was a continuous element in Egyptian thought and was handed on to the Hellenistic and Roman worlds. Those worlds took it over in the form of a portrait, particularly a bust, set in a calyx. The earliest known examples are three Greek stelai of the 2nd century B.C., where a portrait is found linked with leaf-calyces and scrolls. The one Roman example of Republican days is a rosette stele, Greek in form, inscribed with the name Paula (F)laminia; the head is lost. Of later reliefs, one, dated perhaps to the time of Trajan or Hadrian, shows a woman's bust with the calyxbust of a little girl. Most of the sarcophagi with the type belong to the 3rd century A.D.; one of the commonest series is the strigulated, with portraits of husband and wife surmounting a leaf-calyx and set in a roundel. The significance seems certainly to be funereal; the leaf-calyx expresses apotheosis or resurrection. The bronze busts include imperial as well as private portraits; thus Domitian is found with the calyx. The largest set is that of the stone busts, of which one example seems earlier than A.D. 100, the so-called Clytie of the British Museum. She has a single ring of leaves instead of the standard three-leaf calyx of the later busts. Her date is perhaps late Republican, in view of the likeness to the bust on the silver dish from Boscoreale, which we discussed above and found to be probably Cleopatra.[17]

The image of rebirth out of the lotus, out of the leaf-calyx, may be related in turn to a custom, going back to pharaonic times and still active in the Graeco-Roman world: the decoration of coffins and mummies with crowns, leafage, vegetal garlands. On a mummy in the tomb of the Soteres (a family of whom one member was *archon Thebon* under Trajan) an olive wreath had been laid.[18] At Deir el-Medineh, vault 1196 held leafage, and on the coffins of 1407 there had been set garlands of willow-leaves and a bunch of vine-leaves. Much the same occurred at Deir el-Bahari on Roman mummies.[19] In rich burials representations in gold could take the place of withering leaves.[20] We find in the rules of a fraternity that members must put a wreath on the tomb of a buried fellow.[21]

The opening lotus was clearly felt to image the womb in a painless or perfecting birth. Further details of Egyptian plant-symbolism are provided by Ploutarch:

Harpokrates is born about the winter-solstice, incompleted and infantlike in the plants that early flower and spring up; and so they offer him the firstfruits of sprouting lentils and celebrate Isis bring brought to bed after the spring equinox.

By the figure of a figleaf they represent a king and the southern quarter of the world; and the figleaf is interpreted as the watering and stimulation of all things, and it is supposed to resemble in shape the organ of generation.

In the month Mesore they serve up pulse, repeating: The Tongue is Fortune, the Tongue is a Deity. And of all the plants growing up in Egypt they say the Persea is the most sacred to the gods because its fruit resembles a heart and its leaf a tongue.[22]

The native Egyptian ideas of paradise are well exemplified by the rites carried on at Esna under the Romans. At the rites of Union with the Disc, the god's effigy was set in the light and warmth of the sun, so that it might be revivified and a new cycle of life inaugurated. The rite seems to consist of a processional installation of the god in a kiosk set up outside the temple-door. Various offerings were made: of plants in general, scented plants, flowering boughs, open and closed lotus, papyrus-stalks. Here are words from the rite of offering the boughs:

Offer flowering boughs from every kind of tree with sweet scent. Say:

All boughs in flower are for your person, Khnum-Re, Lord of Esna; every odorous plant, every perfumed essence, in big bundles, are for your nose, until you are submerged by them; let your Majesty see them, then the association of gods will be gladdened in its turn, after your person has been satisfied, in this your name of Lord of the Countryside.

Offer flowering boughs. Say: I have gone into the fields, I have walked across the countryside, and here I am entering your residence, at the moment of dawn: your meadow glistens with verdure and streams with flowers; it abounds in vegetation, it overflows with innumerable flowering boughs; its sheaves are in the image of the earth (?) of the sun; all its vegetation greens, opening its buds which expand on your courtyard every day. For you are the master of the fostering earth, who produces what is necessary.—May your beautiful face be gracious to the gardener who loves you, Domitian the Saved. Confer on him all the greenery that covers the earth, so that he may make your eyes sparkle at [the sight of the] flowering boughs, eternally.

Thus the earth at the moment of divine rejuvenation is seen as a paradise of beauty and fertility.

If we now turn to Hellas, we find a very rich tradition of sacred gardens. In myth there is, for example, the eternally fertile garden of Alkinoos; the gardens of the Hesperides; the gardens of gods such as Kalypso in the *Odyssey*, or those of Aphrodite, Dionysos, Eros, Adonis, Asklepios, Herakles—gods of life, of love and rebirth. Hades comes in as the death preluding rebirth, as does also Kalypso the Hiding or Shrouding Mother. Herakles became important as a result of Orphico-Dionysiac syncretism and for other reasons; we find him served by bearded satyrs; he stands for the winner of a place of heroic repose.[23] As earthly counterpart of the mythical sites, there grew up the sanctuaries and enclosures that were especially numerous by the Hellenistic epoch: the enclosures of heroes' tombs surrounded by planes and cypresses, the woods sacred to various deities, the temples with their elaborated *temenea*. (The whole valley of the Nile came to be called the *temenos Neiloio*.) In the orchard of Herakles at Thasos there rose a building composed of portico and halls used for the cult and for ritual meals.[24]

The image of a golden age of unforced nature, when all necessary things were spontaneously produced, merges with the actual
scene of woodlands or gardens enclosing sacred spots. The
imagined or pictured landscape always has some monument—
pillar, statue, shrine, vase, tomb—that gives it its significance.
Nature itself, so to speak, has sudden revelations or moments of
concentrated meaning, its own inner secret expressed in vistas or

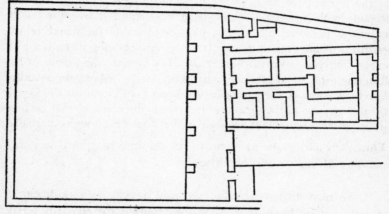

Sacred Garden, oikoi and portico, of Herakles, Thasos.

nooks of intense virtue, of pure harmony become paradisiac.
Typical of this viewpoint is an epigram attributed to Theokritos:

> Turn the lane's corner, Goatherd, with its oaks:
> you'll find a newcarved effigy of fig:
> no legs or ears, and rough with bark, but look,
> the part that does love's job is stiffly big.
> A small brave sacrificial close runs round,
> a freshet always issuing from the rocks;
> greened thick with bay and myrtle lies the ground,
> and fragrant cypresses with vineleaves mix . . . [25]

It was no chance then that the gymnasia-schools of philosophy
became parks or gardens of meditation and discussion. The ideal
setting of thought was that of Platon's *Phaidros*: the shadow of
a great planetree, grass, and gentle breezes, a quietly flowing

stream. The necessary scene of an occasional philosophic with-drawal becomes more and more the continuous background (or inground) of philosophic existence; and we come to the Garden of Epikouros.[26] Further, this setting spreads out again from the sacred enclosure and the garden of meditation, and becomes more and more a desired ingredient of any form of living that aspires beyond the crushing round of business and labour, politics and law. All gardens seek to turn into small samples or symbols of a blessedness that reaches out past the crushing round—into a fully good and worthwhile life on earth or a foretaste of otherworldly bliss.

There is one more important influence that we must bear in mind if we are to understand all that gardens meant in the Roman world. Eastern influences, especially Persian, were strong after Alex-ander and were absorbed into the Hellenistic scheme of things. Already in the late 5th century B.C. the Greeks were growing aware of the Persian Garden or Paradise, as we see particularly from Xenophon. The paradise-park was a piece of unspoiled woodland, which could be used for hunting or as a pleasance. The kings and nobles thus, in a world where tribal equality and brother-hood had long past disintegrated, were able to keep up an illusion of living in the old days of tribal simplicity, close to nature. Kyros is told, according to Xenophon, by his grandfather, "You shall have the use of all my horses and as many more as you like; and when you depart, you may take as many as you please to be satisfied in what you think a temperate way. Also I give you all the various animals now in the park, and I'll collect more of all kinds, so that you may chase them when you've learned to ride, and with your bow and javelin lay them flat on the ground, as grown men do."[27] Elsewhere, Xenophon writes of the Persian king:

Sokrates: In every country where he resides or passes a short time, he takes care to have excellent gardens, filled with every kind of flower or plant that can be collected by any means, and in these places lies his chief delight.

Kritias: By your account it appears also that he finds a great pleasure in gardening; for, as you intimate, his gardens are furnished with every tree and plant that the earth can bring forth . . .

Sokrates: When Lysandros brought gifts to Kyros from the cities of Greece his confederates, Kyros received him with the utmost humanity, and among other things showed him his garden called the Paradise of Sardeis. Lysandros was struck with wonder at the beauty of the trees, their regular planting, the even rows, their positions at regular angles to one another: in a word, the beauty of the quincunx order in which they were set, and the delightful smells they gave out.

He couldn't help extolling the beauty of their order and especially admired the fine skill of the hand that had so curiously disposed them. Kyros noticed and answered, "All the trees you see were arranged by me. I planned, measured, laid out the plantation and I can even show you some I put in with my own hands."

When Lysandros heard this and saw his rich robes, his splendid dress, his gold chains, the number and rareness of his jewels, he cried in astonishment, "Is it possible, Great King, you could condescend to plant any of these trees with your own hands?"

"Do you wonder, Lysandros?" replied Kyros. "I assure you, whenever I've leisure from war and am most at ease, I never dine before doing some exercise in arms or employing myself in some matter of husbandry, till I sweat."[28]

We know more of the Paradise of Sardeis with its greenswards and running waters.[29] The Greeks took the term *paradeisos* over into their language from the Persians for a park or pleasure-grounds; and it was finally used in the Septuagint to translate the Garden of Eden. It passed over into ecclesiatical Latin, and Tertullian used Paradise to signify the abode of the blessed.[30] For Plinius it was only the name of a town in Caelosuria or of a river in Cilicia; and Aulus Gellius annotated:

The word *vivaria*, which is now commonly used for what the Greeks call *paradeisoi* and Varro meant by *leporaria* [warrens], I do not recall meeting anywhere in the older writers. As for *roboraria* [oak-enclosure], which is found in the writings of Scipio, who used the purest diction of any man of his time, I have heard several learned men at Rome assert that this means what we call *vivaria* and that the name came from the oaken planks of which the enclosures were made: a sort of enclosure that we see in many places in Italy.[31]

As the Septuagint was the Greek version of the Hebrew scriptures made in Alexandreia in the 3rd–2nd centuries B.C., it was in Greek Egypt that the word paradise entered Judeo-Christian thought.

The nostalgic element, looking back to early tribal days, which we find in the Persian concept of the paradise-park, persisted in the usages of the word in Graeco-Roman days, but grew much more complex and sophisticated as the inner conflicts of ancient culture developed. The earthly *paradeisos* ends as the otherworld-home of the blessed; but before the umbilical cord with the earth

Hero and Horse before Sacred Tree and entwined Snake (Athens); bronze serpent-stand (Delphoi).

is finally severed, a rich set of overtones and undertones is built up round the word, and the idea, the image, of the actual garden grows correspondingly elaborate. The feeling of the loss of the earth has its intellectual expression in the deepened interest in animals and plants, which begets the first stages of the sciences of zoology and botany. The collections of animals and plants acquire new perspectives as the distance between man and nature increases. The Ptolemies played a leading part in making such collections in the post-Alexander world and in ensuring Alexandreia its supremacy as a place of scientific research. Nostalgic wonder and intellectual inquiry merge.

The worsening social crisis, with its failure to find any effective resolution through the revolutionary conflicts of the last century B.C., intensified both the desire to return to nature and the conviction that nature (the earth as a whole and hence society as well) was hopelessly polluted. After Alexander, and then again after the fall of the Roman Republic, the loss of freedom for the individual was steadily increased. There is no space here to analyse the forms that the subjections took; we are concerned with the multiple effects, which yet come together in certain generally shared attitudes. At some moments of high resilience in classical

Urn of Cossutia Prima, with sacred trees, birds, snakes, interlace, and Eros as charioteer
(B.M.).

Greek culture there had been attempts to define and describe stages of development from barbarism; but again, on account of the contradiction and unresolved conflicts of the *polis*, an ambivalent attitude deepened. Man had risen up from the level of the animals into a noble civilisation; man had declined from a golden age (a utopian version of the days of tribal brotherhood) into stages of corruption and division. The opposed views grew even more irreconcilable after Alexander. Theophrastos, who did so much to found the science of botany, saw that men had reached their present levels by extremely arduous slow and painful struggle. The stages he expressed in terms of the burnt offerings made to the gods: first common wild plants, then aromatics, then acorns and oakleaves, then corn and cakes of flour, then honey, oil and wine, finally the flesh of animals (of which he himself disapproves). The first sacrifices were made by the Egyptians to the heavenly bodies.[32] Dikaiarchos, attempting the first cultural history of Hellas, took up the concept of a peaceful Golden Age, vegetarian in basis, from which human virtue weakened as men passed through the stages of hunting and herding to agriculture and eventually to settled city-life with all its civilised evils.[33] At the same time the interest in actual primitive peoples on the periphery of the Greek world increased, reaching its height in Poseidonios, who linked his theory of progressive stages with evidence drawn from such people, many of whom he visited in his travels.[34]

Could the good life be lived in a city? The very question would have seemed ridiculous to the earlier Greeks who had created and developed the *polis*; but now it lay heavy on the spirits of men. Philon in Alexandreia sets out cogently what had become the commonplaces of almost all thinkers who sought to rise above the corruptions and tyrannies of the post-Alexander world.

The good man is a lover of that mode of life untroubled by business, and he withdraws and loves solitude, wanting to escape the notice of the crowd, not out of misanthropy—for he loves mankind, if anyone in the world does—but out of a repudiation of evil, which the main multitude eagerly clasps, rejoicing at what it should mourn over, and grieving at what it is right rather to rejoice. So the good man shuts himself up, scarcely going over his threshold, or if he does go out, so as to avoid the crowd pressing to visit him, he generally goes out of the city and makes his abode in some country place, living most pleasantly with such companions as are the most virtuous of all mankind, whose bodies indeed time has dissolved, but whose virtues are kept alive by the records left of them—in poems and in prose, histories by which the soul is naturally inspired and led on to perfection.[35]

In his work *On Contemplative Life* he repeats this position, saying that men abandon property and family, but do not depart to another city: "for every city, even that under the happiest laws, is full of indescribable tumults and disorders and calamities, to which nobody would submit if he was even for a moment under the influence of wisdom". Yet elsewhere he subtly undermines these concepts by calling the Logos "a City"—thus showing the realisation that despite all the contradictions the deepest socialising and humanising forces at work lie in the city, in its concentrations and onward drive. The Logos, the reasoning power, is the City, despite the pleasure-lash, the exploitation of man by man, the repressive forms of the State centred there, and so on. The ambivalence of his attitude comes out again thus:

The Sun is also spoken of often in holy writ in a figurative manner. Once as the human mind, which men build up as a City and furnish, compelled to serve the creature [e.g in Babel] in preference to the uncreated God, of whom it is said that "they built strong cities for Pharaoh and Peitho", that is, for Discourse: to which Persuasion is attributed, and Ramses, or the outward sense, by which the soul is devoured as by moths. For the name Ramses, interpreted, means the Shaking of a Moth; and On, the Mind, which they call Heliopolis, since the Mind, like the Sun, dominates the whole mass of our body and extends its powers like the sunbeams over everything.

The Christians took over the philosophic idiom of city-rejection and gave it a yet greater intensity. St Basil, writing about 358, states that the first necessity for a serious Christian is to "sever the soul from *sympatheia* with the body and to become cityless, homeless, propertyless, without love of friends, without any resources, business, or social relations, without knowledge derived from human teaching".[36]

In its negative aspects the city becomes a blasphemy against the earth, a denial of the golden age and of the harmonious relation to nature. At Rome itself, villages and townships had been drawn into the urbanising maw, "and these were so closely compacted", said Dionysios of Halikarnassos, "that if anyone looking towards Rome should estimate its size with his eye he would be much deceived, nor would he be able to distinguish how far the city extends or where it ceases to be city, so are the buildings of the city and the country linked together without a break and stretching out to an unlimited extent."[37] This sense of the confounding of things led to a varied series of revolts and criticisms, ranging from the picture of hopeless vulgarity and contamination of a city like Rome in Juvenal's satires to the furious hatred of the underdog in writings like *Revelation* or the *Potter's Prophecy*, which fiercely look forward to the total destruction of Rome and Alexandreia. One detail in Juvenal is worth citing here. The poet (in the third satire) is seeing off a friend who is leaving Rome; he walks to the gate and they turn into a little park, Egeria's Glen, outside the walls. Once there was a sacred spot here (where the priestking Numa met the goddess who taught him his magic, his songs and spells); now it has been rented by a settlement of poor Jews and the nymph's cave has had its grass and native stone overlaid by costly and gorgeous marble. Economic misery and a vulgar display ousting nature have gone on side by side, even at the heart of the sacred garden.[38]

These points could be much elaborated. Egypt, it is true, had not been marked by a strong early urban development such as came about in Mesopotamia; and even now the Romans did not extend there their full municipal system. However, with the handful of privileged cities and the metropoleis of the nomes, Egypt in effect was a part of the Roman world, and the conflicts and problems of urban life were profoundly affecting it. Not for nothing did it come about that it was in Egypt we find the direct transformation of the term *anachoresis*, which defined the flight of the peasants from intolerable economic conditions, into a spiritual or religious significance, expressing the flight of the faithful Christian into the hermitage of the waste, away from a corrupted world. Away from property and family, as Philon had said of his philosophic fugitive.[39]

13

Flowers, Fruits, Herbs

WE HAVE, then, seen that ideas and images of sacred gardens were strong alike in Egypt, in Hellas, and in the Near East. Certain elements are common to all such traditions, which in the last resort are based on ritual-centres and their associated imagery of a world of leisure, pleasure and plenty: the ancestral spirit-world which is the source of all fertility and which is in some sense made actual for the devotees by the ritual-act. But each tradition develops its own characteristics. The idyllic aspect is strong in Egypt; the heroic and triumphal aspect is strong in Hellas; the link with a free and undivided tribal past is specially clear among the Persians, though paradoxically the park in which that past is preserved has become the privileged possession of king and noble. In the Graeco-Roman concept of the sacred garden the Greek and Persian contributions are definite; but the Egyptian contribution is also present, coming to the fore in such an image as that of the calyx of rebirth.

For the moment let us look again at the rose, the main flower of the ancient garden. The cultivated rose seems to have been red.[1] The account by Kallixenos of the festival of Philadelphos at Alexandreia has given us some idea of the wealth of Egyptian flowers. Suetonius tells us of Nero that "it was his custom to invite himself to supper with his friends; at one of which he expended no less than 4,000,000 sesterves in chaplets and at another something more in roses".[2] Martial writes in hyperbolic praise of Domitian's winter-roses:

> A novel gift: the land of Nile, O Caesar,
> once sent you winter-roses in its pride.
> The Memphian sailor scoffed at Egypt's gardens

when first your city's bounds he trod. Inside,
such beauty of spring, such charm of fragrant Flora,
such glory of Paestan fields, upheaped, he found.
Wherever he turned his wandering eyes or footsteps,
each pathway reddened with roses twined around.
Now forced to yield to what Rome's winter uncloses,
send us your harvests, Nile, and take our roses.[3]

Even Philon has a good word for roses, though what he admires
are their powers, *dynameis.* "Violets, roses, crocuses, with the
other varieties (*poikilia*) of flowers, were made to give health,
not pleasure. Their properties are infinite; they are beneficial in
themselves by their scents, impregnating all things with their
fragrance, and far more beneficial when used by physicians in
compounding drugs. For some things reveal their virtues more
clearly in combination with others: as the union of male and
female serves to beget animal life while neither apart can do what
they can in combination."[4] In fact, there seem to have been very
few varieties of roses.[5] The ancients had almost only fieldflowers
at their disposal. Though the poets write of crocus, violet, grape-
hyacinth, cyclamen, star-of-bethlehem, anemone, iris, tulip,
narcissus, daisy, lily, only the rose was intensively cultivated. So,
in gardens, the main aim was to get new effects, *e.g.* by dwarf
species such as the *chamaie-platanus* or *chamaie-cyparissus*.[6] The
garden thus achieved a miniature park-appearance. In general the
gardeners fell back on laurel, rose-laurel, and ivy. At Pompeii
the flowers are largely limited to the border. We find a small
peristyle, some dozen metres long and half as wide, with several
circular clumps, or more or less regular ellipses, set around a
heap of undeciduous shrubs (probably laurels); or flowers are
sown haphazard in flowerstands on the top of a low wall surrounding a peristyle and separating the portico from the open air.[7]
We can see the large number of conifers in villa-landscapes. The
aim was to create an eternal garden, where nothing withered and
no leaves fell.

We have a few records of Alexandrian gardens. There is a
lease of a garden, dated 22 B.C., for one year at 420 (or 720) dr.
plus certain produce. In 5 B.C., two-thirds of $4\frac{1}{2}$ ar. of vineyard,

rose-garden, beans, and so on, were let for 5 years at 80 dr. a year. At Oxyrhynchos in A.D. 137, a vineyard and reed-plot were leased for 4 years, the lessor providing 5 oxen and 3 steers for irrigation and advancing 3000 dr. for building a new waterwheel, paying public taxes and getting half the produce, plus 50 keramia of wine and 100 one-obol cheeses; the lessee got lodging free of rent and paid for half the irrigation-work, half the fertiliser; there were also leases of a dry vineyard for 3 years at 60 dr. a year and half the produce, and of a rose-garden. In 141 in the Arsinoite nome a narcissus-garden was leased at 60 (plus) dr.[8]

Wreaths had an important role in both Greek and Egyptian

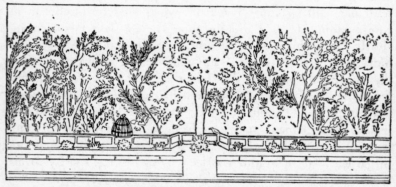

Wall-painting of Garden in villa at Gallinas, near Prima Porta, Rome.

traditions. The life-giving power of renewal or rebirth which was attributed to them made them essential in funeral rites and on occasions of pleasure. The Greeks hung them on doors, by altars, at shrines, to draw and hold beneficent or saving spirits; at festivals and banquets they intensified the enjoyment and protected it. As emblems of a new life, they were presented to victors at the games (olive at the Panathenaia, pine at the Isthmia, laurel at Delphoi, wild olive at Olympia, celery at Nemea). Made of gold or silver leaves they were presented to benefactors of towns and sometimes put in graves to express victory over death.

The discussion of the diners in the 15th or concluding book of Athenaios shows how carefully the genuine or supposed qualities of flowers and herbs were considered in the making and use of wreaths. There was also a complicated magical lore. "I see the slaves are now fetching us wreaths and scents. Why do people say that if the wreaths on the wearers are broken up it shows they're in love? I was very keen to learn the reason for this when I was a schoolboy reading the epigrams of Callimachos, among which is the following. The poet of Cyrene says:

> and the roses, shedding around
> their petals, fell from his wreaths down to the ground.

It's your job, then, Demokritos, most devoted servant of the Muses, to free me from this thousand-year inquiry and explain why people in love hang wreaths on their lovers' doors."[9]

Demokritos in reply cites at length the *Erotika* of Klearchos of Soloi, a pupil of Aristotle. Klearchos says that the dying or loss of the *kosmos*, the orderly beauty of the fresh leaves or flowers, represents the stripping of the beauty of character—*kosmos* as inner order or balance—in the lovers, which love brings about. Lovers of all people love adornment.

Nature, like some divine power [*daimonion*] giving righteous judgment in all things, considers that lovers should not put wreaths on before gaining victory in love: that is, when they've completed the conquest of the beloved and are freed from desire. The removal of the wreath, then, we regard as a sign that the struggle still goes on. Or can it be that the god of love himself, not permitting anyone to be crowned and proclaimed victor over him, strips the wreath from the lovers, while to everyone else he reveals their condition by disclosing that he has overcome them? Hence the others declare that they're in love?

Or is it that whatever has been bound together can be broken up; and just as love is a binding of certain persons wearing wreaths—for nobody is so particular about wearing them as those in love—so people look on the wreath's dissolution as a sign of the lovebond and declare that such persons are in love?

Is it because lovers with wreaths often let them fall away, apparently in passionate excitement, so that we suspect their passion, reasoning conversely, since we infer that the wreath wouldn't drop off its leaves if they weren't in love? Or is it because dissolutions happen mainly in the case of lovers only, and persons (so to speak) bound by a spell, people declare such to be in love? For lovers are certainly spellbound.

He goes on to suggest that a light thing like a wreath cannot bear the weight of Eros, and that in hanging wreaths on doors as on a god's portals they dedicate them to Eros, of whom the beloved is the image, *agalma*. The house becomes a temple. Hence too sacrifices are offered there. They think they've been robbed by the beloved, but it's the *kosmos* of the soul that has gone, so they strip off and dedicate the bodily adornment.[10]

The dialectic of wit here is highly sophisticated; but the underlying ideas are ancient and deep-rooted—the link of wreath and wearer, the magical connection, the binding power of the wreath. The physical effects of flowers and herbs were thought to be understood: roses cooled and acted as a sedative, myrtle dispelled wine-fumes; stocks, marjoram and other plants excited or stupefied, and were to be avoided. Athenaios has a long account of the various flowers used. The extent to which the scents and essences were felt to penetrate the body is pleasantly expressed by Pherekrates:

> You that belch mallows and breathe hyacinth,
> whose speech is melilot, whose grin is roses,
> whose kiss sweet-marjoram, whose clasp is celery,
> whose laugh's horse-celery, whose walk is larkspur,
> fill up, shout the triple paian, as our wont is.[11]

Selina, celery, was a slang term for the vagina; and there is a bawdy meaning also in horse-celery, *hipposelina*. Larkspur is *kosmosandalon*, fancy-shod.

In Egypt there was a special wreath of Naukratis.[12] Pollux tells us that it was composed of marjoram. Athenaios cites a tale from the book *On Aphrodite* by Polycharmos of Naukratis about a voyage from Paphos to Naukratis in the years 688–5 B.C.—though it seems the town was founded in fact about 570–50. The tale states that a violent storm broke out as the ship approached Egypt; the trader Herostratos had with him an ancient Cypriot statuette of Aphrodite; he prayed to the goddess, who caused green myrtle to cover everything beside her and filled the ship with a pleasant smell; though everyone was vomiting with seasick-ness, the sun burst out and the anchorage was seen. Arriving at Naukratis, Herostratos took the statue and the myrtle branches and dedicated them in Aphrodite's temple there, with sacrifices. Then "he invited his relations and closest friends to a feast in the temple, giving each one a wreath of myrtle, which even at that time he called a Naukratite wreath". The tale resembles that of Dionysos and the ship bursting out into vineleaves, and prob-ably was devised in part to explain the alleged power of myrtle to dispel wine-fumes (the myrtle in the tale bringing the redeem-ing sunlight to ease the vomiters on the ship). It stresses the salva-tionist powers of the wreath and links them with the love-goddess. Incidentally, note the part played by the private party of rejoicing in the temple.[13]

Athenaios states that the Naukratite wreath in his view was simply one of myrtle, though others consider it to be of marjoram —"a flower which, it is true, abounds in Egypt". He adds that "the myrtle of Egypt is specially distinguished for its fragrance compared with that of other countries, as Theophrastos records". He rejects the view that the wreath was made of the flowering tops of papyrus. "Myself, I don't know what profit or pleasure is found in wreathing oneself in papyrus with roses, except that people who like that sort of thing would join garlic and roses to make a wreath." It seems from his account that no one in his days was at all sure what the Naukratite wreath had been like. Myrtle, linked with Aphrodite, was indeed a good material for decora-tion: with its starry flowers, the clusters of stamens creamy-yellow enough to contrast with the white petals, and the whole plant richly aromatic. Aphrodite, according to astrologers, pre-sided over wreath-makers, of whom there were large numbers in Alexandreia, making wreaths for both religious and secular purposes.[14]

The ever-flowering wreaths of Egypt come up in the myth about Seth-Typhon we glanced at earlier.[15] Hellanikos sets the acacias with the perpetual flower-wreaths at Tindion. Demetrios in his book on Egypt sets them near Abydos. "The region below has a sort of acacia, a tree with globose fruits on small circling stems. It blooms in spring and the flower is of a beautiful brilliant colour. The Egyptians tell a story that after the Ethiopians, sent to Troy by Tithonos, heard of the death of Memnon, they put their wreaths on the acacia-trees in this region; for the stems on which the flowers grow resemble wreaths." Hellanikos adds a story:

Amasis was an ordinary man of humble rank in the earlier part of his career; but he came to be ruler of Egypt through the gift of a wreath he sent, after twining it with the most beautiful flowers of the season, in observance of the birthday of Patarmis, then ruling Egypt. The latter, delighted at the wreath's beauty, invited Amasis to dinner and there-after treated him as one of his friends. Once he sent him out as army commander when the Egyptians rose in revolt against him; and they, in their hatred of Patarmis, proclaimed Amasis king.[16]

Amasis (570–526 B.C.) seems in fact to have come to power at the head of a native Libyan rising against Apries and his Greek mercenaries—though, once on the throne, he became even more philhellene than Apries. Six months after his death Egypt fell to the Persian Cambyses.

Closely associated with the use of flowers as wreaths and festival decorations was the use of scents, in which the essential life of the flower was felt to be concentrated. Greek authors speak of Egyptian perfumes as a special type. "Go at once and pour perfume for them all, Egyptian and orris. After that I'll bring a wreath for each who's banqueting," writes the comedian Platon.[17] Achaios, a tragedian, writes in *The Games* of Egyptian scents:

On his hand an honour worth its weight in silver
they'll bestow: Egyptian scents and Cyprian gems.

Didymos, commenting, says, "Perhaps he means what is called *stakte*, because the myrrh imported into Greece is brought down first into Egypt." Hikesios in *On Materials* says:

Some perfumes are rubbed on, others are poured on. Rose perfume is suited for a drinking-party, also myrrh and quince; the last is whole-some and good for patients suffering from lethargic fever. Scent from dropwort is wholesome and keeps the brain clear. Scents of marjoram and tufted thyme are suited for a drinking-party, and also saffron crocus if not mixed with too much myrrh. Gilliflower scent is fragrant and very helpful to digestion.

Antiphanes in *Thorikan Villagers, or Digging Through* writes:

—She's really bathing? well then, what?
—Yes, she's got a box inlaid with gold and from it
she anoints her feet and legs with Egyptian scent,
her cheeks and nipples with palmoil, one of her arms
with bergamot-mint, her eyebrows and her hair
with sweet-marjoram, her knee and neck
with scent of tufted thyme.[18]

Anaxandrides in his *Protesilaos:*

Scent from Peron's shop: some of it sold
yesterday to Melanopos, costly stuff,
Egyptian—used on Kallistratos' feet.

Euboulos in *Wreathsellers* writes: "Thrice was she bathed in Egyptian psagdan". Strattis in *Medeia:*

Say that you bring her scent, such scent
as Megallos never concocted yet
or Deinias of Egypt
never saw or got.[19]

Athenaios says "of henna the Egyptian is judged best, next to it is the Cyprian and the Phoinikian, especially the kind from Sidon. The Panathenaic, as it's called, is made in Athens; the Metopion and the Mendesian are made best in Egypt—the former from oil extracted from bitter almonds. Apollonios adds however that the scent's excellence derives in each case from the excellence of those who supply the materials, the material itself, and the manufacturers, rather than to the localities. For example, Ephesos, he says, in earlier times excelled in perfumes, particularly in *megalleion*, but does so no longer. Again, perfumes of Alexandreia used to be superior because of the city's wealth and the interest taken in them by Arsinoe and Berenike. And in Cyrene too the oil of roses was the best in the lifetime of Berenike the Great."[20] It follows that the Alexandrian industries had declined by Athenaios' own days. Under the Ptolemies we hear of an official set over the industry of perfumes and unguents, a superintendent of aromatics and metals.[21]

In astrology, toilets were under Aphrodite, who dispensed cosmetics and scents. When she is in the third place, there occur "activities concerned with pigments and aromatics, vine and flowers".[22] (In the love-songs of the XVIII Dynasty, an important motive derives from the sense of smell, with the theme of the Perfumes of Punt, the land where the migratory birds gather and whence come the odoriferous gum-resins used as incense. Scents have something of a paradisiac quality, coming from magical lands.[23]) Ptolemaios in his *Tetrabiblos* links scentmakers, dyers, persons dealing with wine, poisoners, and athletes:

If Aphrodite rules action, she makes her subjects those whose activities lie among the perfumes of flowers and of unguents, in wine, colours, dyes, spices, or adornments, as for example sellers of unguents, weavers of wreaths, innkeepers, wine-merchants, druggists, weavers, spice-dealers, painters (*zographoi*), dyers, sellers of clothing.

And if Kronos testifies to her, she makes them dealers in goods for pleasure or adornment, sorcerers, poisoners, panders, and those who make their livings from similar occupations.

If Zeus testifies, they will be athletes, wreath-wearers, persons accounted worthy of honours, and men who gain advancement from women.[24]

Of the traditional cosmetics of Egypt, the main eye-paints were malachite and galena, which may have come from Arabia via Punt, while red ochre seems used on the face. Oils and fats provided the chief cosmetics and were needed in a dry hot climate. The oils were doubtless numerous, for example castor-oil was used by the poor; it grew wild and is still so used in Nubia. The solid fats were animal. Distillation is mentioned by Aristotle and Plinius, but its mechanisms were still crude. After alchohol the next medium for absorbing and retaining odours is fat or oil; petals are set in layers of solid fat or soaked in oil, the scent being later removed by means of alcohol. But this method was not possible till the discovery of the process of separating alcohol by distillation from fluids—though a partial application could be made without alcohol, since the impregnated fat or oil would remain scented after the exhausted petals were removed. Theophrastos knew this method for scenting oil. For oil the Egyptian or Syrian *balanos* was mostly used, though olive and almond oil sometimes took its place.[26] Plants were steeped in oil, then pressed, or else boiled in oil.[27]

Theophrastos says that one Egyptian unguent was made from several ingredients, including cinnamon and myrrh; a second, from quince.[28] Plinius says the country was suited above all others for the production of unguents, and that at one time the unguent most esteemed in the Roman world came from Mendes: a complex product, consisting originally of the oil of ben (*balanos*), resin and myrrh, then later adding the oil of bitter almonds, olive oil, cardamoms, sweet rush, honey, wine, myrrh, seed of balsamum, galbanum, and turpentine resin. He states also that the ben nut (*myrobalanum*), which grew in the land of the Troglodytai, in the Thebaid, and in Ethiopia, supplied an oil especially suited for unguents.[29] Egyptian *elate* or *pathe* and the fruit of a palm *adipos* were also used for unguents, as well as *cyprinum* (which Plinius calls Egyptian and which was probably henna with odoriferous leaves).[30] Henna was probably used by the ancient Egyptians as a paste to colour the palms of the hands, the soles of the feet, nails and hair; the Romans used it on hair if not on other parts of the body.[31] There is some evidence further for the use of gum-resins and resins to scent oil and fats.[32]

Perfumed wine was drunk. A 2nd-century letter from Chairemon to Diogenes, for instance, discusses a vineyard, its *mechane*, irrigation, manuring, and perfumed wine.[33]

Perfumers were generally also druggists or herbalists knowing the marvellous virtues of plants. The idea that scents were the products of a paradisiac world appears in a Coptic version of the *Physiologus*, the bestiary that had such a medieval vogue and was born in Alexandreia. "A thirsty eagle goes to Paradise, fills his wings with perfumes and carries them to Aaron; and Aaron takes from the eagle the perfumes that he took from Paradise." The Coptic version seems from the Fayum.[34] The art of scents and flowers shades off into that of medicine and magic. (We have seen how the making of wreaths was entangled with considerations

K

of the physical and emotional effects.) The men who knew the virtues of plants also knew the sympathies or correspondences between the universe as a whole and plants, between plants and man.[35] Thessalos tells us, "Asklepios [Thoth] reveals that the curative herbs of Egypt, Arabia, and Syria, on account of the effects of heat upon them, become *endynamoi* and *drastikoterai*"—filled with a new energy and active power. Thus, scents, curative herbs, dyes were all seen as enclosing or expressing great transformative powers, which in the last resort were linked with the powers that alchemy sought to understand and control.

In Heliodoros' romance, Theagenes is wounded and captured by brigands, but is healed quickly by herbs:

"Tell me, how are you?"

"Easier and better since this evening," he replied, "thanks to this lad's care, which has relieved my wounds' inflammation."

"You'll gain even greater relief," said the person in charge of the prisoners, "by the morning. I'll supply you with the kind of herb that in two days will close up those gashes. I've tested its effect by use. Ever since these people brought me here as a prisoner myself, if any of the chief's followers come in wounded from an affray, their cure takes only a few days' treatment with the herb I mention."[36]

Fumigations, *thymiamata*, played a considerable part in the rites of Graeco-Egyptian magic. Some botanists, whom Galen rebuked for being more magicians than scientists, recommended the practice, which Galen regarded as Egyptian.[37] On the other hand the astrologers Harpokration and Thessalos reproach Nechepso for neglecting astrologic doctrine in his book on botany.[38]

The great recipe of the Paris Papyrus describes a key-rite. The practitioner, after purifying himself with nitre, censes the plant with pine-resin, while going thrice round it with the censer. (The cathartic circumambulations are linked with purifications.) The man then begins censing with kyphi, which we considered in relation to Isis. These actions all take place, it seems, while an invocation, *epiklesis*, is being recited: "I purify you with resin, you like the gods, and I do it to ensure my salvation (safety, well-being). Be perfected also by my prayer . . ."[39]

A similar rite was used in gathering the peony, according to two smaller works that treat of this plant. Here too are fumigation, circumambulation, and censing; but some so-called precious stones are also used. In the Chaldean Rite described by Psellos, stones and aromatics again occur; and a treatise on planetary herbs advises that each plant should be censed with the perfumes appropriate to its planet.[40]

The fumigation seems certainly to have primarily a kathartic value.[41] The peony amassed round it a great deal of magical lore. We are told that its gathering needed a consecrated sealskin, which was attached to the bared root. Kyranides states that a sealskin protected against brigands, maladies, witchcraft, attacks of demons or lightning; it had a corresponding virtue in curing.[42] With its power intensified by consecration, it imparted new virtues to the plant.[43]

The incantation had a high place in Graeco-Egyptian magic. As we noted, Galen rebuked Pamphilos, Xenokrates, Andreas for recommending its use in the gathering of simples.[44] In the magical papyrus of Paris we find two recipes for *botanearsis;* one is described as belonging to the Egyptians and it contains rites and prayers specifically Egyptian, though with Greek elements. Perhaps one or other of the recipes has come from a collection ascribed to Nechepso, a name that authors of magic writings liked to use. An invocation from the Paris Papyrus runs:

You have been sown by Kronos, gathered by Hera, preserved by Ammon, borne by Isis, nourished by rainy Zeus. You have grown, thanks to the Sun and the Dew. You are the Dew of all the Gods, the Heart of Hermes, the Seed of the First Gods, the Eye of the Sun, the Light of the Moon, the Dignity of Osiris, that which makes joyful in all places, the Breath of Ammon. As you raised Osiris, raise yourself. Come up like the Sun. Your Grandeur equals the Zenith, your Roots are as deep as the Abyss, your Virtues are in the Heart of Hermes, your Roots are in the Mouth of Mnevis, your Flowers the Eye of Horos, your Grains the Seed of Pan.

I purify you with resin like the Gods to ensure my safety. Be purified also by my prayer and give us strength like Ares and Athena. I am Hermes. I take you with Good Fortune, the Good Daimon, and at the favourable hour, on the day suitable and favourable for all.[45]

The invocation is more like a litany than a prayer. The herb-gatherer has already made a prayer to the daimon to whom the plant is consecrated; he now identifies himself with a deity and takes possession of the plant as in a magical rite. In the other recipe of the Papyrus there is nothing about a daimon and the gatherer makes his conjuration of the plant together with threats that are to constrain its will. (This idea of using magical forces of constraint was deeply ingrained in the Egyptians, who often turn it towards the gods themselves.) Thus in the *botanearsis* of the Papyrus we find the menace:

I take you up with my fivefingered hand. I (such a one), I carry you off with me so that you may be efficacious in any use whatever. I conjure you by the unpolluted name of God. If you disobey me, the earth that has borne you will moisten you no longer if I don't succeed in carrying out my project.

Then comes a series of magical words, which are endowed with some sort of autonomous or personal force: for the spellbinder ends, "Bring to a good end my perfect *epaoide*" (*epoide*, incantation, charm).[46]

It is characteristic that magical herbs seem always to be gathered in a wild state; a botanist or magician does not grow them in a garden. No doubt their virtue is felt to derive at least in part from their being in a state of pure nature, as if they are relics of a golden age or original divine-garden in a world that man has polluted. The herb remains something that has to be won over, tamed, controlled, so that its powers may be made amenable to human needs. This attitude appears in the incantations cited above. It appears even more strongly in the treatment of certain herbs that are considered very dangerous or difficult to lay hands on. Josephos tells of the plant *baaras* that grows east of the Dead Sea; it shines at night and evades capture, changing its position; the only way to stop it is to sprinkle it with the urine of a woman or menstruating blood.[47] (Perhaps here the paradoxographer is parodying an actual botanical rite.) Such herbs as the *baaras* were thought to have a great apotropaic power, which is indeed demonic; the herbalist had to neutralise the influence by that of a root of the same plant hung at his wrist or by turning its fluid on to an animal.[48]

Dangerous plants were the madragora, the *aglaophotis* or *kynospastos*. The latter hides by day, shines at night like a flame or a star. A hungry dog is tied to it, then is tempted by some food; it wrenches the plant out but dies as soon as the sun has beheld the root. It is buried on the spot with magical rites. Ailian rationalises this by saying that one gives the corpse deserved honours as the dog has died in place of a man. The plant is sympathetic to the moon, antipathetic to the sun, and so cures maladies due to moon-influences, such as epilepsy. From other texts we learn that the *aglaophotis* is the same as the peony, the root of which is used to repulse demons and especially to cure epilepsy.[49] In the treatise on planetary herbs ascribed to Hermes Trismegistos it is the plant consecrated to the moon. Three manuscripts (Vatican, Boulogne, Paris) state that the rite of peony-gathering, which lasts eight days, should start and end in daylight and at the hour of the moon. The *Carmen de Herbis* also knows the peony as the *kynospastos*; it declares that unless the plant is uprooted before sunrise the herbalist will go out of his mind.[50] Plinius knows the *kynokephale* (dog-headed) and says that he who uproots this plant, as also the Tomb-of-Osiris, will immediately die. Ailian mentions two plants that have to be pulled up by a bird attached on a string.[51]

Many of these sorts of beliefs were in late antiquity taken up by mandragora, a magic plant with an increasingly-stressed infernal character.[52] It had in its roots a human form (hence its names *anthropomorphos* and *semihomo*); it shone at night, fled and had to be halted by a surrounding trench; it had to be pulled out by a fasting dog, which then died. Another method, of tying it to a bentdown plant which straightened up, was used to avoid the death. (Both the methods of dog and of plant bent towards the sun were in use in Italy in the 19th century.) Another version of its dangerous power was that its shriek when torn up killed or drove mad; or that its uprooting unloosed an elemental storm as if the whole balance of nature were upset.[53]

14

Trees and Market Gardens

THOUGH Egypt was not a land of trees, it did not lack its wooded nooks and strips. Heliodoros gives us a pleasant picture of the banks of the Nile. "The Nile there had an embankment in the form of a promontory, where the river's flow was broken off its direct course, and, after being diverted in a semicircular detour, turned about to take a course opposite to that it held at the diversion, thus making out of the enclosed land a sort of earth-gulf on the mainland. This tract, surrounded by waters, produced rich meadowlands. Of its own accord it brought forth grass in plenty, providing an inexhaustible supply of fodder for flocks and herds, while overhead it was shaded by Persian trees, syca-mores and other leafy species that flourish by the Nile."[1] We meet here a touch of the earthly paradise in the inexhaustible self-produced nature of the meadowgrass: *nome apautomatizon*. We have already noted the importance of this sort of diction and concept for Nonnos, and shall later have more to say of it.

An account of Egypt in 1873 shows much the same sort of trees as characteristic of the Nilotic scene. "The tree usually em-ployed in forming avenues, where shade is the first object, is the broad-podded acacia. The distinguishing feature of this is the largeness and abundance of its singularly dark green leaves. Its foliage, indeed, is so dense that no ray of sunlight can penetrate through it. The effect is very striking. In one of these avenues, that has been well kept, you will find yourself in a cool gloom, both the coolness, and the gloom, being such that you cannot but feel them, while you see the sun blazing outside." It grows easily. "All that is required is to cut off a limb, no matter how large, or from how old a tree, and to set it in the ground. If it be supplied with water, it grows without fail. This acacia is the *lebekh* of the natives. Another tree used in avenues, and which grows to a greater height and with larger limbs than the *lebekh*, is the Egyptian sycamore. It is a species of the Indian fig. The largeness of its limbs enables you to see the whole of its skeleton. The skeleton of the *lebekh* is concealed by the multiplicity of its branches and the density of its foliage." They seem the oldest trees of Egypt. "The bark is of a whitish colour, and their large branches are covered with little leafless spurlike twigs, of a dingy black, on which are produced their round green fruit, about as big as bantams' eggs." The tamarisk grows as a stunted shrub in the nitre-encrusted depressions of the desert round about Ismailia and elsewhere; where it gets a little moisture, it becomes a graceful tree.

Egyptian Landscape (Pompeian wall-painting).

The small-leaved thorny acacia, the *acanthos* of Herodotos, has a small yellow flower, a complete globe, with a sweet scent, but gives scanty shade. All these trees, together with the palm, remain in full foliage throughout the Egyptian winter.[2]

Groves or gardens of palms are mentioned fairly frequently in the papyri. At Tebtynis in A.D. 47 two arourai of datepalms were leased for 210 dr. a year; other undefined areas were leased for 285 and 440 dr. Ten years later in the Fayum a palmgrove was leased for a year at 44 dr., 1 artaba of dates and other payments in kind. In 89 at Philadelpheia a grove was subleased for a year at 60 dr. and 1 artaba of choice pressed dates. In the next century, in 119, again at Philadelpheia, 1¼ ar. of corn land with palms was let for 4 years at 120 dr. a year. In 126–8 some inhabitants of Soknopaiou Nesos made a proposal for renting palmlands for the unusually long term of 7 years, at Psenuris. In 139 (or 149) at

Hermopolis was drawn up the lease cited earlier for its reference to a wine-press festival. In 145 at Theadelpheia the lessee as part of the rental agreed to build a wall round $\frac{7}{8}$ of a palmgrove. In 168 at Philadelpheia an olive grove with palms was leased for three years at 160 dr. a year, plus an artaba each of olives and dates; a lease of the next year has exactly the same terms. In 167–92 we find an offer addressed to overseers of ousiac leases for date-palms on an imperial estate for a year at 300 dr., with some extras; the overseers are to pay all public charges. (The *ousiai* were great estates, corresponding to the Ptolemaic giftlands; they had been acquired in the early empire by members of the imperial family and a few Roman and Alexandrian nobles; they were absorbed into the emperor's patrimonium or private estate and were defined as a special class of land controlled by a procurator.) During the 2nd century in the Fayum we meet the rental of a palmgrove and cornland at 23 dr., $\frac{1}{2}$ art. of bread, something valued at 10 dr., and a number of palm-fibre baskets; the lease is free of public transport and *epibole*, the levy that seems to have replaced the poll-tax and other assessments in the 3rd century. We also have an official survey of the leases of date-palms and olivegroves.

For the early 3rd century there is a Philadelpheia lease of 5 ar. of palmgrove and 1 ar. of (?) for 4 years at 100 dr. for the first year and 200 dr. after that: presumably there were some difficulties about getting the place into full working order. At Hephaistias in 208:

To Flavia Petronilla also called Titanias with her guardian, her husband Gaius Valerius Pansa, ex-gymnasiarch, from . . . , and Herieus his brother. We desire to lease from you the palmgarden called that of Herennius belonging to you in the area of the village of Hephaistias, at a total rental of 1000 silver dr. and as special items 2 art. of dates on single stems measured by the dromos date-measure of the village and 12 . . . I will pay the rent at the time of the gathering without delay. I the lessee shall be responsible for all acts of cultivation: the gathering, fertilisation, irrigation, circumvallation, a third share of embanking the canals, and a half share of cleaning them: and I will pay 2 art. of . . .

[Signed] I, Gaius Valerius Pansa, have made the lease as above, and as long as there is no higher offer the aforesaid lease shall continue secured to you.

Six years later in the same Arsinoite nome a palmgrove and cornland were let for a year, the grove for 60 dr., 3 art. of dates and 2 art. of (?), the cornland for 10(?) dr., the lessor paying all taxes. About 230, at a place the name of which is lost, a grove brought in 160 dr., 1½ art. of dates on single stalks, 2 palmbrooms, and 5 baskets in a year. In 261 at Dionysias, 7 ar. of olives and palms were let for 3 years, the lessor providing all labour on the olive-trees and getting a third of the produce, and paying 100 dr., 3 art. of choice dates, and ½ art. of Syrian dates yearly; the owner paying all taxes. At Philadelpheia in 267, another area of 7 ar. of olives and palms brought in yearly a rental of 1700 dr., plus 1 art. of dates, ½ art. of black olives, 10 baskets, 4 brooms.[3] Here we see inflation setting strongly in. It is however hard to specify what the rents for palmgroves were over the centuries; for almost always they are lumped in with other kinds of land and much of the payment is in kind. At Tebtynis in 47, however, we find 105 dr. being paid per acre.

For the later periods we may take an application dated 353:

To Aurelios Herakleides son of Herakleides, ex-gymnasiarch, ex-prytanis, senator of the Illustrious and Most Illustrious City of Oxyrhynchos, from Aur. Kastor, son of Patermouthios, of the said City.

I voluntarily undertake to lease for the present 47th, 29th, 2nd year only, from the produce of the 12th Indiction, the date-crop of your two estates, the northern and southern ring, on condition I gather the crop and transport it to my own property in the right manner, and shall pay as the fixed rent of the whole of the said date-crop 8000 talants of silver, secured against every kind of risk. If this lease is guaranteed to me, I will deliver up the rent in three instalments in all, paying for the period from Mesore to Hathyr(?) 2663 talants 2000 dr. . . . [4]

Here we see a purely cash transaction. The Oxyrhynchite senator seems to have no interest in payments in kind.

In Roman as in much later times the palmgroves by the river might fitly be described as the most graceful objects in the

K*

landscape—"rising above the dense foliage of fruit-trees in the gardens or growing in twos and threes in front of a countryhouse or farm like natural pillars. But the palms depend on the atmosphere in a very great measure for their beauty." On a dull day the palm looks dull, grey and sombre as the clouds above. But Egypt has few dull days, and the palm generally varies with the quality of the atmosphere, which changes throughout the day, so that the leaves show a subtle series of merged brilliance and softness: turning deep purple in the calm evening, then a golden green, a bluish tint, then a rose in the setting sun.[5]

Philon speaks of the almond as "the first to flourish of all spring blossoming trees, bringing as it were good tidings of abundance of fruit, and then the last to lose its leaves". He also knows the practice of grafting to improve wild trees. "Those trees of good sorts, making many shoots, he propagates by extending the earth in rather shallow ditches, and those that do not produce good fruit, he tries to improve by the insertion of other kinds of trees into their roots, connecting them by the most natural union."[6]

Market-gardening stands as a link between the pleasure-garden and the festival or party with its wreaths and scattered flowers, and the feast or banquet at which food was served. Flowers, as we have seen, were widely grown for the market and the workshops. The market gardens that grew up round Rome and other large Italian towns were based to a considerable extent on those of Ptolemaic and Roman Egypt: the *paradeisoi* named in the *Nomoi Telonikoi* or Tax Regulations.[7] They seem originally developed on the lands held in fief, *doreai*, and had the treatises, the *kepourika*, which dealt with productive gardens and orchards.[8] Such gardens keep turning up in the papyri. Here is a letter from Horion of the mid-3rd century:

. . . putting off everything, take Kastor with you and certainly get it made at once so that the watering of Sentrepaiou's garden isn't neglected, and stay there with the men. Get 20 dr. from my mother on account and if you're again in need let me know, as the animals keep on going up. If any neglect occurs it'll be you not me to blame. By all means send the receipt . . . Serenos has often cheated us . . . Let

Kastor go expressly to him at Philagris and ask for the 8½ artabai of wheat. Goodbye. Tybi 5. Look everywhere for a little donkey for him.

Horion is often mentioned in the letters of Heronimos as the *phrontistes* or steward of Dionysias, Euhemeria, and Sentrepaiou. Serenos may be the caretaker Serenos whom in another papyrus we find located not far from the phrontis of Hieroninos.[9]

A register of garden lands was kept. We have some columns of a register of the 2nd century A.D. dealing with the Thebaid and illustrating the tax-system in Upper Egypt. The main tax, paid to the administration or the hieratic department, seems the *geometria*, with a supplement of 6¼ per cent. As in Lower Egypt the tax could be paid in instalments, and in some cases the full tax was paid on some part of the whole area. The wine tax was uniformly 8 dr. per aroura without any supplement, and it was not levied on vineyards in the hieratic department. Many holdings were small, and as usual with private property many owners were women. At times land was held in shares, doubtless revealing an undivided inheritance. The estates include vineyards, palmgroves, nut-plantations, balsam-gardens, pigeon-cotes.[10] A Gnomon of taxes on garden lands in the Arsinoite nome, also of the 2nd century, deals with an olive grove, a vineyard, a *paradeisos* of 1½ arourai, and so on. No mention is made here of *geometria*, no doubt because the tax was not collected annually; the wine tax (libation to Dionysos) was 8 dr. as in Upper Egypt, but in the Fayum was exacted, it seems, from each owner or tenant of vineyards without any concern as to the size of his holding, while in Upper Egypt the tax was 8 dr. per aroura without supplementary fee.[11] Various other taxes appear, into which we need not go; for they involve many small intricate problems. Enough to point out the thorough and extensive nature of the exactions to which the cultivator was subjected and which grew increasingly difficult to meet as the economic condition worsened.[12] The tax situation was complicated by the variety of things grown, which included vegetables. A paradise at times held olives as well as fruit trees. The Fayum area where reeds were grown for vine supports was rated as garden land. Doubtless taxes were imposed on any tree that brought money in—gum-acacia, apple, peach, fig, cottontree, and so on—though we do not know the rate.

We may take some representative documents. At Philadelpheia in the 1st century A.D., three men rented the cucumber garden belonging in part to a soldier, Numerius Crispus, near the city, paying 12 dr. yearly for his share. (Doubtless they also signed contracts with the others who owned shares in the garden.[13]) In A.D. 78 two men of Hermopolis applied to the exegetes there for a lease of 5 years of what is apparently garden land belonging to the orphan sons of Sarapion son of Kastor, of Kousai, at a yearly rent of 600 silver dr., excluding the tax of an artaba on each aroura and the naubion-tax (concerned with canal-clearances); the rent is to be paid in Phaophi to whomever the exegetes appoints. "If any part of the land becomes unwatered or is carried away by the river or covered by sand or worn away, from the coming 11th year on, a proportionate allowance shall be made to us from the aforesaid rent." The lease was to be published for ten days to allow for higher bids to be put in. (The tax of an artaba per aroura suggests cornland, but the payment in Phaophi, late September into late October, implies vine culture.) The application was to the exegetes because orphans were wards of the State.[14]

An Oxyrhynchite lease of A.D. 141 deals with land perhaps taken over for nine years; it mentions garden land, vineyard, reed-bed on the south and willowgrove (where the clipping belongs to Primion the owner). The lessee is to have the use of the water-wheel and attached machinery, water-channels and pipes, the watchtower and barnyard. The yearly rental is to consist of

2100 silver dr., plus 450(?) jars of new wine [to be paid in yearly instalments of 50 jars a year?] or else 2500 silver drachmai . . . , the lessor having the option and choice of accepting the highest sum or else taking the 50 jars of wine yearly.

[The lessor shall also receive] 75 bundles of clippings from the vineyard, 300 bundles of choice grapes, the produce of whichever palm-tree Primion may choose, . . . 1 artaba of dried pressed dates, 400 jars of wine, 5 jars of olives, 20 gourds, 40 cucumbers, 2 bunches of vegetables daily of the lachanon raised in season, 20 pomegranates, ¼ art. and 2 choinikes of dried sebesten, free of all risk. Primion shall pay all public charges in money and in kind for the aforesaid property, and he shall also have the right of ownership over the yearly produce till he receives the rental as specified.

If there is need of a new machine, axle, hide and (apparently) mill-stone and tools, Primion is to replace them and take the old ones;

Nilotic Scene with Pygmies (mosaic, Aventine).

all other replacements are in the lessee's hands. The latter, as well as having the use of the irrigation machine for the holding, can use it for any plots he has leased from others, and he may further sell water to anyone he likes. He can also each year throw over the holding as much earth as he likes from the canal on the eastern boundary where the willow-grove lies. In the last year of his lease he is to spend 700 silver dr. over and above his rental at his

own expense for buying fertiliser and fertilising the holding—
which work is to be done under Primion's instructions. He is to
carry out yearly all the oversight, care, and other duties proper
for a vineyard, each in its correct season, without neglecting the
necesary irrigation, for which he is to pay; in the last year of the
lease he is to do a second pruning under Primion's supervision;
but the latter is to pay for any tree-pruner required as well as for
the vintage, the lessee paying a yearly rental of one jar of white
wine . . . Rent is to be paid in Hathyr. If the lessee falls in arrears,
he is liable for half as much again. He is to carry out the work
on the dykes. At the lease's end he is to hand back the holding in
good condition, something [word lost] plastered with a second
coat of plaster, the waterwheel, watchtower, barnyard-walls,
and trees in good condition; and he may not abandon his lease
within the term . . . "Primion shall have the right of exaction from
the lessee and from all his property as if a legal decision had been
given." Fragments indicate that a clause dealt with the right to
sublet.[15]

In A.D. 168 at Philadelpheia three men (one of whom has
only a mother, Nemesilla, named) leased an olive-grove called
Pkmenthiai, south of the city, from a woman Valeria, daughter
of Gaius, through her agent Provinciarius. The rental was 160
dr. in silver, 1 art. of choice selected black olives, and 1 art. of
dates on a single stalk in the 8-choinix measure, "without deduction or risk". The rent in money is to be paid in the month
Hadrian and the rent in kind at harvest-time.[16]

In a year that seems A.D. 222 some land was leased in the Little
Oasis and a confused situation came about. The rental was paid in
money (which suggests garden land); the reference to seeding
could apply to vegetable plots as much as to cornfields.

. . . [When] I leased from Ptolemaios, also called Astoparison, and
from Ammonios, also called Heraklios, from the land on the Oasis
which is owned by Claudia Isidora, [so many] arourai, which they
have on lease from her, carrying out the sowing of the said land for
the present year and providing the local cultivators with both seed
and expenses, then through envy of my proceedings Hermogenes, son of
Petenephotes, and Isidoros, son of . . . , whom I benevolently [aided]

in the management of the business and provided with necessaries, offered in the bid they presented to pay 200 dr. yearly more—one of them, Isidoros, using a false name, . . . genes.

I welcomed this bid of theirs; and as I wanted neither to suffer nor to cause trouble, I claimed to recover from them the loan they'd got from me, and other expenses, being subjected as regards them to a reckoning of accounts between us and certain honourable persons as the result of a confrontation before the strategos of the nome: the sum in question being 3 talants 400 dr.

But as they paid no attention to me and even failed to appear before the court, . . . I offer against their bid to pay 1552 dr. a year more: making the total yearly rent 1 tal. 3000 dr., the stipulations laid down in their said bid being preserved as regards the . . . and period stated in their bid and all its provisions.

I, Aurelios Sarapodoros, am surety for the aforesaid Heron in respect of both the payment of rent and care of operations, and in answer to the formal question we gave our consent. This offer of lease is valid.[17]

The general bearing of Heron's complaint is clear; but the details are obscure. Ptolemaios and Ammonios may have been the primary lessees, as has been suggested, or they may have been Claudia's agents in the area or the overseers of the leasing of part of her land that had been confiscated. Heron bid for the land and seems to have gone to work without a formal lease; probably he had discussed the matter with Ptolemaios and Ammonios and thought that things were settled. If he had got a lease, it is hard to see how his rivals managed to intrude. When they did try to drive him out, he replied, not with a claim about his rights in the land in question, but with a lawsuit raising quite different points of dispute. As these tactics failed to get rid of them, he came in with an attempt to beat them with their own trick, making a yet higher bid. The provision of a surety is of interest, since it has no parallel in other private leases. It could then be used as an argument that the lease here is not in fact a private one or that Claudia is applying on her lands the practices of the imperial estates. If the latter suggestion is valid, we see that already in the earlier 3rd century there is the emergence of landlords seeking to build up large estates with methods borrowed from the imperial system.[17] The honourable persons, *andres axiologoi*, were certainly *logothetai*, assessors, appointed by the strategos to investigate disputed points in an action at law.[18]

In A.D. 239 we meet another lady-landowner:

To Aurelia Demetria, matron with stole, daughter of Aurelios Poseidonios, hypomnematographos, through Aurelios Marinos, ex-gymnasiarch, senator of the city of Arsinoe, from Aurelios Ploutammon, whose mother is Helene, lodging in the village of Euhemeria.

I wish to lease for a term of 3 years, from the present month Mecheir in the 2nd year, near the village of Euhemeria, a vegetable garden of 1 ar., or whatever area it may have, in which is a cistern and water-wheel, at a total rental of 100 silver dr. yearly, subject to no deductions or risks.

It shall not be permitted for me to [abandon the lease] within the term in any way, and I shall carry out all the necessary labour at the proper seasons without doing any harm. For irrigating the land I have taken over from the noble lady a cow valued at 100 dr. Whatever is needed for new equipment, supplies of timber, nails, stone, pitch, carpenter's wages, transport, waterwheel, yokes, and all state-charges, shall be borne by her ladyship, while I, the lessee, shall carry out the work on the dykes and . . . , and after my term is completed I shall return the garden under all kinds of vegetables as I took it over, if it is agreed to lease it.[19]

Again in the earlier 3rd century we find the whole stress on a cash transaction. In the previous leases the landlord tends to be himself implicated in agricultural production, to be living close to the land and its processes, and to mingle rents in cash and rents in kind. Land in *lachanon* (vegetables) used to be leased for 3 to $3\frac{1}{2}$ art. of seed per aroura; now the practice seems to convert this into a money-payment. A vineyard lease of 252 brings out the intrusion of rich Alexandrians into the new forms of exploitation with their more purely financial interests.

To Aurelios Papeis, son of Thithois, from the village of Kerkesoucha in the division of Herakleides, from Aurelios Soulis, son of Herakleides, from the village of Theadelpheia.

I wish to lease $2\frac{1}{2}$ ar. of wooded vineyard, or as many as there are, in the vineyard named the Newly-Planted, which you happen to hold in lease from Aurelios Apollonides, ex-kosmetes, eutheniarch, and senator of the Most Brilliant City of Alexandreia.

I shall give three hoeings for half the fruits, and Papeeis shall yearly provide 5000 reeds and 5 bundles of cordage. Both of us shall share in the provision of *sebakh* or manure. The lessee shall take care of the repairs to waterwheels, while Papeeis shall bear the expense of a new one. I shall set out 50 settings each year in the productive land, and I, Soulis, shall bear the cost of feeding the oxen at the season of irrigation. I shall also provide a young pig worth 20 dr. at the harvest.[20]

As the rich Alexandrian remains the overlord, the lease is in fact a sort of sublease. Papeeis and Soulis remain in a close relationship, both being concerned with productive activities, but over them both stands the distant landlord concerned only with his cash-return. Leases of the old kind naturally continued; for the new kind of landlord did not at all dominate the scene and on account of the nearing monetary crisis he did not have much chance to consolidate his positions.

As the century drew on, it was impossible to maintain the rather belated drawing of the Egyptian countryside into something like the normal monetary network that had operated elsewhere throughout the imperial period. Inflation and monetary chaos set in. In November 260 the strategos at Oxyrhynchos had to issue an order commanding the bankers to accept the imperial coins. True, this moment was one of general disorder through wide-spread revolts and the capture of the emperor Valerian by the Persians; the Blemmyes resumed their raids on the southern frontier for the first time since the early empire.[21] But there must have been a general feeling of the instability of the coinage and of prices. In 261 an honourably dismissed veteran and his servant proposed a contract with yet another lady-landlord, Aurelia Thermoutharion, also called Herais, Matron owning the Right of Three Children. They wanted to lease three olive groves of hers: 5 ar. at Epicharos, 1 ar. at Dareios, and 1 ar. at Geminis—all places lying near Dionysias village. Also the date palms at Thalaautis and in the olive groves.

The lease of all the plots shall run for a term of 3 years from the present 1st year, the rental of the palmgrove being 100 dr. yearly in silver, 3 art. of choice dates, and a half of Syrian dates; and the rental of the olive groves shall be a third of the crops for us the lessees [and two-thirds to the lessor]. We shall pay the rentals for each part in the month Hathyr. The public taxes shall fall on the owner, while all the work on the olive groves and date-palms, the dyking, irrigating, ploughing, digging, gathering of dead wood and branches, casting up embankments of canals and waterchannels [shall be carried out by the lessees] at the correct seasons without doing any damage. The lessees shall also take care of the manuring, the owner furnishing the animals.

Nilotic Scene, with buffoon pygmy fishers (plaque).

At the end of the term we shall deliver the property, after reckoning the harvest, in the same condition as we received it, free of wildgrasses and all filth, if it is agreed to lease it.[22]

Here the transaction involves more payments in kind than in cash, and both parties are productively concerned. The owner supplies animals and presumably is able to make use of the large share she gets of the olive crop. In an Oxyrhynchite contract for labour in vineyard, with the lease of a palmgrove, of 280, that is, after inflation had unmistakably arrived, the operations of tend-ing a vineyard are carefully enumerated—"the pay for all the aforesaid operations being 4500 dr. of silver, 10 art. of wheat, and 4 jars of wine at the vat".

We likewise undertake to lease for 1 year the produce of the date-palms and all the fruit-trees which are in the old vineyard, for which we will pay as a special rent 1½ art. of fresh dates, 1½ art. of pressed dates, 1½ art. of walnut-dates, ½ art. of black olives, 500 selected peaches, 15 citrons, 400 summer figs before the inundation, 500 winter figs, and 4 large white fat melons. Moreover we will, in consideration of the aforesaid wages, likewise(?) plough the adjoining fruit garden on the south of the vineyard.[23]

Here the landlord, Aurelios Serenos (Sarapion), son of Agathinos and Taposirias, of Oxyrhynchos, plays no productive part but takes a large amount of fruit, without any cash payment, for the leasing of dates and fruit-trees. He may be an individual able merely to take advantage of the new situation for a short while, or he may represent the early stages of the new kind of land-lordism that finally triumphs in the baronial estates of the Byzantine epoch.

We can thus learn a certain amount of the changing social history of Roman Egypt from the garden lands. Leases of gardens on crown land or imperial estate are not common; but there are some signs that in the 2nd century the men of finance were hoping to use such gardens in building up large properties. In a few cases they appear to have managed to gain leases of large areas. A fragmentary papyrus seems to record the bids for leases made for olive groves on imperial estates for terms of 6 years; one bid is for a sum of more than 20,000 dr. with supplementary charges; another seems to offer 3900 dr. for 4 arourai, with supplementary charges. The leases include irrigation rights. No doubt in such cases the moneyed owners sublet to smaller men. We have one such case from the Hermopolite nome, dated 120:

Petechon, son of Hareos, to Hermias, son of Sabourion, greeting. I have leased from you, according to the present deed for the current 5th year only of Hadrian Caesar the Lord, from those you hold on

lease 3 ar. from the imperial estates, being part of the holding of
Apollonios, son of Agathinos, to be sown with vegetable seed, at a
rental for each aroura, declared by survey to be available for cultivation by the inspector of the estate, of 3 art. of vegetable-seed by
oilmakers' measure.

This parcel was cultivated in the 4th year of Hadrian Caesar the
Lord by Phibion son of Tothes. I shall measure the rent in the month
Epeiph and you shall carry it all from the common threshing-floor by
halves: new, pure, unadulterated, sifted, measured by the seven-metra
measure of Athena belonging to the estate—you, Hermias, being
responsible for the rent of the estate.[24]

Unfortunately we get no clue as to the extent of the holdings of
Apollonios. Petechon pays Sabourion in kind, but how Sabourion
pays the landlord we are not told. Normally the rentals of the
lands would be in money. Something of the financial system
of payments can be made out from a Fayum document, dated
117–38. It appears that a reassignment of leases has been recently
made in the district; and from the fact that payments are made in
money, we may assume that garden lands are in question. Contractors had taken up leases and sublet the gardens to men who
took over the contracts with the provision of being themselves
responsible for the usual taxes exacted from gardens. The sub-
lessees, however, did not pay up and the state officials took action
against them instead of suing the contractors. On the face of things
it seems that they were favouring the latter, but as we lack the
leases we do not know if there were some special terms which
justified the officials. A document from Karanis shows the tenants
paying both a rent, *phoros*, and the usual garden taxes, but here it
seems the contractors met the rent while the sublessees met the
taxes.

To a letter you wrote to me and to Herodes (also called Tiberios),
royal scribe of the Division of Themistes, you added a *libellus* dealing
with deficiencies in rents and other dues which had been sent to you
by Kestos, ex-assistant in the procuratorial department, and which
included the individual list of moneys owed in the case of certain
lessees who had completed the term of their leases.

In this letter you issued instructions that for the collections in accor-

dance with the regulations there should be more vigorous inquiry
into the amount of property belonging to the defaulters from the
time they entered upon their leaseholds, both as to properties under
pledge as securities and as to property registered with us and as to
whatever . . .

I made all this clear to Herodes (also called Tiberios); and I wrote
to Dios (also called Apollonios) and to Herodes (also called Diogenes),
the keepers of the public records, that they should report the property
registered in their records by the sub-lessees whose names appeared
in the attached libellus, whether in their own names or in the names
of others to whom it was pledged, from the time they entered upon
their leases, and also if any of the property had been alienated.

Likewise I wrote to Kestos to transmit to me the individual lists of
the properties pledged as security by the lessees on taking up their
leases, with a separate list of those properties now put up for sale
[after confiscation by the State], also the conditions on which the
lease was granted, and the terms which each lessee offered when the
bids were made, with a view to sequestrating the revenues of those
indebted [to the ousiac account] . . . or the arrest of those whose
financial status is less favourable.

The keepers of the public records reported that some had no property
and that others had no more than the properties put up for sale. Kestos
transmitted a similar report about the property of those named as
sureties by the above sub-lessees and added a concise summary of the
[leases granted to the lessees] . . . [25]

We get the impressions that the number of small men—the sub-
lessees—falling into insolvency or at least the inability to meet
the taxes was quite large. We see the spread of a commercial
system of landholding, with contractors and sub-lessees, which
ran counter to the official policy of tying down the peasants in
traditional forms of farming. The number of officials concerned
with controlling the system must also have kept on increasing,
with enhanced possibilities of corrupt dealings. Not long after the
document dealing with arrears, in 148, we meet a strategos taking
up the matter of official irregularities:

File 21 in the Metropolis. Theon, strategos of the Divisions of
Themistes and Polemon in the Arsinoite Nome, greets Herakleides,
son of Herodes and grandson of Leon, in the Kilikian Quarter.

In the report presented by Ailios Nikias, auditor of the nome, on impeachments of those appointed by him over taxation—which suits were transferred by the excellent prefect Petronius Honoratus to the imperial procurator at the recent inspection of the nome—he stated that you were overseer of the lease made by Antonios Theon, which has been in default for certain periods.

I send you this order so that you may be cognizant of it and may present yourself immediately to the excellent procurator. I have subscribed to this order. Dated in the 12th year of Our Lord Antoninus Caesar. 15 Hathyr.

I, Arreios (also called Dioskouros), attendant chosen by lot, have handed over this letter.[26]

Corrupt practices continued. In a fragmentary document of 202–3 we find that an examination of land-leases had been ordered. Potamon, auditor of the Antaiopolite Nome, carried his inquiries back at least as far as 178–9, and malpractices by the royal scribes were brought to light during the periodic reassignment of leases. As the rental for the "fiscal lands both on the mainland and islands" was called *phoros*, it is likely that garden lands were in question. What the scribes seem to have done was to ignore higher bids and renew leases at the old rates, while arbitrarily increasing other leases although the tenant had bid less. They must have been bribed by some of the lessors.[27]

Imperial estates enjoyed certain immunities. An inscription, on a bronze tablet, probably came from the Fayum, dated 2nd century: "Immunity from taxation and from angary [the post] for the estate of Agrippina and Rutilia now belonging to Our Lord the Emperor." It had no doubt been set up to warn off soldiers and officials from attempting requisitions on this estate.[28] But failure by a lessee or sub-lessee to meet any obligations brought prompt confiscation and beggary. The following businesslike letter is dated 109:

Aurelios Victor to Ioulios Polydeukes, his most esteemed friend, greetings. Take care to seek out, safely guard, and report to me in full the property of Flavios Harmaiskos, former lessee of the estate of Embre (. . .) and debtor to the fisc. Farewell.[29]

The property was sequestrated till the debt was discharged.

Government overseers managed the farms or gardens, and had their own work inspected by the assistants of an independent commission that was sent out to report on the yearly harvest. The overseers, carrying out their task as a liturgy, were held responsible in some way for the amount yearly due. At Karanis in 157 we find them in a quandary—faced, according to their own account, with paying for taxes for which they were not in fact liable. Considering that the report of the inspectors would make them lose money, they presented a sharp complaint.

To Theodoros, strategos of the Heraklid Division of the Arsinoite Nome, from Ptolemaios, son of Sokrates, and Harpalos, son of Asklas, and the remaining overseers of confiscated property belonging to the administration in the village of Karanis.

A dispute has come up between us and Herakles and Herodes, aides of the inspectors of the olive-harvest in the 20th Year, about the fruits in our jurisdiction, which they have wrongfully declared contrary to their actual condition and in violation of the instructions of our most illustrious prefect Sempronius Liberalis.

These fruits, being mostly withered and untaxable on account of the prevailing scarcity of water, they have rated as taxable. As they were bribed by certain other powerful people whose harvests under our same jurisdiction were more liable to taxation, they reported them as untaxable and free from the demands against them exacted by our most illustrious prefect.

We therefore request that a copy of this indictment be given to them by one of your aides, so that they may have a written copy of it and may appear before this most sacred tribunal whenever he holds his circuit court in the nome and dispenses justice. We rest on this communication. . . [30]

We cannot test these accusations; but in the light of all the documents it seems likely that the big lessees of government lands were trying to crush the smaller men. In the efforts of moneyed landlords to extend their controls and build up their estates (mainly of scattered holdings) in the 2nd and 3rd centuries, a key-part seems played by the imperial domains and particularly by the garden lands that were doubtless the best areas for intensive cultivation and profitable production for the market.[31]

15

Gardens of Death

THE funerary garden was common in both the Greek East and
Italy. In Egypt, as elsewhere, we see it merge with the pleasure-
garden, the *paradeisos*. Often cemetery-gardens were used for
growing vegetables.[1] We have a lease of garden land at Alexandreia, dated 5 B.C., which tells how three persons, a man Hermias,
his son Hermias with Isidora his wife, took over for five years
"three tomb-gardens belonging to Diodoros on the bank by the
Canopos in the so-called Phoinix, which are completely walled
about", at a rental of 20 dr. in silver, together with the best products of the gardens in the seasons whenever they are asked for:

. . . . stalks of cabbage, 800 beet roots, . . . reeds for wicks of various
kinds, 200 stalks of . . . , 100 . . . , 50 cucumbers, 1000 palm . . . ,
300 torches (?) of . . . , 30 bundles of cooking greens, . . . bunches of
asparagus, 10 choinikes of snails, 15 bundles of . . . , 50 bunches of sweet
chives, . . . headed chives (?), 60 bunches of grapes, 2000 wild plums,
2000 figs, 5 baskets of . . . , 100 green, 50 . . . , . . . brooms of palm-
leaves, and . . . Or else they shall pay . . . for whatever they do not
hand over of the above produce in perfect condition.

Even with the gaps it is clear that the gardens were extensive and
well planted with trees and plants. The lessees received 200 dr.
in cash (in Ptolemaic silver) without interest "for planting and
caring for the cemetery-garden, in return for which they agree to
hand over to Diodoros after five years the value of the vegetable
garden in the cemetery . . ." The gardens contain a pump, shadufs,
waterwheels, cistern. At the lease's end the lessees are to hand over
the gardens, doors, and shadufs in good condition "and in addition 200 transplanted plants of the winter cherry".[2]

Such gardens must have been very remunerative. In the Gno-

mon or summary of regulations of the idiologos' department
(drawn up to help a subordinate in the Fayum) about 150–61,
the very first two heads deal with them:

In confiscated estates the fisc does not take into account the tombs.
But when the Divine Trajan learned that owners paid more attention
to tombs in order to outwit the fisc and their creditors, he allowed
them the monuments, but the gardentombs and the like he ordered
to be sold, and directing his attention only to debtors of the fisc . . . ,
he allowed their tombs to remain as they were.

 . . . only Romans may dispose of tombs declared inalienable; for

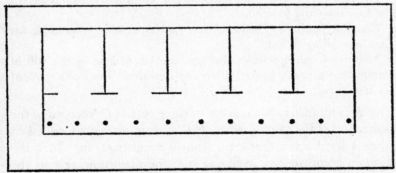

Funerary Garden and taberna of Claudius Entyches at Rome.

the Divine Hadrian enacted that in the case of Romans nothing was
inalienable.[3]

An interesting example of the sort of cases that could come up
with regard to tomb gardens is afforded by a plaque of white
marble found at Alexandreia in twenty-eight fragments. The
Greek inscription has an outlined representation of a crux ansata
and there is a hole in each corner for fixing the plaque to a wall
or the like.[4]

Pompeia Mousa dedicated the garden with a tomb for her [son]
Maximus and Marcus Antonius Theophilus her husband, and their
freedmen and freedwomen and their descendants, to be held in
common, undivided, inalienable, not-to-be-legally-burdened [by
mortgage], and not to be transmitted by will, for all time.

 Ummidius Rufus, the *karpistes*, approached Marcus Mettius Rufus the Prefect when he was passing by, and presented to him a petition, in which he argued that this garden with tomb had been illegally sold. Mettius Rufus accepted the petition and gave it to Claudius Geminus, inasmuch as he was Idios Logos, for investigation. The latter heard the plea and among other things pronounced the following judgment:

Claudius Geminus: "It is clear from everything that they sold the tomb, which is not to be legally burdened, illegally, under pretext of a lease. [They therefore] will be required to surrender what they wrongfully acquired, while the tomb shall remain the property of the bodies lying therein, not legally burdened [for all time].

Dionysios: " ... mus is the [associate] of one of [those who received] the four thousand (drachmai)."

Claudius Geminus: "If this is true, he too must be responsible for the share falling to him."

Manius Mummeius Rufus, having been left as heir by the will of Pompeius Epaphras, looked after and exploited [the tomb garden] for ten years.

This difficult inscription consists of three parts: (a) A record of the dedication of the tomb garden. (b) Clauses in dialogue form taken from a legal action before a Roman magistrate, in which the *karpistes* complains of an illegal sale; the magistrate accepts the contention and orders that the ill-gotten money be given up and the tomb garden remain the property of those buried there; someone (Dionysios) alleges that a further person is involved, and the magistrate rules that he too is liable. (c) A statement of the present occupant, who has had the documents inscribed and who says how he got the land and how long he has held it. The purpose of the plaque can only be to justify action taken in accordance with the magistrate's decision. The man who drew up the text has selected only what he thought was necessary to define the title.[5]

The parties are Alexandrian Greeks with Roman citizenship, though the rare praenomen Manius suggests a man of Italian origin. The phraseology suggests a Roman legal background, though much of the terms echo Greek formulas.[6] There is no stated restriction as to who is to be buried in the tomb, though that would be natural if the Roman institution of *sepulcrum familiare* were concerned. Over the text stands a dedication to the *Theoi Katach-thonioi*, the Gods Under the Earth: which we may take as meant to be a translation of *Dis Manibus*. Further points are that the garden, though inalienable, could be leased, and that the sum involved (4000 dr.—evidently the purchase-price) shows a substantial property.[7]

Claudius Geminus can be identified with the man who was an official of the Thebaid and whose name is found on the Colossi of Memnon. "I, Claudius Geminus, arabarch and epistrategos of the Thebaid, going upstream, heard [Memnon] at the third hour,

Altar to Isis with twined snake, Harpokarates, and Anubis (Rome).

and going down, at the second hour, and, going up yet again, I heard him on 25 Tybi at the third hour." That is, he heard the miraculous cry that the statue was believed to make as the sun came up.[8] By combining the posts of arabarch and governor of the Thebaid, he appears as farmer-general of the internal taxes of Egypt; he was probably based on Koptos, and passed by the colossi on his administrative tours.[9] Mettius Rufus was prefect in 89–81; and we may assume that Geminus had been in the Thebaid before taking up the high office of the Idiologos. That office was mainly fiscal and was especially concerned with *bona vacantia* and *bona caduca* (vacant or heirless estates) such as appear in the inscriptions.[10]

We can then understand the intervention of the *karpistes*. This term is explained in the glossators as *adsertor*, or *vindex* (one who intervenes on behalf of a defendant), or as a prisoner's friend (one who asserted the freedom of a supposed slave in a *causa liberalis*). In all the definitions the common element is that the *karpistes* is a champion or assertor of someone else's rights. If the word has such a meaning here, it means that Ummidius Rufus was defending the religious character of the *kepotaphos*.[11] But such an interpretation is hard to sustain. The connection of the man with a garden suggests *karpistes* as fruitgatherer. (Karpos means fruit.) He could be the tenant of the garden who complains that the sale has jeopardised his tenancy. (We might also recall *karpones*: which means fruitbuyer in Ptolemaic and Roman Egypt. If he were a contractor for buying the fruit, he could also complain that his rights were being threatened.) But the word may simply mean informer, a man who expects profit (fruit) from the act of delation. The relation of *karp-* to garden then becomes unlikely.[12]

But we need not here pursue further the legal intricacies. The curious mixture of piety and profit that appears in the commercially exploited tomb garden is sufficiently brought out by the points we have examined. We have already in our second chapter considered some aspects of the funerary meal with the dead. There is a direct link between the Graeco-Roman tomb garden and the garden shown on pharaonic stelai beside funerary chapels. The *kepotaphia* were the places where the family came together in a banquet in which the dead were considered to take part.[13] Strabon gives us a glimpse of the busy setting of such gardens. Outside the canal that extends to Lake Mareotis "there is still left only a small part of the city; and then one comes to the suburb Nekropolis, in which are many gardens and graves and halting-places fitted up for the embalming of corpses".[14]

At Deir el-Medineh the chapel of tomb 214 is preserved; it served as the vestibule to an important catacomb; the families of the dead inscribed there in the Roman period demotic graffiti that recall the names of the dead.[15] At Gournet-Mouraï were found two doorposts of sandstone of the Ptolemaic period, at the entry of the passage of a funerary chapel, reminding us of the *thyra* that the thieves in a document are described as leaving open.[16]

At Rome and elsewhere in Italy the funerary garden took strong root; local traditions no doubt prepared the ground, but the main idea came from the east. Many inscriptions bring before us the death-garden with its orchard, its triclinium for the meal of communion, its well for watering the trees and plants, its surrounding wall.[17] Martial writes to Faustinus:

> These neighbouring gardens and the narrow field,
> the meadows Faenius owns; and here he buried
> his daughter's ashes, making the name you read,
> Antylla, holy . . . [18]

Trimalchio in his drunken meanderings sets out the ideal of a tomb: ". . . so that your kindness may bring me a life after death.

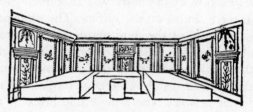

Funeral Triclinium at Pompeii.

I want the monument to have a frontage of a hundred feet and to be two hundred deep. For I'd like you to have all sorts of fruit growing round my ashes, and lots of vines. It's all wrong for a man to prink up his house while he's alive, and not bother about the house where he'll stay a good deal longer." We see the translated paradise in the stucco and painted decoration of the Columbarium of Pomponius Hylas, near the Porta Latina, dated under Tiberius; the conche of the apse and the vaulted ceilings are covered with a fine network of flowering vine-tendrils in which are symbolic figures and birds.[19]

No doubt the idea of communing with the dead in food lay behind the Egyptian tradition of having embalmed bodies at banquets.[20] Mummies were often kept for several months in the house, probably on the same beds as those used on funerary days. Such a bed has been found at Deir el-Bahari, perhaps once provided with a canopy (as a sky-emblem, making the deathbed a cosmic centre or image). The lionfeet are raised on a cavetto; on the sides are painted scenes of a winged disk, gods, the owner of the bed and his wife, plus a meaningless debased text in hieroglyphics. The man has yellow hair and fair skin; his wife, Senenteris, is dressed in Greek or Egyptian style—the tunics are late in fashion, without girdles. The bodies are shown in side-view, the faces frontally. Deir el-Bahari, we may note, was in the 3rd century a centre of nationalist attitudes.[21]

However, already in the Greek period burials were getting shallower: for example in the Memnonia. Perhaps more and more people wanted to bury their dead in holy earth. So much ground was already used, people were poorer, and scruples as to the way in which preservation of the body was attempted grew weaker. Often burials were almost on the surface. The mourners dug less deep or built a house of the dead above the ground.[22] Tombs became more vulnerable. Also they stank. The Greeks seem to have used the term *apophorai* for the pestilential emanations.[23] Further, burials became careless. People preferred to make them near the ruins of temples where the crude brick of the broken walls was abundant; and no doubt the site gave a feeling of ancient sanctities.[24]

Perfumes were put in tombs, probably as a counterforce to the stinks and because of their magical powers of revival. Incense in the form of balls or discs has been found in the graves of priests at Philai.[25] An interesting example of the Greek reaction to the malodorous cemeteries is provided by inscriptions from the nekropolis of Hermopolis the Great. Here we meet a brick structure—like many other tombs in the grounds: square in plan, with pyramidal roof.[26] The type occurs already in pharaonic Egypt and supplies yet another case of continuity in ideas and attitudes.[27] The pyramidion is painted red; the sides were once white; on the front (the eastern face) is hollowed a square niche, rather shallow, for an eikon of the dead man on wood or for a small offering to him (*e.g.* little phials of scent). Far back in the New Empire funerary chapels were surmounted by a white-painted pyramid, and the form was carried on in the Saite age. In the Thebaid it

persisted right into the Graeco-Roman world. In the 3rd century
A.D. a man in his will at Oxyrhynchos laid down that his heirs
were to raise a pyramid over his tomb.[28] Small pyramids of this
kind have been found in the Fayum.[29]

Under the niche of the brick-tomb that interests us are two
epigrams, the first in iambics, the second in elegiacs.

> Epimachos' son am I. Don't pass unthinking,
> but halt. Not here is oil-of-cedar stinking
> to annoy you. Pause before the tomb a spell
> and hearken to a dead man smelling well.
> My grandfather, exercised in his hometown's offices
> nobly, begot Epimachos, a man wellfitting
> his blood; he followed his father in acquitting
> himself as notary to the town's approval.
> Such was my father. Yet more fame he obtained
> through countless victories that his horses gained.
> But I, who am I?
>   The stadion reminds me.
> Still young, not more than twelve years old, I wasted
> and faded out, assigned a wretched doom
> by Fate. Death made me undergo and try
> the common lot, with Cough for aid. Don't sigh
> or weep, my friend. Tears always I've detested.
> and so "no weepers" Philhermes still I prayed.
> Like a brother he loved me, though no brother he
> by nature, born my cousin, but, when tested,
> he passed my father in loving care for me.
> Philhermes then on my behalf I bade
> to eschew all funerary lamentation:
> not bury me to unbury me again,
> but bring me only once to this my tomb:
> no cedar-oil or malodorous translation.
> There's no one who avoids me then as men
> avoid the other dead who lie around me.
>
> Though Fate brought me before my time to Hades
> laments afford no joy to me, I hate
> repeated funeral rites and moaning ladies.
> All men with Death encounter soon or late.

Perhaps it was a portrait, statue, bust, which thus speaks. The deadly Cough, *Bex*, suggests that the boy died of phthisis. Another epitaph from the same nekropolis mentions *Bex*, and a marble statue of a toga'd youth from the Fayum—an Egyptian or Graeco-Egyptian—suggests the same disease with its narrow shoulders and thin body. Perhaps it was sculptured after a death-mask. The Weepers are the *threnetriai* or hired women mourners, whom we know of as far back as Herodotos; they lasted long, for a papyrus of the 4th century A.D. deals with payment to

Theoxenia of the Dioscures (Larissa); Apotheosis of Aeneas (or Caesar) from altar of Lares Augusti (Vatican), note chariots, tree, eagle, and sky-veil or tent.

both male and female weepers, especially the latter. There were even such mourners for the funerals of animals. By the second century A.D. the craft of embalming was in decadence, Terebinthine (*kedria* from cedarwood) was injected into the corpses; or perhaps all that was done was to soak them in *kedria* or varnish them with the oil. So the smell of corruption, worsened by the smell of kedria, floated over the nekropoleis: at least in the countryside. At Alexandreia, the cemetery at Kom el-Chigafa was underground. In general the mummies were set on beds and then put on the ground floor of the funerary houses, which were as close-packed as the houses of living; and there is no evidence that the entries were at all carefully sealed.[30]

The son of Epimachos surely had exequies in Greek style. He would have been burned; the ashes would then have been sprinkled with scented oil. Hence his claim that he smelt good. (Cremation appeared late in Egypt and was not known till the Greek occupation. Mummification was a definite rite with strong beliefs attached to it; not the sort of thing that could easily yield to quite different funerary practices which were unconcerned with the lengthy preservation of the body.[31]) The Egyptian rite had two stages: first, the lamentations and so on immediately after death, then *apophora*, carrying-away or translation, when the corpse was given to the taricheutai and after their treatment was put into the final death-house.[32]

The son of Epimachos belonged to a family which was proud of its Greek culture. He laments that he did not enter the gymnasion and take his place in the stadion; he stresses that his father as agoranomos, government-notary, was a less important figure than he was as the breeder or trainer of horses. We are not told if the horses ran in the circus or hippodrome; but in any event they were racers.

A death that smelt good was a death that held fast to the flower-garden of saving and transformative scents. The Greek opposes his intact scents to a preservative magic that seems to have ended in stench, in expressing decay, not renewal.

L

16

Paradises

THE Hellenistic garden, to which Egypt, mainly through Alexandreia, made an essential contribution, provided the models on
which the Roman garden was developed. Latin words for gardener are instructive. The old word for garden, *hortus*, persisted;
but not till the 2nd century A.D. did the term *hortulanus* appear.
The Greek term *topiarius* was used for gardener—for the man
who made and carried on the pleasure-garden. Old words such
as *olitor*, *arborator*, *vinitor* (defining those who dealt with olives,
with trees needing pruning, with vineyards) did not die, but
seem to have corresponded to specialised and commercialised
forms of gardening. We thus gain a series that represent stages in
development: the *hortus*, the original *heredium* of an estate, remained the domain of the farmer's wife; specialised plots were
tended by trained slaves who produced for the market; the pleasure-garden came in under strong Greek influences. *Topiarius*
has a Greek radical with a Latin suffix; we may deduce that the
men who cultivated the Roman pleasure-garden were Greeks.[1]

Cicero, writing to his brother Quintus in September 54 B.C.,
described the work being done on the latter's house at Laterium:
"The villa, just as it stands, has such a philosophic effect as to
rebuke the craziness of all the others. Still, the proposed additions
will be delightful. Your *topiarius* won my praise. He has so enveloped everything with ivy, not only the villa's foundation-wall,
but also the spaces between the columns of the walk, that I declare the Greek statues seem to be in the topiary business (or art)
and to advertise ivy. As it is now, the dressing-room is the coolest
and mossiest retreat in the world."[2]

What then was the *ars topiaria*? It has been generally taken

as the art of making plants creep up columns or of cutting them
into various forms. Thus Plinius writes: "Today the cypress is
trimmed, is made into thick hedges, where, thanks to the hook,
it shows a ceaselessly sprouting foliage. It is also drawn into topiary
decorations (*in picturas operis topiarii*), continually attiring in verdure (*vestiens*) hunts, fleets, and other *imagines* of things with its
fine short greening leaf."[3] A close scrutiny shows that he doesn't
define the cutting of plants into various shapes as the topiary art,
but says that the cutting is made to express or reflect that art.
Trimmed trees were in fact called *nemora tonsilia*; and Plinius
tells us that the shape-trimming was invented by the *eques* C.
Mattius less than forty years before the publication of his Natural
History.[4] The *topiarii* used the trimmed effects, but only as a part
of their methods.

The root of the word *topiarius* is *topos*. *Topographia*, or rather
topiographia, was the painting of landscapes. The first landscape-
painter or topiographer of whom we know was the Egyptian
Demetrios, who came to Rome three-quarters of a century before
the art of gardening appeared there.[5] We know little of this
artist; but we may take him to be the man whom Diodoros calls
the son of Seleukos, a *topographos*, who lived in Rome about 164
B.C.; Valerius Maximus describes him as *pictor Alexandrinus*, without naming him. How he came into history was through acting
the generous host in his poor dwelling for the fugitive king
Ptolemaios VI.[6]

Painted landscapes were *topia*. The *topiarius* was a landscape
gardener. Vitruvius in his sketch of the history of landscape painting in Rome remarks that the promenades or walks needed to
be decorated on account of their length "with various sorts of
topia representing images drawn from the definite characteristics of
certain sites (*ab certis locorum proprietatibus imagines exprimentes*).
Thus it was that ports were painted, promontories, riverbanks,
sources, canals, sanctuaries, sacred woods, mountains, flocks,
shepherds."[7] He returns three times to this stress on the particular
and definite nature of the sites represented. Behind his terms we
can see the Stoic idea of the particular, *to idion*. The Stoics wanted
art to reproduce not "real scenes", but the typical elements of

things.[8] These typical elements of places were *topia*; they composed the sacro-idyllic landscape that pervades Hellenistic painting as we see it at Rome and Pompeii.[9] *Topia* were used also as components of the compositions in which gods and heroes played their parts, as in the paintings of the Esqueline.[10]

In Vitruvius' list of themes, water plays a considerable part; he mentions ports, promontories, rivers, springs, canals, and puts them first. Springs are universally sites of worship; and in Egypt the Nile was paid an enormous reverence. Cult-practices had set to work creating *topia* long before there was any detached art of the garden and of the landscape. Thus, a section of the Nile with a natural promontory, such as that we found Heliodoros describing, could beget its sacro-idyllic landscape. At Karnak a sacred lake was attached to the temple of Mut (worshipped there in the form of a woman with a vulture's body as head); but it seems sure that the name Icheru designated originally a crescent-shaped lake formed by an ancient bend of the Nile, in which were established the cults of lioness-goddesses. We may ask then if "these lakes with their lunar aspect were ritual inventions of man or indeed natural forms associated with leonine powers by a mythological speculation and disposed after the event to receive the sanctuaries of these goddesses".[11] The interplay of landscape and ritual-forms is clearly to be detected, one moulding the other.

The making of waterways, pools, or lakes in the pleasure-garden, with its sacro-idyllic basis, was highly important. Cicero sought to follow the Platonic tradition in setting his dialogue on the *Laws* in a grove under a shady ancient oak by the river Liris; the second book opens with the characters passing over water on to an islet, which Marcus describes as the spot he chooses for quiet meditation, reading or writing. Atticus declares:

Would you believe that the pleasure I find here makes me almost despise magnificent villas, marble pavements, and sculptured palaces? Who would not smile at the artificial canals which our great folk call their Niles and Euripi, after he has seen these beautiful streams? Therefore, as you just now in our conversation about Justice and Law referred all things to Nature, so you seek to preserve her domination even in those things which are constructed to recreate and entertain the mind.[11]

There is an amusing contradiction here; for Cicero belittles the *topia* of landscape-gardening to enhance the *topia* of his literary art, which refers back to Nature in the same way as the gardens did.

At Rome there were two Euripi, one in the great Circus, the other in the Gardens of Agrippa. The second, which used the bed of an ancient canal, concerns us here; for it was much imitated. But, as Cicero shows, the type already existed.[13] A good example has been found in the garden of Loreius Tiburtinus at Pompeii, where it took the form of a T. The short arm ran along the portico and terrace of the house, some 10 metres; the long arm, some 25 metres, followed the axis of the garden; the width was about 2 metres—ten times less than the river in Varro's garden. Running water fell in a cascade from an artificial grotto built under the terrace at the point where the two canals met; on the main branch there was another fountain; and further on there rose an aedicula.[14] At Tivoli, in Hadrian's elaborate pleasure-garden there was a Canopus with apsed Serapeum at one end. Among recent art-works excavated there have been a Mars, rivergods, four caryatids (imitating those of the Erectheion on the Athenian Akropolis) and two caryatid-Sileni.[15] Clearly, no effort was made to reproduce the Canopus in any realistic way.

Why were the Nile and the Euripos the two waterways so widely chosen for the pleasure-gardens? Because they were the themes of *topia*. The Nile was the great festival river, the river of hunts, fishing, and pleasure, where each noble house on the banks had its own pond and canal, and where waterflowers were cultivated.[16]

The Euripos, the channel between Boiotia and Euboia, was a hydrographic marvel with its periodic reversal of the current. Seneca records the use of such changes in the garden-canals:

Today, which man do you regard as the wiser—the one who invents a process for spraying saffron perfumes to a tremendous height from hidden pipes; who fills and empties euripi by a sudden rush of water;

who so cleverly constructs a dining-room with a ceiling of movable panels that it represents one pattern after another, the roof changing as often as the courses—or the one who proves to others as well as to himself that Nature has laid upon us no stern and difficult law in telling us that we can live without the marble-cutter and the engineer, that we can clothe ourselves without traffic in silk fabrics, that we can have everything indispensable to our use, provided only that we are content with what the earth has placed on her surface?[17]

Hence the quest for grottos, nymphaea, amalthaea, fountains, and the like in the composition of pleasure-gardens. "In Pompeian gardens, we meet fountains constructed to create light-effects by spreading the water out in a sheet over the steps of a miniature cascade or by making it fall from a great height. In studying the types of these fountains we notice that many of them proclaim the sacred themes of the pure landscape, of which we see the primordial importance for the aesthetic of the garden. Some of them show a form close to that of the lararia; others attach themselves to a different theme of staging—these in a general way are the fountains with persons: Seilenos, satyrs with wine-skin, nymphs with shell, dolphins; and on the other hand, kraters contrived as waterbasins, which are all linked with Dionysiac motives."[18] The scattering and pulsation of light, the flowing and sprinkling of water, the pouring-out of wine: all these themes are associated in the festival nature of the sacro-idyllic garden, with its enhancement of life, its aim of transforming earth and at the same time tempering the divine ecstasy so as to harmonise it with everyday existence. Hence the importance of the Dionysiac element.

Let us glance again at Hadrian's villa, which might be described as an attempt to synthesise a large number of topia. The emperor baptised the lovely valley to the east of his villa as Tempe, the romantic place of poetry. He added names of provinces and famous cities or buildings: Lyceum, Academia, Prytaneum, Poecile, Canopus. The result is often taken as a sort of huge album of travel-pictures and memories. But there was also an Underworld in the park. Hadrian had been initiated into the Eleusinian Mysteries. The world-picture of the garden may represent the journeys of the emperor in his guise as Herakles. Canopus had its important place in the scheme because it was considered the pleasure-scene above all. It expressed the *topia* of the Nile, the region of god-given fertility and play, the landscape of the Pygmies.[19] The Nilotic imagery reappears in the garden of the so-called House of the Silver Wedding at Pompeii, where were found two crocodiles, a large frog and a toad. A gem from Egypt, of the late Roman or Byzantine period, shows a snail

Nilotic Scene with Pygmies (Rome).

emerging from its shell and moving left with two horns erect. At this period mythological subjects tend to be replaced by magical or gnostic motives; and the snail-gem is an amulet, representing the emergence of life; the shell is the womb. We may recall the apsidal conche. Plinius tells us the snail was used as a remedy for female complaints and functional troubles; to hasten birth. It is still so used in Egypt. The Christians turned the snail-shell into an emblem of the tomb, the womb of second birth.[20]

A passage in Philostratos' *Eikones* describes the prevailing image of the Nile:

About the Nile the Dwarfs are sporting, children no taller than their name [*pecheis*: from *pechys*, forearm, cubit] implies; and the Nile delights in them for many reasons, but particularly because they herald his coming in great floods for the Egyptians. Anyhow they draw near and come to him smilingly out of the water, dainty smiling infants, and I think they are not without the gift of speech as well. Some sit on his shoulders, some cling to his curling locks, some sleep on his arms, and some romp in his bosom. And he yields them flowers, some from his lap and some from his arms, that they may weave them into wreaths, and, themselves sacred and fragrant, may have a bed of flowers for sleeping on. And the children climb up one another with sistra in hands, instruments the sound of which is familiar to that river.

Crocodiles, however, and hippopotami, which some artists associate with the Nile in their paintings, are now lying aloof in its deep eddies so as not to scare the children. But that the river is the Nile is indicated, my boy, by symbols of agriculture and navigation, and for the following reasons.

At its flood the Nile makes Egypt open to boats. Then, when it has been drunk up by the fields, it gives the people a fertile land to till. And in Aithiopia, where it takes its rise, a deity is set over it as steward, and he it is who sends forth its waters at the right seasons. This deity has been painted so as to seem heaven high, and he plants his foot on the sources, his head bent forward like Poseidon. Toward him the river is looking and it prays that its infants may be many.[21]

The summerhouses or *diaitai* were especially useful for the topiary artist in his landscape-compositions. Rising isolated amid greenery, they provided points of centralisation, making precise the sacro-idyllic aim. Examples are the Hermaeum of the Palatine with its *velum* and the little temple which in the Domus Augustana is shown in the midst of a basin, bound to the rest of the garden by a bridge.[22]

In the Roman system we can see a trend to unite house and garden as much as posible.[23] While on the one hand the ancient world glorified the city as the great achievement that permitted the highest flowering of human powers, there was also a growing sense of sin at living in a way that cut men away from nature. The city gave leisure to some, but intensified toil for others; the skills and crafts that it stimulated seemed more and more to minister only to corrupt and depraved tastes and needs. The garden thus became a token of the blessedness which men had lost, a rebuke and yet also a consolation, bringing a touch of redemption into the very midst of depravity and corruption. The climax of these attitudes appears in Nero's vast Golden House, which was an attempt to introduce the countryhouse, the pleasurepark, into the very heart of Rome, and which stirred him to declare that now at last he was living like a man. On a smaller scale the city-householder who had even the most modest garden felt that he was not quite abandoned to a denaturalised world, that he had his humble stake in paradise; and he longed to be buried in a setting where the paradisiac elements would dominate. If he could not have a large garden or even any garden at all, he might at least hope to have the sacro-idyllic landscape painted on his walls. Hence the effort to create an illusory effect of houses opening out into that landscape, which surrounds the inhabitants and provides a sort of protective screen between them and the actual world of chaffering and toil. The private house is isolated in a no-man's-world of paradise. This blessed space is at once removed from actuality and yet at the heart of all living experience, expressing as it does the deepest aspirations of the individual alienated from society, himself, and nature, and yet desiring above all things a worthy union with powers beyond himself, powers harmoniously in accord with his own hopes and potentialities of development.

Hence the way in which this paradise is both earthly and otherworldly. The two aspects combine and conflict in an endless series of complex relations. In the Dionysiac sphere this process continues with its richest tensions; but as hope of a good life on earth finally recedes, the otherworldly aspects triumph and Christianity defeats the Dionysiac synthesis.

The inner conflict is well stated by Philon. He says that the original paradise did not resemble "the parks now seen among men". For "the parks of our day are only lifeless woods, full of all sorts of trees, some evergreen with a view to the undisturbed

L*

delectation of the sight, others budding and germinating in the spring and producing fruit, some eatable by men and sufficient not only for the necessary support of nature as food, but also for the superfluous enjoyments of luxurious life, and some, uneatable by men, of necessity bestowed on beasts." But the trees of the first paradise were endowed with souls and reason, "producing for their fruit the different virtues, and bestowing a life free from disease".

On the other hand, Philon cannot resist the idea of the whole universe as an organic lifegiving plant. At the beginning of the second part of *Noah's Plantations* he calls God the perfect planter or gardener, and sees the world as the all-productive plant of which air, water, earth, fire are the main shoots. Here paradise appears as the perfect functioning of nature, not as some abstracted sphere.[24]

Again, Philon expresses the notion of organic correspondences in a commentary on a Biblical passage (*Numbers* vii 5), where his arguments are not Hebraic but belong to the complex of ideas built up at Alexandreia with alchemy at its core. The text deals with "the composition of spices for the purposes of fumigation", with four spices to be used.

The Lord enjoins here that each of the separate portions shall be equal to each, with a view to the proper composition of the whole.

As I imagine, these four ingredients composing the whole perfume are emblems of the four elements of which the whole world is made. He likens the *stakte* to water, the *onycha* to land, the *galbanon* to air, the pure transparent frankincense to fire. For *stakte*, deriving its name from the drops, stagones, in which it falls, is liquid; and *onycha* is dry and earthy; sweetsmelling *galbanon* is added to represent air, for there is fragrance in the air; and the transparency in frankincense serves to represent fire.

Similarly he has separated the weighty things from the light, uniting the one class by a closely-connecting combination, and bringing forth the other in a disunited form: as where he says, "Take to yourself sweet odours, *stakte*, *onycha*", these things being weighty he mentions disconnectedly, as symbols of earth and water. Then he begins afresh with the other class, which he cites in combination, saying, "And the sweet spice of *galbanon* and the transparent frankincense," these again being in their nature emblems of the light things, air and fire.

And the harmonious composition and mixture of these things is truly his most ancient and most perfect holy work: namely, the world: which, speaking of it under the emblem of perfume, he thinks is bound to show gratitude to its creator. So, in name, the composition which has been carefully fabricated by the apothecary's art may be offered up; but in fact the whole world created by divine wisdom may be consecrated and dedicated, being made a burnt offering of early morning and of evening. For such a life as this becomes the world: namely, continually, unceasingly, to give thanks to its father and creator, so as to stop short of nothing but evaporating and reducing itself to its original element, in order to show that it stores up and conceals nothing, but dedicates itself wholly as a pious offering to God who created it.[25]

This important passage shows how the ideas and practices gathered round flowers and scents and wreaths had helped to bring about the fundamental alchemic concepts of a dynamic universe in ceaseless transformation. Such concepts were in radical opposition to the notion of an aboriginal paradise absolutely separated from earthly gardens. Rather the products of those gardens are seen to symbolise and express the creative processes (physical, biochemical, biological) whereby the universe came into being and is ceaselessly recreated. Philon was aware of the contradiction between such positions and the idea of an absolute deity; intuitively he saw the universe as organic and selfenclosed, but intellectually he felt the need to insist that God was not contained by the universe.

Now let us look at some accounts of gardens. Achilleus Tatios has the following picture, which we may take as embodying the essential Graeco-Roman elements with an Egyptian colouration. (Tatios is described as an Alexandrian; and though this particular passage is set in Tyre, much of his romance has Egypt as its background.) "After the funeral I hurried to the girl, who was in our *paradeisos*. This paradise was a meadow, a thing of great delight to the eyes. A tall enough wall ran round it, and on each of the wall's four sides was a portico standing on a group, *choros*, of pillars, within which was the plantation, *panegyris*, of trees.

The branches in full foliage intertwined with overlapping leaves and fruits conjoined. Such as the close intercourse, *homilia*, of the trees." Note the words used. The lines of pillars form a *choros*, a dance-formation; the plantation is a *panegyris*, a festival assembly, and reveals an *homilia*, another word of assembly that suggests intercourse and conversation.

"Some of the bigger trees had ivy and smilax attached, the smilax drooping from planes and filling all the spaces between the boughs with its soft leafage, the ivy twisting up the pines and embracing the trunks, so that the tree supplied its support while it supplied the tree with a garland. Beside each tree grew vines, creeping on reed props with luxuriant growths; now in full fruitage they hung from the reedjoints and formed as it were the tree's ringlets. The higher leaves were in gentle movement, and the sun's rays, coming through as the wind stirred them, gave the effect of a pale dappled shadow on the earth. Flowers too of various colours displayed each its own beauty, setting the ground aflame. Narcissus and rose with their blossoms (the cup of the flowers) were there, alike in shape but varying in hue, the rose being the colour of blood above and milk below, while the narcissus was wholly of the undercolour of the rose. There were violets too, with cupshaped blossoms you couldn't distinguish, but their colour was that of a shining calm at sea. In the midst of all these flowers bubbled a spring with its waters caught in a square man-made basin. The water served as mirror for the flowers, so that there seemed a double grove, a real one and a reflection. Birds were there too. Some, tame, sought for food in the grove, pampered and domesticated by the rearing of men. Others, wild and winging, sported round the treetops, some chirping out in birdsong, others brilliant in gorgeous plumage. The songsters were grasshoppers and swallows, the first singing of Eos'marriage-bed, the second of Tereus' banquet. There were tame birds, too, a peacock, a swan, a parrot. The swan fed round the sources of the spring, the parrot was hung in a cage from a branch, the peacock spread his tail among the flowers, and the brightness of the flowers shone up against the hues of the birds, whose wings were themselves flowers."[26]

Important points to note are: (*a*) the imagery of the love-embrace and the Dionysiac revel in the creepers, in ivy and grapes; (*b*) the stress on luxuriance, on the growth of nature as a sort of onset obliterating all things else—this also, we shall see, is a Dionysiac aspect; (*c*) the intermingling and fusion of the elements, the double grove, the contrasting and merging of birds and flowers in a sort of delicate restless transformation; (*d*) the aesthetic link of these images with the light-effects of flicker and dapple.

Each of these ingredients of the total picture can be shown to

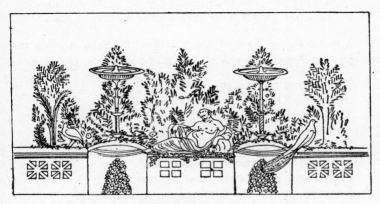

Silenus in Garden (Pompeii).

have earlier roots in Greek poetry; but the coherence and intensity with which they now come together represent something new. The development begins in Hellenistic days, but matures under the Romans. It stands for the aesthetic side of a great new cultural movement, breaking finally away from classical bases; its scientific side appears in alchemy.

Nonnos is the poet who brings all these tendencies to their first full climax. Here we shall take a few instances. First, the flower-fusion. Of a girl he writes: "Her mouth was the blossom of roses, when the rose begins to uncurl its petals." Again, "Her body's beauty rivalled the meadowflowers. She gleamed with the complexion of a narcissos. Roses sprang from her cheek, her eye's dark gleam was a violet, her ringlets curled and tendrilled more

than ivy. Such a meadow was she in her whole appearance."
Comparison has passed over into identity.[27]

But Nonnos goes further still. The girl is a flower. The flowers
are girls. "He saw all the flowers blooming with girl-colours",
synchroa koures, fellow-coloured of the girl. A naiad "dived in
the spring one-coloured with her body", *synchroon hydor*.[28]

> The form of your body cheapens
> precious marble. I'd not bring you lampstone like
> a blazing lamp, your eyes send lustre out.
> I'd not give you roses bursting from the flowercups
> of a rosy cluster, your cheeks have the skin of roses.[29]

There is a ceaseless flow between nature and human being in his
imagery; and garden work becomes one with lovemaking.

> For my mother the Cyprusborn
> and not for Deo I'll celebrate harvest-home.
> Accept me as labourer to help on your fertile lands.
> Take me as planter for your Foamborn,
> so I'll plant the lifegiving tree and the halfripe berry,
> detect and feel the newlysprouting bud.
> I know how apples ripen, how to plant
> the spreading elm that leans against the cypress,
> join the male palm rejoicing with the female,
> or make, if you wish, pretty saffron grow with bindweed.
> No gold for my gardening. I've no need of wealth.
> My wage is two apples, a bunch of grapes of one vintage.[30]

The sexual metaphor is sustained throughout. The two apples,
mela, of the last line are the two breasts; and to gather the grape-
harvest is to copulate. The pastoral idyll, which comes to a head in
Daphnis and Chloe, has ancient roots in Egypt. In the lovesongs of
the New Kingdom the lover at times appears as a countryman,
with the young girl in the role of bird-catcher or flowergatherer
which sets her in an appropriate frame of blossoms and greenery.[31]

We may glance here at two more aspects of Nonnos' garden-
imagery. First, the garden centred with the dome as a cosmic
symbol. He describes the house built by Kadmos (with the account
of Phaiakia in *Odyssey* VII in his mind). There is a brazen thres-

hold with tall-pillared double doors opening into a vestibule,
"and a dome spanned the roof with rounded head seen in the
middle." Near the courtyard is a four-acre enclosure of fruit-
trees.

> The male palm stretched his leaves
> over the female palm and pledged his love.
> Pear growing by glorious pear, all of one age,
> whispered in the morning breeze and with dangling clusters
> beat on the pollard growth of a luscious olive.
> In springwinds the myrtle waved leaves by the shrinking
>   laurel,
> while still the fragrant breath of morning fanned
> the foliage of the luxuriant cypress. There,
> on the figtree, mother-of-sweets, and the pomegranate
> rich in its juices, red fruit over purple fruit
> were growing, and apple flourished at apple's side.
> On the learned leaves of Apollo's grief-fond iris
> many a plantgrown word was stippled . . .
> The pattern traced out its own *alas* on the iris
> and thus the tears of the god on the flower were figured.
> Such was the shady garden. Nearby a stream
> divided. One runnel gave water to be drunk,
> the other was cut by a gardener in a network
> of curving channels and carried from plant to plant.
> One runnel chuckled at a laurel's root
> as if Phoibos sang a delicate song to Daphne.[32]

Once more we have the love-imagery of twining or leaning
plants, which are *symphytos*, of-one-age, growing-as-one. The
transformation-motive appears in the hyacinth which of its own
nature creates the pattern, *typos*, that reflects and expresses the
ailinon or cry of Apollo mourning for his slain boylove whose
blood stains the flowers. Apollo, the god of poetry, pervades
the scene, changing it and incarnated in the forces of nature;
he is also the poet himself who sings the scene, not from outside
it, but as a voice of nature singing in the water.

Another passage shows nature stimulated by the act of love:
Zeus is mating Hera. Once again we get the dome as a cosmic
symbol.

So with a whirl he gathered the golden clouds
like a wall and arched them eddying, a veiling dome
rounded above. A type of the bridal chamber
so made the purple manycoloured rainbow
crowned it.

In this bridal scene male bindweed wraps his leaves round the
female saffron, "as though he breathed desire, a dainty mate
among flowers". The saffron covers Zeus, the bindweed his wife;
and "lovely iris, leaping upon anemone, portrayed the sharp love
of Zeus with a significant silence", *noemon sige*. The significant
silence is that of the pantomime, whose art thus invades nature
and is one with it; the plants mime the lovemaking of the gods
and are fertilised by it. Also, the link of flowers and copulation
reminds us of what Diodoros said of the Festival of the Valley.

Nonnos indeed sees the universe, as one aspect of its united
opposites, composed everywhere of male and female elements.
"No one untrembling! the lovemaddened lamprey drawn by
passion for the serpent's bed was shivering at the god-desecrating
breath of these seafaring serpents." Fire is born from the collision
of male and female stones—Nonnos adds a fairly rational explanation of the winds as resulting from the condensation and evapora-
tion of moisture. Male and female palm embrace. Flowers are
male and female. Music too has male and female tones.[33]

Secondly, we may link this outburst of natural forces with
Dionysos. From one aspect almost the whole of the *Dionysiaka* is
an expression of the wild onrush, with its countless transformations; but one particular moment is that when Lykourgos, the
enemy of Dionysos, attacks the vine and is strangled by it. That
episode came to stand out as expressing the forces resisting the
Dionysiac march, the world of power that denied the deep
energies of growth in man realised as a part of nature. We can
gauge Nonnos' originality by comparing his treatment of it with
that by a Greek-Egyptian poet of the 3rd century A.D. Our papyrus is the author's own copy and was left incomplete.

The countryside has been laid waste by a miracle. Lykourgos is
scared. Dionysos makes his advent and assails the king with
thunder and lightning; he distracts his soul with madness while

mainads and satyrs attack. Lykourgos, fighting imaginary serpents, kills his two sons in his delusions. Kytis his wife tries to hold him back and is rescued by the god. Lykourgos regains his senses. Bound with vines, he is carried to the underworld where he must keep on filling a leaky vessel with water. The last unfinished lines were to be an epilogue. There seems a reference to a Dionysiac ceremony, so that the hymn was no doubt meant to be recited at a particular festival. Three lines of prose at the end perhaps represent a sketch or memorandum for further verses. Here is a sample of the thing:

> For not long after, Madness at Dionysos' command
> stirred up Lykourgos again with real frenzies.
> He thought to kill snakes but snatched life from his sons.
> Now Kytis would have fallen upon them, but in pity
> Dionysos took and set her past reach of doom,
> because she'd warned her lord in his storms of rage.
> But stubborn he'd stayed. Now with his mad fit ended,
> through experience of suffering he knew the god.
> But Dionysos held fast to unflinching wrath.
> Lykourgos stood, still frenzied with distress,
> then the god spread vines and fettered all his limbs.
> With neck and ankles straightened, he underwent
> the most pitiable doom of all earthly men.
> And now in the Land of Sinners his phantom endures
> the unending labour of using a broken pitcher
> to draw water. The stream pours out in Hades.[34]

The poet is unoriginal, drawing on previous epic and tragedy—though the names of sons and wife are new, and the punishment in Hades for the king (imitating the Danaids) seems his own invention. There is no sign of the proliferation of fancy that such a theme excites in Nonnos. In his account of the sin of Lykourgos, the king attacks Ambrosia with an axe; the earth opens and swallows the nymph; she "changed her form to a plant and became a vineshoot, which coiled its selfwinding cord round the king's neck, and throttled him with tight noose, fighting now with menacing clusters as once with the thyrsos". She cries out that though a vine she will attack. "Even as one of the world of plants, I'll wound you, I've no brazen chains but will choke with inextricable leaves." People will say, she declares, that "Bassarids kill murderers even when they're part of the world of leaves". Lykourgos is to "fear even vegetable warriors: vines can shoot foes and grapes can stab them."

Lykourgos and Ambrosia (mosaics).

So vining pointedleaved Ambrosia cried out
with clusterbearing voice as Lykourgos she whipped.
The wild man, caught in fresh green bonds, immovable,
smothered all round in the galling fetters of leaves
he couldn't tear, roared out and defied the god.
Lacking strength to escape, in vain he shook his throat
wound round with the tiny tendrils in strong constraint.
His voice could find no ferry through a gullet throttled
with wreathing growths. The Bacchants thronged around,
his neck confined in the middle of stifling clusters.[35]

Note, as usual, the inner driving force, the self-twining of the vines. But Nonnos does not use the motive only in connection with Lykourgos. When Zeus woos Semele he goes through a series of shapeshiftings, then shakes a dappled fawnskin. "All the earth laughed. A vining garden ran around her bed there with self-sprouting leaves. The walls budded with flowers of the dewy meadow, at Bromios' getting. Zeus who lurked inside rattled his thunder on the unclouded bed, foretelling the drums of Dionysos in the night."[36]

The leafing force used against Lykourgos is the force ceaselessly used by Dionysos and his followers in battle. Again and again the motive recurs. The Dionysiac side "hurl on the foe volleys of deadly garlands, mainadising for war". The bronze-clad Indians are "cleft by the grapebunch spear of an unarmed Bacchant"; their chests are wounded by sharp ivy. The Bacchants are unhurt by axe or sword, but slay "their curlyheaded foe with little bunches of leaves". And so on.[37] Dionysos attacks the Giants themselves "with a volley of leaves".[38] The thyrsos of fennel is described as especially deadly.[39] Nooses of ivy are used as against Lykourgos.[40] There is a vivid account of a man fighting a tree; and another of an ambushed man who spies on a miraculous scene of dancing animals from inside a tree like a jack-in-the-green:

> He peered out through the top of a thick cluster.
> He made a rounded spyhole through the leaves:
> he let himself see as much as a man who stares
> out of the eyeholes cut within his helmet
> or one who trained in the tragic choros utters
> a terrible roar from his farsounding throat
> and strains his eyesight through the holes in the mask
> worn as the delusive likeness of a man's face.[41]

Finally we may note that Nonnos uses the motive of the enveloping selfgrown vine for the Triumph of Dionysos:

> Dionysos, threatening the sea,
> danced into the fray with thyrsos and vineleaves, seated
> in the chariot of Mountainranging Mother Rheia;
> and round the rim of the Mygdonian car
> was a selfgrown vine that covered the god's whole body
> and girdled its shadowing clusters under ivy entwined.
> A lion, shaking his neck folded under the yokestrap,
> scratched the earth's surface with sharp claw and loosed
> a harsh roar from his snarling lips, while slowly
> an elephant advanced to a neighbouring spring.[42]

Nonnos had been anticipated by the mosaic-artists as we can see by looking at the floors of North Africa. Here, amid many representations of Dionysiac struggles and triumphs, the motive of enveloping plantlife is well established by the later 2nd century. Thus, on the mosaic of Asinius Rufinus at the port Acholla (after A.D. 182) Herakles fights with monsters amid vegetal wreaths and interlaces. On other pilasters of the same basilica the *protomai* of animals rise out of vegetal corollas. (The motive is first found in Africa on the coffers of the cornice of the temple of Apollo at

Triumph of Dionysos, with Pan and Mainad (mosaic, El-Djem).

Mactar, built in the early 2nd century.)[43] Herakles and Bacchus, we may note, were the *dei patrii* of Lepcis; there, where the Basilica and Forum were completed in 216, two Severan pilasters frame the main episodes of their myths, in interlaces of two vine-plants issuing from a single krater.[44]

Acholla has a Trajanic Triumph of Dionysos; and Byzacène has Egyptian and Sudanese landscapes in mosaics of the same period, while Lepcis Magna in the earliest level of the painted decorations of its Hunting Baths shows a leopard hunt and Nilotic scenes. At Sousse mosaics show pairs of Bacchantes entwined in interlaces of vegetal scrolls. In the Baths of Acholla the central picture shows the theme of Ambrosia and Lykourgos; but here we do not see vegetation as a dynamic factor at the expense of the human actors; the composition is based on an earlier mosaic at

Acholla, a nymph and amorous satyr; later the workshop that had
decorated the Baths carried out the mosaic at Cuicul with Bacchantes and various phases of initiation.[45] As the Hadrianic period
proceeds, vegetal arabesques more and more displace geometrical
motives; an impressionistic approach yields to a more direct
realism.

At the villa of Oudna the decorations date mainly from the mid-
2nd century. In the chief oecus is a Dionysiac composition, with a
central scene of three persons representing the discovery of the
vine. The god, the king, the slave presenting the grapes are all

Triumph of Dionysos, with scrolls (Sousse).

enveloped by the boughs of four great vines issuing from craters set
at the pavement angles which take over the whole field, twining
in scrolls and enclosing a small host of birds and winged genii
(Bacchoi resembling Loves). The leaf-garlands, framing animals,
decorate the peripheries of other pieces and represent a variant of
the flowery style that dominated under Hadrian. In the main
mosaic we see a farm scene in Alexandrian style.[46]

In the 3rd century romantic tendencies grow stronger; the
crisis of the latter half of the reign of Marcus Aurelius, both economic and military, has been overcome but leaves a disquiet. At
the outset of the 2nd century ornamentation had been calm and
discreet, controlled by a clear background, from which were

detached the fine lines of geometric forms or vegetal interlaces; now come rich and complex compositions, heavy and swirling: "fleurons of tormented acanthus, entanglements of braids and garlands, which hardly let the field show through".[47] Into this dominant world of plantforms are inserted the human figures, suggesting medieval tapestry or oriental faience. For example, in the oecus of the house of Asinius Rufus at Acholla, Hercules fights with monsters. The theme is chosen in accordance with the emperor Commodus' use of the hero's myths; but hero and monsters

Drunken Dionysos upheld by Mainad, etc., with scrolls (Carthage).

alike are deluged in a mass of wreaths, vines, acanthoi, and bacchic thyrsoi.[48]

This subordination of the figured theme to the décor is imposed at the same time on to the monumental sculpture, from the Capitol of Mactar to the pillars of the Basilica of Lepcis. Doubtless to make the exuberance of his main pavement emerge, the mosaic artist has however kept in the other pieces the calm geometric themes of the Hadrianic period. But the principles of the composition of Hercules' Labours reappear unchanged in mosaics of Lepcis Minor and of Thysdrus consecrated to the Muses. At Carthage the House of the Aviary is decorated in the same spirit; the great pavement of the peristyle, which has furnished its name, evokes a tapestry by its disordered seedplot of boughs, in the midst of which evolve birds, lizards, even a small gazelle; another composition makes us think rather of the ceramic panels of Moslem art, with its entanglement of fleurons of acanthus and vine-scrolls that cover the whole field with a uniform web.

In the treatment of figures, the mosaic artists of this period renounce realism to return to the colourist impressionism of the Flavian epoch.

The Hercules of the house of Asinius Rufinus is thus already a mono-chrome silhouette animated by the play of light.[49]

The flow of interlacing vines and boughs in art had its link with the floral scrolls, peopled by various creatures, which, immensely popular under the empire, originated in the late classical and Hellenistic periods—though with complex roots in primitive ideas of the sacred tree, and drawing energy from the small detailed genre-realism of the 4th century B.C. Dionysiac attitudes contributed much to the development of these scrolls. Among early examples we find a gold diadem on which ten small figures sit on the stems making music while Dionysos and Ariadne recline above the scroll's centre. Also we find the great Mother, at times flanked by beasts, with her nether limbs dissolving into two coiling tendrils, the stems of which she clutches. Sometimes she holds animal-headed coils; and her male counterpart is Dionysos-Sabazios. Pergamon played an important part in expanding the motive of the peopled scroll, but a Hellenistic plaster-model for a helmet from a metal worker's cache at Memphis gives us a glimpse of the way that it was rooted in Egyptian crafts as well.[50]

Loves and Dionysiac figures are strongly linked with the scrolls, and the Dionysiac side is well represented in the mosaics of North Africa: e.g. at Ouled-Agla, Carthage, Sousse, El-Djem, Oudna. Thus the Triumph of Dionysos at Sousse has putti, birds, baskets of grapes in the whorls of the vine-scroll border, and at El-Djem has vintaging putti, beasts, and other Bacchic figures among the branches of four vines, which spread in towards the centre from corner-vases. The Christians took the motives over. At Cherchel (5th–6th century) a vine-scroll springs from a chalice and frames animals in its medallions. In the Basilica of Justinian at Sabratha in Tripolitania (probably done by craftsmen from Byzantion or Syria) the great mosaic of the nave shows two vinescrolls rising from a huge calyx of stylised leaves (suggesting a womb-symbol of the Great Mother) and interlacing up the centre while throwing off shoots either side. In three of the central medallions are phoinix, peacock, caged quail (resurrection, immortality, soul-caged-in-flesh); in a fourth medallion, and between the lateral boughs, many sorts of birds fly about and feed on the fruit in a representa-

tion of the freed spirits in paradise. The Dionysiac turmoil has
passed away; the hope of conquering and transforming earth
has died; the great vines dominate all space in a calm majesty.[51]

We see then from the African mosaics that art had already by the
3rd century in some respects broken away from classical concepts
and was looking towards a complex future. Only with Nonnos
in the 5th century did poetry make a commensurate leap. Coptic

Pilasters (Haterii tomb).

art continues the tradition; its textiles show a strong tendency to
"dissolve reality into half-floral ornament. Hands and feet and
floating draperies take on leaf-like aspects. Finally, towards the
end of the Byzantine period and in the early years of Islam,
human figures often disintegrate into all but meaningless geometrical or highly conventialised floral parts and become vague
spectres of personages, real or mythical, now entirely unrecognisable." In a textile probably of the 6th century the roundel of a
charioteer shows wheels turned into flower-sprays and the sun-
rays from the driver's halo have become a palmette.[52]

17

Gardens and Architecture

WE HAVE already considered many ways in which the garden and its complex of ideas affected the house. By introducing a new stress on the surroundings—though in a townhouse the garden would be in an inner courtyard—it in turn stressed the interior of the house on the walls of which the landscapes were painted. The garden thus helped to develop the sense of an architectural structure as a whole, a thing of inner volumes and movements as well as of outer geometries. A new dynamic sense was born, in which building and environment, inner spaces and outer proportions began to make up a new sort of unity. It was no accident that edifices like Nero's Golden House, which sought to work out fully the aesthetic of the sacro-idyllic landscape, also showed this new sort of unity, which in time led on to Byzantine and Romanesque forms. Other factors combined to make possible this development, including the working-out of the full potentialities of concrete as a material; but at the core of the new architecture lie dynamic concepts directly and indirectly linked with the garden. In the first phase of the use of concrete by the Romans (roughly 250 B.C. to A.D. 50):

the conception of architecture that still dominates the scene is the time-honoured notion of a building as four walls and a roof, each in clear and simple relationship to the other. The turning-point and the moment which was to alter the course of architectural history came with the realisation that, working in concrete, one was no longer bound by those familiar conventions. The walls and vault of a concrete building were not separate entities; they were parts of a single, rigid envelope enclosing a certain tract of space and within the limits imposed by the intrinsic strength of this envelope the enclosed space could be any shape that the architect might choose.[1]

The break-through came under Nero, between A.D. 60 and 70;
by about 130 the revolution was a fact and a new system had been
established. What had happened was a sort of turning inside out
of the traditional Greek ideas that looked on architecture as
essentially concerned with the exterior tangible mass, which held
nothing vague or difficult to grasp. The effect depended on calculable subtleties of proportion and on the rhythmic alternation
of solid and void. Though Hellenistic and early Roman architecture was aware of the demands of the interior, it introduced no

Landscape: note herm, pillar, velum, central dome (Baths of Constantine).

radical changes; it adapted the Greek system of conceiving a building in terms of its constituent structural members—for example,
with the basilica, in which it met the problem of covering a large
space. All the issues that are raised

are stated and resolved with all the candour of a Greek temple. Compare that with a building like the Pantheon. The Pantheon, as it now
stands, is substantially the work of Hadrian; and it has often been
remarked that it is perhaps the first great surviving building to have
been planned almost exclusively as an interior. The porch, it is true,
is a concession to the conservative idea of what a temple ought to be.
But nobody who has stepped inside the door and felt the lift of the
great coffered dome, with the light flooding in from the single central

oculus—nobody who has had this experience can doubt for a moment that what the architect was really concerned with was not the brick-faced mass of the rotunda, but the space which it contained. What is more, he was out to conceal the essential structure. The essence of the design is that of a huge concrete dome carried on a ring of enormously solid masonry; and had the design been stated architecturally in these simple terms, the result could hardly have failed to be overwhelmingly oppressive.[2]

Pompeian Landscape: circular shrine.

As things are, the architect has managed to conceal the structural problem and liberate his forms as though they floated on light and air, as though they were dynamic expressions of a single form within which there is a highly complex play of light and shade.

We have already noted something of the part played by the dome as a cosmic symbol in the sacro-idyllic garden—with the parasol of Dionysos owning much the same significance. It was no accident that the Pantheon gained its revolutionary achievement through the concentration of architectural thought on the dome as opposed to the box. The change in structure is a change in fundamental views of the universe. A firm calculable structure yields to a circling form moulded by the play of light and shadow; the stress is on the plastic and the dynamic. The enveloping plant forms of the great Dionysiac moment implicated the dome as the spinning and yet comprehensive pattern. The god was closely connected with the circular form. Hesychios defines *skias* as "a small vaulted rotunda under which Dionysos is seated". The Dionysiac temples of Palatika in Macedonia and of Gortyna in Crete, as well as the Monument of Lysikrates in Athenai, were circular; so was the temple of Sabazios-Dionysos on Zilmissos Hill in the land of the Bessoi (as described by Macrobius). A painting in the Thermae of Titus shows the god enthroned under a small domed circular building and surrounded by Nymphs.

The association of a sacred tree with a circular or domical sanctuary, a mortuary *tholos*, was very ancient. In hellenistic art the sacred tree is linked with domical *tholos*, rustic shrine, and ancestral *tegurium* or hut. There is a strong suggestion of the Golden Age when men, animals, and gods all lived together in a harmonious utopia.[3] The whole complex naturally moves over into the sacro-idyllic and funerary garden, and appears in Pompeian paintings and the stucco ceilings of Roman tombs. Thus in the Domus of Vesonius Primus (owner or manager of a clothfulling mill) a great tree is shown, its branches mingled with the supports of a domical baldachin which covers an open-air altar in a sacro-idyllic scene of love and happiness.[4] Coins depict the heroon of Melikertes at Corinth as a domical shrine with a tree on either side.[5]

The domical structure, thus, from one angle is bound up with the set of ideas which linked the paradise as park or garden with the tribal past (idealised as the Golden Age). We may compare the *kalybe* or hut, in which Apollo was said to live at Delphoi, and the huts, tribal tents, or portable canopies used in Syria as the tabernacle of a god. Coins show that such structures continued to be used for dwellings or festival-homes of the gods even after temples in the classical style had evolved with porticoes and gabled façades. Some of them were conical, others pyramidal, and a few had hooped roofs; but the dominant form was domical or owned a cupola under a projecting conical roof. The Christians in turn took over the form to cover tombs, relics, ritual thrones, in their baldachins or ciboria.[6]

We may pause to consider the term *ciborium*. When first the Christians used it is not clear; but the word seems certainly the same as the Greek *kiborion*, which was used for a cup that imitated the seed vessel of the Egyptian bean.[7] The Christian ciborium evolved as a column-supported canopy over the altar. The name strongly suggests a connection with Egypt, and Strabon gives us the clue. He tells us, of the *kyamos* or bean from which the *kiboria* comes, that it provides leaves and flowers in many parts. "So the beanfields afford a pleasant sight as well as enjoyment for those who wish to hold feasts there. They hold feasts in cabinboats, in which they enter the thick of the *kyamoi* and the shade of the leaves. For the leaves are so large that they are used both for drinking-cups and for bowls, as they even have a sort of concavity suited to this purpose; and in fact Alexandreia is full of them in the work-shops where they are used as vessels." The festival in the enveloping *kyamos*-thicket reminds us at once of the paradisiac garden— of the moment of surging leaves which are here seen in their friendly embracing form. Strabon explicitly points to the way in which the *kyamos*-bushes with their *kiboria* shaded the rejoicers, just as the baldachin or ciborium later did. There must then surely be a link between these pagan feastings and the latter application of the term *kiborion* to the sacred canopy. Here however the colouration is entirely Dionysiac; the exact process by which the *kiborion* moved from the pagan scene of drink and love to the Christian altar, the *mensa* of the sacred communion with the martyr-dead, is lost to us.

The emotional importance of the tabernacle as opposed to the temple is brought out by its frequent use on coins, *e.g.* the skygod as eagle in a domical shrine of Laodicea-ad-mare, the similar structure over a pair of altars at Pisidia, with stars and moon to make explicit the heavenly or cosmic meaning.[8] The arch which commonly appears over altars of the Dioskouroi or other deities is also a sky-symbol as well as a numismatic convention for the curved canopy. The altar of Zeus at Pergamon had a huge baldachin over it. An Alexandrian coin shows a tent-canopy of Canopos.[9] The Tychai or Fortunes that came to personify cities in the Greek world took over the symbolism. The shrines of the Tyche of Tyre and apparently of Antioch, as well as that of the veiled

Pompeian Landscape: circular shrine.

goddess of Arca, were portable tabernacles with domical covers. The way in which such figures drew in local traditions is suggested by the Tyche of Damaskos, whose domical *kalybe* has an outcurving flange, suggesting a curved roof built on a framework of pliable materials. This type was carried on by the Christian carvers of the Syro-Palestinian and the Palestinian-Coptic schools to express a ritual shelter.[10]

We have already noted the cosmic tent of Alexander.[11] It seems clear that it was from the Persian sky-tent as taken over by him the Roman and Byzantine emperors gained their jewelled and golden baldachins. The tradition seems to drive deep roots with Nero. There is no reason to doubt that his Golden House held a revolving astronomically-decorated cupola of wood and that the scheme carries on to the domical throne room of Khosro II, where a similar structure, built by craftsmen from the Roman Empire, "went round perpetually day and night like the world". The dome became an essential part of palace-architecture. The *velum* or tent, sometimes called a carpet and fan-pattern, appeared as a celestial symbol on imperial domes and other kinds of vaults: a traditional decoration on Roman, Christian and Renascence domes.[12]

The tent was inevitably carried into funerary imagery. On the ceiling of the pagan tomb of M. Clodius Hermes in the cata-

Niobe at the circular tomb of her children (sarcophagus, Lateran).

combs of S. Sebastiano is painted a tent. We see an apotheosis of the heroic dead rising skyward through the opening at the top of the domelike tent with its four fringed lobes. We see why the Christians used the term *skene*, tent, to designate the martyrion of S. Babylas at Antioch as an ideal home in his afterlife.[13]

We find the same traditions among the Semites. They probably all had an ancient dome-tent of leather, the *qobba*, as a portable dwelling of divine baetyls. The *qobba* was a palladion or ark. It led the way in migrations, was carried into battle, and served as the emblem of clan-authority as well as being set over the graves of ancestors and great men. Though it later lost its baetyls, it survived as the clan palladion and emblem of authority, being the prototype of the *kubbe* of Islam that Mohammed and his successors bore on the march and in battle.[14] The Semitic traditions were carried into Alexandreia by the Jews there settled, as is made clear by Philon.

In his *Life of Moses* he states at some length that the tabernacle symbolised the structure of the universe. His remarks on the covering set inside on the four pillars to hide the innermost sanctuary are specially interesting. "In choosing the materials for the woven work, he selected as best out of the vast number possible four, as equal in number to the elements, earth, water, air, fire, out of which the kosmos was made, and with a definite relation to those elements: the byssos or bright white coming from the earth, purple from the water, while dark red is like the air, which is naturally black, and scarletlike fire, since both are bright red. For it was necessary that in framing a temple of man's making, dedicated to the father and leader of all, he should take substances like those with which he constructed the whole."[15]

This passage helps us to understand the processes of thought that turned the faction-colours into cosmic emblems; its notion of the colours as dynamic elements links with alchemy and is in the key of the new system of creative thought we are considering. Though there is a primitive core in the attitude, the elaboration belongs to the alchemic positions that were being developed in particular at Alexandreia. That they were now becoming a general property of the intellectual world is shown by Josephos, who describes Moses' tabernacle as an "imitation of universal nature", its holy-of-holies with four posts "like the heavens devoted to God", and the highpriest's dress as representing essential parts of the universe.[16]

We have already noted the function of the royal tent in ancient Egypt. At Alexandreia the post-Alexander synthesis of the images and practices we are reviewing reached its height. That city "must have been the most important disseminating centre of this *skene* imagery, for all evidence indicates that there the canopy symbol was taken over into the decorative arts of the palace, where it was stylised into a domical, or conical, tentpattern with cusped edges and radiating lines, which in the past has been frequently misinterpreted as either a fanpattern or confused with the shell-decoration." Rather, perhaps we should say, the shell of rebirth was merged with the sky-tent of apotheosis. The Ptolemaic Ipsium tomb at Alexandreia has Egyptian motives (*e.g.* sun-emblems) round the edge of the heaven-canopy in its paintings. The canopy appears again in the decoration of Pompeian niches and apses, *e.g.* in the Forum Baths, and is carried on via imperial vaults into the Christian tradition. The strong effect of the tent-image explains the melonlike corrugations in the constructions of Roman and

Advent of Apollo under circular shrine (silver plate from Corbridge).

Byzantine domes, the constant representation of cupolas with the convex gores of the heavenly skene on early Christian martyria, and the persistent use of tent-striations on the cupolas of church and palace through the middle ages. The canopy had its love-relations too. In the romance of Xenephon of Ephesos, partly set in Egypt, the heroine is laid on a bridal couch over which "is variegated (*epepoikilto*) a Baylonian *skene*", on which are embroidered Loves, "some twining wreaths and some bearing flowers", as well as Aphrodite and garlanded Ares on his way to mate the goddess.[17]

M

The pharaonic Egyptians had made buildings that remind us of the Neronic audience-hall. Diodoros, describing the Thebaid, tells of a hall "with its roof supported by pillars, constructed in the style of an Odeion", that is, with a rectangular plan and a circular roof (if it was like the Odeion of Perikles). Nearby stood another hall with a table holding couches for 20 statues of "Zeus and Hera" as well as of the king. "Here, it would seem, the king's body is buried. In a circle about this edifice are many chambers that hold fine paintings of all the animals considered sacred in Egypt. An ascent leads through these chambers to the tomb as a whole; at its top is a circular border of gold crowning the monument, 365 cubits in circumference and 1 cubit thick (? wide); on this are inscribed the days of the year, one in each cubit of length, and beside each day the risings and settings of stars as nature ordains them, and the signs indicating the effects that the Egyptian astrologers hold they produce. This circle, they said, had been plundered by Cambyses and the Persians on conquering Egypt."[18] Philon knows the Odeion or music-hall as something essentially circular:

So too with the ear. Nature turned it with her lathe and made it spherical, drawing circles within circles, lesser within larger, so that the sound might not escape and be dispersed outside it, but that the thing heard might be collected and enclosed within the circles, and, being as it were poured through them, be conveyed into the receptacles of the mind. We see here a paradeigma for the theatres seen in prosperous cities; for the system of theatres exactly imitates the structure of the ear.[19]

Here we have the side of Philon that leans to organic and dynamic positions, to a scheme of vital correspondences. The image of the enclosing spirals is close to the garden-image of winding and enveloping tendrils. The triumphant liberation of life is one with the processes of organic construction.

The question of the dome, the *tholos*, the circular construction, opens up a vast field. Here we must keep to the Egyptian aspects. As nothing is left of the Alexandrian palaces—the area having been continuously and populously occupied—we are driven to secondary evidences: the eastern traditions, the royal epiphanies, the Alexandrian tombs with their domical vestibules. To these we may add the evidence of what is called the fourth Pompeian style for the proposition that the domical vestibule like the tent of advent was a symbolic feature of palace architecture in the Hellenistic East, and especially in Alexandreia. We may assume that royal and aristocratic tombs and funerary chapels drew their fundamental forms from palaces; for in afterlife the king was anxious to continue in the style to which he had been accustomed.[20]

We find in Egypt the appearance in the last century B.C. of a new kind of rockcut tomb with domical vestibule or chapel,

Eagle shrine (coin, Laodicea ad Mare); domical tent-shrine, altars of Dioscures (Sagalossa, Pisidia); domical tent-shrine (Alexandreia).

which presupposes an earlier kind of entry-hall in palaces where the master of the house had honours paid to him. For instance, at Sidi Gabbari; in the catacombs of Mex, known as the Baths of Cleopatra; in the tomb of Taposiris Magna; in the tomb near Hadra (first half of 3rd century); in the catacomb of Kom ech Chugafah with its large domical rotunda plus triclinium, chapels, and burial chambers opening out from it.[21] Tombs with apses appear in the nekropolis of Moustapha Pacha near Alexandreia.[22] The loculus seems to have originated in the Near East and to have passed to Alexandreia in the 3rd century.[23]

Let us look closer at some of the examples. In the nekropolis of Ezbet el-Makluf we meet circular hypogaia with a series of *loculi* or niches opening out in a single row along the wall.[24] The type is rare: the only other known examples are in the Tomb of the Mercenaries and in a tomb at El Rubiyat.[25] The latter is however not dug in rock but is built of cut stones. The conclusion to be drawn is that "the tombs of the Ptolemies, and notably that of the last Cleopatra, had the character of circular mausolea, which would have influenced the similar great tombs of Roman architecture". The catacombs of Kom ech-Chugafah were once an edifice of four storeys; but the storey above ground has disappeared and the lowest one underground is now waterlogged. The other two storeys however give us a sufficient idea of the system, in which the circle dominated.[27] After the entry comes a staircase that leads to a landing; to the right and left are semicircular niches with benches, decorated in the upper part by a great "shell" in relief—a pattern found again on the ceiling of the stairs to the second storey. Only the living used the steps; the dead were lowered on ropes down the lighting-pit, then taken in through large openings in the walls, and thus finally settled in the rooms of the lower storeys. We enter a circular room, in the midst of which is a well covered by a sort of cupolaed kiosk made out of a parapet and eight pillars attached to the vault of the room; out of the room open the chambers with sarcophagi, loculi for urns, and small wallholes for lamps. In the big hall, left of the entry is a funerary triclinium where the relatives of a dead man gathered for a meal in communion with him on days consecrated to the cult of the dead—such as, under the Romans, *dies violae*, *dies rosae*, and so on. The hall is 8m. 50c. by 9m., its roof upheld by pillars; the three beds of the triclinium, like the pillars, are cut from the rock. (The beds would have been furnished for mattresses, when in use, with a wooden table set between them.)

As we go down to the next storey from the triclinium, we gain a view from the top of the steps of the central part of the tomb. The staircase-vault has again a great "shell" decoration in relief; lower, the steps divided into two sections before a large niche in "shell" form. At their foot we face the vestibule of the funerary chapel proper, its front upheld by two Egyptian columns with papyrus-bundles and flower-capitals. Among the decorations are two niched statues worked according to the principles of Egyptian art, though the type and coiffure recall the plasterheads of the 1st and 2nd century, and the Fayum paintings.[28] Left and right, on bases that imitate the form of an Egyptian naos, are two large bearded serpents with the double crown, *pschent*, but also with the caduceus of Hermes and the thyrsos of Dionysos. The room has three niches with sarcophagi. The sarcophagus in the back niche has a festoon of flowers on its front, and above is a woman's figure lying down, perhaps the dead woman; other decorations include masks of Seilenos and Medousa and a festoon of ribboned grape bunches. The covers of the sar-

Funeral altar of Julius Secularis : showing shell-tent and paradisiac scene.

cophagi do not lift; holes are made from the other side of the niches, in the surrounding galleries, so that bodies could be laid inside—probably for the last prayers of the rite. The walls have reliefs composed of Egyptian themes (Osiris, Isis, Apis, Anubis, Thoth, Horos and so on); but the artist seems drawing on ancient models without any clear understanding. One section however is of interest to us. A priest with two tall plumes, clad in panther skin thrown over a long robe, offers a lotus-bud and a cup with an ewer to a woman whose wig is surmounted by a solar disk and who lifts her two hands, the palms turned to her face: she is surely a dead woman in apotheosis. To the right of the entry is dog-headed Anubis dressed as a Roman soldier; to the left is Seth-Typhon or Makedon with wolfhead. The date of the system is between the end of the 1st century and the first half of the 2nd.

From the gallery around the chapel run others giving access to chambers like the central chapel but without ornament. Galleries and chambers seem added at successive periods as new families took over or perhaps funerary entrepreneurs; another possibility is that a burial college ran the place for its member.[29]

These tombs are important in showing the development of the dome as a cosmic symbol; but the garden has naturally disappeared. However it reappears in the symbolism of the Christian martyrion. The martyrion of St John Baptist at Alexandreia seems certainly domical, and was accompanied by the sacred tree.[30] A similar system of dome and tree appears in the martyrion of St Athenogenes on an ampulla from Alexandreia. The Holy Sepulchre and the tomb of Lazarus were often shown as a *tegurium*, a domical *tholos* or the like, in a *paradeisos*. Early western pilgrims referred to the atrium in front of the Anastasis, the Church dedicated by Constantine at Jerusalem, as a *hortus* and *paradisus*.[31] A good instance of the symbolism is provided by a Sardianian tomb near Cagliari (late 3rd century) where Jonah is devoured by sea-monsters and his soul, shown as a babe, is borne by the Lamb to an ideal *tegurium*, which is both mausoleum and paradisiac home, with two trees, the olive of peaceful bliss and the palm of triumph (the entry into Jerusalem).[32] The domical *tegurium* is a shepherd's hut and the abode of the Good Shepherd, bearing the dove instead of the imperial eagle; the utopian image of a Golden Age is clear, with an explicit rejection of the existing world and its state-power. The golden-age aspect is indeed well brought out in the legend of the martyr Athenogenes; one day a hind entered his rustic cabin with its dome and offered itself as a disciple.[33]

We cannot follow this complex matter further, but may note that "the early association of the *skene* baldachin with the *sphairos* [sphere, globe] and griffins, as evidenced by a fresco from Herculaneum, is further evidence of its derivation from the palace decorations of Alexandreia, where the cosmic tent and globe were insignia of a Sun-king's domination over heaven and earth".[34] Sphere and tent, world and sky, are commonly combined in Pompeian decorations. In the so-called House of Diomedes, a sort of tree-of-life supports a globe on which stands an eagle, which in turn is under a baldachin with dome on the interior and a *fastigium* on the exterior. Another fresco shows an

Ciborium (mosaic in church of St George, Thessalonika).

arabesque tree-of-life supporting a sphere which in turn is under a *skene*-baldachin.[35]

The development of the dome, so fateful and fruitful for architecture, could not have come about without its deeply-felt symbolism. It was not merely an emblem of heaven. It represented the womb of a rebirth, a renewal of all things: new heaven, new earth. It cannot in the last resort be separated from the paradisiac garden, from the tree of life, the scents and colours of regeneration and joy. The summerhouse or rustic shrine of the sacro-idyllic landscape is the humble precursor of the martyrion which has drawn into itself also all the rich symbolism of heroon and tent-of-advent. While it is impossible with the material at our disposal to reach finality on the exact process of fusion and re-definition between the early Greek heroon and the matured Christian martyrion, we can be sure that Alexandreia played an essential part at most of the phases, and that immemorial elements from Egypt as well as from Syria were drawn in.

From one angle the *paradeisos* of joy and revival was also the place of Dionysiac advent and fertilisation. The sacro-idyllic landscape was the scene of Dionysos' childhood, advent, and triumph, before it became the scene of the martyr's new life. The complex imagery of garlands and crowns, especially strong at Alexandreia, had its centre here; and Pompeian gardens and walls show how the Dionysiac idea could pervade the systems.[36]

18

The Triumph of Alexander and Dionysos

IN OUR inquiry we have continually found the Dionysiac idea intruding. The attitudes which we have been exploring and which are concerned with leisure, with enjoyment, with the effort to grasp and express the fullness of life, cannot be understood apart from that idea, which plays an important unifying role. Now we must pause to take a larger historical view, to consider some aspects of Dionysos and his cult, and to assess the way in which that cult helped to provide men with their understanding of the processes of history. First, the pre-Alexander significance of the cult. Dionysos seems to be a very ancient god, with his roots in the Minoan-Mycenean world. His cult gained a new and expansive life in the 8th–6th centuries B.C., when above all it was used to express the demands of the peasantry as against the rule of the nobles. The typical myth of Dionysos and his wild followers being resisted by the king of a city has this situation at its heart. Hence the way in which the Tyrants and then the democracies fostered the Dionysiac cult and found in its ritual forms the basis of great new art-expressions, tragedy and comedy. Those art-expressions were bound up with the democratic *polis*, above all Athens, and died out when that *polis* broke down.

In making this schematic analysis, which needs a detailed analysis in order to come to life, we are not claiming that any political programme was linked with the uprush of the Dionysiac cults, which in their expansive period drew on elements from tribal groups on the periphery of Greek *polis*-civilisation, especially in Thrace. The Dionysiac fertility-cult was a convenient form in which to embody aspirations that wanted larger and more fluid unions than the aristocratic clan-cults could provide. As such it

M*

became a centre around which popular ideas and emotions could gather—where they could crystallise in new art forms and where the triumph of the new forces could be explored and affirmed.[1]

What then was to happen to such a cult with the breakdown of the *polis*? It was too deeply rooted in popular emotions to wither away. Instead, it was still used to express the needs that people felt for a fuller life, in the new situation. In the process it was again taken over by the State and was partly distorted; but it continued to embody and express the popular needs in various important ways.

The triumph of Macedonian power under Alexander meant the crushing of democracy (in the weakened forms it had taken). At

Triumph of Dionysos, with Victories and Captives (Rome, Coll. Torlonia).

least once, in the early days, the hope of throwing off the new political oppressions was linked with Dionysos. An inscription from Eretria, probably dated 308 B.C., records:

The priest of Dionysos, Theodotes, son of Theodoros, and the polemarchs Sosistratos, Protomenes' son; Aischylos, Antandrides' son; Ithaigenes, Aischylos' son, have made the following proposal:

Since at the festival procession on the Dionysia the [Makedonian] garrison has gone away and the people have regained their freedom, and the ancestral laws and the democracy are restored once more, therefore the Council and the People have decreed, in order to keep this day in memory, that all the Eretrians and those who dwell among them shall wear a crown of ivy at the festival procession of Dionysos; the citizens shall be provided with the crowns at public expense, and the treasury shall pay for the supply of crowns . . . The dances shall begin . . . like the dances in honour of Dionysos [when the] wine is sent . . . [2]

The tone suggests the political propaganda of the Antigonids; but the advent of liberation during a Dionysiac festival is none the less interesting.

But in general the Dionysiac ideas began gathering round Alexander as the hero of a new dispensation. The Hellenistic kings, especially in Egypt, tried to use the cult for their own glorification, with the climax in the propaganda of M. Antonius and Cleopatra. Next, then, let us consider the way in which Alexander became a sort of Dionysos.

In his lifetime, partly through his own heady eagerness to dramatise his actions on a grand scale, partly through political exigencies, partly through flatteries and the popular impulse to

Triumph of Dionysos (Vatican).

interpret great happenings in mythological terms, he was linked or identified with various heroes or deities. In Egypt, according to Ploutarch, he was impressed by the sayings of the philosopher Psammon, especially that "everywhere the being who commands and rules is divine", and that "God is the father of all men and in particular adopts the best".[3] Also among the flatterers who treated him as divine were Egyptians.[4] And it was his Egyptian expedition that took him to the oracle at Siwa where he gained his conviction of being son of the highgod. As for the roles he played, we can at least say that he wanted to assume the fullest kingly and heroic honours traditional in the conquered areas. So we find him Achilleus in the Troad, Son of Ammon at Siwa, Pharaoh-god at Memphis, the Great King (a divine vicar) in Persia. And finally he demanded divinising honours from the Greek cities of the

Korinthian League.[5] In turning to Siwa he was following the example of the hero Perseus, his model, and of Herakles, his ancestor.[6] He himself seems to have mixed a romantic belief in his hero-powers with a sardonic humour about his divinity, as in his comments on the praises that he had surpassed Herakles, after the capture of Aornos.[7] Still, he called his son by Barsine, Herakles.

Ephippos, a contemporary witness, who seems rather hostile to Alexander, stated explicitly (according to Athenaios):

Alexander also used to wear sacred clothing at his dinners, sometimes the purple robe of Ammon and slippers and horns like the god, sometimes again the robe of Artemis, which he also often wore on his chariot with Persian dress, revealing the arrows and hunting-spears on top of his shoulders, and sometimes again the costume of Hermes—most of it indeed he wore almost all the time, the purple chlamys and chiton with white stripe and the broadbrimmed hat, kausia, with the royal diadem, but on special occasions he wore the winged sandals, and on his head the petasos and in his hand the herald's staff of Hermes. Often too he wore the lionskin with club like Herakles.[8]

Ephippos may be exaggerating, but he can hardly be inventing the whole thing. In any event, the omission of Dionysos is striking.

Ephippos indeed seems to regard Dionysos as Alexander's foe. In telling how the king collapsed, in the beginning of his fatal illness, through a drinking bout, he adds that Dionysos was wrathful with him for "laying siege to his own city of Thebai" (where he was supposed to have been born).[9] It was inevitable however that he would be given a Dionysiac role. Dionysos and Herakles had become in popular thought the two great conquering figures who broke their way into Olympos.[10] Chares, who had been Alexander's chamberlain, gives us one clue. In his account of the king's marriage, which lasted five days, there were banquets and nuptials announced by trumpets, Greek and Indian conjurings, recitations by rhapsodes, cithara-playing with and without song, singing to the flute, flute-playing—the Pythikon first, then music for choroi. "From that time the Flatterers of Dionysos, as they had been called, came to be known as the Flatterers of Alexander because of their lavish gifts, which gave him great pleasure. There were dramatic shows by the tragic

actors Thessalos, Athenodoros, and Aristokritos, and the comic
actors Lykon, Phormion, and Ariston." There was also a harpist.[11]
Protogenes is said to have painted Alexander, apparently after his
death, about 300, the addition *ac Panem* meaning "(as Dionysos)
with Pan" or referring to two different pictures.[12]

In any event it was not long after his death that the Dionysiac
accretions began. They mainly concerned the passage through
Karmania, where, in the fullblown version, there was a seven-day
procession in flamboyant Bacchic style, with Alexander as Dionysos; and the discovery of a mountain identified with the Nysa of
Dionysos' upbringing by the Nymphs as a child. Thus, steadily
the great conquering march of Alexander into India was imagined
as a Dionysiac triumph; and Dionysos himself with his myths of

Dionysiac War (or Circenses): Rome.

wandering conquests, which already in Euripides' *Bacchai* are
defined as a march out of the east into Hellas, was seen as the
invader and conqueror of India.[13] The crucial steps in this development appear to have been taken early: for instance Kleitarchos,
whose dates seem 310–300, wrote of Dionysos' conquest of the
Indians.[14] The great procession at Alexandreia with its Dionysiac
basis and its picturing of Nysa, which we summarised earlier,
occurred about 274.

A Dionysos, son of Ammon, was produced, and we hear of
Dionysos invading Africa.[15] (The Siwa-Dionysos is doubtless
only Osiris.) The decisive turn in confirming the link of the god
and Alexander seems taken in Egypt.[16] We do not find Dionysos
on the coins of the successor-kings of Baktria; but the Ptolemies
clearly did all they could to stimulate the Dionysiac image, which
gained new momentum from the victorious march of Ptolemaios
III. There was a strong Hellenistic tendency to link Dionysos and

Herakles, *e.g.* as founders of Nikaia.[17] And we have seen how in North African mosaics and cults the connection was carried on under the Romans. The two hero-gods stood out as the supreme types of men undergoing labours for the benefit of their fellows, world-travellers conquering everywhere, city-founders, civilisers. The imagery of their triumph early reached Rome. Significantly, it was Marius, leader of the Populares in a revolutionary situation, who broke with the old triumphal customs and mounted the Curia in purple robes; he directly imitated the Triumph of Dionysos. After the Cymbric triumph he always used a cantharus for drinking from, as it was from such a cup that Liber Pater (Bacchus) drank on his return from India with his thiasos. (Plinius says that Liber Pater invented the royal diadem and the triumph.) Pompeius Magnus and Caesar carried the tradition on. Pompeius wore a chlamys said to have belonged to Alexander: and when he was aged about forty to forty-five, his flatterers said he was thirty-four (the age of Alexander at his death). In his triumph were carried placards comparing him with Alexander, Herakles and Dionysos. Caesar on the last day of his triumph in 45 came out into the Forum on sandalled feet, his head crowned with flowers, and went home accompanied by a vast crowd and by the light of elephant-borne torches, as the New Dionysos.[18]

This is a vast theme, and we must keep to the most relevant aspects. Ptolemaios XIII took the title of Neos Dionysos; but long before that, Ptolemaios IV seems to have been called Dionysos by court and people; we are told that he had the ivyleaf tattooed on his body, and he got Satyros to fabricate a genealogy showing his descent from the god. We have an order of his that seems to refer to the instructors in the Dionysiac Mysteries rather than those who merely performed the rites:

Those in the country districts who impart initiation into the Mysteries of Dionysos are to come down the river to Alexandreia, those residing not further than Naukratis within ten days after the promulgation of this decree, those beyond Naukratis within twenty days, and register themselves before Aristoboulos at the registry-office within three days of the day of their arrival, and they shall immediately declare from whom they received the rite for three generations back, and give in the Sacred Logos, sealed, each man writing upon his copy his own name.[21]

This document suggests how widely spread the cult had become in Egypt and that some effort of regularisation was being made. However the sacred *logos* does not refer to texts, as it has often been taken, but the accounts of the cult, which had to be sealed as often was done with documents of financial importance; the registry was probably that of the chief judge, archidikastes, which might well have been concerned with the qualifications of the priests of Dionysos and their financial administration. Intruders had apparently wormed their way into the favoured cult. Another text seems to imply a lifelong and hereditary priesthood. An Alexandrian inscription, set up by Poseidonios and other *thiasitai*, records a sacred banqueting-hall, *hestiatorion*, built in honour of Philopator, Arsinoe and their infant son.[22] Ptolemaios V took the name Epiphanes, which suggests the god of an advent, especially Dionysos; but the Greek word may be merely a translation of an Egyptian term: "he who comes forth".[23] In his reign there was a native rebellion; and thenceforward special attention was paid to placating the Egyptian priests and fostering their cults. Dionysos in such a scheme tends to have his identification with Osiris emphasised.

There is one more historical episode, however, which we must glance at: the attempts of M. Antonius and Cleopatra to build up something of a religious war against Rome and the West, or at least to stimulate and extend certain religious ideas in their support.[24] Cleopatra bore Antonius two children, Alexander Helios and Cleopatra Selene. Isis was considered to have borne the Sun; as the New Isis, Cleopatra did likewise. Her son was to be the new Alexander, marching West instead of East. In the *Potter's Oracle*, a document originally Egyptian, which we have in Greek fragments, a king is to come from the Sun and be established by Isis. In a prophecy given in Sibylline verses, which certainly belongs to Cleopatra's period, a Queen is to shear Rome's hair, she will completely wreck Rome's power; a new dispensation of peace, happiness, brotherhood and plenty will come about as the result of the East's revanche. *Homonoia* (harmonious brotherhood) will reign. Cleopatra is here called the Widow, perhaps because she wanted to stress her position as Caesar's widow, but more likely because she had broken the Ptolemaic rule of a wedded pair ruling Egypt—she is thrice called the widow in the account of her fall given in other Sibylline verses written by an Alexandrian Jew. (The poem in question also has at least a strong Jewish tinge, for it uses the Isaiah image of the heavens being rolled up like a papyrus-roll.) A widowed condition also suggests Isis after the murder of Osiris: a prelude to the joyous resurrection. What is constant in the prophecy is the hope of cataclysm and renewal. Another Sibylline prophecy says that when a triumvirate rules at Rome and Rome hesitates over the conquest of Egypt, mankind will be destroyed by a heavenly cataract of fire and there will come the rule of a holy king for ever. Another such prophecy states that a warrior king will come from the Sun to pacify the earth and precede the Golden Age.

Antonius seems to begin by connecting himself with the Sun: his coins after Philippoi have his own head and the Sun radiate. At this stage he was doubtless only trying to link the supreme man with the supreme god. It was in the autumn of 39, when he went with his wife Octavia to Athens, that he began striking *kistophoroi*. Sokrates, a contemporary, says he now proclaimed himself Dionysos. (The Ephesians had hailed him as Dionysos in 41, but that does not prove he then claimed the title.) The coins he now struck bear out what Sokrates says. They are not normal *kistophoroi*. They bear the mystic *cista* or chest of the god, ivy and serpents, but they also bear Antonius' head wreathed with ivy and Octavia's bust on the cista—or else jugate busts of the two of them, with a figure of Dionysos on the *cista*. Henceforth Antonius was Dionysos. Possibly the enigmatic 4th Eclogue of Virgil was written at this time, hailing the child that Octavia was to bear as the saviour who would restore the Golden Age—though more likely it commemorated the hopes of 40 B.C. when, pregnant by her recently-dead husband Marcellus, she married Antonius and seemed to seal the concord between him and her brother. In any event the child she bore to Antonius was a girl; and he turned his thoughts to conquest of the East. Hence his proclamation of himself as the new Dionysos at Athens. In 37 he broke with the West, sent Octavia away, sent for and married Cleopatra. He could not but have had in mind that she had borne him a son. Now he sought to base his political position on their union and to use the symbolism of Cleopatra-Isis and Alexander-Helios in connection with his own Dionysiac role. (In 34 he proclaimed the boy overlord of Parthia.) That the Romans saw the

Personal Apotheosis: Hateria on the funeral bed and the tomb-temple of the Haterii (shown in construction), Rome.

threat of Cleopatra as a threat of eastern revanche is proved by Virgil when in the *Aeneid* he makes the whole of Asia—Bactria, India, Sabaea—follow her and Antonius to Actium.[24]

Cleopatra was represented as Hathor-Isis and she assumed the title of Nea Isis as well as Thea Neotera. The Neotera who appears in the Oxyrhynchite list of temple-property (cited in chapter one in connection with Typhon) may well be Cleopatra rather than Isis-Aphrodite. The Aphrodite also called Cleopatra whom we meet under Alexander Severus seems again to be a survival of the conjoint cult. Her suicide had its religious aspect, but we should probably see her there not as Isis but as the Queen of Egypt choosing a death through the twin cobras of the traditional crown. (She appears in a relief at Hathor's Dendera temple as Hathor-Isis; beneath the symbols of these goddesses she has a vulture headdress topped by a chaplet or uraei, but no uraeus or double-uraeus in front. No doubt when she assumed royal garb, she wore the crown with the front of double-uraeus.) Representations at Hermonthis show her son Caesarion as the true son of Re, and her interest in Egyptian cult is shown by her presence at the installation of a Bouchis bull.[25]

What political schemes Cleopatra and Antonius had for the organisation of a world-empire, we can only guess. No doubt Cleopatra would have liked to apply generally the methods of Ptolemaic Egypt. This would have meant something like an anticipation of what eventually did happen in the 4th century A.D.— a personal semidivine rule, with a large bureaucracy, and so on; but without the complexity gained by the struggles over the preceding three centuries, and so, above all, without Christianity. This point is not irrelevant to our inquiry here; for it indicates something of the weakness in the Dionysiac synthesis in the post-Alexander world—a desire to achieve the fullness of life by a spontaneous release, a pure reunion of man and nature, without social or political struggle. Though at moments of great social convulsion it might help to beget such visions of *homonoia* as we have found in the Sibylline verses, it could not sustain their ideal and succumbed to glorification of power—of the existing embodiments of power in the State. At each great spasm of change it

rushed up to embrace the new leader—Marius as well as Alexander
—but had only its imagery of an earthly paradise to present in
place of a political and social programme. Though at root an
expression of peace and brotherhood, it became a glorification of
war. Alexander's conquests were a mimesis of the Baccheia; and
Dionysos Thriambos was the name of the god triumphing in war
over India—an old epithet, it seems, with a new meaning.[26]

We have already looked at some of the examples of the theme
of the Dionysiac Triumph in art. Many more might be cited, but
we must keep to a few which are of special interest.[27] On textiles

Dionysos as Indian Victor (Lateran).

we find the triumph set among branches, leaves, vine-tendrils.[28]
North African mosaics show the same setting.[29] A Coptic sculpture shows the god standing under an arbour of vine.[30] But the
god of fertility and enjoyment was also an initiatory god who
brought men a new life, a new consciousness. In the Delphic
hymn of Philodamos, in Alexander's day, the representation of
Dionysos standing in a lion-chariot is compared with the light of
the rising sun; an inscription from Sousa, probably of the 1st
century A.D., identified Dionysos, Apollo, and the Sun; and
Nonnos tries to moralise his picture of the Indian war by making
it a struggle of light and darkness. Hermes sings: "I liken light-
bringer Bacchos to the Sun shining again, and the bold black Indian to the dense darkness."[31]

The association of Alexander and Dionysos continued. Thus, in
the painting in the house of M. Lucretius Fronto at Pompeii the

god's triumph is still very much that of the king.[32] And the imitation went on in life. We can perhaps best end this chapter with a passage from Philon in which he describes the god-masquings of Caligula:

He began at first to liken himself to those beings who are called demigods, such as Bacchos and Herakles and the Twins of Lakedaimon . . . Like an actor in a theatre, he was continually wearing different dresses at different times: at one time taking a lionskin and club, both gilded over, in the guise of Herakles, then wearing a felt hat in the character of the Spartan Twins, Kastor and Pollux, while at times he adorned himself with ivy, a thyrsos, and fawnskins, so as to appear as Bacchos . . . In his envious ambition he appropriated all the honours of the whole body of demigods at once, or as I should say, appropriated the demigods themselves: transforming himself, not into triplebodied Geryon, so as to attract all beholders by the multitude of his bodies, but, what was most extraordinary, changing and transforming the essence of one body into every variety of form and figure, like the Egyptian Proteus, whom Homer represented as being susceptible of every kind of transformation, into all the elements, and into animals and plants belonging to the different elements.

He goes on to say that the emperor has however not imitated the virtues of Herakles and Dionysos. "Have you imitated Bacchos in any respect? have you been the inventor of any new blessings to mankind? have you filled the whole habitable world with joy as he did? are all Asia and Europe inadequate to contain the gifts you have showered on men?" No, but he has even dared to assume the characters of high gods like Hermes, Apollo, Ares, again without embodying any of their good qualities. Philon returns to the image of transformation, this time directly relating it to the theatre. "Like a mummer transforming himself on the stage, putting on all sorts of masks one after another, he sought to deceive the spectators by a series of fictitious appearances."[33]

This account, in which the masquing emperor is seen as a sort supreme pantomime, serves excellently as a lead-in to an account of Nonnos, in whose poetry the processes of transformation are considered to be a cheat and yet to provide the sole clues for a full understanding of reality.

19

The Dionysiac World

"THERE was a certain cave near Thebai in Egypt. As it followed its winding course in the depths of the earth, it formed a natural spiral; for it didn't take a straight course at the opening and then branch off into straight-running corridors, but twisted about under the mountain and made a huge spiral, ending in a most difficult maze." So writes Kallistratos. "In it was set up an image of a Satyr made in marble. He stood on a base in the attitude of one preparing to dance, and lifting backward the sole of his right foot, he not only held a flute in his hand but was also being the first to leap up at its sound." He adds that "the appearance of a Satyr is unkempt, as of a mountain-spirit leaping in honour of Dionysos". Pan stood at his side, embracing Echo, "afraid, I suppose, that the flute might set some musical sound in motion and draw the Nymph into an echoing response to the Satyr". He himself, on seeing the statue, could well believe in the tale of Memnon's statue breaking into a sound at the coming and going of Day.[1]

We might take this Satyr in his spirals and his maze as an emblem of Nonnos' poetry, with its deep earthy song and its endlessly involved filigrees of music, image, symbolism. In it a Greek spirit is singing deep in an Egyptian world. Kallistratos, who is certainly not earlier than the later 3rd century and who may well be a century later, is not so far in this account from Nonnos' own sensibility. The spiral grows *autophyos*, in a selfmade way, and the statue is of stone that grows its wreath. It "was wreathed with ivy, though the sculptor's art did not gather real berries from a meadow—rather the stone itself for all its hardness spread out into sprays and circled the hair, creeping back from the forehead till the ends met at the sinews of the neck".

Alexander and Dionysos had become indissolubly merged as conquerors of India. The identification of Dionysos and Osiris, intensified by the Ptolemies for dynastic reasons, ended by making the Indian Triumph also a part of Egyptian religion. Diodoros tells us that Isis and Osiris were entombed at Nysa in Arabia, so that Dionysos is called Nysaios. On Osiris' stele is inscribed: "I am Osiris the King who has fought wars in every land, as far as the uninhabited regions of India and the far borders of the

Pans in grotto, nymphs dancing above (at Munich); satyrs vintaging (plaque).

North, even to the springs of the river Istros (Danube) and again to the other parts of the earth as far as Okeanos."[2] In an inscription found in Chalkis, dated about A.D. 250–300, we read:

I am Karpokrates son of Sarapis and Isis . . . of Demeter and Kore and Dionysos and Iacchos . . . brother of Sleep and Echo . . . I devised the ways to hunt all kinds of children . . . I established rulers for cities at all times. I preside over the upbringing of children. I established hymns . . . and dances of men and women, the Muses aiding me. I invented the mixing of wine and water . . . of flutes and pipes. I am always at the side of litigants so that nothing unjust may be done. I always share the thiasoi of Bacchoi and Bacchai . . . I cleansed the whole earth: mountaindwelling seadwelling riverdwelling divining-by-throne divining-by-stars . . . hornshaped Agyieus Bassareus of-the-heights Indianslaying thyrsos-shaking Assyrian-hunter wandering-in-dreams giver-of-sleep . . . [3]

Internal analysis shows that it was not translated from Egyptian, but was the work of a Greek-speaking Egyptian or a Greek who had adopted the Egyptian standpoint. Karpokrates seems a corruption of Harpokrates (Isis' son) through *karpos* (fruit). However what concerns us here is the way in which a sort of missionary effort to affirm faith in the Egyptian high gods brings in the Indian invasion and triumph.

Nonnos then had every reason for taking up the theme of the Indian war as a profoundly significant theme for the Graeco-Roman world in general and Egypt in particular. He was born at Panopolis (Chemmis) in the Thebaid, a suitable township for such a poem and a place not far from the Satyr in the spiralling cavern. We can deduce his date only from the internal evidence of his work. Besides his long poem of Dionysos, he paraphrased the Gospel of John in the same metre and style. His date seems best settled as 5th century. Arguments have gone on as to whether he belongs to the late 4th and early 5th or whether we may call the years 450–90 his period of activity. On the whole the later years seem the more likely. Much of the discussion of his dates is rather circular; it depends on comparisons with authors whose own dates are doubtful or who may have borrowed from him rather than have provided him with material. Thus, we have an epigram by Kyros of Nonnos' own town Panopolis, which begins: "Would that the father had taught me to pasture shaggy sheep." Nonnos has two lines with the same opening, "Would that the father had taught me . . ." Kyros is an historically known person, who, through his poetic talents, rose to high office at Byzantion, but, on the retirement of his patronness Eudokia in A.D. 445, became a bishop. His epigram has been dated 441–2. But it is quite likely that Nonnos was imitating Kyros and not the other way round.

The first reference to Nonnos is by Agathias Myrrhinos (A.D. 570); then there is nothing for some centuries till Eustathios (1175) in his commentary on the *Iliad* as well the author of the

Etymologicum Magnum cite the poet of the *Dionysiaka* without naming him. There is no name on our chief manuscript of the poem, and it is only on a papyrus codex of two books, written out perhaps in the 7th century, that the attribution is made.

We may add that there is no sign of a poet of the Nonnan school before Anastasios (491–518) except perhaps Pamprepios and Tryphodoros (who wrote mainly on Homeric themes and whose *Sack of Troy* is extant). Pamprepios raises the most interesting questions. He also was born in Panopolis, was a poet-philosopher, and played an important historical role; he was an avowed pagan, and it seems safe to attribute to him the *enkomion* of another Panopolite, Patrikios Theagenes, who flourished at Athens. This poem is very strongly Nonnan and may be dated 465–75. Altogether, we may assume a strong literary and philosophic development in Panopolis throughout the 5th century, with a nationalist flavour, in which pagan systems of symbolism were carried vitally on. (Kyros' epigram is non-Christian, calling on the Muses; and when he became bishop, he is said to have shown gross ignorance of theology.) It would be rash however to consider Nonnos an obstinate pagan, who was later converted. Pamprepios shows that a rebellious paganism was still possible in literary circles, drawing force no doubt from a sense of national traditions—just as we see at Canopos how the ordinary folk could resent the Christians destroying the pagan shrines that had been such profitable centres of pilgrimage, unless they were given martyr-remains that could serve as an alternative attraction. But Nonnos does not strike one as at all fanatical. What absorbs him is the interpretation of symbols and the problem of defining the moment of transformation. A case may even be put up for arguing that he wrote on St John before Dionysos. We must realise how the fascination by symbolic images, which had long gone on, had both prepared the way for Christianity and also produced an eclectic type of mind that could accept Christianity and yet cling to the old symbols without any sense of incongruity.

Panopolis (Chemmis) was the sort of place where pagan elements might well linger on; and Nonnos could find many stimulations for his Dionysiac enthusiasms in its traditions. With

Koptos, as we saw in connection with hunts, it was the centre of
the cult of Min, the phallic god identified with Pan. Min's temple
was round, with a grove of trees; and phallic rites were part of the
worship. Originally it seems that the king and the queen had had
intercourse during the rites; and various sorts of fertility-acts may
have continued into Nonnos' day. And as for the transition from
Dionysos to Christ (or back again), we have only to recall that
even in the Vatican nekropolis have been found the burials of
initiates who worshipped Isis and Bacchus at the same time,
and in the catacombs of Pretextatus is the tomb of Vibia, an adept

Min, god of the lifted hand, with plumes (a late form); his round temple with streamers;
his grove.

of the Phrygian Dionysos, Sabazios, who was identified with the
Lord Sabaoth.

An interesting sidelight on the possible late continuance of
Dionysiac organisations is thrown by a Coptic relief carved on
limestone in which is a fossil (Nummulite) from the area round
Cairo. The central section consists of a tympanum framed in an
arch that is combined with a truncated pediment—an architectural form not uncommon in Coptic art. Inside is a two-wheeled
chariot drawn by two bulls with their heads turned round to the
onlooker, a circular ornament in the middle of their foreheads.
The seated driver holds the reins in his left hand, a raised whip
in his right, and drives towards a domed circular building, a

tholos or *skias* showing four columns. On the right side, balancing the *tholos*, is a heavy staff of fruit and a three-berried bunch such as Coptic artists used to represent the grape, while some bell-shaped flowers suggest a climbing plant. There can be no doubt that the youthful figure is Dionysos with his bulls and grape-vine—the climber reminds us that the god was connected also with smilax, ivy, and the like. Coptic art provides many examples of Bacchic representations of the vine, in stone, ivory, and textiles. On a gold plate excavated at Siverskaia in the Caucasus there are Bacchic scenes with a background of ivy and vines; a Coptic sculpture shows the god leaning on a *cippus* or small altar, with a luxuriant floral motive; and terracotta vessels from the Fayum and Lower Egypt show him with his body, or a part of it, replaced by the grapevine.

On the relief, on either side of the tympanum, are two busts (originally medallions). These are not allegorical flanking figures, Nymphs or Victories, but portraits with a realistic touch. Funeral portraits were often set on monuments with Bacchic scenes; and the two women in our relief can only be Dionysiac votaries, perhaps priestesses of a thiasos. The style of the relic suggests the 5th–6th century; the sculpture of the god has been dated 6th–7th as well as a head of Bacchos. While there can be no precision in such dating, the works can hardly be earlier than the later 5th century—that is the period which best suits Nonnos. It is hard however to imagine Dionysiac thiasoi at such a time. Hypatia was murdered by the Christians and the Sarapieion at Alexandreia wrecked in the earlier 5th century. Clearly pockets of paganism lingered on for long, especially in the countryside. Justinian in the 6th century had to enact the closing of the temples as well as of the neoplatonic schools; a law of 535 lays down that churches in Africa and their belongings are to be taken from Arians and pagans, and restored to the orthodox; some time before 543 Nerses was occupied with stamping out the remnants of the Isaic cult. The last evidence we have for celebrations of the Diony-siac mysteries is at the time of the emperor Julian and the poet St Paulinus of Nola; but in favourable spots they may have carried on for a generation or so.[4]

Nonnos was an extremely skilful metrist, who carefully keeps to the rules he has devised for stabilising the hexameter in a period when the ancient systems were disintegrating. He managed to reconcile the quantitative bases of verse with the new accentual forms. The musical accent had now yielded before stress; long and short vowels were no longer strictly distinguished in speech and their sounds were growing blurred. To devise a definite and

Siverskaia plate.

melodious system in such a situation was a considerable achievement. The system was naturally not wholly his own work. But we must still allow him a large measure of credit for his remarkable metrical achievement, which for the most part scholars, their ears attuned to the ancient hexameter, have praised grudgingly.[5]

The name Nonnos was common in Asia Minor as well as in Egypt. It has been claimed as originally Egyptian; but we have no clear proof.[6]

The main theme of the *Dionysiaka* is the Indian Invasion; but Nonnos is nothing if not discursively leisurely in his narrative. He begins with the battle of Zeus and Typhon, which takes two

books; then we get the wanderings of Kadmos and the foundation of Thebai in Greece, with the death of Aktaion: three more
books. By the end of the 8th book Dionysos has been born.
Other legends intrude, such as that of Ino and the carrying-off of
Ampelos (Vine) by a bull, his death and rebirth as the vine. By
the 13th book a host is gathering to follow Dionysos, but the 16th
takes us aside to the seduction of Nikaia by Dionysos in her sleep.
Then, though the god has made captive the Indian nation by
getting them drunk, the war begins properly with the 17th book.
After various vicissitudes Dionysos arrives in heaven in the last
lines of the 48th book. There is no need here to detail the episodes; for we are concerned with the essence of what is defined.

First, a word on Nonnos' predecessors. We have already noticed
a poet writing on Lykourgos without any of his magic in the 3rd
century. From the next century we have a piece of the *Bassarika*
by Dionysios, in which the Indian expedition is treated. The poet
uses the same name for the Indian king, Deriades, as Nonnos does
later. Both in style and in material he is superior to the previous
poet, though he lacks the magical undertones of Nonnos. Three
men kill a stag and skin it at the command of a fourth; they dress
the corpse of a foe in the skin. A woman awakens Dionysos.
Coming to the four men, he decrees that the corpse shall be eaten
by its compatriots, then he leaps into the midst of the enemy army
and tells Deriades that they cannot escape unless they rend an
animal apart and eat its raw flesh. He offers them the body in the
stag-skin. The Indians rush to eat the flesh, but Deriades says that
he'd rather eat up Dionysos himself. The whole thing is a strange
twisted application of the cult-practice of rending wild animals
and devouring raw flesh, here used to bring a curse on those who
carry it out. A Dionysiac practice turned into a blasphemy: as
when Aguae rent her son Pentheus in the delusion that he was an
animal. Here is Dionysos' speech to the Indians:

> Slaves of women, Indians, consider now this way.
> Most to Deriades I speak this of my knowledge.
> In your sore straits you won't resist the onrush
> of gleaming wine and avoid your wretched fate
> unless in the hurrying night you rend apart

the raw flesh of a living beast and devour it.
This tall and straighthorned stag, the best of all
that followed from holy Hellas, a wonder to see—
come haste in a good conflict to tear its flesh;
and when the night gives birth to brightness, at once
let's cast the beast's remains in silver coffers
for removal under the broad beams of the sun.[7]

What looks forward to Nonnos is the theme of a mysterious significant cheat or delusion.

Papyrus fragments show many war-pieces of contemporary bearing. The common theme is the fight with the Blemmyes in the south, who were taking advantage of the weakened empire to renew attacks and who appear in the romances, e.g. Aithiopika. In Nonnos they are the allies of the Indians. A poem of the early 4th century deals with the Persian war of Diocletian and Galerius: that is, the conflict of east and west. Our fragment opens with the end of a fiery speech and the soldiers (Persians) rushing to arms; their vast numbers are stressed. Mythology and history are mixed. The soldiers are maddened by Enyo's lash; their gathering is compared to the Persians at Thermopylai and to the host that Nereus assembled on rafts hurrying over the sea. Thus the two emperors are described—those held in the west are their colleagues Constantius Chlorus and Maximian:

> . . . hung blossoming garlands from the sterns of ships.
> (Other kings would have rushed with aid from Italy;
> but one was held by battle in Spain and round
> the other went flames in Britain's Isle outblazing.)
> So one from Crete, the second from seagirt Delos—
> Zeus over Othrys, Apollo to Pangaios—
> goes forth, gird on their armour, and make tremble
> the mob of Giants. Then comes our elder Lord
> by the younger King, east with the Ausonian host,
> like blessed gods: the one a match in might
> for Zeus above, for longhaired Apollo the other . . . [8]

Such themes must have given a fresh stimulus to the image of the Dionysiac march on India. Of the same date, and perhaps by the same hand, is a poem on the Creation of the Universe, which shows a Grecized Egyptian cosmogony. It starts with God and the four elements out of which a Kosmos is to be made. God begets out of himself a second god Hermes (Thoth) as demiurge, who harmonises the strife of elements and creates heaven and earth. (In a gap he seems to decide to create life and change himself into the sun.) He looks for a place to set life when it is created, decides to build a city, and rejects the extremes of north and south. (Obviously he was to pick on Egypt, which even the Greeks accepted as the first inhabited region. Perhaps the main point of the poem was the narration of the historical foundation of some particular city.) With the golden regulating wand given by Zeus, and "clad in wonderful fourfold shape" (himself the four elements), he shuts his eyes and bids the elements cease from strife and fall apart.

Victory of Dionysos (sarcophagus, Vatican).

"Then you shall come together in a better way; for I'll create mutual love and friendship among you, in your day of separation, toward a better destiny." So, "united they forgot their immemorial conflict." He makes a sphere by whirling the sky round and divides it into seven zones under seven star-leaders. "Their wandering revolves the constellations; one under another they rove in close array." The earth is fastened in the centre. There is still only Night "faintly gleaming under the thin rays of the stars". After a gap, Hermes goes through the grey skies with his Son, Logos, "the swift herald of his Father's pure purpose". They go to earth "seeking a temperate climate where he might found a city . . ."[9]

The *Dionysiaka*, as we have noted before, is a poem in which the parts are more important than the whole; and yet for all its sprawling lack of dramatic structure the work is held together by certain pervading concepts. On the one hand there is the image of triumphant Dionysos, in which had long been packed the popular hope and demand for the fullness of life. This image, born out of the simple fertility-rite in the political struggles that welded the democratic *polis*, had become entangled with the world of absolutist power; and was thus rent by a ceaseless ambivalence. It expressed the submission to the absolutist State and the obstinate hope of turning the ruler into the beneficent god of a world of peace and plenty; it expressed also the wish to wrench from the power-world the controls that prevented any such hope coming true. It represented the desperate clinging to the sources of joy and renewal in experience—sources that could not be wholly closed up under even the most parched and oppressive of existences.

On the other hand the poem sees Dionysos as more than the sustainer of all that makes for joy and liberation; it sees him as the deep force driving life onwards and begetting an endless series of transformations. Under the surfaces endless new possibilities are seething and coalescing, and no one can predict exactly what forms will emerge. Despite all the absolutist controls and the dogmatic impositions, there is an incalculable element that makes for joy and liberation, for new forms and balances of energy. Life consists of surfaces, with their complex rationalisations and habitual acceptances, and also of underdepths, in which all that the surfaces assert may be contradicted. Which is reality? which is illusion? This is the question continually posited by the poem.

Nonnos builds up his world out of a large number of ingredients; mythology from all sorts of sources, including previous poets, local legends, folklore. He draws on magic, astrology, and other intellectual fields of study of his day.[10] He is capable of high lyrical verve and can construct charming genre-pictures. Here however we shall keep our analysis to the two main points outlined above, which give his poem its unity and reveal his originality, his profound significance as the poet of his epoch.

For him the association of things or persons goes beyond the level at which the simile serves. Vital association implies iden-

tity or a conflict issuing in transformation. Hence the simile
plays a slight part in his aesthetic, and his similes, few and scattered,
could be omitted without any damage to his essential effects.[11]
We have only to think what a loss for the Homeric poems
would be the omission of their similes to realise something of
what has occurred. In a sense, the progress of poetry is a continual
absorption of the simile into the metaphor; and Nonnos represents one of the decisive turning-points. Here, as in all things,
he appears as the poet of the breakdown of the ancient world
and of the transition into the medieval. We have already noticed
something of this quality of his in the way he fuses girl and flower.
Here are some more examples:

> Who has dimmed the red that glowed upon your face
> and changed the roses to brief anemones?

> Your body
> is a single anemone flushed and flowering for ever.

> I'll change my shape,
> mix with the birds and flit a philomela.
> I'll be a swallow beloved of the zephyr of spring,
> messenger of roses and of the blossoming dew,
> a bird that chatters its sweet song under the tiles
> and flashes about its nest with dancing wing.[12]

His lyricism is based in turning the simile into a magical identification. "The breezes piped a tune with their wings all night."
Wind, birds, and musical instrument are fused; the fluttering of
the wings, the shaking of boughs in the breeze, the quavering of
notes are grasped in a single image.[13] Nature is alive and shares
in human or animal delights and fears; there is a continual movement from one sphere to the other:

> The doublepipe made music and quickened the dancers
> with its rollicktune in time to the leaping steps.
> And the trees all murmured, the rocks gave out a boom,
> the revelforests shook with conscious nods,
> and the dryads sang. Bearpacks joined the dance . . . [14]

Mythology comes alive, an aspect of immediate experience:

> If I go to the misty sunset, my comfort's the Moon
> who felt as I feel, for Endymion stretcht upon Latmos.[15]

There results a sense of elusive mystery in life, which at the same time yields a conviction of inner reality and grasps the moment of transformation:

> Both of them there were haunted with shadowy dreams,
> their eyes glimpsing the wing of a nightingale sleep.[16]

This is all something quite new and is based in a new vigour, a rebirth, of language. Ovid in his *Metamorphoses* had told at length

Dionysos leaning on Ampelos (Vienne, Isere); Ariadneo Dionysos, Ampelos (plague).

many myths of the changes of people into birds, animals, plants; and his conclusion shows that he had a serious Pythagorean philosophy of transformation and rebirth or reincarnation behind the tales. But the thought is far behind them. At best the tales illustrate it; they are not a poetic incarnation with the meaning powerfully present at several levels. But for Nonnos transformation is not merely an idea; it lies at the core of all experience, a matter of everyday life as well as of myths. He is the poet of alchemic process.

Interestingly, the precondition of Nonnos' imagery is found,

N

not in literary works, but in the epitaphs on tombs, which, even
if written by hack-poets, represent a sort of popular verse, embodying ideas that have arisen directly from the people concerned
or are felt to be likely to make a special appeal to them. And the
ideas involved are those of transformation, even if there is a
simple and crude material basis for the fantasies. The following
are versions of Greek epigrams from Nîmes and Rome:

> Vibius, may all things about you turn violets,
> marjoram, water-narcissus and roses too.

> On Akyleinos, good earth, lie light and grow
> such delicate flowers as you in India bear,
> in Arabia. Grow them by his breast below.
> Then dew that comes from his fragrant skin
>   will show
> the gods with loving-kindness hold in care
> the child within, who thus deserves libation
> and sacrifices, but not lamentation.

The remark about dew shows that the poet conceives the flowers,
their scent and dew as direct products of the child—indeed that
they represent the child in a new form. The child as flower and
dew deserves worship of a kind. This type of conceit is usually
employed for children or women. From near Astypalaia we get
an inscription, "May there be teeeming of flowers from his
bones." From Karales we get:

> May your bones, Pomptilla, turn violet and lilies,
> may you burgeon out in flowers of roses too,
> sweet crocus and the unaging amaranth.
> May you blossom into beautiful white lilies
> so Time, far ahead, may own some flower of you
> to match the narcissus and lamented hyacinth.

Narcissus and hyacinth have myths of the metamorphosis of
young persons; Pomptilla's "white lily" is probably meant to represent some new flower that will express her as the rosy lotus
was said to embody Antinoos. Again on a stele of Sardeis, com-
memorating Menophilos, a lily is cut: the text states that "the

flower is his youth, which a daimon has ravished". (The lily was used to cure snake-bite and toadstool-poisoning; it effaced wrinkles with its renewing powers.) A Latin example from Rome carries the idea on further:

> O, if the gods will hearken to my prayer,
> a new flower growing from your tomb I'll view,
> with greening bough, with amaranth-blossom too,
> with the violet's rosy or purple glow. And there
> the passer-by those flowers will descry,
> read the inscription, and let out a sigh:
> "This Flower's the Body of Flavia Nicopolis."

In these epitaphs the dead body becomes a flower, which in some sense or other is the youth or girl in a new form of life. Nonnos turns the transformation by death into one already present in life because of the unity of human and natural process. From this aspect it is worth noting that three epitaphs from Alexandreia have the phrase, "Let all the earth shed tears." Mourner and earth are felt as one.[17]

Nonnos has thus an incessant delight and wonder at the spectacle of life with its endless changes; and this emotion is one of love. As he says, "Love is neighbour to Wonder", Eros lies close to Thauma. *Thaumata* can mean conjurer's tricks: which brings out the link of magic with the countless changes of juggling Nature. (The preceding sentence indeed referred to a *thambos* overcoming Zeus as he looks at Semele, and *thambos* is a sort of magical stupefaction.)[18]

Hence the paradox of his world, in which all is unstably in change and yet some deep consistent forces of renewal assert themselves and vindicate the strength of love:

> and the deepbosomed spring,
> filled with the showering tears that were freshly shed
> upon her sorrowing face, grew dark, lamenting
> the heavy grief of ungrieving Dionysos.[19]

The world is topsyturvy. The poem opens with the vision of violent cosmic conflict and confusion. Typhon cries: "Smash the House of Zeus, O my hands! Shake the foundations of the uni-

verse and the blest ones with it. Break the selfturning divine bar
of Olympos. Drag down to earth the pillar of heaven", and so
on.[20] The elements irrupt on one another, earth and water, water
and fire.

> In the depths of the mountaintorrent a straying boar
> encountered a dolphin of the sea . . .
> The manyfooted squid dragged his coils on the hills
> and pounced on the hare. The dripping Tritons wagged
> their green forked tails against their flanks at the edge
> of a secret wood and hid in the mountain vaults
> where Pan had his home . . . [21]

Patera with triumphant Dionysos and Herakles (found Rennes) with gold coins, Hadrian
to Julia Domna, round rim.

(The last lines suggest the Thebaid scene of Kallistratos and its link with Nonnos' birthplace, the City of Pan.) Chaos forever threatens order. The war of the elements reappears in Dionysos' campaigns and reaches its climax in his final battles.[22] At one moment Okeanos threatens to rise up and break all the heavenly systems, reversing the catasterisms or metamorphoses that have changed persons or things to constellations.[23] A favourite formulation of Nonnos is that *the universe is adrift*. The problem is to restore its meaning and purpose: for instance,

> I'll make you rescuer
> of the world's harmony and Harmoneia's husband;
> and you, Love, primal foundation of fecund marriage,
> bend your bow—and the universe is adrift no longer.

The universe ceases to be a lost wanderer, *aletes*.[24]

The universe is continually broken and cast adrift; but Nature heals and mends all broken things.

> Then Nature, controller of the kosmos, of ever-renewed
> Matter, closed up the gaping rents in the broken earth.[25]

Nature is *tamie* of the kosmos. *Tamia* is properly housewife, but here is equivalent to *tamias*, steward, treasurer, controller. Matter is defined as *palingenes*, self-renewing. Thus Nonnos reveals his essentially materialist, or at least pantheist, position, and joins hands with Philon on his organicist side. The divine forms are principles of the perpetual power of life and of more life in Nature. *Tamie* is seen to suggest its root-meaning of cutting-up or distributing, *tamnein, temnein*; Nature is the inherent power of matter to divide, break up, and yet combine in new forms, *palingenes*. I do not mean that Nonnos had a consistently worked-out philosophy; but such views lay at the heart of his vision, his system of imagery.

The revival after the moment of chaos and destruction is also expressed in terms of myth. Thus, after Zeus has struck down Phaethon for usurping the sunchariot and endangering the universe, he restores order on the eternal principles:

> He bound the recalled harmony with a like-aged bond
> and gave the sun his horses, the skychariot
> brought to the place of rising . . .
> All the earth once more laughed. Rain cleared the fields
> come from lifebreeding Zeus and with moist showers
> quenched the wandering fires, all that the fiery horses
> spat whinnying from burning throats over the earth.
> Helios rose and drove his car on its ancient road;
> crops sprouted and the orchards laughed once more,
> receiving the lifegiving warmth from the sky as of old.[26]

Beyond everything lies the image of Dionysiac plenty: an end to
which the universe aspires and which is yet present as the innermost significance of all experience: something that has to be realised by the individual in all its existential immediacy and at the
same time brought into being in the outer world: a condition
of peace, happiness, and sustained harmony with nature—which
implies also harmony with oneself and one's fellows. Take for
instance the opening of the twenty-second book when the host
reaches the Indian Nile, the Hydaspes:

> All the earth laughed, the rocks gave out a boom,
> the naiads alleluia'd, the nymphs in mazes
> circled over the silent streams of the river and sang
> a melody of Sicilian tune.

The relation to the pastoral is correctly stated.

> All the woodland rang,
> the wise trees uttered a music like the hoboy,
> the hamadryads cried out and the nymph was singing,
> peeping up halfglimpsed over her leafy cluster.
> The spring, though water, turned white and poured a stream
> of snowy milk. In the hollow of the torrent
> the naiads bathed in the milky currents and drank
> the white milk. The rugged rock spilled out
> wine from red nipples and deeply stained itself
> as on the unplanted hill the must welled up
> in showers sweet to drink. The pleasant gifts
> of honeydropping bees selfdribbled from holes
> without the need of hives. From newsprung bushes
> of spikehaired thorn the softbloomed apples sprouted.

Oil poured of itself on the twigs of Athena's tree
and bathed it in unpressed drops.
                                    And hares embraced
the dancing dogs, and lengthy serpents joined
the jolly dance, downcurving heads and licking
the prints of snakyhaired Dionysos.

Here is the vision of the lion lying down with the lamb which
had been vainly promised in the evangel of Antonius and Cleopatra, and then in that of Augustus. True, in the 5th century it
is further away than ever from earthly fact, yet it seems
closer as a potentiality because of the deep historical changes,
ultimately more far-reaching than the creation of the empire,

Triumph of Dionysos (sarcophagus, Rome).

which were going on—just as the idiom of the outcast and hopelessly oppressed has triumphed in Christianity, yet has seemed
only to provide a gilding for the absolutist State. Something
unparalleled has happened, though it is going to take a long
time for the final act of the new drama.

Further, we may note that the picture of the redeemed earth
gives us an essential clue for the obsession of Nonnos with
epithets that define self-growth, self-movement, self-circling or
spiralling, self-fulfilment. The self-movement represents the spon-
taneity of the universe released from all fetters and realising itself
in joy, in fullness, in Dionysiac redemption.

More, this spontaneous release, where all things find themselves in harmony, is a condition of realised rhythm, of dance.
Hence the way in which the whole action of the epic, which we

saw in connection with the pantomime, is one of a vast continuous dance-drama. To make one's point fully effective, one would have to quote most of the long poem. Conflict is resolved in Komos, in Revel.

> Zeus quickly turned his golden chariot
> to the aithereal stars' round rim; beside him
> with skywhip Victory drove her Father's team.
> So the god came once more to the heavens; the stately Seasons
> welcomed him, opening the gates aloft. With Zeus
> victorious, the other gods homed, doffing
> the shapes with wings they'd assumed, in their own forms.
> Unarmed and daintily-robed Athena came.
> Ares turned Komos, and Victory was song.[27]

War has become revel and Victory is now simply song. Again:

> Women's voices resounded, echoing the Revel
> of Salvation, Inachian women and Mainads
> cast their heedless fury to the winds.[28]

Indeed the war itself is one involved dance. All nature dances. The Seasons dance. Zeus dances into Semele's chamber. Bearing Dionysos, she continually dances on the hills.[29] Dionysos is the teacher of dances, the ever-dancing. Life is for ever

> proclaiming the rites of danceweaving Dionysos:
> there was no one in the city who would not dance:
> the countryfolk wreathed the streets with leafage of spring.

There is no dance proper without Dionysos. Without him the Seasons joylessly

> plaited garlands only of meadowgrass for the gods.
> Wine lacked. The grace of the unbacchus'd dance
> was halved and vain. The company were charmed
> only when a dancer circled in twists and turns
> with a tumult of steps, with nods his only words,
> a hand his mouth and fingers for his voice.

The Dionysiac dance is the dance of life and its highest moments come in the art of the pantomime, which gives the dance its full consciousness as the interpretation and exaltation of life.

20

World Within World

WE HAVE already had cause to cite a few examples of Nonnos' use of the notions of delusion and counterfeit forms. But if we are to penetrate at all fully into his definition, we must explore this part of his poetry more thoroughly; for here it is that he gives depth and complexity to the general vision of Dionysiac energy and liberation. However, we cannot make this exploration without a close attention to texts and to the use of certain keywords. In the following exposition I shall do my best to make things easy for the reader without Greek. The resulting insight into Nonnos' mind, and indeed into the mental processes of his epoch, is worth the tortuous inquiry. Once the general drift of his ideas are grasped the investigation has a considerable fascination.

First, for convenience' sake, I should like to set out the main terms and the equivalents I use for them. In order that the reader may follow Nonnos' consistent use of the terms, it is necessary not to change the words used in translation, even if the result at times lacks the elegance of the original and obscures the close connection of some of the words.

eidos: form	*eikon*: image
morphe: shape	*demas*: body (living)
eidolon: phantom	(*soma*: corpse)
indalma: apparition	*phasma*: phantasm
mimema: imitation	*mimelos*: imitative or mimic
typos: type	*antitypos*: antitype
poikilos: motley	*poikilonotos*: motleybacked
(dappled, spotted, varying, variegated, changeful)	*stiktos*: stippled
daidalos: intricate	*polydaidalos*: much intricate

N*

prosopeion: face
(also dramatic mask
or persona)

allophyes: transformed.

Then there is another group of words dealing with cheat and delusion:

nothos: bastard or counterfeit
dolos: crafty
(epithet in many
compounds)
apatelios: deceitful, illusive
pseudaleos: delusive
opsis: vision

pseudomenos: imposter
dolos: craft or trick
doloplokos: cheatwoven

epiklopos: deceptive
emphron: conscious
opope: appearance

Dionysos as Indian Conqueror (scenes above include his birth and handing-over to the Nymphs): sarcophagus from the hypogaeum of the Licinii Crassi on the Via Salaria.

We may begin with *poikilos*. (I shall attempt to exemplify a term by passages where it is the main component, but inevitably the whole complex we are considering tends to come together.) *Poikilos* has a very ancient sacred association. Sappho's ode to Aphrodite begins with the word *poikilothron* : "Motleythroned immortal Aphrodite." An archaic Arkadian inscription states: "If any woman wears a robe that is brightly-coloured, it shall be consecrated to Demeter Thesmophoros. If she does not consecrate the garment, let her, being unfriendly as regards a sacrificial garment, be outlawed, and let whoever is Demiourgos pay out

30 dr. If the Demiourgos does not pay, or if he does not have authority over the impious act, ten years shall be the duration of the curse in this latter event." The robe that must be consecrated is one that is *zteraion loipon* (braided or embroidered). The term here translated as "let her be outlawed" means literally "let her perish [for all we care]" and has been taken to mean a death penalty; outlawry is however more likely. In any event we see how in Arkadia of the 6th–5th century B.C. a motley-coloured dress was taken as necessarily sacred, at least in a festival context. (*Zteraios* in the inscription has essentially the same meaning as *poikilos*.) There seems a strong and wide-spread conviction that a woman too brightly dressed, or showing a *poikilos* robe, at a ritual moment, would affront a goddess as her rival. Thus again at Patrai in the 3rd century B.C., embroidered robe or cloak, *lopion poikilon*, was forbidden, as well as purple or cosmetics in the cult of Demeter. At Andania, Lykosoura and Kios, women must not wear gilded robes or ornaments of gold on ritual occasions.[1]

Poikilos, we saw, gained a fresh force in the aesthetic of the paradise, expressing the twinkling and variegation of the leaves and flowers, the play of light over the scene. The sacred dress is one with the sacro-idyllic landscape, which is the embroidery of Aphrodite and the Seasons.[2] (Its earliest meaning, *e.g.* in Homer, Hesiod, Pindar, seems many-coloured, dappled, mottled: applied to snake, fawnskin, leopardskin, embroidery, metalwork. Something of the spin-image perhaps comes in with *iynx*, the bird used in wheelmagic, and in *sphaira*, ball or sphere. The Poikile at Athens was so called from its wall paintings by Polygnotos. Meanings of changing, varying, manifold come in: applicable to song or prose-style. Intricate, complex, abstruse, subtle, changeable, unstable, are natural extensions.[3]) For Nonnos it helps to sum up, with *daidalos* (which suggests the complexities of art-process and product), the moment of transformation and of deep realisation, when different levels of life collide. Thus:

[Dionysos shapeshifting:] sometimes a motley-shaped baby, sometimes like a mad youth.

Figuring with wordless hand a motley-eloquent silence.

A cheatwoven vision of sleep, that paints motley phantasms, spoke in a shadowformed counterfeit shape.

A motley necklace in dazzlehues of adornment . . . bewitching your mind by crafty hope of triumph.

[Dionysos shapeshifting:] If as leopard he spring up in air from his pads with stormy leap, changing his much-intricate form, I'll hymn the Son of Zeus.

You sceptred imposter . . . when you re-enter the motley-backed vault of the highranging stars, let craftyminded Prometheus leave his chains and come to you.

Why craft instead of battle? Are you afraid that you change your much-intricate form?

[The distracting moon displays] motley-shaped phantasms.

The motley meadow is patterned with bright stars.

How may I liken the motley starface to an intricate fawnskin?

His shape was changed and I wept over a fawn . . . you have beheld no alien type of your dead son . . . I alone beheld my son a bastard corpse. I lamented a transformed, stippled and voiceless image of his shape . . . Change my mortal shape to a deer, and when I am changed to the same horned shape as your deer, do not yoke me . . .[4]

The first two examples show compound forms, *poikilomorphos* and *poikilomythos*; the third uses a verb, *poikillousa*. What is brought out is the way in which the epithets *poikilos*, *daidalos*, *stiktos*, with their suggestion of changing evanescent colour and patterns of light, provide an essential aspect of the moment of transformation for Nonnos.

Some passages from Philon will help us to understand. First he is allegorising Jacob's Coat of Many Colours. "He is properly said to put on a *poikilos* coat, for politics is a *poikilos* and multiple (*polytropos*) thing, liable to a myriad changes (*metabolai*)."[5] Behind the colour-image lies a sense of the increasing complexity that has come over social life and which begets incessant transformations in men and in society: the new quantities leading into new qualities, the aggregations into new formations. Elsewhere, however, in analysing the "variegated and stippled" coat at length, he introduces his pessimistic attitude to all relationships and thus achieves much the same idiom as Nonnos in his delusion-complex.

He clad himself in the much-variegated (*pampoikilos*) web of political affairs, in which a minimal amount of truth is contained, but many large portions of false, probable, plausible, conjectural matter, out of which sprang all the sophists of Egypt, bird-interpreters, ventriloquists, portent-readers, adepts at decoying, spellbinding, bewitching, whose insidious crafts it is no easy task to escape. So Moses shows philosophic insight (*physikos*) in introducing this coat all bloodstained; for the whole life of the political man is stained, warring and warred against, receiving blows and shots from the mishaps that befall it . . . Why then invest ourselves with the gauds of political importance, as with some costly garment, and bear ourselves proudly in it, deceived

Dionysos in the land of the Maides (from Mt. Orbelos).

by the fairness of what meets the eye, and not noting its insidious and dangerous ugliness, which is out of sight, hidden away? Let us cast off this showy tunic and put on the sacred one woven with the *poikilmata* of virtues.[6]

One aspect then of the moment of change, with its variegations, is its revelation of unexpected and treacherous depths.

Philon brings out another aspect of variation in his analysis of the serpent as pleasure. Pleasure is called *poikile* because "she glides with many a coil about every part". Pleasure, "being then a thing so *poikile*, was it not fitly compared to a tortuous animal, the serpent?"[7] Philon goes on to compare the serpent-pleasure with its variegations "to that part of us corresponding to the turbulent mob of a city", which "pines for the dwellings in Egypt. That is, in the corporeal mass, it encounters pleasures that bring death", the death of the soul. Here we find a Nonnan link of variegation with circular or spiral movement—though in the Dionysiac scheme of things these bring new life to the soul, not death. Joy is their essence, despite the dangers lurking in the moment of change. Philon himself stresses the basis of the coiling or spiralling pleasures in the variegations of art:

Pleasures become *poikilai* through sight, those afforded by every kind of painting and sculpture, and by all other artistic productions which in one art after another delight the sight; by the changes (*diaphorai*) also that plants undergo as they sprout up, blossom, and bear fruit; by the manydivided fine shapes of animals. Similarly the ear gets pleasure from the flute, the harp, every sort of instrument, the melodious voices of unreasoning creatures, swallows, nightingales, other birds made musical by Nature, the euphonious speech of beings endowed with reason, musicians exercising their histrionic powers in comedy, tragedy and all that is put on the stage.[8]

Here the link of art with nature is used to urge its degradation; for Nonnos the link is its supreme virtue, expressive of the unity of all being.

Now let us turn to *eidos, morphe, demas, prosopeion*.

The naked form of Athena.
Changing his widespread form, he shapeshifted into another nature.
Putting off the form of the dreamface.
She changed her body and stood there in the form of a Bacchant.
[Hermes] put off the higher form of selfborn Phanes and resumed his original shape.
Megaira cast off the terrible serpent shape and waited like in nature to an owl.
They have human shape and shaggy horned goathead. Twelve Pans there were with this bastard form.
[She changed magically] the former form of their human appearance; a shape longeared in nature appeared in them.[9]
Athene changed her craftwoven form . . . He grasped that the human shape which bore the deceitful image of Morrheus was the imitation of an antitypal face.

Set up a new star of Seafaring Loves and make in the aither an image of an antitypal bull.

Dionysos disguised himself by craft in a deceptive form; he donned a counterfeit shape.

[Persephone] once amused herself in a shining bronze plate [mirror] which reflected her face like a judge of beauty; she confirmed the type of her shape by this silent selfacting herald, testing the delusive body in the shadowy mirror and smiling at the imitative image.

Beroe smeared no reddish ornament for the skin on her round rosy face, no rouge put a lying blush on her counterfeit cheeks; she consulted no shining bronze mirror with its antitypal reflection of her looks, she laughed at no unbreathing form of a mimic appearance to estimate her beauty.

A transformed counterfeit image of the unseen Megaira . . . He saw the shadowy deceptive image of the shape of Artemis; with his eyes he beheld the empty phantom, and the antitypal phantasms made him desire to go hunting.[10]

We see how unstable form is conceived to be; at the same time it provides the sole clue to reality and to illusion. (*Poikilos* too had developed a submeaning of unstable.) The gods who represent the principles of the life-process are precisely those who are most given to shapeshifting and change. Yet because they do represent the principles, they also stand for stability of structure, for the possibility of our understanding how and why the changes occur, and of sifting out the cheat from the reality. The naked form of Athene did not bring about a shapeshifting; it blasted the eyes of the beholder, but gave him a deepened consciousness. "The brilliancy of the eyes she transplanted into your mind." Each type or definite image, *typos*, has its *antitypos*, its corresponding image or opposite which somehow balances it, establishes its dynamic identity. The antitype creates the full reality of the type, completes the type, reflects it, and yet opposes it.[11]

As always, the analogy of the pantomime pervades the conceptions. Thus, Mimas (note the name) performs a "rolling-gaited well-measured wardance, whirling a dancetype sword" and "brandishing a spear in mimic armoured leap of the dance". Fighters "clanged naked swords on beaten shields with resounding clashes, with antitypal *skarthmoi* (leapings); they imitated the rhythm of the dance-at-arms with quick circling movements of the feet, revelling on the battlefield." (Note the circling whirls and spiralling movement, which is linked in turn with the death-roll or backtumble.) Zeus, "disguised in bastard body of a mimic archeress with unrecognisable limbs", woos Antiope "in a tricking type, with a mimic love of a dancing bridal". Love, dream, and mime intermingle: Dionysos, dreaming of Beroe, "beheld the apparitions of his troubles and sent his mind flying in mimic dream till he mixed with her in a shadowy marriage". He prays to have again "the same vision of a dream, desiring the deceitful phantasm of an embrace".

Instead of saying that arrows are like a flight of cranes, Nonnos

Triumph of Dionysos (Rome, Coll. Torlonia).

writes, "It was the mimic type of a flight of cranes." (This idiom can lead to a sort of kenning, in which an arrow becomes a "wellfledged bastard bird", and Zeus as a bull swimming the waters is a "mimic seaship alive with nimble knees".) Instead of saying that the stripped skin of Seilenos looks like a live man, Nonnos writes, "the breeze often swells it out in a mimic type of him". The forces of nature beget a pantomimic activity everywhere, for all things correspond together and suggest one another; human and natural process are inextricably entangled. "This was the type with his hands", Nonnos says of the expressive gesture. When Poseidon comes as water, as "a liquid seducer", he is "a bastard Enipeus [river] with mimic ripples". Poseidon becomes a river; but the river is not really a river; the ripples are mimic ripples. A mask worn by satyrs is the "terrifying bastard form of a lying voiceless face". The image of Persephone in the mirror, which expresses both her self-consciousness and her selfdeception, is also a "selfacting herald" who mimes the part of the fascinated woman, charming her "silently". This point is brought out by relating the *typos* to the shadow: "As a shadowy type of a man, inanimate moving, accompanies him close-appearing without a mark, running as he runs, standing when he stands, sitting when he sits, and at table sharing the meal with mimic hands..." The silent mimicking shadow is the perpetual pantomime.[12]

Life is thus seen as a continual sliding-away of the face of things and the advent of a new form, a new reality. But the moment of change, of birth and rebirth, is not a simple or painless thing; it involves pang and confusion; it begets a strange light of consciousness in which the danger and the cheat underlying the old surfaces is abruptly and frighteningly brought out.

There are many aspects of these ideas and the images by which Nonnos expresses them that we could investigate. There is the mimic act that merges men with nature. Maron, lifted by two dancing satyrs, is "the antitypal imitation of the crescent moon". Herakles wears "a motley robe, type of the sky, image of the universe". Seilenos, changing, owns "the same-natured imitation of the much twisting stream."[13] Dionysos "changed his turnabout form and assumed an intricate phantasm of all sorts of shape", he became "a wild firestorm shooting tongues of crooked flame through dancing smoke", then running water "rolling a deceitful wave", then the "same-natured imitation of a leonine face", then "like something with much-intricate form of shadowy foliage", he shaped himself into an alien appearance and ran up like a selfmade sapling into the sky; "his head changed and he tree-grew a bastard head-of-hair with mimic leafage". After that he "wove a mimic type with stippled limbs" and leaped like a panther; changed his body again and rose as a moving firebrand, then a lion. Deriades went on fighting the voiceless phantasms with vain hopes. "He always wanted to grasp the intangible phantom with hands unable to touch it; he thrust his lance in the countenance of the antitypal lion and cried threats against many-formed Bacchos.[14]

Inevitably there is an element of magic in the changes. Thus.

Envy "put on the lying shape of antitypal Ares, with mimic armour: the shieldfront he scored with a liquid compounded from a drugging (*pharmakoeis*) flower for bloodsmears; he dipped his tricking fingers in vermilion dye, staining his hand with isotype redstuff a bastard reddening gore . . ." The magic is linked with the recipes of transformative dyes which at Alexandreia played so large a part in the early developments of alchemy. And continually the spiralling, twisting movement intrudes: "the flame twisted selfspiralling (*autoeliktos*) round Morrheus' neck, as if conscious of what it did". As Amphion's music builds Troy, "at the tune a hill, twisting itself on to a selfrolled course, danced, though only a

Triumph of Dionysos and Herakles (Rome).

work-of art". Atlas "could scarcely hold up the selfspiralling firmament of stars."

Such imagery shows Nonnos' closeness to the thought of the alchemists. Thus Zosimos, who seems to be writing in the early 4th century and who was a citizen of Nonnos' town Panopolis, stressed the sexual analogy in defining the union of opposites in all process. "Above what is heavenly, below what is earthly; by the male and the female the work is accomplished." And, "Mary said: Join the male and the female, and you will find what you are seeking."

The passages I cite will have brought out how difficult it is to translate Nonnos in a way that will truly reflect the movement and meaning of his thought. The verses can be made easy and flat by ignoring the particular force of each term and using a generalised diction; but then his originality disappears and the precise definitions of his imagery, with its basis in a world of alchemic correspondences and fusions.[15] We might go on to show how the conflict of forms at the moment of change is related to the truth-and-illusion of dreams, which are prophetic of things to come: "the phantoms of a mimic dream leaped through the undeceiving Gate of Horn"—and yet lack all stability.[16] Desire cheats and yet drives life on. "I'll tell you the multifarious ways of crafty desire." It merges with dream. "Gamos, whom love got in shadowy dreams, fulfilling the illusive desire of the mimic embrace, after from sleeping Zeus he had sprinkled the wet seed over the earth with the selfmarrying swordpoint."[17]

There is a wide complex of images based on the epithet *nothos* (translated here bastard or counterfeit). Some instances have already been cited; and as the series merely reinforces what has been said above, I shall cite no more. There is again a large number of *auto*-terms, which bring out how deeply rooted in Nonnos' worldview was the idea of spontaneous inner movement as an aspect of Dionysiac liberation.[18] We must however say something more of the crucial terms *type* and *antitype*, the image and its correspondences. The word *typos* means a blow or its effect, a mark or impression. It thus came to mean any wrought figure or statue, a man's form (himself), the general form or character of a thing, then (by Platon's time) the idea of a thing; an original type or model, a pattern or sample; an outline, sketch, draught—with special meanings such as the form of expression or style, the kind of a disease, an action for debt, and (by the Byzantine times of Nonnos) an ordinance or decree. Theophrastos had used it of the impressions on the senses; and this meaning, together with the meaning of image, actual or mental, lies at the heart of Nonnos' use. The root-meaning of a blow was never quite submerged, and the *typos* is linked with the seal, *sphragis*. We may note also that the word *charakter* has the root-meaning of something cut-in, stamped, impressed; and came to signify a characteristic mark or a likeness, an image. The creative impact or blow transforms as well as handing on a likeness; it can turn things into their opposite. Philon says of Jobel that his name, "translated into Greek means transforming the nature of things and making them other

than they are; for he changed (*metecharatten*) the godformed beauty
of wisdom, endurance, justice, and virtue in general into opposite
types, obliterating all that was impressed before."[19] In another
work he links the idea of contrary impressions or forces with the
Garden of Eden. "The Man stamped with the spirit that is after
God's image differs in no way, it seems to me, from the Tree
bearing the fruit of immortal life . . . The earthy man has a disposition of versatile subtlety, fashioned and concocted of elements of all sorts." It was then to be expected that God would set
in the *paradeisos* (the whole kosmos) the middle-mind "played upon by forces driving it in opposite directions and given the power
of choice."[20] (The importance of the image of the blow or seal
in this world is brought out by the Christian idea of Baptism as a
sphragis or *signaculum*, impressing the new life on the convert and
obliterating the old.[21])   *Antitypos* developed as the opposite
term to *typos*. It expressed repulsion by a hard body; *typos
antitypos*, the blow against blow of hammer and anvil. It took on
the sense of echo and reflection, of correspondence (to the stamp),
of mental impression. The sense of repulsion survived, giving the
word a suggestion of the springy and elastic as well as of the rigid
and inelastic, the stubborn and obstructive; it expressed harshness
in sounds, *harmoniai*, and in colour. The sense of "opposite"
developed early.[22]

Philon has already worked out much of the idiom that we find in
Nonnos, but moralisingly and without his dynamic quality. Thus
he argues that the *typos* of sense-impressions conveys the truth;
the mind "takes hold and absorbs the sustenance provided" by
the impressions. Pleasure is the distorting factor that makes the
ugly look beautiful and deceives men.[23] The difference in thinking
may be exemplified by citing a few lines in which Nonnos makes
Hera address Iris:

> Change your body, take on yourself the ugly shape
> of Sleep's Mother, blackgirdled divine Night.
> Become darkness with false name, since I as well,
> when need drives, turn with antitypal limbs
> into Themis, Kythereia, Artemis.[24]

Nonnos delights in the way that life changes into its opposite,

seeing in it the essential creative force of ever-reborn matter.
The accumulation of his key-phrases can become bewildering:

> He realised that the deceitful image
> of the human shape of Morrheus bore the *mimema*
> of an antitypal face and recognised
> the deluding trickery of wise Athena.
> But Dionysos was glad at the sight of the goddess
> and in his heart knew her as a guising battle-ally.[25]

As usual, the best commentary on Nonnos' ideas is to be found in
Philon. The following passage helps us to understand the significance of the multiplicity of forms and changes in the Dionysiac

The Dionysiac Earth (sarcophagus).

world. The picture presented to us by the world, Philon says, is
not constant, but "subject to manifold and multiform changes",
and so, "since the *phantasia* [mental picture] is variable, judgment
of it too must be variable". He goes on with an account, in which
he is partly confused between the variability of the life-forms and
that of sense-impressions (especially in terms of their real or appa-
rent transformations):

In the first place there are the countless differences in living creatures,
concerned not with a single aspect but with practically all: differences
in origin, structure, and equipment (or constitution), in food and
mode of life, in predilection and aversions, in sense-activities and
movements, in the distinctive qualities arising from the innumerable
ways that body and soul are affected.[26]

Setting aside the question of those who form the judgments, consider examples of the objects of such judgments: *e.g.* chameleon and polypus. The former, we're told, changes in colour and grows like the kinds of soil over which its habit is to crawl; the latter grows like the rocks to which it clings in the sea, and we may fairly suppose that this power of being many-coloured is given them by saving Nature as a remedy against the danger of capture.

Again, have we not seen the dove's neck change in the sun's rays into a myriad different hues, sometimes scarlet and dark blue or fiery or like red-hot coal, again yellow and then ruddy and all other kinds of colour, so many that it would be difficult to give even the names in full?

Indeed it is said that in the land of the Skythians known as Geloans, a remarkable animal is actually though rarely found, called an elk, equal in size to an ox, but with a face shaped very like a deer. The account of this creature states that it always changes its hair's colour into that of the places, trees, and whatever it stands near; owing to the similarity of colour, we are told, it is unnoted by passers, and this fact, rather than its bodily strength, makes it hard to catch. These and similar phenomena are clear proofs of the impossibility of apprehension.[27]

Thus, with some rather devious logic, Philon works himself to the sceptical position about knowledge. The same sort of material sends Nonnos to his attempt at constructing what we may call his Dionysiac dialectic of *typos* and *antitypos*, of endless variability and of decisive moments of change with their complex problems of truth and illusion. (In the alchemic world colour is as real as form and Dionysos is the central "matter of the stone".)

An example from Nonnos, dealing with the same sort of phenomena as those discussed by Philon, will bring out his subtlety, the way in which his concept of craft is linked with the moment of material (also spiritual) change: "The manyfooted squid with changeful mind, weaving his trailing web of winding whirls, stuck fast to his familiar rock and the apparition of his limbs became a flow-printed shape." The term for changeful mind is *aiolometis*, *aiolo-* signifying quickness of movement, glitter and change of hue, shifting, varied, wily. *Aiolometis* thus takes up into the inner organism all the elements that we have noted in connec-

tion with *poikilos;* and the image is carried on by the stress on spiralling change, *skoliai helikes,* into the final touch of imprint or form
(*typos* as structure) dissolving into the flow of process. The
shape is *charadraie,* an epithet that suggests both *charagma* (imprint
or character) and *charadra,* a stream that cuts its course or pattern
down the hillside.[28]

But though from one angle Nonnos does effectively reveal an
alchemic and Dionysiac universe of revelling and changing forms,
which aspire to pure freedom and harmony, from another angle
he flattens and disperses the picture. Otherwise his poem would be
among the greatest ever written. Though it is true that he shows
the involved struggle of the moment of transformation, he is not
at all clear as to the nature of the truths and illusions that clash
there. And this is because his whole fable, his narrative of the
Indian war, is devoid of meaning. At best it is an allegory of the
wars between east and west from Alexander to early Byzantine
days, with their Persian threat; at worst it is a dull farrago of
interminable Bacchic onslaughts which lack all drama because we
know the wretched Indians cannot defeat the god.[29] If the *Dionysiaka* were to have true epic greatness, it would have to express, in
however symbolic a form, the real conflicts of the age, the conflicts that underlay the breakdown of ancient civilisation and the
growth of the first stages of the new medieval society. Instead, it
is an allegory of an allegory; and the incidental charms and in-
sights, the profound linguistic energy that underlies the imageries
we have discussed, cannot offset the fundamental flaws. The
changes spiral in a void, and we see the weakness inside the *auto-
concepts* dominating the situation. All things burst in strange new
vivid energies, and the Dionysiac Triumph (in the context of a
meaningless Indian War) can stimulate but not contain them.

Nonnos thus, willy-nilly, explains to us why no pagan synthesis
could satisfy his world, however brilliant, however intellectually
or aesthetically worked out. Such a synthesis could not stand up
against Christianity; for it was compromised with the State and
all the oppressions and inequalities on which that State was ultimately based. Dionysos for Nonnos was the symbol and incarnation of the free energies of the universe, but he was also the expres-

sion of the imperial conquering State. Christianity had at its core a total opposition to that State and expressed this with poignant drama in the story of Calvary, whatever the mythological or religious overtones. Though by Nonnos' day Clement of Alexandreia had long made the creed safe for bankers and the Church had circuitously come round to a point of agreement with the imperial State, the original values were deeply embodied in its writings and rituals: the insistence that the first should be last and that to be perfect you must sell all and give to the poor; its saviour was a poor man historically murdered by the State-power; its ethic absolutely opposed to blood-sacrifice. No glimmer of all this appears in the *Dionysiaka*. It was natural then that Nonnos, seeking a

Triumph of Dionysos and Herakles (Woburn Abbey).

Christian theme, should turn to the gospel in which the plain meanings are most luminously dissolved into symbols.

But in putting strongly the weakness of Nonnos' positions, I do not wish to rob of force what I have previously said of his virtues. And in essence what was there said applies to the whole Dionysiac idea as we have seen it coming up in all significant phases of ancient life in the Hellenistic and Roman periods. The demand for the fullness of life was none the less valid and valuable because of the limitations which deprived it of the power to formulate political programmes. Without the programmes, the demand could not stabilise itself and had to divert its glorifications of life into glorifications of power. That is, it became passively and

distortedly political. Yet there was in it the root of something
without which all programmes could not but be betrayals of
human hope and aspiration. The tragic condition of man in this
epoch is expressed by the fact that the Dionysiac idea contaminated itself by political subserviency, so that the Christian idea had
to reject all the imagery of earthly paradise and look only to the
otherworld, if it were to maintain its ethic of absolute resistance
to the "world" and its powers. Hence the close interlocking and
the violent opposition between the two ideas, which we have been
able to bring out in our comparisons of the thought of Philon and
Nonnos. (Philon, though a Jew, was impelled like the Christian to
cut the paradise finally from its earthly basis.)

But let us end on a more positive note. Here are some lines in
which Nonnos shows his romantic power, evoking a Venusberg.
(He did not fade out in an early medieval world; his work re-
entered the European tradition through the Italian Baroque poets.)

> I saw Sleep, Aphrodite's usher. I saw the deceitful
> stream of the Loves' gold fountain at your bridal.
> The fountain where young girls get a treacherous potion
> and loosen the girdle that they've lifelong worn,
> in a dream of marriage filching their maidenhead.
> I have seen, I have seen the slope where a woman abruptly
> becomes a bride, in treacherous sleep, by a love-rock.
> I have seen the mating mountain of Cypris where
> lovers steal girls' maidenheads and scamper off.[30]

And a last glimpse of the god who turns the everyday earth into a
paradise: Dionysos swimming—

> He lifted up his head and spread his chest;
> paddling his hands, he clove the golden calm.
> Waveless the banks upspurted selfgrown roses,
> the lily sprouted, the Seasons wreathed the shores
> while Bacchos bathed; and in the sparkling stream
> the flowing locks of his dark hair were reddened.

Notes

1. HOLIDAYS

1. Fuad 37. Zambon 63 sees an allowance of free days in Oxy. 724, a teaching contract, but misconstrues *heortika,* not festivals but festival gifts: WGP sv; cf. Eitrem (1) 46 n.l. See here n. 8 ch. 2.

In general: Westermann; Zambon; REg 288–92; Youtie (1) on whose analysis much of this chapter depends.

2. Oxy. 725.

3. Clause: Zambon 62; Westermann 303; Oxy. 275. Illness: BGU 1125; SPP xxii 40; Oxy. 725 and 1647.

4. Oxy. 1647. Cf. 725 (A.D. 183) for formula. Other weaver contracts are Oxy. 275 and 322; Tebt. 385 and 442; BGU. 855; Grenf. ii 59; PSI 241. BGU 1021 is with a *ktenistes* of 3rd c. Other trades: BGU 1125 and 96; Oxy. 724; PSI 287. In Tebt. 384 (A.D. 10) apprenticeship with a weaver is combined with a loan from him; cf. Flor. 44.

For Psobthis: Oxy. 458 (cf. Oxy. 719.10).

5. Oxy. 1721 (cf. 1638); main clause is not reached. Ophelas occurs in Oxy. 963.

6. Youtie (2) 43 on O. Strasb. 654; (1) on Heidl. inv. 1818. For paranome: this kind of contract binds the antichretic servant; his services are in place of interest on a loan, his time wholly at the master's disposal (with no need of instruction): Mich. ii 121. r. iii III; intro. Reinach ii 105; Oxf. 10 intro. Penalties: Mich. v 355; PSI x 1120; SB v 7612, etc. (Exception at Dura: YCS ii 1931 6,16: 7 days for illness.)

Hired worker could make his own terms, but subject to the condition of the labour-market, etc. Contracts show no allowance for festivals or illness. Thus, PSI viii 902 (Mich. v 355) 1st c. lays down for every day lost the payment of 2 dr.

7. Athen. xi 784b.

8. Nenconi; CW xxxvii 1943–4. Necklace is *peritrachelon;* usual form *peritrachelion,* but see PSI 1116, 6 and Oxy. 1273, 6. *Daktylion* is also perhaps mentioned. For workers in gold and silver: Reil; Neuberger 29. Athen. *l.c.* and ii 71b; he often cites Sopatros. Other cups he links with Egypt in book xi are the karchesion, kiborion (narrow at bottom), and ethanion: "In the Egyptians' houses are a bronze *phiale,* a bronze *kyathos,* a bronze *ethanion*" (Hellanikos).

9. Dyers: Grenf. ii 87. Others: Youtie (1).

10. Fuad 37; BGU 1125.

11. Other metal-trade contracts: PSI 871; Reinach ii 113; BGU 1124.

12. *Aedia* is used in papyri to express unpleasantness, *e.g.* from brawls or clash with authorities. See Mich. iii 204 and v 243: Boak says there, "It might possibly refer to cases of actual want, but is much more likely to apply to members (of the gild) who have got into trouble with the public authorities and are under arrest or in danger of prosecution." Illness is a late but certain use of the word. See Youtie (1) on this and *karos*, with medical refs.

13. Youtie (1). Aristoteles and Souidas refer to hangover or alcoholic stupor. Here in the next line seems *astheon*; see Lond. iii 1170 verso, where this word is used in reporting absence of carpenter.

14. Tesenesis: various spelling in pap. Closest to this is Tsenesis: Preisigke (2) sv Senesis. The name means Daughter-of-Isis in Egyptian.

15. Budge 253–5; Lanzone pls. lxxiii–iv. Bes was modified under the New Kingdom: *Book of Dead*, clxv 21.

16. See further Budge 254f.

17. Baedecker 266.

18. Griffith 31n. Counters: BM 24668f. For Dogs: cf. *latrunculi* etc. in ch. 2. Note E. Brummer Coll. (Sotheby Nov. 16–17 1964) no. 16, gaming-pieces, heads of Isis, Bes, and dog.

19. Budge 39. Hermes directs the Moon: Plout. *de isid.* xli.

20. Griffith 31f (made slightly less archaic and with Dogs, the literal meaning, for "pieces"). Anherru is brother by Menkh(?)-art: Griffith 31n; the Pharaoh is Ramses II.

Griffith: "The battle of the clans in Krall's fragmentary Hist. Rom. p. 36 is also arranged 'at fifty-two' . . . Prof. Petrie suggests a connexion with the number of weeks in a year. Perhaps we can trace the effect of a foreign (Jewish?) calendar on Egyptian type-numbers." But there seems no need to posit an intrusion. Note that Diodoros says that Typhon divided the body of Osiris into 26 pieces: i 21. Cf. Celtic boardgame: In tale of Peredur, *Mabinogion,* pieces move themselves on a magic board. "The chessboard (*gwyddbwyll*) of Gwenddolen; when the men were placed on it, they could play of themselves. The board was of gold and the men (*gwyr*) of silver," Guest 75; Murray 34; Cook, *Zeus* ii 682f. Geasa game in Celtic folktales: Christiansen. Van Hamel in *Arkiv f. Nord. Filologi* l 1934 218 says the Eddic poem *Voluspa* depicts the gods playing in the Golden Age a game with which the world is governed; Ragnarok, world-end, comes at the game's end; and a new era is inaugurated by a human couple's retrieving of the board.

21. Erman, 147, 392, 404, 409, 415.

22. Perdrizet (1) 114, no. 641; DS v 1053 fig. 7593; Neugebauer 69. For Hygeia: Perdrizet (2), and Edelstein, *Asclepius* II, index p. 274. Cumont takes it as favourable. Perdrizet (1) 115; Bataille (1) 288.

23. Hermias: UPZ 163 (pap. dem. Berl. 3114); W. Chr. 51. Ammonios: P. dem Berl. 3141 and 3111. Psen-Mont: *ib.* 3103. Bataille (1) 288. For influx of pop. cults: Jouguet (1). For the early Greek population at Memphis egyptianised by the time of Alexander's conquest: Swiderek (2).

24. Amm. Marc. xix 12.3-15; Schubart (1). For spies, cf. A.M. xiv 1.6 at Antioch, A.D. 353.

25. BGU 387; Otto i 332 n2.

26. Oxy. 1272. Sarapion her guardian writes for her. Terrace: *pessos*, see Munich. 11; Lond. 210 (*J. Philol*. xxii 272), 978, and 1023; Flor. 5. For Thefts etc. see DLRE chs 11-12. Abydos: Jesi (1); *Mém. de la Mission fr. du Caire* iv 406-689. Note cups called bessa, Athen. xi 27 (784b): besa, Eustath. on *Od*. i 1405b,16; besion, *Stud. Pal*. x 67 (2-3rd cs); besoton, cup, P. Holm. 163; Hesych. prob. in P, Mag. Par. i 750. Athen. says narrow on top, wide below.

27. SPP xxii 1922 183, 176; REg p. 657; Bilabel 15; Eitrem (1) 48; Ross-Georg. ii 41,9. Cf. Heid. inv. no. 1818 (verso 11); Bilabel 5-7 days? Note *rhodopheristes*: Ryl. 224(a), 2nd c. A.D.

28. RE sv rosalia (Nilsson) with refs. col. 1115; also Nilsson (1) 134; Laum i 85-7; BCH 1914 47 and 1931 58—also 1930 376; Carcopino 77ff (esp. 90-2). Date: ? 12 Mecheir: *Stud. Pal*. xxii 183.76 (Krüger).

Further refs.: Heuzey, Waltzing iii 533-43, Caetani-Lovatelli, Perdrizet (9), Azevou-Picard, Seyrig (2), Collart (4), Gernet, Lemerle. Other names (all CIL): *rosae et escae*, v 2090, 2176, 2315; *dies rosae*, vi 10234; *dies rosationis* vi 10248; *rosar(ia)* x 3792, xi 1436 (*rosarium* in xi 3895 means rosegarden); *ad rosas et profusiones*, v 4990; mentioned with Parentalia v 4016, 4440, 4489, 4871, 5907, vi 9626 (*parentalis rosae*), 10248: Marquardt iii 311f thinks the R. a variety of P.; mentioned with *violaria*, vi 10234, 10248. Many general expressions, *e.g*. xi 132 (strew roses on mon.). Flower-laying on tomb esp. common for collegia, celebrated annually out of income of specific bequest, a dinner with many roses. Dates, May to August: CIL v 7906, *rosas suo tempore*; x 3792, vi 10234, vi 10239, x 444, xi 132. Note 3rd Isidora epigram, cited ch. 10 here. Link with emp. worship: *Inschr. Perg*. 374 (pp. 265f).

29. Schleidan; Joret. For 3c., *Vit. Elegab*. xix 7, *vit. Gall*. xvi 2; *vit. Car*. xvii 4.

30. Entry: Plout. *pomp*. 57; Herodian i 7.3 and 6; Cass. Dion. lxxv 1.4 (Boissevain). For Commodus, Sept. Sev.: Herodian iv 8.8. Processions: Lucan ii 624-8; Ov. *fasti* iv 346; Herodian v 6.8.

31. Tac. *hist*. ii 55; cf. Tertul. *de corona* 13.

32. Athen. iv 29. But see ch. 8 here, n37.

33. Hoey 26 n55; Cic. *verr*. ii 5; Nock (1) 290.

34. Hoey 27 n56; Floralia n57; Magna Mater n58-9.

35. Bilabel 18.

36. Nilsson (1) ii 134.

37. Macellum: Hoey 31 and n83. Survival: RE sv *rosalia* 1114; *N. Heidl. J.* viii 1898 1ff; Murko ii 142-54; Nilsson (2) 682 and (1) 149; Abbott 40-2.

38. Mart. x 19.21.

39. Philostr. 53 (34); cf. Plat. *symp*. 196a for love as *hygros*.

For Dionysiac rels. see Nilsson and Cumont (6) 45.; inscrs. from Bithynia and Macedonia refer to the festival. Roman or Italian in origin: perhaps from Cisalpine Gaul: Lattimore 139f and Perdrizet (9); some inscrs. suggest a burning rite,

Avezou-Picard, but it can hardly have been the roses burned—perhaps the refs. are to lamps, though there may have been censings. For lamps: Collart (4) 65 n5 and CIL vi 10248.

40. *Ib.* 1 (29). Tiara: Xen. *anab.* ii 5.23; Pearson 222. Cf. the *Vigil of Venus* for the close rel. of Roses, Venus, Spring, Birth and Rebirth. Bilabel's attempt to relate the R. to cult of Horos (Dendera) or Isis (Isis-Hathor or Apollin. magna) is surely wrong. Wreath of roses worn by her priest on sistron (Apul. *met.* xi.6) has no special meaning—cf. epithet *rose-breasted Isis* (Nubia: CIG 5115). Medallion: Gauckler (2) p. clxvi (1) ii 29 no. 71b; D. Levi (2) 148, 472, and fig. 173. *Xenia*: Foucher (2) 293ff, dated early Severan. Blood: Cumont (6) 45. Note Elegab. and roses: HA *elegab.* xix, xx, xxviii. "Divine": *Geopon.* xi 18 5; Merlin 137 n6.

41. See refs under n27 here. In BGU 1 plus 337 (W. Chr. 92) about A.D. 140 at same temple, Choiak 8 is marriage of Isis Nepherses "9 days, 4 art. daily". The Birthday, 26 Epeiph.

42. Apul. *met.* xi 8; fate, Joh. Lyd. *de mens.* iv 45 (Wünsch); Alföldi 46 and n107 (bibliog.); Roman *Navigium Isidis*. Note link of Kikellia (28–9 Choiak) where worshippers lamented Osiris, and Navigium: Merkelbach (1) 39–41, 57–9.

43. Hopfner (2) ii 180; Cumont 91.

44. Plout. *de isid.* 52 puts the *zitesis* in winter solstice; cf. Ach. Stat., Isag. ad Arat. *Phaen.* 23 (Maass 54f). For Hathyr 17–20, Plout. 39; Bilabel 39; Wilcken UPZ i 401; Geminus viii 16 (Manit. 106). Philoc. *Kal.* (A.D. 354): Mommsen, CIL I i (2nd) 256, puts Isia in Oct. 28–Nov. 1, cf. Hopfner (2) i 26, ii 182. For annus vagus: Frazer, *Adonis* (3rd) ii 24; Grenf. ii 637 (A.D. 237); Oxy. ii p. 137f; Oslo ii p. 147. In general: Merkelbach (1); Leclant; Bonneau, esp. 365 and 248 for displacements; Gressmann. For harvest fests., Sarapeia (25 April, Philo-kalos).

Geminos of Rhodes, 1st c. A.D., says in his day the rite was a month from the solstice: 17–20 Hathyr. Refs. for Choiak fest.: Merkelbach (1) 32 n2; add Ovid. *met.* ix 693; Seneca (?) *apocol.* xiii 4; Juv. *sat.* viii 29f; Lactant. *div. inst.* i 21. Parker in effect states that the lunar calendar was used for temple-liturgies in Egypt till end of paganism.

45. Oxy. 731; DLRE.

46. DLRE 263; Fay. 118.

47. Oxy. 525: *Nyktelion Isidos.* "Lotus" is uncertain.

48. Heliod. i 18.

49. *Ib.* vii 8 and 11. K. is a *prophetes.* In the first passage Arsake brings necklaces and gold in "in a specially pompous progress of her own".

50. *Ib.* v 14.

51. Last 3 chapters. For Plout. and Egypt: J. G. Griffiths (2) and Avdiev cited CE 1963 251.

52. Refs. in n27 here.

53. R. iv 725 (Roeder); RE (2te R) ii 4 1896 (Kees); also Hopfner. Evil:

Plout. 73,33; Diod i 21-22 and 88. Condemnation: Hopfner (2) i 134; Kees 1920. Stormgod: JEA 1963 19. T. and Hor: JEA 1962 82. In Gen. Griffiths (1); Montet; Schott.

54. Bilable 13-28.

55. Hopfner (2) i 22, 135, 139; 115 for Antaiopolis; ii 267 for Eileithyiaspolis. Also Kees 1902; Griffiths (1) 25, 144f.

56. Plout. de isid. 30f; Diod. i 88. For red as colour of T. and evil things in general: Hopfner (2) i 24. See also Griffiths (1) 120.

57. Str. xvii (814f); Plout. de isid. 50 and sept. sap. conv. 5 (150f); Ail. NA x 24, 28; Hopfner (2) ii 74, 80, 138 and (3).

58. Nagel 33; W. M. Müller 108; Griffiths (1) 128, 144 (Libyans 145).

59. Griffiths 123; Beckerath 34; Hölscher, pt. ii, pl. 21a and p. 5; Ranke (20th dyn. in particular) i 321 (nos. 29-31), 322 (nos. 1-6), 317 (nos. 11-23). Statue: Oxy. 1449.

60. Hopfner (1) 47; Derchain; Griffiths 116f against a rel. to the Island-in-the-midst of the Contendings. Bebon: Plout. de Isid. 22 (576A-B); RE ii 2718-9. See also n115 ch. 13 here.

61. Oxy. 1380; Griffiths 117 n4.

62. P. Osl. i 337.

63. Ib. 316.

64. Eitrem, P. Osl. 1925 133; Griffiths 118 n3. In Plout. de isid. 357c (16) the child not the pillar is set on fire. P. Osl. i 9 bids Seth fear his son (?Hor): Griffiths 118 n3, Hopfner (1) 605.

65. PGM i 4.174; Lond. 46.145-6.

66. Bones: PGM i 5.266; "I am he": ib. i 4.185; threats, ib. i 5. 281; sun, Hunt.

67. Lond. 122.91-3.

68. Reitzenstein (2) 184.

69. Puech (1) and (2); Cullman.

70. Doresse, sv Seth in index.

71. Roeder, par. 99c, pl. 72g; C. Bonner (2) 203; Doresse 74, 104f.

72. Eitrem, Pap. Osl. 1925, fasc. 1; Doresse, opp., p. 127. For donkey-head: Guentch-Ogloueff.

73. Setheus as primordial god, creator, etc., Doresse 81; earthshaker, C. Baynes 19-21.

74. E. Peterson 200 n3. In G.-R. magic, Seth has the asshead recalling the long snout and ears of the African creature with which he is at times identified in pharaonic iconography.

75. Hermes Tris. frag. xxv 8.

76. Frag. of Aigyptiaka, in Steph. Byz.: FHG iii fr. 108.

77. Lefort 83.

78. Doresse 127-34.

79. As suggested by E. Petersen 200 n3.

80. Bilabel 7.

81. Str. xvii (815); Baedecker 240. This location is important, as Tentyris (which like near Apollinopolis was at this time a centre of Hor-worship, with the hawk as sacred animal) was apparently near the goldsmith-apprentice: Youtie (1) and Ail. NA x 24.

82. Heliod. ix 9; he stresses the mystery-aspect and describes the city as "engaged in sacs. and ceremonies". Cf. Plout. *de isid.* in general. For Isis and flooding: D. Müller. Semasia: Bonneau 375. Isis-Sothis: Merkelbach, with Leclant 390. Some refs. for flooding: Zenon Cair. 59176 (255 B.C.) seems earliest pap. ref.; mosaics of Thmouis and Praeneste, Pompeian paintings, sarcophagus of Filocyrius, with Hermann (2) 30–69.

83. Diod. i 36; Shorter 10f etc.; Nilometer in Strabon: DLRE 13.

84. Dion. xxxii 38.

85. On Tybi 11; Epiphan. *haer.* i 51 (30); Hopfner (2) 607.

86. Oxy. 486 and 1211: the Nile is the hierotatos as in Oxy. 486. For strategos: cf. Otto ii 79. The wine is *euodes*; wafers are *lagana*; cones, *strobiloi* (cf. Oxy. 1144); cakes, *plakountes*; spice etc., *pan aroma choris libanou*. For *bais* cf. BGU 362 vii 13; Tebt. 295. 11 (note); and Oxy. 519 (*palmai*).

Note the Sarapiastai who celebrated the Neiloia (IG xii 2.511: from Methymna) were also linked with cult of Dionysos: Kumanudis 457 no. 4.

For komasterion: Tebt. i 123 recto (a) 19–20 (cf. (c) 4 and ? (d) 12); Preisigke WB explains it as building for use of processional priests; Hunt (Oxy. 519) suggests it was used for Flood-festivals; in the Tebt. pap. it merely serves as a wine-shop (date A.D. 45–7).

87. Oxy. 519; DLRE 163f—in Oxy. 1050 (DLRE 164) Neilos may be a man (as some others later mentioned), but coming straight after the priests he may well mean someone acting the part of the River (the Egyptian god Hapy). "The two great festivals of the Nile took place one in the middle of June and the other in the middle of August. During the first of these the goddess Isis was supposed to shed tears into the Nile to make the river rise . . . The great Harris Pap. No. 1 (ed. Birch 1876 pl. 37f) proves that the Egyptians made gifts to the Nile at the time when it was due to rise. Ramses III had statues and figures of the Nile made in gold, silver, lapislazuli, malachite, iron, copper, tin, lead, stone, and wood, and 5098 statues of the Nile-goddess made in wood, and he had spells written on 272 'books of the Nile' and cast into the river during the thirty-one years of his reign", Budge 236f. Hapy was shown as a man painted blue or green, with a cluster of aquatic plants on his head. Nile-worship in general: Lumbroso 1–8. Arsinoe: BGU 362 xv 11. Strategos: cf. Otto ii 79. Nile-water: Deonna (4) 133.

2. MORE ON HOLIDAYS

1. There is also "as a special honour on the following occasions: Sarapeia on Hadrianos 26 and festival of Harpokrates on Tybi 16, 1 keramion (of wine)

for each day. At the robing of the gods: Hathyr 7, Phamenoth 9 and Epeiph 26, 1 keramion daily. At the Isle of Women, 6 keramia."

2. SB 7365; REg no. 347.

3. Lond. 1169; REg no. 350; Fiesel, *Nach Gesells. d. Wiss. Gött. P.-H. Kl.* 1925 62.

4. Heliod. v 13 and vi 7. Thoth with his ibisform was identified with Hermes, but the stress was on his intellectual pursuits, his position as patron of scribes; the relation to writing gave him great magical powers; hence the role of Hermes Trismegistos in G.-R. days.

5. BGU 362; REg no. 404 (thrice).

6. Wormald. Doorkeeper: Otto i 395.

7. PGM i 180–98. For Anubis cf. Apul. *met.* xi 11. There are also two officials whom Wormald calls rubbers-down and suggests were connected with purifications.

8. Fayum doc.: Ross. Georg ii 41, commentary O. Krüger; cf. SPP xxii 183. I treat this cursorily as I do not want to get too involved with religious questions apart from Dionysos. See Eitrem (1) 45–8 in general. He suggests Meribollia may be Melobolia (cf. *ballachrades,* throwers-at-figs: Eitrem (2) 291), but there is no evidence for apple-throwing. Demetria occurs in a Zenon pap. (Edgar i 59028 in 258 B.C.), later in SB 7199 (2nd c. A.D.): cf. Bilabel 35 (citing Giess. 18, Heptakomia, and 49, Oxy.), and sc. Kallim. *h.* vi 1. Gardens: for Isis and vines, IG xii 5 no. 539.86; Peek *Isishymn. v. Andros* 18; and gardens: hymn from Gomphoi, Peek 135, and hymn of Mesemedes (Powell, *Coll. alex.* 198). Dates: Amesysia may come in or near Thoth, seems here just at end of Mesore; Demetria perhaps Phaophi; Gardens implies autumn. Rhodophoria: see ch. 1 here. Delia belongs to Anthesterion if we base things on Greek calendar. Eitrem suggests combining Panteleia and Stephanephoria (line 83: ? Charmosyna) as *pantelitia* occur only at these two fests., but notes Souchia falls 2 Epeiph (acc. to Vienna calendar) and Sarapeia, 26 Choiak (line 71; cf. Hopfner (2) index sv dies). Constituents of sac. seem uniform; Roses for R., pantelitia for P, mela (? line 45) for Melophoria. But Memphite Wine, essential for Kepouria, and wreaths for S., appear in the others too. Conventional too the supply of wine (1 or 2 keram.) and hens (2 or 4), sucking pig (missing only at Sarap. and Merob., may be also at odd fest. with name lacking.) Swineflesh forbidden to Eg. priests as food, and Egs. in general seem continue abstaining from it— note lack at Sarap. (but contrast Sext. Empir. cited Hopfner 383) and Merob. But Egs. sacrificed pig once a year at full moon to Isis and Osiris: Herod. ii 47. So delphakion might come into Isis fest. (Edgar cites Zenon letter 59078; cf. PSI 431.) For *delph.* at Demeter fest., Giess 49.16 (3rd c. A.D.)—and here (line 48) for "Amesysia of the Egyptians", showing it wasn't purely Eg.

Eitrem (1) again for *sponde* etc., with fuller details and refs. See also Oxy. 916–17, 525, 653, 913, and 1283 with discussion; Ryl. 216. 128n; Schubart (5). Modern Eg.: Blackman 172. Some refs. for cited docs.: libation (6c) Hamb. 23.24; (7th) Pal. xx 218.55. *Protolena*: Ostr. Strassb. 653. Cornbride: Blackman

171, 307; JEA xix 31 (cf. *Golden Bough*, 3rd, v 2, 109; J. Harrison, *Proleg.* 83ff).
Trygetika: P. M. Meyer on P. Giss 56.20, and Hamb. 23.34; Flor. 369.14. Pigs:
Berl. Leihg. 23.15 (Theadelpheia, A.D. 252); Byz., Berl. 310 and Strassb. 40.
Winepress: Flor. 369 (Hermop.).

Apomoira: Eitrem (1) 29f. Note revenues of Anthylla, famed for wine, given
to queens of Eg., under both Eg. and Persian rule. There are various complications about the *oktadrachmos*: Eitrem 31ff. Ships: Ross. George. ii 18 (A.D. 140),
Lond. iii 948 (M. Chr. 341) A.D. 286.

Children: Eitrem 39f; Hamb. 23; Oxy. 730. Jobs: Lond. 131. Fay 102, Leipz.
97; REg 186. Payment: Berger; Oxy. 1207 and Giess. 49; PSI 788, A.D. 125;
Amh. 88 (M. Chr. ii 150) A.D. 128; Würzb. 14, A.D. 132; Hamb. 23 (A.D. 569);
Grass: Oxy. 730 (A.D. 130); fowls, Oxy. 1207 (? 175-6). *Sponde tes misthoseos*:
Eitrem 40f. *Thallos*: 41-5 Porridge: UPZ i 98.44: Leid. i 97ff (188 B.C.), W's
comment. p. 428, add. p. 654; Alex., *Hist. Alex. Magni* i 32, Kroll 33. The
athera prob. given to the Good Daimones guarding the house as well as to the
inhabs. as a fest. gift: note *olyra* (*athera*) as "good medicine": Plin. xxii 121.
Woman named Sponde with homebred slave, Hygia: *Eph. arch.* 1900 31;
Thallos father of Stephanos, Athens 5 c. B.C., Lys. xix 46. Sentence cited:
Eitrem.

Some of the problems about *heortika* are brought out by Merton 96 (Oxy.),
letter of *geourchos* to subordinate (prob. *pronoetes*) "Have the goodness to grant
a respite to the people of Pempo and return to the city for 2 or 3 days for the
festival-presents, and I will let you depart home again and collect them."—
"Deliver to Iacob son of Psaei of Meskanounis, from the Landowner."

Not clear from grammar if he wants I. to stop making collection of rents,
dues, and come for *heortika* for the villagers, or I. is to collect the h. in addition
to rents; but prob. the former.

For *synetheiai* paid to landlords as to govt. officials: Lond. 1771, and (though
the word lacks) 1694-5. For *heortika*: see further Oxy. 1890, 1950-1, 2032.72;
Strassb. 40.49. And the *synetheia* in Lond. 1036 (6c) in lease: fest. of Thynis
(? village of that name); J. Schwartz no. 55, L. Baudi 359.

Lond. 1171 (8 B.C.), farm-accounts, refers to Amasesia, a festival (cf. Amh.
93; Fay. 95): note Amesesis (?) in Georg. Synkellos (Bonn, 180) as a king
of Egypt.

For late exs. of fests.: Oxy. 1950 (A.D. 487) order from holy church to pronoetes of St Philoxenos to give to asst. in office of exactor 4 double jars of wine
for fest. of Tybi; 1951 (5c) order to butler to supply 2 double jars to a bed-
maker for same purpose; 1890, lease of milling-bakery, 11 months, in a monastery, the rent part cash, part kind, the oddments including "3 chickens and 30
eggs for festivals"; 1945 (517) order from Comes and a peribleptos (cf. 994,
1946, 2047) for wine issue to monks on Christmas Day and to the prisoners
on Tybi 1 (Dec. 27).

9. Nero: Oxy. 1021. Hadrian: Giss. 3. Pert.: BGU 646. Max.: SB 421.
See DLRE. 162. Eleph.: W. *ost.* i 13.

10. Giss, 3; P. J. Alexander; David.-G. no. 2; M. and W. Grundz. i *Hist. Teil* 2 *Chr.* (1912) 491; Kornemann (1). Unknown god: Norden 1–124.

11. Kornemann (2) 284.

12. *Ib.* 286.

13. Bourguet 72f.

14. Lofoscade 16–17.

15. Merton 75. The writer has a copy of the will; four of the six witnesses will be present at the opening.

16. Tebt. 407.

17. Merton 73, mutilated. The revenue seems to consist of rents owed by artisans of certain trades. Two persons are mentioned, one with Greek, one with R. name, latter seems "an ex-keeper of sacred crocodiles". Apparently T. was called on to make statement of her revenue under various headings and her contribs. to exchequer over certain period: part of normal routine or result of special occasion. For Athena-T., Oxy. 438, 579, 1117, shrine 43, 1028, 1188, 1627, PSI 215, JEA xx 1934 20ff. *Plethos:* OGI i 56.24; Mich. v 244 and ii 123 (recto iii 41 and xxii 44); P. Jews 1913 16f; Lösch 42(3). There seems a ref. to gilded shrines, line 18, cf. BGU ii 387 (cf. BL i p. 43); i 149; Bacchias i (Yale 363) and ii (Yale 902, 906), iii (Lund 3.6), iv (Lund 3.5), v (Lund 4.2), vii (Yale 378–9).

18. DLRE 162f; also for Games.

19. See n 27 ch. 1 here. BGU 362. I have cut details of wreaths, illuminations ("etc."). Other items mention a Holiday (name lost) and visit of imp. procurator. Zeus Kapetolios was worshipped in various cities of the eastern provs. For Capitolia: Wissowa PW iii 1529; Arsinoe, W. *Grundz.* i 1.116. Capitolium at Sabratha: Haynes 117. Genesia of divine emperors (2nd c.): Oxy. 521.

Oxy. 1185 (scraps of docs.): for the jingle: Souid. sv *an oinou*; Diogenian and Zenob.; cf. sc. Aristoph. *peace* 123; Plout. *an virtus* ii (439d); Aristoph. *clouds* 981–3. The metric can easily be restored. Tax-appropriations: Martin (1) 137.

20. Amh. 70; W. *Chr.* 149; DLRE 64. And Oxy. 1333.

21. Lond. 1028.

22. DLRE 287.

23. DLRE 167. We know little of the regulations: Mitteis (1) 384. The interpretation that the man wanted to leave Egypt and attend a festival elsewhere is less likely.

24. Hoey.

25. DLRE 261. And Oxy. 122. War: Oxy 705, DLRE 287–8. Clubs: full account in DLRE 172–5: add Edgar (2); Jouguet (4), SB 5627. Ptol. exs.: Hibeh ii 214, PSI 528 (more or less contemporary), SB 6319. Lease: Flor. 369. Party: Fuad viii 25.

26. *Treatise of Cherubim* ii 27–8.

27. DLRE 5f, Breccia (1) 139–41. Many refs., *e.g.* Seneca *ep.* v 11; Lucan x; Juvenal *sat.* vi, xv etc.

28. A. M. xxii 16.14. Ptol. III also founded a temple of Osiris: gold plaque in BM. Not a centre of Aphrodite: Roeder.

29. Rostovtzeff (1) pl. li, (2) pl. xv: I follow his description. For boats: (1) 615 n35. Date: (1) 276 and (3) pl. xxxviii 1 (text). For Nile-landscape as sacred theme: Deonna (4) 133—and for mosaic at Rome with *xenia*, theatral mask, and river-landscape. Nogara 5. For Caryatids and Telamones bordering the landscape: Deonna: "Their action takes on here a more precise character when one considers that they have the aspect of Isis and Osiris." Cf. Nogara.

30. DLRE 262.

31. Oxy. 113.

32. Oxy. 530. A carrier Onnophris appears again in Oxy. 531. See DLRE ch. 14, *e.g.* Oxy. 2149, Oxy. 112 (Birthday Festival of the God), BGU 596 etc. Diogenes: Oxy. 933. Hermopolis: Leipz. 39.3, 40. iii 16; Asia Minor: Hirschfeld 868. Cf. *nykterinos strategos* of Alexandreia. The office is *munus personale*, Dig. l. 4.18.12. Linen merchant: *Othoniakos*, cf. CIG 3582.2 (where Boeckh prob. wrongly takes it as a proper name). For *presbeutes*: Oxy. 33: BGU 932. Troilos: Fuad viii 6 and Oxy. 1069. First letter may mean: "the post left and the camels were away from home". The two letters show differences in hand and may have been by different scribes, or T. may have written both, with different pens, etc. Both show much same level of literacy, not a high one. Tools: *synerga*.

33. DLRE 150; W. *Grundz.* 419; David-Groningen no. 84.

34. Oxy. 2147 for gymnasion: DLRE 150 There are several non-Egyptian exs. of the gym. used for feasts: gymnasiarch of Akraiphia gave breakfast, *ariston*, for all (cits., strangers, freeborn boys, even slaves) and the inscr. mentions other feasts of his for the people, prob. in gym. (IG vii 2712) A.D. 40; gymnasiarch of Aigina gives feast for club of anointers (prob. all who frequented the place for gym. purposes) early 1 c. A.D. (IG iv 4); public feast on Amorgos, *c.* end 2nd c. B.C., in gym. with beef carcass (IG xii 7.515); similar feast about same time in gym. of Paros (*ib.* 5.129); at Panamara, priest and priestess give dinner to whole city in gym.; near Stratonikeia, gymnasiarch invites cits. to feast in his building (BCH 1891 206 no. 146; CIG 2719); Sardeis, gymnasiarch often sac. victims to gods and distrib. the meat to all cits. in his house and the gym. (IGRom. iv 1757). See Forbes (1) 39.

35. Oxy. 110 and 747. Party is *xenia*.

36. Fuad viii 7; Oxy. 524 and 111; cf. 181, 3c. Crawford comments that it is still (1949) the custom in Egypt to give 24 hours' notice for a party.

37. Oxy. 927, cf. Fay. 132. It is on verso of strip cut from two docs. gummed together; one seems to mention Alex. Sev.; so we may date the invitation mid or later 3 c.

38. Oxy. 926 and 1214. Reading of address not at all sure. For *epikrisis*: P. Oxy. ii pp. 217ff and DLRE 59.

39. Athen. xv 668c; Smith, *dict.* i 558; Athen. 668d and ef; Abbott, 297.

40. Phil., *creation* xvi, and Dion K. xxxii 13, cf. Paus. vii 22.2–4.

41. Predynastic: Cat. exhib. King's Coll. London July 1909; cf. E. R. Ayrton

and W. S. Loat, Eg. Explor. Fund 1911; grave H 41; Murray fig. 1. Scribe's tomb: Lepsius ii 61, tomb 16. Ben-hassan: Murray fig 2. Robbers: Murray 13f. In gen. Murray 14–19 and 19–21 (Ur), fig. 3 (dogs, jackals). Gezer, R. A. S. Macalister, *Hist. Civil. in Palestine* 1921 91 fig. 4; Gadd 46 n2.

42. Plat. *phaidr.* 274d; *rep.* 374d. Pollux ix 98; Austin (1).

43. Prop. iv 8.45f.

44. Murray 17.

45. Austin (2); Emery 46 pl. 32 (date, between A.D. 291 and 7 c).

46. Procul. xiii 2 (early 4 c); players rebuked Macrob. *sat.* i 5; it seems to be *petteia.* Roman games: Murray 29–34,27.

47. *Röm. Mitt* 1896 238; *BM Guide GR Life* 1920 206 fig. 245 (Muses are 6, Helios 2); a set was fd. in child's tomb, Pantikapaion. Inscrs.: Smith, *dict. antiq.* ii 73; BM Guide 207; Murray; *Num. Chron.* (4th) vi 232; *Not. d. Scavi* 1887 118; Picard (2) 278. Contorniates: *BM Guide* 207.

48. Souid. sv *Tabla;* Plin. xxxvii 13.

49. In general, Bataille. Choachytai: P. dem. Brux. 3 (p. 12). Hunger: Cumont (2) 352f. Meuli, 185–228.

50. Bataille 269, citing Lefebvre. *Ib.* 270: "The *ch.* acted as funerary priests during the Festival of the Valley. As for that, Peyron (P. Turin. p. 85) and Brugsch (*Letter to de Rougé*, p. 44) made out of the diabasis of Amun a festival of the dead. Steindorff did not agree (UPZ ii p. 86). Still it could hardly fail to have that character to some extent, at least in what concerned the *ch.*" Cf. Foucart, 38, 43, 103.

51. SB 364; Weill-Jouguet.

52. BIFAO 1939 xxxviii 161.

53. *Ib.* 164, pl. xvi; Bataille 187, 271.

54. Ryl. 153; DLRE 66.

55. Oxy. 494.

56. P. Leip. 30; W. *Chr.* 500.

57. Lefebvre 26; Grenfell-Hunt, *Fay. Towns* 41 (Karanis).

58. Lond. i 77 (p. 231).

59. Drioton (1).

60. Bataille 268f. Tickets: Spiegelberg (1) 3ff; Blackman. Karnak: Drioton (2).

61. Spiegelberg (2); P. dem. Cair. 31170–2, 31175–6; Blackman.

62. Lefebvre 132 for water in the rite of Opening the Mouth, plus incense and natron, in the reliefs of Petosiris' tomb. P. seems to have been highpriest of Khmunu (Hermes) at Hermop. under Persians and to have survived into reign of Ptol. I: Bevan 81, fig. 16–17.

63. Deonna (2).

64. Stele: G. Maspero (1) 113. Greek: Jouguet (2).

65. SB 335, 5037, 5718: cf. P. dem. Cair. 31172 (p. 282). Also Christian ideas combining Egyptian, Syrian, Mesopotamian elements in the need to overcome thirst-causing heat in the beyond: A. Parrot (1–4). In general: Bataille 265. Cf. the Orphic formula: J. Harrison *Themis* 513.

66. Schreiber. At Ras Shamra, installations to bring water for the dead, going back to time of Eg. alliance (1440-1360 B.C.): Schaeffer. For liquid offerings in Theban nekropolis under Ptols., Bataille 266; incense etc., 266f.

67. Spiegelberg (2); Bataille 267.

68. Vandier (1).

69. Bataille 293; cf. *Book of Dead*, ch. cxxv.

70. Diod. i 92. Baris: Nile-scow, Herod. ii 96. For Charon, cf. Diod. i 96; no evidence for the name as Egyptian.

71. In general, Bataille 268n. Liturgic drama: Drioton (3); de Walle (Herod. ii 63); Sethe (1) on enthroning of Sesostris I. After lamentations and procession to Nile in Pharaonic times, the river-crossing: the coffin with mummy on a bier set in a boat. "A woman on each side, representing Isis and Nephthys respectively, lamented during the whole crossing the misfortune that had befallen them." Other boats took the wailing family, mourners and friends; on west bank the bier was put on sledge drawn by cows; the procession went to the nekropolis, the priests wafting incense on the bier and intoning ritual chants. At the tomb "rites were performed by the priests, such as the Opening of the Mouth, followed by the farewell to the deceased uttered by the widow kneeling before the coffin and holding it in her arms." Then coffin was lowered into vault with the dead man's possessions; shaft blocked "and the congregation took part in a funerary banquet in communion with the departed one": Sauneron (1) 102.

Mounu: Vandier. At funerals of Pharaonic days there was the dance of the Muu, dancers wearing odd reed-crowns.

72. Sc. *Il.* i 425; Diod. i 97.9. Flowers: *Il* xiv 346. For Pharaonic period: Foucart and Sethe (2).

73. UPZ 162/3/1-3 and /8/19-20.

74. Bataille 90: for further details.

75. P. dem. Ryl. xlii (pp. 27, 116), lx (pp. 30, 117); Bataille 91.

76. Bataille 91 and 149.

3. DANCE OF LIFE AND DEATH

1. DLRE esp. ch. xiv. The folk of Euergetis are mentioned Oxy. 814 (1st c.) *Biologos*: also at Aquileia (Jacobs, *Anth. Pal.* iii p. 970); L. Robert (1). In Oxy. 519 and 1050 *mimos* and *homeristes* are close together. For order of officials: P. Oxy. vii p. 157; Preisigke (3) 31; Flor. 21. For gratuities to artists: Eitrem (1) 26f.

2. DLRE 61 and *Aith.* iii 1-3. Oxy. 526, Dancer (male) *orchestis*.

3. Michailides 307f.

4. For ex., Cumont (3) 85f,61. Conjurer: Oxy. 1050.19. Firmicus ii 307.13. Wise animals: Phil. *de animal.* 23ff.

5. *Tetrabib.* iv 4. Counting houses prob. mean fiscal offices. Leaders: Cumont (3) 47 nl for vagueness of astrologers as to lesser civic positions.

6. *Tilling of Earth by Noah* viii.

7. Neugebauer (1) 121: Vett. Valens v 10 (231.5–31), omitting some technicalities.

8. Trouble: *Hist. Aug. Anton.* v 5; Malal. xi 280; John of Nik. 74; BGU 372 and W. *Chr.* 19 (p. 31). Munatius: 17 April 150 (Ryl. 75) and 13 Sept. 151 (Oxy. 237). Petronius: 28 Aug. 147 (*Ann. Epig.* 1904 no. 218), 3 Nov. 148 (W. *Chr.* 212).

9. Dion xxxii 55–9; Plin. xxiv 164 on herb gelotophyllis, which, mingled with wine and myrrh, produced immoderate laughter. Dion seems recalling Eurip. *Bacchai* 669f, 1278f, 708–10. A.M. xiv 18–19.

10. Athen. i 37 (20e); cf. Plout. *quaest. symp.* viii 8.3 (711. 44); Seneca *contra excerpt.* iii praef.; Zosim. i 6; Suet. (Roth) p. 301.25. Bathyllos, freedman and favourite of Maecenas, danced a comic pantomime (themes: Pan and Echo; Satyr and Amor), but this type did not last long.

11. Athen. i 27 (15d) citing also Xen. *anab.* Hyporchema, choral hymn to Apollo, akin to paian: see Sandys, Loeb *Pindar* p. 575; H. W. Smith, *Greek Melic Poets* lxix–lxxv; Plout. *quest. symp.* ix 15.2 (748b) as link of poetry and dance; accomp. by flute with or without kithara; not confined by Pindar's time to religious themes. It seems that thus Apollo plays the part in the pantomime's dance that Dionysos did in the tragic (though the relation is not close and dynamic). See also Athen. xiv 628. Further on pantomime: Albizzati 27ff; Butler 26ff; Weege 156ff. L. Robert (2) on inscrs. of Greece and Asia Minor; Bieber (1) 305 n22 takes it as a Roman influence penetrating east as early as Sulla. Also Wüst (2).

12. *Salt.* 16.

13. *Ib.* 27; cf. 2, "countless other things to hear and see that are worth while, if one wants them: fluteplayers who accompany cyclic choruses, singers of conventional compositions for the lyre, and, in particular, grand tragedy and comedy, gayest of the gay". Tragedy: Bieber (1) 237, 241, 250f.

14. Monoidiai; cf. Aristoph. *frogs* 1331ff. Cf. the *Persians* of Timotheus, describing Marathon, recited with kithara-accompaniment—prob. first at the Panionian Panegyris, 397 B.C.; done again 207–6—Wilamowitz-M. (1) 10f, (2) 27, 55ff.

15. Purser 334b.

16. *Salt.* 30–2; games at Naples, instituted by Aug., A.D. 2: Geer, n.19. It seems that *emmeleia* and *sikinnis* provided elements; the *kordax* prob. went into the mime proper.

17. L. Robert (2).

18. *Salt.* 31. *Poikiloterai,* more varied; *metabolai,* changes.

19. *Salt.* 2. Libanios tried to moralise the pantomime: both his work and Louk.'s reply to the attack by Aristeides: Mesk. Louk. prob. wrote at Antioch, 165–2, while Verus was there (Verus being much taken up with the dance): D. S. Robertson. Ironshoe: shoe with heavy sole, once of wood, now iron (Lib. *pro salt.* 97), worn by fluteplayer or scabellarius who marked time: DS

sv *scabellum* fig. 6142; Suet. *Cal.* 54; Poll. vii 87; Liban. iii 385.13. Beare does not see the link with tragedy; sees the link with drama in the setting, 224.

20. *Salt.* 5.

21. *Salt.* 80.

22. *Ib.* 83. Scripts. Poems by Ovid, not meant for the theatre, were used, and even orations were set to music and adapted to dancing: Ov. *trist.* ii 519; v 7.25; Plin, *paneg.* 54; Tac. *dial.* 26. But poets also wrote librettos, *fabulae salticae, e.g.* Silo (Senec. *suas.* ii 19), Lucan (*vit. vaccae* in Teuffel, par. 298.4), Statius (Juv. vii 92). For use of tale of Kinyras and Myrrha: Jos. *ant.* xix 1.3. For pantomime masks: Kokolakis 36f; Webster 3.

23. Macr. *sat* ii 716. Pylades said to intro. orchestra in place of single flute: Louk. 68; Ov. *rem. am.* 753ff. Wüst, 1754–5, on fondness of Egyptians for mime.

24. *Salt.* 36f; *Il.* i 70. *Salt.* 19 and 58–60.

25. *Salt.* 67. Other shows have a single activity, "the dancer however has everything at once, and that equipment of his, we may see, is varied (*poikile*) and comprehensive, the flute, the pipes, the feet-taps, the cymbal-clashes, the actor's melodious voice, the concord of the singers", 68. A barbarian says to the dancer, "I did not grasp, my friend, that though you have one body you have many souls", 66. Occasionally a second actor: cf. Odysseus above, and Quint. vi 3.65. At times the one dancer acted 5 parts; prob. some sort of choral recitative while he changed clothes. If he made no change, he was said *palliolatim saltare* (Fronto, Naber, 157.3), using a single cloak to represent all sorts of things, swan's neck, Venus' hair, Furies' whip, etc.

26. Exception must be made for Claudian, an Egyptian, who revived epic via the panegyric and who partially succeeded because of what we may call his Egyptian Romanticism which was derived from the same sources as later that of Nonnos. For Apuleius: J. Lindsay (7) intro.

27. *Dionys.* xix 138–42, 153–8. Yet Reich and Wüst do not mention him.

28. *Ib.* 198–200 and 225f. In Nonnos, Maron is a personification of the vine and wine, as are Staphylos, his wife Methe (Drunkenness) etc. For an account of a dance-mime: Apul. *met.* x 30–4, esp. "sometimes she seemed to dance only with her eyes".

29. *Dionys.* 263–87.

30. *Ib.* 287–95.

31. Maspero (2); Michailides 308.

32. Sauneron (1) 57: also citing H. Wild for Egyptian steps: feet still, arms and hips making sinuous movements; feet moving forward in simple walk or on toes, arms raised en corbeille or in Roman salute; running, leaping (erect or bent), splits (forwards) or sideways arabesque, grand battement, pirouette, backbend, cartwheels.

Salt. 62; Herod. i 47. *Salt.* 63–4, 70; Athen. i 20d. Agrippa: *Aug. Hist. verus* 8. Athen. i 21f: "Telesis or Telestes the dance-master was the inventor of many figures rendering to perfection words by means of the hands." Cf. Pollux iv 99 and Hesych. sv *telesia*. Hand-movement: *cheironomia*.

33. Deonna (1) figs. 4–5 and p. 7: Evans (1) 362, 364, 369; (2) iv 2.501 and figs. 445–8; (3) 122ff. Charpouthier 51.

34. *Ib.* figs. 7–9, 23–4, and p. 7 nn 2–4.

35. *Ib.* figs. 17–18.

36. *Ib.* fig. 20, cf. 21. Lanzone 408 and 410, pl. clix 6 and clx; CE 1943 40f; Hopfner (3) 139.

37. *Ib.* fig. 22. Lanzone 402 pl. clx, 2 (Dendera); Prinz 16, 21, no. 3 pl. viii, 2 (Philai, Ptol. era); Bénédite, pl. i; Malten JDAI 1928 95.

38. Deonna (1) figs. 25–7 and p. 9; cf. figs. on tomb of Ramses ix, fig. 35.

39. Sauneron (2).

40. Amélineau 309. See Deonna for the carrying on of the tradition into the medieval world. Assyria: *Aith.* iv 17—cf. Phrygian mode: Louk. *salt.* 34, and the *Persikon* of Xen. *anab.* vi 1.10; cf. Aristoph. *thesm.* 1175. *Paktis* as flute: AP ix 586.

41. Buschor 165, fig. 184; Deonna fig. 55.

42. Herod. vi 126; PW sv *Hippokleides*; DS sv *Cernuus* 1078 n3; Gauheis 13; Depping 153; CR 1907 169; AJA 1908 227; Plat. *euthyd.* 294e; Xen. *symp.* ii 11 and 22; Weinreich 128; Weege 9.

43. Athen. iv 3 (for marriage, cf. *Od.* iv 17–19; RA 1947 i 85; PW sv *Kybisteter*); Ail. VH ii 183 and Letter 16 (Hercher); Stob. xix 75 (like Ail., links sword-dance and fire-breathing).

44. *Oneirocrit.* i 76 (65); Charpouthier 60 n4.

45. Capart i 55, ii p. lxviii (6th dyn.).

46. Moret 262 n2; Deonna 82f, also for Cretan refs.

47. *Il.* xvi 745–50; Picard (1) 85 n1; Chamoux 333.

48. Deonna (1) 29f. The tumblers appear on Achilleus' Shield, *Il.* xviii 590–606, and at a marriage festival, *Od.* iv 17–9.

49. Deonna 76f.

50. *Ib.* 77; and Louk. *salt.* 71.

51. The tumbling Seilenos becomes the everturning waters: xix 314ff, esp. 348; cf. satyrs in water, x 148ff and the dance xl 239ff.

52. *Dionys.* xix 341f.

53. *Ib.* x 158–61.

54. *Ib.* xl 241f.

55. *Ib.* xxii 317.

56. *Ib.* xxxvi 213, *autokylistos*; his fate is *geiton*, neighbouring, bordering; 218, *kymbachos*.

57. *Ib.* xxx 145, xxii 315–17, xvii 152f, xxii 315ff.

58. *Ib.* ii 434f, xxviii 128 and 139.

59. *Ib.* xliv 64, xlvi 187.

60. *Ib.* xxxix 336–9, xliii 46–51.

61. *Ib.* xvii 211–4.

62. *Ib.* xxxvi 453, xxviii at end, xliii 162. See further Deonna 92–5.

63. Deonna 37f. Phlogios: xxx 118–25. Phaethon: *ib.* 115 and xxxviii 99. Note Phlogios is son of Strophios (Turner, Spinner).

64. This point did not miss the acute Deonna, 108–10. Ino-Leukothea leaps *kybistesasa* into the sea, Dionys. x 121. Note the *k.* on Ach.'s Shield with Okean round it. (I have dealt at length with the leap in my *Clashing Rocks.*) In this section I draw on Deonna, but had already myself made the analysis as part of the general inquiry into Nonnos' imagery which is set out in the final chapter.

4. THE GYMNASION

1. A.A. *or.* xiv 264 (Dindorf). Dion, *or.* xlviii 9 and xxxii 44: cf. Philostr. *vit. soph.* ii 26. Forbes (1) 32. Anacharsis: Herod. iv 76; Dion seems drawing on same source as DL i 104. Drug: *pharmakon.*

2. Louk. *de gymn.* 15.

3. Herod. ii 91 and 156. He links Chemmis with Danaos and Lynkeus.

4. Diod. i 81.

5. Yoyotte (1) 268. For ancient attacks on songs: Erman (2) 234; Griffith (2).

6. Vitr. v 11; cf. Dion. Hal. *ant. rom.* vii 70–2. Plout. *quaest. rom.* xl; Plin. *epist.* x 49. Spartans: Nepos: *epam.* v 4; cf. Polyb. i 6.6. For Roman revulsion further: Ennius in Cic. *tusc.* iv 70; Plin. NH xv 19; Tac. *ann.* xiv 20; Plout. *cat. mai.* xx. Also, Oehler. Mayor on Juv. iii 68.

7. Varro RR ii proem; Cic. *ad att.* i 4, *in verr.* ii 14.36. Grimal (1) 262ff; for Val Catena, *Oest. Jahrb.* 1907 56 fig. 2. Suet. *ner.* 12. Herodian i 12.4 (Commodus).

Athletics were included in Roman games from 186 B.C. and grew very popular under empire, but as carried on by professionals. Nero tried in vain to get the nobles to appear in the stadium; only a few exceptions, Tac. *ann.* xiv 20; 47.4; sc. Juv. iv 53. Any exercise was a matter of hygiene, ancillary to use of steambaths. Architecturally, the Roman palaestra was subsidiary to the thermae, which, compared with Greek original, expanded out of all proportion to the actual connection with sports. The R. gym. was simply a pleasure-garden. (Palaestrae tacked on to hot baths at Pompeii and Herc.)

8. II *Macc.* iv 12–15 and 18–20.

9. SEG i 466; Jones (1) 10. Cf. Paphlagonia: IGRom. iii 1446.

10. Sarapieion pap. of Ptol. in W. (2) i; Bevan 295.

11. Col. Zen. 66; Bell (1) 137 n7; Préaux (1) 69 n10. *Hellenizein* may mean "speak Greek", the letter being written and translated by a scribe.

12. Lond. i 43 (p. 48).

13. Bilinski (1) 102; Méautis; DLRE 166; Aisop 20 Perry. Non-Greeks, but not Egyptians, were admitted to Ptol. gym.: Delorme 427. Exclusion of Jews: Lond. 1912 (Claudius A.D. 41); Bell (2) 25—though BGU iv 1140 seems to declare an Alex. Jew or his father had a gym. education, but is not sure.

14. Appian BC i 102; Plout. *ant.* 54 and 80; SHA *carac.* vi 2.

15. Str. xvii 1.10.

O*

16. Elis: Delorme 71. In gen. C. Peterson GG 10 n7. Text: Koraes 145, Delorme 137.

17. SB 4314; Peak (2) 1887 and (3) 192. Cf. inscr. (2 c.?) *Archiv* iii 1906 138 no. 21 (line 17); Launey ii 837 n7.

18. Neroutsos Bey 72.

19. BA xiii 2; Appian BC v 11.

20. Tebt. 700 (iii p. 39) col. ii line 37. For ded. of a *bathra* in a g(ymnasion) of Alex. by an agonothetes (163–45 B.C.) see JEA 1961 145 and *Berytus* xiii 142 no. 7.

21. PSI iv 340.

22. Polyb. xv 30.6 and Ptol. *synt. math.* 197 (Heilberg-Teubner). Romme thinks there were two circles.

23. Mekios 36. Apart from what is said in the text, note the following gymnasia. *Luxor*: insc. found here (but provenance unsure) mentions gym.—decree in honour of gymnasiarch and kosmetes as benefactor: his portrait to be ded. "in the most conspicuous part of gym." Henne; SB 7246; SEG viii 694; JEA 1961 145 on date. Dedication of a Ptolemaion and throne for the tutelary deities Herakles and Hermes by Areios, strat. of *Pharbaithite nome*: SB 1164. (For thrones in gymns., Picard (3) and CRAI 1959 151.)

Psenamosis: two decrees of the *georgoi* under a Ptol. (late): SEG viii 529. *Ptolemais* (?): Frag. decree of a gym. (mentions *boule*): SEG viii 641 and JEA 1961 145. *Thmuis*: statue-base, SEG. viii 504. *Theadelpheia*: gymnasiarch Leonidas, 150–49 B.C. deds. a gate and entry to gym: SB 6157–8. *Arsinoe*: prob. two gym., as ref. to the Big Gym.: BGU iii 760 (Ptol.). *Aphroditopolis*: frag. decree in honour of hipparch Herodes, 1 c. B.C.: SEG viii 531. *Sebynnytos*: gym. and gym. club called Herakleion: SB 1106 (Ptol.). Where *Cairo* now is: Ptol. (2nd c.) gym. with club *Archiv* ii 1903 548 no. 26. Far up Nile: *Omboi*: 2nd c. B.C. decree of 136–5: Archiv v 141; and *Elephantine* (3rd c. A.D.): Philol. liii 1894 82. *Hermopolis*: Ryl. ii 101; CPR 20; Amh. ii. 124; Flor. 57, 79; Lond. 1166 (A.D. 15); Amh. 64 (A.D. 107); Amh. 70: W. *Chr.* 149 (114–15 A.D.); *Philadelpheia*: PSI 391A. *Samareia*: Enteuxis 8 (privately built).

In trouble between Crocodilopolis and Hermonthis, 123 B.C., the reps. from C. were the young men attached to the gym., W. *archiv* v 1913 410–16, cf. vi 389. *Oxyrhynchos*: Oxy. 2127, 2147, 42, 477, 705, 1102, 1697, 1703, 1705; Gym. Square, 1116, cf. 1449.

Further for *Alexandreia*: SB 5069; Tebt. ii 316; BGU iv 1084; PSI vii 477; JEA xii 1926 246; Dion. Kass. li 6.1.

See further note 35 below.

24. APF ii 528.26; SEG viii 504, 531, 694.

25. PSI iv 391a; *Archiv* vi 392; *Aeg.* xi 1931 488 no. 2; Launey ii 840. Also BGU vi 1922 1256; Launey 859; cf. PSI 340. And PSI 418.

26. Enteuxis 8; SB 7245; Jouguet (3); Guéraud; Launey ii 846, 853; Delorme; Jones (2) 472 n4.

27. Brady (1); Rostovtzeff (4) 1588 n23; Launey ii. Delorme denies.

28. Roussel (1) 37; SEG viii 53; SB 7746.

29. SEG viii 357; SB 7456.

30. Preisigke SB 2264. Also in Kyrene: AI iii 1930 189; but here was a Dorian area: the epheboi are called *triakatioi*: Hesych. sv. In war-emergency gym. could be used for drill and tactical studies; St John Chrysos. (Migne lx 217–8) alluded to general going to gym. to improve knowledge of tactics (*e.g.* reviews, parades, musterings, camping ground, fort, base of operations).

31. Jouguet (4) 67, 150; Bickermann (1); Brady; Rostovtzeff (4) iii 1395; Marrou (1) 109 and 386 n16; W. *Chr.* 143, 146. Duration: two to three years?: W. *Grundz.* 142.

Apo gymnasiou (Jouguet (4) 79–86) is in practice the same as *apo ephebeias* (BGU 1903 2). Jouguet 83 admits there may be a difference, but what could it be? Also, synonymous with *hoi ek tou gymnasiou* (Rost. (4) 1059; Brady (1) is in doubt); but Oxy. 2186 seems to settle the matter: *ek tou g.* seems limited to the Ptol. period (APF ii 548.26; v 415–16.13, 17; SEG viii 504, 531. 641, 694). But there, dated A.D. 260, is a list of nine generations *ek tou g.*: Marrou (1) 110.

32. Oxy. 2345 (two frags.). In some other respects, cf. Oxy. 2186 and PSI 457. See DLRE 59–61.

33. Jouguet (4) 152.

34. Early ages: Tebt. ii 316; BGU 1084. Age of admission, 14: Flor. 57; W. *Chr.* 141 (boy, 14 yrs. 17 days at *epikrisis*). Admission voluntary. Subdiv. of *symmoria*: *plagion*: BGU 1084; JEA xii 246; San Nicolò (1) 34. Term *synepheboi* still used in Amh. 11 124. Documents cited: Oxy. 1266 and 1109. Cf. Oxy. 257, 1202, 1306; Ryl. 101 etc. Mertens for the different officials dealing with *epikrisis* at different periods and for the differentiation of the *epikriseis*; *tagma*, 115, 124, and Oxy. 1202. For tax-reduction: Wallace 127, Mertens 111. For *koinon* and tagma: Mertens p. viii.

35. Lond. 1912; Bell (2) 53. Caesarion, Cleo.'s son by J.C. was enrolled in Alex. ephebeia; also M.A.'s son by Fulvia, Antyllus: Dion Kass. li 6.1 and Plout. *ant.* lxxi.

List of gymnasiarchs in van Groningen (1), Kosmetes at Alex. IGRom. i 1074; SB 5225. Hermopolis: CPR 20; Ryl iii 77, 86, 116–17, 181, 282; Amh. ii 124; SB 5676. Arsinoe: BGU ii 362; W. *Chr.* 193. Arsinoite nome: Flor. 21. Oxy.: Oxy. 477, 519, 1645, 1703 (one of the k.'s sons belonged to the *ex ephebias hieronikai*). Fayum; CPR 228; W. *Chr.* 176. Two undefined places: IGRom. i 1097; SB 5676.

36. Amh. ii 70; CPR 20.

37. Oxy. 632; Van Groningen (1). And Oxy. 42. See DLRE for discussion of the decline, esp. chs. 23–5. Last refs., Oxy. 42 (A.D. 323); gymnasiarch. Oxy. 2110 (A.D. 370); about same time St Basil refers to gymnasiarchs, *ep.* lxxiv 448a, and Himerios to palaistra, *or.* xxii 7. About 400, Synesios refs. to paidotribes, esp. xxii. These brief refs. hardly suggest a flourishing institution. Sport seems lacking in student life of 4 c., though some ballgames played for pastime (Lib. *or.* i 22). The shows still continued: St Greg. Naz. (384–90) denounces the frivol-

ous who waste time and money at stadion, palaistra, circus: *carm.* ii 11, 4.154–7 (carrying on idiom of 2nd c. Christians, Tatian, Tertullian, Cyprian).

38. Traces of the palaistra-organisation are slight in Egypt, though Herondas (i 28) speaks of the "wealth, palaistrai, power" of the country. Naukratis: a p. ded. to Apollon: SB 355. Alexandreia: Polyb. xv 30.6 (plural). Hermopolis: boys of p. acted as guard of honour for strat., gymnasiarch, kosmetes, and other officials, 2nd c., Amh. ii 124; they were called palaistrophylakes, but differed from the slaves with that name elsewhere. At Alex. paidotribes and grammar-teachers exempt from taxes: Hal. line 260ff, 259–3 B.C.; letter 257–6 by a paido-tribes of Alex. speaks of opening a p., PSI iv 340; letter from unknown place speaks of boy sent to a p. (using diminutive *palaistridion*).

39. Frequenters of palaistra: Cumont (3) 79. Protagoras: DL ix 54. In New Comedy, man seeking another always tries the gym., *e.g.* Plaut. *amph.* 1011, *epid.* 198.

40. Prodikos: Ps.-plat. *eryx* 399a. Sokrates: Epiktetos iv 4.21. Note the start of the *Lysis, Euthydemos,* and ps.-plat. *Axiochos.* Karneades: DL iv 63; Plout. *de garr.* xxi (513c).

41. DL v 2 and 10; vi 13, Grimal 75f., 264, 384.

42. Plout. *amat.* ii (749c). Vitruv. vi intro. 1; cf. Galen *protr.* v; Forbes (1) 34; Salvian *de gub.* vi 11. Louk. *pereg.* iii and *dial. dead* i 1.

43. See Vitruv. v 11 for spacious exedrae and seats for students. Hellenistic and Roman architects often had an akroaterion (auditorium) in gym. plans: Forbes (1) 34 for exs.

44. Forbes (1) 35f for exs.

45. *F. de Delphes* iii 1 273.

46. At Teos: SIG (3rd) 578 11.32–4; Ziebarth 56.

47. Forbes (1) 36f for refs.

48. IG ii (2nd) 1006; Forbes (3) 158.

49. Cic. *de fin.* v 1.1; *de orat.* ii 5. Dion, xxxii 7.

50. Forbes (1) 40.

51. BGU viii 1767–8: some village in H. nome, and Hiera Nesis.

52. Burials: Forbes (1) 41. Ceremonies, *e.g.* Seleukeia by the Kalykadnos had the physician Asklepiades crowned with gold in gym., Wilhelm.

53. Sarapion: REg no. 425. The baths represent the public works initiated or stimulated by Hadrian on his visits. Hermes: Oxy. 1015.

Epheboi at Ephesos sang hymns and paians: Sokolowki (1) no 121, lines 12–7.

54. Oxy. 1104, cf. Oxy. 55.

55. Oxy. 896. For "painting" garden: *Archiv* ii 449; sv Hesych. as *poikilos.* (Painters: Louk. *herod.* 4; *epigr.* 41; PSI iv 346, 407; SIG 682.3; pap. in *Abh. Berl. AK.* 1904 2.6; E.M. 412.53. zographia tou stylou: IGR i 1272.) A.D. 306, Oxy. 1430; See Pap. Oxy. xii pp. 85–7 for dates and currency.

56. *Aithiop.* ii 27; K. goes on to tell about the Nile.

57. FGH 87F 10; Athen. v 210F. For the Clubs of Anointers, a sign of de-cadence: Forbes (3) 186, 190, 195, 202, 215, 243f.

58. Diog. cyn. *ep.* xxviii 4: *Epistolog. Gr.* 242.

59. Mamertinus, *Paneg. Lat.* xi (lii) 9; Forbes (1) 39f.

60. Philostr. *vit. apol.* iv 42. For Christian preaching in gym. in wall-painting: Forbes (1) 41; Rostovtzeff (5) 154.

61. Grimal 262ff.

5. ATHLETICS

1. Plat. *rep.* iii 406 a–b; Souid. iii M, 989. Jüthner (1) 50 and (2). For Athen. aristocrats and baths: Ps.–Xen. *ath.* ii 10. In gen., Bilinski 94. For education at Miletos *c.* 200 B.C. see Forbes (3) 223, as an example of the high cultural level that could not be held: SIG (3rd) 577.

2. Plat. *rep.* iii 404a, 407b, 410–11. Arist. *pol.* iv 13.3, cf. v 4.8. Also Tyrtaios, Xenophon. In gen., Bilinski and Forbes (3) 90 f.

3. Plout. *de sanit. tuenda* xvi 20. Galen, *protr.* ix–xiv—see discussion Bilinski 121–6. Contrast Dion Chr. *or* xxix.

4. Forbes (3) 199ff. Women profs.: Ditt. SIG 802A; Marrou (1) 115. Olympia: Paus. v 16.3.

5. *Special Laws: women not behaving immodestly* i.

6. BCH xv 1891 264 no. 5.

7. BCH 1891 25 no. 3; 1908 414f no. 2. Forbes (3) 214.

8. Siska.

9. Hermes: R i 2368.

10. E.g., Kyrene, 244 A.D.: *J. des Sav.* 1927 319. Deds. to Hermes, Herakles, Apollon at Delos: BCH xv 250; xxxvi 387ff. Cf. Paus. ii 10.7 (Sikyon); vi 23.5 (Elis). Hermai: PW sv 702. Note statue for sacred synod of Herakleistai (local gild of athletes, 2nd c. A.D.) at Pagai, Megaris: IG vii 192; RE viii 503.

11. Kaibel, epigr. gr. 295; Ziebarth (2) 83 n1. At Athens boys entered pal. at 7, the gym. about 14. Cf. epigram on lad of the Milesian pal. who died at 8: *Rev. philol.* xxxiii 1906 6.

12. Michailowski. Heavy-lidded: Watzinger II 1B pl. xi. 3 no. 14.

13. Battered: BCH 1930 pl. vii. General trend of young heads: some in Glyp. Ny-Carlsberg (nos. 162, 262, 115): Arndt, *La G. Ny-C.* pl. 117, 95, 118. *Ausgrab. v. Pergamon*: vii 1 no. 136, p. 154; vii 2 nos. 178–9, 181, p. 184ff. Egypt: Watzinger.

For H.-portraits *e.g.* Demokrates in gym. near pal. at Sparta (late 1 c A.D.): Kaibel 949, cf. 950–73 (Athenai) and Paus. i 12.2; also h. of kosmetes in gymn. of so-called Diogenes, Athenai. For decs. in Roman garden-gym.: Cic. *ad att.* i 10.3. For Palaistra as d. of Hermes: Philostr. *imag.* ii 32. In Hellenistic times meaning of gym. and pal. gets blurred; at times pal. is for young boys, gym. for ephebes and adults; pal. private school, and gym., the municipal organisation; or we can take gym. as comprehensive term, made up of pal. (practice-ground) and stadion: Marrou 392 n15.

14. *Tetrab.* iv 10 (204–5); Cumont (3) 75.

15. *Ib.* ii 8 (87); iii 8 (124); iii 13 (123). Cf. end of bk. iii; diseases, iii 12 (152); animals iii 8 (123); type iii 11 (144).

16. *Ib.* iii 13 (162). Gentlemanly: *holos kalous te kai agathous.*

17. See n23 ch. iv here. *Aithiop.* x 31.5 and *Dionys.* x 336f.

18. Thouk. i 6.4 (girdle); Paus. i 44.1; Plat. *rep.* 452D.

19. Jüthner, RE ix 2.2545 (*infibulatio,* though *inf.* is in fact the more crude way of fastening prepuce by metal brooch).

20. Bowl-crop, *skaphion*: Arist. *thesm.* 838. Knot: *cirrus.* Cap: Poll. x 64; Giraud 210f; Mart. xiv 50. Track: BCH 1899 566.5; Louk. *anach.* 27. Earcovers: DS i 1. 521a.

21. Oil: Galen, *san. tu.* ii 2, iii 7 (Orib. vi 13). After: iii 2 (Orib. vi 16, cf. 17–20). Dust: Philostr. *gym.* 56 and 29. Galen (ii 12.162) thinks the dust too much for the very young; Louk. 29 says it is to make the body more secure in wrestling.

22. Philost. 56.42; Suet. *nero* 45.

23. Philost. 18. Phil. frags. in Euseb. *praep.* viii 13.

24. Herod. viii 59; Louk. *asin.* 10. Gymnastes: Philost. 20; Epiktet. *ench.* 29. Philon (*Dreams* i 21) on gym. trainer who gives man a hand and invites him to gym. and, standing firmly, obliges him to wrestle.

25-26. Sc. Arist. *knights* 492. Aristot. *eth. nik.* ii 6.7; Plout. *de san.* 133.9.

27. Aristot. *pol.* v 4.7; Galen vi 487K; Philost. *gym.* 3 and 37.

28. Early diet (may be gold-age idealisation) DL viii 1.13. Meat: Paus. vi 7.10; Plin. NH xxiii 63; DL *l.c.*; Philost. 43. For similar modern dilemmas: *Times* 31 Oct. 1964 (Bizarre Diet no help to Athletes).

29. Pork: Gal. vi 661; beef, Plat. *rep.* i 338c; goat, Athen. ix 402a; fish, Philost. 44; no wine, Gal. xv 194; no cakes. Epiktet. *l.c.*; bread, Gal. vi 180K and Philost. 43 (cf. Plaut. *pers.* i 3.12 and Juv. ii 53). Day: Gal. vi 168f. Meat: Gal. viii 843K, i 28K; Arist. *eth. nik.* ii 67; Athen. x 412; Thouk. iv 34; Aristoph. *peace* 34; Plin. NH xviii (63); Cic. *tusc.* ii 17.40. Some trainers had own systems: Gal. vi 208: Theon with warm baths and lesser food after exercises; walks, Plin. NH xi (283). Violent exercises: Gal. vi 117, 123, 222; v 898; Philost. 47. Costume: Hor. AP 414; Plat. *laws* viii 840.

30. Bags: Louk. *lex.* 5; Philost. 43. Mattock: Theok. iv 10.

31. Philost. 43. The pentathlon required a more all-round development, Aristot. *rhet.* i 5.

32. Heats: Paus. vi 13.2. Olympic stadion: some 210 yds: Delphic 194; Pergamene 230. Armed: after 450, no greaves—2 stadia at Olympia and Athenai, 4 at Nemeia; Philost. *gym.* 7; sc. Aristoph. *birds* 292. Philost. 7 for myth of fire-lighting in origin of Olympics. Running: Krause; *Il.* xxiii 72 etc. Cicero: *tusc.* ii 23.56.

33. Dionys. x 402–24; cf. xxxvii 620ff where one runner slips in the huge heap of dung from slaughtered cattle. For problems of deadheat: Harris 22f.

34. *Aithiop.* iv 1–4. Philon: *Special Laws, Coventing.* For foul: Stat. *theb.*

vi 550ff. Stadia were late at Rome; Julius Caesar built one at time of his fivefold triumph, Suet. *Jul.* 39, cf. *Aug.* 43, 45 and *Domit.* 4, 5.

35. Tod; Harris (1) 24; IG vi. 213; IAG 16.

36. IG xiv 739; IGR i 444; IAG 77.

37. Harris 21–4; Gough AJA lx 1956 361.

38. Marrou (1) 120f; Paus. i 35.3 (*balbis*); *Il.* xxxiii 431, xxiii 824–46, ii 774 and 523; *Od.* viii 129 and 186–200, xvii 168. Stat. *theb.* vi 703. Quint. *inst. or.* ii 13.10; Louk. *philops.* 18; Philost. *imag.* i 24; Mart. xiv 164; Pind. *Isth.* i 34. Truce: Paus. v 20. Stand: Philost. *l.c.* and *Ausgrab. in Olympia* v 35. For Ptol. disc-votive, DLRE 164.

39. Long fingers of jav. men: Philost. *gym.* 31. Nonnos xxxvii at end has contest of javelins but as mimic battle.

40. Eustath. *Il.* xxiii 621; Simonides; sc. Pind. *isth.* i 35 and sc. Soph. *elek.* 691; Pind. *nem.* vii 70–3.

41. Dionys. xxxvii 552ff: *autotelestos*. I draw much on W. H. D. Rouse's Loeb translation. Tricks: *mangana* (once with strong magic relation). Rafter-image more precise in *Il.* xxiii 712. Significant (conscious): *emphron*, a favourite word of Nonnos.

42. *Ib.* x 339ff.

43. *Aithiop.* x 31–2, cf. Philost. *imag.* ii 6. Philon: *alleg. sac. laws* iii 6 (wrestler seeking respite to collect breath), cf. *Moses* i 19. Wrestler who wins by tricks: frags. in Bodleian coll. (*Gen.* xxviii 30). For sex-imagery: Louk. *asin.* 8–10; AP xii 2.206. The *Aithiop.* account uses the old theme of Hellene against barbarian.

44. *Insc. Ol.* 54, 55; SIG (3rd) 1073; cf. *Il.* xxiii 700ff. AP xi 85; Harris 22.

45. IG xiv 739; IGR i 444; Harris 23. For dead heats: Sen. *ep.* lxxxiii 5; Kaibel 939; SEG xi 61; Peek.

46. JRS iii 267 no. 12.

47. Philost. 9; see Theok. xx for a match and Bilinski 97–101 for his rel. to athletics. Champion: Dion Chr. *or.* xxix.

48. DLRE 66f.

49. *Ib.* 164.

50. C. H. Roberts (1) 269f. For the champion from Egypt, boxer, Kleitomachos: Polyb. xxvii 7a; Bilinski 90.

51. *Dionys.* xxvii 500ff.

52. *Cherubim* 24 (81): other passive sufferers are freemen racked on wheel for crimes, wood, stone, gold, silver beaten or divided in the forge.

53. *Husbandry* xxv–vii (111–21). For cestus loaded with lead or iron: aen. v 405ff.

54. Antyll (ap. Orib.) vi 31; vi 30, 26, 32; Gal. *san. tu.* ii 9. Bag: Antyll. vi 33; Philost. *gym.* 57. Oboe: Jüthner, Philost. 301n. Note use of *auletes* in army and navy. Dion (cited) xxxii 68.

For jump: Philost. 55; Antyll. vi 34; Gal. iii 10.145.

55. Antyll. vi 22.3 and 27.2. Gal. says the methods were developed for

educating lads from 14 yrs., perhaps even younger: *san. tu.* ii 1.81; ii 2.91. Marrou (1) 124f.

56. Oxy. 466: Jüthner (1) 26–30; Marrou (1) 123f; Gardiner in his JHS articles; CR 1929 210–2. Theophr. *char.* vii for talkative man at palaistra.

57. *Dionys.* vii 186ff; cf. Klymene, xxxviii 118ff. Race: xi 43ff.

58. *Dionys.* xxxvii 703ff. A weight-putting contest precedes. The landing missile rolls on, "bearing an *autossyton hormen*", 693.

59. Athen. i 19a for *sysphairistes* of Alexander. Ball games were common in Rome: Suet. *aug.* 83 and *vesp.* 29; (Capitol.) *m. aurel.* 4; Lamprid. *alex. sev.* 30; Plin. *ep.* iii 18; Sen. *brev. vit.* 13; Hor. *sat.* i 5, etc. Ball-room in thermae: Hor. *sat.* i 6.125; Mart. vii 32 and xiv 163; Petron. *sat.* 27. Also big villas: Plin. *ep.* ii 17 and v 6. Game in Campus Martius etc. Exercises: Antyll, ap. Orib. i 528. Further: Marrou (1) 115; Grundel; F. A. Wright 108–22.

For this chapter in general: Gardiner, Forbes, Jüthner, Shröder, Frost, Reisch, A. de Ridder, Marrou, Tod, Harris, Moretti, Bilinski, Klee, L. Robert (3) and (4).

6. CHARIOTEERS

1. Positive aspects: Michailides 311. Artemidoros: Le Blant 12. (For a tribal aristocracy: chariot-races and gambling as the main amusements of Vedic India: H. Lüders.)

2. Cumont (3).

3. *Moses* iii 27.

4. *Or.* xxxii 4 (with cento of Homeric phrases); 31. Cf. Juvenal's *panem et circenses,* but prob. no direct borrowing.

5. Klee 118; Bilinski 90.

6. Polyb. xxvii 7a.

7. Trypanis 232ff; Maas 447. Kall. also wrote elegy on a Nemean victory by an unknown (Sosibios and even Queen Berenike have been suggested); Bilinski 90–2.

8. Bilinski 92. The epigram in the 3rd c. lengthens, grows slacker in form, but gains in illustrative vivacity; aspires to a Pindaric tone: cf. esp. inscrs. of Lindos and Sidon: Peek (2), Moretti 47–8; *Fouilles, Lindos,* ii inscr. 698–9. Theokritos shows the agonistic element in the pastoral. For rel. to Apoll. Rh., Hagopian; Bilinski 98. Theokritos xxii (best anc. account of boxing), iv. ii, xxiv–v (Herakles). Rels. to New Comedy, Bilinski 101.

9. *E.g.* Panaitios: Gellius xiii 28.3. Plout. *de san tu. praec.* 133D. Epiktet. ii 18.22 iii 20.9; 26.22. *Vet. Stoic. Frag.* iii 128 (fr. 47), 173 (689). Cf. Philon in numerous places. J. Lindsay (2) 191f; Sawhill; Spicq; Hijmans on *askesis.* New Stoa's exclusion of sports: Sen. *ep.* lxxxviii 18. List of Olympic victors 396 B.C.: Oxy. 2381.

10. Frag. Telestes (46H). Krates: Bilinski 104.

11. Dion Chr. viii 30f; DL vi 71; Dudley 217.

12. *Taphe Menippou* (Buech. fr. 519); cf. Louk. *conviv.* 19 (pankration of Cynic and buffoon).

13. *Or.* xxxii 8f. Spurious: *nothos.*

14. *Anach.*, opening.

15. Gardiner (3) 296; Sen. *ep.* xv.

16. Bilinski 106f; Photiadis. For Diogenes as the Athlete of Pontos, who defeated hunger, hardship, cold: Dion Chr. ix 11–12; Herakl. *ep.* iv 3 on Herakles.

17. *Ars. rhet., Protreptikos athletais*: Bilinski 110f.

18. L. Robert (4) 121; Méautis 152; Friedländer ii 145–60. Also: IG xiv 1102; P. Lond. 1178 and Gerstinger 57; L. Robert (5); Marrou (1) 130–2. Contests seem to continue in the schools, *e.g.* 2nd c. Termessos, Peisidia: RE IIR v 1 767f sv *Schulagone.* High-rankers in foot-races: *Insc. v. Pergamon* 460; cf. *I. v. Ol.* 239. IG ii–iii (2nd) 3769.

19. Mazzarino (1) and (2); Van Groningen (3) 37, cited; *apo gym.*, P. Cornel 18.13. In general, Mertens p. xii and 112.

20. Diocles: Gruter, Inscrs. 337; Friedländer 2, anh. iii 492. Prize: St Paul, 1 *Cor.* ix 24; Prudent. *peristeph.* v 538; Suet. *ner.* 53. Backers: Juv. vii 113, 243; Suet. *claud.* 21; Capitol. *ver.* 6; Mart. x 74.5; Renan in paper to Soc. des Inscr. Nov. 1878. Horses: Friedländer (2). Betting: Juv. xi 202 (Mayor's note); Mart. xi 1.15. Horses in Eg.: REg 348.

21. *Dionys.* xxxvii 116ff: *autokylistos* and death somersault, 257. Cf. xliii 270ff. The start in R. days was by presiding mag. waving a *mappa.* Seven laps: Varro in Gell. iii 10. For treachery in the arena: Lattimore 145f.

22. Firm. ii 296.11; cf. Manil. v 85–9.

23. Fr. in Euseb. *praep.* viii 13.

24. *Or.* xxxii 46, 74f, 77–9 (cf. 94), 81.

25. *Ib.* 82. Parodies: Brandt. Athletic, theatral, charioteering themes common. IG xii 8.87 for *spoudaiogeloios* at Imbros: writer of satiric parodies.

26. Sen. *ep.* lxxxiii 7. Textile: Michailides 302. For acrobat: Camiros vase, Salzmann, *Necrop. de C.* pl. xxxvii; de Witte, *Arch. Z.* 1870 52.

27. Oxy. 288.

28. Ryl. 86. Prob. each order of municipal officers had a koinon inside the wider *koinon* of *archontes.* The combined municipal and priestly office does not appear in latter papyri. Note BGU 362 (W. 96); Thead. 34.14 etc. Later such disbursements as here in Ryl. 86 needed authorisation of *boule*: CP Herm. 66–7; and it is likely there was an earlier subordination to *koinon* of *archontes.*

29. REg p. 229. BGU 563, *polea* prob. refers to a tree.

30. PSI 1401. Ryl. 236; for Heroninos, Flor. 118–277; Syros to H. 241–58. Sale of Cappodocian horse to cavalryman, A.D. 77, for draught purposes: PSI 729. Diogenes; Oxy. 1287 (on back of 1267). For extract, cf. BGU 861, 870.

31. Oxy. 140; Milne 266; W. *Chr.* 352.

32. Oxy. 145 and 152.

33. Sales etc.: Lond. 1005. Oxy. 153 and 146. Another stable-contract: Oxy. 140. Account: Oxy. 922. *Gerates*: may mean "old"; Pleb may equal Plebeius.

Asses are *zoia*. cf. Am. 150.23–4 and 146.3; also Oxy. 140.22; Soph. *lex*. Karaneots: ? natives of Karanis (but cf. line 5: *Arsinoitou*); there may be a village Karaneia nearer to Oxy. *Pelaton* may be *pelagon*. Loukiou: Oxy. 998. Post-express: Oxy. 900. A 610–11 contract for control of stable: Oxy. 138.

34. Gruter, *Inscr.* 336–9. Earlier factions: Juv. xi 196; Tert. *de spect.* 9; Suet. *dom.* 7.

35. AA 57; SB vi 8989; HCSP li 1940 35–41. Foremen: cf. AA 40.

36. AA 58; HCSP I. c. 41–5; SB vi 8990. For price: AA p. 237, and cf. Princeton pap. roll iv 31 (with note). Chief: cf. Lond. v 1904 (where *phakto-narios* is ambiguous). See Meinersmann and Liddell-Scott-Jones sv. For Benetoi: Oxy. 152 and 145.

37. *Or.* xxxiii 41f, cf. 33. For Nike and chariot on gems from Egypt: JEA 1963 149f.

38. Michailides 304f; DS sv *contorniati*; Picard (2) 262. In general, Audollent; JRS 1963 122. Inscription *Nika* (for Greens): Lefebvre no. 37.

39. 3 *Macc.* iv 11; v 1–2. I leave religious matters for future volumes. John of Nik., 119.

40. Picard (2) 261–2 and (4); Wuilleumier; Hanfmann; Merlin and P.; Gauckler p. 10 nos. 18, 11 (mos. of Thermae of Thina).

41. Merlin. For Dionysos and Seasons: Foucher (2) 296.

42. J. Lindsay (2) 116 and (3). Some Wallachian towns in early 19 c. had quarters marked with colours; Constantine VI of Byz. noted the hair-colours in names of Pecheneg tribes, corresponding to the sky-regions towards which the tribe in question was oriented.

43. *Dionys.* xli 376–8. Olympos and 7 zones: ii 170f.

44. *Rich man's sal.* 937P; and *exhort.* xii (93P). Charioteering Christ: Rief-stahl 538f, adding, "Coptic apocryphal writings on the Assumption of the Virgin represent Christ as appearing in a chariot to receive the soul of his dying Mother. It is usually the chariot of the Cherubim, but sometimes a chariot of light, or just a chariot." Cf. James 183–227. Also, Egyptian amulet, "I adjure you by the chariots of the sun", Kendrick (2) 269.

45. Cumont (2) 461–5. Symbolism as old as sarcophagus of Haghia Triada: Strong, 126, 226.

46. Haynes 104f. In gen., L'Orange (1).

47. Picard (4) 91f; BAC 1924 171–6.

48. L'Orange (2) figs. 31–4 and 36 (diptych). Note Queen Kandake's moving throne-room mounted on wheels, inspected by Alex.: Ps.-Kall. iii 22. Philon in *Change of script. names* xv, cites as outstanding marks of greatness (vainglory likened to the rays of sun): "formally enrolled decrees, erection of statues and images, purple robes and golden crowns, chariots and teams of four horses, and processions of the multitude".

49. Gasiorowski. Textiles: Kendrick, i nos. 58–9, pl. xiv. Eyes: panel with half-length figure of Hermes, also Apollo: *ib.* nos. 52–3, xiv. Fayum: Wasmuth i pl. 4 etc. Uniting of factions: RA 1911 xi 76ff; *Ath. Mitt.* 1880 308.

50. Philon, *God unchangeable* 35 (Arnim ii 458). Stob. *eklog.* i 153.24 (Arnim ii 471); Sambursky (1) 31.

7. INTERNATIONAL ORGANISATION OF ATHLETES

1. General: Glotz (1), San Nicolò 61–5, Poland (1), Ricci (1), Holleaux 51–60, Forbes (2).

2. JOAI xiii 1910 Beibl. 70f n54.

3. Lond. 137; CR vii 1893 476; *Hermes* 1897 509; *Philol.* 1898 422; JOAI 1911 Beibl. 123; SB 4224; Poland (1) 150; Suppl. Ep. Gr. vi 58–9, vii 825.

4. JOAI vii 1904 Beibl. 47; *Forsch. in Ephesos* iii n5; Forbes (2). At Tralles the hieronikai joined the gerousia and neoi in a decree honouring the city's secretary; in another, with the gerousia, in hon. of gymnasiarch: CIG 2931 (3c), 3203, IGRR iv 1429; Laum, *Stift.* ii n87; REg 1929 428; Broughton 751.

5. Forbes (2) 242 n29–30. Astrol.: H. 64.12; Cumont (3) 79. And Ditt. *or.* 714; Friedländer (1) 8th ed. ii 502 n5. Actor-boxer: Herzog; O'Connor 80 no. 40; Flickenger 191f. Pompeii: Beiber (1) 232 fig. 775. Parodies of boxers on stage, *ib.* 143. Smyrna under Domitian had large synod that included mystai and technitai of D.; officers, agonothetes and xystarch, first often, second always athletic: CIG 3713, 3176, with comment. of Boeckh, cf. E. Ziebarth (3) 89.

6. OGIS 713; Mitteis, *Chr.* n381 (Lips. 44) and *Grundz.* 290.

7. Forbes (2) n31 and p. 242.

8. Term xystos first met in Olympic inscr. dated 85 B.C.: Inscr. Ol. 436; Glotz (1) 1027f. Paus. vi 23: Elis, enclosure where Ol. contestants did their 30 days' training.

9. Lond. 1178; Charlesworth (1) 11 n7, Domitian estab. the 4-yearly Greek-style Agon Capitolinus (IG xiv 1055) that lasted 4 centuries.

10. L. Robert (5) on bronze of Mitylene under Sev. Alex.; cf. IG xiv 747.6, pankratiast Archibios of Alex. For use of term on coins: Robert (Aigai, Kos, Philadelpheia in Lydia, Daldis, Sardeis). Olympionikes occurs, e.g. SB 1070 and 5725 (tombstone), PSI 456, Fuad viii 40. For paradoxonikes (victor in wrestling and pankration), Plout. *comp. Kimon and Luc.* 2.

11. SB 5725. And Firm. ii 330.25; 330.20; 348.21, cf. 220.10 and i 215.27; Cumont (5) 78. Vitruv. ix *praef*, cf. Diod. xii 82; sc. Aristoph. *clouds* 70; Plat. *symp.* ii 5; Plin. ep. x 119, 120; Paus. vi 13.1; Plat. *rep* v 465d (Olympic victor enjoys a blessed life); Louk. *anach.* 10, cf. Pind. *pyth.* x 27, Cicero *tusc.* i 46.111. Boxer: Plin. NH vii 152. Contrast rule at Olympia, no statue of athlete to be over life size: Louk. *On Eikones*, 11.

12. IG xiv 1054–5.

13. *Ib.* 1052 (18 Jan. 154); IG xiv 956B; CIL vi 10153.

14. IG xiv 1109.

15. IG xiv 1110; IG v i. 699 and xiv 1109–1110.

16. Forbes (2) n77, n62. Great Tyche of xystos on gem: CIG 7305; Furtwängler in R. i 2183. Emperor worship: Lond. 1178; Liermann 70 n13.

17. Forbes (2) n 45–7.

18. *Cod. Iust.* x 54.1.

19. Oxy. 59.

20. Fees: Lond. 1178. Aphrod.: CIG 2758.

21. Lond. 1164 i; DLRE 68. Far back Athenai had *sitesis en Prytaneioi* for victor in the four great games: Plout. *arist.* 27; *de soll. an.* 13 (970B); Schöll. Oxy.: Oxy. 908 and BGU 1073–4; W. *Archiv* iv 564 and Viereck. Claims for privs., *Stud. Pal.* 73ff.

22. PSI 1422 with intro. Amelotti; Amelotti (1) in gen.

23. Oxy. 2477; JEA 1963 180f. Dated March-April 289. For the imperial Tyche in general: Oxy. 2106; Ryl. 607: Lugd.–Bat. ii 14.2f and v p. 125; Seidl 16f (2ter Teil).

24. Lond. 1178.

25. Insc. Ol. 436.

26. IG xiv 956; Ricci 192.

27. CIG 2756; CIG 2758; Oxy. 1050.

28. TAPA lxvi 1935 208–21.

29. Forbes (2) 247f.

30. PSI iii 236. Hibeh ii 274 is the end of a petition-draft to some important Roman, perhaps patron of athletic synod in early 3rd c.

31. IG xiv 1102; more in Forbes (2) 248 n98–9.

32. *Cod. Theod.* xiii 3.8; Pharr. See Forbes (2) n. 114–22 for more refs.

33. CIL vi 10153.

34. Lond. 1243, cf. 1178.

35. Oxy. 1284. *Enkyklion*: Oxy. 99; Teby. 350. In Tebt. 347 sponde is 2 dr. on 18; Oxy. 1283; PSI 109. It is possible the *enk.* has been rising a lot in the 3rd c., but in BR 933 (iii p. 69) of A.D. 211 the old rate seems still recognised (n116 of Oxy. 1284). Alex. agonothetes: Ditt. OGI 713 (*Archiv* ii 567). Deed of gift: Grenf. ii 68 and 71; *enk.* on gift, Tebt. 351.

36. *Hermes* 99.41; Firm. i 177.2 and 223.22 (cf. ii 345.3; also Manetho iv 449 and vi 16).

37. Harris 20f. Note adj. *peripolistike* of synodos, *e.g.* IAG 68.

38. Cf. IAG 75; *Ephesos* ii 72 as in Harris.

39. PSI 1412; Koskenniemi, *Aeg.* xxxiii 1953 322–4.

40. Athen. v 196ff; Mahaffy (1) par. 74 (2) 216ff; Ditt. *Sylloge* (3rd) n390; PSI iv 364; Freib. 7 (250 B.C.); Zen. pap. 54 (246 B.C.); Hal. i line 263 (end of reign Ptol. II); *Mitth. Arch. Inst.* xliv 1919 25 (?242 B.C.); Pap. Gradenwitz 6 (222 B.C.) For the Basileia: Hal. *l.c.* and Kohler, *Inscr. Att.* ii 1367. A third festival has its name torn off in Hal.

Why the Ptolemaia in midwinter? It seems not to be the usual period. E. Meyer supposes the proper time June–July, but here postponed through troubles from Magas' attack in summer 274: *Untersuchungen* 66. Date of first fest.: Frazer (3)—281–79 B.C. Ptol. games at Ptolemais and other towns: Ditt. *Or.* 49–51; Preisigke WB sv *agon.* Philadelphos exempted winners from salt-tax:

Hal. i pp. 158–61. Contests (incl. music) at Eleusis near Alex. Oxy. 2465. Augustus celebrated his triumph by estab. 5-yearly games at Nikopolis; Str. xvii 1; Dion Kass. li 18. Philon (*Flaccus* xi): "It was fitting that in imitation of the sacred games those who had superintended the collection of arms should keep a new triennial festival in Egypt"—note emotional link of games and revolt.

41. Hautecoeur 20f. For link with funerary symbolism, an Apulian vase representing the exposure of Achemoros, *ib.*

42. Plout. *alex.* xx 8. For Alex.'s use of it: *ib.* xxxvii 4 and Q. Curt. *hist. alex.* ix 7.15; banquets, Ailian VH viii 7 and ix 3. Association: Plout. *eumen.* xiii 3–4. Symbol: DS sv *tentorium* v 117. (Warlike eastern kings spent much time in tent: hence assoc. with victory: Xerxes in *Esther* i 5.6; invasion of Greece, Broneer. Whether the Achmainid tent from Assyria or Central Asia is not clear. Assyrian reliefs show round and domelike tents app. used ritually; kings' tents seem mostly rectangular uncovered pavilions with apselike canopy at one end: A. L. Layard, *Mons. of Nineveh* 1853 i pl. 77; ii pls. 24, 50; P. E. Botta, *Mons. de N.* 1849–50 pl. 146.)

43. NH xxxiv 8.

44. Sacred banquet: Cook, *Zeus* ii 1170; DS iii 1006–1012; Warde Fowler. *Relig. Exp. of R.* 1911, 263, 268, 318; *J.d.kl. Arch. Inst.* xxxii 1917 114; *R. di filol,* xxii 1893; RE xii 1924 1108; RA xv 1867 403 etc.

45. Smith, *Dict. Ant.* ii 16. The Dioskouroi were esp. connected with theoxeniai (Eur. *hel.* 1666; Pind. *ol.* iii; Bacchyl. in Athen. vi 400; CIG ii 2338, 2374; Athen. iv 137E, Athenai). They were assoc. with victory in battle—hence in games. Dionysos probably comes next as entertainer or entertained (Paus. i 2.5; vi 26.1; Athen. xi 465a; miraculous wine, Paus. vi 26.3), sv *theodasia,* Hesych. Heroxenia: important in popular Thasian religion: Sokolowski (1) no. 64 and 69; see further Salviat, and Nock HTR 1944 144ff.

46. Moret (2) 91, 295; 80, 295; 238–52 and 253–5. Smith (3) 112f, also citing Sethe. Pharaohs enthroned under sky-canopy: *Z. f. Äg. Sprache* lxi 1931 43f; Prichard 144–6.

47. Smith (3). See further ch. 11 here.

8. MEN AND ANIMALS IN THE ARENA

1. H. N. Fowler.

2. Or. xxxi 121–2; cf. Philostr. *vit. apoll.* iv 32.

3. *Ib.* 110, where Dion praises Nero for competing at the Elean Festival; also the men of Elis for ignoring letters recommending an athlete (? from Romans of high rank) "till he had competed", 111.

4. Perdrizet (3) no. 112 (pl. xxvii) and (4) xc; *ib.* no. 445 pl. xc and 442 pl. lxxxix.

5. Ryl. 15; *Archiv.* v 558. *Monomachesein* seems to occur earlier. Metre seems Ionic, as in poem from Marisa discussed *Rh. Mus.* lxiv 433 and perhaps Oxy.

219: DLRE 63 (cockfighting). Wilamowitz, *Gött. Nachr.* 1896, 230, 277, calls it an Hilarodia and sees Ionia as the home of this sort of poem. There is a second col. that probably continued the theme.

6. CIL x 1685; Dessau 1397; Friedländer (1) iv 230ff; Robert (6) 267 nl.

7. Lips. 57; REg 385.

8. Robert (6) 199. For glads. complaining of lack of fights: Epiktetos i 29.37 and Sen. *de prov.* 4.

9. Dessau 5088-9, 5117.

10. CIL xii 3329.

11. *Ann. epigr.* 1962 no. 48 (p. 13).

12. Vett. Val. 74.29 to 75.3; Perdrizet (3) 76; PGM iv 1390 (i p. 118).

13. CCAG viii 2; Neugebauer (1) 109. Recorded by Antigonos of Nikaia.

14. Neugebauer (1) 146f, 187; Cumont (4) takes the name as Egyptian, but see N. 187. In general: Robert (6) no. 70 and 258; Friedländer ii 65f; CIL iii 6573, 6994.

15. Robert (6) 158 n2.

16. DLRE 11f.

17. Roussell (2); San Nicolò (1) i 193 202-4. Lesquier, 353, sees as quasi-military. Not to be taken as Roman *venatores*: W. *Grundz.* i 1 387, against Rostovtzeff (6) who sees the service as a liturgy.

18. DLRE 8.

19. *Change of script. names* xxix.

20. *Aith.* x 28-30. Thessalian bull-fights: Jennison 26f.

21. Oxy. 2470. Slender legs could be girl's. Boots no colour. Broad red streak spreads up from near bottom right hand, turns back, reappears at top right edge of pap. It is not outlined with pen-strokes like rest of composition.

22. *Protrep.* xii-xiii; Bilinski 124f. Tertullian, *apolog.* 38 (cf. Pud. 7 med.), "atrocity of arena and vanity of x".

23. *Rh. Mus.* 1881 96.2; 1889 311; Haupt. *opusc.* iii 445; Kaibel 55.

24. Philon, *post. cain* 161. Cf. trad. in Phaedrus; Euseb. *praep.* v 34.2. Parodies in general: Brandt.

25. Della Corte (1) 25ff for refs. and (2) no. 220. Already in 1875 Fiorelli recognised the ref. to Actium.

26. *Aug.* 96.

27. *M. Ant.* 65.

28. Della Corte 29. CIL iv 6757. Aureus: Grueber ii 505f; Bahrfeldt JId'AN xii 94; date, Tarn (9) 150. Lion: Grueber ii 395n; *sib. or.* xi 290. Alex.: Osl. ii 14.9; Crönert *symb. osl.* vi 5.7; Korte thinks not proved Sibylline. Battle of Stars: v 512 to end; Tarn (9) 143f; Rzach (2) 2140 takes it as Hellenistic (parts may be—prophecies can always be made topical by interpolations or "corrections"); Kugler sees only astronomy; Nilsson (3) rels. to summer solstice. The cited lines are 518f, 521. Romance: i 12.8 (Kroll). Capricorn: Suet. *Aug.* 94.

29. Della Corte 35ff.

30. Edgar 281 pl. xviii. BM Cat. Ptol. 1883 pl. ii 10f; Mattingly pl. i 5, 6, 19; BM Cat. Alex. 1892 no. 339 pl. xxvii 508, 863; cf. Matz 748.

31. Perdrizet (3) 39; Rostovtzeff (1) 277; della Corte 35ff.

32. Collignon (1) and (2) holds the spirit is Ptol. but patera was made at Alex. or in Campania, perhaps 1st c. A.D.

For Cleo. iconography: E. Breccia (2); L. Curtius; P. Ducati 89, pl. xlv 3. Carcopino generally agrees with Della Corte about the plate but sees Cleo. there in the form of Isis-Panthera. Della Corte is certainly wrong in seeing the snake she holds as her death instrument.

33. Della Corte 44f; *Not. Sc.* 1922 478.

34. Della Corte 65ff.

35. *Ib.* 34.

36. Della Corte makes the Claudius suggestion. One difficulty which he ignores is that the B. Ass could not be later than the conquest of Egypt, yet he takes it to refer to Cleo's failure to win over Octav. The work could however have been made in the period between Actium and the capture of Alexandreia, the Ass being merely the recalcitrant, who denies the Dionysiac love-ethic.

37. J. Lindsay (3); CAH x 99 (Tarn and Charlesworth); K. Scott; Altheim 367. Note that Octav. would hardly have played Apollo to someone else's Jupiter.

38. Smith (3) 111.

39. Strong (2) 569, 578; CAH Plates iv 176 abc, 178b; Ovid *fast.* v 563–8. Cf. coinage of 17–6 B.C.: Apollo on platform ornamented with prows and anchors: CAH x 478. Dionysos leaves: Plout. *Ant.* 33, 78.

For Seth as the Ass-ravisher: Griffiths (5) and Barb (1–3). For lamps: Wald-hauer, pl. xlvii nos. 495, 498. Seth has an ass-head as far back as the Middle Kingdom: Daressy, BIFAO xiii 88 and *Ann. Serv.* xx 165f; he is symbolised by an ass yet earlier, Bonnet (1) 172; *Dramatic Ramasseum Papyrus* 29–33. Anat: Pap. Chester Beatty vii, vs.1.5ff; Dawson, JEA xxii 107. For further refs., Griffiths and Barb, esp. Barb (2) 370 n33 for the womb-fear, and Deonna (4).

9. HUNTS

1. Aymard 45f; Plout. *alex.* 11; Justin xvi 3; Q.C. viii 1.11 etc. Citation: Aymard, 320, 321f, with refs. Polyb. xxxi 25, congratulates his young friend Scipio Aemilianus on his royal love of hunt, which as an Achaian gentleman he shared: he saw other young Roman nobles having time only for law and politics. In Arkadia, at Tegea we see the aristoc. trad. kept up: hunting in the mountains and a gym.-official the *kynagos*: Forbes (3) 191.

2. *Moses* i 11 (60–2); he argues that kings should have experience as shepherds. Note the association of the Mysteries in his mind.

3. *On special laws, carcasses.* Xen. *kyr.* 13; Plat. *laws* vii 833c, 824a; Aymard 470.

4. Corps: Ditt. *Or.* 99 n2; 143; cf. 20; W. *Ostr.* i 162 and *Grundz.* i 387; ii nos. 451–2; Kroll (2). Expeditions: Ditt. *Or.* 82, 86, 54, 72, 76; Rostovtzeff (6). Hunts: Cair. Zen. 59524 gazelles; 59186 waterbirds; BGU 1252, royal monopoly. Dogs: Kallix. cited and REg xxi 1908 147 n2; Aymard; Athen. v 201b; Philon, *Dreams* i 9.

5. Soldier: Witkowski (1) no. 16 (2nd c.). Zoos: Cair. Zen. 59075. Alex.: Plout. *alex.* 4. The Ptols. had a superintendent over the king's animals; they had their paradise as the Caesars their vivaria. Philadelphos sought exotic animals and had rare African specimens, e.g. a gigantic python (Diod. iii 36.3; 37, 67; Athen. v 32 (260f–261c); Hubbele). To please the king a Syrian sheik sent young onagers, with dogs and horses, to dioiketes Apollonios (Cair. Zen. 59076; Edgar ASAE xviii 1938 231 no. 13). The parks and enclosures of the Hellenistic kingdoms affect Rome in late Republic: Jennison and Aymard.

6. Pap. Jur. Inh. 10230 (p. 77); pastophoros(?): P. dem. Berl. 3111; cf. Dawson. Note *ibiotapheion* in UPZ 153–5; ibis cemetery, JEA 1963 132.

7. P. dem. Ryl. iii 11 (p. 122).

8. Bataille 34, 231; UPZ 157.25; 180a/41/8; P. dem. Brux. 5/a/15; W. *Ostr.* 1486.

9. UPZ 18a a/41/8. Ghoran: BCH xxv 1901 402. Bataille 232; Petrie (1) 171–3. There seem milk-offerings in brickchamber at Abydos (? Mid. Kingdom). Sites: cats esp. at Boubastis, Speos Artemidos: dogs, ichneumons, locally; hawks and shrewmice, Bouto; ibis, Hermopolis. These relate to Persian age; general preservation of animals does not seem earlier, though catacombs at Dendera (first half XVIII dyn. on) have hosts of dogs, hawks, ibis, gazelles, cats, ichneumons, snakes. Mnevis bulls of Heliopolis were buried in stone chambers; Elephantine had cemetery of sacred rams; crocs. at Lahun (Herod. knows one at Hawara), also in cave opp. Manfalut. Fish (almost all *lates*, up to 5 ft. long) at Ghurob.

10. Oxy. 1188. Harpebekis, cf. Tebt. 5.70. Osorphnas: W. *Grundz.* 105f. For wood, DLRE sv index Trees, esp. 93–6, 330f; add Oxy. 53 and C. P. Herm. 7 ii 28, iii 7.

11. Firm. Mat. ii 229.21; Ptol. 123.18. Perdrizet (5) and L. Robert (7) no. 73.

12. Diod. i 48.

13. Bataille 131, 314.

14. Ail. NA v 39; Weinreich (2) 90, 101f.

15. Yoyotte (1) 133; Speelers.

16. Säve-Söderbergh pl. iv; Stracmans 25.

17. Erman (1) chs. 21–2.

18. Junker 37; Derchain (2) 14. The orig. opponent of Horos here was Rekhyt. For oryx as foe of the Eye: Derchain (2) 28ff.

19. Derchain (2) 38.

20. Plin. xxv 138.

21. Polyb. xxiii 1.8. In gen. Préaux (1) 35.

22. Householder and Prakken. Trog. land was on the west side of the Red

Sea and ran south from Heroonopolis, at least as far as Saba and perhaps to Notu Ceras (Str. xvi 4.4–18); the n. and s. limits vary with diff. authors (*e.g.* Markianos of Herakleia, GGM i 523, puts it all along Red Sea Coast, the Sea ending near Deire; Ptolemaios, iv 7.10, includes whole country as far as mt. Elephas). Here it prob. reps. west coast of Sea to s. of port of debarkation (Myos Hormos or Berenike). Myrrhland may be taken as Punt: Householder 112. Koloboi here seem natives of coast between harbour of Antiphilos and prom. of Pytholaos, esp. s. part (immediately n. of Myrrhland). Ptolemais Epitheras estab. 270–64: Kortenbeutel 27, 34.

Inscrs. "saved from T.": SB 4033 (Lepsius 133), SB 4049 (L. 157), SB 4050 (L. 158). OGIS 70 (L. 170), OGIS 71 (L. 122); "from the land of the Sabaioi", Cougny i 156 (L. 124), disputed. For Epekoos: Weinreich (3).

At Redesieh the temple is built of native Nubian sandstone, many frags. about; it lies on the caravan route to sea, which the dedicator may well have travelled; if he had been somewhere like a port or Koptos he could have got better stone. See Householder for narrowing date down (not 170–68 when also troubles: invasion of Epiphanes, brawls of Physkon and Philometer etc.). The expeditions not known after Euergetes. Ptol. and Arsinoe in l. 12 are not sure. For Ptol. II and Red Sea: Tarn JEA xv 14. Ptol. XIV (51–4 B.C.) gave 34 tusks for Great Door of temple of Apollo at Didyme (each tusk estimated at average 14.4 kilograms, as against modern African average of about 9): JHS xxxi 305f.

23. Plin. viii 96. In politics as in art the question of Egypt was in the air. A.M. xii 15, 21 and 24. Pompeius: Plin. viii 70–1; Lucilius *sat.* (Marx) 159; Aymard 81; Jennison 54. See lastnamed for details. Rhino. of Domitian: Blanchet.

24. Bell (3) no. 6. Nos. 7, 8, and perhaps 19 also from Meios; 7 is in cursive.

25. *Ib.* no. 19. First words are conflation of *Mark* ix 41–2 (*Matt.* x 42 and xviii 6).

26. *Ib.* no 31; some of the phrases are uncertain. Chickens are *strouthoi*, gen. sparrow or ostrich; but T. seems to expect them to be fattened up. Nikandros, *Alexipharmaka* lx 535, has *strouthos katoikas* as hen; in pap. *strouthoi* appear as domestic livestock, for which, along with pigs and pigeons, fodder is bought: Lips. 97 xxviii 18; cf. Oxy. 920.8, where 8 dr. are paid for a big *strouthos*.

27. Lond. 2677 (information from B.M.); date of fest., Edgar, *Zenon pap. Cairo,* iii no. 59312, line 26n. Hides: furriers worked up skins provided by hunters for the Alex. markets: Cumont (3) 91–2; Athen. v 196; Manil. iv 180. They were looked down on as dirty: Cumont (3) 91. Firm. i 166.28, "arts either sordid or squalid through the heavy smell and to which ceaseless attention is required from the operators, such as skin-dyers, fullers". Skins: also Lumbroso (2) 130; Reil 132; Heichelheim (1) 164. Tariff-list (? imports via Red Sea) includes hides: Dig. xxxix 4.16.7.

28. Ptol. royal hunters demand *opsonion*: PSI 350 (254—3 B.C.); farming-

out: Hamb. 57; BGU 1252; Préaux (2) 197 n1 and 198. Special bodies;   Rostovtzeff (7); soldiers allowed hunt if they pay prescribed rate to tax farmers: *Klio* xv 376.

Eve of festivals: Lond. (unpub.) 2677; Préaux (1) 35. Ptol. system of hunt: Cair. Zen. 59292, 59328, 59747; PSI 350 and 527; Rostovtzeff (11) 112.

Roman *demosioi kynegoi*: Ryl 98a and app. p. 423; further, SB 235–91; and Rostovtzeff (8); Lond. ii. 459 (p. 163) 3rd c.; cf. P. Oxf. no. 4 (150 A.D.); Wegener in P. Oxf. p. 21.

Theadelpheia: P. Bibl. Univ. Giss. 12.

29. PSI 458 and Ryl. 98a. *Merismon therion*: Tebt. 355, 683; Lond. 844. Also Wallace 317. For Persian-of-Epigone status, DLRE 20–2. More on hunts: Fay. 313; Tebt. 612 (prob. a monopoly).

30. PSI 222; another petition, BGU 1252; Winter (1) 62n.

31. DLRE 107.

32. H. 65.5; 54.2; 93.40; 90.2. For more refs.: Cumont (3) 57–62. Violent death by beasts common: spider and scorpions appear: Cumont and Oxy. 2061–3 (spells). SB 1267 (A.D. 8): girl bitten by scorpion.

33. Vett. Val. ii 41 (p. 130); Neugebauer 96. *Ibid.* ii 41 (129); N. 112. Cumont (3) 57.

34. *Ib.* vii 5 (pp. 284–5); N. 128f. Reading not sure.

35. Perdrizet-Lefebvre no. 174.

36. Aymard 342f, 459. In a mos. of Carthago, a mounted hunter prepares to lasso (*Inv. mos. Tunisie* ii suppl. 615a), beast not shown. In Libya, onagers and stags: Aymard 462 nos. 4–6. Bear and boar, 462–3.

37. *Algerie inv. mos.* at Oued-Atmenia (Aymard, 271, 352); de Ridder (2) 175 pl. 116; JHS liii 1933 208. Stags: Aymard, 116 n5, 124, 130, 133, 136.

38. They peopled the Nile as far as Sais. Refs.: Daressy; Roeder (2); Vandier (2); Meulenare. Opet: De Wit and J. G. Griffiths (3); Ipy, *Pyr.* 381a and Sethe, *Pyr. Komm.* ii 111. Citation: Säve-Söderbergh.

39. Meulenare.

40. *Dionys.* xxvi 236. Makeshift: *mimelos*.

41. A.M. xxii 16.14; xxxii 21–4. Plin. xxviii 31: "The blood is used by painters", and "the hide from the left side of the forehead, worn as amulet in the groin, is an aphrodisiac; the same reduced to ash restores hair lost through mange. A drachma of a testicle is taken in water for snakebite", etc.

42. A.T. iv 2–3; cf. *Job* xli 19. Also the trap in *Daphnis and Chloe*.

43. Hunt-mixture: the 4th c. mos. at Piazza Amerina, Sicily, shows lions, tigers, rhinoceros, even griffon. For latter: cf. Heliodoros x 26. Mosaic with capture of ostriches at Kef: Picard (2) 259; also Aymard 75, 192 n3, 195.

44. Goodchild (2). Geon: Philon *alleg. interp.* i 21 (68) and 27 (85). For Pharos: Goodchild (3) and AA 1959 342; JTS xi 291 no. 21. I. A gem (Dalton 14 no. 78) shows Apollonios of Tyana on one side and harbour scene on other with a three-storied building topped by a Helios figure. Not Aigai where Apoll. lived a while and some coins show a lighthouse, but Alexandreia. The second

statue here may be on one of public buildings of city inland, but prob. on Pharillon.

45. Philon (*Euseb. praep.* viii 13) says the crocodile is the most odious of beasts and addicted to devouring men. "Born and brought up in the most sacred way, and though dwelling in the depths, it feels the benefits it receives from mankind." For among the people who honour it, it multiplies, but hardly ever shows up where it is liable to be hurt. "So there are places where even the most timid, when sailing by, jump out of their boats and swim about with their children."

I make no effort to catalogue refs. to the crocodiles or other animals, but use what seem significant examples. For Strabon: DLRE 10. Ammianus: xxxii 15-20. *Theos krokodeilos*: Tebt. 298 (A.D. 107-8) etc.

46. *De isid.* 2 (50). Ach. T. (iv 19) mixes wit and mythological horrors (cf. iii 7, Andromeda's dragon).

47. *Aith.* v 1. Ichneumons: Lond. 904. Construction of palisade in canal to protect pigs—against crocodiles: Mich. Zenon 84. Robbers blame crocodiles?: Cair. Zen. 59443, 59379. Beasts in swamps: Firm. ii 337.28; Val. 126.33.

48. Edgar, *Cat. gén. des ant. eg. du mus. du Caire,* iv 1, and ASAE xix 1920 130 no. 48; Wilcken *Archiv* vi 453; Powell, *New Ch.* i 107; G. Herrlinger 52f no. 54. Two metres: Kaibel, epig. gr. 325, 462, 502, 546, 550. Scylax is the name of Trimachio's dog, *sat.* 64.

Indian dogs: Aymard, 238, 244f; Xen. *kyn* ix 1. See Philostr. *imag.* i 28 (335 K): boarhunt on horses (cf. P. younger, 3).

49. Ryl. 238. For Alypos, *e.g.* Flor. 127, 137, 142, 162, 176.

50. A.T. ii 34.

51. Gnomon 36; RT i 328, 425. Mines etc.: BGU 1024, RT (3) 111 n1 and 2.

52. Oxy. 1101. The encroachment of the military on judicial matters is attacked in imperial constitutions of the period: CJ i 46.2; CT xii 1.128 (A.D. 392); ii i.9 (393). Cf. Liban. *de patroc.* 4f, 23 etc.; Lond. 408.

10. LIONS, BIRDS, CATS

1. Athen. xv 677 d–f: Hesych. sv *stephanoma*, adds "and herbaceous" to the comment on leafy plants. Hadrian and boar: Dion Kass. lxix 10 (note medallion of Arch of Constantine is conn. with boarhunt: A.D. 134-8. No surety of a link. Cohen ii (Hadrian) 502f; Strack ii no. 491). His barbarian hunter Mastor, a favourite, refused to help him commit suicide: Dion Kass. lxix 22; *Vit. Hadr.* 24.8. H. perhaps kept record of hunts and kills, imitating Alex.: Aymard 175; Perdrizet (6). His poem: CIL xii 1122; Riese AL 903; Buecheler CE 1522; Herrlinger 49 n51; Bardon 419. Love of horses: *Vit. H.* 20, 25, Dion K. lxix 10; Aymard 174-9. Artworks: della Seta 107 fig. 292, and 106f; Richter 290f.

2. Oxy. 1085. Adrastos was the hero saved by his horse Arion on the expedition of the Seven against Thebai: Apollod. iii 6.7; Homer *Il.* xxiii 346f. The Egyptian Claudian tells us how to snare Libyan or Ethiopian lions (*laud. stil.*

iii 339). "Blazing torches, twigs on undermined turf wellstrewn, the voice of a tender kid alluring their hunger, a dug pit deceiving them", cf. Aymard 445.

For Pankrates: Athen. 478a and Plout. *de mus.* 1137F.

3. Milne (1) 45f. A new road was built from A. to Berenike on Red Sea, for trade. Dion Kass. lxix 11; Spartian. *vit hadr.* 14; Paus. viii 9.4. Bithynion: Smith, *Dict. GR Biog.* i 192a; Eckhel vi 532. Kaibel IG Ital. 978a.

Antinoion at Hermopolis: DLRE 196; A. "*synthronos* of the gods in Egypt": IG *ad res rom. pert.* i 31, 32; Neos Iacchos at Tarsos (BMC Lycaonia 189 no. 159), Iacchos at Adramyteum (BMC Mysia 4 no. 13).

4. Spartian. *l.c.*; Dion K. *l.c.*; Paus. *l.c.*; CIG 1124, 1129, 1147; Tertull. *de cor.* 13, Oxy. 2132; CIA iii 1202 (mid-3rd c.).

5. Levezow. For the elephant-hunts: Kortenbeutal 16–41; Wilcken (6); Préaux (2) 34–7, 357; Rostovtzeff (3) i 383 and in 183 (13) 740–3 (6) 301ff.

6. *Charid.* 6, 7, 12, 23, 20; Tondriau. Cf. Nock (3) 31 n50; JEA xi 136; Charax fr. 13 (Jacoby ii 486); DL x 5; Scott (5); CLE 879 (Tibur).

7. Near opening Bk. ii—goes snobbishly on: "and hence, by still greater necessity, the children of noblemen," cf. i 14 etc.

8. Drowning: Herod. ii 90; Jos. *contra ap.* ii 7 (86), with Spiegelberg 4 and Hopfner (2) 217, Griffiths (4) 115. Moira destroys a 3-yr.-old boy drowned in well: SEG iv 573 (Notion, 2nd c. B.C.).

Shell: Plaut. *rud.* 704; Graindor (1) 103; Picard (7). Bratschtova 53f sees shell-dec. as Anatolian in origin and dating from Hellenistic epoch. Twisted cols.: Chapot, Graindor etc. for exs. (2nd c.) Apamea, Ephesos (*c.* 106–7 or later construction) etc. Dura-E.: *Fouilles* 1926 pl. xlv, 141.

Samothrace: CIG 2158, IG xii 8.188; JHS 1928 180 no. 3; Picard (7) sees the twists on right, so may assume also on left. Ziebarth (4) on Kyriakos of Ancona; F. Chapouthier, *Dioscures* 1935 176 fig. 17.

Aion: Vermaseren nos. 102–3 (cf. 94,100), sv index Aion for exs. outside Egypt. Statuette: Wiedemann 311; relief, Breccia (3) D. Levi 275 fig. 5, Pettazoni 27 pl. ii 4. Egyptian origins: Pettazoni. Note Mithraion, 3rd c. B.C.: Smyly 36ff; Mithres as name, Oxy. (A.D. 214), W. *Grundz.* 1912 129, Schubart (3) 343, 353; Chapot 48ff noted rel. to Aion. Bes: E. Brummer col. no. 30 (Sotheby 16 Nov. 1964).

For Isidora: SEG viii 473–5; SB 7540; Graindor (1); *Archiv f. relig. wiss.* xxxv 313. Rome: Kaibel (2) 570,7–8—cf. whirlwind in Phrygian inscr., Ramsay 684.3–5 (Dokoumion), and Apol. Rh. i 211–23 (*aorai*); guardian nymphs (2 c. B.C.?) IG xi 5, 1017.8–9. Kyrilla: SB 4230 (Cairo), cf. SB 7016 (near Pelousion) where however interpretation is uncertain. For Charis: cf. Thea Charis Bassaris (B. is the name), Verona CIL v 3382; IG xiv 2307. The other Isidora: Peek (3), cf. Kuenzle.

For vine-column: J. Toynbee (1) 25f, 28.

9. Wild hunt; Jeanmaire (1) 151, 214, 270, 274, 431, 496. Autonoe: *Dionys.* xlvi 322ff. Bastard: *nothos.* Type: *typos.* Image etc.: *eikos, morphe, stiktos, allophyes.*

10. ASAE xv 1915 pl. iv; Perdrizet (7) 93.

11. Lenzen pl. 5b.

12. *Ib.* pls. 1–2.

13. Lauer figs. 19, 92–3, 95; pl. 19a.

14. Lenzen pl. 626a; Pierce ii pl. 160a. Cf. Lenzen pl. 6b; Pierce ii pl. 158c.

15. Lenzen pl. 4a.

16. Lenzen 9; Rizzo pl. xl. Cf. Nonnos xxv 220–2.

17. Oppian *cyn.* iv 320–53; the wine must be 11 yrs. old.

18. Aymard 464. Felines: Eisler 58 n4; Bérard (Cherchel).

19. Philostr. *vit apoll.* ii 2 (Pamphylia).

20. CRAI 1946 548; REA xlix 1947 248 and lii 1950 278. Soldiers went some 100 km. beyond the limes after beasts: Inscr. in Saharan Atlas: Picard (6) 58–60 n47.

21. Strab. xvii 815; Plin. viii 96; Dion li 22; SHA *antonin.* 10 and *gord.* 33.

22. A.T. iv 3–5. Heliodoros has elephants in battle: ix 17f. Hunts, Aymard 325, 447; Picard (2) 250.

23. Sen. *ep.* lxxxv 41; cf. *de ben.* i 5; Suet. *galb.* 6 and *ner.* 11; Plin. viii 2.

24. Ail. NA xi 25; Manil. iv 236.

25. Jennison ch. iv. Heliod. describes giraffes with some odd touches: stresses swaying gait and says two right legs move at once, then two left. "It rolled its eyes, the rims of which were pigmented, with a grim look." Cf. Plin. viii 18 (27) 69. Not mentioned as killed in arena till Commodus, Jennison 132.

26. Hunt-idyll: P. Gilbert (2) 153f; Capart (2) 17 pl. 423; W. S. Smith 178 (songbirds). Strab. xvii 804; Cair. Zen. 59186; Athen. ix 388, 393; Clem. *paed.* ii 1.

27. Athen. ix 48, Egyptians as skilled catchers of birds and fish: Keimer.

28. Athen. ix 39. Kallimachos the poet wrote in his prose works one on birds; tells tale of partridge fluttering near nest to draw hunter off. The amorous male breaks eggs to stop hen from hatching, so she hides eggs: *ib.* ix 41–2; he also dealt with duck and diver, ix 52; *porphyris* (*porphyrion*) eats in dark and warns husbands of wives' adultery (latter tale not by Kall.): ix 41.

29. Athen. xiv 654c (also *tetrax, tatyras*). Olymp.: fr. 36. Phil. *rewards* 15 and Mart. vii 87. Birds speaking: Manil. v 378; AIL NA v 36. Alexandrians: Lumbroso (1) 105; Phil. *de anim.* 23–8; Taming: Sen. *ep.* lxxxv 41; Firm. ii 313.23; Maneth. iv 245. Gazelle fed by she-goat: Cair. Zen. 59429.

30. Tollington i 253; Louk. *de merc. conduct.* 34.

31. Yoyotte (1) 36f; Jeanmaire ch. viii. Sen. ep. cxxi 19; Plin. x 73 (94) 202. Pompeii, relief etc.: Keller i 79. Cats v. moles: Palladius iv 9. Romans used weasels, polecats, v. mice: Keller i 169; Petron. *sat.* 46; Pallad. iv 9, *mustelae* v. moles (Jennison 129f); Plin. viii 55 (81) 218, ferrets v. rabbits; cf. Strab. iii 2.6. Caricatures: BM pap. 10,016; BM Guide Eg. Coll. 1909 28f. For Eg. folk-art in general: Kantor, "The folk art copied some motives of major art but altered them in a manner that sometimes suggests a satirical or at least a comical

intent." Tait: "The genet-cat may walk up a papyrus on an O.K. tomb-wall; but here [on a relief chalice] a huge, clumsy calf balances his way down". 112. Fable of fox and goat on ostr. from Deir el-Medineh, New Kingdom: Glanville pl. 10. fig. 12.

32. J. Lindsay (4) 102f. Egyptian cats: Denis.

33. *Animals fit for sac.* (beginning).

34. Col. viii 8.8; Athen. ix 50.

35. Rostovtzeff (1) 277 and (9) 56 fig. 31; W. Helbig no. 1569. Wells and shadufs, *phreata* and *keoneia* or *mechanai*: Flor. 16; Ryl. 99; Oxy. 2137; Schnebel 71. Farm towers: Hermes liv 1919 423 and Rostovtzeff (10) 374.1.

Philon on Askalon where doves were taboo: frag. Euseb. *praep.* viii 13.

36. Lease: Flor. 361. Mem.: Ryl. 228.

37. Oxy. 1127; Goodsp. 30 xxx (col. xxi, xxiii, xxxiii); CPR 120; BGU 889.

38. Oxy. 1278; cf. perhaps BGU 985.11. For guardianship of children under age by mother: Oxy. 898; W. *Grundz.* 253; in gen. DLRE 49f, 321f. Here the mother, though daughter of a gymnasiarch, seems a *peregrina,* herself acting through a *kyrios.*

39. TAPA lxiv 89; SPP xx 74; Flor. 10. Lentils fed to pigeons on estate of Epimachos (A.D. 78–9): Lond. 131 recto; Swiderek 100.

40. Zinche 436f; sparrows, wagtail, pelican, herons, geese, flamingoes, doves, hoopoe, hawks, larks, quail, plovers, small owl, rook. Rawnsley, 57, on wagtails.

11. PLAYS AND PLAYERS

1. Tragedies still read and well known by intellectuals, *e.g.* Clement: Tollington i 173f. For examples of literary mimes etc. see DLRE ch. 15.

2. J. H. Reynolds no. 606.

3. ILA ii 819.

4. Philostr. *vit. soph.* (Kays 260); Louk. *pisc.* 33, *menipp. nekyomant.* 16, *navig.* 46. Bayet, *Libyca* iii 1955 103–21.

In astrologers: low opinion *e.g.* Rhet. 173.18; Firm. i 151.4. High praise: H. 50.31; 56.12 (Teukros 44.9); Firm. ii 319.21, iii 307.8. Ptolemaios iv 4 (179f): "When two planets are found to rule action, if Hermes and Aphrodite take the rulership, they bring about action expressed by the arts of the Muses, musical instruments, melodies, or poems, and rhythm, especially when they have changed places. For they produce workers in the theatre (*thymelikoi*), actors, slave-dealers, makers of musical instruments, members of the choros, makers of strings, painters, dancers, weavers, and wax-moulders."

5. Fuad viii 16; D. S. Crawford on *thyrones.* Hesych. sv, says *sanides* and *eisodoi* (? doorway); *sanides* are movable parts of door—not clear if H. means *th.* are either or both. *Thyron* is found as loan word in anc. Coptic meaning shield (*thyreos*). But *thyra* could also mean frame (*i.e.* here stage-sets). For doors in mimes: L. Robert (1) 250; G. Guidi 52, 36, fig. 32. *Thyromata*: openings into

which backcloths etc. were set: Bieber (1) 114–5 etc. Shields as theatre-decorations, *ib.* 219.

6. Oxy. 2190; 2127; 2128.

For Hellenistic theatre-building: Bieber (1) ch. ix. The scheme of design of the proskenion theatre (house with forebuilding equal in height to first storey): occurs in Asia Minor as far back as temple of Ishtar in Assur (destroyed *c.* 2700 B.C.), also in "soulhouses" of Egypt, XI–XII dyns. (some 150 models known) and in rock-tombs V–XII dyns.; in Greece from 4th c. B.C. Bulle sees the form as originating in Alexandreia: 303ff. He notes the wooden Aboukir sarcophagi as showing the same spirit as the proskenion with engaged columns as merely decorative supporting wall. Bieber (n13 p. 291) says the house sarcophagi from Crimea (which Bulle relates to the Saite exs.) may derive from Miletos. Studniczka points out the symp. tent of Ptol. II in the procession prob. had low colonnades as porches on 3 sides before the central main building. It is likely indeed that all the main Hellenistic capitals played a part in the development, but we may still hold that Alex. had a key-role.

7. Michailides pl. vi; pl. viii a, c; pl. vii (textile). See list in Webster 97–112.

8. *Ib.* 305f, pls. xi, xii; Africa, Picard 270.

9. *Giants* vii; and *Exhort.* iv (52p).

10. *Aithiop.* i 3.1 and x 39.2. Pollux iv 151; Dikaiarch. *Geog. G.M.* i 103— for sense, Plout. *mor.* 789. Also Budé ed. *Aith.* iii 125f. The idea that the *l.* appeared only at end of play because Pollux mentions it last hardly helps. See Amisos mask: Bieber (1) fig. 364. Heliod. repeats *epetragoidei:* vii 14.7.

11. *Ib.* ix 24.4; ii 8.3; v 12.2.

12. Generally following Pickard-C. Also C. Luders; Oehler (2); Klaffenbach; Hahland; Reisch (4); Poland (1) 129ff and (2–3); Ziebarth (2) 79ff.

13. IG (2nd) 1132, Ditt. (3rd) 399, IG 1134.

14. Diod. iv 5.

15. OGIS 50, BCH ix 140 no. 2, Michel *rec.* 1018, Strack 35. Trouble of gild at Teos, Str. iv 1.29.

16. *Klio* viii 1908 413; Rehm, *Milet* i 3.383; P.–C. 306.

17. Kraeling 442; JRS xviii 1928 173—prob. A.D. 105–14. Other inscrs. P.–C. 301. A. Muller, 411 n5, thinks independent societies still existed. Note CIG 3082: *hoi apo tes Ionias kai Hellespontou (technitai)* honour a Greek, Tiberios Klaudios, enrolled in Quirina, who must have become a citizen under Claudius at earliest (cf. Oxy. 2471.3). Within the world-society (BGU 1.2; Suet. *aug.* 45; San Nicolò (1) Bd. i 54), local organisations functioned: BCH ix 124 with members in Ephesos contrasted with *hoi epi Romes.* Note further *synagonistai* in Oxy. 2476 (examined later in this ch.), of doubtful meaning: used early of local associations, *e.g.* CIG 3068b (Teos where soc. has a *koinon* of its own): Poland (3) 10 accepted Boeckh's theory of artists of another soc. temporarily working with Teans. If the *oikoumene* was the only soc., no other soc. could thus exist; but the word may have kept its use through the survival of local groups inside the world-one.

18. Oxy. ii p. 208; Oxy. 1050 (2–3c), 473 (Ant. Pius), 2127. Other eastern decrees, P.–C. 308f. Also Oxy. 473, 2127, 1050.

19. *Ath. Mitt.* xiv 1889 316; Poland (2) 594. See Philostr. (n4 above) on Eudianos of Smyrna at Rome. Lüders 185 no. 102: victories of flute-player, incl. at Eusebeia inst. by Antoninus (to commem. epithet *Eusebes, Pius*). Nemausus, Nîmes, as centre early in century: CIG 6785–6.

20. More details P.–C. 311; the gild was not a thiasos, a band of devotees of one particular deity.

21. *Ib.* 312, more details. Archiereus as well as hiereus found. In some places D. and emp. shared the same highpriest. Epimeletes at Eleusis: IG (2nd) ii 628. Nomodeiktes to settle disputes between members. Sauneron (2) 137, Esna.

22. CIG 2529; P.–C. 307.

23. Hypodid.: Phot. sv., cf. Plat. *ion* 536; C.–P. 313.

24. Costumier: *himatiomisthai—skeuopoioi* in Ptolemais inscr. as in Aristoteles' *Poetics*. Trumpeters: Poll. iv 87, 91. Subgroups: C.–P. 301, 306. Plat. *rep.* iii 395 suggests tragic and comic separate; Cicero *orat.* 109 speaks of some excelling in both. Unlikely a general distinction of registered members and metechontes (Teos): P.–C. 301. Philon, *Migr. of Abraham* 20, "whole dramas full of panegyrics".

25. C.–P. 314 for exs. *Paradoxoneikes* occurs in Plout. A 3rd-c. inscr. from Athenai has list of victories of herald; outstanding victors of a whole festival might be called victors *dia panton*: CIG 1585–6, 1720. In general DLRE ch. 14.

26. Oxy. 2475–7.

27. Oxy. 2475–7; cf. BGU 1074, which has also a letter from Sept. Sev. and Caracalla, and interposes a letter from claimant to Senate (cf. 2475 here). For 2477: Rea. The hand is not unlike 2475–6, but more cursive and hurried.

Hadrian's *diatagma*: only new item is *synthesia* (right to assemble as a gild: REg 400); cf. Diod. iv 4.5.4. "Payments to temples of emps.": payments to sacred games called Sebasta or for imp. shrines? If 289 was first year of 7th Pythiad, games were founded 265. Antioch is called colonia and metropolis: could be in Syria or Peisidia (RE iv 1901 531, 553): cf. Moretti no. 85. Perseus: Herod. ii 91. Note Nonnos on P. : xiii 461, xviii 291, xxv 31, xlvii 450 and 502.

28. Upps. 18; REg. 78.

29. *Abraham* xvi (72–3). Platon, *rep.* 514b, also has *thaumatopoios* for worker of puppets; he refers to a screen above which the *th.* exhibit their wonders. The puppet-world becomes for him the image of the real world—its reality to the observers. Herod. ii 48.

30. Suet. *Caesar* 84; tragic poet at Pompeii, Bieber (i) fig. 594. Kyrene: Wieseler 99f, pl. xiii, 2; Pacho 49f; Pickard–C. (2) 245 fig. 120; Bieber (1) 239. Rome: Bieber 239 (2) 120f; Lippold no. 2366.

31. Grimal 254–7, 344 (cited), in gen. 337ff; Vitruv. v 6.9; von Cube; Beyen 268ff; Sogliano *Mon. Ant.* viii 1898 233–416; *Not. Scav.* 1907 560ff. Note the many oscilla in these gardens: Altheim (2) 65ff. For "satyric play" of Ariadne,

Grimal 349, cf. mime in Xenophon, *symp.* ix 2–7, and motive of Seilenos un-
veiling a nymph, a very common garden theme: Labrousse.

32. CIL vi 461; Dessau ILS 3361; Grimal 340f.

12. GARDENS AND THEIR TRADITION

1. Drioton (4) 257: Ténand 130.
2. P. Gilbert (1) 55.
3. Gilbert (2) 142f, fig. 33.
4. Budge (2) pl. xxxi.
5. Early exs.: Petrie (2) 26 pl. vii (93–5); ILN 2 July 1921 6.
6. Morenz 45f; Gilbert (2) 144.
7. Tait 95f; Spanton 1ff; Goodyear 18; Keimer (1–3).
8. Tait 98; Naville (1) iv pl. 109.
9. Tait 99.
10. Tait 103 no. 1; pl. xiii 4: with more botanical details.
11. Tait 104f, nos. 2–4; 107 nos. 5–9 for variations. In 5 "In the stern a naked
blackwigged girl, wearing a necklace, leans her weight back against a puntpole
held behind her, her left hand grasping the pole above her head and the right
hand reaching down the pole to full extent. Her legs are to right, the left knee
bent and pushing against the sternpost, her shoulders to front; her head turns
back to left. The other woman's left shoulder is foreshortened in a common
Egyptian manner; but this expert hunter is spatially conceived as she propels
this boatload with such nonchalance and an air of disdain", Tait 107.
12. Nos. 10 and 35, 26, 27, 29, with p. 131. Bes: nos. 28 etc. (p. 122), 40–1;
p. 128.
13. No. 16 (pp. 113–15): cf. 24, baby sungod on lotus; 25 (with Hathor);
19, with Horus and Isis and conquest-scene, cf. 20. Cf. generally the Buddhist
symbolism of lotus-rebirth.

Note further ibex (no. 15) with calves etc.; p. 123, naked girl playing lute;
girl swimming, p. 126; ? oryx, no. 38, with chariot; rite of baptism p. 129;
ibex; chariot; djed-pillar; Horus, pp. 133–4, 130; winged cobras 129–31.

14. Tait 133; Roeder (3) 65, 36, and (4) 79, 123; ASAE lii 347: discussion
319–74.
15. Lefebvre (1) i 140; Roeder (3) 36, 169, 196; MDAIK iii 1932 6; ASAE
lii 361.
16. Tait 138. As will be seen, I rely wholly in this matter of the chalices on
Tait's illuminating essay.
17. Jucker; also D. E. Strong 217.
18. Bruyère vi 2 p. 52; xv. Soteres: A. Reinach 50; Bataille 188f, 220 (but
see de la Ferté 12–15 on Louvre portraits).
19. Bruyère vii 2, 85; BIFAO xxxvi 150.
20. Rhind 26 fig. 2.
21. Fraternity: Boak (1) 218. Further, charge for *anthinou* (?), Tebt. i 182

(late 2nd c. A.D.); 12 ob. for *stephanion*, Fay. 103; 16 ob. for *staphanikon*, Wessely SPP xxii 56. Bataille 243f.

22. *De isid.* lxv, xxxvi, lxviii.

23. J. Bayet (1) 403ff; RA xvii 1941 102f; Grimal 70 n4.

24. Launey (2); Grimal 81. Satyrs: Athens vase 14.902. Note Aphrodite of the Garden (on banks of Ilissos, opp. Stadion, Athenai): statue by Alkamenes: Louk. *eikones* 4 and *on eikones* 8.

At Thasos a votive relief seems to concern a group of banqueting thiasotai; two docs. attest a communal meal in 5th c. B.C. Also at Thera the chapel of Dionysos seems a stibadeion for communal meals and ecstatic experiences. Pouilloux 88, 366; Devambez; (docs.) BCH li 1927 197 and Plout. 811de. Stibadeion: Picard (9); BCH lxviii–lxix 1944–5 240. For Delos: Vallois (1) 72; F. Robert (2). Further Frickenhaus; Welter 30ff; Roebuck 42ff.

25. Ep. 4.

26. Heliodoros i 16f. Planting of planes on agora seems to go back to Kimon (Plout. *kim.* 13.7 (487c)) but the ambulationes of which Plout. speaks may be later. Note the discovery of a garden round the Hephaisteion at Athenai, dating from the early 3rd c. B.C.; maintained at least till the Augustan period. (The water system broke down in the late 1st c. A.D.)

27. Xen. *kyr.* i 3.14; Pollux *onom.* sv; Grimal 74f.

28. Xen. *econ.* iv 14 and 20; Cic. *cat. mai.* 59; Assyrians, Assur. W. Otto, *Handbuch d. Arch.* 1939 i fig. 72.

29. Plout. *alk.* 24 (204c).

30. Tertul. *apol.* 47; *carm. iudic. dom.* 195 etc.

31. Plin. v 23.19 (82), v 27.22 (93); Gellius ii 20.4; Aymard 68ff. The Assyrians had entertained the people with animals, the gifts of other princes or the booty of their own conquests; but they looked on the beasts as royal quarry, which they hunted in great enclosures stocked for the purpose. These preserves, maintained by the Persians, fell into Alex.'s hands: Barnett.

32. *On Piety*, reconstructed from Porph. *de abst.* ii 5–7; Üxküll-Gyllenband 38f.

33. See Wehrli i 1944, frags. 47, 49.

34. K. Reinhardt (1) 392ff, 408ff and (2) cols. 719–25, 805–14. Also in general Lovejoy and Bass, and E. D. Phillips.

35. *Abraham, Treatise of life of wise man* iv; and *Cont. life* ii.

36. *On fugitives* xviii; *dreams* i 14. Basil *ep.* 2 (Loeb).

37. *Antiq. rom.* iv 13.

38. Cf. Martial iii 47; Sen. *ep.* xc—also cii 21, the soul "does not consent to a lowly birthplace like Ephesos or Alexandreia", etc.

39. DLRE 254. For Greek Gardens of Gods, see further J. L., *Clashing Rocks* (1965).

13. FLOWERS, FRUITS, HERBS

1. Olck. Discussion in Athen. xv 682: number of petals etc.

2. Suet. *ner.* 27. Dill estimates for his period at £35,000.

3. Mart. vi 80.

4. *On Providence* ii 71; Variety: Athen. v 25 (196); Mich. Zen. 45; Cumont (3) 55. The single species, *rosa canina,* and cabbage types, *rosa centifloria,* both flourished.

5. Joret.

6. Grimal app. ii nos. 69 and 28.

7. *Ib.* nos. 42, 48, 61. Plin. NH xxii 76.

8. BGU 1118-19; Oxy 729 and Ross. Georg. ii 18 lix.

9. Athen. xv 669cd. "Wreaths messengers of holy silence", Chairemon in Dionysos, etc.: Athen. xv 676ef.

10. *Ib.* 669-670f. Agalma also means delight, darling. Binding: cf. Plat. *tim.* 41a. Klearchos wrote at least three works on Platon. For farfetched comments, cf. Athen. 553e.

11. His play *The Persians*: Athen. xv 685a; cf. Aristoph. *clouds* 910. Celery: Aristoph. *lys.* 227; sc. Theok. xi 10; Loeb Athen. vol. iv pp. 500f, ns. 5 and f, v 405 n.f. Larkspur: Athen. 681bc; Paus. ii 35.5.

12. Athen. xv 671e, citing Anakreon; 675ff. Pollux, sv *Nauk. steph.*

13. Athen. xv 675-6. Date: Kahrestedt RE viii 1145; How and Wells on Herod. ii 178; Athen. 283 de. Statuette: R. sv *Aphrodite* 407-8. Cf. tale from the physician Philonides' *On Perfumes and Wreaths,* on rel. of wreaths to bandages for hangover etc.: Athen. 675. For rose used medicinally (ear-ache), Oxy. 234 (late 2nd or early 3rd c.): "Dilute some gum with balsam of lilies and add rose-extract; twist some wool with oil in it round a probe, warm, and drop in."

14. Theopompos on pap. wreaths given to Spartans arriving in Egypt: Athen. xv 676d.

Myrtle: Athen. xv 682 cd, on embracing sprays of Parthian plant; see ch. 20 n28 here.

Aphrodite: Firm. ii 299.14; Maneth. iv 492 and 300; Cumont (3) 95 n1; Manil. v 144; Athen. xii 527e; Phil. *leg. ad G.* ii 12. Alexandreia: Cumont (3) 94 ns. 4-5. Apollonios ordered 300 at a time, PSI 333.8; Juv. xv 50.

15. Athen. xv 679-80; see ch. i here on Hellanikos FHG i 66, J.; Steph. Byz. places T. in Libya; Hellanikos seems to take the site from Thrakian Chalkidike. The tree is *acacia albida, A. arabica*: Theophr. HP iv 2.8 (Hort i 298), black acacia (gum arabic). For N. Greece: note patronymic Mestos, derived from Makedonian river, on a Dionysiac inscr. (2nd c. B.C.), Hermop. magna: *Bull. Soc. arch. d'Alex.* xi 1908 187.

16. Athen. xv. 680c. Contrast Herod. ii 162-9; How and Wells i 252. Patarmis: ? Patarbemis (Herod. ii 162). The season is spring.

17. Athen. xv 665c, cf. 66c and 553e.

18. *Ib.* 689b; *stakte* 688c. Also 679ef. For the use and powers of saffron: Deonna (4) 45.

19. *Ib.* 689-90.

20. *Ib.* 688.

21. Firm. i 169.3; Str. xvi 780; Ditt. *or.* 132 (130); Firm. i 304.24; Lumbroso (2) 134; Reil 144; Collart (2); Heichelheim (1) 161.

22. Cumont (3) 92 n3–4; Firm. i 188.16 (cited); Manil. v 255; Firm. ii 304.22.

23. A. Hermann ch. 3.

24. *Tetr.* 178–9.

25. *Meteor.* ii 2; NH xv 7 and xvi 21.

26. Lucas (1).

27. Plin. xiii 2 and xv 7.

28. HP 353, 355; other ingredients not named.

29. NH xiii 6 and 2; xii 46 and xv 7.

30. NH xii 62 and 47; xiii 2 and xii 51.

31. NH xxiii 46.

32. Lucas 46; also 47–53 for frankincense, myrrh, galbanum, ladanum, storax etc.

33. Merton 79, unknown prov.

34. Cumont (3) 93 n3–4; Manil. v 353, 643. Van Landschoot, 344f for eagle; von Lemm 361–6. Alex. origin: RE xx 1 1941 sv *Phys.* 1104 (bibliog. 1075f). Also F. Sbordone: p. xii for date (1 c. A.D.).

35. *Ib.* 92 n5; Manil. iv 671.

36. *Aithiop.* i 8, cf. i 27.

37. Delatte (1) 85.

38. CCAG viii 3 (p. 137); viii 4 (p. 257). Cf. the Orphic hymns for penetration of incense in late Greek rites.

39. *Pap. de Paris*, 1. 2967ff. Circumambulation: Delatte (1) 73–5.

40. Psell. *quaenam sunt* 7; Petersburg MS; Delatte 86.

41. Hopfner (4) i par. 539–50; Pfister sv *Rauchopfer* in RE; Eitrem (2) 241ff citing Vegetius, *mul.* iii 12: *suffimentorum composito fascinum pellet, lustrat animal, fugat daemones, submovet morbos.*

42. Ed. Ruelle 41 no. 12; 121 no. 3.

43. Delatte 84f on apotropaic aspects. Further discussion and refs. 86f.

44. Galen, *de simpl. med. temp.* vi t. xi (Kühn 792ff).

45. Lines 2978ff. Prayer: l. 2975. More prayers: Delatte 101ff.

46. Lines 262ff. Barbarian words (often called Chaldean, Syriac, or Persian, to quiet Christian conscience as to pagan magic), Delatte 93ff. Further details about peony: Delatte 109ff, also the Christianising of the spells. Peony, *paeonia*, is of order of Ranunculaceae (incl. Aconites, Hellebores, Actaeas). Homoeopathic proving showed it as a remedy for anal affections (abscess, fissure, fistule etc.). "The dreams of the provers were of a terrifying nature; and it is interesting to note, as Geyer, one of the provers, did, that both Dioscorides and Plinius cured nightmare with Paeonia, the former with the seeds, the latter with the root. Geyer was ignorant of this fact until after he had experienced the nightmare-causing power of the drug. As the tissues are sensitive to pressure and injury, the mind is also sensitive; cramping pains in abdomen, preceded, and esp.

followed, by anxiety, trembling of legs and arms, as though they were frightened; he became apprehensive if anyone spoke to him, and unpleasant news affected him exceedingly", J. H. Clarke, *Dict. of Practical Materia Medica,* 1962 ed. R. Hooper in his *Lexicon-Medicum* 1820, 4th ed., says the roots, flowers and seeds have been esteemed as anodyne and corroborant, esp. roots. Used since Galen against epilepsy; sliced roots hung round neck as amulet. He discusses recent uses but says most modern writers now reject it.

47. Jos. *de bell. iud.* vii 180.

48. Eitrem (2) 44, 446; Plin. xxviii 77: Delatte 87–8, also 144f for *battaritis* of Byz. historian Kedrenos (PG. Migne cxxi 581).

49. Ailian NA xiv 27; cf. Diod. in Photios cod. 223 (215 a 33).

50. Hermes: CCAG viii 3 154. In cod. Vindobonensis 13647 is described a plant *lunatica* or *arabica*: identified with *baaras*. Another night-shiner is *nyktalope* or *nyktegreta* of ps.-Demokritos: Plin. xxi 62. In general: Delatte (1) 144–8. *Carmen*: ed. Haupt, *opusc.* ii 1876 475ff, in Greek hexameters.

51. Plin. xxx 18; Ailian NA ix 32 (no ref. to what happens to bird); Delatte 146. Servius, *aen.* vi 136 on death for cutting of bough in cult of Diana Nemorensis; cf. Balder and mistletoe, etc.

52. Steier in RE xiv 1028ff, esp. 1037; refs in Delatte (1) 147 n2; Italy, Delatte 148.

53. Cf. Apoll. Rhod. iii 865. Nature grieves when the *herbe de l'or* is cut in Brittany in defiance of the rites: Delatte 148. See further my *Clashing Rocks*.

14. TREES AND MARKET GARDENS

1. *Aithiop.* viii 14.

2. Zinche 411–13. For trees in G. R. Egypt see DLRE index sv *Trees.*

3. Mich. 128 (A.D. 47); BGU 591 (57); Hamb. 5 (89); Corn. 10 (119); *Pap. gr. de la Bibl. nat. et univ. de Strasb.* 1959 267 (P. gr. 1134) (126); Flor. 369 (139); Oslo ii 36 (145); BGU 604 and 603 (168–9); SB 5670, Bucoli (167); CPR 47 (2c.) cf. BGU 862. Survey: BGU 657. Ryl. 172 (208); SPP xx 21 (CPR 45) 214; SB 7441 (*c.* 230); SPP xx 70 (261); PSI 33 (267).

Epibole: e.g. REg no. 329; W. *Ost.* 1472; SB 7596.

Application: Oxy. 1632: see Oxy. xiv p. 27 for reckoning.

4. Ryl. 172. In general, see Oxy. 1631–2 and Hohlwein for list; also Wallert. Fuad viii 33 (2nd or 3rd c.), a list of taxes on gardenlands (on account of Athenodoros) has tax of *steleche. Stelechis* is gen. taken as dry-stalk or trunk. It occurs twice in SB 7188: *Aeg.* v 1924 129ff; once with *phoinikina* and once in context opposed to *dendra* (perhaps as olive trees); if *dendra* means just trees, then *steleche* could mean only palmfronds as distinct from whole tree. Also note the money here paid seems cash-commutation for tax in kind, and the govt. could not have demanded a regular delivery of the trunks of such slow-growing trees as palms: Crawford *l.c.* pp. 67f.

5. Whateley 320f. Late trad. of Delian palm as Egyptian: Wallert 148 n2,

cf. Tschudin 29–32. Wallert defines two kinds: date and dûm (with rare medemia argun) attested by offerings at various epochs. Both kinds are associated with Thoth (also Min); date, with Re and Hathor; dûm, with Thoueris.

6. *Moses* iii 22, and *Tilling of earth* (start).

7. Col. 36 line 11; Rostovtzeff (11); Préaux (1) 165.

8. Grimal 92f; Plin. (bk. xix) cites K. of Caesennius; see also xix (veg.) 64 and 177 (K. of Savinius Tiro). For commercial flowergrowing: Mallet 234; Glotz (2); Cumont (3) 55; Preisigke WB, *kepouoi*; San Nicolò (1) i 74.

9. Ryl. 239. Dionysias: Flor. 123, 253; Euhemeria, 136; Sentrepaiou. 146, 234–5. Recipient here, Euporos, unknown. For Serenos: Flor. 245, 248.

10. Lond. 109; REg. no. 323.

11. SB 6951; REg no. 320; cf. Tebt. ii app. i. See also Lond. 195 (Ryl. ii p. 255) Fayum 1st c.; Oxy. 1185 (*c.* 200), 8-dr. tax; Ryl. 215a iii, Thmouis (2nd c.) etc.

12. REg. pp. 515–21; Wallace. Hamb. 41–53; Lond. 917; Fay. 55; Oxy. 1437; Tebt. 478, 503; Ryl. 192b.

13. Hamb. 99. Some more exs.: Mich. 123 R iv 26 (Tebt. A.D. 45); PSI 82 (Oxy. vineyard, 65); Amh. 85–6 (78); Lond. 163 (Karanis, vineyard 88); Flor. 86 (Hermop. *lach.* 91); W. O. 787 (Upper Eg., *lach.* 96); Flor. 356 (Hermop. *lach.* 1–2 c.).

14. Amh. 85; Mitteis *Chr.* 274; Naubion sv index DLRE; Phaophi: Schnebel 276.

15. Ross. Georg. ii 19. Lessor is a Persian of Epigone.

16. BGU 603. Some more exs.: Lond. 840 (Hermop., rec. of 1432 dr. rent for gardenland?) 129; Oxy. 707 (suit as to lease of vineyard and orchard on 6-yr. term; no rent for 4 yrs. if lessee plants new vines on part and builds wall round property; 2000 dr. advanced for new waterwheel) 136; Lond. 438 (Kerkesoucha, *lach.*, 30 art. of seed for 1 yr.) 142; Lond. 168 (Psenarpsenesis, 3-yr. lease 1 ar. olives, prob. produce shared) 162; Upps. 24 (Theadelpheia, 125 dr. for winter garden) 169; Lond. 920 (Fayum. garden and storeroom); Oxy. 1692 (vineyard and reeds) 188—cf. Oxy. 1631; Lond. 151 (Karanis, 3 measures of oil as rent on olive grove) and Ross. Georg. ii 36 (Fayum, vineyard at 100 dr.) 2nd c.

17. Oxy. 1630; DLRE sv C.I. in index esp. 280–2 and 360 n35. Smaller Oasis at this time joined admin. to Oxy. nome.

18. Mitteis (2) 122; Ryl. 116.10n; Lond. 196; P. Cattaoui verso.

19. Flor. 16. Cf. Ross. Georg. ii 17, Hermop., surety for woman leasing gardenland on imp. estate (surety agrees to pay the rent in money to public bank); Oxy. 1123, woman as lessee of crownland at Petenouris and Panechmothis, 158–9; Lond. 604, 604B. Women were exempt from forced cultivation of crownland: Oxy. 899, BGU 648. In Oxy. 1123 the woman takes over from her dead father; the lease seems to go to heir, but no evidence of compulsion of heir to take over: cf. Baden 18 and Tebt. 325.

20. Upps. 23. Alexandrians DLRE 284-7; lach. lands—see REg p. 82 and Flor. 16. Vineyards: sv index DLRE, and esp. 243f; Oxy. 1631: Schnebel 239ff.

More exs.: CPR 34 (Dionysias, 5 ar. private olive ground, 3 yrs.) and CPR 244 (Fayum, sublease on shares for 5 yrs, lessee gets third produce, lessor pays taxes) 2-3rd cs.; Flor. 340 (Ars. nome, $\frac{1}{4}$ of 20$\frac{1}{2}$ ar. gardenland at 40 dr. ?, 1 year) early 3rd c. Flor. 16 (Euhemeria, 1 ar. private *lach.* land 3 yrs., 100 dr. a yr.; lessor pays taxes, provides ox worth 100 dr. for irrigation) 239; Upps. 23 (Theadelpheia, sublease 2$\frac{1}{2}$ ar. vineyard, 2 yrs. on share, lessor giving 5000 reeds, 5 bundles twine, paying for new wheel, supplying animals for operations; each gives half the fertiliser; lessee repairs old waterwheel, feeds oxen, plants 50 sets yearly, digs land thrice, provides pig worth 20 dr., and gets $\frac{1}{2}$ produce) 252; SPP xx 58 ii (Herm. nome, survey of temples' property; gardens leased to Paniskos) 265; Princeton 39 (lease garden of cucumbers, gourds, melons, 1 yr. at 300 dr., and delivery of certain amount of produce to lessor, who pays taxes) 3rd c.

21. DLRE 295.

22. SPR xx 70.

23. Oxy. 1631.

24. REg. 58 and Ryl. 168. Petechon is illiterate.

25. BGU 1047 iii 10—iv 18; cf. Rostovtzeff (12) 183; reassessment, col. ii 11. Karanis: REg p. 127. Sublease on crownland at Tebt., A.D. 110-11, Tebt. 373 (10 yrs. sublease); application for lease at reduced rental, Tebt. 325 (A.D. 145); petitions for reduction of rent, Giss 6 (A.D. 118). Redistribution of crownland: Flor. 20; W. *Chr.* 359 (Theadelpheia A.D. 127). See also Tebt. 376 (W. *Chr.* 350) A.D. 162, sublease.

Much revenue came from rent of gardenlands in add. to the taxes (*e.g.* BGU 558-9, 657; Oxy. 653). The *phoros hierou Aphrodites* in Mich. docs. perhaps reps. rent on gardens, which was used to pay syntaxis for the temple of A.: REg p. 521; Eitrem (1) 32.

26. Meyer, *Gr. Texte* 3.

27. Giss 48; W. *Chr.* 171. Under Sept. Sev. there was a reform of admin. machinery and methods of taxation; Claudius here may have held the office of catholicus: *Grundz.* 157. Reassignment: *diamisthosis.*

28. SB 4226.

29. BGU 106, cf. Ryl. 84. Also BGU 599 (W. *Chr.* 363) Fayum, 2nd c., 3 aur. of ousiac land in olive culture near Euhemeria.

30. SB 4416. More exs. of leases on imp. estates: Ryl. 157, Herm. nome, div. of vineyard-lease, A.D. 135; Ryl. 97, Oxy., olive grove (prob. imp.) at 15 measures of oil and gratuity, *epichyma*, of 2 kot. per measure, 139; Ross. Georg, ii 17 (see n19 above); W. O. 657, Elephantine, overseers give rec. for 91 dr., 165. In Ryl. 99, Hermop. nome, land seems leased at intervals of 5 yrs, and to be gardenland as cash-rent is paid to the "official bank in Hermopolis in the customary instalments", 3rd century. It seems then that gardenland was still

profitable. There was competition in the bidding, the bidder offering 12 dr. a yr. more than the previous lessee.

31. Wine and oil was early found more profitable than cereals: *e.g.* Lond. 195 (Ryl. ii p. 255), Fayum, 1st c., where the doc. (taxes on gardenlands) implies the land was being used for various kinds of garden crops, though the whole area was called by name of vineyard. One ar. of olive, constituting a *paradeisos,* and 1 ar. of *lachanon,* each paid 25 dr. per ar. for *geometria,* while the rest, 61¼ ar., was taxed at 50 dr. "Taxes on the estate called. . . , of the emperor Tiberius Caesar Augustus . . . vineyard . . . ar., consisting of . . . wine press 4 ar., productive figs (?) . . . ar., aromatic balsam . . . 52¼ ar., greek reeds productive 4 ar., olivegrove in bearing 1 ar., vegetable garden 1 ar." Then "Estate of M. Antonius Pallas, formerly of Gallia Polla and once of Lucius Septimius" (with allotments once "owned by Eros and Charmos" and by Philoxenos son of Theon). And Estate of [name lost] with various allotments that had once belonged to others (Sotas, Timotheus, Mendeios, Aniketos): a brickyard, ½ ar. here. We seem to see small owners being swallowed up. Note the woman Gallia Polla.

15. GARDENS OF DEATH

1. See Klein; Stemler. For Rome: Laum; Wamser 14 *Bull. Comm.* xli 1934 211.

2. BGU 1120, with further usual legal terms about care etc. See also Schubart (2).

3. Gnomon 1-2; BGU v 1; Meyer, *Jurid. Pap.* 93; more refs. REg p. 711; Üxküll-G. (2) 11. From Theadelpheia. W. H. S. Jones, 57, points out light thrown by BGU 1120; only the graves, not the *kepotaphia,* excepted.

4. Mus. GR inv. 26528; P. M. Frazer (1) and (2); L. Robert (8).

5. Dialogue form is rare in inscriptions; commoner in papyri. Nearest ex. is *antigraphon hypomnematismou* of the idiologos, A.D. 120, though there the procs. are in indirect speech: *Jahreshefte* xxi–xxii 1922 Beibl. 1271; SEG ii 848; SB 8757. Exs. from Asia Minor and Syria: Frazer (1) n5–6.

6. Frazer (1) 119f and 121. Tomb as sacred place: Lattimore 106ff; Hirschfeld (4); Arkwright; de Zulueta etc.

7. *Ib.* 121f, and REg 257ff.

8. Bernand 159f, no. 67, with refs.; Frazer (1) 122 and Robert in *Bull. epigr* 1959 498. Frazer suggests as alternative the Cl. of the Memnonia may be strat. of *Herakleidou meris* in A.D. 124: Amh. 66.

9. Hirschfeld (2) 352; RE sv. *I.L.* 901–2. He prob. took the post after Lysimachos, A.D. 88: P. Fouad Inv. 211; BIFAO xli 1942 43.

10. P. M. Meyer (3) 149; Frazer (2) 157 n7.

11. Frazer (1) 125–7 and (2) 158.

12. Pringsheim 305, for *kapones.*

Karpistes: De Visscher (1); Frazer (1) 158 n13. De Visscher sees *karpos* (in karpistes) as *karphos*: Latin *festuca*, the rod used to touch slaves in manumitting them.

13. Cumont (2) 353, 380. Schreiber (2) 217; Bataille 183, citing P. dem. Lond. 1024 (UPZ 189) on gardens sold in nekrop. of Memnonia.

14. Str. xvii 1.10: west of city, though inscriptions come from east, it seems.

15. Bruyère v 2.44; Spiegelberg (2) 15 pls. i, 4.

16. Bataille 183; cf. Bruyère viii 3.21 fig. 6; UPZ 187; cf. Revillout, Ä.Z. xviii 1880 112.

17. CIL vi 29964, 10876, 17992, 29967, 29970 etc. Outside Rome: iii 2072, 2279; v 2176; xi 2895; xiv 396. See Grimal 80 fig. 2; 341 fig. 28; 63.

18. Mart. i 114.

19. *Sat.* 71. And Strong (2) 567; CAH plates iv 180b. For grave as *aeterna domus*: Lattimore 167, 318.

20. Bataille 225; 244 (Boak and fraternity banquet) 267. Also Loukian *de luctu* 21; Sil. Ital. xiii 474.

21. W. E. Needler.

22. Tuna: Perdrizet, (8) 725; Karanis: *Fay. Towns* 41; Philadelpheia; *CR Ac. Inscr.* xv 1887 229; Ghoran: BCH xxv 1901 401.

23. CE 1938 373.

24. Winlock 14.

25. Reisner i 85. Flowers and tombs in general, Lattimore 129, 135; Rose.

26. Perdrizet (8); SEG viii 621, SB 7871, with Goosens CE xiii 1938 373; xv 1940 132; Préaux (3).

27. Bruyère i 1.4; iii 3.9; N. M. Davies; G. Maspero (3) 342 fig. 108; Steindorff-Wolff pl. 16. In Syria and Palestine from Hellenistic to Roman times, pyramid a common memorial form and grave monument. Vallois, i 394f (with refs.), says in Syria the pyramidal towers were tombs or heroa; Lagrange, 206, says they were often used as grave stelai and called *naphcha* (soul or person). Vallois sees only a sun-symbolism in the Egyptian pyramid, whereas in fact it is essential a sky-ramp and world-centre or mountain.

28. Leipz. 30.

29. Möller; Gabra 80, 104 (Hermop.).

30. Perdrizet (8). Mourners: Herod. ii 85 (comm. of Wiedemann and note by H. Brugsch in 5th ed. of Stein, i 1.93); Genesis 1.3. 4th c.: BGU i 34; Schubart (3) 470.

Embalming: Herod. ii 86; Diod. i 91; Plin. xvi 11; xxiv 11; *Thes. ling. gr.* of Steph. (1841) iv 1402; *ib.* of Berlin, iii 734–7. For consumption: Robert, *Coll. Froehner* 121.

31. Bataille 181; Cumont (3) 140 n4.

32. Exped. Sieglin i; Wreszinski pl. 8. Note tomb of Haterii (DS fig. 3360; cf. Helbig. Toutain i 499) where so many details, torches, colonettes, behind the bed of the dead woman are Alexandrian, and where the wall-decs. (garlands and shells) recall paintings etc. of houses of Hermopolis nekropolis.

P*

16. PARADISES

1. Grimal 93–102. Hortulanus: Macrob. *sat.* vii 3; Apul. *met.* iv (143), ix (235); Orelli *insc.* 4200.

2. *Ad Q. frat.* iii 1.5.

3. NH xvi 140.

4. *Ib.* xii 13.

5. Wörmann (1) 219ff.

6. DL v 83; Diod. *exc. vat.* xxxi 8; Val. Max. v 1.1. B.R. Brown follows Dawson in denying he was an Egyptian and calls him a mapmaker!

7. *De arch.* vii 5; Grimal 97 n5 and 98 n1.

8. Grimal 98; *topia* 99 n3. Stoics: Arnim, *stoic. vet. frag.* ii 75, ii 25f; Sextus *adv. math.* vii 242.

9. Rostovtzeff (9).

10. Grimal 100f on Plin. xxxv 116–17; 103 and 321 on Cicero's Amalthaeum.

11. Yoyotte (2); Derchain (3) on the clay from *išrw* in Pap. Reisner I; also rel. to lioness-goddess Mehyt.

12. *Laws* ii 1. The oak is the starting-point, suggesting to Atticus the oak Cicero described in his poem in hon. of Marius.

13. Grimal 127.

14. J. Lindsay (5).

15. ILN 5 Oct. 1957; Grimal 336. Further: Crema 466; Aurigemma 100–33; Hanfmann (2) pl. i.

16. Grimal 92.

17. *Ep.* xv 15.

18. Grimal 318f.

19. *Ib.* 335f; 76 (Cicero's Lyceum and Acad.); 270 (*gestationes*), *Vit Hadr.* 24. Tempe: Gusman 323. Roman ideas of Canopos: Sen. *ep.* li 2; Juv. i 26, vi 84, xv 44, Amm. Merc. xxii 16.14.

20. Warcher; *Not. Scav.* 1910 315ff. Snail: el-Khabab (1) 155; Plin. xxx 3–4; RE sv Schneke; Deonna (1) 142 and n8; Debono; Cabrol sv *Coquillage.*

21. *Imag.* i 5, cf. Louk. *rhet. prec.* 6. For statue of Nile with dwarfs: Loeb ed. of Philostr. *imag.* fig. 1. Deity at source: cf. Philostr. *vit. apoll.* vi 26 (Pindar, Bergk fr. 282). Poseidon: Overbeck, *Kunstmyth. Poseidon. Gemmentafel* iii 3. Steward: *tamias.*

22. Grimal 336f, 275, 164; *Not. Scav.* 1929 20f. The term *diaeta* is post-Aug., *e.g.* Plin. *ep.* ii 17.15; Suet. *Claud.* 10; Stat. *silv.* ii 2.83; Orelli *inscr.* 4373 etc. Egyptian rels.: Grimal 277.

23. Grimal 259, 272, 289.

24. *On Creation* liv. Men as trees: *Incorrupt. of world* vi.

25. *Heir to divine things* xli. Metaphysical opposition: *de migr.* 179 and 181, cf. *allegr. interp.* i 39 (91), taking up Stoic phrase (*S.v.f.* ii 774 and i 532).

26. A.T. i 15. Tithonos, human spouse of Dawn, gained immortality but still aged, was changed to grasshopper. Tereus held a cannibal feast, then was

changed to owl, the cooked boy Itys into pheasant, Philomela into nightingale, Prokne into swallow. For scene: cf. Philostr. younger, *imag*. 3 (Hunters) for closeknit roof etc., based on Philostr. *vit. apoll.* xlix 23fK (ii 7).

27. *Dionys.* i 4 and 19; Cf. Dionysos sophist. A.P. v 81.

28. *Ib.* xvi and xlii 108. *Chroa (chroia)* means both the skin and its colour.

29. *Ib.* xlii 424ff.

30. *Ib.* xlii 303. Deo is Demeter. Vintage: Aristoph. *Peace* 1338f.

31. A. Hermann ch. 3.

32. *Dionys.* iii 131ff. Mother-of-sweets: *hedytokoios*. Stippled; *poikilleto*.

33. *Ib.* xxxii 78. Male-female: i 281, ii 495, iii 142, xxxii 88, xix 79; Lind (7) 62.

34. Ross. Georg. i 1925 11; *Archiv* viii 254; Loeb. *Lit. Pap. Texts* 129. "With real frenzies", *ortheisin maniesin*. Phantom: *eidola*.

35. *Dionys.* xxi 26ff; the attack continues to line 90. Cf. xxi 297: "Ambrosia who'd attacked the bold Lykourgos, the battle of the twigs and the war with vines."

36. *Ib.* vii 344ff.

37. *Ib.* xvii 320ff. *Areï baccheutheisa.* Note prophylactic power of ivy; its perennial green (immortality); Pythagoreans counted it among the plants on which they set their dead: Cumont (2) 220, (6) 42, (7) 10; K. Lehmann (2) 220; Hor. *odes* i 29–30. Mosaics: Gauckler 291 no. 890; D. Levi (2). i 485–6; Hinks (2) 72–3.

38. *Ib.* xxv 87.

39. *Ib.* xxxv 339f.

40. *Ib.* xxxv 363–6; cf. xxxvi 267f; 335ff.

41. *Ib.* xv 44ff; xxii 55ff. Likeness here is *indalma*.

42. *Ib.* xliii 20–5.

43. Picard (8) 38, pl. xii. Acholla has a Triumph of D.

44. Picard (2) 335 n69–70.

45. L. Leschi, *Mon. Piot* 1935 xxxv 139; RA 1949 ii 150. Lepcis: Ward Perkins, Picard (2) 341–2. For an Antonine mingling of sea themes with Dionysiac (Picard (2) 343) with growing stress on interlaces etc: BAC 1954 113 pl. iii.

46. Picard (2) 344f, pl. opp. p. 66, and n93 on p. 401.

47. Picard (2) 346.

48. Rufinus renovated his house in yr. of his consulship, 184: *Kartago* iv 1953 123ff; rel. to imp. mystique, Picard (2) 346 as against M. P. Romanelli.

49. Picard (2) 346f.

50. J. Toynbee (1) for full discussion and illustrations. At Rome the motive spent itself under Domitian and died out in Italy for near 100 years; was revived in early 3rd c. through a conscious return to Flavian palatine motives and the impact of models from the East, esp. Asia Minor. For Memphis helmet (? 2nd c. B.C.): Ponger, *Kat. gr. u. röm Skulptur, Allard Pierson Mus.,* Amsterdam 1942 86f. For Dionysos Sab., L. Curtius (2) and *Ath. Mitt.* li 117ff. In Boscoreale treasure: *Mon. Piot* v pls. ix–x.

51. Toynbee 41. Sousse: *Africa Ital.* vi 1935 147 fig. 34. El-Djem: *in.* v 1933 34, fig. 20; vi 1935 148 fig. 35. Cherchel: *Inv. mos. Afrique*, iii no. 435. Sabratha: Haynes pl. 21; Peirce ii pls. cxv, cxviaa, cxviia.

52. Riefstahl, with discussion of other charioteer textiles. A floral border for pictures is attested for the 2nd c. B.C. by a pap. epigram (JJP v 1951 237) on a work of Apelles.

17. GARDENS AND ARCHITECTURE

1. Ward Perkins (2).
2. *Ib.*
3. E. B. Smith (1) 27. This chapter leans heavily on his work. *Sat.* i 18.
4. Rostovtzeff (9) 44 fig. 24.
5. Donaldson 61; F. Robert 156ff. Hautecoeur 18 on hellenist. heroa: that of Philip, Arsineion of Samothrace, Mausoleum of Halikarnassos, Roman trophies; circular plan 19ff.
6. Smith (1) 67f. Coins of Byblos show Thea Ouraneia (statue) in a sort of shell-niche; in one type the roof seems pyramidal. At B. Egyptian influence was strong: Hill 59. See also 63 on Macrobius *sat.* i 21.5. And Heisenberg for rel. to Aelia Capitolina and the Holy Sepulchre.
7. Strab. xvii 1.15 and 2.4; *Herb.* (attrib. Apuleius) 67; Horace *odes* ii 7.22. Latin: *umbraculum.* Italian: *baldachino.*
8. Smith (1) figs. 102, 104; Sassanian, fig. 143. For Pergamon, cf. fig. 36 (church); and 228 (Parthian sanctuary), also L'Orange (3) 75.
9. *Numi agg. Alexandrini*, Coll. G. Dattini 1901 pl. xxxix/1132; Smith (1) fig. 105.
10. Smith (1) 69 figs. 110–11 etc.
11. Note starlike rosettes app. on vaults of Mykenean tombs; later the cosmic tent of Ion at Delphoi with heavenly embroideries. By classical period, several trads. of cosmic sacred tent round shores of E. Medit.
12. For Nero's Golden House: Lehmann; Herzfeld; Alfoldi (2); L'Orange (3); Smith (1) 82 etc. There is no need here to enter into the controversy as to how far Nero considered himself a sungod; his precise attitude is irrelevant to the general trend, which is undeniable.
13. Wirth 190 pl. 50; Smith (1) 53.
14. Smith (1) 83ff: ephods, tabernacle etc. Also Seyrig; Lammens (1–3).
15. *Moses* ii 15 on; cf. *spec. laws* i 66. Also *Isaiah* xl 22 and lxvi 1 (tent). More exs. of Philon's use of tab. as emblem: *Worse against better* xlvi; *Change of script. names* v; *Moses* iii 9; *Ten fests.* (the last).
16. Jos. *antiq.* iii 123ff.
17. Citing Smith (3) 118f; Lehmann (1). Ipsium: Pagenstecher (2) 194 fig. 119; Lehmann (1) 13 fig. 35; Ronczewski; Smith (1) 119 (sacred tent of Alexandreia, fig. 108). Striations: Smith (1) figs, 7, 79, 132 etc.
18. Diod. i 48.5 and 49.5 (based on Hekataios); Bataille 136–8.

19. *Post. of Cain* xxxi (104).

20. Smith (3) 149.

21. Gabbari: Delbrueck 79, 102 and Thiersch, pl. iii. Mex: Pagenstecher (2) 134ff pl. 1; Taposiris Magna, *ib.* 54 pl. iii and Breccia (1) 121ff; Hadra: Pagenstecher 84, 153. Infl. of Alex. dome at Tall Hinnon, Palestine: Smith (1) 57-9, figs. 75-81. Relations to Hadrian's villa: Smith (3) 145. Ciborium and domical vestibule in middle ages; *ib.* 152ff.

22. Andreani (1) and (2).

23. See F. Robert, 86f, 424f, 377f, 393f, 398, 126f; Heuzey 214f. Thermai: Reinach, *peint.* 109.4. See also Coptic relief described in ch. 19. For the god's epiphanies, Grabar 144ff; *Orphic hymns* xxix and l; Soph. *antig.* 1146ff, 1131 ff. Hut: Schreiber (2) 200.

24. Adreani (3) esp. 88-90 and figs. 44-5.

25. Néroutzos 102ff; same period. Ebers pl. 1.

26. Adreani (3).

27. Breccia (1) 104-14; von Bissing; Schreiber (2).

28. Von Bissing.

29. In so-called Hall of Caracalla, a large amount of skulls and bones; Botti thought refugees from C.'s massacre. No proof. For Anfucy: Breccia (1) 115-20. This is Ptolemaic, but lacks circular structures in its two important hypogaia. The paintings are of much interest, using Egyptian themes, also imitating stonework and foreshadowing the 1st Pomp. style.

For the apse at Luxor in imp. cult: de Villard. Earliest known ex. is perhaps that of Trajanic camp at Odruh in Arabian limes: Brünnow 439 fig. 531. There was a canopy at Luxor.

30. Smith (1) 53 figs. 30-1: mosaics at Gerasa. Grabar i 71-5.

31. *Ib.* 27 figs. 8-10, 23. Lazarus: Ferretto 236 fig. 40. Not all the early reliquary chapels, oratories, martyria were domical central structures with circ., polyg., sq., quatrefoil, trefoil plans. Between 4-6 cs. with the great expansion of the martyr cult, domical tombtypes were taken over from Roman sepulchral architecture and enlarged. Starry dome: Smith (1) figs. 14, 71, 73. Note shrine of St Menas in Maryut (W and SW of Alex.): earliest structure, catacomb of earthcut chambers with radiating loculi like Alex. catacombs (based on Ptol. and Roman tombs). Then "a small building like a tetrapylon" (*Enkomion*): prob. a four-square domed tomb, like the four-way arch or square chamber, type used early in Syria and Egypt (*e.g.* cemetery of El-Bagawat in Kharga oasis, square structures with spherical vaults). See further Warde Perkins (3): the later structures do not concern us here.

32. De Rossi; Smith (1) figs. 17-21.

33. Ampulla: *Germania* iii 1919 57, Abb. 3, *die gr. Äg. Samml. v. Sieglin* iii 1913 Abb. 106/2. Wulff no. 1403 pl. xlix; Kaufmann 143; Strzygowski 39 fig. 24. For inner sanct. of Ptol. temple reproducing anc. Eg. type of hut shrine: Smith (2) 121 pl. xxxii 4.

34. Smith (1) 119 fig. 48; Zahn pl. 41.

35. Niccolini nos. 96, 177.

36. Childhood: Grimal 323; garlands as the typical Alexandrian form of art-motive, 299, 304f; general 339f, 237–53.

18. THE TRIUMPH OF ALEXANDER AND DIONYSOS

1. I have written a work largely dealing with these issues, *The Clashing Rocks*, to appear 1965.

2. *Ditt. Syll.* (2nd ed.) 277 (S. 3rd, 323); IG xii 9.192; Michel *Rec.* 343. Boeckh (CIG 2144) dates to second war of Macedonians and Romans; Wila-mowitz, to liberation by Antigonos and Demetrios c. 313 B.C. (polemarch Aischylos has same name as an Eretrian who was member of faction devoted to those two: DL ii 140); Holleaux (*Ét. Ep. Hist.* i 41–73), c. 308, when troops of general Ptolemaios retreated from town and Boiotian League to which Eretria was joined had restored democracy. Polemarchs were magistrates of the B. League. See further T. Reinach REG xiii 1900 201; A. Wilhelm, *eph. arch.* 1892 129; Ziebarth in IG l.c.; Sokolowski (1), no. 46.

3. *Alex.* 38.

4. Max. Tyr. *logos* i 20 (3292).

5. Arr. *anab.* iii 3. 1–2; Str. xvii i.13; Kallisth. fr. 14.

6. Hyperides, *contra demosth.* xxxi 10 (20 Blass); Dinarch. *contra dem.* i 94; Timaios in Polyb. xii 12b; Ail. VH v 12; Gnomol. Vatic. 236 (Sternbach, *Wien. Stud.* x 221); Val. Max. vii 2 ext. 13; Athen. vi 251b; Plout. *pol. praec.* viii 804b (sneer of Pytheas); *Vit. x orat.* 842b. In general: Cerfaux 141 (Greek elements of heroisation, 141–3) with bibliog. 23ff; Tarn (6–9), Wilcken (3–5), Tondriau (2–3); Nock (3); Vallois (2) etc. Sparta: Ail. VH ii 19. Thirteenth god: Nock 22.

7. Plout. *apoth. reg., alex.* 27; Scott (3) 321. An interesting theme is the opposition of Diogenes-Alexander, but I have no space to treat its working-out.

8. Athen. xii 537e. Stripe: Q.C. iii 37; Plin. xxviii 102; Plout. *alex.* 51. Athen. links him with Commodus; goes on to sacs. to Dionysos when a satrap feasted the army (? during the return in 324). Note project to model Mt. Athos as statue: Plout. *de alex. fort.* 2 (335 de). Coins show Herakles into Alex., not vv: Gebauer 2. Not long after death, with horns of Ammon, *e.g.* coins of Lysima-chos: Hinks 9 and Macdonald pl. vi. 1; E. Neuffer, 40, thinks he wore the horns. For his features on the head of his tetradrachms: Macdonald pl. v. 13. (*c.* 300). Deinokrates, who wanted to make the Athos sculpture, appeared before Alex. at a banquet nude, with lionskin and club: Vitruv. pref. to ii.

9. Athen. x (434ab). Hostility of Asklepios: Arr. *anab.* vii 146; Pearson (1) 67.

10. Isokrates sees H. as man who gets worship as culture-hero of more than human achievement: Elter.

11. Athen. 538b–539b, cf. Ail. VH viii 7. Festal tent: Pearson (1) 53. Chares says heavy drinking at funeral of Kalanos due to Indian love of wine: Athen, x 437 ab; Plout. *alex.* 70; Ail. VH ii 41.

12. Plin. xxxv 81, 87, 105f; Berve ii 329 and i 94; Nock (3) 23. Note *Apollinem ac Dianam* in Plin. xxxv 108. Iconog. of Alex.: Perdrizet (4) i 104.

13. Karmania: Plout. *alex.* 67; Nock (3) 23; Wilcken (5) 205; Baege; Arr. *anab.* vi 28; Tarn (11) 416; Carfaux 154f; Pearson (1) 215ff; etc. Poetasters on the expedition, Tarn (6) ii 55–62; Q.C. viii 5.8, mentions Agis of Argos and Kleon of Sicily among these "who opened heaven to him, boasting that Hercules and Bacchus and Castor and Pollux would give way to the new god". Athen. xii 537d for Alex. knowing Euripides' *Andromeda* by heart: Dionysos' favourite play, Aristoph. *frogs* 52–4—scene in park at Babylon. Strabon on Alex. and Arabs, who had two gods, Zeus and Dionysos: xvi i.11.

Nysa as foundation of Alex.: FGH Müller ii 404; Diod. ii 38; Nock (3) 27 n31. As world wanderers, both Herakles and D. were said to have raised pillars in far east. For a recent effort to find in the Hindu Kush where Alex. struck the trail of Dionysos: Maraini.

14. Fr. 17 Jacoby ii 747, with note. Bacchic triumph: Q.C. iii 12.18, and viii 10 (Nysa: linking D. and Herakles), cf. ix 8; ix 2; ix 9; x 2; also Strab. xv 1.33 and 55; 58; Diod. xvii 72 (burning of Persepolis as a D. Triumph).

15. Alexander Theos: Nock (3). Dionysos of Ammon: Nock (3) 27f for refs. Ammon annexed to D. cycle; Carcopino (4) 301; Kern, *Orph. frag.* xliii 13.

16. Leon, Hermippos, Dionysios Skyt. and prob. Kleitarchos wrote in Egypt.

17. Quandt 17, cf. Cicero *inst. deor.* ii 62; D. with turreted crown, Lenzen 17ff.

18. Marius: Perioch. Liv. lxvii, cf. Dion K. xlviii 4; Val. Max iii 5–6; Plin. vii 191; Bruhl. Pomp.: Appian *mithr.* 115; Plout. *pomp.* 45–6; Plin. vii 95, cf. xxxvii 13. Caesar: Dion K. xliii 22, cf. Serv. *ecl.* v 29. Triumph of D. in general: Stat. *theb.* iv 656; *Latomus* 1964 pl. xv; L. Foucher 217–21.

19. Nock (3) 30–8 with refs.

20. Bevan 234; also called Gallus, castrate of Gt. Mother.

21. BGU 11774; Schubart (4); W. *Archiv* vi 413; Cichorius; Jesi (2). Satyros: Theoph. ad Autolyk.; Bruhl 84f. Alex. demes: Oxy. 2465, Bevan 99, Perdrizet (12) 236. Further for decree: Reitzenstein (4) 191, (5) 103ff; Cumont (1) 196; Nock 31, 74; Eitrem (1) 341. There may have been a separate decree for Alex. or the registry may have already had them under control. Seal: REg 577 and Seidl (2) 6. Lifelong status: BGU 1211.11. Perhaps the groups were *synodoi* earlier estab. by private initiative—see further Otto i 253, 257; San Nicolò i 21.

22. *Bull. Alex.* xix 126.

23. Nock (3) 38–41. Rosetta stone: Ditt. OGIS 90; Bevan 262; Murray, *Five Stages* 187; Wendland 123, etc.

Drinking contest of D. and Herakles: D. Levi (2) 15, 21; Morey 27; Hanfmann (2) pl. xxi.

24. This section mainly based on Tarn (9). I do not go into the difficult matter of Virgil's eclogue, but incline to set it at the Peace of Brindisi, though I

think the inner contradictions are rather the result of V.'s own confusions than of rewriting. Refs. for the Sibylline verses in Tarn, 136–143; translations J. Lindsay (3) 278f. See further Tarn for birth of Helios-Aion on Dec. 25th 144; Parthian rels. of Sun and Moon names, 158f. Coins: Grueber ii 502ff. Virgil: *den.* vii 685–8, 705f. For *homonoia*: Tarn (1) 2nd ed. 73ff, 84, 113, 116, and (10); Kramer. It had both a revolutionary aspect (Pergamon revolt and Iamboulos' utopia) and a conforming one (the State as the reconciler) as developed by later Stoics etc. (Goodenough etc.).

For the Asian revanche, note the prophecy of the Mad Praetor (2nd c. B.C.): Phlegon *mir.* 320. For Widow: Rzach (1) and (2); Lanchester. In general, Geffeken; Norden (2); Weber. Note that in Roman law Antonius could not marry a foreigner, so his marriage with Cleo. by the Makedonian rite meant nothing; in the Greek East these considerations would not however apply.

Early as Scipio Africanus (tale of his fathering by snake), ideas from Alexander's Sonship into west: Elter ii 1.40.17. Also Bruhl 86f. For expansion of Dionysiac cult: Quandt. Note Rhodian coins, 43 B.C. and later, showing Helios with ivywreath: BM C. Caria, 2631 pl. xlii 3, text fig. 1.

No need for refs. as to the eclogue, but I note d'Anto's essay, and think he is generally correct. The stress is on Octavia and her offspring (a child, peace) rather than on the males.

25. Hathor-Isis: Otto and Bengtson 74 n1. Isis: Plout. *ant.* 54; Dion K. 49: Vandebeek 75; Tarn (9) 139. Arsinoe II was also called Isis (SB 601–2; OGIS 31—*Mitt. Athen.* xix 234 admits *Isidi* is possible): Kleo. III had a priest as Isis Megale Meter Theon (Dem. Leid. 185: *Rev. Eg.* i 1880 91; ZAS xxxvii 38; Otto (1) i 158. Neotera: Oxy. 1449, Nock (3) and HTR xli 1948 213–15. Moretti (2) identified N. with Nephthys, cf. JEA xlvi 96 no. 13.

Suicide; J. G. Griffiths (4). Dendera: Jéquier pl. 57.; Bevan fig. 62; Otto and Bengtson 74 n1; Griffiths (4) 118. Hermonthis: Otto ii 280; Jéquier pl. 57. Bull: Tarn (12) and Fairman (2) ii 13. On bearing Caesarion she struck coins of herself as Isis with child Eros: RE xi 754.41.

For a caricature of her and M.A., JEA i 99 pl. xiv.

Note that Clem. Alex., *protr.* i 2.6. says, "God in the Bosom" is a term used by the adepts of the Mysteries of Sabazios. "This is a snake passed through the bosom of the initiates." Cf. Louk. *alex.* 15. It is thus a ritual-mime of immortality. But one cannot press the point and argue Cleo. was uniting rite and actual death; the Egyptian aspects are the key-thing, but there may be a lingering subnote of Dionysiac rebirth. (Inscription to M.A. as "his god" by one of his *synodos*: OGI 195.)

26. Bruhl 84f; Theoph. HP iv 4.1; Macrob. *sat.* i 19.1; Arr. *anab.* vi 27. *Thriambos*: sv Souidas (4 poss. origins); Diod. iv. 5; Athen. i 30b; Voigt 1076.

27. Lenzen 14–17 for development of frontality in treatment; C. Robert, etc. Epiphanies of D. etc. see n3 ch. 17 above. Epiphany as procession: Foucart (2) 163f, (3) 176f, (4) 130, 141, (5) 111. BCH vii 35. Whittemore 549f. Women in Dionysiac epiphaneiai: Whittemore 551. For a *kore propolos Dionysou* of

Alex. origin: CIG xiv 1366; Cumont (1) 198, cf. Foucart (5) 238 no. 65, 239; also nos. 8, 25, 38, 65 etc.: nos. 6, 7, 9, 26, 43.

28. Lenzen; Liapounova.

29. *Musées de l'Alg. et de Tun.*: Aloui, suppl. 1910 pl. xi; Sousse 1902 pl. vi; Oran, pl. vii. Cf. Nonnos xvii 19, 21.

30. Strzygowski no. 7292a pl. iii.

31. Matz 760; *Dionys.* xxxviii 80–2; Lenzen 22f.

32. In general RE v 671.42ff; 674.56 (agreement of Dionys. Skyt., source of Diod. i 17–20, and Apollod. *lib.*); diffusion, Christ-Schmidt ii 967.

33. *Virtues and office of ambassadors* xi–xv. D. as hero: *Dionys.* vii 94ff.

19. THE DIONYSIAC WORLD

1. Kallistratos, *descr.* 1. His date: Reisch, intro, pp. xxii–xxiii; W. Meyer. After Alex., it was common to put together different statues of related subjects, For satyr, cf. that in Villa Borghese, Brunn-Bruckmann no. 435. For Dionysos and Poetry: Lauer and Picard.

2. Diod. i 27.5.

3. Harder; Nock (4). Dedicator Ligyris (?form of Ligyrios) may be author.

4. *Date of Nonnos*: Keydell; Lind (3): Ludwich, *praef.* of edition, pp. v–x (asserting N. drew on Greg. of Naz. and finding a ref. to his period in Eunapios, *vit. soph.*); Christ-Schmid-Stählin, vii 2 965–71; Friedländer (3); Lubker 715,338; Krumbacher i 8 266.

Note that Planudes in his copy of Nonnos' *Gospel of John* (Cod. Marc. 481) names its author Ammonios (Alex. philosopher of second half 5 c.) or Nonnos. Seems a connection of the two men: Maas (2). See Lind (3) for possible links of N.'s Christian position and 5c. controversies. Pamprepios: Korte; Page no. 140 etc. (I hope to treat Pamprepios at length in a further volume.)

Note that Berytos was intact when N. wrote; it was destroyed by earthquake in 529. Eudokia's *Violarium* mentions N. but is a 16c. fabrication.

Min: reps. in Capart, *Les départs de l'art* 257; Sethe, *Urgeschichte* 17; Lanzone pl. 332. Temples: Lefébure. We cannot doubt the existence of phallic rites in Roman Egypt, since they have continued into the 20th century. "The penis made of whipcord or leather, and several feet in length, is still a prominent feature at all the great festivals in Egypt, and especially in the Delta," Budge (1) 431n. We have a votive epigram (3rd c. B.C., Upper Egypt?) to Pan Euagros as Min: Householder. Intercourse: Fairman (1) 85. Burials: Carcopino (3) and Cumont (1) 61,228 n62.

Kanopos was given the remains of St Kyros after the temples of Sarapis and Isis were made monasteries, as many people stuck to paganism and regretted the old days.

Coptic Dionysos: Whittemore (1) for full discussion. Architect. form: cf. Deir el Abyad (White Monastery), Mosque of Bawit. Also Duthuit pl. xxx c, xxxv ab; Drioton (5) pl. i; Quibell pl. xxxvii 2; Gayet pl. iv 7. In less dynamic form: in the Italian Renascence. Siverskaia: Reinach, *rels*. iii 496.3, cf. Quardt 108, 112, 128 etc. Sculpture: Strzygowski (2) pl. iii. Head: Drioton (5) 87–9. TCs: Perdrizet (10) pl. iii–iv. See also Brooklyn mus. no 189. Bull-chariot: note Bacchos and Ariadne in bull-drawn biga, terracotta metope from Paestum: Reinach iii 485.3. Also his *stat*. i 391; v 2,476.5; *vases* i 18.3–4; 81.7, 159a; 182.1; 488.1–2; ii 196.1; rel. iii 49 (rams); *peint*. 108.2 (centaurs)—for various animals. Cf. Quandt 111, 187, 199, 223; Cumont, *Doliche* 200f.

Whip as solar symbolism (syncretism): Whittemore 547f. Julian: *or*. vii; Cumont (1) 204. Paulinus, *carm*. xix 169ff (PL lxi 525). Justinian: Pargoire 12; Diehl 552ff; P. N. Ure, *J. and his age* 1951 150; Procop. *de bello pers*. i 19 (Bonn 104). For Dionysiac survivals, 62nd Canon, Council in Trullo, 692; Zonaras, etc.

5. Wilfstrand esp. 35–74; and RE sv *Nonnos* 912.

6. JEA 1962 149; xli 138 no. 42; xlii 111 no. 34; J. and L. Robert, *Bull*. 1955 no. 57; Hanssens for Eg. origin.

7. Kenyon, *Album Grat. in hon. H. van Herwerden* 1902 137; *Archiv* ii 351, vii 3, ix 222; *Phil. Woch*. xxiii 1903 23, and 1929 1101; Milne (2) no. 40; *Rev. de Philol*. xxvii 1903 82; *Byz. Zeit*. xxix 383; *Eranos* 1930 102; Knaack; RE xvii 1 1936 902f; Page no. 134. Also, *Gött. Nach*. 1923 24–6.

Note Antinop. ii 58: hex. poem with some suggestions of Nonnos (account of serpent: cf. *Dionys*. i 185, v 144, vi 155, vii 328, xii 319, xxv 402, xxxv 209, xxxviii 354, xl 476, xliv 106, xlv 137, 310), but the proparoxytone endings in lines 11, 14, and elision, l. 12, are non-Nonnan.

8. Reitzenstein (3) 47; Cumont (5); Bidez; Page no. 135. The argument as to myth. figures in contemp. epic had a long history, cf. Petronius *sat*., Lucan etc. The attribution of this and the next to Soterichos is very conjectural.

9. Reitzenstein (3) 53; Bidez; Page no. 136.

10. Lit. sources: Koehler; Castiglione (2–3).

Astrology: Stegemann; W. Koch; Rose in Rouse i 42f, 240–3.

11. Some similes: xxii 171 (torrent), 334 (anvil), 348 (moon); xxix 157 (curdling figjuice); xxxii 153 (seastorm); xxxiv 252 (shepherd); xxv 245 (dream); xli 256 (moon); xlii 6 (star), 185 (ox, gadfly); xliii 270 (circus). Lind (7) 60 likes the similes and cites some further. For N. and the epyllion: d'Ipollito. Contrast Q. Smyrn. with his inordinate number of similes.

12. *Dionys*. viii 209f; xxxiv 12; ii 131–5. Cf. the ship-phrases with Norse scaldic kennings: B. S. Phillpotts, *Edda and Saga*, 27.

13. *Ib*. ii 181.

14. *Ib*. iii 66.

15. *Ib*. iv 194.

16. *Ib*. v 410f.

17. Braune; Keydell (4) and d'Ipollito on infl. of Ovid whose *Met*. ends with Pythag. ideas; physical evolution (4 elements); volcanoes and earthquakes; met. of animals; evolution of people in history; moral not to eat flesh; then legends of Latium ending with tale of general who grew horns; arrival of

Aesculapius in Rome, murder-apotheosis of Caesar. Epitaphs: Kaibel (2) 548.3–4 (cf. Perdrizet BCH xxiv 1900 300); 569.5–10; 194.7; 547a 1–6 and Coppola. CIL 1184.12–8 (cf. CLE 1313). SB 366, 373, 391 (tears). Lattimore 131f, 136, 180 in general. Note Brelich, 39–44: Dionysiac basis in link of flowers and dead; though there is little evidence for it in epitaphs, there is an element of truth in the idea. Sardeis: Cumont (2) 26 n5; cf. *Aen.* vi 883–5; lily-cures, Plin. xxi 19 (74) 126. Note Plin. xxi 19 (75) 128–9 for narcissus; Deonna (4) 43. The violet was a flower of immortality, born of Attis' blood; it was put on tombs so that the dead might share in his resurrection: Cumont (6) 45. For hyacinthos and its cures: Plin. xxi 26 (97) 170. Cf. the stress on scent in poem on p. 305.

18. *Dionys.* vii 279.

19. *Ib.* xxxii 296; cf. i 156f (snow and fire).

20. *Ib.* ii 258ff.

21. *Ib.* vi 265ff.

22. *Ib.* xliii 70ff, 186ff; water and fire, xxiii.

23. *Ib.* xxiii 284ff.

24. *Ib.* i 396ff, cf. xxiv 319f; xxxii 54; xxxvi 97ff; xxxviii 349f.

25. *Ib.* ii 650ff.

26. *Ib.* xxxviii 412ff.

27. *Ib.* ii 700ff.

28. *Ib.* xlviii 739–41: *komos zoarios*.

29. War: xxviii 167ff; xxviii 275, 296; xxix 237; xxx 118. Seasons: end of xi. Zeus and Sem.: viii 371 and opening viii.

30. *Ib.* opening xiii; viii 88f. Heedless: *lathiphron.* Cf. xiv 36ff; xlvi 96; opening xlvii; xxxi 223; xxxiv 38; xxxv 145 etc.

Indian Dionysos. There is a strong case for an identification having been made between Dionysos and Rudra. Megasthenes, in his visit to India, saw a Dionysiac cult in that of Rudra-Shiva and transformed the mythical exploits of countless Rudra of the forests into the military progress of Dionysos across the mountains of India. The identification seems to have become general; the representations of Dionysos on the bilingual coins of the Greek kings of the Indus show Shiva rather than Dionysos.

Rudra has his bands, his *marya.* He is "surrounded and served by the Yakshas and by a host of genii of nature and of diverse forms . . ." (Barth, *Les religions de l'Inde* 149). In general Grégoire 155ff. The armies of Rudra, haunting the forests. attack men with swords and arrows; these become the Dionysiac host. For coins: Tarn, *Greeks in Bactria*, 392.

20. WORLD WITHIN WORLD

1. D. M. Robinson and Beattie; B. for *zteraion* and rels. to twisting, braiding, embroidering. The *seir-* root is in *kalasiris* (Herod.), the long tasselled robe of Egyptian men. For Sparta: Beattie (2), Sokolowski (1) no. 28, LGS ii 63, Boeckh CIG 15. Patrai: Sokolowski (1) no. 33 (cosmetics using, *psemythious-*

thai, seems related to Egyptian *psimthi*). Note sc. *Oid. Kol.* 681. Andania: LGS ii 58; IG v 1, 1390. Lykosoura: LGS ii 63; IG v 2, 514. Kios: Sokolowski (2) 6. At Patrai flute-playing also forbidden: cf. Smyrna (Dionysos Bromios) Sokolowski (2) 84, 17; Eur. *phoin.* 791; Ploɯt. *mor.* ii 277f, iii 406a.

For Arkadia, further: Woodhead; Jeffery; Buck 196 no. 16; Guarducci; LGS ii 58, 15–26; Sokolowski (2) nos. 6, 16, 35, 77, 79, 84 and (1) 28, 33, 56, 91; *La parola del passato* 1957 443; Wächter 15–24.

2. *Kypria* in Athen. xv 682df; sacred robe in Nonnos: xli 295; ii 166f, *aithera daidallousa*; xl 416.

3. Liddell-Scott sv. *Poikilma* for embroideries, *Il.* vi 294. Cosmic: Plat. *rep.* 529c; cf. sphaira, *phaid.* 110b. Poikile: Paus. i 151; v 11.6.

4. *Dionys.* vi 179 (*eikelos*); xix 200; xxix 326f; ii 595, 602 (cf. v 580); i 23f (same phrase of Proteus xliii 246); ii 570–6; xxxvi 339f; xlvi 102; xl 385, *charassetai*; xxxix 61f; xlvi 326ff (Aktaion), *alloios* and *allophyes*.

5. *Jos.* vii (32).

6. *Dreams* i 37–9 (213ff).

7. *Alleg. interp.* ii 18–19 (71–8).

8. *Ib.* (75).

9. *Dionys.* v 338; vi 176, *allophyes morphouto*; xxvi 37; xxxiii 349f (xl 6, 8: she assumed "a manly shape, the form of Morrheus"); ix 157; xxxi 100f; xiv 69, 71; xiv 176f. Cf. xxix 309, hornstrong shape; xxxi 53, deceptive shape of serpent, etc.

10. *Ib.* xl 74–8; xli 245f; xlv 119f; v 594ff, *automatos*; xlii 74ff; x 35, 42–4. For mirror: cf. vi 207.

11. *Ib.* v 341f.

12. *Ib.* xxviii 289f, 296 (*helisson* and *eilipodes*); xxix 219ff; xlii 333–5, 341–2; xxx iii 291, 302f. Cranes: xxxvi 36—xvi 63; xix 321. Hands: xix 227. Poseidon: i 124. Mask: xxvii 230. Persephone: xxix 169–73.

13. *Ib.* xviii 115; xl 416; xix 248.

14. *Ib.* xxxvi 294ff, *allophanes morphouto*. Zosimos: see discussion Ho Ping-Yu 195; Berthelot i 163, 165; iii 196; Sherwood Taylor JHS 1930 109.

15. Sun and Moon: xl 375–7: Sun, "you bring forth the threefold image of the motherless Moon, while dewy Selene milks her antitypal light from your fruitful beam"; xviii 71f: "a much-intricate brightness likecoloured to the Sun and antitypal Moon". More exs. of type: xii 184f; xvii 236, 240; xvi 65 etc. Ares etc.: viii 39; xxx 79; xxv 420; xxxviii 532.

Typos as legal term: RT(1) 397 n6; cf Ryl. 75 (late 2 c.), principle of judgment; Oxy. 893, ordinance.

The Stoics had developed the notion of the *typos*. Kleanthes' definition, which Zenon seems to have taken over, was that "presentation is an impression, *typosis*, on the soul or on the *hegemonikon*" (dominant part of soul): Sext. Emp. *pyrrh. hyp.* ii 70. We are told that Kleanthes took *typosis* in a literal way, a definite impress like that of a signet-ring on wax, but Chrysippos rightly saw this as mechanistic. One impression would simply destroy another. So he worked out a more dialectical notion of *heteroiosis*: presentation as a change or modification, an "othering" of the soul: Sext. Emp. *adv. math.* vii 372; Sambursky (1) 25f. This comes closer to Nonnos with his *typos-antitypos,* one blow affecting and transforming another; cf. his terms like *allophyes* in defining transformation.

The Stoics saw the universe as *autarkes,* self-sufficient, spontaneous in its totality, but interlinked causally in its parts: Sambursky, 51, 114. Nonnos attributes to each part the potentiality of the whole. Where he again, however, approaches the Stoics is in their notion of tensional movement: see the passage of Philon at end of ch. 6. There the image of tensional movement is circular and spiral; Nonnos' Dionysiac spirals also are tensional movements linking all things and creating structure as well as the collisions of transformation.

For the alchemic notion of united opposites as creating movement and transformation: Kleopatra's *Making of Gold*: "One is the Snake that has venom after two matings" *synthemata*: J. Lindsay (2) 427. Note the snake-spiral here as well.

We may note that the Stoics had the clue to the point of dialectical break in the circle that created the spiral, but could not develop it. Sambursky notes Clement of Alex. telling "of the distinction between the asymmetrical cause-effect relation and the symmetrical relation of mutual cause and interaction", 82 (*Strom.* viii 9). But we can hardly expect the Stoics, the ancient mathematicians, and Nonnos to have solved problems that are still beyond Quantum Mechanics. These points however help us to grasp the great dynamic behind Nonnos' imagery. The idea of Olympiodoros (the last important leader of the neoplat. school at Alex., early 6th c.) that "everything is contained in everything" (Arnim iii 302: cf. Anaxagoras, fr. 4, Diels 59B4), has certain links with Nonnos' notion of spontaneous growth and the inner forces of transformation.

Note *helix* was used of screw-windlass for launching ships (also treadmill to raise water), planetary orbits, volute on capital of column, convolutions of ear or bowels, spiral of shell—or of a child's ball, a staff (cf. twisted column). Note also Lind (5) on Nonnos xix and use of *graphein, katagrapho* in figurative sense of drawing pictures on air; also xxx 108–117; and xix 219 *charasson*.

16. Dreams: xlvii 148ff, "Ikarios' soul drifted like smoke to Erigone's room; a light phantom, with mortal shape, of a shadowy dream-apparition (*opope*); xviii 171ff, D. "busy in deceitful image of a dreambattle", sees a prophetic form of his "mimic battle" with Lykourgos: a lion leaps from a rock on him as he dances, he flees under water, the lion chases the thyrsos-bearing women, but a bacchante muzzles it with vinecord, Artemis tries a rescue, lightning strikes the lion and makes him "a blind vagabond on the roads".

17. *Ib.* xlii 208, cf. 216f; xl 403ff.

18. *Nothos,* some exs.: in simple sense, xlviii 18, xlvi 35, viii 91, xlv 79, i 295, i 31, iii 384, xxxi 139. Counterfeit, linked with dreamprocess, magical and divine transformation: iii 318, lii 323, xiii 215, xvi 63ff (well-fledged bastard bird: arrow. "I'd rather be the liquid type of Danae's loves"), xii 49, xxxiii 291. In the normal formulas of transformation: xlii 385, v 416 and 528.

Delusion: x 11f, x 35–44. Hardly more than imitative: xxvi 117f with *typos technemon.* More exs. of counterfeit with varying shades: i 521, xxxvi 68 and 72f, xliv 287ff, xlv 258f, vi 198, xlii 37, viii 325, xxx 89, xxix 125, xxxi 218 and 220, ii 109, xxxix 337, xlvii 717f ("she put off her bastard shape and resumed her divine form"), iv 71f ("she put off the type of a heavenly face and assumed a body like a girl of the vicinity"). What exactly is (xiii 242) the "bastard passion for the strange land"? The account of Phaethon (xxxviii 174ff) shows the mime: "With skilled joinery he made a wooden axle, bent a rounded type for the cheating car, fashioned yokestraps, made a threetwined leash of withies from the blossoming garden, and put a new sort of bridles on four young rams. Then he made a bastard wellconstructed Morning Star, wheel-round, from a bunch of white flowers, and fixed it before his spoke-wheeled waggon, to stand for the type of the Evening Star. He set burning torches to stand about his hair on every side and mimicked his father with fake-rays as he drove round and round the coast of the seagirt isle."

19. *Post. Cain* xxvi (93); 94 stresses the seal-image. The term for opposites is *enantioi typoi.*

20. *Noah's work* xi (44–5). Stamped: *charachtheis.* Cf. *Alleg. Int.* i 18 (61–2): "The dominant part in us that has received it (wickedness) is actually in the *paradeisos,* but on the other hand is virtually not in it; for the typos of the wicked is alien to a place of divine sunrising." People in unconsecrated places are really in the most sacred ones "when forming images (*phantasioumenoi*) of all that pertains to virtue"; others, though in consecrated spots, are profane in mind when their mind takes on inclinations to the worse "and bad *typoi*". More on character, *ib.* iii 32 (97ff); cf. image in iii 34 (104), and end of 64 (183). The platonic idea of earthly things as a mimema of heavenly (*e.g.* Philon *ib.* i 14 (45)) does not exist in Nonnos; mimema is always for him contained within the organic process. Hence the archetype, so important for Philon, does not occur in his poem.

21. The phrase is originally military: Chrysost. in 2 *Cor. hom.* ii *ad fin*; cf. *Nota Militum*, Augustine *de bapt.* i 4.

22. Liddell-Scott for both *typos* and *antitypos*; *ant. mimema*: exact counterpart, *Or. Syb.* i 33, viii 270; in mental relation, Plot. ii 9.6. As opposite: as far back as Theognis 1244 (craft opp. of *pistis*). Some more ex. of antitype in N.: ii 344f; xvii 203f; xvii 65f (landscape); viii 201ff.

23. *Alleg. interp.* iii 19 (60ff).

24. *Ib.* 31 (116–20).

25. *Ib.* 50 (77–81).

26. *Drunkenness* xli (170); changes, metabolai.

27. Equip., *kataskeue*; food and mode, *trophai* and *diaitai*; act. and movements, *energeia* and *kinesis*; dist. qual., *idiotai*—cf. Stoic stress on *to idion.*

28. Bacchus as Matter of the Stone: S. Hutin, *Hist. of Alchemy* 1962 30. Squid: *Dionys.* i 278–80. The extent to which Nonnos is drawing together and generalising elements already present in Greek thought is brought out by com-

paring his idioms with that used by Apollodoros in his fourth book of *Parthian History* where he describes the embracing sprays of plant that he calls a sort of myrtle but which may have been jasmine. "When separate sprays meet *automatos*, they stay united in an embrace like that of animate (conscious, *empsychon*) beings." Athen. xv 682d. (The reading is difficult: Loeb ed. vii 115nb.)

29. *E.g.* efforts to make D. the god of light v. the dark Indians; apostle of Hellenic culture v. barbarians. But such ideas can only have a hopelessly vulgarised force in N.'s imperial world.

30. *Dionys.* xlviii 752ff.

31. *Ib.* x 169–74. Some faint tinges of archetype, *e.g.* wine is "the earthly type of heavenly nectar," xii 159, xvii 75f.

FURTHER NOTE

Only a Concordance could bring out the full complexity and inter-relatedness of Nonnos' diction. Here however are some further instances of the key-words.

First, *auto*-forms: i 308, thunderbolts; ii 434, hand; v 185, dolphins: vi 186, tail cf. xxi 210; vi 369f, ship; xii 312, mist; xxv 376, precinct; xli 279, cosmic house; xxxix 336, dolphin and xxxix 397, fire, *autoeliktos*; xxxv 295 wheel (like Tantalos traversing skies); xlii 97, nectar; xliv 43, miraculous sweat on image; xlvi 140, gates; ii 259, bar of Olympos, *autoeliktos*; iv 427, dragon's teeth; viii 103, selfborn Athena; iii 367, Nile; v 166, sunfire; v 370, rumour; viii 87, Dionysos; ix 157, Phanes; vii 73, Time; xii 297 and xxxvi 364, vines (*helix*); xxxvi 306, tree; vii 228 and xii 58, a birth; xiii 101, birth from urine; xii 185, orchard of vines; xii 185, selftaught, also viii 29, and xxiv 231, poet; xl 508, nautilus (antitypal *mimema*); viii 173, selfbidden; viii 309, thunder self-announcing symbol, cf. ix 240; xvi 286, breeze; xl 119 selfslain; xliv 129, boughs; xlvii 18, grapes.

See Philon, *alleg. inter.* iii ix (30), where a universe *automatizon* means the absence of all deity. Note also that *automatizein* can mean to prophesy spontaneously: JHS 1962 145.

Some exs. of *doloplokos*: i 413, tune; ii 7, plan; ii 27f; ii 602, magic; iv 76, tongue; transformation, vii 210. Also viii 108, 121–7; viii 336; xvii 12, drug; xxxiii 148; 201; xxxv 313; xl 165; xlii 120; 208; 217; xlv 248; xlviii 7; xlvii 334; xlv 158; xlvi 45 (with magic), xxxvii 395.

Poietos: xliii 406; cf. xxxviii 205; xxxi 71; xxxi 151.

Apatelios, epiklepos: xvii 25; xxxi 214; xxxiii 298.

Pseudo-: ii 570; iii 323; v 157; v 568 and 597; viii 39 and 325; xxxi 218; xxxiii 366; xxxvi 343; xxxviii 173.

Emphron: xiii 487 (spear); xxxv 1 ("Muse, fight anew the wise war with conscious thyrsos"—wise having much same sense); xxxvi 72 (bear); xxxvii 395 plan (as web).

For Calendar, Money, Glossary (officials etc.): see *Daily Life in Roman Egypt.*

Bibliography

AA: see Youtie (3). AC: *L'Antiquité Classique*. Albizzati: *Rend. di Pont. Accad. Rom.* v (1926-7: 1928). Alexander, P. J.: HCP 1938 144. Alföldi, A. (1) *A Festival of Isis in Rome under the Christian Emps. of 4 c.* 1937 (2) *R. Mitt.* I 1935 128. Altheim, F., *Hist. of Rom. Relig.* 1938 (2) *Terra Mater.* Amann, E., *Dict. de theol. cath.* xi 1931 793-5. Amélineau, *Les Moines ég., La vie de Schnoudi* 1889. Amelotti, M., *Studia et Dic. Hist. Iuris* 1955 123-56. Andreani, A. (1) *Ann. du Mus. GR. d'Alex.* 1933-4 (2) *ib.* 1934-5 (3) *ib.* 135-9 (1940) (4) *Rep. d'arte dell'Egitto GR* i 1961. Anto. V. d', *Latomus* 1964 258ff. AP = Anthologia Palatina. Arkwright, JHS 1911 259-75. Arnim, J. von, *Stoic. vet. frag.* 1921. Audollent, A., *Defixionum Tabellae* 1904. Austin, R. G. (1) *Antiquity* 1949 257-78 (2) *Arch. Camb.* Dec. 1938. Avezou and Picard, BCH xxxviii 1914 38-62. Aymard, J., *Essai sur les chasses rom.* 1951.

Barb, A. A. (1) *J. of Warburg and C. Inst.* xvi 193-238 (2) *ib.* xxii 367-71 (3) *Hommages W. Deonna* 1957 (Abraxas). Baedecker, *Eg. and Sudan* (8th) 1929. Baege, W., *Diss. Phil. Hal.* xxiii 1 78ff. Baehni, C., *Musées de Genève,* fev. 1953. Bardon, H., *Les emps. et les lettres rom.* Barnett, R. D., *Listener* 26 Aug. 1954 (Assyr. Lion-hunt). Bataille, A. (1) *Les Memnonia* 1952 (2) *Inscrs. gr. du temple de Hatshepsout* 1951. Baudi, L.; *Aeg.* xvii 1937 349-451. Bayet, J. (1) *Hercule rom.* (2) *Mél. ec. fr.* xxxviii 1920 106ff (arcadisme rom.). Baynes, C., *A Coptic Gnostic Treatise.* BCH: *Bull. Corr. Hellénique.* Beare, W., *The Roman Stage* 1955. Beattie, A. J., CQ 1947 66-72. Beckerath, J. v., *Tanis u. Theben* 1951. Bell, H. I. (1) *Egypt* 1956 (2) *Jews and Christians* 1924 (3) *Abinnaeus Archives* (with Martin etc.) 1962. Bénédite, *Temple de Philai.* Bérard. J., MR 1936 151ff. Berger: *Z. f. Rechtwiss.* xxix 1913 394. Bernand, A. and E., *Inscrs. gr. et lat. du Col. de Memnon* 1960. Berthelot and Ruelle, *Coll. des. anc. Alchimistes grecs* 1888. Berve, H., *Das Alexanderreich auf prosopograph. Grundlage.* Bevan, E., *Hist. of Eg. under Ptol. dyn.* 1927. Beyen, H. G., *Pomp. Wandd.* i. Bickermann, E., *Das Edikt den k. Caracalla* 1926. Bidez, *Rev. Phil.* xxvii 1903 81. Bieber, M. (1) *Hist. of Gr. and R. Theater* 1961 (2) *Denkmäler zum Theaterwesen in Alt.* 1920. Bilabel, F., *Gr.-äg. Feste, N. Heid. J.* 1929. Bilinski, B. (1) *L'agonistica sportiva nella gr. ant.* 1959 (2) *Meander* 1951 347ff (3) *ib.* 1955 257ff (4) *Protrept. de Galeno.* Binsfeld, W., *Grylloi* 1956. Bissing, F. von, *Basreliefs de Kom el-Choufaga.* Blackman, A. M., JEA iii 1916 33. Blackman, W. S., *The Fellahin of Upper Egypt.* Blanchet, A., *Rev. de Num.* 1941 5ff. Boak, TAPA lxviii 1937. Bogner, H., *Philologus* lxxxix 1934 320-33. Bonneau, D., *La crue du Nil* 1964. Bonnet, (1) *RE d. äg. Religionsgesch.* 1952 sv Seth (2) *Studies in Magical Amulets.* Bourguet, A., *De rebus Delph. Imp. Aetatis* 1905. Brady, T. A. (Gymn. in Ptol. Eg.) *Phil. Stud. W. Miller* 1936 15ff. Brandt,

P., *Corpusculum poesis epicae gr. ludibundae* ii 1888. Bratschkova, M. (Muschel in d. ant. kunst) *Bull. de l'Inst. arch. bulgare.* xii 1938 1ff. Braune, J., *Nonnos u. Ovid* 1935 (*Greifswalder Beiträge*). Breccia, E. (1) *Alex. ad Aegyptum* (2) *Encicl. Ital.* sv Cleopatra (3) Cronos Mitraico in *Mél. Maspero* ii 1935–7 (4) *Terracotte.* Brelich, A.: *Aspetti della morte nelle iscr. sepol. d. Imp. rom.* 1937. Broneer, O., *Univ. Calif. Pubs. in Class. Ant.* i 305ff. Brooklyn Mus. *Pagan and Christian Eg.*, 1941. Broughton, T. R. S., *Roman Asia* (Econ. Surv. Rome iv). Brown, B. R., *Ptol. Paintings* 1957. Bruhl, A., M.R., xlvi 1929 75–95. Brunn-Bruckmann, *Denkmäler gr. u. röm. Sculptur.* Brunnow, R. E. (with A. von Domaszewski), *Die Prov. Arabia* i 1904. Bruyère, B., *Fouilles IFAO, Rapps. prélim.* 1924ff (Deir el-Medineh). BSAC: *Bull. soc. d'arch. copte.* Budge, E. A. W. (1) *From Fetish to God* 1934 (2) *Greenfield Pap. in B.M.* 1912 (3) *BM Guide to Eg. Galleries* 1909. Bulle, H., *Abh. Bayen, Ak. wiss. p.h. Kl.* xxxiii 1928. Buschor, *Gr. Vasen* 1940. Butler, *Post-Aug. Poetry.*

Cabrol, *Dict. ant. chrét.* Caetani-Lovatelli, *La festa della rosa.* Capart, J. (1) *Une rue de tombeaux à Saqqarah* (2) *L'art égyptien, les arts graphiques* 1942. Carcopino, J. (1) *In mem. Lui V. Parcan* 1934 (2) REA lv 1953 196f (3) *Ét. d'hist. chrét.* (4) *La Basilique pythag.* 1954 (5) *Aspects mystiques de la Rome paienne* 1952. Castiglioni (1) *Rend. d. R. Inst. Lombardo di Sc. e Let.* lxv 1932 309–37 (2) *Ann. d. R. Scuola Norm. sup. di Pisa, Filos. e Filol.* xx 2 1907 (3) *Studi crit . . . a Carlo Pascal* (Actaeon e Artemis). Cataudella, Q. (1) CE vii 1932 332 (2) *Atene e Roma* xii 1916 40–68. CCAG: *Catal. Codicum Astrol. Gr.* CE: *Chronique d'Ég.* Chamberlayne, L. P., *Studies in Philol.* xiii 1916 40–68. Chamoux, *Les. Ét. Class.* xviii 1950. Chapot, V., *La Colonne torse et le décor en hélice dans l'art ant.* 1907. Charbonneaux, *Libyca* ii 1954 59ff. Charlesworth, M. P., *Docs. illustr. reigns of Claudius and Nero* 1939. Charpouthier, *Études cret., v, Mallia* 1938. Christiansen, R. T., *Studies in Irish and Scand. FTs* 1959. Christ-Schmid, *Gesch. gr. Lt.* (6th ed.). Cichorius, *Röm. Stud.* 1922. CLE: *Carmina Latina Epigraphica* (Buecheler 1895–7; Lommatzsch, 1926). Cube, G. von, *Die röm. Scaena Frontis in pomp. Wandbildern vierten Stils.* Cohen, *Médailles imperiales.* Collart, P. (1) *Pap. Bouriant* (2) with Jouguet in RL 101–21 (3) *Nonnos de Panopolis* 1930 (4) BCH lv 1931 58–69. Collignon, M. (1) *Mon. Piot* xxii 1918 163ff (2) *CR Acad. Inscrs.* 1916 337ff (Eg. statuettes rep. Alexandreia). Coppola, *Rend. Acc. Lincei* vii 1931 388–437. Corte, M. della (1) *Cleopatra, M. Antonio e Ottaviano* 1951 (2) *Case e Abitanti di Pompeii* (2nd) 1954. Costa, G., *Bilychnis, Riv. mens. di studi relig.* xxxvi 1931 143–55 (Nonnos). Cougny, *Appendix Nova Epigram.* 1890. Cullmann, O., *La problème litt. des écrits ps.-clémentins.* Cumont, F. (1) *Relig. orientales* 1929 (2) *Recherches sur le symb. funéraire* 1942 (3) *L'Ég. des astrologues* 1937 (4) *Rev. d'instruct. publ. en Belgique* xl 1899 1–12 (Palchos) (5) REA iv 1902 36 (6) *Lux perpetua* 1949 (7) *La stèle du danseur d'Antibes et son décor végétal* 1942. Curtius, L. (1) *Röm. Mitt.* 1933 182ff (2) JDAI xliii 1928 281–97.

Dalton, *Cat. Christian Antiq. B.M.* Damiani, G. F., *L'ultimo poeta pagano* 1902. Daressy, RT xxxiv 1912 189–93. David, M. and B. A. van Groningen, *Papyrological Primer* 1952. Davies, N. M., JEA xxiv 1938 25ff. Dawson, *Aeg.* vii 1926 130. Debono, *Cah. d'hist. ég.* ix 1957 44. Delatte, *Herbarium.* Delbrueck, R., *Hellenist. Bauten im Latium* ii 1907–12. Delorme, F., *Gymnasion* 1960. Denis, A., *Cats of the World* 1964 (ch. 1). Deonna, W. (1) RA 1960 ii (2) *Rev. hist. religs.* cxix 53–81 (soif des morts) (3) *Le symbolisme de l'acrobatie ant.* 1953 (4) with M. Renard, *Croyances ... de table* 1961 (5). *Rev. belge de phil. et d'hist.* xxxiv 1956 641f (laus asini). Depping, G., *Merveilles de la force et de l'addresse* 1869. Derchain, P. (1) AC xxv 408–11 (2) *Rites ég., i, le sacrifice de l'oryx* 1962 (3) CE no. 76 228–9. Diehl, C., *Justinien* 1901. DL: *Diog.* Laertes. DLRE: *Daily Life in Roman Egypt* by J. Lindsay. Donaldson, T. L., *Archittura numismatico* 1859. Doresse, J., *The Secret Books of the Eg. Gnostics* 1960. Drioton, E. (1) *Bull.Mus. de Fr.* 1930 27 (2) *Ann. Service* xliv 1949 149f (3) *Rev. du Caire* xxxviii, Jan. 1942 (4) with Vandier, *L'Égypte* 1938 (5) BSAC x 1944. DS: Daremberg-Saglio *Dict. des Ant.* Ducati, P., *L'arte in Roma.* Dudley, D. R., *Hist. of Cynicism* 1937. Duthuit, G., *La Sculpture copte* 1931.

Ebers, *Die hellenist. Portraets aus den Fayum* 1893. Edgar, C. C. (1) JHS xvi 1906 (2) *Racc. Lumbroso (Aeg.* 1925) 369. El-Khabab, Abd ed-Mohsen (1) JEA 1963 147ff (2) *ib.* 1961 119. Elter, A., *Donarem pateras* ii 1 Bonn. Progr. 1907. Eisler, *Orph. dion. Mysteriengedanken.* Eitrem, S. (1) *Symb. Oslo.* xvii 1937 (2) *Opferritus u. Voropfer.* Emery, W. B., *Nubian Treasure* 1948. EP: *Études de Pap.* Erman, A. (1) *Relig. d. Aegypter* 1934 (2) *Life in Anc. Eg.* 1894. Evans (1) JHS xvii (2) *Palace of Minos* (3) *Scripta Minoa.*

Fairman. (1) in *Myth, Ritual and Kingship* ed. S. H. Hooke 1958 (2) *The Bucheum* Ferretto, G., *Note storicobibliog. di arch. crist.* 1942 Ferté, E. C. de la, *Les portraits roman-ég. du Louvre* 1912. Flickinger, *Gr. Theatre.* Forbes, C. A. (1) CP xl 1945 32–42 (2) *ib.* 1955 238ff (3) *Gr. Physical Education* 1929 (4) *Teachers' Pay in Anc. Greece.* Foucart, P., (1) BIFAO xxiv 1924, (2) *Culte de Dionysos en Attique* 1904 (3) *Rev. de Phil.* i 1877 (4) BCH. 1885. (5) *Assns. relig. chez les gr.* 1873. Foucher, L. (1) *Hadrumetum* (2) *Latomus* xx 1961. Fowler, *Amer. Sc. of Athens, Corinth* i "Topography". Frazer, P. M. (1) JRS 1958 (with B. Nicholas) 117 (2) *ib.* 1962 156 (3) HTR liv 141–5 (4) *Opuscula Athen.* iii 1960 1–54. Frost, K. T., JHS 1906 (boxing).

Gabra, S. (with Drioton, Perdrizet, Waddell). *Rapp. sur les fouilles Hermop.-Ouest* 1941. Gadd, C. J., *Iraq* i 1934. Gardiner, E. N. (1) JHS 1905 14–31, 263–93 (2) *ib.* 1906 4–22 (3) *Gr. Ath. Sports and Fests.* 1910 (4) *Athletics of the Anc. World* 1930 (5) JHS 1903 54–70, with more in 1904, 1906–7, 1925. Gasiorowski, S. J., JEA vii 1ff. Gauckler, P. (1) *Inv. Mos. Tunisie* 1910 (2) *Bull. arch. du Com. des Ét. hist.* 1904. Gauheis, *Gaukler im Alt.* Gayet, A., *Mons. coptes Musée de*

Boulaq iii 3 1889. Gebauer, *Ath. Mitt.* lxiii–iv 1938–9. Geer, R. M., TAPA lxvi 1935 (Gr. Games, Naples). Geffcken, *Komposition u. Enstebungzeit d. Orac. Sibyllina* 1902. Gernet, REG xlvi 1933 308. Gerstinger, H., *Anz. Ak. Wien.* 1954. Gilbert, P. (1) CE xxxvi 1961 26–55 (2) *ib.* xxxv 1960 140ff. Girard, P., *L'éducation athénienne.* Glanville, S. R. K., ed. *Legacy of Eg.* 1942. Glotz, G. (1) DS sv *Xystos* v 1027–31 (2) REG xxxiii 1920 188. Goodchild, R. E. (1) *Cyrene and Apollonia* 1959 (2) ILN dec. 14 1957 (3) *Antiq. J.* xli 218–23. Goodenough, *Polit. Philos. of Hellenistic Kingship* (YCS i 1928 75ff). Goodyear, *Grammar of the Lotus.* Grabar, *Martyrium* 1946. Graindor, P., BIFAO xxxii 1932 97–119. Gressmann, H., *Tod u. Auferstehung d. Osiris* 1923. Griffith, F. L. (1) *Stories of the High Priests of Memphis* 1900 (2) JEA iii 195. Griffiths, J. G. (1) *Conflict of Horus and Seth* 1960 (2) CE no. 76 1963 249 (summary) (3) JEA 1961 168f (4) *ib.* 113–18 (5) J. of Warburg and C. Inst. xxii 1959 367. Grégoire, H. (with Goosens and Mathieu), *Asklépios Apollon Smintheus and Rudra* 1949. Grimal, P., *Les jardins romains* 1943. Groningen, B. A. van (1) *Aeg.* 1926 189 (2) see David (3) *Gymnasiarches des metropole de l'Ég. rom.* Guent-Ogloueff, M., BIFAO xl 1941 127ff (noms propres incantoires). Guéraud, *Enteuxis* 20 no. 8. Guest, C., *Mabinogion* ed. W. Stokes 1868. Guidi, G., *Africa Italiana* iii 1930. Gundel, W., *Gnomon* 1928 449f. Gusman, P., *La villa imp. de Tibur* 1908.

Hadas, M., *Hellenistic Culture.* Hagopian, D., *Pollux' Faustkampf mit Amykos* 1955. Hahland, W., *Wien. Jahresh.* xxxviii 1950 67ff. Hanfmann, G., *The Seasons Sarcoph. in D. Oaks.* Hanssens, J. M., OCP xxvi 29–41. Harder, R., *Karpokrates von Chalkis u. d. Memphit. Isispropaganda* 1944. Harris, H. A. (1) JHS 1962 19–24 (2) *Gr. Athletes and Athletics* 1964. Hautecoeur, L., *Mystique et Architecture.* Haynes, D. E. L., *Antiqs. of Tripolitania* (foreword 1955). Heichelheim, F., RE sv *Monopolie.* Helbig, W., *Die Wandgem.* Henne, BIFAO xxii 1923 191. Hermann, A. (1) *Altäg. Liebesdichtung* 1959 (2) (Nil. u. Christen) *J. f. Ant. u. Christ.* 2 1959 30–69. Herrlinger, G. (1) *Totenklage um Tiere in d. ant. Dichtung* (2) *Ant. Tier-Epikedien* 1929. Herter, H., *Bursians J.* 1937 cclv and cclvii 80f. Herzfeld, J., BCH 1927 74. Herzog, R., *Philol.* lx (1901) 440ff. Heuzey, *Mission en Macedoine* 1876. Hewitt, J. W., CJ 1925–6 644ff (comic aspects of Gr. ath. meet). Hijmans, B. L., *Askesis* 1959. Hinks, R. P. (1) *Gr. and Rom. portrait sculpture* 1935 (2) *Cat. of Gr., Etr., and R. Paintings and Mos. in B.M.* 1933. Hirschfeld, O. (1) *Die kaiserlichen Vewaltungsbeamten* 1905 (2) 2nd ed. (3) *Sitz. Berl. Ak.* 1896 (4) *Koenigs. Stud.* 1 (1887) 85–144. Hoey, A. S. HTR xxx 1937 13–35. Hohlwein, N., EP v 1939 1–74. Holleaux, M. *Études d'epigr. et d'hist. gr.* ii 1938. Hölscher, *Mortuary Temple of Ramses III.* Ho Ping-Yu and J. Needham, *J. of Warburg and C. Inst.* 1959 173–210. Hopfner, T. (1) *Plut. über Isis u. Osiris* 1940–1 (2) *Fontes Hist. Relig. Aeg.* 1922–5 (3) *Die Tierkult d. alt. Äg.* 1914–18 (4) *Gr. äg. Offenbarungszauber* 1921. Householder, F. W. (with D. W. Prakken) TAPA lxxvi 1945 108–16. Hunt, A. S., JEA xv 1929 155ff.

James, M. R., *The Apocryphal NT* 1926. Jeanmaire, *Dionysos*. Jennison, G. *Animals for show and pleasure in anc. Rome,* 1937. Jéquier, *Les temples ptol. et romaines*. Jesi, F. (1) *Aeg.* 1958 171–83 (Bes) (2) JNES xv 1956 236–40. Johnson, A. C. *Roman Eg*. 1936. Jones, A. H. M. (1) *Past and Present* no. 27 1964 1ff (2) *Cities of east. provs.* 1937 (3) *Gr. cities from Alex. to Justinian* 1940. Jones, W. H. S., *Fresh light on roman bureaucracy* 1920. Joret, C. *La rose dans l'ant. et au m. âge* 1892. Jouguet, P. (1) RBPH ii 1923 (2) REG ix 1896 433–6 (3) *Racc. Ramorino* 1927 381ff (4) *La vie municip. dans l'Ég. rom.* 1911 (5) *Macedonian Imperialism and the Hellenisation of the East* 1928 (6) CR *Acad. Inscrs.* 1902 350. Jucker, H., *Das Bildnis im Blätterkelch*. i and ii 1961. Junker, *Onurislegende*. Juthner, J. (1) *Philostratos über Gymnastik* 1909 (2) RE vii 2054–7 (3) *Über ant. Turngeräte* 1896.

Kaibel, G. (1) *Galen Protreptr.* (2) *Epigram. Gr.* 1878. Kantor, AJA lxi 1957 53. Kaufmann, C. M., *Ikonog. d. Menas-Ampullen* 1910. Kees, *Griffith Studies* 402–5 (apoth. by drowning). Keimer (1) *Rev. EA* ii 210 (2) *Bull. Inst. Ég.* xxxvii 1956 215–19 (3) *Aeg.* vii 169 (4) ASAE lii 59. Keller, *Ant. Tierwelt*. Kendrick, A. F. (1) *Cat. Textiles from burying-grounds in Egypt* (2) *Studies . . . Crum* 479–84. Keydell, R. (1) RE 1936 904–20 (2) *Hermes* lxii 1927 393ff (3) AC i 1932 193ff (4) *Gnomon* ix 1935 605. Klaffenbach, *Symbola ad hist. colleg. artif. Bacchiorum* 1919. Klee, *Zur Gesch. d. gymn. Agonen*. Klein, F. N., *Die Lichtterminologie bei Philon von Alex. u. in d. hermet.*, Schriften 1962. Knaack, RE sv *Dionysos* no. 95. Koch, W., *Astrologie* xii 1930 321–41. Koehler, R., *Über d. D. d. Nonnos* 1853. Kokolakis, M., *Pantomimus and the treatise peri orcheseos* 1956. Koraes, JEA 1961. Kornemann, E. (1) *Klio* vii 1907 278–88 (2) *Anax*. Körte, A., *Archiv.* x 1–2, 18–70. Kortenbeutel, H., *Der Äg. Süd.-u. Osthandel* 1931. Kraeling, *Gerasa*. Kramer, H., *Quid valeat homonoia in litt. gr.* 1915. Krause, *Gymnastik u. Agon. d. Hell*. Kroll, W. (1) with Skutsch, *Firm. Mat. lib.* viii 1897–1913 (2) *Klio* xviii 224 (3) Vett. Val. *Anthol. libri* 1908 (4) *Hist. Alex. Magni*. Krumbacher, K. *Kultur d. Gegenwart*. Kuenzle, *Riv. fil.* xi 1933 76f. Kugler, F. X., *Sibyll. Sternkampf u. Phaethon* 1927. Kumanudis, *Athenaion*.

Labrousse, MR. 1938 80ff. Lagrange, M. J., *Ét. sur les relig. sémitique* 1903. Lammens, (1) BIFAO xvii 1920 39ff (2) *L'arabie occid. avant l'Hégire* 1928 101ff (3) *Mél. Univ. S. Joseph* xi 1926 39. Lanchester, in Charles, *Apocrypha and Pseudogr. of OT* ii 372. Landschoot, A. van, in *Studies . . . Crum* 339–63. Lanzone, *Dizionario di Mitologia egizia*. Lattimore, R., *Themes in Gr. and Latin Epitaphs* 1962. Lauer, J. P. (with Picard) *Les Statues ptol. du Sarap. de Memphis* 1955. Laum, *Stiftungen in d. gr. u. röm. Ant*. Launey, M. (1) *Recherches sur les armées hellenistiques* ii 1950 (2) BCH lxi 1937 401f. Le Blant, E., *Mém. acad. inscr. et BL* xxxvi 2de. 1899. Leclant, J., *Latomus* 1964 385–92. Lefébure, *Muséon* xvii 1898 193ff, 349ff. Lefebvre, G. (1) *Le Tombeau de Pétosiris* 1924 (2) *Rec. inscrs. gr. chrét. d'Ég.* 1908. Lefort, L. T., *Les vies coptes de saint Pachome* 1943. Lehmann, K. (1) *Art. Bull.* xxviii 1945 1–27 (2) with others, *Dionys. Sarc. in*

Baltimore 1942. Lemerle, BCH lx 1936 336–43. Lemm, O. von, *Bull. Acad. imp. des sc., St. Petersb.* vi 4 1910. Lenzen, V. F., *The Triumph of Dionysus on Textiles* 1960. Lepsius, C. R., *Denkmäler auf Weg. u. Aethiopien* 1849–56. Lesquier, *L'armée rom. d'Ég. d'Aug. à Dioclet.* 1918. Levezow, K., *Über d. Antinous dargestellt in d. kunstdenkmälern d. Alt.* Levi, D. (1) *Hesperia* xii 1944 269ff (2) *Antioch Mos. Pavements* i 1947. Levi, M. A., *Parola del Passato* ix 1954 293–5. Liapounova, X. (1) *Musée de l'Ermitage, trav. du dept. orient.* iii 1940 149ff (2) with Matye, *Khudozhestvennyie tkani kopskogo Egipta* 1951. Liermann, *Analecta epigr. et agon.* Lind, L. R. (1) in Rouse, Loeb *Nonnos* i (2) CP xxviii 208f (3) ib. xxix 69–73 (4) ib. xxx 78 (5) *Class. Week.* xxix 17–20 (6) ib. 21 (7) AC vii 1938 57–65. Lindsay, J. (1) DLRE (2) *Byzantium into Europe* 1952 (3) *Marc Antony* 1936 (4) *Arthur and his Times* 1958 (5) *Writing on the Wall* (7) *Golden Ass* 1960. Lippold in Arndt-Amelung, *Einzelaufnahmen ant. Skulpt.* Lofoscade, L., *De epistulis . . . imperatorum magistratumque rom.* 1902. Loisel, G., *Hist. des ménageries* 1912. L'Orage, H. P. (1) *Apotheosis in anc. portraiture* 1947 (2) *Studies in iconog. of cosmic kingship* 1953 (3) *Sirta Eitrem.* 1942 68–100. Lösch, *Epist. Claud.* Lovejoy, A. O. with G. Bass, *Primitivism and related ideas in antiquity* 1935. Lubker. *Reallexikon* (8th ed.). Lucas, A. (1) JEA xvi 41ff (2) ib. xviii 1932 52–7 (3) ib. 125–32 (4) ib. xvii 13–8 (cedar) (5) *Anc. Eg. Materials and Industries* 1948. Lüders, C., *Die dionys. Kunstler* 1873. Lüders, H., *Das Wurfelspiel im alten Indien* 1907. Ludwich, A. (1) ed. of *Dionys.* of Nonnos i 1909, ii 1911 (2) *Hermes* xii 1877 273–99. Lumbroso (1) *L'Egitto* (2) *Recherches.*

Maas, P. (1) *Mél. H. Grégoire* i 1949 (2) *Byz. Zeit.* iv 1923 265–9 (3) *Gnomon* v 1928 250–2. Macdonald, G., *Coin Types* 1905. Mahaffy (1) *Empire of Ptols.* (2) *Gr. Life and Thought.* Mallet, D., *Première étab. des grecs en Eg.* (Mem. Miss. arch. du Caire xii) 1893. Maraini, F., *Where Four Worlds Meet* 1964. Marrou, H., *Hist. of education in ant.* 1956. Martin, V. (1) *Les epistratèges* 1911 (2) *La fiscalité rom. en. Ég.* 1926. Maspero, G. (1) *Hist. des peuples de l'Or.* (2) *Hymne au Nil* 1912 (3) *Guide Mus. Caire* (4th ed.) Mattingly, *Coins R. Emp. in BM* i 1923. Matz, F. (Gott auf dem Elegantenwagen) *Ak. Wiss. u. Lit. Mainz, Abh. d. geestes. u sozialwiss. Kl.,* Jhrg. 1952 no. 10. Mazzarino, S. (1) *Aspetti sociali del quarto secolo* 1951 (2) *La democratizzazione della cultura nel basso imp.* (XI congrès internat. des sc. hist., rapp. ii 1960 35ff). Méautis, *Hermoupolis-la-Grande* 1918. Mekios, K. M., *To hellen. gymn. en Aig.* Merkelbach, R. (1) *Isisfeste in gr.-röm. Zeit.* 1963 (2) *Roman u. Mysterium* 1962. Merlin, A. (with L. Poinssot) *Mon. Piot* xxxiv 129ff (*Mos. prophylact.*). Mertens, P. *La Service de l'état civil et le contrôle de la pop. à Oxy.* 1958. Mesk, *Wien. Stud.* xxx 1908 59–74. Meulenaere, H. de, CE xxxviii 1963 217–9. Meuli, *Gr. Opferbraüche* 1946. Meyer, P. M. (1) *Jurist. Pap.* 1920 (2) *Gr. Texte* 1961 (3) *Fest. Hirschfeld* 1903. Meyer, W., *Der accentuierte Satzschlus in d. gr. Prosa vom IV bis XVI J.* Michailides, G., *Bull. Inst. de l'Ég.* xxxi 1949. Michailowski, BCH 1930 131–46. Mitteis (1) *Röm. Privatrecht* (2) *Lehre v. d. Libellen.* Möller, G., *Archiv* vii 1923 66. Montet, P., *Le drame d'Avaris* 1940. Milne, J. G. (1) *Hist. of Eg. under R. rule* 1924 (2) *Cat. Lit. Pap. BM.* Morenz, S., *Der Gott auf der Blume* 1954. Moret, A. (1) *Mystères égypt.*

1913 (2) *Caractère religieux*. Moretti, L. (1) *Inscriz. agonistiche greche* (2) *Aeg.* xxxviii 1958 203–9. MR: *Mel. école fr. de Rome*. Müller, A., *Lehrbuch d. gr. Bühnenalterthümer*. Müller, D., *Ägypten u. d. gr. Isis Aretalogien* 1961. Müller, W. M., *Eg. Myth*. 1918. Murko. H., *Wötrer u. Sachen* ii 1910.

Nagel, G., BIFAO 1920 33ff. Naville, *Deir el Bahari*. Needler, W. E., CE no. 76 1963 249. Nenconi, G., *Riv. di studi orient*. xix 1941 98. Néroutsos Bey, *L'anc. Alex*. Neuberger, A., *The tech. arts and sciences of the ancients* 1930. Neuffer, E., *Das Kostüm Alex. d. Grosse* 1929. Neugebauer (with van Hoesen). *Greek Horoscopes* 1959. Niccolini, *Pompeii*. Nilsson, M. P. (1) *Beitr. z. Religionswiss*. ii 1917 (2) *N. J. f. d. kl. Alt*. xxvii 1911 (3) RE i A 2 1708 (4) RE sv *Rosalia*. Nock, A. D. (1) *Gnomon* June 1934 (2) *Conversion* (3) JHS 1928 21ff (4) *Gnomon* xxi 1949 221–8. Nogara, *I mosaici del Vaticano*. Norden, E. (1) *Agnostos Theos* 1923 (2) *N. J. kl. Alt*. xxxi 1913 656ff.

O'Connor, *Chapters in Hist. of Actors and Acting in Anc. Gr*. 1908. Oehler, J. (1) RE sv *gymnasion* 2055–6 (2) *Epigraph. Beiträge z. Gesch. d. Dionys. Kunstler* 1908. Olek, RE sv *Gartenblau*. Otto, W. *Priester u. Tempel im hellenist. Äg*. 1905–8. Otto and Bengtson, *Zur Gesch. d. Niederganges d. Ptol.*

Pacho, *Rel. d'un voyage dans la Marmarique, La Cyrénaique*. Page. D. L., Loeb *Lit. Pap*. Pagenstecher, R. (1) *Exped. E. von Sieglin, Malerei u. Plastik* 1923 (2) *Nekropolis* 1919. Pargoire, J., *L'église byz*. 1905. Parker, R. A., *Calendars of anc. Eg*. 1950. Parrot, A. (1) *Bull. Mus. de Fr*. 1936 131 (2) *Rev. Hist. Relig*. cxiv 1936 60–92 (3) *ib*. 158–96 (4) *ib*. cxv 53–89 Pearson, L. (1) *Lost Histories of Alex. Gt*. 1960 (2) *Historia* iii 1955 429–55. Peek (1) *Gnomon* ix 1933 (2) *Studies . . . Robinson* ii (3) *Bull. Soc. R. Arch. Alex*. viii 1932 53,1. Peirce, H., with R. Tyler, *L'art byz*. 1932–4. Perdrizet, P. (1) with G. Lefebvre, *Les graffites grecs du Memnonion d'Abydos* 1919 (2) REG 1914 266–80 (3) *Bronzes gr. dÉg. coll Fouquet* 1911 (4) TCs *gr. ibid* 1921 (5) REA xxiii 1921 90ff (6) JHS 1898 273 (7) *Rec. Champollion* 1922 (8) *Mél. Bidez* ii 719 (9) BCH xxiv 1900 299–325 (10) *Cultes et mythes de Pangée* 1910. (11) *Ann Service* ix 1908 (12) REA xii 1910. Perkins, J. B. Ward (1) 19th J. Toynbee, *Archaeologia* xcii 1949 (2) *Listener* 1 Nov. 1956 (3) *Brit. School Rome* 1949 26ff. Petersen, E., *Rev. biblique* lv 1948 199ff. Petrie, W. M. F. (1) *Relig. Life in anc. Eg*. 1924 (2) *Abydos* pt. 2, 1903. Pettazoni, R., AC xviii 1949 265ff. Pharr, C., *Theod. Code* 1952. Philippart, V. H., *Rev. Belge de Philol*. ix 1930 5–72. Philips, E. D., *Antiquity* 1964 no. 151 171–8 Photiades, P. (Diatribes cyniques de pap. de Genève) *Mus. Helvet*. 1959 137ff. Picard, C. (1) RA 1947 i (2) *Civilisation de l'Afrique rom*. 1959 (3) BCH lxxxiii 409ff (4) MR lviii 1941–6 90ff (5) see Lauer (6) *Castellum Dimmidi* (7) RA 1939 79–83 (8) *Civitas Mactar*. Pickard-Cambridge, A. (1) *Dramatic Festivals of Athens* 1953. (2) *Theatre of Dionysus*. Pincherle, *Gli oracoli sibillini giudaici* 1922. Poland, E. J. (1) *Gesch. d. gr. Vereinswesens* 1909 (2) RE 1934 sv *technitai* (3) *De collegiis artificum Dionys*. 1895. Posener, G.,

Dict. of Eg. Civilisation 1962. Préaux, C. (1) *Grecs en Égypte* 1947 (2) *Econ. roy. des Lagides* 1939 (3) *Mus. Helv.* x 203–21. Preisendanz, K., *Akephalos* 1926. Preisigke, F. (1) see WGP (2) *Namenbuch* (3) *Städt. Beamtenwesen.* Prichard, J. B., *Anc. Near Eastern texts* 1950. Pringsheim, *Gr. Law of Sale.* Prinz, *Altorient. Symbolik* 1915. Puchstein, *Epigram. gr. in Aeg. reperta* 1880. Puech, H. C. (1) *Rev. Univ. Bruxelles* 1934 137–58, 298–314 (2) *Eranos* xx 1952 57ff. Purser, L. C. *Smith Dict.* ii 334–6 sv *pantomimus.*

Quandt, G., *De Baccho ab Alexandri aetate in Asia Minore culto* Diss. phil. Hal. xxi 2 1913. Quibell, *Excavs. at Saqqara* 1907–8 (1909).

R: Roscher, *Dict.* RA: *Rev. archéol.* Ramsay, W. M., *Cities and Bishoprics of Phrygia* 1895–7. Ranke, *Personnamen.* Rawnsley, H. D., *Notes for the Nile* 1892. RBPH: *Revue belge de Philol. et d'Hist.* RE: Pauly-Wissowa *Reallex.* REG: *Rev. études gr.* Rea, J., JEA 1963 180f. REg: *Roman Egypt,* Johnson. Reich, H., *Der Mimus* i 1903. Reil, T. (1) *Beitr. z. Kenntnis d. Gewerbes im. hellenist. Ag.* 1913. Reinach, A., RA 1914 30–53. Reisch, E. (1) RE sv *akontion* (2) *De musicis gr. certaminibus* 1865 (3) RE sv *baltis* 2 2819. Reisner, G. A., *Arch. Survey of Nubia* 1907–8 rep. Reitzenstein, R. (1) *N.J.f.d.kl. Alt.* xxi 1908 365–7 (2) *Poimandres* (3) *Zwei religionsgeschichtl. Fragen* 1901 (4) *Archiv f. Rel.* xix 1918 (5) *Die hellenist. Mysterienrel.* 1927. Reynolds, J. H. (with Ward Perkins), *Inscrs. of R. Tripolitania* 1952. Rhind, *Pap. found in tomb at Thebes* 1863. Ricci, C., *La cultura d. vita nell' Eg. g.r.* 1924. Richter, G. M. A., *Sculpture and sculptors of Greeks* 1930. Ridder, A. de, (1) DS sv *lucta* iii 2 1340a–1347b (2) *Bronzes ant. du Louvre* ii. Riefstahl, E. in *Studies . . . Crum* 531–40. Riemschneider, M., *Aus d. byz. Anheit d. DDR* (Stil d. Nonnos) i 1957 46–70. Rizzo, G. E. (1) *La pittura ellenistico-romana* 1929 (2) *Dionysos Mystes.* Robert, C., JHS xx 84–6. Robert, F., *Thymélè* 1939. Robert, L. (1) REG xlix 1936 235–54 (2) *Hermes* 1930 106–22 (3) *Ét. epigr. et philol.* 1938 (4) *Ét. anatol.* 1937 (5) RA 1934 i 52ff (6) *Les gladiateurs dans l'orient grec.* Roberts, C. H. in Glanville. Robertson, D. S., in *Essays . . . to W. Ridgeway.* Robinson, D. M., CP 1943 191. Roeder, G. (1) *Bronzefiguren* (2) R. iv 878–908 (3) *Hermopolis* 1929–39 (4) MDAIK ii 1931 (4) RE sv Kanopos. Romanelli, M. P., AC vii 230. Romme, A., *Acad. roy. belge Bull. Lettres* xxxviii 1951 264. Ronczewski, R., *Gewölbeschmuck in röm. Alt.* 1903. Rose, H. S., *Ann. arch. anthrop.* xi 25–30. Rossi, de, *Boll. di arch. crist.* iii 130–44, pls. vi-viii. Rostovtzeff, M. (1) *Social and Econ. Hist.* RE 1957 (2) *Rome* 1960 (3) *Soc. and Econ. Hist. Hellist. World* 1941 (4) JHS xxxix 146 (5) *Mystic Italy* 1927 (6) *Archiv* iv 301–4 and v 181 (7) JEA vi 177 (8) *Klio* vi 171 (9) *Röm. Mitt.* xxvi 1911 (10) *Anatolian Studies . . . W. Ramsay* 1923 (11) *Large Estate in Eg.* 1922 (12) *Stud. z. Gesch. d. röm. Kolonats* 1910 (13) *J. Econ. and Business Hist.* iv 1932. Rouse, W. H. D., *Nonnos in Loeb ed.* Rousell, P. (1) *Mél. Maspero* ii 1924 (2) REG 1930 361–71. Rowe, E. A., *Ann. Service* xl 1940 1–67, 291–9. RT: R. Taubenschlag. Rzach, (1) *Mél. Nicole* 498 (2) RE ii A 2 2129ff.

Sambursky, S. (1) *Physics of the Stoics* 1959 (2) *Physical World of the Greeks.* San Nicolò, *Äg. Vereinswesen* 1913. Sauneron, S. (1) in Posener (2) *Les fêtes relig. d'Esna aux derniers siècles du paganisme* 1962. Säve-Södenbergh, T., *Horae Soederblomianae* iii 1953. Sawhill, O. A., *Use of athletic metaphors in . . . St John Chrysostom* 1928. SB: *Sammelbuch.* Schaeffer, F. A., *Ugaritica* 1939. Schleidan, M. J., *Die Rose* 1873. Schnabel, M., *Die Landwirtschaft im hellenist. Äg.* 1925. Schneider, A., RE 1927 sv *skenikoi agones.* Schöll, *Hermes* vi 137. Schott, S., *Büche u. Sprüche gegen den Gott Seth, fasc.* 1–2, 1929 and 1939, in *Urk. d. ag. Alt., Sechste Abt.* Schreiber, T. (1) BSSA xv 1914 12 (2) *Die Nekropole von Kom esch- Schkafa.* Schröder, B., *Der Sport im Alt.* Schubart, W. (1) ZASA lxvii 1931 114 (2) *Archiv* v 57 (3) *Einführung in d. Pap.* 1918 (4) with Kuhn, *Pap. u Ostr. d. Ptol.* 1922. (5) *Amtl. Ber. aus d. Kunstsamm.* Nov. 1913, col. 57. Schwartz, J., *Les archives de Serapion* 1961. Scott, K. (1) CP xxiv 1929 133 (2) TAPA 1929 117–35 (3) YCS ii 1931 201–78 (4) CP xxvii 1932 317–38 (5) *ib.* xxxiii 384–8. Seidl, E. (1) *Der Eid* (2) *Münch. Beitr.* xxvii. SEG. *Sel Epig. Graec.* Seta. A. della, *I mon. dell'ant. class., i Grecie* 1931. Sethe, K. (1) *Der dramat. Ramesseumpap.* 1928 (2) *Amun.* Seyrig (1) *Syria* xv 1934 159ff, pl. xix (2) *Rev. Hist. Relig.* xcvii 1928 275–7. Shorter, A. W., *Intro. to Eg. Religion* 1931. Skeat, T. C. JRS xliii 1953 98–100 (Kleo.'s date 17 Mesore 30). Siska, H., *De Mercurio ceterisque deis ad artem gymnicam pertinentibus* 1933. Smith, E. Baldwin (1) *The Dome* 1950 (2) *Eg. architecture* (3) *Archit. Symbolism of Imp. Rome and Middle Ages.* Smith, W. S. (1) *Hist. of Eg. sculpture and painting in OK* (2) *Art and Architecture.* Smyly, J. G., *Gr. Pap. from Gurob* 1921. Sogliano, A., *Le pitture murali campane in Pompeii* 1879. Spanton, *Anc. Eg.* 1917. Speelers, L., *Rev. de trav. rel. à la phil. assur. et ég.* xl 158ff. Spicq, C. (1) *Ephem. Theol. Lovanienses* 1937 209–29 (2) *Rev. biblique* 1947 229–42. Spiegelberg (1) *Äg. u. gr. Eigenn. aus Mumienetiketten* (2) ÄZ liv 1918 86–92 (3) *Demotica* ii (4) *Äg. Mitt., Sitz. München* 1925 3–6. Stegemann, V., *Astrologie u. Universalgeschichte, Stud. u. Interpret. zu d. D. d. Nonnos* 1930. Steindorff-Wolff. *Die Theban. Gräberwelt.* Stemler, *Die gr. Grabinsch. Kleinasien* 1909. Strack (1) *Untersuch. z. röm. Reichsprägung* (2) *Die Dyn. d. Ptol.* 1897. Stracmans, CE lxxi. Strong, A. (1) *Apotheosis* 1915 (2) CAH x ch. 17. Strong, D. E., JRS 1963 217. Strzygowski, J. (1) *Hellenist. u. kopt. Kunst* 1902 (2) *Kopt. Kunst* 1904 Studniczka, *Abh. Sächs. Akad.* xxx 1914 66ff. Swiderek, A. (1) *La propriété foncière dans l'Ég. de Vespasien* 1960 (2) *Eos* li 55–63.

Tait, G. A. D., JEA 1963 93ff. Tarn, W. W. (1) *Hellenistic Civilisation* 1927 (2) *Greeks in Bactria and India* 1938 (3) JEA xv 1929 11 (4) JHS 1928 215 (5) CAH x 108 (6) *Alex. Gt.* 1948 (7) AJP lx 1939 41–70 (8) JHS xli 1–17 (9) *ib.* 1928 206–19 (10) *Alex. Gt. and Idea of World Unity* (11) CAH vi (12) JRS 1936 187ff. Taubenschlag, R. (1) *Law of GR Eg. in Light of Pap.* 1944 (2) ii 1948 (3) *Strafrecht* 1916. Ténand, S., *Bull. des Musées* viii 1936. Thursch, *B.S. Arch. Alex.* no. 3. Tod, M. N., CQ xliii 1949. Tollington, R. B., *Clement of Alex.* 1914. Tondriau, J. L. (1) *Studi . . . Calderini-Paribeni* i 1956 15–22 (2)

Rev. Phil. xxiii 1949 41–52 (3) *Mél. Grégoire* iv 1953 453–5. Toynbee, J. C. M. (1) with Ward Perkins, *Brit. School Rome* xvii 1 1950 37ff (peopled scrolls) (2) *Num. Chron.* 1947 126–49. Trypanis, C. A., Callimachus' *Aitia* etc. Loeb. Tschudin, P. F., *Isis in Rom* 1962.

Üxküll-Gyllenband (1) *Gr. Kulturentstehungslehren* 1924 (2) *Gnomon* 1934.

Vallois, R. (1) *L'architecture hellenique et hellenist. à Delos* i 1944 (2) REG xliv 1931 121–52. Vandebeek, *De interpretatione Graeca van de Isisfiguur* 1946. Vandier, J. (1) *Relig. égypt.* 125 (2) CE xxxvii 1944 51ff (3) *Rev. du Louvre* xii 1962 197–202. Vermaseren, M. J., *Corpus inscr. et mon. relig. mithriacae* 1956. Viereck, *Klio* viii 413. Villard, V. M. de., *Archaeologia* xcv 1953 85–106. Visscher, F. de (1) CE xxxv 271–7 (2) *Fest. H. Lewald* 175ff. Voigt, R i sv *Dionysos.*

W. and W. *Chr.*: Wilcken. Waldhauer, O., *Kaiserliche Hermitage: Die ant. Tonlampen* 1914. Wallace, S. L., *Taxation in Eg.* 1938. Walle, van de, CE 1930 37–50. Wallert, I., *Münchner Äg. Stud.* i 1962 (palm). Waltzing, *Ét. hist. sur les corps. prof. chez les romains* Wamser, *De iure sep. romana.* Warcher, *Pompeii* 1930. Wasmuth, *Kunsthefte.* Watzinger, *Exped. E. von Sieglin.* Weber, W., *Der Prophet u. sein Gott* 1925. Webster, T. B. L., *Mons. illustr. New Comedy* 1961. Weege, *Der Tanz in der antike* 1926. Wehrle, F., *Der Schule der Aristoteles.* Weill-Jouguet, *Mél. Maspero* ii 93ff. Weinreich, O. (1) *Epigramm u. Pantomimus,* Sitz. Ak. Wiss. p.-h. Kl. Heidelb. 1948 (2) *Stud. z. Martial* 1928 (3) *Mitt. d. K.D. arch. hist. ath. Alt.* xxxvii 1912 1–62 (epekoos). Wendland, P., *Hellenist.-röm. Kultur* 1912. Westermann, W. L., CP ix 295–315. WGP: Preisigke-Kiessling *Wörterbuch d. gr. Pap. kunden* 1925–31. Whateley, M. L., *Among the huts of Eg.* 1871. Whittemore, T., in *Coptic Stud.* . . . *W. E. Crum* 1950 541–53. Wiedemann, *Wein. Z. f. d. Kunde d. Morgenlandes* xxi 1924 310f. Wieseler, *Theatregebäude.* Wilamowitz-Möllendorf, V. von (1) *Wiss. Veröffent. d. deut. Orientges.* Heft 3 (1903) (2) *Timotheos, Die Perser.* Wilcken, U. (1) *Chrestomathie* (2) *Urkunde d. Ptol.* 1927–35 (3) SBA 1928 576–603 (4) *ib.* 1930 159–76 (5) *Alex. d. Grosse* 1931 (6) *Z. f. Äg. Spr.* lx 86ff. Wilfstrand, A., *Von Kallim. zu Nonnos* 1933 Wilhelm, *Neue Beitr.* iv 54. Winlock, MNY 1914. Winter, J. C. (1) *Life and letters in pap.* 1933 (2) *De mimis Oxy.* 1906. Wirth, F., *Röm. Malerei* 1934. Witkowski (1) *Epist. priv. gr. quae in pap. aet. Lag. servantur* 1906 (2) ed. 1911. Witt, C. de, *Inscriptions du Temple d'Opet in Karnak* 1958. Wormald, F., JEA xv 239–42. Wörmann (1) *Die Lanschaft in der kunst d. alt. Völker* 1876 (2) *Über den landschaftl. Natursinn d. G. u. R.* 1871 (3) *Von Apelles zu Böcklin* i 1914 (4) in *Gesch. d. Kunst alt. Zeiten u. Völker* (2nd) 1924. Wreszinski, *Atlas altäg. Kulturgesch.* Wright, F. A., *Gr. Athletics* 1925. Wuilleumier, P., MR, xliv 1927 191ff. Wulff, *Altchrist. u. mittelalt. Bildwerke* i 1909. Wüst, E. (1) RE sv *Mimus* xv 1727–64 (1932) (2) xviii 3 (1949) 847ff.

Q

Youtie, H. C. (1) in Coleman-Norton, *Stud. in R. Econ. and Soc. Hist. in hon. A. C. Johnson* 1951, 178 (2) *Textual Crit. of Doc. Pap.* 1958 (3) with Boak, *Archives Aur. Isidorus* 1960. Yoyotte, J. (1) in Posener (2) RdE xiv 108ff.

Zahn, W., *Ornamente alle klass. Kunst.-Epochen* 1870. Zambon, A., *Aeg.* xv 1935 1–66. Ziebarth, E. (1) *Aus d. ant. Schule* 1910 (2) 2nd ed. 1914 (3) *Das gr. Vereinswesen* 1896 (4) *Ath. Mitt.* 1906 413f. Zinche, B., *Eg. of the Pharaohs and of the Khedive* 1873. Zulueta, de, JRS 1932 184–97.

Additions to Bibliography. Abbott, G. F., *Macedonian FL* 1903. Aurigemma, *Villa Adriana* 1961. Beattie (2) CQ 1951. Buck, C. D., *Greek Dialects* 1955. Crema, L., *L'Architett. Rom.* xii (1, Encic. class. sez. 3) 1959. Devambez, P., BCH lxx 1946 164–72. Frickenhaus, *Jahrb..* 1917 114–33. Guarducci, M., *Annuario* 1959–60 239–42. Hanfmann (2) *Roman Art* 1965. Heisenberg, *Grabeskirche und Apostelkirche.* Hill, G. F., JHS xxxi. Ippolito, G. d', *Studi Nonniane, L'Epillio* 1964. Jeffery, L. H., JHS 1949 30. Morey, C., *The Mosaics of Antioch.* Perkins, Ward (4) *Procs. Brit. Acad.* 1947 169. Picard (9) CRAI 1944 130. Pouilloux, J., *Recherches sur l'hist. et les cultes de Thasos* 1954. Robert, F. (2) RA xli 1953 1.8–40. Roebuck, C., *The Asklepieion and Lerna* (Corinth xiv) 42ff. Salviat, F., BCH 1958 193–267. Sbordone, F., *Physiologus* 1936. Sokolowski, F. (1) *Les Lois Sacrées des Cités Grecques* 1962, (2) *Les L. S. de l'Asie Mineure* 1955. Wächter, *Reinheitsvorschr. im griech. Kultur* 1910. Welter, G., *Troizen i. Kalaureia.* Wilamowitz-M. (3) *Antigonos.* Woodhead, A. G., SEG xi 1112. For background further: the list in DLRE.

Indexes

AUTHORS

(Cited or referred to, Egyptian and non-Egyptian)

Valerius Maximus, 309; Varro, 131-2, 260, 311; Virgil, 354, 356; Vitruvius, 99, 158, 246, 309, 310; Vopiscus, 54

Xenophon, 193, 259-60, 339; Xenophon of Ephesos, 339

Zenodotos, 99; Zosimos, 389

DEITIES AND CULTS

Adonis, 14, 257; Aion, 221-2; Akephalos, 24; Animals, Sacred, 21, 195-6, 230, 356; Antinoos, 39, 215-19, (festivals) 39, 160, 203, 218; Amenophis, 57, 61; Amen-Re (Ammon etc.), 57, 60-2, 199, 222, 249, 349; Amesysia, 32, 34, 402-3; Anubis, 6, 23, 32, 46, 58, 62, 222, 343-4; Aphrodite, 14, 21, 26, 33, 41, 64, 110, 178-9, 219-20, 224, 257, 270-1, 274, 339, 356, 380-1, 395; Apis, 343; Apollo, 21, 35-6, 101, 104, 157, 186, 190, 320, 326, 334, 339, 357, 367; Ares, 64, 110, 199-200, 277, 339; Arsinoe, 240; Arsinoiia, 203; Asklepios, 156, 221, 257, 276; Atargatis Bethennunis, 21; Athena, 37, 170, 277, 294, 384-5, 391; Artemis, 41, 115, 156, 223, 383; Artemis Szzanathcona, 39; August Days, 37-8; Augusti, 19, 21, 35-7

Basilissa (Berenike), 41; Bastet, 230; Bes and Besia, 4-11, 217, 222, 252-3; Bebon, 22; Bouchis Bull, 356

Ceres, 12

Delia, 31; Demeter and Demetria, 21, 32, 321, 360, 380-1, 402. Dionysos: Alexander, 349-51, 357-8; Antinoos, 218; Antonius, M., 353-6; Architecture (parasol, dome), 168, 172, 184-7, 333-5; athletics, 111, 114-15, 119, 126; Caligula, 358; creative energy, 322-3, 326-30; cult, 21, 347-8, 364: dance, 68, 76-7, 81-6, 126; democracy, 347-9; Dionysia, 69; gardens, paradise, 246, 257, 312, 315-30, 346, 357; gladiators, 175 (against); gymnasion, 51; Herakles, 257, 326, 351-2, 374, 388; Hunt, 223-6, 360-1, Indian Dionysos, 453; Indian War, 169, 171, 185, 351, 357, 360-1, 365-7; light-bringer, 357, 457; Loves, 14; Lykourgos, 322-6; Mysteries in Egypt, 352-3; Nile, 405; Nysa, 168-72, 351, 360; Nonnos (see Nonnos; Organisation of athletes and actors, ch. vii), gild of artists, 239-45; Osiris, 351, 353-7, 360-1; Oxyrhynchos, 160; Ptolemaia, 165-71; Ptolemies, 352-3; puppets, 245; Rosalia, 13-14, 398-9; Sabazios, 334, 367; scroll, 222, spiral, 222; sponde, 32-3, 35, 285; Thriambos, 357; Triumph, 225-6, 324, 326-7, 248-9, 352, 357; Triumphator, 352; theatre, 175, 237; vintage, 33; world-image, 172-4; see also Gardens, Nysa. Dioskouroi, 173, 336, 341, 358

Eros, 257, 270

Gardens Festival, 32; Germination of Divine Plants, 12

EMPERORS, KINGS, ETC.

PERSONS IN OR OF EGYPT

HIGH OFFICIALS

PERSONS OUTSIDE EGYPT

PLACES OUTSIDE EGYPT

GENERAL